By Lynne Olson

THOSE ANGRY DAYS: ROOSEVELT, LINDBERGH, AND
AMERICA'S FIGHT OVER WORLD WAR II, 1939–1941

CITIZENS OF LONDON: THE AMERICANS WHO STOOD
WITH BRITAIN IN ITS DARKEST, FINEST HOUR

TROUBLESOME YOUNG MEN: THE REBELS WHO BROUGHT
CHURCHILL TO POWER AND HELPED SAVE ENGLAND

A QUESTION OF HONOR: THE KOSCIUSZKO SQUADRON:
FORGOTTEN HEROES OF WORLD WAR II (WITH STANLEY CLOUD)

FREEDOM'S DAUGHTERS: THE UNSUNG HEROINES OF THE
CIVIL RIGHTS MOVEMENT FROM 1830 TO 1970

THE MURROW BOYS: PIONEERS ON THE FRONT LINES OF
BROADCAST JOURNALISM (WITH STANLEY CLOUD)

THOSE ANGRY DAYS

Published in the United States by Random House,
an imprint of The Random House Publishing Group,
a division of Random House, Inc., New York.

RANDOM HOUSE and colophon are registered trademarks of Random House, Inc.

Grateful acknowledgment is made to Houghton Mifflin Harcourt for permission to reprint
excerpts from *The Wartime Journals of Charles A. Lindbergh* by Charles A. Lindbergh,
copyright © 1970 by Charles A. Lindbergh and renewed 1998 by Anne Morrow Lindbergh
and Reeve Lindbergh, and excerpts from *War Within and Without: Diaries and Letters of
Anne Morrow Lindbergh, 1939–1944* by Anne Morrow Lindbergh, copyright © 1980 by
Anne Morrow Lindbergh. Reprinted by permission of Houghton Mifflin Harcourt.
All rights reserved.

PHOTO CREDITS: All images are from the Library of Congress with the exception of pp. 15
and 38, which are from Manuscripts and Archives, Yale University Library, and p. 152,
which is reprinted courtesy of Century Association Archives Foundation.

LIBRARY OF CONGRESS CATALOGING-IN-PUBLICATION DATA

Olson, Lynne.
Those angry days: Roosevelt, Lindbergh, and America's fight over World War II,
1939–1941 / by Lynne Olson.
p. cm.
Includes bibliographical references and index.
ISBN 978-1-4000-6974-3
eBook ISBN 978-0-679-60471-6
1. World War, 1939–1945—United States.   2. World War, 1939–1945—Diplomatic
history.   3. Roosevelt, Franklin D. (Franklin Delano), 1882–1945—Political and social
views.   4. Lindbergh, Charles A. (Charles Augustus), 1902–1974—Political
and social views.   5. Isolationism—United States—History—20th century.
6. Intervention (International law)—History—20th century.   7. United States—
Politics and government—1933–1945.   8. Political culture—United States—
History—20th century.   9. United States—Foreign relations—1933–1945.
10. United States—Military policy.   I. Title.
D753.O47 2013
940.53'10973—dc23   2012025381

Printed in the United States of America on acid-free paper

www.atrandom.com

9 8 7 6 5 4 3 2

Book design by Barbara M. Bachman

THOSE ANGRY DAYS

ROOSEVELT, LINDBERGH, AND AMERICA'S FIGHT OVER WORLD WAR II, 1939–1941

Lynne Olson

RANDOM HOUSE | NEW YORK

For Stan and Carly

Though historians have dealt with the policy issues, justice has not been done to the searing personal impact of those angry days.

—ARTHUR M. SCHLESINGER JR.

In a democracy, a politician is supposed to keep his ear to the ground. He is also supposed to look after the national welfare and to attempt to educate the people when, in his opinion, they are off base.

—JOHN F. KENNEDY

You can always count on Americans to do the right thing— after they've tried everything else.

—WINSTON CHURCHILL

CONTENTS

INTRODUCTION

===

On a soft April morning in 1939, Charles Lindbergh was summoned to the White House to meet President Franklin D. Roosevelt, arguably the only person in America who equaled him in fame. The images of the two men had been indelibly impressed on the nation's consciousness for years—Lindbergh, whose solo flight across the Atlantic in 1927 had mesmerized and inspired his countrymen, and Roosevelt, whose energetic, confident leadership had helped jolt a Depression-mired America back to life.

When Lindbergh was ushered into the Oval Office, he found FDR seated behind his desk. It was their first face-to-face encounter, but no one would have guessed that from the president's warm, familiar manner. Leaning forward to clasp Lindbergh's hand, Roosevelt welcomed him as if he were an old friend, asking him about his wife, Anne, who, the president noted, had been a high school classmate of FDR's daughter, Anna.

His head thrown back, with his trademark cigarette holder tilted rakishly upward, Roosevelt exuded charm, joie de vivre, and an unmistakable air of power and command. During his thirty-minute chat with Lindbergh, he gave no sign of the many grave problems weighing on his mind.

He was, in fact, in the midst of one of the greatest crises of his presidency. Europe was on the brink of war. The month before, Adolf Hitler had seized all of Czechoslovakia, violating the promise he had made at the 1938 Munich conference to cease his aggression against other countries. In response, Britain and France had promised to come to the aid of Poland, the next country on Germany's hit list, if it were invaded. Both Western nations, however, were desperately short of arms, a situation that FDR was trying to remedy. But he was faced with a dilemma. Thanks to the provisions of neutrality legislation passed by Congress a few years earlier, Britain and France would be barred from buying U.S. weapons once they declared war on Germany. As Roosevelt knew, his chances of persuading the House and Senate to repeal the arms ban were close to zero.

But he mentioned none of that in his conversation with Lindbergh. Nor, in the course of his genial banter, did he betray any hint of the considerable suspicion and distrust he felt for the younger man sitting opposite him. Five years before, Roosevelt and Lindbergh had engaged in what the writer Gore Vidal called a "*mano a mano* duel," in which the president emerged as the loser. FDR hated to lose, and his memories of the 1934 incident were still raw and bitter.

The clash had been prompted by Roosevelt's cancellation of airmail delivery contracts granted by his predecessor, Herbert Hoover, to the nation's largest airlines. Charging fraud and bribery in the contract process, Roosevelt directed the U.S. Army Air Corps to start delivering the mail. Lindbergh, who served as an adviser to one of the airlines, publicly criticized FDR for ending the contracts without giving the companies a chance to respond.

Less than seven years after his history-making flight, the thirty-two-year-old Lindbergh was the only person who could match the fifty-two-year-old president in national popularity. They were alike in other ways, too. Both were strong-willed, stubborn men who believed deeply in their own superiority and had a sense of being endowed with a special purpose. They were determined to do things their own way, were slow to acknowledge mistakes, and did not take well to criticism. Self-absorbed and emotionally detached, they insisted on being in control at all times. A friend and distant relative of FDR's once described him as having "a loveless quality, as if he were incapable of emotion." Of Lindbergh, a biographer wrote: "The people he called friend were mainly, to him, good, functional, temporary acquaintances. He seemed to have taken much more than he gave in the way of warmth and affection."

The conflict between the president and Lindbergh quickly became front-page news. A former airmail pilot himself, Lindbergh warned that Air Corps fliers had neither the experience nor the right type of instruments in their planes to take on the extremely hazardous job of delivering the mail, which often involved night flying in blizzards, heavy rain, and other extreme weather. To the administration's embarrassment, his assessment proved correct. In the four months that Army pilots flew the mail, there were sixty-six crashes, twelve deaths, and, as one writer put it, "untold humiliation" for the Air Corps and White House. On June 1, 1934, following rushed negotiations between the government and airlines to come up with new delivery agreements, the commercial companies resumed mail delivery.

For the first time in his year-old presidency, FDR found himself bested in the court of public opinion. According to the historian Arthur M. Schlesinger Jr., "the fight dented the myth of Roosevelt's invulnerability. It quickened the pace and intensity of criticism of the administration. . . . [It] also uncovered in Charles Lindbergh a man who perhaps appealed to more American hearts than anyone save Franklin Roosevelt."

The following year, Lindbergh took his family to live in England, then France. During his three-year stay in Europe, he made several highly publicized trips to Nazi Germany, where he inspected aircraft companies and air force bases—and made clear he thought that the German air force was invincible and that Britain and France must appease Hitler.

And now he was home, ostensibly to join General Henry "Hap" Arnold, head of the Air Corps, in an effort to build up America's own airpower as quickly as possible. But was he plotting something else? The last thing Roosevelt needed was a campaign to stir up public opposition to the idea of arms sales to Britain and France. He had invited Lindbergh to the White House to get a sense of the man, to try to figure out how much of a problem he might pose in the turbulent days to come.

During his session with Roosevelt, Lindbergh was well aware that the president was scrutinizing him closely. Writing later in his journal, he noted, "Roosevelt judges his man quickly and plays him cleverly." Although he thought FDR "a little too suave, too pleasant, too easy," Lindbergh still enjoyed the encounter. "There is no reason for any an-

Photographers swarm around Charles Lindbergh as he leaves the White House after a meeting with President Roosevelt in April 1939.

tagonism between us," he observed. "The air-mail situation is past." He would continue to work with the administration on ways to improve the nation's air defenses, but, he added, "I have a feeling that it may not be for long."

He was right. In early September, just five months later, Hitler invaded Poland, and Britain and France declared war on Germany. The following spring, German troops swept through Western Europe, vanquishing France and threatening Britain's survival. As unofficial leader and spokesman for America's isolationist movement, Lindbergh emerged as Franklin Roosevelt's most redoubtable adversary in what would become a brutal, no-holds-barred battle for the soul of the nation.

UNTIL MAY 1940, MOST Americans had viewed the war in Europe as if it were a movie—a drama that, while interesting to watch, had nothing to do with their own lives. But the shock of Germany's blitzkrieg demolished that belief. It forced the country to struggle with two crucial questions: Should it come to the aid of Britain, the last hope of freedom in Europe? Or should it go even further and enter the war?

For the next eighteen months, the debate over those issues raged throughout the nation, from the White House and halls of Congress to bars, beauty parlors, offices, and classrooms in the biggest of cities and smallest of towns. "The war was everywhere," one historian recalled. "It lay behind everything you said or did." Millions of Americans were swept up in the struggle, knowing that whatever its outcome, their lives were likely to be profoundly affected. At stake was not only the survival of Britain but the shape and future of America.

What was the United States to be? A fortress country that refused to break out of its isolationist shell, still clinging to the belief that it could survive and thrive only if it were free from entangling foreign commitments? The adherents to that view pointed to the aftermath of World War I as proof of its validity. We had been tricked, they argued, into coming to the aid of Britain and France in 1917, thereby losing more than fifty thousand of our young men and providing our allies with loans that were never repaid. We were supposedly making the world safe for democracy, but in fact democracy had cravenly given way to Adolf Hitler. Britain, France, and the rest of Western Europe had repeatedly demonstrated an inability to settle their own disputes. If those countries refused to stop Hitler when they could have, why should we bail them out again? We must be ready to fight for the defense of our own nation, but for nothing and no one else.

For their part, those who argued for U.S. intervention maintained that America could no longer evade international responsibility: the times were too dire. Britain's survival was absolutely essential for our security and welfare. If the British were defeated and Hitler controlled all of Europe, he would then move to dominate Africa and infiltrate South America, thus posing a serious threat to the United States. America, the interventionists argued, would have little chance to survive as a free, democratic society.

Others in the interventionist camp emphasized what they viewed as America's moral obligation to stop Hitler—the embodiment, as they saw it, of pure evil. How could we stand on the sidelines, they argued, while Nazi Germany enslaved sovereign countries, went on a rampage against Jews, and threatened to wipe out Western civilization as we know it?

The passions engendered by the debate were as high as its stakes. The CBS correspondent Eric Sevareid remembered the period as "bitter" and "heart-burning." Arthur Schlesinger said the dispute was "the most savage political debate in my lifetime." He added: "There have been a number of fierce national quarrels—over communism in the later Forties, over McCarthyism in the Fifties, over Vietnam in the Sixties—but none so tore apart families and friendships as this fight."

One of the families most deeply affected was that of Lindbergh's wife, Anne, whose mother was an outspoken advocate for American involvement in the war and whose brother-in-law, a Welshman named Aubrey Morgan, happened to be one of the British government's top propagandists in the United States. While Anne Morrow Lindbergh supported her husband in his isolationism, her sister, Constance Morrow Morgan, worked with *her* husband in New York attempting to sway American public opinion in favor of Winston Churchill and the British.

AS MOMENTOUS AS IT WAS, the passionate prewar battle over America's destiny has largely disappeared from the national memory. "The intense feelings and bitter conflicts of the time were engulfed in the vast events which followed Pearl Harbor," Anne Lindbergh noted decades later. "Today, hardly anyone gives much thought to what was once called 'the Great Debate.'"

Certainly, little has been written that brings to life this suspenseful, tumultuous, and vital period in U.S. history, with its host of colorful, larger-than-life characters. "Though historians have dealt with the policy issues," Arthur Schlesinger wrote, "justice has not been done to the searing personal impact of those angry days." General George Marshall, who became Army chief of staff on the day Hitler invaded Poland, observed to his official biographer: "People have forgotten the great hostility of that time."

Marshall, like many others in Washington, found himself intimately involved in the dispute. Throughout the period, the nation's capital was a nest of intrigue and infighting. In early 1941, a harsh debate between isolationist and interventionist congressmen ended in an unseemly brawl on the floor of the House. On the lawn outside the Capitol, demonstrators threw a rope around a tree branch to hang the straw-stuffed effigy of a senator who favored aid for Britain. The wife of a Washington columnist who endorsed such aid received a package in the mail one morning. Opening it, she found a tiny black coffin containing a paper skeleton. The skeleton was labeled "Your husband."

The upper reaches of the Roosevelt administration, including the president's cabinet, were also riven with deep divisions about which direction the country should take. Many high-ranking officers in the Army, Navy, and Air Corps fiercely opposed FDR and his proposals to help the British. Convinced that America should stay clear of the war, a number of them worked to sabotage the policies of their commander in chief, leaking top-secret information to isolationist members of Congress and to Lindbergh and other key leaders in the antiwar movement. Just before Pearl Harbor, Hap Arnold, the Air Corps chief of staff, was implicated in the leak of one of the administration's most closely guarded military secrets—a contingency plan for all-out war against Germany.

George Marshall would later say that he had been frequently approached during this time by subordinates who wanted him "to take open action contrary to the administration." Marshall, who believed strongly in civilian control over the military, never did so. Nonetheless, his role in the pre–Pearl Harbor struggle was far more complex than has been commonly portrayed. Focused on transforming an emaciated U.S. army into a powerful force, the man who is widely—and rightly—regarded as the country's greatest military figure in World War II was hostile to the idea of sharing with the British the few modern military resources America then possessed. And until late 1941, he disapproved of U.S. entry into the conflict. While Marshall himself never openly rebelled against FDR's policies, he supported and protected those on his staff who did.

The president, meanwhile, was hardly a passive bystander in the struggle. In September 1939, he told an associate that it was going to be "a dirty fight." His prediction was accurate, of course, and he played a major role in making it so. Convinced that the isolationists, particularly Lindbergh, posed a major threat to the country and himself, Roosevelt and his supporters, assisted by a covert British intelligence operation, embarked on a campaign to destroy their credibility, influence, and reputations. As part of that effort, FDR authorized FBI investigations of his political opponents, who were branded by administration spokesmen and much of the press as subversives, fifth columnists, and even Nazis. In return, his foes portrayed Roosevelt as a dictator who had destroyed free speech in America and was rushing it into war without the consent of the people. According to Lindbergh, democracy "doesn't exist today, even in our own country."

That image of the president as a sinister "super-Machiavelli," intent on ramrodding America into the conflict by insidious and unlawful means, doesn't hold up. But neither does the more beneficent idea, put forward by many historians, that Roosevelt, knowing full well that America must enter the war but hamstrung by strong isolationist public opinion until Pearl Harbor, had no alternative but to edge the country toward intervention by indirect and often devious methods.

In fact, by December 1941, the American people had been thoroughly educated about the pros and cons of their country's entry into the conflict and were far less opposed to the idea of going to war than conventional wisdom has it. And it's far from clear that Roosevelt himself, while certainly determined to help Britain, ever intended that America go to war, at least in the sense of sending troops. Indeed, there is ample evidence, as the historians William Langer and S. Everett Gleason noted, that the president "recoiled from the prospect of war, was determined to spare no effort to keep this nation out of it, and devoutly hoped that, by one means or another, he would succeed."

Although FDR exhibited bold leadership in the first years of his presidency and again after America was catapulted into the war, he was notably cautious and hesitant in the two years before the Japanese attack on American soil. Eloquent and forceful in his repeated calls for action to help Britain and end German aggression, he often procrastinated in making such action a reality. He was intimidated by congressional isolationists, whose strength he tended to exaggerate, and was loath to challenge them.

George Marshall later remarked that from 1939 to 1941, he had doubted the president's ability to lead America in a national emergency. Observing FDR's swift, decisive actions following Pearl Harbor, Marshall finally concluded that his commander in chief was in fact a great leader. "I hadn't thought so before," the Army chief of staff said. "He wasn't always clear cut in his decisions. He could be swayed."

This vacuum of leadership at the top was filled, to a large extent, by several private citizens' groups, which mounted campaigns—some of them quietly encouraged by the president—to educate and mobilize American public opinion in favor of intervention. The work of these organizations, according to one prominent interventionist, allowed Roosevelt to "move gingerly in the direction of saving his sleeping country."

One of the most striking—and unsung—aspects of the fight over U.S. involvement in the war is the critical role played by ordinary Americans in its development and outcome. Millions of individuals, convinced that the survival of their country was at stake, became involved in the debate, which, for all its anger and mudslinging, was a true exercise in democracy. Grassroots activism flourished throughout the nation as volunteers on both sides circulated petitions, phoned their neighbors, ran ads, and lobbied their congressmen.

These citizens' movements would have a considerable impact on U.S. foreign policy and ultimately on the course of the war itself. At Yale, antiwar college students—among them a future U.S. president, the first head of the Peace Corps, and a Supreme Court justice—founded the America First Committee, which would fast become the nation's most influential isolationist organization. Interventionist groups, for their part, played a critical role in the administration's controversial decision to send fifty old destroyers to Britain in exchange for the lease to America of British bases in the Western Hemisphere. Interventionists also helped persuade Roosevelt to make fateful changes in his cabinet, and they were the chief force in persuading a highly dubious Congress in the summer of 1940 to approve the first peacetime draft.

Two months before the draft bill was passed, a coalition of political amateurs hijacked the largely isolationist Republican Party and, at one of the most exciting conventions in American history, engineered the presidential nomination of Wendell Willkie, a dark-horse interventionist who had announced his candidacy only seven weeks before. Although Willkie would turn out to be the strongest opponent FDR ever faced in his political career, the president called the Republican's nomination a "godsend for the country" because it removed the war as a campaign issue and signaled to the world that America's top political leaders stood together against Axis aggression.

Thanks in large part to these efforts by private citizens, the American people were made aware of the need to ready themselves, both militarily and psychologically, for the looming war. By the time of Pearl Harbor, attitudes toward entering the war had shifted dramatically. According to polls, a substantial majority of the U.S. population now regarded "defeating Nazism" as "the biggest job facing their country"; a similar majority preferred U.S. entry into the war to a German victory over Britain.

After all the bitter conflict of the previous two years, America was finally ready to claim its future.

THOSE ANGRY DAYS

CHAPTER 1

"A MODERN GALAHAD"

The cab stopped in front of the Smithsonian's Arts and Industries Building and Charles Lindbergh stepped out. He stared for a moment at the Victorian-era museum, with its turrets and multicolored brick facade, then strolled around its perimeter, hoping to find a side door. Seeing none, he returned to the front entrance, considering how to slip past the tourists outside without being recognized.

By now, avoiding public attention was as natural to Lindbergh as breathing. He put his head down, covered his nose with a handkerchief, blew into it—and walked into the museum unnoticed. Once inside, he ducked into the first room on the right, which featured a display of dresses worn by the nation's First Ladies, and stationed himself by the salmon-pink silk gown that once belonged to Martha Washington. From there he had a perfect view of the *Spirit of St. Louis,* hanging from the ceiling in the main hall.

It was March 1940, and Europe was at war. Lindbergh was at the epicenter of the struggle over America's role in the conflict. But for almost an hour that day, he took time out from the frenzy of the present to find refuge in the past. Lost in reverie, the lanky blond aviator gazed at the *Spirit of St. Louis,* suspended by cables above the tourists staring up at it. He had long felt a mystical closeness to this tiny silver plane. When he landed in Paris on May 21, 1927, at the end of the first solo transatlantic flight in history, his first thought had been how to protect it from the hordes of frenzied Frenchmen racing across the field to greet him.

To Lindbergh, the *Spirit* was "a living creature," with whom he had shared a transcendent experience and whose loyalty to him was unquestioned. In his mind, they were inseparably linked: he always referred to the plane and himself as "we." (Indeed, *We* was the title of the first of two books he wrote about the flight.) More than once in recent years, he dreamed he had crept into the Smithsonian at night, cut the *Spirit* down, transported it to an airstrip, and taken off. Once aloft— away from his troubled, complicated life—he experienced nothing but joy. He could ride the sky "like a god . . . I could dive at a peak; I could touch a cloud; I could climb far above them all. This hour was mine, free of the earth."

A supremely rational, practical man by nature, he was unexpectedly lyrical, even fanciful, when he later described his visit to the Smithsonian in his journal. He noted the kinship he felt with the mannequin representing Martha Washington as they studied the *Spirit* together: "I rather envied her the constant intimacy with the plane that I once had."

But then, he wrote, he suddenly noticed two young women staring at him. He was well acquainted with that look. Not quite certain it was him, they soon would come closer to find out. Up to that point, it had been a wonderful visit: just him, Martha, and the *Spirit of St. Louis*. Determined to preserve the enchantment of the moment, he spun around and walked out.

WHEN THE TWENTY-FIVE-YEAR-OLD Lindbergh touched down at Paris's Le Bourget airfield on that late spring evening in 1927, there was so much awaiting him, his wife later observed: "Fame—Opportunity— Wealth, and also tragedy & loneliness & frustration. . . . And he so innocent & unaware." Several decades after the flight, the Lindberghs' daughter Reeve mused: "Sometimes . . . I wonder whether he would have turned back if he'd known the life he was headed for."

Although his flight had attracted considerable attention even before he'd taken off, Lindbergh was convinced that any fame that followed would swiftly vanish. Soon after he arrived in France, he presented letters of introduction to Myron Herrick, the U.S. ambassador, unsure

Charles Lindbergh and the Spirit of St. Louis.

whether Herrick even knew who he was. He had no inkling of the remarkable international response to what had been, in essence, a stunt flight—a stunt that the press and public, especially in America, had transformed into something infinitely more.

The New York *Evening World,* for example, had made the astonishing declaration that Lindbergh had performed "the greatest feat of a solitary man in the records of the human race." The day after the flight, the usually staid *New York Times*, under the banner headline LINDBERGH DOES IT!, devoted its entire front page and four more pages inside to stories about the young airman and his triumph.

In hindsight, the reason for the extraordinary reaction was clear: America, nearing the end of a decade marked by cynicism, disillusionment, and political apathy, badly needed a hero. As one historian put it, Lindbergh became "a modern Galahad for a generation which had forsworn Galahads."

The 1920s in America had been a feverish time, noted for government corruption and graft, a spectacular boom in the stock market, organized crime on an unprecedented scale, a widespread rebellion against convention, the loss of idealism, and an emphasis on enjoying oneself. All this was fodder for the country's booming mass-circulation tabloid newspapers, which specialized in prodigious coverage of the latest national sensation, be it a murder trial, a heavyweight boxing match, or a dramatic but failed attempt to rescue a man lost in a Kentucky cave. Under heavy competitive pressure, the other, more respectable newspapers more often than not followed the tabloids' lead, as did the national magazines and a mass media newcomer called radio.

In early 1927, the media, insatiable as ever, had shifted their focus to the $25,000 prize offered by Raymond Orteig, a wealthy French-born businessman living in Manhattan, to whoever made the first nonstop flight from New York to Paris (or vice versa). Although several airmen had already failed—and died—in the attempt, a new crop of aviators had recently announced plans to enter the competition. Most were well known, with expensive, technologically advanced planes, considerable outside financial backing, and armies of assistants, including staffers whose sole job was to publicize their bosses' participation. And then there was Charles Lindbergh, an unknown, virtually penniless airmail pilot from Minnesota who managed to scrounge just enough funds from a group of St. Louis businessmen to finance the construction of a stripped-down little plane he named *Spirit of St. Louis,* in honor of his benefactors.

To aviation experts, Lindbergh's plan appeared more than quixotic; it seemed suicidal. Never having flown over any large body of water before, he would now try to cross the Atlantic, steering by the stars, a method of navigation relatively unfamiliar to him. He would carry neither parachute nor radio. Even more foolhardy, he planned to make the thirty-three-plus-hour flight alone. No one had ever attempted such a hazardous journey solo; as one wit noted, not even Columbus had sailed by himself. Lloyd's of London, which issued odds on virtually any enterprise, regardless of its danger, refused to do so for Lindbergh's venture. "The underwriters believe the risk is too great," a Lloyd's spokesman declared.

America has always loved an underdog, especially one as polite, unassuming, self-disciplined, and boyishly handsome as Lindbergh—a stark contrast to the bootleggers, gangsters, playboys, arrogant bankers, dizzy flappers, and corrupt government officials who made up a sizable percentage of the era's top newsmakers. It was not surprising, then, that when he took off from Long Island's rain-slick Roosevelt Field in the early morning of May 20, 1927, the entire nation anxiously followed his progress. Newspapers throughout the country printed extra editions, and radio broadcasts issued frequent flash bulletins. During a prizefight at Yankee Stadium, forty thousand people, at the urging of the announcer, rose as one and prayed silently for the young flier. In his May 21 newspaper column, the humorist Will Rogers wrote: "No attempt at jokes today. A slim, tall, bashful, smiling American boy is somewhere over the middle of the Atlantic Ocean, where no lone human being has ever ventured before."

When word came that Lindbergh had made it, America went mad. "We measure heroes as we do ships, by their displacement," said Charles Evans Hughes, soon to be chief justice of the U.S. Supreme Court. "Colonel Lindbergh has displaced everything." President Coolidge dispatched an admiral's flagship to Europe to bring Lindbergh and the *Spirit* home. In Washington, the president presented him with the Congressional Medal of Honor and Distinguished Flying Cross. In New York, more than four million people—75 percent of the city's population—lined its streets to honor Lindbergh in the biggest ticker-tape parade in New York's history. A few months later, *Time* magazine named him its first "Man of the Year."

After his tumultuous homecoming, Lindbergh spent three months touring all forty-eight states in the *Spirit*. An estimated thirty million people flocked to see this new national idol, labeled a "demigod" by one newspaperman; wherever he appeared, huge crowds fought to get near him. Intensely uncomfortable with the adulation, Lindbergh sought to use his fame to increase public interest in commercial aviation. Instead of accepting the millions of dollars he was offered to endorse products or appear in movies, he became a technical adviser to two start-up airlines—Pan American Airways and TAT, which eventually became Transcontinental and Western Air and ultimately Trans World Airlines (TWA). Working with both to help establish passenger service, he flew all over the country and later the world, surveying possible air routes, testing planes, and playing a key role in creating the first modern airports.

Try as he might, however, this intensely reserved, solitary man was unable to reclaim his privacy and restore equilibrium to his life. His engaging modesty, coupled with his refusal to capitalize financially on his celebrity, only whetted his countrymen's appetite for more information about him. "In his flight, and even more in his fame, he proved that personal heroism, decency, and dignity were yet possible in the world," wrote Kenneth S. Davis, a Lindbergh biographer. Americans were in no mood to leave such a paragon alone, and neither was the press.

Wherever he went, he was besieged. Strangers came up to him to shake his hand or pat him on the back, women tried to kiss him, crowds gathered in hotel lobbies and outside restaurants, waiting for him to appear. At a picnic he attended with members of his National Guard unit in St. Louis, he watched with disgust as several young women crept under a restraining rope to grab corncobs he had just chewed on.

The furor only increased when, in May 1929, he married Anne Morrow, the shy, pretty twenty-two-year-old daughter of the U.S. ambassador to Mexico. The Lindberghs were stalked everywhere by the public and press, even on their boating honeymoon off the coast of Maine, where they were followed by motor launches filled with reporters and photographers. "Like criminals or illicit lovers, we avoided being seen in the world together," Anne Lindbergh later wrote, "and had to forgo the everyday pleasures of walking along streets, shopping, sightseeing, eating out at restaurants."

A loner all his life, Lindbergh was singularly unprepared for all this. The only child of a small-town Minnesota lawyer and his schoolteacher wife, he had lived an isolated, rootless existence since early childhood. When he was four, his father, a stern man with a strong populist bent, was elected to Congress, and for the next ten years, Charles shuttled back and forth between Washington and the family farm near Little Falls, Minnesota.

His parents had an extremely unhappy marriage, punctuated by violent quarrels, and Charles responded by rigidly controlling his emotions and withdrawing into his own solitary world. In school, he had virtually no friends, took part in no sports or extracurricular activities, was silent in class, and did not date. After his flight to Paris, his high school classmates, when questioned by reporters, had few if any memories of him.

As an acquaintance of Lindbergh's later put it, his historic achievement and its aftermath plunged him "into waters that he did not understand and could not navigate." He adamantly resisted the idea that he and his wife were public property. While he readily answered que-

Anne Morrow Lindbergh with her newborn son, Charles Jr., who was kidnapped and killed in March 1932.

ries from reporters about his flights and aviation in general, he curtly turned aside any questions about his personal life and refused to sign autographs or pose for photos. His recalcitrance only fanned the publicity flames. "Because he kept a distance," *Time* noted, "the public became more hysterical."

As a result, the Lindberghs lived under constant siege at their secluded home, set in several acres of woods near Hopewell, New Jersey. Tabloid reporters went through the Lindberghs' garbage, pilfered their mail, and offered bribes to their servants for tidbits about their private lives. One journalist even applied for a servant's job with the couple, presenting them with forged references.

Then, on the evening of March 1, 1932, harassment gave way to tragedy: the Lindberghs' twenty-month-old son, Charles Jr.—known as Charlie—was kidnapped from his nursery while his parents were having dinner downstairs. Two months later, the toddler's body was found in the woods near the Lindberghs' home. H. L. Mencken called the kidnapping the biggest story "since the Resurrection," and the extraordinary media frenzy that followed seemed to prove his point.

The grieving Lindberghs were convinced that the excesses of the press were responsible for their son's abduction and murder. "If it were not for the publicity that surrounds us, we might still have him," Anne bitterly wrote in her diary. Even before the tragedy, Lindbergh had come to hate the mass-circulation newspapers, viewing them as "a personification of malice, which deliberately urged on the crazy mob." That conviction was only strengthened when two news photographers broke into the morgue where his son's body lay, opened the casket, and took pictures of Charlie's remains.

The media circus surrounding the kidnapping continued for another four years, with millions of words and photos devoted to the lengthy investigation of the crime, the arrest, trial, and conviction of a German-born carpenter named Bruno Richard Hauptmann, and Hauptmann's eventual execution in April 1936. For much of that period, the Lindberghs took refuge at the Englewood, New Jersey, estate of Anne's widowed mother, Elizabeth Morrow.

Five months after Charlie's death, the couple's second son, Jon, was born. When Hauptmann was convicted, the Lindberghs received so many letters threatening Jon's life that armed guards were hired to keep a twenty-four-hour watch outside the Morrow home. Several intruders, including an escaped mental patient, were caught approaching the house at various times.

A few months after the Hauptmann trial, three-year-old Jon, accompanied by a teacher, was on his way home from preschool when the car in which he was riding was forced off the road by another vehicle. Several men holding press cameras jumped out of it and ran toward the car containing Jon, taking flash photos of the terrified little boy as they came near.

After this latest press outrage, Charles Lindbergh decided that he and his family had no alternative but to leave America. "Between the . . . tabloid press and the criminal, a condition exists which is intolerable for us," he wrote his mother. A few days before his departure, Lindbergh told a close friend that "we Americans are a primitive people. We do not have discipline. Our moral standards are low. . . . It shows in the newspapers, the morbid curiosity over crimes and murder trials. Americans seem to have little respect for law, or the rights of others." It was not the first time—or the last—that he would equate his personal situation with the current state of American democracy.

The murder of his son, along with the disgraceful behavior of the media, left Lindbergh with a psychological wound that would never heal. Reeve Lindbergh, who was born thirteen years after the death of her eldest brother, recalled that her father never talked about him. The pain, she believed, was too overwhelming. "I can imagine how much this baby must have meant to my father, who had been raised as an only child . . . this Charles, this namesake," she wrote. "I know that the loss was immeasurable and unspeakable."

One day, after piloting a small plane through a violent thunderstorm, Lindbergh turned with a smile to his shaken wife, who had been in the plane with him, and said: "You should have faith in me." Then the smile faded. "I have faith in you," he said. "I just don't have any more faith in life."

Shortly before midnight on December 21, 1935, the Lindberghs were driven to a deserted dock in Manhattan and spirited aboard an American freighter bound for England. Before leaving, Lindbergh gave an interview to a reporter for *The New York Times,* one of the few news outlets he still respected. The day after the Lindberghs' departure, the *Times,* in a story that took up much of the front page, described for its readers how "the man who eight years ago was hailed as an international hero . . . is taking his wife and son to establish, if he can, a secure haven for them in a foreign land."

In the English countryside, the Lindberghs did indeed find the privacy they craved. For slightly more than two years, they rented Long Barn, a rambling old half-timbered house in Kent owned by Harold Nicolson—a member of Parliament, ex-diplomat, and author, who had written a biography of Anne's father, Dwight Morrow—and Nicolson's wife, the novelist Vita Sackville-West. During that time, the Lindberghs' third son, Land, was born.

In her diary, Anne observed that the years spent at Long Barn were among the happiest of her life. For the most part, the English press and public left the Lindberghs alone. Jon could play in Long Barn's extensive terraced gardens and roam the meadows beyond without an armed guard shadowing him. Anne and Charles, meanwhile, could take a drive through the countryside with "a wonderful feeling of freedom, [knowing] that we can stop anywhere, that we will not be followed or noticed."

In the summer of 1938, the Lindberghs moved from Long Barn to an old stone manor house on the tiny, windswept island of Illiec, off the coast of Brittany. "I have never seen a place where I wanted to live so much," Lindbergh confided to his journal. Considerably more isolated than Kent, Illiec proved to be another refuge for him and his wife.

WHILE BRITAIN AND FRANCE might have been havens of safety for the Lindberghs, those countries' own security was in the gravest peril during that time. Fascist Italy and Nazi Germany were on the march, and the threat of another war drew relentlessly closer. Two months before the Lindberghs sailed for England, Italian forces invaded the East African country of Abyssinia. Five months after that, Germany occupied the demilitarized Rhineland—a flagrant violation of the Versailles Treaty and a defiant challenge to Britain and France, its chief European adversaries in World War I. Neither country lifted a finger to stop the incursions, nor did the League of Nations, which from its creation in 1919 had consistently failed to confront aggressors and keep the peace. How could it be otherwise, considering that the United States had refused to join the League, Germany withdrew after Hitler came to power, and Britain, the League's leading member, had slashed its armed forces and armaments as soon as the war was over?

When Hitler annexed Austria in March 1938 and thousands of Austrian Jews were arrested and sent to concentration camps, the British and French governments once again turned a blind eye. France was not quite so accommodating, however, when it came to the Führer's next target, Czechoslovakia: the French were bound by treaty to come to Czechoslovakia's aid in the event of a confrontation with Germany.

But the British had no such treaty obligations. Knowing how pathetically small his armed forces were, British prime minister Neville Chamberlain was determined to remain on good terms with Hitler and find a peaceful solution to the Czech problem. After four years of half-hearted rearmament (consisting mostly of the development and production of fighter planes), Britain still had no army worthy of the name, no modern bombers in production, and virtually no stockpiling of essential supplies and raw materials. "It would be murder to send our forces overseas to fight against a first-class power," the chief of the Imperial General Staff informed the prime minister.

In late September 1938, Chamberlain and French president Édouard Daladier, at a meeting with Hitler in Munich, surrendered to the German leader a huge chunk of Czechoslovakia—the Sudetenland—along with its vital fortifications and major centers of industry. Enraged by the sellout, Winston Churchill, the leading foe of Chamberlain's appeasement policy, called it "the grossest act of bullying treachery since Benedict Arnold."

NOTWITHSTANDING CHARLES LINDBERGH'S longing for privacy, he began to play an increasingly public role during this period. He was invited by officials in Britain, France, and Germany to inspect their aircraft factories and other aviation facilities. What he saw convinced him that neither Britain nor France had the spirit or capability to fight a modern war against the Germans. And by underscoring British and French deficiencies in airpower and exaggerating German achievements, he unwittingly helped to encourage the capitulation to Hitler at Munich.

As Lindbergh observed, France's government and people were riven

by feuds and factions, and its cities were in disrepair. Political corruption and labor unrest were endemic, as was a strong streak of apathy
and cynicism. The British, for their part, were passé, Lindbergh
thought: they "had never adjusted themselves to the tempo of this
modern era. Their minds were still attuned to the speed of sail rather
than to that of aircraft." He wrote in his journal: "I cannot see the future for this country. . . . Aviation has largely destroyed the security of
the Channel, and [Britain's] superiority of manufacture is a thing
of the past."

Although grateful to Britain for providing a haven for his family, he
was exasperated by what he saw as its mediocrity, inefficiency, and
complacency. Even the British penchant for drinking tea drew his ire.
"The whole idea seems a little effeminate to me," he noted shortly
after arriving in England. "It is hard to explain why, except that I grew
up with that idea. I thought tea was only for society women and 'Eastern dudes.'" Later he would write: "It is necessary to realize that England is a country composed of a great mass of slow, somewhat stupid
and indifferent people, and a small group of geniuses. It is the latter to
whom the empire and its reputation are due."

Lindbergh, however, made these pronouncements without really
knowing the British. Indeed, for most of their lives, Charles and Anne
Lindbergh had very few dealings with ordinary people, a situation that
Anne lamented in later years. Sequestered as they were at Long Barn in
the mid-1930s, they made the acquaintance of only a small number of
Britons. When they did socialize, it was usually with those in upper-
crust social and political circles—aristocrats, higher-ups in Chamberlain's government, the royal family, and prominent businessmen—most
of whom were appeasement-minded and pro-German. These Britons
believed that the Germans had been badly treated by the Allies after
World War I and that a strong Germany, Nazi or not, was necessary as
a counterweight to the Communist Soviet Union. (One person with
whom Lindbergh definitely did not fraternize was Winston Churchill,
who would later declare about his countrymen: "The British have always been the biggest damn fools in the world. They are too easygoing
to prepare [for war]. Then at the last minute, they hurry around and
scrape together and fight like hell.")

While convinced that Britain's glory days were over, Lindbergh was
sure that Germany's had just begun. At the invitation of Colonel Tru-

Charles Lindbergh with German officials in Berlin. On the right is Colonel Truman Smith, the U.S. military attaché in Germany.

man Smith, the American military attaché in Berlin, he had spent considerable time in that country from 1936 to 1938, gathering information about the German air force.

A Yale graduate who spoke fluent German, Smith was considered one of the U.S. Army's foremost experts on Germany. During an earlier posting there in the early 1920s, he had been the first American official to interview Adolf Hitler, then an obscure political agitator in Munich. While most foreign observers at the time regarded Hitler as an inconsequential rabble-rouser, Smith believed that the future Führer, whom he described as "fanatical" and "a marvelous demagogue," had struck a chord with the German people, still bitter and resentful after their country's defeat in the Great War. Smith was convinced, he told his superiors, that Hitler and his newly formed National Socialist Party were "already a potential if not immediate danger to the German republic."

Reassigned to Berlin in 1935, Smith kept close tabs on Germany's explosive military expansion, which was in direct contravention of the Versailles Treaty. But while he was able to collect relatively up-to-date facts and figures about the German army's size, armaments, and commanders, he knew little about aviation matters and lacked good intelligence about the equally massive buildup of the Luftwaffe.

Smith figured that Luftwaffe chief Hermann Goering would leap at the chance to show off his prized air force to the world-famous Charles Lindbergh. That turned out to be true. When Smith, on behalf of Goering, asked Lindbergh to come to Germany in 1936, he sweetened the invitation with the promise that "the strictest censorship would be imposed by the German Air Ministry with respect to your visit." (The pledge was not strictly kept; reporters and photographers were allowed to photograph Lindbergh and attend his public events in Germany but were not permitted to interview him.)

During that trip, as well as on several subsequent visits, Goering and his subordinates gave Lindbergh an effusive welcome, unveiling their latest-model bombers and fighters, taking him on tours of bustling aircraft plants around the country, and staging demonstrations of aerial diving and precision bombing. As the Germans hoped, Lindbergh was thoroughly impressed by what he considered the Reich's overwhelming airpower. Many years later, Anne Lindbergh would acknowledge: "There is no doubt that Goering did 'use' [my husband] to

Charles and Anne Lindbergh with Luftwaffe chief Hermann Goering in Berlin.

show off his air production, anticipating that stories of its strength would spread abroad and delay opposition to Hitler's aggressive program."

In his reports, which were passed on to the U.S., British, and French governments, Lindbergh concluded that German military aircraft were greatly superior in both quality and quantity to those of any other European country, or, for that matter, the United States. Furthermore, he warned, "Germany now has the means of destroying London, Paris and Prague if she wishes to do so. England and France together have not enough modern war planes for effective defense or counter-attack."

But there were serious flaws in Lindbergh's findings, as Truman Smith would later acknowledge. Lindbergh did not know—and as a result, the reports failed to mention—that the superiority of the Luftwaffe in the late 1930s lay solely in its ability to support German ground forces in attacks confined to the European continent. It had not yet developed a long-range bomber fleet with the capacity to launch raids on London (or any other distant target) from Germany. Indeed, Goering had been informed by his subordinates in late 1937 that none of the Luftwaffe's bombers or fighters could "operate meaningfully" over England. "Given our present means," Goering was told, "we can hope at best for a nuisance effect. . . . A war of annihilation against Britain appears to be out of the question."

Lindbergh's omission of that key point served to support the conviction—and fear—of the British government and people that "the bomber will always get through." For years, the country's top leaders had been warning their compatriots that in any future war, massive bombing attacks would decimate the nation in a matter of days.

While the American's gloomy findings were not a major factor in Chamberlain's decision to appease Hitler at Munich, they certainly bolstered the British leader's belief that Germany's air strength was prohibitively strong and that it was far better to give Hitler what he wanted in Czechoslovakia than to be pitchforked into a war Britain was not ready for. The French, more strongly influenced by Lindbergh's assessment, came to the same conclusion. Shortly before the Munich conference, the deputy chief of the French general staff declared that if the Sudetenland were not surrendered to Hitler, "French cities would be laid in ruins, [with] no means of defense."

The British military attaché in Paris, who was clearly skeptical of Lindbergh's report, wrote his superiors: "The Fuhrer has found a most convenient ambassador in Colonel Lindbergh, who appears to have given the French an impression of [German] might and preparedness which they did not have before." In the view of Group Captain John Slessor, director of plans for the British air staff, Lindbergh, while "extremely likable" and "transparently honest and sincere," was "a striking example of the effect of German propaganda." The American airman had told him, Slessor noted in his journal, that "our only sound policy [was] to avoid war now at almost any cost."

Lindbergh's impressions of Germany's military strength were undoubtedly colored by his personal affinity for the Germans, an attitude in sharp contrast to his feelings about the British and French. "All his life he had had to depend on absolute accuracy and complete expertise; nothing could be left to chance," a friend once noted. "Everything in his view of life had to be calculated and tidy. He could neither tolerate nor understand an amateur approach to anything." As Lindbergh viewed the situation in the late 1930s, the British and French were amateurs in aviation and other military matters, while the Germans were experts whose efficiency and perfectionist attitude rivaled his own. "I cannot help liking the Germans," he wrote in his journal in March 1938. "They are like [Americans]. We should be working with them and not constantly crossing swords. If we fight, our countries will only lose their best men. We can gain nothing. . . . It must not happen."

Both he and Anne, who accompanied him on his trips to Germany, greatly admired what they saw as the vitality of the country, its youth and vigor, its "refusal to admit that anything was impossible or that any obstacle was too much to be overcome"—so different from the spirit in France and Britain. Germany seemed prosperous, orderly, and bustling, with "a sense of festivity" and "no sense of poverty."

What Lindbergh valued most about his visits, however, was the Germans' respect for his privacy. "For twelve years I found little freedom in [America], the country which is supposed to exemplify freedom," he mused in his journal. "I did not find real freedom until I came to Europe. The strange thing is that of all the European countries, I found the most personal freedom in Germany, with England next, and then France." There was seemingly little consideration of the fact that in a dictatorship like the Third Reich, which had extinguished all dissent and crushed all opposition, no German would have been foolish enough to violate the privacy of an official guest of the state. Lindbergh's freedom, in other words, had come at the expense of the liberty of others.

The Lindberghs' knowledge and understanding of Germany were, to put it mildly, superficial. They had no chance to observe what was really going on in the country; they saw what the Nazis wanted them to see. Neither spoke or read German. Almost all their dealings were with German officials and military men. They didn't mix with ordinary Germans, and they certainly were given no opportunity to witness firsthand the regime's increasingly vicious persecution of Jews.

A dispassionate man who simplified virtually every problem he faced and who never gave much thought to the complexities of human nature, Lindbergh resolutely shut his eyes to what columnist Walter Lippmann called "the ice-cold evil" of Hitler's dictatorship. Lindbergh would later write: "I shared the repulsion that democratic peoples felt in viewing the demagoguery of Hitler, the controlled elections, the secret police. Yet I felt that I was seeing in Germany, despite the crudeness of its form, the inevitable alternative to decline." To a friend, he observed that while the Führer was clearly a fanatic, he was also "undoubtedly a great man, and I believe has done much for the German people. . . . [He] has accomplished results (good in addition to bad), which could hardly have been accomplished without some fanaticism."

Described by one journalist as a "hypersensitive man who was insensitive to others," Lindbergh was similarly detached in his response to reports of the Nazis' mounting savagery to the Jews. When he learned about Kristallnacht, the brutal Gestapo-led pogrom in November 1938 that resulted in the murder of hundreds of German Jews and the vandalizing and burning of countless synagogues, homes, and businesses, all he did was question Nazi stupidity. "I do not understand these riots on the part of the Germans," he wrote. "It seems so contrary to their sense of order and intelligence in other ways. They have undoubtedly had a difficult Jewish problem, but why is it necessary to handle it so unreasonably? My admiration for the Germans is constantly being dashed against some rock such as this." Speculating about the reasons for Lindbergh's lack of empathy for Hitler's victims, an acquaintance commented: "Perhaps it is because he has been cut off for so long from common people, that he is incapable of being outraged by their degradation under fascism."

Uninterested in moral questions, Lindbergh believed that France and England had no choice but to come to terms with Germany, no matter how distasteful those terms might be. "If England and Germany enter another major war on opposite sides," he declared, "Western civilization may fall as a result," leaving the door open for incursions by the Soviet Union and Communism.

In the United States, meanwhile, news of Lindbergh's visits to the Reich had begun to erode the sympathy and admiration still felt for him by much of the American public. The playwright and literary critic Wolcott Gibbs acidly wrote in *The New Yorker* that Lindbergh "has, if any man ever had, a reason to hate democracy and admire a system that can protect privacy just as efficiently as it can destroy life and hope."

When Goering presented Lindbergh with a medal on October 18, 1938, just three weeks after the Munich agreement, the attacks back home grew sharper. The medal ceremony had taken place at a reception preceding a stag dinner hosted by Hugh Wilson, the U.S. ambassador to Germany, at the American embassy in Berlin. Neither Lindbergh nor Wilson had been told in advance about the medal—the Service Cross of the German Eagle—which, according to Goering, was meant to honor the aviator's services to world aviation and to commemorate his 1927 flight. Although Lindbergh was surprised by the decoration (a young U.S. Army officer standing next to him that night described him as "flabbergasted"), he thought little about it. His wife, however, had a far different reaction. When Lindbergh and Truman Smith, who was also at the dinner, showed the medal to Anne later that night, she looked at it and flatly dubbed it "the albatross."

Indeed it was. The medal presentation had occurred just days before the Kristallnacht outrages, which deeply shocked the U.S. public. Not since World War I had Americans shown such open animosity toward Germany, reported the German consul general in Los Angeles. Hans Dieckhoff, the German ambassador in Washington, cabled Berlin: "A hurricane is blowing here." As a sign of his displeasure with the Nazis, President Roosevelt recalled Hugh Wilson from Germany, whereupon Hitler ordered Dieckhoff back from Washington.

Considering the strong anti-German feeling in the United States, it was not surprising that news of Lindbergh's medal aroused considerable controversy. At this point, the flier's open contempt for the U.S. press came back to haunt him. Long resentful of his scornful attitude toward them, journalists not only played up the medal story but, in some instances, invented details that further tarred his reputation. *Liberty* magazine, for example, wrote that he had flown to Berlin for the sole purpose of accepting the decoration. Even *The New York Times*, so sympathetic to him in the past, incorrectly reported that he had proudly worn the medal for the entire evening of the dinner. In fact, he never put it on.

"We know Charles never denies anything the newspapers print, and we know too that some outrageous things have been printed about him. But this thing seems to us to be different," a distant relative of Anne wrote to her. "For the first time, it actually puts Charles on a side, it allies him with something this country believes is wrong and bad, and it may give impetus and encouragement to some weaker men who lean to the wrong side."

Ignoring appeals from his friends to set the record straight, Lindbergh repeatedly declined to give his version of what had happened that night. As *Life* magazine pointed out, "His refusal to talk about the medal has magnified its importance out of all proportion." Astonishingly, Lindbergh insisted for the rest of his life that his acceptance of the medal had never been a problem for him. In 1955, he wrote Truman Smith that he always regarded "the fuss about it as a tempest [in a] teapot."

That statement simply underscored Lindbergh's political myopia. In fact, from late 1938 on, the medal incident was used by his critics as a cudgel with which to bludgeon him. Chief among his foes was Harold Ickes, the hard-nosed, cantankerous secretary of the interior, who was widely known for his slashing invective against those he considered his and FDR's adversaries. "I cannot be tolerant of fools," Ickes once remarked to Roosevelt, "and there are altogether too many fools everywhere." According to T. H. Watkins, Ickes's biographer, "a world without something in it to make him angry would have been incomprehensible to him."

A disgruntled Republican senator who had been the target of one of Ickes's verbal assaults called him "a common scold puffed up by high office." To one cabinet colleague, Ickes was "Washington's tough guy." To another, he was the "president's attack dog." Encountering the pudgy, bespectacled Ickes at a dinner at the British embassy, the assistant secretary of state Adolf Berle refused to shake hands with him, later describing the interior secretary in his diary as "fundamentally, a louse."

Ferociously combative, Ickes was also a stalwart champion of civil rights and liberties. As a young lawyer in Chicago, he had been president of that city's branch of the NAACP. As secretary of the interior, he had banned all segregation in his department and was responsible for arranging Marian Anderson's 1939 concert at the Lincoln Memorial after the black singer was barred from performing at Washington's Constitution Hall. Following Hitler's rise to power, Ickes was outspoken in his criticism of Germany and its treatment of the Jews.

Lindbergh's acceptance of the German medal put him high on Ickes's already crowded enemies list. Shortly after Kristallnacht, during a speech to a Jewish group in Cleveland, the cabinet secretary blasted Lindbergh for accepting "a decoration at the hand of a brutal dictator, who with that same hand is robbing and torturing thousands of fellow human beings." Anyone who took a medal from Germany, he added, "automatically forswears his American birthright." From then on, Ickes boasted that he had been "the first man in public life to utter a criticism of Lindbergh."

In letters and cables, friends and family members informed the Lindberghs that movie audiences in New York and other cities were now hissing whenever images of Charles appeared in newsreels. Lindbergh, according to his brother-in-law, Aubrey Morgan, had become a "convenient channel" into which the American public could pour its increasing anger over what was happening in Germany. "You have become the scapegoat," Morgan wrote Lindbergh. "The press certainly went out of their way to make you the real villain and Machiavellian intriguer behind the European scenes."

Anne was greatly shaken by the attacks on her husband, believing they were deeply unfair. Lindbergh, by contrast, exhibited what his wife called "his immobile, tolerant unconcern." In her diary, she noted: "Their scorn does not touch him any more than their praise once did." Indeed, in early April 1939, just a few months after the medal incident, he abruptly decided that he and his family should return to the United States, giving up their privacy and plunging back into the maelstrom of celebrity from which they had escaped more than three years before.

His decision came after Hitler's seizure of all of Czechoslovakia on March 15, 1939. A short time later, Neville Chamberlain, finally realizing the futility of his appeasement policy, announced to the House of Commons one of the most dramatic reversals of foreign policy in modern British history. Britain, he declared, would go to the aid of Poland, widely reported to be Hitler's next victim, if it were invaded. France made a similar pledge.

Realizing that Europe was on the verge of war, Lindbergh concluded there was nothing more he could do on the Continent to ward off the conflict. His place, he thought, was back home. "I felt I could exercise a constructive influence in America, trying to convince its citizens of the need for strict neutrality in the event of war," he wrote in his journal. "[T]hen at least one strong Western nation would remain to protect Western civilization."

CHAPTER 2

"WE WERE FOOLS"

≡

When the ocean liner *Aquitania* docked in New York on April 14, 1939, dozens of reporters and photographers laid siege to Charles Lindbergh's cabin, camping out in the hallway and on the stairs leading down to the deck. Unfazed by Lindbergh's refusal to meet them, one photographer broke through the cabin door, snapped a quick photo of the startled flier, and ran. A few minutes later, Lindbergh, whose wife and children would arrive on a later ship, strode swiftly down the gangplank, surrounded by a horde of uniformed policemen. Journalists swarmed ahead and behind the entourage, falling over one another in their frantic attempts to get a photo or comment from the man in its center. "There must have been over a hundred of them," Lindbergh wrote in his journal, "and the planks were covered with the broken glass of the flashlight bulbs they threw away. I have never seen as many at one time before, even in 1927, I think. It was a barbaric entry to a civilized country."

Several days before, as the *Aquitania* steamed across the Atlantic, Lindbergh had exchanged radiograms with General Henry "Hap" Arnold, who wanted to arrange a meeting with him as soon as possible. The day after Lindbergh's arrival, the two men met secretly at West Point. The furtiveness of their encounter was as much Arnold's doing as it was Lindbergh's: the general, noted Arnold biographer Murray Green, was "walking on eggshells because Lindbergh by that time had become a dirty word at the White House."

General Henry "Hap" Arnold, chief of the U.S. Army Air Corps.

For three hours, they talked over lunch at a nearby hotel, whose dining room, at Arnold's request, had been cleared of other guests. When the dining room closed so the staff could prepare for dinner, Lindbergh and Arnold continued their discussion in the grandstand at a West Point baseball game, surrounded by rooting cadets.

The head of the Air Corps could not have cared less about the controversy surrounding Lindbergh. Nor was he bothered by the political ramifications of the aviator's visits to Germany. A man who "seemed to seek out trouble" and who, like Lindbergh, thrived on danger and adventure, the fifty-two-year-old Arnold had often been severely reprimanded for his own iconoclasm. He was a headstrong, tactless maverick with a penchant for criticizing his superiors and going outside the chain of command to get what he wanted. Indeed, earlier in his military career, he had been threatened with court-martial for secretly lobbying members of Congress in support of legislation he favored.

As for Lindbergh, all Arnold cared about was that he had provided the Air Corps with badly needed information about the size and strength of the Luftwaffe—information that Arnold himself had asked him to gather, "as a great personal favor and act of patriotism." Even more important, Lindbergh's dramatic reports of German airpower had helped influence President Roosevelt's decision to order a massive increase in U.S. aircraft production just five months before. For Arnold, who was determined to build the most powerful air force in the world, FDR's proposal was nothing less than a military Magna Carta.

A pioneer and visionary, the stocky, broad-shouldered Arnold had big dreams about the future of aviation, which at that point was still relatively new. Only thirty-five years had elapsed since Orville and Wilbur Wright first flew over the sandy beaches of Kitty Hawk, North Carolina. The Wright brothers had taught Arnold how to fly, and he had gone on to become one of America's first four military pilots. When he took charge of the Air Corps in 1938, it was in pitiful shape—a pale shadow of the mighty Luftwaffe or Britain's Royal Air Force. Arnold himself called his service "practically nonexistent." Ranked twentieth in size among the world's air forces and still under Army control, it had a few hundred combat planes, many of them obsolete, and fewer than nineteen thousand officers and enlisted men.

From the time he assumed command, Arnold was obsessed with the idea of proving that airpower was superior to any other type of armed force. He was brusque and impatient with the many top government officials in Washington who failed to share his unswerving faith in the Air Corps' future dominance and who thought that "we damned airmen were too cocky, too big for our boots."

Among the skeptics was Franklin Roosevelt, a sea-loving man who once had been assistant secretary of the Navy and had always favored that service. In the aftermath of the Munich agreement, however, the president's advisers persuaded him that Germany's supposedly overwhelming aerial strength posed a major threat not only to the security of Europe but to America and the rest of the world. Although the reports of the Luftwaffe's might, including those made by Lindbergh, proved to be highly exaggerated, they convinced Roosevelt "for the first time," in the words of a War Department memo, "that American airplane production should be greatly stimulated with all possible speed."

On November 14, 1938, the president ordered the Army to draw up a two-year plan for the production of ten thousand new aircraft, most of them bombers. He was captivated by the idea of waging war from the air, telling his cabinet that it "would cost less money, would mean comparatively few casualties, and would be more likely to succeed than a traditional war." And if he sold a large percentage of the new planes to Britain and France, thus enabling them to defend themselves against Germany, maybe America could avoid being sucked into the conflict now threatening Europe. For Arnold, the idea of shipping off aircraft desperately needed by his own Air Corps was anathema; over the next three years, he would do all he could to oppose it, even to the point of insubordination.

In his quest for the biggest and best air force possible, Arnold was determined to utilize the star power of Lindbergh. At their West Point meeting, he asked the flier to lead an effort to speed up the development of faster and more sophisticated U.S. warplanes. Acceding to Arnold's request, Lindbergh, a colonel in the Army Reserve, returned to active duty a few days after his return to America. Although an outspoken advocate of U.S. neutrality, he was also firmly convinced that America had to build up its military strength as quickly as possible in order to be able to defend itself properly. After several weeks of touring the country's aircraft factories and aeronautical research centers, he concluded that their potential was "tremendous" but that in their current state, they were far inferior to those in Germany. Again at Arnold's bidding, he served on a board that, after a brief study, made strongly worded recommendations for a greatly accelerated and expanded program of aeronautical research, development, and manufacture.

For a cause like this, Lindbergh—as Arnold had hoped—was not averse to using his celebrity. He became the Air Corps' point man, involving himself in countless discussions with members of Congress, bureaucrats, diplomats, business executives, scientists, and engineers about what needed to be done—and spent—to make America No. 1 in airpower.

LINDBERGH, WHO HAD SPENT a year in an Army flying school in the early 1920s, loved being back on active military duty. He was given an office across the hall from Arnold's in the Munitions Building, a huge structure on Washington's National Mall that housed Army and Air Corps personnel. At the end of each day, to avoid any photographers and reporters who might be hovering near the front entrance, Arnold's aide escorted Lindbergh out of the building through a back exit to a waiting taxi.

After just a few days in Washington, Lindbergh realized that many others shared his feelings of alienation from the outside world. His associates in the Munitions Building and elsewhere in the armed services were an embattled, demoralized band, who were treated as pariahs by their profoundly antiwar, antimilitary countrymen. No longer did the American public want to "make the world safe for democracy," as President Woodrow Wilson had promised in 1917, when the United States entered World War I. In the words of the historians William Langer and S. Everett Gleason, "Americans, having once believed, erroneously, that war would settle everything, were now disposed to endorse the reverse fallacy that war could settle nothing."

Once the Great War was over, the belief had taken hold that America had been tricked into it by British propaganda and by U.S. bankers and arms merchants who had acted on the European allies' behalf. According to a 1937 Gallup poll, 70 percent of the American people thought it had been a mistake for the country to enter the war.

The misty idealism of the pre–World War I period had given way to a hard-eyed, determined isolationism, which precluded accepting any of the inherent responsibilities that came with America's position as the world's leading economic power. Giving voice to the national mood, Ernest Hemingway wrote in 1935: "Of the hell broth that is brewing in Europe we have no need to drink. . . . We were fools to be sucked in once in a European war, and we shall never be sucked in again."

In towns close to military bases, it was not uncommon to see signs on storefronts reading: DOGS AND SOLDIERS—KEEP OUT. The atmosphere in the nation's capital was so antimilitary that most officers, including Lindbergh, did not wear their uniforms in public. When the services' top brass testified before congressional committees, they also appeared in mufti, so as not to antagonize Capitol Hill's powerful isolationist bloc.

Long starved of support by both the White House and Congress, the U.S. Army in 1939 ranked seventeenth in the world, sandwiched between those of Portugal and Bulgaria. While the Navy was by far the strongest of the services (despite the fact that nearly half its vessels dated back to World War I), the Army was, as *Life* noted, "the smallest, worst-equipped armed force of any major power." With fewer than 175,000 men, it was in such bad shape that, in the words of one military historian, it would not have been able to "repel raids across the Rio Grande by Mexican bandits." Weapons were so scarce that only one-third of U.S. troops had ever trained with them; those weapons that did exist were almost all of World War I vintage.

Conditioned to ask for only the smallest increases in their budgets, the country's military leaders were accustomed to seeing even those paltry requests slashed. With most Americans opposed to the very idea of rearming, there was little likelihood of getting enough money to replace deteriorating weapons and equipment, much less to create a modern, mechanized force to match the power of Germany or other potential enemies.

While every president in the post–World War I era had kept the military on a short leash, Roosevelt was the object of particular distrust and dislike in the upper reaches of the armed forces. "Although Roosevelt had his defenders among officers, opinions generally ranged from aversion to disdain and loathing for him, especially on the part of the older generation," the historian Milton Goldin has noted. Largely conservative in political outlook, many American officers faulted FDR for starving national defense for the previous six years while spending billions of dollars on what they considered wasteful domestic programs, which, as they saw it, pampered the unemployed and poor.

A substantial number of military men were also highly critical of FDR's increasingly antagonistic attitude toward Germany. While decrying Nazi brutality and repression, they, like Lindbergh, admired Germany's military and economic achievements and its evident restoration of national pride. Many, too, had great respect for the professionalism and skill of the German army and saw nothing wrong with the Wehrmacht's massive growth in the 1920s and 1930s—an expansion expressly forbidden by the Versailles Treaty. In 1934, General Douglas MacArthur, then Army chief of staff, told General Friedrich von Boetticher, the German military attaché in Washington, that he believed the treaty was a "gross injustice" and that Germany had every right to enlarge its army.

Like many of their countrymen, a large percentage of the American military felt that Germany had been unfairly treated after the war and that England and France shared much of the blame. Indeed, a sizable number of senior officers were far more antagonistic toward their former allies than toward their former enemy. Many felt that America had been tricked by Britain and France into entering the Great War, which, in their view, had neither served nor advanced U.S. interests. They strongly believed in the idea of a Fortress America and shared Lindbergh's adamant opposition to the idea of getting involved in another European conflict.

Anyone who thought that the American military in the late 1930s and early 1940s was "an incubator of militarism prolifically hatching designs for war . . . would have been surprised by the strong element of isolationism and the absence of militancy in their deliberations," the historian Forrest Pogue observed in his biography of General George Marshall. As General Malin Craig, Marshall's predecessor as Army chief of staff, saw it, another war "would mean the end of civilization."

The antiwar views of senior American military figures were faithfully transmitted back to Berlin by von Boetticher, who had established close contacts and friendships with a number of officers in the Army's high command. A cultured man, whose mother had been born in America and raised in Britain, the short, stout von Boetticher had first begun cultivating U.S. officers in the 1920s, as part of his job as a key intelligence officer for the German army. Assigned to Washington as military attaché in 1933, he rented an imposing Victorian mansion in the increasingly fashionable neighborhood of Georgetown, where he entertained lavishly. In June 1938, for example, he hosted a garden party in honor of Hap Arnold's son, who was bound for the Naval Academy in Annapolis.

Von Boetticher had built something of a reputation as a military historian, and his expertise in the American Civil War gained him entrée to both civilian and military social circles. Indeed, the U.S. Army War College invited him on several occasions to lecture to its students about the battles of Bull Run and Chantilly. Among von Boetticher's friends was the Virginia newspaper editor and historian Douglas Southall Freeman, author of a Pulitzer Prize–winning four-volume biography of Robert E. Lee. Another was Colonel George Patton, then commandant at Fort Myer in northern Virginia, who, like the German attaché, was a Civil War buff. Patton frequently accompanied von Boetticher on expeditions to Civil War battlefields near Washington, where the two men would tramp the ground for hours and debate the battles that had raged there.

Thanks to his close connections with high-ranking U.S. officers, von Boetticher had been given free rein to travel around the United States, visiting military research installations, regular army commands, and plants producing aircraft, weapons, and other military equipment. After a nationwide tour of warplane manufacturers in the summer of 1939, he reported to Berlin that "there was not the slightest indication of [the U.S.] preparing for war."

General Friedrich von Boetticher, German military attaché in Washington (on right), and Colonel T. Nakamura, Japanese military attaché (on left), observe U.S. Army war maneuvers in upstate New York in August 1939, a month before the beginning of World War II. U.S. Brigadier General Walter C. Short is in the center.

Franklin Roosevelt, for his part, considered such inertia an enormous mistake. He desperately wanted to convince his fellow Americans that the United States must come to the aid of Britain and France if war erupted in Europe, as he was sure it would. But up to that point, he had done almost nothing to persuade them of the need for action. How could he make them listen to him now?

ROOSEVELT WAS THEN NEARING the end of his second term. When he first took office in 1933, his optimism, eloquence, and aggressive activism had helped restore hope and confidence to a demoralized country. In his first inaugural address he had promised "action now"—a pledge that he fulfilled beyond anyone's expectations. Because of Roosevelt and the dizzying array of domestic programs launched by his administration, the lives of Americans had been transformed, and the federal government had assumed vast new power and authority.

But he had shown no such resolution in his approach to foreign policy. Throughout his political career, FDR had tacked back and forth between isolationism and internationalism. He had started out as a supporter of international cooperation and collective security; in the aftermath of World War I, he had backed Woodrow Wilson and the League of Nations. But he was, above all, a consummate politician. Keenly aware that most Americans were against the League, he adjusted his public views accordingly. When he sought the presidency in 1932, he assured voters that he opposed U.S. participation in the organization.

During his entire first term and much of his second, Roosevelt subordinated foreign policy to his efforts to stimulate domestic economic reform and recovery from the Depression. Not until 1939 did his administration begin to consider active involvement in the darkening situation in Europe. In the midst of the 1936 presidential campaign, Roosevelt had declared: "We shun political commitments which might entangle us in foreign wars. . . . We seek to isolate ourselves completely from war."

Equally determined to keep the United States out of future conflicts, Congress passed a series of so-called Neutrality Acts in the mid-1930s that, among other things, banned U.S. arms sales to countries at war and made it illegal for U.S. citizens to join a warring power's military service or travel on a belligerent ship. While Roosevelt supported the idea of an arms embargo, he believed that only aggressor nations should be prohibited from buying munitions and that he, as president, should have the authority to decide which belligerents fell into that category. But Congress refused to give him such authority, and facing the prospect of an isolationist filibuster, he signed the bill.

And so, as Hitler and Mussolini prepared for war in Europe, Roosevelt and his administration were stripped of the power to provide any future material support to countries on the list of the dictators' future victims. The Axis leaders, meanwhile, were reassured that the United States, in what the historian Richard Ketchum called "its almost pathological desire to stay uninvolved in Europe's quarrels," would sit quietly by while they snatched up any country they wanted.

In 1938, after Hitler annexed Austria and then did the same to Czechoslovakia's Sudetenland, the Roosevelt administration deplored such aggression (in private, the president called it "armed banditry") and urged peaceful settlement of the crises. But it made no commitments and offered no meaningful assistance to achieve such settlements. "It is always best and safest," Neville Chamberlain acidly remarked, "to count on nothing from the Americans but words."

After the Munich agreement, Roosevelt had little doubt that appeasement would fail, that war would soon follow, and that the United States could not escape unscathed, no matter what the isolationists claimed. But he shrank from passing this thought on to the American public. When Harold Ickes urged him to do so, he replied that the people would not believe him.

In his tenure as president, Roosevelt, who had been so effective in educating Americans about domestic issues, had never done the same for foreign affairs. As his biographer, James MacGregor Burns, put it, "He hoped they would be educated by events." As it turned out, they were, but not in the way he wanted. With the president making little or no attempt to persuade Americans that it was in the country's best interests to help stop the dictators, the increasingly dire events in Europe only confirmed their determination to stay as far away from that hornet's nest as possible.

As a result, when FDR tried to redirect U.S. foreign policy in early 1939 toward a greater involvement in the European crisis, he was acutely aware that public opinion did not support him. Convinced by this time that the arms embargo had been a mistake of epic proportions, he wanted Congress, at the very least, to revise it so that nations at war—i.e., Britain and France—would be permitted to purchase arms from the United States, as long as they were paid for in dollars and transported on the buyers' own ships. But he declined to press for such an amendment. Instead, he was persuaded by Senator Key Pittman, the ineffective, alcoholic chairman of the Senate Foreign Relations Committee, to abdicate presidential leadership and stay silent on the matter while the committee debated a number of recently introduced neutrality measures. The president and Secretary of State Cordell Hull were "anxious to do what they can to help," an official of the British embassy in Washington reported to the Foreign Office, "but are obsessed by the risk of going too far ahead of public opinion and thus losing control of Congress."

Weeks, then months, passed with Pittman scheduling no hearings and the committee taking no action. When the chairman finally bestirred himself to announce he would begin to consider the various pieces of legislation, Senate isolationists threatened a filibuster over any attempt to "repeal or emasculate" existing neutrality laws, and Pittman fell back into his usual somnolent state. In May 1939, two months after Hitler seized all of Czechoslovakia, the Nevada Democrat informed the administration of yet another postponement in the committee's examination of revising the Neutrality Act, claiming "the situation in Europe does not seem to merit any urgent action."

Though fully aware of the absurdity of that statement, the White House was unable to convince Pittman and his congressional colleagues otherwise.

CHAPTER 3

"WHERE IS MY WORLD?"

═══

Not long after Charles Lindbergh came back to America, his wife and two small sons made their own return voyage. In a letter to Anne shortly before she left France, Lindbergh informed her that because of the swarm of journalists that followed him wherever he went, he would not be at the dock to greet her. He instructed her to lock the doors of her stateroom when the boat docked in New York and to cover the boys' faces as much as possible to thwart the taking of news photos. She did as he asked, much to the chagrin of the reporters and photographers who crowded around the gangplank of the French ocean liner *Champlain* as she and the boys disembarked.

From the moment of her arrival, Anne Lindbergh felt like a stranger. She had spent much of her life in and around New York, but its ceaseless bustle, brightness, and jangle now disoriented her. Unlike Europe, she thought, New York contained "nothing solid or real or quiet." She desperately missed her life in France, "the sense of tasting and touching and relishing life as it goes by." Above all, she yearned for the peace and security that France—and, before that, England—had given her and her family. Anne, now thirty-two, was plagued by a deep sense of foreboding about the future. It was not a new sensation. Ever since the murder of Charlie, she had had the feeling that disaster lay just ahead, that "very near to the surface of this lovely glaze of a safe, peaceful, normal life lies the terrible, the unbearable." She was living, she be-

Anne Morrow,
in her teens.

lieved, in "a half-mad world where nothing is safe, nothing is sure, anything can happen."

But another, more specific fear overlaid that general sense of impending doom—a premonition that the United States was about to tear itself apart over the issue of war in Europe. The country was embarking, in her view, on "a long period of struggle and hate and jealousy and false names." She added: "I see no place for me in that . . . I who do not want to fight, who do not want to force myself—even intellectually, even spiritually, even emotionally—on another human being."

Nonetheless, she soon would find herself in the middle of the "hate and jealousy" she had so accurately foreseen and dreaded so much.

THANKS TO THE GREAT wealth of her father, Anne Morrow Lindbergh had grown up in a gilded cocoon, as remote from the economic and social realities of early-twentieth-century America as anyone could possibly be. Years later, she would describe her two sisters and herself as "the sleeping princesses." There was, she said, a "haze of insulation which permeated our early years, our indefinable sense of isolation from the real world."

One of the most influential men on Wall Street in the 1920s, Dwight Morrow was a senior partner in the international banking firm of J. P. Morgan, which, by the turn of the century, had emerged as the most powerful—and controversial—financial empire in the world. Unlike most of his colleagues, Morrow was never fully satisfied with his life as a multimillionaire financier. A graduate of Amherst and a voracious reader, he considered himself an intellectual and harbored dreams of returning to academia as a history professor. But his desire for money and influence—an appetite shared by his forceful wife, Elizabeth—trumped any thoughts of taking refuge in a cloistered, impecunious university environment.

The Morrows and their children lived, at various times, in a spacious apartment just off Fifth Avenue in Manhattan and a grand Georgian mansion on seventy-five acres in Englewood, New Jersey. Each summer, they traveled to their house on an island in midcoast Maine; in the winter, they spent a couple of weeks in Nassau. Not infrequently, Morrow swept his family off to Europe, where he met with bankers and heads of state while his wife oversaw the children's sightseeing.

Shy, sensitive, and bookish, Anne felt eclipsed by her more outgoing sisters. The eldest, Elisabeth, was bright, blond, and beautiful—"the belle of the ball," as Constance, the youngest of the three, described her. "Men fell at her feet." Constance, for her part, was exuberant, funny, warm, and arguably the smartest of the Morrows—she would later graduate summa cum laude from Smith College.

Anne was hardly undistinguished herself. At Miss Chapin's, the private girls' school she attended in New York, she was student council president, captain of the field hockey team, and a frequent contributor to the school's literary magazine. Petite and pretty, with sad eyes and a radiant smile, she had more than her share of male admirers.

Yet no one would know any of that from reading her diary entries and letters of the period. Convinced she was a failure, "the complete loss in our family," she constantly apologized for her self-perceived shortcomings and felt especially inferior to her energetic, demanding, dominating mother. A prominent clubwoman, Elizabeth Morrow was also a poet, a writer of children's books, a trustee of Smith College, her alma mater, and, at one point, its acting president. "She carries action and life into whatever room she walks," Anne wrote in her diary. "I carry shyness and silence and inaction. It spreads in pools around me wherever I go."

For all her insecurity and outward conformity, Anne Morrow was desperate to assert herself, to break free of her rigid, tight-knit family circle. She tried to resist her parents' wishes that she attend Smith, like her mother and sister before her. In the end, however, she enrolled there. "The chain was just too strong for her to break," Constance later observed. "None of us really had a choice."

Still, it was at Smith that Anne's distinctive literary talent was first discovered and encouraged to flourish. Urged on by Mina Kirstein Curtiss, her creative writing professor, she contributed poetry and essays to the college's literary publications and won Smith's top awards for writing. Over and over in her poetry, she alluded to her desire to burst out of her cocoon, describing herself in one poem as "a brown-haired Quaker maiden" who yearned to be "a scarlet Spanish dancer."

Anne Morrow Lindbergh with her mother, Elizabeth Morrow.

In December 1927, during her senior year, Anne traveled to Mexico City to spend the Christmas holidays with her family. Earlier that year, her father had been appointed U.S. ambassador to Mexico by his close friend, President Calvin Coolidge. Unlike his recent predecessors, who saw their main duty as serving the interests of U.S. oil companies in Mexico, Dwight Morrow was determined to improve the contentious relationship between the United States and its southern neighbor. To help achieve that goal, he invited America's golden boy, Charles Lindbergh, to fly to Mexico City on a goodwill tour and spend Christmas with the Morrow family. Lindbergh accepted.

Although she didn't know it yet, Anne was about to find her means of escape.

ONLY SEVEN MONTHS HAD passed since Lindbergh's history-making flight, and he was at the apex of his fame. But, with the Morrows in Mexico, he acted more like an awkward schoolboy than a much-feted international celebrity. Although relaxed and confident in aviation circles, "this shy, cool boy," as Anne described him in her diary, had few social graces when it came to mixing with strangers, particularly young women. He was the most eligible bachelor in the world, but, as far as anyone knew, he had never gone out on a single date. Wary and aloof, he regarded conversation, Anne wrote, "as though it were a business transaction or a doctor's pill that he has to take."

None of that mattered to twenty-one-year-old Anne, who, when asked in high school what her life's ambition was, had replied: "I want to marry a hero." For all Lindbergh's gaucheness and lack of sophistication, she, like countless other young women, had become besotted with him, even before they met. A few months after their first encounter, she wrote in her diary: "Colonel L . . . is the last of the gods. He is unbelievable, and it is exhilarating to believe in the unbelievable."

In the fall of 1928, after Anne's graduation from Smith, Lindbergh renewed contact with her. On their first date, he took her flying over Long Island. He was as relaxed and natural in the air as he was awkward on the ground, and the two began to open up to each other. "I discovered that I could . . . say anything to him, that I wasn't a *bit* afraid of him or even worshipful any more," Anne exulted in a letter to Constance. "That Norse god has just gone." He confided in her his dreams and hopes for the future of flying; she told him of her ambition to become a writer. Less than a month later, they were engaged.

Beneath Anne's shy facade, Lindbergh discovered a love of nature, curiosity, and thirst for adventure that matched his own. She, for her part, "was given confidence, strength, and almost a new character" through her relationship with Lindbergh. "The sheer fact of finding myself loved . . . changed my world, my feelings about life and myself," she later wrote. "The man I was to marry believed in me and what I could do. . . . He opened the door to 'real life' and although it frightened me, it also beckoned. I had to go."

Yet, as much in love with him as she was, she was clear-eyed from the start about the vast differences between them. "He doesn't seem to touch my life anywhere, really," she noted. "I have more in common with *anyone*—the most distant of distant people—than with him."

The differences began with their fathers. Charles A. Lindbergh Sr., who died in 1924, had been a radical populist Republican congressman who devoted his political career to a campaign aimed at breaking up the power and influence of the House of Morgan and other Wall Street banks, which he called "speculative parasites." Although he didn't see much of his father, Lindbergh greatly admired and respected him. By all accounts, the two were very much alike—in their chiseled good looks, independence, stubbornness, dislike of cities, and preference for rural and small-town values.

At heart, Lindbergh was a country boy, while Anne was a city girl. He was a college dropout who hated school and rarely picked up a book. Having been raised in an intellectual family, she prized education and reading. When she first told him she wanted to become a writer, he was astonished, exclaiming, "You like to *write* books? I like to *live* them." She was emotional and sensitive; he was logical, practical, and often tone-deaf when it came to the feelings of others. "He is terribly young and crude in many small ways," Anne wrote to Elisabeth before their wedding. "Sometimes he will say something that wrenches terribly."

Anne had been swept away by "this amazing, overwhelming, and extremely forceful man," but she was well aware, even in her starry-eyed state, that their life together would never be easy. In a letter to a friend, she wrote that "if you write me and wish me conventional happiness, I will *never* forgive you. Don't wish me happiness—I don't expect to be happy, but it's gotten beyond that, somehow. Wish me courage and strength and a sense of humor—I will need them all."

FROM THE BEGINNING OF their marriage, Lindbergh made his young wife an equal partner in his life's work—or so it appeared. After learning to fly a plane, operate a radio, and navigate, she joined him in his aerial explorations, traveling all over the world to map prospective air routes for the fledgling airline industry. She loved flying—the beauty and adventure of it—but even more important, the freedom it gave her and Charles. The sky turned out to be the only place she could truly be alone with him.

While her life seemed to have changed completely, she had in reality merely exchanged one cocoon for another. Isolated from normal human contacts by the constant pressure of Lindbergh's fame, she had been warned by him to use extreme care in everything she said, did, or wrote. "The worst problem," she told Constance, "is how to keep up a polite conversation and yet say *nothing* personal, bearing in mind every second that everything you say . . . may be repeated and made into a 'story.'"

What she hated above all was the total lack of privacy. "Oh, it is brutal," she lamented to her mother. "We never can catch people or life unawares. . . . It is like being born with no nose, or deformed—everyone on the street looks at you once and then *again;* always looks *back*—that second look, to leer. . . . That look, as though we were a public amusement, monkeys in a cage." Whenever she and Lindbergh attended parties or other gatherings, she later told an interviewer, those present immediately lost their naturalness as soon as the Lindberghs entered the room: "They seemed to freeze, as though we carried a Medusa's head."

Anne's dream of becoming her own person had also died aborning. She found she had exchanged the overpowering influence of her mother for domination by her husband—a control that she outwardly accepted while rebelling inwardly. In keeping with her fondness for romantic fairy-tale imagery, she later wrote that she had seen Lindbergh as "a knight in shining armor, with myself as his devoted page. The role of page came naturally to me." But as the years passed, she increasingly resented that role, exploding at one point in her diary:

"Damn, damn, damn! I am sick of being this 'handmaid to the Lord' . . . the 'worthy helpmeet,' a rather pale and good shadow in C.'s world. . . . Where is my world, and will I ever find it?"

The murder of the Lindberghs' son only sharpened the differences between them. She was devastated by the loss of Charlie, her "gay, lordly, assured little boy." Lindbergh was distraught, too, but, unlike Anne, refused to show it. He disliked open displays of emotion and scolded Anne whenever she revealed her anguish. One day, during the stresses of the Hauptmann trial, he told her she was too controlled by her feelings and was, indeed, "a failure."

Plunged into despair, she taught herself to cry without making a sound, to turn a blank face to the world. "I feel completely frustrated," she exclaimed in her diary. "I am hemmed in on all sides and pounding against the walls . . . I must not talk. I must not cry . . . I must not dream. I must control my mind—I must control my body—I must control my emotions. I must put up an appearance, at least, of calm for C."

Years later, Anne would write a novel entitled *Dearly Beloved,* two of whose major characters were clearly modeled on herself and Charles. About them, she wrote: "She didn't know him at all. Oh, of course, she did; it was only that she couldn't talk to him. She had another language: feelings, poetry, music. . . . He lectured; she listened. And her worries, her failures—she never brought them any more. Just hid them, like a bad arithmetic paper in school. He couldn't bear her failures. . . . He would nail her down with the good strong nails of his logic. Bang, bang, bang, with the good hard hammer of his mind. Nailed to her faults forever."

About Charles, the Lindberghs' elder daughter, Anne, would note, "There were only two ways of doing things—Father's way and the wrong way." Anne's sister, Reeve, remembered their father as "the most infuriatingly impossible human being I have ever known." While blessed with humor, charm, and a "shy courtesy," he was also "an angry, restless, opinionated perfectionist . . . obsessed with his own ideas and concerns."

Close to a nervous breakdown in the mid-1930s, Anne Lindbergh gradually began to find a way out of her misery, thanks in part to Harold Nicolson, Dwight Morrow's biographer. A deeply literate and cultured former British diplomat, who had written several highly regarded novels and works of nonfiction, Nicolson stayed at Elizabeth Morrow's estate in New Jersey while researching the book about her husband, who had died in 1931. While there, he struck up a friendship with Anne, whom he described in a letter to his wife as "shy and retreating . . . with a tragedy at the corner of her mouth."

Impressed by a *National Geographic* article Anne had written about a flight she and Charles had made in 1931 across Canada and Alaska to Japan and China, Nicolson praised her writing and encouraged her to continue it. Anne, elated by his praise and his recognition of "something inside me . . . that I have tried to ignore for fear of being hurt," turned the article into a book. In June 1935, the publishing house Harcourt, Brace published *North to the Orient,* which won almost universal critical praise for its lyrical prose and became the country's top nonfiction bestseller.

Its success prompted Anne to begin work on a second book, this one about a journey the couple took to Greenland, Europe, and Africa in 1933. From the beginning, Lindbergh had enthusiastically supported her writing and pushed her to succeed. At the same time, he made clear that he and his needs and desires took precedence over their children and her books. She was in perpetual conflict, angry and resentful, but "having been brought up to be 'a good girl' and to want to please everyone," she usually acceded to his wishes. "Who am I to say, 'No, I want my own life'?" she wistfully observed.

In the fall of 1935, however, she asserted herself enough to find a "room of her own," a tiny Manhattan apartment she rented as a peaceful refuge to use for her writing. Less than two months later, Lindbergh abruptly informed her he had decided they must move to Europe, to get away from the prying press; she must be ready "to go by the end of the week—at 24 hours' notice." On December 21, the Lindberghs sailed for England.

ANNE HAD FEARED THE turmoil of another major disruption, writing in her diary that "all my life seems to be trying to 'get settled' and C. shaking me out of it." To her delight, however, she found herself more settled in the havens she and Charles established in England and France than in any other place she had lived during her marriage. She finished her second book, entitled *Listen! The Wind,* at Long Barn, the house in rural Kent that she and Charles rented from Harold Nicolson and Vita Sackville-West. In late 1938, the book was published to widespread acclaim—*The New Yorker* called it "a small work of art"—and it, like *North to the Orient,* reached the top of the bestseller list.

Until the Lindberghs' sojourn in Europe, Anne had never shown much interest in the burning political and social issues of the day. Only when Charles became involved in the debate over whether Hitler should—or could—be stopped did she begin expressing her views, which, for the most part, were a parroting of her husband's opinions. At a Paris dinner party, for instance, she argued that the Western allies had been so unfair to Germany in the post–World War I peace settlement that the Germans understandably felt the need to violate the Versailles Treaty, build up their forces, and take back the territory they had lost. To her mother, she wrote that Hitler "is a very great man, like an inspired religious leader—and as such rather fanatical—but not scheming, not selfish, not greedy for power."

At the same time, however, her diaries were sprinkled with expressions of doubt about the correctness of such views, which differed so dramatically from those she had been brought up to hold. Unlike Lindbergh's father, who had been a staunch isolationist before and during World War I, her parents were strong adherents of internationalism. "The talk I heard around the family table," Anne later recalled, "was full of enthusiasm for Woodrow Wilson's Fourteen Points; the right of 'self determination' for nations, and 'a new order of world peace.'"

In October 1938, she declared she had been "converted to the practical, hard facts" of political life by Charles, yet also lamented the Nazis' use of terror, "their treatment of the Jews, their brute-force manner, their stupidity, their rudeness, their regimentation. Things which I hate so much that I hardly know whether the efficiency, unity, spirit that comes out of it can be worth it."

After Germany swallowed up all of Czechoslovakia in March 1939, she wrote in her diary: "This time you have gone too far. You are wrong. You are standing on a wrong and you (Germany) will ultimately fail because of it. . . . All nations break their word eventually, but the Germans break their word the moment it leaves their lips." A month later, the Lindberghs returned to the United States.

FOR ANNE, LEAVING EUROPE turned out to be a much greater wrench than she could have imagined. Later she would write that she had not realized "how wrapped up in Europe" her plans, dreams, and hopes for the future were, "how Europe is the mecca, the spiritual home, of so much I love."

Yet her return to America provided one consolation: a reunion with her mother and the rest of the Morrow family. For all her conflicted, rebellious feelings about Elizabeth Morrow, Anne remained very close to her. At her mother's invitation, she, Charles, and their two sons lived at Elizabeth's New Jersey estate while they looked for a home of their own.

There had always been a certain amount of tension between the strong-willed Elizabeth Morrow and her equally domineering son-in-law. While she was impressed by his accomplishments and fame, she had never thought he was good enough for Anne. "Lindbergh is really of a lower social stratum," a friend of the Morrows told Harold Nicolson, "and they treat him with aloof politeness." In reality, the friend added, the Morrows' son-in-law was "no more than a mechanic, and had it not been for the Lone Eagle flight, he would now be in charge of a gasoline station on the outskirts of St. Louis."

But it wasn't just social snobbery that fueled Elizabeth Morrow's sometimes difficult relationship with Lindbergh. She was bothered by what she considered his rigidity—his insistence, for example, that people made too much of special occasions like birthdays, anniversaries, and weddings. Such celebrations, he thought, were unduly sentimental, and he frowned on Anne or anyone else taking part in them. But most of all, Elizabeth disapproved of the way Charles treated her daughter. "Charles isn't capable of understanding her—the beauty of her soul and mind," she once wrote. She felt he had forced Anne to adopt a dual identity—the person she really was and the person Charles wanted her to be. "He loves her, but he wants to *reform* her—make her over into his own practical scientific mold. Poor Charles! What a condemnation of him!"

To Anne's distress, the relationship between her husband and mother grew even more strained after the Lindberghs' return from Eu-

*Constance Morrow
Morgan.*

rope. Elizabeth, who strongly believed that the United States must
help Britain and France, disagreed sharply with Lindbergh's isolationist
views. Anne found herself in the middle, once again caught in the
"eternal struggle of what I must be for C., and what I must be for
Mother, and what I must be for myself."

Elizabeth, as it turned out, was not the only close relative of Anne's
to be a fervent interventionist. Her beloved younger sister, Constance,
known as "Con," had married a Welshman, who was about to become
one of the British government's key propagandists in the United States.
Con, in turn, would soon emerge as an active partner in that effort.

DESPITE THE SEVEN-YEAR DIFFERENCE in their ages and great dissimi-
larity in their personalities, Anne and the petite, blond Con had always

been extraordinarily close. Anne might have had ambivalent feelings—love vying with envy and a sense of inferiority—about her mother and elder sister, but she never felt ambivalent about happy-go-lucky, confident Con, the only member of the Morrow family to have a relaxed, teasing relationship with Lindbergh. "She rags him about his fame complex," Harold Nicolson noted. "He just grins at her. She says, 'Well, Colonel Lindbergh, it's no use turning on the Lindbergh smile famous on two continents in order to impress your little sister-in-law. It doesn't work.'"

Con was the person to whom Anne confided her most private thoughts and emotions. "We understand each other so perfectly," she wrote in her diary, noting "the intense pleasure of talking to Con about everything." In a letter to Lindbergh before they were married, Anne bemoaned her difficulty in communicating to him exactly what she thought, adding, "Do you feel it—this wall? Why can't I write you as I could write Con?"

Con and Anne had drawn even closer after the 1934 death of their sister, Elisabeth, who had suffered from heart disease since childhood. Two years before she died, Elisabeth had married Aubrey Morgan, a Cambridge University graduate and an heir to a Welsh department store fortune. Witty, outgoing, and cultured, Morgan became a valued member of the Morrow household and remained so after Elisabeth's death. A good friend of both Anne and Charles, he accompanied Charles each day to the Hauptmann murder trial. When the Lindberghs moved to Britain, he sailed ahead of them so he could meet them when they arrived and take them to the privacy of his family home in Wales, where they stayed for several weeks.

Elizabeth and Con Morrow joined the Lindberghs in Wales for a short visit. While there, Con informed Anne that she and Aubrey were engaged. Jolted at first by the news, Anne came to the conclusion, as she wrote in her diary, that "yes, it is right—right for her, right for him." A man who loved to laugh, Morgan was described by his friend, the noted British historian John Wheeler-Bennett, as "warm, fearless, and utterly delightful, full of initiative and imagination . . . and a contempt for all pomposity, official or unofficial." That description summed up Con as well. The two had gravitated toward each other in their grief over Elisabeth's death, and in the process, had fallen in love. Years later, Reeve Lindbergh would write: "Although many people . . .

have considered the story of Elisabeth and Aubrey a romantic one, I for one have never thought that dying young counted for much in the way of romance. . . . The story of Con and Aubrey, on the other hand—now, there was romance for you!"

Soon after the couple's marriage, Anne wrote Con: "How wonderful that C. and you, and Aubrey and C., and Aubrey and I, and you and I get on so well. . . . It does make for security ahead." But that sense of well-being was threatened almost as soon as the Lindberghs returned home from Europe. In the summer of 1939, Sir Robert Vansittart, the British government's chief diplomatic adviser, privately recruited Aubrey Morgan and John Wheeler-Bennett to play major roles in a

Aubrey Morgan, Anne and Charles Lindbergh's brother-in-law and one of Britain's chief propagandists in America during World War II.

campaign to convince Americans they must come to the aid of Britain in the event of war—the very thing that Charles Lindbergh was determined to prevent.

EVEN BEFORE THE WAR began, the British were acutely aware that it could not be won without the help of the United States. To get that help, they knew they would have to appeal not only to the U.S. government but to the American people as well. They also knew what a formidable task that would be, given the considerable anti-British feeling that existed among Americans.

There was, to begin with, the vestigial suspicion and dislike of Britain as the tyrannous great power from which the United States had won its independence. "Anglo-American relations began in conflict, and that conflict has never been far beneath the surface," noted a British diplomat in Washington. Senator Burton Wheeler, who would soon emerge as the most influential isolationist lawmaker in Washington, recalled how, as a child in suburban Boston, he loved to watch the reenacted battles between costumed American rebels and British soldiers every July 4. "No colonist in 1775 ever cheered louder than I did when a redcoat bit the dust," Wheeler remembered. "We had been steeped in the lore of the Revolution, and I still bore a grudge against John Bull."

In the country's early years, Thomas Jefferson's Republicans and their successors, Andrew Jackson's Democrats, had cast themselves as populists, in direct opposition to the Eastern elites, who, in the public's mind, were too closely associated with the snooty British and their rigid class system. Virtually every U.S. populist movement since that time has contained significant strains of nativism and antielitism. In the early 1900s, Benjamin Tillman, a prominent populist senator from South Carolina known as "Pitchfork Ben," was fond of thundering: "America for Americans, and to hell with Britain and her Tories!"

Throughout the late nineteenth century and well into the twentieth, a sizable percentage of U.S. farmers blamed greedy British investors and ruthless Wall Street bankers for their many economic problems, including high railroad shipping rates and an inability to get cheap credit. According to one historian, Midwest and Great Plains farmers felt themselves "the innocent pastoral victims of a conspiracy hatched in the counting houses of New York and London."

Britain's imperialist policies also drew considerable fire, with some critics claiming that the British were far worse in their treatment of those they had colonized than Nazi Germany was to Jews and others under their subjugation. One such detractor was Senator D. Worth Clark, an isolationist Democrat from Idaho, who declared on the floor of the Senate in 1939: "Paint me a picture of the six years of persecution of the Jews, the Catholics, and the Protestants in Germany, paint it as gory and bloody as you please, and I will paint you one ten times as brutal, ten times as savage, ten times as bloody in the years of British destruction, pillage, rape and bloodshed in Ireland." Notwithstanding the hyperbole of Clark's statement, there was no question that many if not most Irish Americans were hostile to Britain, as were a good number of German Americans.

In the late 1930s, an Irish American congressman named Martin Sweeney proposed that the United States adopt a new national anthem, sung to the tune of "God Bless America" and containing these lyrics:

God save America from British rule:
Stand beside her and guide her
From the schemers who would make her a fool.
From Lexington to Yorktown,
From bloodstained Valley Forge,
God save America
From a king named George.

To be sure, the British government had not helped its cause in the United States by its seemingly blind determination to appease both Hitler and Mussolini. The news of Neville Chamberlain's sellout of the Czechs to Hitler at Munich was greeted in America with shock and outrage. After a trip to New York in December 1938, Anthony Eden, who had resigned as British foreign secretary over Chamberlain's appeasement policies earlier that year, remarked that the prime minister had managed to "lose American sympathy utterly. While I was there, most of my time was spent in asserting that Neville was not a fascist."

A few months later, Robert Bruce Lockhart, a bestselling author and former British diplomat, saw for himself what he called "the melodramatic and almost hysterical attitude of the Americans toward Britain." During a three-month lecture tour in the United States, he encountered considerable anti-Nazi sentiment, but, to his surprise, discovered that "criticism of the British government was even more bitter." In one city, he saw women wearing tiny white piqué umbrellas as lapel pins—a mocking salute to Chamberlain's trademark umbrella that had come to symbolize appeasement.

It was essential that the British act soon to combat such hostility and anger, but they had to tread extremely carefully. A good part of Americans' antagonism toward Britain in the late 1930s stemmed from the British government's sophisticated—and successful—propaganda campaign some twenty years before to draw America into World War I. Many Americans came to believe that their country had entered the war not because its own national interests demanded such action but because it had been tricked by the scheming, duplicitous British. And they were determined not to let it happen again.

BEWARE THE BRITISH SERPENT! screamed the headlines of posters plastered on the walls of buildings in Chicago and other Midwestern cities in late 1939. In smaller type, the posters declared: "Once more a boa constrictor—'Perfidious Albion'—is crawling across the American landscape, spewing forth its unctuous lies."

Prominent Britons who, like Bruce Lockhart, traveled throughout the country on lecture tours found themselves the objects of considerable anger and suspicion. Arriving in San Francisco, Duff Cooper, who had resigned as first lord of the Admiralty in protest over the Munich agreement, was greeted by a crowd of unruly protesters waving giant cardboard lollipops emblazoned with the slogan "Don't Be a Sucker for British Propaganda." After his own tour, the British literary critic William Empson ruefully wrote: "There were times when I felt quite sure that if I had stood on my head and sung 'Three Blind Mice,' [my American hosts] would have wondered why the British government had paid me to do *that*."

Highly sensitive to American ill will, the British government had forbidden any more official propaganda or special pleading campaigns in the United States. The only remnant of its World War I effort was a small press bureau, known as the British Library of Information, that continued to function, albeit somnolently, in New York. Unbeknownst to his superiors at the Foreign Office, Sir Robert Vansittart, who had been one of the most outspoken antiappeasement figures in the British government, decided to turn the library into a press intelligence unit, whose first assignment would be to closely monitor American public opinion and then, in the future, try to influence it. To do that, he needed Britons who not only knew the United States but who got along well with Americans and were in a position to sway their views.

In Vansittart's opinion, Lindbergh's brother-in-law, Aubrey Morgan, fit the bill perfectly. So did John Wheeler-Bennett. Left a fortune by his father, a wealthy London importer, the gregarious Wheeler-Bennett had lived in the early 1930s in Germany, where he witnessed the rise of Hitler, wrote several books on diplomacy, and, being violently anti-Nazi, barely escaped arrest by the Gestapo. Soon afterward, he became a lecturer on international relations at Oxford and later took on the same role at the University of Virginia.

Wheeler-Bennett's maternal grandmother had been a Virginian, and from childhood he had been enamored of the United States, particularly the South. Distantly related to A. P. Hill, a noted Confederate general, he became an expert on the Civil War and spent much of every year teaching in Charlottesville. His students at the university included the president's son Franklin D. Roosevelt Jr., who in January 1939 invited him to spend a weekend at the White House, where FDR pumped him for information about the Munich agreement.

Both John Wheeler-Bennett and Aubrey Morgan were appalled at "the spirit of lethargy" they found at the British Library of Information. On his own initiative and using his own money, Morgan set up a team of writers to gather information about America's mood, much of it found in U.S. newspaper articles and radio broadcasts, and to write reports on the material, which were then sent to Whitehall and the British embassy in Washington. Employees of this new survey department, known as the "clip club," included some good friends of Morgan's, his private secretary, and his twenty-five-year-old wife.

Morgan himself began to make contacts with prominent American journalists and pro-British members of the East Coast establishment. Soon, as the historian Nicholas Cull has noted, "a river of intelligence was flowing into his office. It would be a relatively modest task to switch the direction of this tide and transform [it] from a receiving office for information on public opinion into a full-blown propaganda agency."

For the British, this new offensive had come none too soon. The "gathering storm," as Winston Churchill called the war threatening Europe, was about to break at last.

CHAPTER 4

"YOU HAVEN'T GOT THE VOTES"

On the surface, it seemed like the start of a typical Labor Day weekend. Americans were making their final trips to the beach and other favorite summer spots, getting ready to put up their sailboats, store their fishing rods, and head back to the routines of home and work. At thousands of country clubs and roadhouses across the country, the last music of the season played late into the night. Large crowds, taking advantage of the long holiday weekend, flocked to the 1939 New York World's Fair.

Earlier that summer, Charles and Anne Lindbergh had finally found a home of their own—a big white clapboard house on the north shore of Long Island, perched high on a hill overlooking Long Island Sound. After a violent thunderstorm the previous night, Friday, September 1, dawned dazzlingly bright, and Anne decided to take a walk on the beach below the house. Before she did, she turned on the radio for the latest news broadcast—and learned that Germany had just invaded Poland. In a daze, she headed for the beach, where she walked for hours, trying, as millions of other Americans were doing, to comprehend the momentous news.

On September 3, after two days of dithering, the British and French governments finally lived up to their pledges to Poland and declared war on Germany. That night, President Roosevelt went on the air to proclaim America's neutrality in the conflict. Yet he also made clear that he had no intention of asking Americans to be "impartial in thought as well as in action," as Woodrow Wilson had done at the start of World War I. "This nation will remain a neutral nation," FDR declared, "but . . . [e]ven a neutral has a right to take account of facts. Even a neutral cannot be asked to close his mind or his conscience."

After this subtle indication of support for the Western allies, Roosevelt went on to pledge: "I hope the United States will keep out of this war. I believe that it will. And I give you assurance and reassurance that every effort of your government will be directed to that end." At a press conference the following day, he tried again to soothe the country. "There is no thought in any shape, manner or form, of putting the nation, either in its defenses or in its internal economy, on a war basis," he told the reporters crowded around him. "We are going to keep the nation on a peace basis."

According to the noted playwright Robert Sherwood, who would become a top FDR aide less than a year later, these statements "were probably the weakest words that Roosevelt ever uttered. He was outdoing even Warren Harding by getting the country 'back to normalcy' before war had really started."

But what else could he do? He was boxed in by the antiwar mood of both the public and Congress. Stickers declaring KEEP THE U.S. OUT OF WAR adorned car windshields all over America within days of the British and French declaration. A French journalist based in New York observed: "This country is literally drunk with pacifism. The war as an absolute evil in itself has become a mysticism. One no longer dares to pronounce the word nor to think of it except with pious horror. To spare our boys has taken on the value of a national mission."

Yet Roosevelt, while pledging to keep the country out of war, was still determined to come to the aid of Britain and France through repeal of the arms embargo provision of the neutrality law. Persuading Congress to authorize "cash and carry" for arms shipments to the Western allies would become the administration's primary objective for the fall of 1939 and the first wartime decision to face America. As the president knew only too well, it would be an excruciatingly difficult battle.

LESS THAN TWO MONTHS before, on a hot July night, Roosevelt had invited key senators from both parties to the White House in a last-ditch effort to persuade them to amend or repeal the Neutrality Act before war broke out. After the senators poured drinks for themselves from an array of liquor bottles on a side table, Roosevelt and Secretary of State Cordell Hull argued that the world was on the brink of catastrophe and pleaded with the lawmakers to allow America to throw its weight on the scales before it was too late.

Leaning back in his chair, Senator William Borah shook his leonine head in cool disdain. The seventy-four-year-old Republican from Idaho had heard all this before. A member of the Senate since 1907, he had been that body's fiercest and most influential proponent of isolationism since he helped spearhead the congressional battle against Woodrow Wilson and the League of Nations in 1919. When Wilson, stymied by the Senate, embarked on a speaking tour of the nation to make his case for the League, Borah and a band of like-minded senators followed him everywhere, arguing the opposite to huge crowds. Thanks in no small part to Borah's persuasive oratory, public opinion turned against the League, and Wilson, his health broken by a stroke, saw his cherished dream go down to defeat.

Now Borah looked at Roosevelt, then at Hull. "There is not going to be any war in Europe this year," he snapped. "All this hysteria is manufactured and artificial." Struggling hard to keep his voice calm, the secretary of state said he wished the senator "would come to my office and look over the cables coming in. I feel satisfied he would modify his views." Borah dismissed Hull's comment with a contemptuous wave of his hand. He had, he replied, "sources of information in Europe that I regard as more reliable than those of the State Department." They had told him "that there is not going to be any war."*

Dumbfounded by what the columnist Joseph Alsop later termed Borah's "inconceivable arrogance," a white-faced Hull lapsed into silence. Roosevelt, for his part, retained his customary jaunty good humor, at least outwardly, even when his vice president, John Nance Garner, announced to him: "Well, captain, we might as well face the facts. You haven't got the votes, and that's all there is to it."

As Roosevelt was well aware, he hadn't had the votes for much of

---

* When Joseph Alsop later asked Borah who those sources were, the senator reached into his desk drawer and pulled out a copy of a highly opinionated political newsletter called *The Week,* written and edited by Claud Cockburn, a leading British Communist.

anything in Congress over the past several months. Largely because of his own political miscues, a powerful coalition of Republicans and conservative Democrats had been successful in defeating several major pieces of legislation advocated by the administration. In early 1939, when Democratic congressional leaders urged their dissident colleagues to stick together and support FDR, one of the rebels responded: "Congress has done all the cooperating in the past. It's up to the President to do some now."

The extent of the president's loss of influence had been immense. When he first took office in 1933, he could do no wrong. The American public, facing economic catastrophe and yearning for strong leadership, supported virtually every program he proposed, and Congress marched behind him in lockstep.

In later years, the New Deal did draw increasing fire from business and industry executives, Wall Street bankers, and other well-to-do Americans, who condemned its penchant for heavy government spending, stricter federal regulation of business and banking, and encouragement of labor unions. The president's conservative foes claimed he was a revolutionary, intent on destroying "the American way of life."

Even so, Roosevelt appeared invincible. For all the vitriolic sniping at him by his critics, he was extremely popular with a majority of Americans, as demonstrated by his historic landslide victory over Republican Alf Landon in 1936. Landon carried only two states, and his fellow Republicans suffered calamitous losses in Congress, winning just 89 seats in the House and seeing their Senate roster drop to 17. So many Democrats were elected to the Senate that twelve of their freshmen had to be seated on the Republican side of the chamber—an unusually large number and another humiliating indignity for the GOP.

With FDR's lopsided majorities in Congress, who could possibly stand in his way? Even as he savored his overwhelming triumph, the president was acutely aware of the answer. Over the past two years, the Supreme Court, dominated by conservative justices, had struck down several key New Deal initiatives. A number of new government programs, including Social Security, were edging up the list for judicial review. Not only was the administration's second-term legislative agenda in peril, so, it appeared, was the entire New Deal. Buoyed by his huge election mandate, Roosevelt was determined to stop that threat in its tracks.

On February 5, 1937, the president outlined to congressional leaders a piece of legislation that would end up undercutting his influence and authority and severely damaging his administration, the country, and the world for years to come. The biggest mistake of his presidency, the measure—and the battle over it—would greatly strengthen FDR's political enemies and leave him so unsure of his standing in the country that from then on, he would be reluctant to move more than a few millimeters ahead of public opinion.

Under the legislation, the president would be given the power to enlarge the Supreme Court by appointing as many as six additional justices, increasing their number from nine to a maximum of fifteen. The ostensible purpose of the plan was to improve the court's efficiency; more than half the current justices were seventy or older—too old, FDR argued, to keep up with the heavy caseload.

Every person in the room knew that his rationale was bunk. What the president had in mind was to appoint a new crop of justices whose views agreed with his. Why not be honest about it? Why try to deceive Congress and the public with an explanation that no one would believe? After all, he was not alone in thinking that something needed to be done about the Court and its relentless obstruction of reform efforts, its seeming determination to grant Congress no power to intervene in social or economic matters through legislation. For more than a year, there had been calls from Capitol Hill and elsewhere for enactment of a statute or constitutional amendment to curb the Court's power.

Aides and cabinet members had urged Roosevelt to make the Supreme Court a campaign issue in the 1936 election, to explain to voters how the highest judicial body in the land had continually thwarted the will of the people as expressed by Congress. The campaign was the perfect forum in which to seek a mandate for reform, FDR's supporters contended; regardless of what he said about the Court, there was no way he could lose the election.

Roosevelt, loath to do anything that might narrow his victory margin, refused. Only an unequivocal landslide, he felt, could give him the popular sanction he needed to take on the Supreme Court. And that he had achieved in November. FDR had always been "filled with unbounded self assurance," his chief speechwriter, Samuel Rosenman, noted, but now it had blossomed into an "overconfidence which, even for him, was spectacular and dangerous." Again and again, Roosevelt told his aides, "The people have spoken." With them on his side, he felt he needed no one else.

Sitting in stunned silence as they read the bill, congressional leaders begged to differ. They were dumbfounded by Roosevelt's springing this extraordinarily controversial measure on them as if they had nothing to do with its becoming law. They were the ones who would have to harry and hound their congressional colleagues into passing it. He had not consulted them, had not worked to build a broad coalition behind the bill before introducing it. In the most flagrant way possible, he had made clear he considered them nothing but errand boys.

For some time now, it had seemed to members of Congress that FDR was taking them for granted. "[M]any Congressmen resented the feeling of being lackeys or rubber stamps of a chief executive who had taken over the legislative function," noted one journalist. This growing dissatisfaction only served to sharpen the culture clash that had existed between Congress and the administration since the president's earliest days in office.

On Capitol Hill, there was none of the brisk pace and frenzied, electric atmosphere found elsewhere in New Deal Washington. Congress still carried on in the drowsy, genteel manner of the late nineteenth century, as evidenced by its polished brass spittoons, snuffboxes on senators' desks, potted palms, and the McKinley-era black sofas and armchairs that adorned the Capitol's public rooms. Westerners like William Borah still wore string ties on the Senate floor, and in the summer, southern congressmen sported white suits, looking for all the world like plantation owners, as some of them indeed were.

On slow afternoons, several of the more elderly senators could be seen napping in armchairs outside the Senate chamber. A similar atmosphere prevailed in the Senate pressroom, where "news was scarce, and there was not much work to do," recalled Joseph Alsop, then a young Capitol Hill correspondent for the *New York Herald Tribune*. "One or two of the older men would nod off to sleep on the ample sofas, and the rest of us would draw huge leather chairs up around the fire and trade tales and gossip."

There was no such lethargy in the executive branch. Throughout the 1930s, government agencies were hotbeds of energy and experimentation, often hovering on the brink of bedlam, where "men rush in and out and fume at the slowness of the elevators." Young, Ivy League–educated economists, lawyers, professors, and specialists in various arcane disciplines flocked to Washington to join the agencies' staffs.

Many of these intellectuals were openly patronizing and contemptuous of congressmen and the staff members of their committees, who were largely patronage appointees and had considerable difficulty keeping up with erudite, fast-talking administration witnesses. According to a 1942 study, only four of the seventy-six congressional committees had "expert staffs prepared professionally even to cross-examine experts of the executive branch."

Congress had nobody but itself to blame for this backward state of affairs. Conservative southern Democrats, who held most of the leadership positions on Capitol Hill, had no interest in increasing staffs or taking any other measures that would help Congress effectively monitor the executive branch and stay abreast of a complex, rapidly changing world. "They didn't want the institution to change," remarked the journalist and author Neil McNeil, an expert on U.S. congressional history. That didn't mean, however, that House and Senate leaders looked kindly on the administration elbowing Congress aside. "It's no fun to work with [the president]," Rep. Joseph Martin, the House minority leader, once told a reporter. "He don't ask you, he tells you."

Attorney General Robert Jackson, who had known Roosevelt when he was governor of New York, once speculated that the president had transferred to Congress a good bit of the combative attitude he had shown toward the New York legislature, which was heavily Republican. As governor, FDR treated the legislature as "a target instead of a collaborator," Jackson said, and was always "trying to outmaneuver it."

Faced with the Supreme Court bill, some of the congressional leaders finally rebelled. After their meeting with the president, Rep. Hatton Sumners of Texas, chairman of the House Judiciary Committee, announced to his colleagues: "Boys, here's where I cash in my chips." In the Senate cloakroom, Vice President John Nance Garner, a former congressman from Texas, revealed to senators his opinion of the bill by holding his nose and pointing his thumb toward the carpet.

Since Sumners's committee would play a vital role in the measure's consideration, his immediate opposition was an ominous portent of things to come. Soon after introduction of the legislation, the White House began receiving disturbing reports of other congressional Democrats, reliable past supporters of the president, also coming out in opposition. According to Marquis Childs, an influential Washington newspaper columnist, the court reform bill was "the signal that released all the smoldering animosity that had been obscured" by Roosevelt's landslide. "Within the space of a few hours," Childs wrote, "the lines were drawn for a battle that served in large part to nullify the thundering majority of two months before."

And there was even more bad news for FDR. The leader of the Senate fight against the legislation was to be Burton Wheeler, a feisty progressive Democrat who just a few years earlier had been a strong Roosevelt supporter. To the Republicans' delight, members of the president's own party had decided to take the initiative in the battle against him.

The gregarious, cigar-smoking Wheeler was once described by *Life* as "one of the wiliest and toughest operators in American politics." A bare-knuckle political fighter with a "cool and deadly" smile, the senator had adopted as his motto: "If I don't get them, they'll get me." Considering his earlier life, the maxim made perfect sense.

The tenth son of an impoverished Quaker shoemaker in Hudson, Massachusetts, Wheeler had worked his way through law school at the University of Michigan, then headed west, looking for a place to practice his new profession. He ended up in Butte, Montana, a tough, hardbitten copper mining town that seemed to come straight out of the dime Wild West novels that Wheeler had devoured as a boy.

The main power in Butte—and the rest of Montana—was the Anaconda Copper Co., known to Wheeler and other state residents simply as "the Company." Much like the snake that shared its name, Anaconda was known for its tight grip on those in its coils; it basically controlled the economic and political life of the state. Those who defied the Company did so at their peril, as Wheeler discovered when, first as a young lawyer and then as a state legislator, he campaigned for better working conditions for Anaconda miners. Threats of bodily

Senator Burton K. Wheeler.

harm and political reprisals did nothing to dissuade him. "Anything the Company was for, he was ipso facto against," Marquis Childs noted.

In 1922, Wheeler was elected to the Republican-controlled U.S. Senate. He immediately launched an investigation into the involvement of Attorney General Harry Daugherty, a close crony of the recently deceased President Warren G. Harding, in the selling of pardons, acceptance of kickbacks from bootleggers, creation of illegal stock market pools, and intimidation and blackmail of government critics.

Daugherty, who was still in office, fought back against this Democratic upstart. Federal agents ransacked the offices of Wheeler and other members of his investigating committee. They also kept his house under surveillance and shadowed Wheeler and his wife. In 1924, he was indicted for allegedly using his senatorial influence to help a former legal client acquire oil leases. The case, however, had all the earmarks of a frame-up, and a Senate committee promptly exonerated him; soon afterward, a jury acquitted him after deliberating for just ten minutes.

In the end, Harding's successor, Calvin Coolidge, forced Daugherty to resign, and Wheeler emerged as a national political figure. Years later, a novel based on the freshman senator's fight against government corruption, entitled *The Gentleman from Montana,* was sold to Hollywood. The movie that resulted was the 1939 hit *Mr. Smith Goes to Washington*, starring James Stewart.

In 1930, Wheeler was the first Democrat of national stature to call for the election of Franklin Roosevelt, then governor of New York, as president. At the 1932 Democratic convention, he played an important role in getting Roosevelt the nomination, and during the campaign, he traveled throughout the West on FDR's behalf. In 1935, he was asked by Roosevelt to lead the battle for Senate passage of a controversial measure to curb the power of utility holding companies. The nasty, hard-fought struggle ended in triumph for both the Montana Democrat and the administration.

By early 1937, however, the ambitious Wheeler, who had designs on the presidency himself, had become disenchanted with the man he had helped elect. He complained of increasing difficulty in getting access to Roosevelt and of the administration's favoring his political enemies in Montana with patronage that should have gone to him. He noted that the last time he had run for reelection, the president had traveled the state without ever mentioning his name. Wheeler was an inveterate grudge collector, and he had collected a sizable number against FDR.

During Roosevelt's presidency, Wheeler had become part of the ruling crowd for the first time in his life. But the role of insider didn't really suit him. He was always more comfortable in opposition, whether to the Company, to government corruption, or, in 1937, to what he considered the president's growing lust for power, which, in his view, threatened Congress as well as the Supreme Court. "I've been watching Roosevelt for a long time," Wheeler told the presidential aide Thomas Corcoran. "Once he was only one of us who made him. Now he means to make himself the boss of us all. Your Court plan doesn't matter: he's after us."

Relishing the battle ahead, Wheeler marshaled his forces against the White House and Senate Democratic leadership. It was a clash of extraordinary intensity, one that would last for months and arouse the passions of the country. Joseph Alsop would later call the Court fight the "greatest national debate to take place in Congress during my career there" and "the greatest single political drama I have witnessed in Washington."

As winter gave way to spring, the hemorrhaging of congressional support for the president's proposal picked up speed. What began as a clash between the president and Supreme Court had evolved into a venomous, no-holds-barred fight between the executive and legislature. After weeks of debate, the Senate defeated the bill on July 22, 1937, with 20 members in favor and 70 against. Most of those voting in opposition were Democrats.

When the congressional session had begun in January, Roosevelt, fresh from his landslide victory, had towered over the Washington landscape. Now, as Congress prepared to adjourn, he was so politically weakened that, as one historian put it, "the chances of congressional passage of anything he proposed were diminished by the very fact that he had proposed it."

Having handed Roosevelt the worst trouncing of his presidency, Wheeler reveled in his triumph. "I must confess," he later wrote, "that it gave me quite a thrill when we defeated the President. We could not have had a smarter or more powerful antagonist." As the victor, Wheeler could afford to be magnanimous. The deeply humiliated president felt otherwise.

On the surface, he was his usual imperturbable, confident, genial self. In reality, however, he was shaken, resentful, angry, and determined to get even. Francis Biddle, who served as solicitor general and attorney general under Roosevelt, once described him as "an Old Testament Christian, who believed that his friends should be rewarded and retribution visited on his enemies, for . . . once his will was marshaled behind a defined vision, it became sinful for others to interfere with its fruition."

According to the journalists Joseph Alsop and Turner Catledge, FDR "had made up his mind that if he had to suffer, the men in Congress whom he held responsible would suffer doubly later on." Urged on by his closest advisers, he decided to lead an effort in the 1938 congressional primaries to defeat a select group of conservative Democratic senators and congressmen who had opposed the court-packing proposal. (Wheeler, who was not up for reelection that year, had his income tax return audited for the first time in his life.)

In previous elections, Roosevelt had relied on his enormous personal popularity with the voters to achieve his electoral goals. By 1938, however, the situation had changed dramatically. The country was in the midst of a severe recession, and, in a Gallup poll taken earlier that year, barely half of those responding said they would vote for the president if he were running for reelection that year.

They still liked him as a person, the voters made clear, but they were increasingly wary of his programs, his advisers, and, above all, his manner of governing. There was particular concern about what was seen as his attempts to gain too much power, with half of those questioned in the poll saying they thought he should have less authority.

Unsurprisingly, then, Roosevelt's exceedingly bitter campaign to purge his congressional opponents resulted in disaster. Only one of the men he targeted was defeated in the Democratic primaries. Even worse, the Republicans made a dramatic comeback in the general election, nearly doubling their numbers in the House and picking up eight new Senate seats. While the Democrats still held large majorities in the two chambers, both were far more conservative than they had been in the previous five years.

This was the lowest point of Franklin Roosevelt's presidency—and it coincided with the period in which Hitler and Mussolini stepped up their march to war. No matter how much FDR may have wanted to intervene in the darkening European situation, he felt powerless to take any concrete action. "Punch drunk from the punishment" he had suffered in Congress and at the polls, as Interior Secretary Harold Ickes put it, Roosevelt lost his previously unquenchable confidence that the American people would always stand behind him. From then on, his actions and decisions would be dictated by an unwonted wariness and caution, a determination never to get too far ahead of public opinion, which at that point was still profoundly against American involvement in a European war.

WITHIN DAYS OF BRITAIN's and France's declarations of war against Germany, isolationist members of Congress and their allies launched a drive to arouse public opposition to administration attempts to aid the Western allies. Hundreds of thousands of antiwar letters, postcards, petitions, and telegrams poured into the offices of senators and congressmen. Some members received so much mail that hand trucks were needed to deliver it.

While many in both houses of Congress were ardently opposed to U.S. intervention in the war, the real stronghold of isolationism was the Senate, where a handful of members held the whip hand in foreign affairs. They included Burton Wheeler and several other prominent progressive senators from the Midwest and West, chief among them William Borah, Hiram Johnson of California, and Gerald Nye of North Dakota.

Ironically, although all but Wheeler were Republicans, they had strongly backed most of FDR's early domestic legislation, breaking with the administration only when they thought it was not bold or radical enough. Colorful, quirky, and rebellious, the GOP progressives, in their fight for social and economic justice and against the concentration of economic power, had repeatedly defied the three Republican administrations preceding Roosevelt's. Exasperated by their refusal to fit the conservative Republican mold, one GOP leader called them "sons of the wild jackass"—a term the progressives proudly adopted as their "password and badge of honor."

Of this group, Wheeler was the only newcomer to the isolationist cause. Although he had always been antiwar, he had touted the importance of collective security after World War I and had supported the League of Nations. His opposition to Roosevelt's campaign to help Britain and France stemmed less from hard-core isolationist beliefs than from his intense dislike of the president and his determination to prevent FDR from garnering any more power. He shared the view expressed by Hiram Johnson that Roosevelt "wants to knock down two dictators in Europe, so that one may be firmly implanted in America."

Borah and Johnson, the two ranking Republicans on the Senate Foreign Relations Committee, were the grand old men of American isolationism. Like Wheeler, they were combative, contrary, independent-minded mavericks from the West, who had always felt like outsiders in the gentleman's club of the Senate. In 1919, they and the other senatorial foes of the Versailles Treaty and League of Nations had been dubbed the "Battalion of Death" and "the Irreconcilables" for their ferocious opposition to the League.

Born soon after the Civil War, both senators were blinkered by the late-nineteenth-century world in which they had grown up—a world without warplanes and submarines, which viewed America as an invincible fortress and the idea of a threat from Europe as absurd. Borah, who took great pride in never having traveled outside the United States, joined Johnson in refusing to accept the idea that, as the most powerful economic power on earth, their country could no longer act, in the words of Oliver Wendell Holmes Jr., as a "snug, over-safe corner of the world." As determined to stop American involvement in World War II as they had been to torpedo Woodrow Wilson, both, however, were in their early seventies and in declining health. They would take an active role in the fight against FDR's proposed revision of the Neutrality Act, but afterward, the leadership baton would pass to Wheeler.

While even the bitterest foes of Borah, Johnson, and Wheeler regarded them as effective, serious senators, the same could not be said for the fourth member of the Senate's isolationist leadership, Gerald Nye. Roosevelt called the North Dakota Republican "unscrupulous." Joseph Alsop wrote that Nye, a former country newspaper editor, "had no principles whatsoever." A pugnacious, publicity-seeking gadfly, he had made his debut in the Senate chamber in 1925, wearing

Senator Gerald Nye.

high-top yellow shoes and a gaudy tie and sporting a soup-bowl hair-cut. Although he eventually adopted a different hairstyle and took to wearing more conservative ties and shoes, he never strayed far from his small-town roots or populist-progressive politics.

In 1934, after a flood of revisionist books and magazine articles had whipped up a public outcry about the causes of World War I, Nye was appointed to head a Senate investigation into the role of U.S. and European bankers and munitions makers in maneuvering the United States into the war. Like other agrarian populists, Nye had long denounced the power of big business and Wall Street. For him, the munitions probe was a tailor-made opportunity to convince the public that "merchants of death" and "economic royalists" had duped the U.S. government and people into entering a conflict that was none of America's business, solely for the purpose of making unconscionable profits.

Some American companies did indeed make huge amounts of money from World War I. But during its hearings, the Nye committee refused to consider the possibility that the United States might also have had legitimate commercial and geopolitical reasons for getting involved. Specifically, no one mentioned that America's cherished isolation from Europe's affairs was made possible in large part by the supremacy of the British fleet. If Germany had won control not only of Europe but of European waters and the sea-lanes of the Atlantic, the threat to America's economy and security would have increased exponentially.

The columnist Walter Lippmann called the findings of the Nye committee "a falsification of history." But in the years leading up to World War II, they had far-reaching effects. Heavily influenced by the committee's conclusions, many Americans came to believe that wars were fought almost exclusively for the economic gain of a few greedy capitalists. It stood to reason, then, that if armament sales and trade with belligerents were curbed, America could keep itself out of war. Such simplistic ideas led to the passage of the neutrality legislation, in which Nye played a key role.

Nye enjoyed being in the limelight and quickly capitalized on his newfound fame. A private lecture agency arranged speaking tours for him throughout the country, during which, for handsome fees, he railed against the "merchants of death." As Roosevelt cautiously stepped up his efforts to lead America away from isolationism in the late 1930s, Nye launched increasingly vehement attacks against the president.

When Roosevelt announced on September 13, 1939, that he was calling Congress back into special session to take up revision of the neutrality law, Nye and the other isolationist senators were lying in wait. The following night, William Borah, known as the best speaker in the Senate, was scheduled to make a nationwide radio broadcast, kicking off a massive nationwide publicity campaign against "cash and carry."

As formidable an opponent as FDR knew Borah to be, the president was far more worried about another foe. As he had feared for months, Charles Lindbergh was now set to enter the lists. The battle for America's soul was about to begin.

CHAPTER 5

"THIS WAR HAS
COME HOME TO ME"

After the Western allies' declaration of war, Lindbergh was initially undecided about what his role should be in the upcoming debate. Before leaving Europe, he had vowed to do everything in his power to keep America neutral, but since his return, he had devoted most of his energies to building up U.S. airpower. Now that war was finally here, he still hesitated, knowing that his involvement would catapult him back into the whirlpool of celebrity he hated so much. Finally, on September 7, he made up his mind. As much as he disliked politics and public life, he wrote, "I do not intend to stand by and see this country pushed into war."

Earlier that summer, he had been invited to dinner at the home of William R. Castle, a former diplomat who had been Herbert Hoover's undersecretary of state and closest foreign policy adviser and who was now a fervent opponent of U.S. involvement in the war. Present, too, was Fulton Lewis Jr., a young conservative radio commentator for the Mutual network. As the three men chatted, Lewis, realizing that the famed aviator "had something on his chest," suggested he come on the air as a guest speaker to "tell the American people how you feel about things." After thinking about the offer for a moment, Lindbergh replied: "I don't believe I could do that. But I'd like a rain check on the invitation." A week after the war began, he cashed in the check, arranging with Lewis to make a broadcast on September 15.

He was urged on by Colonel Truman Smith, who'd been a good friend of Lindbergh's since Smith, the former U.S. military attaché in Germany, had invited him to visit Berlin in 1936. In April 1939, Smith had been ordered to return to the United States after being diagnosed with diabetes. Facing a mandatory disability retirement, he was rescued by then deputy chief of staff George Marshall, who had served as a mentor to Smith earlier in his career. Marshall restored him to active service as his chief analyst and adviser on German affairs, a position Smith kept when Marshall was appointed Army chief of staff on September 1, 1939.

Pro-German and fiercely anti-Roosevelt, Smith agreed with Lindbergh that Britain and France should seek accommodation with Germany rather than risk another war. He contended that the Third Reich posed no threat to America and that it should be allowed to pursue its expansionist policy of *Lebensraum,* which, if implemented, would mean German conquest of all of Central and Eastern Europe as well as the Soviet Union. While serving as a key adviser to Marshall, Smith actively worked with Lindbergh against the administration's foreign policy.

A few days before his broadcast, Lindbergh showed a copy of his speech to Hap Arnold, to whom he had become personally close. Indeed, just two weeks before, he had had dinner with Arnold and Marshall at Arnold's home. In his journal, Lindbergh noted that the air chief seemed very sympathetic to the ideas in his speech and said that he was "fully within [his] rights as an American citizen" to make it. Nonetheless, he advised Lindbergh to stop his work for the Air Corps while taking part in political activity. Lindbergh did as Arnold suggested, returning to inactive status in the Army Reserve.

Arnold's relaxed attitude about the broadcast was hardly shared by other Roosevelt administration officials. Alarm bells were soon ringing in the White House, since Lindbergh was arguably the only man in the country who could rival Roosevelt in commanding the public's attention. Over the previous four months, Lindbergh had managed to mend his somewhat tattered reputation through his well-publicized campaign to increase and improve U.S. airpower. "He is just as loyal an American as he ever was, just as interested in his profession, just as desirous of doing something worthwhile in the world," *The New York Times* assured its readers.

Ever since his historic flight, the reclusive Lindbergh had been a figure of mystery to the American people. In all those years, he had never publicly revealed his political opinions or discussed his private feelings. Nor had he ever spoken on American radio, not even at the time of his son's kidnapping. Knowing that a Lindbergh broadcast would draw a huge audience, the White House scrambled to stop him.

The day before the broadcast, Truman Smith came to see him. Smith passed on an oral message from Hap Arnold, who received it from War Secretary Harry Woodring, who in turn got it from unnamed White House officials. If Lindbergh canceled the speech, the message said, the administration would create a new cabinet post for him. He would be named secretary of the Air Corps, a position that would make him the coequal of Woodring and Charles Edison, the secretary of the Navy.

Lindbergh stared incredulously at Smith, then burst out laughing. So did Smith, who said, "You see, they're worried." Hap Arnold knew that Lindbergh would turn down the proposition, Smith added, but since it had come from the war secretary's office, the Air Corps chief felt obliged to pass it on.

Lindbergh did reject the offer. On the night of September 15, he went before six microphones in a room at Washington's Carlton Hotel to share with the American people his opposition to any U.S. involvement in the European war. Thanks to enormous public interest in the speech, all three national radio networks carried it.

While he made no direct mention of the upcoming congressional fight over the Neutrality Act revisions, Lindbergh, his reedy, high-pitched voice containing a hint of a Midwestern twang, declared that sending munitions to the Western allies could never ensure victory. To "take part successfully" in the conflict, the country would have to send millions of American boys overseas—millions that "we are likely to lose . . . the best of American youth."

In his view, the war was not a battle of good versus evil, democracy against totalitarianism. It was just another in a long history of internal European feuds, "a quarrel arising from the errors of the last war," that Americans could—and should—do nothing to resolve. Lindbergh advised his massive radio audience to view the world situation as he did—with utter detachment, never allowing "our sentiment, our pity, our personal feelings of sympathy, to obscure the issue [or] to affect our children's lives. We must be as impersonal as a surgeon with his knife."

It was the duty of the United States, he added, to act as a repository of Western civilization, which was on the verge of being torn apart in Europe. "This is the test before America now. . . . As long as we maintain an army, a navy, and an air force worthy of the name, as long as America does not decay within, we need fear no invasion of this country."

In laying out his central argument, Lindbergh took a moment to sound a disturbing note of racial supremacy. The real threat to Western civilization, he declared, came not from Germany but from the Soviet Union or some other "Asiatic intruder." Instead of fighting one another, European countries—and the United States—should band together to "defend the white race against foreign invasion."

Lindbergh's advocacy of racial purity, which would become a hallmark of his speeches and writing over the next two years, was similar to the racial theories of Hitler and other Nazis. But it was also a widespread belief throughout the United States and Europe during the nineteenth and first half of the twentieth centuries. It had its origins in eugenics, a pseudoscience advocating the improvement of human hereditary traits by selective breeding. As the proponents of eugenics saw it, whites of Northern and Western European descent—"the exemplar of the highest type of civilization yet evolved"—were inherently superior, mentally and morally, to "the black, brown, and yellow races." (Russians were included in the nonwhite category: the infusion of Mongol blood meant that the "racial characteristics of the Russian [had become] fundamentally more Asiatic than European.")

At the peak of its popularity, eugenics was promoted by governments, treated as a legitimate academic discipline by prestigious universities, and supported by influential individuals, among them Theodore Roosevelt, Woodrow Wilson, H. G. Wells, George Bernard Shaw, and John Maynard Keynes. By the 1930s, however, it had begun to fall into disrepute, primarily because of its identification with Nazi Germany, which used it as justification for the Reich's horrific racial policies, including the extermination of "defective" populations such as homosexuals, the retarded and mentally ill, Gypsies—and, most infamously, the Jews.

Nonetheless, racist theories like those espoused by Lindbergh in his speech were still being put forward in the late 1930s by other well-known and influential Americans. They also were deeply embedded in the culture of the U.S. military. Books by prominent white supremacists such as Lothrop Stoddard had long been mandatory reading at West Point and other Army institutions of higher learning. Taught that the white Aryan race had always taken "the leading part in the great drama of the world's progress," officers were encouraged to see themselves as the guardians of true Americanism, as embodied by Anglo-Saxon society.

Perhaps because such attitudes were so commonplace, little public attention was paid at the time to Lindbergh's references to race in his broadcast. As the White House had foreseen, however, the speech was a national sensation, not so much because of what was said (which was not very different from the arguments made by other isolationists) but because of who said it.

Anne Lindbergh had reportedly edited the speech, and the line "We must be as impersonal as a surgeon with his knife" was said to be hers. But if that was so, it was not a sentiment she shared. Unlike Lindbergh, she was never dispassionate about this war. On the day it was declared, she was consumed by visions of catastrophe—destruction of the British and French air forces, Paris and London under endless bombardment, her French and British friends killed, "all the things we love . . . destroyed." As she watched Charles make the broadcast in the Carlton, she prayed that the Lindberghs' friends in Europe would realize how difficult it was for him to deliver the speech, to turn his back, in effect, on the countries that had given them sanctuary. Deep down, she knew they never would.

She was fearful, too, of her own response. Could she follow Charles as his "loyal page" in the battle that had just begun? She was not entirely sure of the answer. "That is the nightmare—separation from him," she wrote in her diary. "Suppose I should fail him? . . . I feel bitterly alone."

AFTER JUST ONE SPEECH, Charles Lindbergh—a man with little knowledge of and virtually no experience in politics and foreign affairs—found himself the most controversial figure on the U.S. political scene. In a matter of hours, he also had become the foremost champion of isolationism.

Thousands of letters and telegrams poured in immediately after the broadcast from "all kinds and types of people," Anne wrote Evangeline Lindbergh, her mother-in-law, "—grateful mothers & fathers, school professors and teachers, businessmen, and farmers. . . . C's speech has answered a real need, a clear call in the confusion." Among the letter writers was Hap Arnold, who told Lindbergh that his ardently isolationist boss, War Secretary Harry Woodring, thought the address "very well worded and very well delivered," as did Arnold himself.

Another of Lindbergh's correspondents, however, was profoundly dismayed by what he had heard that night. A few weeks earlier, Albert Einstein had written to Lindbergh, asking him to deliver a letter to President Roosevelt on behalf of Einstein and two other noted physicists, Leo Szilard and Edward Teller. The letter warned FDR that scientists in various countries were on the brink of producing an explosive nuclear chain reaction—a development that could lead to a bomb of extraordinary power. Noting that German scientists were among those hot on the trail of such a weapon, the letter urged Roosevelt to set up formal contact with physicists working on chain reactions in America.

Einstein had met Lindbergh in New York a few years earlier and, clearly unaware of his isolationist bent, suggested to his colleagues that the famed flier would be the perfect intermediary between them and the White House. When Lindbergh failed to respond to Einstein's letter, Szilard wrote him a reminder on September 13. Two days later, Lindbergh delivered his speech, and the reason for his silence became obvious. "Lindbergh," as Szilard ruefully noted to Einstein, "is not our man."*

Most of those who wrote to Lindbergh had a different view, with many urging him to present a specific program for keeping America out of the war. After consulting with Truman Smith, William Castle, and others, Lindbergh decided to give a second nationwide radio address on October 13, in the middle of the fierce congressional debate over revision of the Neutrality Act. This time, he went on record as

---

* A month later, the letter finally made it to the White House, prompting Roosevelt to begin the process that led to America's development of the atomic bomb.

opposing the sale of U.S. planes, ships, and most other munitions to Britain and France, adding, however, that the Allies should be allowed to buy defensive weapons such as antiaircraft guns. Since Lindbergh himself had said repeatedly that the only effective defense against an air attack was a strong air force, he was basically ceding the advantage to Germany.

Lindbergh also claimed that Britain and France were responsible for starting the conflict, asserting that if they had "offered a hand to the struggling republic of Germany" at the end of World War I, "there would be no war today." And, reiterating his belief in white solidarity and superiority, he declared: "Racial strength is vital; politics is luxury. If the white race is ever seriously threatened, it may then be time for us to take our part in its protection, to fight side by side with the English, French and Germans, but not with one against the other for our mutual destruction."

Once again, he touched off a storm of reaction, but this time, much of the comment was intensely critical. "To many a U.S. citizen," *Time* wrote, "he was a bum." Social and business circles that had previously welcomed Lindbergh now gave him a chilly reception. They included the partners of J. P. Morgan and Co., who invited Lindbergh to lunch one October day at the Morgan headquarters on Wall Street.

During Dwight Morrow's tenure at the House of Morgan, he had advised Lindbergh on his business dealings, and his colleagues at the firm had also befriended Morrow's son-in-law, welcoming him and Anne into their homes and taking care of their finances while they were in Europe. But at the lunch, the partners made clear that they strongly opposed his stand on the neutrality law. The Morgan men, as one of them later noted, had long been "pro-Ally by inheritance, by instinct, by opinion, and so were almost all the people we knew on the Eastern seaboard of the United States." After the lunch, Lindbergh noted in his journal that "obviously, my stand was extremely unpopular. . . . We all parted in a courteous (no personal feelings, you know) but tense atmosphere."

The British reaction to Lindbergh's speech was even more negative. As Anne had feared, Britons deeply resented his spurning of a country that had given him and his family refuge at a time when they needed it most. In late October, audiences at a London musical revue loudly cheered a song containing these lyrics:

Then there's Colonel Lindbergh
Who made a pretty speech,
He's somewhere in America,
We're glad he's out of reach.

Particularly painful to Anne was a column that Harold Nicolson wrote about her husband in *The Spectator,* a British current affairs weekly. Billed as an explanation of Lindbergh's behavior, Nicolson's piece contended that his "almost pathological" hatred of publicity and the press had led to a distrust of freedom of speech "and then, almost, of freedom [itself]. He began to loathe democracy." In the ten-plus years since Lindbergh's historic flight, Nicolson wrote, his "virility and ideas" had become "not merely inflexible but actually rigid; his self-confidence thickened into arrogance and his convictions hardened into granite." Nonetheless, the British writer declared, people should realize that Lindbergh had never really grown up and thus should not judge him too harshly: "To this day he remains [a] fine boy from the Middle West."

The condescending, wearily patient tone of Nicolson's article masked real fury on the part of its author. A member of Parliament since 1935, Nicolson belonged to a small group of antiappeasement rebels in the House of Commons who believed that Britain was on the brink of catastrophe and that the Chamberlain government must do considerably more to defeat Hitler. He had no sympathy or patience for the views of this American he had once considered a friend.

Lindbergh, for his part, curtly dismissed Nicolson's comments as "rather silly." He commented in his journal: "Like so many others (I expected something better from him), he attacks me personally rather than the things I advocate with which he disagrees. Naturally, the English did not like my addresses, but I expected a somewhat more objective criticism. . . . However the country is at war, and one should be prepared to overlook and excuse many acts from [its] citizens."

Anne could not be as dispassionate or loftily Olympian. When she first read "that biting little article," she felt as though "my breath was knocked out of me." The friendship of Nicolson, whose house in Kent had given her such happiness and whose warmth and encouragement helped her launch her writing career, had meant a great deal to her, and his disparagement of Charles was deeply hurtful.

Far more damaging to Lindbergh was a slashing attack by the celebrated political columnist Dorothy Thompson, America's leading journalistic critic of Hitler and his regime. Syndicated by the *New York Herald Tribune,* Thompson's column was carried by more than 150 newspapers nationwide and read by an estimated eight to ten million people a day. The massive size of her readership, combined with her weekly radio program on NBC and a popular monthly column in the *Ladies' Home Journal,* had made Thompson one of the most influential molders of American public opinion in the late 1930s and early 1940s.

"People who had probably never read a book in their lives quoted her familiarly from day to day," observed the journalist Vincent Sheean, a friend of Thompson's. "She was as much a star as any baseball player or film actress." Sheean's point was underscored by the popularity of the 1942 movie *Woman of the Year,* whose main character, played by Katharine Hepburn, was a fictionalized, thinly disguised version of Thompson.

Dorothy Thompson had first met Lindbergh in 1930, three years

Columnist Dorothy Thompson testifies before a Senate committee in September 1939 in favor of repealing the ban on selling arms to Britain and France.

after his flight to Paris, at a dinner party in northern California. Before dinner, Thompson had watched in horror as the young flier, playing one of the practical jokes of which he was so fond, stealthily poured mouthwash into a bottle of rare Burgundy being decanted on a sideboard. Prohibition still reigned in the country, and to Dorothy, "a very good Burgundy was a rare and precious thing," Vincent Sheean noted. "She never forgot [what Lindbergh had done]; it formed, or helped to form, her impression of him."

But irritating as his prank had been, it was his cool, unemotional rationalization of German aggression that really maddened her. Unlike Lindbergh, Thompson had not merely made a few quick, closely supervised trips to the Reich before announcing her views of the country to the world. As a foreign correspondent for two U.S. newspapers, she had lived in Germany and Austria during Hitler's rise to power, had witnessed firsthand the sheer evil of his regime. She had watched as Nazi thugs broke into the houses of Jews, leftists, and other so-called enemies of the Reich, beat them with steel rods, knocked their teeth out, urinated on them, and made them kneel and kiss swastika-adorned flags. Nazism, she wrote in the early 1930s, "is a complete break with reason, with Humanism, with the Christian ethics that are at the base of liberalism and democracy. . . . It is the enemy of whatever is freedom-loving and life-affirming."

In 1934, Thompson was expelled from Germany without warning, on direct orders from the Führer. It was the first time the Nazis had ever ejected an American reporter, and it made Thompson an international celebrity overnight. She began her newspaper column in 1936, and for the next four years, most of what she wrote took the form of caustic attacks on Nazi Germany, as well as on the indifference of other countries to the Nazi threat. "The spectacle of great, powerful, rich, democratic nations capitulating hour by hour to banditry, extortion, intimidation and violence is the most terrifying and discouraging sight in the world today," she declared. "It is more discouraging than the aggression itself." In another column, Thompson wrote that the "civilized world has had its face slapped and turned the other cheek so often that it's become rotary."

Her preoccupation with the international situation extended to her personal life as well. At dinner parties and other social gatherings, she could talk of virtually nothing else. "If I ever divorce Dorothy," her husband, the Nobel Prize–winning novelist Sinclair Lewis, once quipped, "I'll name Adolf Hitler as co-respondent." She was particularly angered by her own country's inaction. "She plainly feels that America's neutrality is a kind of cowardice," noted *The New Yorker,* "and she has repeatedly implied that if the United States manages to keep out of the war, it will be without her approval."

Unlike Lindbergh, Thompson passionately felt that the war was indeed a fight between good and evil and that America had a moral obligation to intercede. "Believe it or not," she wrote, in a direct slap at the flier, "there are such things in the world as morality, as law, as conscience, as a noble concept of humanity, which once awake, are stronger than all ideologies."

The fierceness of those beliefs undoubtedly contributed to the savagery of her assault on Lindbergh. He was, she wrote in her column, "a somber cretin," a man "without human feeling," a "pro-Nazi recipient of a German medal." She charged that Lindbergh had "a notion to be the American Fuhrer." While acknowledging she had no proof for this theory, she maintained that "Colonel Lindbergh's inclination toward Fascism is well known to his friends."

Eleanor Roosevelt, who had her own widely syndicated newspaper column, applauded Thompson for what she called her perceptive views about Lindbergh: "She sensed in Colonel Lindbergh's speech a sympathy with Nazi ideals which I thought existed but could not bring myself to believe was really there." There were others, however, who thought Thompson's incendiary remarks had gone too far. Even Harold Ickes, who had attacked Lindbergh with similarly tough language a year before, wondered whether she should have written what she did. Although he "heartily approved of what she had to say," Ickes went on to note: "Whether it was tactful to say all of this at once is questionable."

Thompson's column, as well as other press criticism of Lindbergh's October speech, undoubtedly contributed to the torrent of hate mail that descended on him and his wife, including several letters threatening to kidnap and kill their two small sons. Always in the back of Anne's mind was the searing memory of what had happened in March 1932—"that terrible, insane, evil world of The Case." She now wrote in her diary: "We are thrown back again into that awful atmosphere. . . . One can't take a chance. I feel angry and bitter and trapped again. Where can we live, where can we go?"

Although Lindbergh shared his wife's concern, he was determined to continue his fight against American involvement in the war. "I feel I must do this, even if we have to put an armed guard in the house," he wrote in his journal. Then came this bitter postscript: "It is a fine state of affairs in a country which feels it is civilized: people dislike what you do, so they threaten to kill your children."

The Lindberghs weren't alone, however, in feeling the lash of angry public opinion. For days after her anti-Lindbergh column, Dorothy Thompson received so many menacing letters that she told friends she feared for her safety. "I pray that the first bomb that is dropped on the U.S. will hit your Son," one letter began. Another said: "Why not get out of the U.S., as we do not care to have your kind around?" Much of the mail was addressed to "Dorothy Thompson, Warmonger." But Thompson refused to be cowed by the hostility directed at her. She would attack Lindbergh in three more columns that year, followed by six in 1940 and four in 1941.

Robert Sherwood.

ROBERT SHERWOOD WAS ANOTHER major U.S. writer profoundly affected by what Lindbergh had to say about America and the war. But unlike Dorothy Thompson, Sherwood did not publicly skewer the aviator—at least not then. His only comment about Lindbergh's addresses came in the form of a mild letter to the editor of *Time,* which had cryptically stated in an article that Lindbergh, in his second broadcast, had "represented Nobody, yet everybody." Sherwood protested: "I beg to say he did not represent me."

One of the best-known literary figures in New York and a founding member of the Algonquin Round Table, the forty-three-year-old Sherwood was the author of several popular Broadway plays. His latest, *Abe Lincoln in Illinois,* which had opened a few months before, was a smash hit and would soon win him a second Pulitzer Prize. (He would collect two more Pulitzers, as well as an Academy Award, before the end of his career.)

Sherwood had fought in World War I and, haunted by his experiences, had emerged from the conflict an embittered pacifist. Yet by the fall of 1939, he had also become convinced that Hitler represented a mortal danger not only to Europe but to the United States and the rest of the world. The playwright was struggling with the question of how to respond to such a threat when he tuned in to Lindbergh's two speeches. The shock and outrage he felt propelled him into action. Over the next year, he would become one of the foremost activists in the fight for intervention—a crusade that would ultimately land him in the White House as a key aide to the president. And, as with Thompson, his chief bête noire would be Charles Lindbergh, a man he had once considered a hero.

Sherwood had always needed heroes to believe in. Beneath his veneer of sophisticated charm and wit lay an unrepentant romantic and idealist. "Sherwood remains an incorrigible optimist," noted *The New Yorker.* "He has a faith in the ultimate triumph of the democratic principle."

The son of a Wall Street stockbroker, Sherwood came from an affluent, well-connected New York family. His father had gone to Harvard, where he helped found the humor magazine *The Harvard Lampoon* and was a member of the Hasty Pudding Club, the university's famed theatrical society. Following in his father's footsteps, Sherwood also attended Harvard, becoming the Hasty Pudding's star playwright and president of the *Lampoon*. He was still at Harvard when World War I broke out. Believing that America had an obligation to aid the Allies, he tried to enlist in the U.S. Army but was turned down because, at six foot seven, he was considered too tall. Undeterred, he dropped out of school and joined a Canadian regiment—the Fifth Royal Highlanders, also known as the Black Watch. The unit was sent to France in early 1917.

That August, the Black Watch, along with other Canadian forces, played a major role in the battle of Vimy Ridge, suffering heavy casualties. Among the injured was Sherwood, who, having been gassed the month before, fell into a booby trap during the fighting and was severely cut by barbed wire. His wounds became badly infected, and he developed respiratory and heart problems from the gassing, which resulted in several months of hospitalization.

Although horrified by the bloodbath he had witnessed, Sherwood still believed that the war's terrible sacrifices were justified by the Allied victory, which he was sure would result in a world of justice, altruism, and peace. When that didn't happen, he felt duped and betrayed. He returned to New York disillusioned, cynical, and a rabid opponent of the League of Nations. In 1920, he cast his first presidential vote for Warren Harding, thus, as he later put it, doing "my bit in the great betrayal. . . . [W]hat I and all other Americans got from Harding's victory was a decade of hypocrisy, corruption, crime, glorification of greed and depravity, to be followed logically by a decade of ascendant Hitlerism."

That insight, however, would come many years later. In the present, Sherwood, like other veterans, underwent a difficult readjustment to civilian life. Seeking an escape from his nightmares, he threw himself into the heedless good times of the twenties. At the age of twenty-three, he got a job at *Vanity Fair,* a slick, sophisticated monthly that published literary essays, short stories, and poetry, as well as in-the-know articles about the theater, art, and high society. There he met twenty-five-year-old Dorothy Parker and twenty-eight-year-old Robert Benchley, another product of Harvard. The three staffers became inseparable, so much so that when Sherwood left *Vanity Fair* to write for a humor magazine called *Life,** Parker and Benchley quickly followed him.

The trio lunched every day at the dining room of the Algonquin Hotel, near *Life*'s office in midtown Manhattan. Soon, other writers and editors joined them. In time, the group came to be known as the Algonquin Round Table, regarded by its members and much of New York as the embodiment of urban wit and sophistication. In addition to Sherwood, Parker, and Benchley, its regulars included playwrights Marc Connelly and George S. Kaufman; columnists Heywood Broun and Franklin P. Adams; critic Alexander Woollcott; *New Yorker* editor Harold Ross; and novelist Edna Ferber. Other luminaries, like writer Ring Lardner, comedian Harpo Marx, and actress Helen Hayes would occasionally stop by.

Abstract ideas were of little interest to most of these literary celebrities, nor did they talk much about politics, economics, or social problems. For much of the 1920s, they were blithely disconnected from the real world, absorbed in incessant, feverish socializing. Sherwood was no exception, usually following lunch at the Algonquin with a night out at a theater, a nightclub, or a late-night Round Table poker game. His weekends were often spent at boozy parties at the Manhattan apartments or country houses of other Round Table members, where croquet was played as if it were a blood sport.

Much as he enjoyed the company of his Round Table colleagues, however, Sherwood felt more and more out of step with their superficial, self-absorbed way of life. Still trying to come to grips with his experiences in World War I, he wanted to do something meaningful, but he was not quite sure what that might be.

Then, in the summer of 1925, during a raucous country house weekend on Long Island, Edna Ferber pulled the twenty-nine-year-old Sherwood aside for a heart-to-heart talk. The Pulitzer Prize–winning author of such novels as *So Big, Show Boat,* and *Giant,* Ferber was one of the few Round Table regulars who took her writing seriously. Ignoring "crap games to the right of us, chemin de fer to the left of us, and Irving Berlin in front of us," as Sherwood remembered, she told him: "The best thing that could happen to you would be to have

---

* In 1936, the now struggling *Life* was bought by the magazine publisher Henry Luce, who closed it and used its name for the new photo magazine he was about to launch.

you snatched out of the Algonquin and exiled to Kansas City for two years. At the end of that time, you'd come back with some fine work."

The conversation with Ferber proved to be a defining moment in Sherwood's life. Although he did not go to Kansas City, he did take the rest of her advice. Distancing himself from the Round Table, he began writing plays, churning out more than a dozen over the next decade, most of them dealing in some fashion with what he considered the mindless, nonsensical folly of war. Like many of his early efforts, Sherwood's first major hit, *Road to Rome,* cloaked its angry antiwar message in a smoke screen of witty, urbane dialogue designed to appeal to New York audiences; the critic Charles Brackett described the play in *The New Yorker* as "a hymn of hate against militarism—disguised, ever so gaily, as a love song."

A number of his plays, including *Waterloo Bridge, Reunion in Vienna,* and *The Petrified Forest,* were made into movies. So was *Idiot's Delight,* which opened as a Broadway play in 1936 and earned him his first Pulitzer Prize. Both anti-Fascist and antiwar, *Idiot's Delight* was Sherwood's last play to feature characters who raged against evildoers but who failed to do anything meaningful on behalf of what they believed.

As Europe drew closer to the brink in the late 1930s, he struggled to find a balance between his hatred of war and his growing conviction that Hitler and Mussolini must be stopped. "Oh God," he wrote in his diary in 1937, "how I hope to live to see the day when those unspeakable barbaric bastards get their punishment."

Increasingly obsessed by the worsening European situation, Sherwood gave up his writing to focus on reading "practically every word of foreign news in the papers—columns, editorials—and listening to news broadcasts as much as I can." After the sellout of Czechoslovakia at Munich, he finally abandoned his pacifism: "I feel that I must start to battle for one thing—the end of our isolation. There is no hope for humanity unless we participate vigorously in the concerns of the world and assume our proper place of leadership with all the grave responsibilities that go with it."

Not long after Munich, his change of heart energized him into writing another play. This one would feature neither his trademark witty cynicism nor his customary gently nihilistic approach. Reaching back to the past, it would focus instead on one of America's most cherished heroes, who, like Sherwood and millions of other Americans, had been a man of peace forced to grapple with the dilemma of appeasement or war.

Abe Lincoln in Illinois follows Abraham Lincoln in his pre-presidency days, as he agonizes over what position to take on slavery. Should he remain quiet and let that evil institution metastasize throughout America, or should he stand firm against it, thus accepting the possibility of civil war, the idea of which he hates as much as slavery itself?

In tracing Lincoln's tortuous journey from neutrality to his acknowledgment of the need to take action, Sherwood features a brief reenactment of the famed Lincoln-Douglas debates in 1858. When Senator Stephen Douglas insists that each state should be allowed to mind its own business and "leave its neighbors alone," Lincoln retorts that such an attitude is "the complacent policy of indifference to evil, and that policy I cannot but hate." He explains: "I hate it because it deprives our republic of its just influence in the world; enables the enemies of free institutions everywhere to taunt us as hypocrites, causes the real friends of freedom to doubt our sincerity."

The implied comparison of America's dilemma in the 1850s to that in the late 1930s was clearly understood by the play's audiences. Heywood Broun of the New York *World* called *Abe Lincoln in Illinois* "the finest piece of propaganda ever to come into our theater. . . . To the satisfied and the smug, it will seem subversive to its very core. And they will be right. . . . It is the very battle cry of freedom."

But having sounded that battle cry, Sherwood, caught up "in a frenzy of uncertainty," was still ambivalent about what steps the country should take to combat Hitler. Even when Germany invaded Poland, he did not add his voice to the public discourse. It wasn't until he listened to Lindbergh's speeches that he decided he must step from behind his playwright's persona and speak out as Robert Sherwood.

A great admirer of Lindbergh since his 1927 flight, Sherwood believed that the young aviator's decency and dignity had provided a beacon of light for the country amid the corruption and materialism of the 1920s, which Sherwood later described as "the most sordid of periods." When others criticized Lindbergh and his wife for their trips to Germany, he had defended them. In early 1939, he wrote in his diary: "It makes me sick to think of the way the Lindberghs have become excoriated as pro-Nazis—shows how unbalanced people have become on that awful subject."

But when he heard Lindbergh declare that the United States should do nothing to help the Western allies and that they, not Germany, were responsible for the war, he felt shocked, horrified, and "rather sick." While he did not doubt the sincerity of Lindbergh's beliefs, he was appalled that the man he had once regarded as a hero was so oblivious to the evil of Nazism and the threat it posed to the world. As he listened to Lindbergh's broadcasts, he was convinced, as he wrote later, that "Hitlerism was already powerfully and persuasively represented in our own midst." Shortly after Lindbergh's first speech, Sherwood wrote in his diary: "Will Lindbergh one day be our Fuehrer?"

A few days later, when the famed Kansas newspaper editor William Allen White sent Sherwood a cable asking him to join a nationwide campaign to lobby Congress for revision of the neutrality law, Sherwood immediately said yes. He told White he would "give all the help I can, physical, moral and financial. . . . If the Allies should be defeated, then the next war will follow quickly, and it will be fought in this hemisphere."

Several weeks after that, in a long, soul-searching letter seeking White's advice on what further role he should take in the burgeoning debate over the European conflict, Sherwood observed that he still hated war with all his might. But, he added, "the terrible truth is that when war comes home to you, you have to fight it; and this war has come home to me."

CHAPTER 6

"I AM ALMOST LITERALLY WALKING ON EGGS"

═══

Robert Sherwood was hardly the only person to turn to William Allen White for counsel. From William McKinley on, most U.S. presidents had done the same. Indeed, seeking White's opinions had become an American habit. He was, as one historian put it, "as close to being a national institution as an elderly newspaper editor could be."

Rotund and bespectacled, the seventy-one-year-old White had spent most of his life in the little Kansas town of Emporia. His newspaper, the *Emporia Gazette,* had never boasted a circulation above seven thousand, yet the name of its Pulitzer Prize–winning editor was instantly recognized by millions of people throughout the country.

White was also a biographer, political kingmaker, novelist, writer of articles and short stories for *The Saturday Evening Post* and other major national magazines, and an outspoken enemy of the Ku Klux Klan. But what appealed most to his countrymen was his homespun political and social commentary and the values it espoused—the need for tolerance and community, for example, and the importance of local institutions such as churches and schools in building democracy. His writings were akin to the paintings of Norman Rockwell, depicting innately decent people who eschew conflict and come together for the common good, all of which helped give readers and viewers a sense of pride and comfort about themselves and their country.

William Allen White.

An old-style Republican progressive who'd been a close friend of Theodore Roosevelt, White had a somewhat complex relationship with the current occupant of the White House. He'd long advocated many of the social and economic reforms that Franklin Roosevelt had implemented; at the same time, he was a staunchly loyal Republican who had never voted for a Democratic candidate for president, even when he preferred the Democrat's stand on issues. On a stop in Emporia during the 1936 presidential campaign, Roosevelt, who considered White a friend, laughingly declared to the crowd he could count on the editor's support "three and a half years out of every four."

That support extended to Roosevelt's foreign policy as well. Like Robert Sherwood, White hated the very idea of war, and it would have been logical to assume that he was an isolationist, coming from the Midwest as he did. But he was also a man of the world, an incessant traveler who had visited six of the seven continents and who had long advocated closer U.S. cooperation with the rest of the globe.

He had earlier supported strict enforcement of the Neutrality Act, hoping it would keep America out of the approaching war in Europe.

But when Germany invaded Poland, he changed his mind, backing Roosevelt's proposal to revise the law to allow Britain and France to buy arms. Well aware of White's popularity in Middle America, the president asked for his help in selling the plan to the public.

White was initially reluctant because of his age. But he finally yielded to FDR's famed persuasiveness, becoming head of a group with the tongue-tying name of the Nonpartisan Committee for Peace Through Revision of the Neutrality Law. Recruiting Sherwood and more than a hundred other prominent Americans as members, the committee worked to mobilize public opinion through editorials, newspaper advertisements, and radio broadcasts. After urging supporters to flood Congress with letters and telegrams of support, White went to Capitol Hill himself to buttonhole Republican senators and congressmen.

When he arrived, it was apparent that the isolationists, at least initially, had gained the advantage in the fight. Lindbergh's first radio speech had had a dramatic impact, as had broadcasts by Burton Wheeler, Gerald Nye, and other noted antiwar figures. "If America really means to stay out of foreign wars, she needs to remember how easy it is to get in," Nye declared in one of his radio addresses. "We need the neutrality law. We need restraints upon a President."

Such appeals to antiwar sentiment had resulted in a torrent of several million telegrams, letters, and postcards to lawmakers, almost all demanding that the arms embargo remain untouched. Of 1,800 pieces of mail received by one Republican senator, only 76 were in favor of repealing the embargo. Although he had been inclined to support the president's proposal, the senator said, he now would probably vote against it. Other members of Congress made similar statements.

Yet despite these gloomy portents, the situation remained extremely fluid, as Roosevelt realized when he looked at the latest public opinion polls. Most Americans were still adamant about staying out of the war, but at the same time, most (85 percent in one survey) wanted the British and French to win. In another poll, 24 percent of those questioned were in favor of supplying aid to the Allies, while 30 percent opposed giving help to any warring country. Thirty-seven percent, meanwhile, said they favored neither the Allies nor Germany but would approve the selling of arms to belligerents on "cash and carry" terms.

This lukewarm middle group, combined with those unequivocally in favor of aid, would give the president the public backing he needed. As he saw it, the only way to ensure that support was to downplay the importance of saving the European democracies and to argue instead that replacing the embargo with "cash and carry" was the best way to keep America out of the war.

In his campaign to garner congressional support, Roosevelt, who was acutely aware of how vulnerable he still was after the political disasters of the previous two years, moved as carefully and cautiously as possible. "I am almost literally walking on eggs," he told an acquaintance. Before calling Congress back into session, he took pains to lay the political groundwork, asking Senate and House leaders for their opinions and briefing individual members to try to win their backing. At the same time, governors, mayors, and prominent businessmen sympathetic to the Allies' cause were recruited to help in marshaling votes, while William Allen White's committee was handed the job of rallying public opinion. Influential interventionists such as former secretary of state Henry Stimson were called on to make radio addresses to counter those of the isolationists.

Most important was the creation of an entirely new coalition of pro-administration legislators. Just as the president's chief opponents were now the progressives who previously had backed his domestic programs, many of his new supporters in this topsy-turvy period were conservatives who in the past had savagely attacked the New Deal.

Roosevelt was particularly assiduous in courting southern Democrats, whose region was traditionally pro-military and pro-British. Among them was Senator Walter George of Georgia, one of the chief targets on the president's 1938 purge list. To manage the revision bill in the Senate, the White House chose Senator James Byrnes, a wily South Carolinian who, according to an acquaintance, "could charm snakes without a flute and with his eyes closed." The administration also handed out a substantial number of patronage plums to southerners.

Once his spadework was done and Congress had reassembled in emergency session, Roosevelt traveled to Capitol Hill to deliver his appeal in person. In the wake of the outbreak of war in Europe, Washington was bristling with extra security against potential saboteurs and spies, and the Capitol and its grounds had taken on the appearance of an armed camp. Several dozen policemen and an expanded Secret Service detail swarmed around the president as he entered the building and, clutching the arm of an aide, walked slowly and awkwardly to the dais of the House chamber.

Showing no sign of his usual cheerful, buoyant manner, Roosevelt stood unsmiling at the podium, barely acknowledging the ripple of applause that greeted him. One reporter described him as looking "tired and worn." But when he began to speak, there was no hint of weariness in his voice. Until that moment, Lindbergh, Borah, and his other opponents had dominated the discussion. Now it was the president's turn in the spotlight, and he was determined to make the most of it.

To the assembled lawmakers and the millions of Americans listening to the speech on radio, FDR bluntly declared: "I regret that the Congress passed the [Neutrality] Act. I regret equally that I signed that Act." He argued that revising the law was the best way to guarantee peace and safety for the United States in the tumultuous period ahead: "Our acts must be guided by one single hardheaded thought—keeping America out of this war!"

FDR urged the isolationists not to regard themselves as the only members of "the peace bloc," adding, "We all belong to it." Again, he emphasized: "This government must lose no time or effort to keep the nation from being drawn into the war"—a comment that drew the loudest applause of the day.

As the president's limousine left the Capitol grounds following the speech, a crowd of protesters, waving small flags, demonstrated against both his appearance before Congress and his proposal. "We're mothers!" one woman shouted. "We don't want our boys to go to war!" Overall, however, public reaction was overwhelmingly favorable. Within a couple of days, the White House received tens of thousands of telegrams and letters applauding the speech, while members of Congress reported a shift in their mail that favored repeal of the embargo. According to polls taken immediately after the president's address, slightly more than 60 percent of the American people now backed repeal.

When the congressional debate began a few days later, "nerves were strung fiddle-tight," Time noted. Hundreds of people, most of them opponents of the bill, crammed the galleries of both houses. Herbert Agar, a well-known southern newspaper editor who watched several days of the Senate debate from the press gallery, said of the onlookers' reaction: "One might have thought the President had asked permission to sell the United States to England." Agar, an ardent interventionist, observed foes of the measure "storming the corridors of the Senate [office] building, screaming about 'merchants of death,' 'the House of Morgan,' 'British propaganda,' and similar phrases from long ago— not a pretty picture of democracy at work in the making of foreign policy."

Immediately after the president's speech, a group of more than twenty isolationist senators had vowed to fight the proposed repeal "from hell to breakfast." Throughout the intense six-week debate that followed, they made good on their pledge. The most eloquent foe was William Borah, who, although physically frail, showed once again why he was regarded as the best orator in the Senate. His voice shaking with fury, the aging Borah told his fellow senators that passage of the legislation would be the first step on the slippery slope to active intervention in the war. Aiming his next comment at the American public, he warned: "If you believe what is now being preached throughout this country, you will soon be sending munitions without pay, and you will send your boys back to the slaughter pens of Europe."

Dismissing Borah's admonitions, the pro-administration senators who spoke for the bill followed Roosevelt's lead in never mentioning the need to help Britain and France and in insisting that repeal of the embargo was the best guarantee of peace for America. By doing so, the historian Robert Divine observed, they continued "the elaborate pretense that the sale of arms to the Allies was but an accidental by-product of a program designed to keep the United States clear of the war."

Although congressional isolationists prolonged the debate for as long as possible, theirs was clearly a losing fight, especially when the administration, in a nod to isolationist sentiment, agreed to retain the Neutrality Act's provision prohibiting American vessels from entering war zones. In the Senate, southern conservative Democrats joined their northern liberal colleagues to vote for the embargo's repeal; the final tally was 63 to 30 in favor of the legislation. The House followed suit with a similarly top-heavy margin. In both houses, most of the negative votes came from the Midwest and West.

Afterward, an elated Cordell Hull declared: "We have won a great battle." But some isolationists argued that the administration's triumph was in fact a Pyrrhic victory. "Because of our battle, it is going to be much more difficult for FDR to lead the country into war," Senator Arthur Vandenberg, a Michigan Republican, wrote in his diary. "We have forced him and his Senate group to become vehement in their peace devotions—and we have aroused the country to a peace vigilance which is powerful."

A number of proponents of the embargo's repeal, meanwhile, expressed dismay at the repeated arguments of the president and his congressional allies that its enactment would help keep America out of the conflict. Dorothy Thompson, for one, complained that the American public had been promised "more security than it is wise for them to think they can have. Not a single people in the world today is safe."

Roosevelt waved aside all such criticism. He responded coolly when the literary agent George Bye, a friend of the Roosevelts, passed on a letter from an acquaintance that said in part: "Why don't you tell our idol FDR to quit beating around the bush, to get on the radio and be honest with his people? . . . Of *course,* we cannot afford to let France and England get licked. Of *course,* we should prepare to help them— first with munitions and then, if that is not enough, with everything we've got. Why stall around? Why let these pussyfooting Senators kid the American public into the belief that we could stay out of another war? Why not talk brutal realism to the American people *before* it is too late?" Clearly unmoved, the president instructed his secretary to respond with a boilerplate expression of thanks: "Say I was delighted to get it."

After the twin disasters of the Court fight and congressional purge, Roosevelt had yet to recover his once buoyant assurance that the American people stood behind him. Throughout the next two years, to the consternation of his allies in the intervention fight, he would repeatedly refuse to assume the mantle of bold leadership he had donned in the early 1930s. And whenever he did take a step toward greater involvement in the war, he invariably did so, as the historian Richard Ketchum observed, "with an uneasy backward glance to see if the opposition might be gaining."

CHAPTER 7

"PARANOIA CAN BE CATCHING"

With the repeal of the arms embargo in September 1939, life in the United States quickly returned to normal. Congress adjourned, the president went on vacation, and Americans relaxed, confident in the belief they had put the specter of war behind them.

Events—or rather the lack of them—reinforced that view. The Allies' declaration of war against Germany apparently hadn't meant what it said. This putative conflict was, as *Life* pointed out, "a queer sort of world war—unreal and unconvincing." There had been no fighting in Western Europe, no German air raids over Paris and London, no Allied air assaults on the Ruhr. Having supposedly gone to war over Poland, Britain and France did nothing to help save that tortured country except send a few token patrols across the Maginot Line and fly a few reconnaissance flights over German territory. In Britain, the phantom combat was called the "bore war"; in France, it was the "*drôle de guerre*." Senator Borah tartly dubbed it the "phony war," the name by which it became known in the United States.

Most Americans had little doubt that even if the war did heat up, the Allies would easily win and their own country would escape involvement. According to the *Denver Post,* "the smallest domestic problem is now more important to the American people than the most momentous European crisis."

In his State of the Union speech in January 1940, Roosevelt warned his countrymen about the perils of complacency, observing that "it is not good for the ultimate health of ostriches to bury their heads in the sand." But he was hardly a role model for action himself. When the Soviet Union, now a quasi-ally of Germany, invaded Finland in November 1939, the president protested strongly, as did the American press and public. But the United States sent no material aid to the Finns in their David-and-Goliath struggle against the Soviets, even after the Finnish ambassador declared that the U.S. decision not to sell arms to his nation "would be tantamount to signing a death warrant." Although not unsympathetic, Secretary of State Cordell Hull could only reply that the U.S. government would "not engage in acts or utterances that might materially endanger its peace and safety by causing it to be drawn into war."

Such inaction infuriated Robert Sherwood, who wrote in his diary, "How long can the conscience of the U.S. remain dormant?" Inspired by the Finns' desperate resistance, Sherwood began work in January 1940 on his first play since *Abe Lincoln in Illinois*. Entitled *There Shall Be No Night,* the drama, about a Finnish family caught up in the conflict, was meant as a protest against "the hysterical escapism, the Pontius Pilate retreat from decision" that, in Sherwood's view, marked American public opinion about the war.

Written in a white-hot frenzy, *There Shall Be No Night* opened on Broadway in April and toured the country soon afterward. The public's widely varying reactions to it vividly demonstrated Americans' increasingly divided opinions about the war. In New York, protesters passed out leaflets headlined "Warmongers Capture the Alvin Theater" and describing the play as a "weapon pointed straight at the hearts of the American people." In Philadelphia, picketers blocked the entrance of the theater in which it was playing, and in Chicago, the isolationist *Chicago Tribune* refused to print one word about it. Nonetheless, it sold out in every city on the tour.

In Washington, the syndicated columnist Raymond Clapper disapproved of Sherwood's propagandizing—a "rank and inflammatory job"—but noted that the production "played to capacity audiences, which are traditionally undemonstrative here, and sent them away moist-eyed. Most . . . were swept off their feet." One of those "moist-eyed" Washington playgoers was the president, who sent Sherwood a fan letter soon after he saw the drama. But Roosevelt's enthusiasm did not translate into concrete help for Finland, which, unsupported by any Western country, was forced to capitulate to the Soviets in the early spring of 1940.

During this period, one historian wrote, "American foreign policy remained almost in a state of suspended animation, paralyzed by its avowed neutrality." FDR and his advisers were sure that the phony war would not last—Germany was clearly consolidating its strength—but they felt powerless to do anything substantive to alter the course of events.

In March, Roosevelt sent Undersecretary of State Sumner Welles on a mission to Europe to explore the possibility of a negotiated peace. The only thing to come of Welles's talks with Chamberlain, Daladier, Mussolini, and Hitler was an expression of anger by Britain and France over what they saw as U.S. meddling. To his colleagues in the British Foreign Office, Sir Robert Vansittart bitterly referred to the undersecretary as "an international danger. . . . His chief crime towards common sense and humanity is that he has now gone so far as to want us to make peace with Hitler." Welles, for his part, acknowledged that only a U.S. pledge to provide all-out support for the Allies in the event of real war might have given Hitler pause. But, as everyone knew, the chances of that happening were nil.

Indeed, since the beginning of the war in September, the Roosevelt administration had made little effort to shore up America's own defenses, much less mobilize to help Britain and France. In the view of the historians William Langer and S. Everett Gleason, Roosevelt seemed to have "considered repeal of the arms embargo a sufficient program for the moment [and] thought that this measure was about all that the public would accept." Even the president's plan to build ten thousand warplanes a year, which had so delighted Hap Arnold in late 1938, had been slashed by almost 70 percent.

With fewer than two hundred thousand men, the U.S. Army was still in pitiable shape, and General George Marshall urged Roosevelt to ask Congress for a substantial increase in military appropriations for the 1941 fiscal year. Marshall was doomed to disappointment: the administration's request was slightly more than half the amount originally proposed by the Army's top brass. In the late 1940s, Marshall would tell his biographer, Forrest Pogue, that if the United States had embarked on a full-fledged rearmament program in the fall of 1939, it probably could have "shortened the war by at least a year" and saved "billions of dollars and 100,000 casualties." The former Army chief put much of the blame for lagging U.S. war production on Roosevelt's reluctance to press Congress for a greatly expanded defense agenda.

But even if Roosevelt had been more aggressive in his requests, it's highly doubtful they would have won congressional approval. FDR's standing on Capitol Hill was still considerably diminished, and congressional leaders made it clear early in the 1940 session that they would probably make deep cuts in even the modest military budget that had been proposed. Pointing to the lack of fighting in Europe and focused on upcoming elections, members of Congress paid little heed to Marshall's warning that time was running out for America. Due to "chaotic world conditions," the Army chief of staff declared, the United States was certain to face critical military challenges in the near future, for which it was dangerously unprepared.

On April 3, the House Appropriations Committee slashed the administration's proposed military spending by 10 percent. Six days later, thousands of German infantry and parachute troops, supported by warships and hundreds of aircraft, descended on Scandinavia, vanquishing Denmark in a day and laying siege to Norway. Barely a month after that, more than two million German soldiers poured into Holland, Belgium, and France, crushing the first two countries in little more than a week and trapping British and French forces at Dunkirk, on the northern coast of France.

THE PHONY WAR WAS clearly over, and Americans were in a state of shock. In New York's Times Square, vast crowds watched in stunned silence as illuminated news bulletins atop the Times Tower headlined one nightmarish Allied defeat after another. The vaunted French army, supposedly the finest in the world, was collapsing like a house of cards, and the British Expeditionary Force faced extinction on the beaches of Dunkirk. Decades later, Americans who lived through the high drama of those weeks still found it difficult to put into words the panic and bewilderment they felt over what Roosevelt called the "hurricane of events."

The German blitzkrieg seemed unstoppable. Soon, it appeared, America, whose immunity from foreign aggression had seemed a certainty just days before, "would be left, as the last great democracy on earth, to fight the war of the Western Hemisphere against a united German continent of Europe." In his diary, Harold Ickes grimly observed: "There is no doubt in my mind that this country is in the most critical situation since we won our independence."

Not since the worst days of the Depression had the country's citizens been so uncertain, fearful, and confused. Aubrey Morgan's survey group at the British Library of Information reported to Whitehall that there was "near hysteria in many sections of the U.S. press and deep anxiety in practically all." According to a poll conducted for *Fortune* magazine, 94 percent of Americans were willing to spend whatever was necessary to make U.S. defenses secure.

On May 16, with public opinion solidly behind him, Roosevelt went before a joint session of Congress to request $1.18 billion in new military appropriations and to call for the production of fifty thousand planes a year, as well as creation of a two-ocean navy and a 280,000-man army. For the first time in years, lawmakers greeted Roosevelt with ovation after ovation as he ticked off his list—a congressional reception almost as rapturous as when he first took office in the depths of the Depression. All thoughts of penny-pinching had vanished, at least when it came to national defense.

In its swift approval of the president's proposals, Congress gave FDR $500 million more than he had requested. When he came back two weeks later to ask for another $1 billion plus, members voted yea again. Over the next few weeks, the appropriations requests kept coming; by the first week of October, Congress had authorized a staggering $17.6 billion in new military spending.

The U.S. public was equally enthusiastic. Scarcely recovered from their initial panic, Americans put on a dramatic show of patriotism in the spring and summer of 1940. Flag sales soared by more than 200 percent, and department stores had a hard time keeping patriotic-themed jewelry in stock. At Tiffany in New York, a particularly popular item was a flag pin in rubies, diamonds, and sapphires, which sold for $900. Also available in stores were Betsy Ross umbrellas, featuring red and white stripes and a field of blue stars; red-white-and-blue suspenders; and bandannas imprinted with the words of the national anthem, to be worn either as a halter or a scarf.

In this great flood of public and congressional support for bolstering the nation's defenses, one key fact was barely mentioned: it would take months, even years, before the astronomical amounts of money appropriated by Congress could be translated into planes, armaments, and other urgently needed supplies. There were shortages of virtually everything necessary for war production: factories, raw materials, machine tools, and the men to operate them. As Admiral Harold Stark, chief of U.S. naval operations, tartly put it, "Dollars cannot buy yesterday."

Adding to the sense of crisis were alarming reports by Roosevelt, Marshall, and other senior government figures that German infiltration of Central and South America now posed an imminent danger to U.S. national security. The State and War Departments had long been concerned by the large number of German nationals living in Latin American countries, as well as by Germany's many military and trade missions in the region. In addition to helping Latin American nations equip and train their armies, the Third Reich also controlled several key national airlines. Among them was the Colombian airline SCADTA, which operated planes within three hundred miles of the U.S.-run Panama Canal.

There was considerable fear in Washington that in some particularly vulnerable Latin American countries, Nazi-backed coups might overthrow the current governments and establish regimes that would become vassal states of Germany. In late May, after receiving reports of possible future coups in Argentina and several other nations, Roosevelt ordered plans drawn up for the dispatch of a U.S. expeditionary force to South America. (The coups never took place, and the plans never got beyond the drafting stage.) There was also concern, voiced by Marshall and others, that a German force might one day be transported from the west coast of Africa to the east coast of Brazil, a distance of some 1,600 miles across the Atlantic. The Germans would then be in a position to move northward toward the Panama Canal.

In his May 16 speech to Congress, Roosevelt had mentioned the possibility of German aircraft making their way from South America to Central America and into Mexico, which then could be used as a staging area from which to attack the United States. A few weeks later, *Life* ran a story that described in hair-raising, hypothetical detail how "fascist" forces could occupy Brazilian ports, raid the Panama Canal, bomb Caribbean islands, destroy America's Atlantic fleet, occupy Cuba, and invade the U.S. mainland. The article, complete with illustrations, envisaged "a victorious Fascist Army" marching up Market Street in Wilmington, Delaware, while Fascist tanks and infantry overpowered small, underequipped U.S. forces near Pittsburgh. After the fall of Washington, New York, and the major East Coast industrial centers, U.S. envoys, in the *Life* scenario, would meet with Fascist officials at Philadelphia's Independence Hall to sue for peace.

After reading such stories and hearing repeated warnings from political and military leaders about a looming Nazi threat to the Western Hemisphere, many if not most Americans became convinced that such a danger did exist. In a *Fortune* poll, 63 percent of those surveyed believed that if Germany succeeded in conquering Britain and France, it would then try to seize territory in the Americas.

Assistant Secretary of State Adolf Berle was one of the believers. In late June, a Hearst newsreel cameraman told Berle that Hitler planned to conquer Britain by July 10; then, supported by a massive fifth column, German troops were to invade the United States three days later. Astonishingly, Berle believed him. He later wrote in his diary that the cameraman's prediction was "so graphic" that "it frightened me completely," adding wryly that "paranoia can be catching."

Other Americans, however, held quite a different view. Isolationists in Congress and the military believed that all this talk about German infiltration and subversion was simply a smoke screen by the administration to disguise what its critics felt were its plans to lead America into the war against Germany. "President Roosevelt tried to curdle our blood by talking about Nazi plans to invade South America . . . when in fact there never was any such menace," the retired general Albert Wedemeyer, who had been one of the staunchest isolationists in the Army, contended after the war. Senator Hiram Johnson declared at the time that Roosevelt, "with diabolical cleverness," was trying to "create a terrible public clamor and hysteria" so as to "follow the line followed by us in 1917, which took us into the European conflict."

Strongly opposed to what they saw as Roosevelt's increasing bellicosity, a number of high-ranking military officers began conducting their own private guerrilla campaigns to do what they could to shut the president down.

IN LATE MAY, A short, rotund man paid a call on Burton Wheeler in his Senate office. He was Rear Admiral Stanford Cooper, a former director of naval communications who, having created the Navy's tactical signaling codes, was known as "the father of naval radio." After telling Wheeler that what he had to say was confidential, Cooper declared: "The man at the other end of Pennsylvania Avenue is going to get us into war." The president was "blowing smoke" about the dangers of a German attack in South America, the admiral said, and was "using the specter of a Nazi invasion of the U.S. as a pretext for our joining the Allies."

Cooper urged Wheeler to go all out in opposing Roosevelt: "You can't stop him by making one speech. You've got to make a lot of speeches. You licked him on the Court issue and you can lick him again." When Wheeler asked him how other Navy officers felt about the war, Cooper replied: "Most of the older heads feel as I do—that we should keep out—but a lot of the younger men who look forward to promotions think the President knows more about the Navy than we do." Before he left, Cooper agreed to provide the Montana Democrat with facts and figures backing up his arguments.

A couple of weeks later, after Wheeler delivered a scathing radio speech against what he called the administration's scare campaign, he received a visit from another military man—this time, a clean-cut Air Corps captain, whose name Wheeler never revealed and who told him that he was only a messenger. According to the senator's son, Edward, Wheeler had no doubt that the envoy had been sent by Hap Arnold.

For more than eighteen months, Arnold had mounted a rearguard action to stop Roosevelt from transferring to the Allies the modern aircraft that his own air force so desperately needed. Convinced that the United States should not become entangled in the war in Europe, the air chief had been involved in a number of confrontations with the exasperated president, who at one point threatened Arnold with exile to Guam if he kept defying FDR's wishes.

Arnold was sure, his wife later told his biographer, Murray Green, that the administration was bugging his home telephone. White House staffers "apparently were going to wage war against Hap," she said. "In other words, try and force him out." If it hadn't been for the steadfast support of George Marshall, who had been a friend of Arnold's for more than thirty years, "it is doubtful," Green wrote, "that Arnold would have survived in his job."

A seasoned veteran in the art of leaking information to members of Congress, Arnold had known Burton Wheeler for several years; indeed, he had helped Wheeler acquire an Air Corps base for Montana several years before. Now, as Wheeler saw it, Arnold had designated this young captain as his mouthpiece in his continuing battle against Roosevelt.

"Are you going to keep up this fight?" the captain asked Wheeler. When the senator said yes, the officer told him that the Air Corps was in no shape to go to war and that Wheeler must do everything he could to prevent it. "We haven't got a single, solitary plane that's fit for overseas service," the captain added. He promised to pass on detailed information about the air force's weaknesses in the near future.

LIKE THE ADMIRAL AND the captain, Charles Lindbergh believed that the administration intended to do far more than shore up the military strength of America, that it was in fact preparing the country for war. And, he feared, Americans seemed to be going along with the plan. "The press is hysterical," he wrote in his journal on May 16. "The newspapers give one the impression that the United States will be invaded next week!"

In mid-May, over lunch at the Army and Navy Club in Washington, Lindbergh told former undersecretary of state William Castle that Roosevelt's call for fifty thousand planes was "childish," that "we could never manage such a force" and that the cost "would be prohibitive even for a very rich country." As Castle recalled, Lindbergh was "furious at the President's speech because he said it showed a lamentable lack of knowledge of the entire air situation."

Determined to halt what he saw as a march toward intervention, Lindbergh made another nationwide radio broadcast on May 19, three days after the president's speech to Congress. While he agreed that America's military forces should be reinforced, he argued to his listeners that the United States "must stop this hysterical chatter of calamity and invasion that has been running rife the last few days." There was no danger of attack, Lindbergh said, unless the country (i.e., the administration) incited it by meddling further in the European conflict: "If we desire peace, we have only to stop asking for war." Insisting that the Western Hemisphere was secure against foreign assault, he urged: "Let us turn again to America's traditional role—that of building and guarding our own destiny."

After listening to her husband's speech, Anne Lindbergh wrote apprehensively in her diary, "This will raise the roof! It will be taken as anti–New Deal and anti-intervention." Her fears were well founded. The first to weigh in was *The New York Times*, which sharply rapped Lindbergh in an editorial: "The 'hysterical chatter' [of which Lindbergh spoke] is the talk now heard on every side in the democracies, with France and Britain in danger of defeat by Germany. Colonel Lindbergh is a peculiar young man if he can contemplate this possibility in any other light than as a calamity for the American people."

The *Times*'s reaction was mild, however, compared to that of the administration. Although Roosevelt had been angered by Lindbergh's speeches the previous fall, he had been content to let interventionists like Dorothy Thompson take the lead in criticizing him. Now his reticence was at an end. Enraged by Lindbergh's continued criticism of his actions at a time of great national crisis, the president set in motion a well-orchestrated administration campaign against him. "If I should die tomorrow, I want you to know this," FDR wrote to Treasury Secretary Henry Morgenthau. "I am absolutely convinced that Lindbergh is a Nazi." To former secretary of state Henry Stimson, Roosevelt observed: "When I read Lindbergh's speech I felt that it could not have been better put if it had been written by Goebbels himself. What a pity that this youngster has completely abandoned his belief in our form of government and has accepted Nazi methods because apparently they are efficient."

Roosevelt, however, voiced none of these criticisms in public. Instead, he employed a series of prominent presidential surrogates to make his points against Lindbergh. The first to speak out was Senator James Byrnes, the shrewd South Carolina Democrat who had become a key Roosevelt lieutenant on Capitol Hill. In a national radio broadcast on May 23, Byrnes mounted a savage attack against Lindbergh, equating him with appeasers in Britain and France and likening his speech to "fifth-column activities" that allegedly had taken place in the European countries overrun by Hitler.

Throughout the West, there was a widespread belief that Germany's stunning victories in Denmark, Norway, Belgium, the Netherlands, and France could not be explained solely by the political and military weaknesses of those nations. The triumphs must also be due to the effectiveness of Nazi agents and their sympathizers in undermining the countries before the Wehrmacht invaded—a belief that was later found to have very little basis in fact. Nonetheless, Roosevelt and many of those around him fully accepted the premise and applied it to the United States.

In his assault on Lindbergh, Byrnes reported: "Fifth columns are already active in America. And those who consciously or unconsciously retard the efforts of this government to provide for the defense of the American people are the fifth column's most effective fellow travelers." The senator reminded his listeners that Lindbergh had accepted a medal from the German government less than two years before and accused him of having urged Britain and France to appease Hitler "by offering no resistance to Germany's aggression."

Three nights later, during a fireside chat on national defense, FDR weighed in with his own denunciation of what he saw as fifth-column activities in the United States. After assuring the American people that he would do everything in his power to keep the country safe, he warned about this powerful strategy for "weakening a nation at its very roots." He went on: "These dividing forces are undiluted poison. They must not be allowed to spread in the New World as they have in the Old."

Roosevelt had long been preoccupied with the idea of internal subversion. As assistant secretary of the Navy during World War I, he had been instrumental in hiring hundreds of special Navy investigators to guard against sabotage of naval installations. In September 1939, his press secretary, Steve Early, suggested to reporters that the massive number of letters and telegrams sent to Congress opposing repeal of the arms embargo had been prompted by cabled instructions from Berlin to "its friends in the United States."

A few months later, in his 1940 State of the Union address, Roosevelt warned Americans about the "apologists to foreign aggressors," whom he described as "those selfish and partisan groups at home who wrap themselves in a false mantle of Americanism." In his May 16 speech requesting huge increases in defense spending, the president spoke of the new "treacherous use of the Fifth Column," mentioning the possible recruitment of refugees coming to the United States as enemy agents.

When Roosevelt used the term "fifth columnist," he clearly meant it to include Lindbergh and other critics of his foreign policy. The president "did not view isolationists with the detachment of a scholar," historian Richard Steele noted. "He believed the worst of them." In FDR's view, his isolationist opponents "were not only wrong, they were contributing mightily to apathy and disunity, thus jeopardizing national survival."

In his May 26 fireside chat, Roosevelt contended that attacks on the government's rearmament plan and its other foreign and military policies were not part of "a wholesome political debate of honest and free men," as Lindbergh and other isolationists maintained. Instead, those assaults were connected to the "clever schemes of foreign agents," meant to "create confusion, public indecision, political paralysis, and eventually a state of panic." In essence, the president was claiming that any criticism of his policies was detrimental to national security. To preserve the country's unity and safety, he said, Americans must combat this new fifth column with all their might.

THAT KIND OF TALK greatly worried Attorney General Robert Jackson, who thought the president was being overly alarmist. Jackson informed the cabinet in late May that even before FDR's broadcast, "a hysteria was sweeping the country against aliens and fifth columnists." He had received several reports of Americans "breaking into other people's houses and confronting them with a flag, demanding that they salute it." Many citizens, Jackson said, had the view that "anyone you don't like is a member of the Fifth Column."

An ardent champion of civil liberties, Jackson had vivid memories of the vigilante mania that had taken hold of much of the country during World War I. As city attorney of Jamestown, New York, he had stood fast against what he saw as busybody snooping and spying, reckless accusations of disloyalty made against blameless town residents, and "suspicion of everyone who was not a native son and 100 per cent American." He had been labeled pro-German and un-American because he refused to prosecute those who he believed had been unjustly targeted.

Now, Jackson feared, that same nativist, anti-alien hysteria was on the rise again. Throughout the country, *Time* reported, Americans were developing "morbid fears of invisible enemies and were chasing ghosts and phantoms. . . . From Baton Rouge, La., to Lake George, N.Y., tales of spies and saboteurs floated wraithlike but menacing in the troubled air." A book entitled *The Fifth Column Is Here,* claiming that the United States contained more than a million fifth columnists, became an instant bestseller.

In Georgia, Jackson told the cabinet, the governor "was hunting down every alien," ordering them to be fingerprinted and registered for a possible roundup. A German American clubhouse near St. Louis had been burned down by arsonists, while a similar club in Chicago was destroyed by a bomb. In Grand Rapids, Michigan, a foundry worker, convinced that his neighbor was a fifth columnist, shot and killed him. FBI offices across the country were deluged with reports of suspected espionage and sabotage—more than 2,900 reports alone on the day after Roosevelt's fireside chat, almost twice the number received in all of 1939.

After listening to Jackson's concerns at the cabinet meeting, Harold Ickes wrote in his diary: "America isn't going to be any too comfortable a place to live in during the immediate future; and some of us are going to be ashamed of the excesses that will be committed against innocent people." He later noted: "Some of our super-patriots are simply going crazy."

Declaring that American liberties were endangered more by "our own excitement" than by enemy conspiracy, Jackson was determined to impose federal control over all investigations of alleged subversion. With that goal in mind, he offered little objection to legislation passed by Congress in late May ordering the mandatory registration and fingerprinting of all resident aliens. Although the American Civil Liberties Union strongly protested the Alien Registration Act (also known as the Smith Act after its main sponsor, Rep. Howard Smith, a conservative Democrat from Virginia), Jackson's fear of local witch hunts of aliens and others outweighed his concern about possible abuses.

The Justice Department was assigned to oversee the registration program, and Jackson vowed that his agency would do everything possible to protect all foreigners living in the country, some of whom were Jewish refugees from Germany and German-occupied nations. Under the direction of Solicitor General Francis Biddle, more than 3.5 million aliens were registered over the next few months. Overall, Americans accepted federal jurisdiction over alien-related activity, and the vigilante movements died out.

But the Smith Act contained another provision that, in the long run, would threaten civil liberties far more than did the alien registration clause. This section made it a criminal offense to advocate the overthrow of the government or to belong to any organization that did so. In effect it was an antisedition law, the first such peacetime legislation enacted in the United States since the Alien and Sedition Acts of 1798.

Zechariah Chafee, a Harvard Law School professor and the most eminent First Amendment scholar in the country, strongly protested passage of the act. When it was still being considered by Congress, Chafee observed that the best way to preserve free speech was to prevent repressive legislation from being enacted because, once such laws were approved, "patriotic judges and panic-stricken juries" would make sure they were enforced as strictly as possible.

Chafee had in mind what happened during World War I, when two laws—the Espionage Act of 1917 and the Sedition Act of 1918—were used to suppress not only those promoting rebellion against the government but also people who simply criticized the government and its conduct of the war. Enforcement of the statutes touched off what one scholar called "an orgy of repression" in the United States that took particular aim at radical speech and ideas.

The Supreme Court upheld the two laws, but later dissenting opinions by Justices Oliver Wendell Holmes and Louis Brandeis ended up having a powerful influence on postwar American jurisprudence. Heavily influenced by Chafee's writings, Holmes argued that "a clear and present danger" to law and security must exist before speech can legally be curbed by the state. In other words, unless speech can be proven likely to spark immediate violence or any other lawless action that would harm the nation, it should not be punished.

In later years, the "clear and present danger" doctrine espoused by

Holmes became widely accepted in U.S. courts, and a much broader view of free speech took hold in the country as a whole. But by 1940, as the specter of war once again faced the United States, a reevaluation of rights and liberties, especially those relating to the First Amendment, had begun. The fear engendered by Hitler's assault on Western Europe and the resulting reports of fifth columnists caused many people, including liberal intellectuals who had decried the First Amendment injustices of World War I, to urge curbs on politically provocative speech in what the historian Geoffrey Perret called "the Holy War against fascism." Among the few dissenters to that view was the American Civil Liberties Union, which had been organized after World War I to protect individual rights. Roger Baldwin, one of the ACLU's founders, bemoaned the fact that support for freedom of speech was "more and more confined to the small circles of defenders of civil liberty on principle," as well as, of course, to those under attack.

For a time, Robert Jackson and Solicitor General Francis Biddle were also among those who resisted the drive toward suppression of dissent. Decrying the attacks being made on Lindbergh and other isolationists, Biddle wrote: "Why shouldn't Lindbergh say 'England is defeated; we must keep out,' if he wants to? Isn't that part of our theory of freedom of speech? Isn't that the thing that we must fight back with other ideas?"

Both officials, however, came under considerable pressure from fellow liberals and their boss, the president, to change their views. Jackson, for his part, believed that Roosevelt "had a tendency to think in terms of right and wrong, instead of terms of legal and illegal. Because he thought that his motives were always good for the things that he wanted to do, he found difficulty in thinking there could be legal limitations on them."

In his memoirs, Biddle noted that FDR never seemed particularly troubled by violations of civil liberties: "It was all very well, he believed, to be liberal, but you must not be soft." That was especially true in wartime, Biddle observed. "If anything, [Roosevelt] thought rights should yield to the necessities of war. Rights came after victory, not before."

In his relationship with the Federal Bureau of Investigation and its controversial director, J. Edgar Hoover, the president made that position abundantly clear.

ROOSEVELT'S CLOSE TIES WITH Hoover began in early 1934 when he invited the thirty-nine-year-old director to a meeting at the White House. Hitler had taken power in Germany the year before, and the president asked Hoover to look into "the Nazi movement" in the United States, "especially its antiradical and anti-American activities." That vague, briefly worded instruction gave Hoover considerable investigative leeway, and he took full advantage of it.

Thanks to the FBI's use of such questionable methods as wiretapping, break-ins, and bugging, Hoover was already the bane of civil liberties advocates that he would continue to be for the rest of his long career. In response to Roosevelt's 1934 request, his agents began gathering a voluminous amount of information on what was loosely re-

FBI director J. Edgar Hoover shows off his machine-gun prowess to an admirer.

ferred to as the Fascist movement in the United States. It comprised a wide variety of nativist, xenophobic organizations, led by a colorful assortment of right-wing demagogues. Most of the groups were anti-Communist, anti-Roosevelt, and anti-Semitic, with some openly supportive of Hitler and Nazi Germany.

But the FBI chief was much more concerned about what he saw as the Communist threat, and in 1936 he warned Roosevelt of an alleged Communist plot to take over several American labor unions. Again, the president gave him vaguely worded instructions, this time to probe both Fascism and "the general [Communist] movement and its activities as may affect the economic and political life of the country as a whole." According to Hoover, FDR told him not to make any record of his directive.

As was his wont, Hoover interpreted the president's imprecise mandate as broadly as possible. By 1939, the Justice Department reported that the FBI had collected "identifying data" on more than ten million persons and had compiled extensive dossiers on those whose beliefs, associations, actions, or ethnic origins seemed suspicious to the FBI or its informants. Included were persons thought to have Nazi, Fascist, or Communist sympathies or who had ties to other countries, including those who subscribed to foreign-language newspapers. Hoover told a congressional committee that he was compiling lists of such people for possible detention "in the event of any greater emergency."

The FBI's far-ranging, seemingly uncontrolled investigations and surveillance were increasingly troubling to the ACLU and a scattered number of other civil libertarians, among them several members of Congress. Since the probes were carried out in secret, how could anyone be sure that they were directed only at those who posed a true threat to U.S. security?

In early 1940, Roger Baldwin complained to Robert Jackson that Hoover and the FBI apparently believed they had the authority to investigate any individual or organization they defined as unpatriotic, including pacifists, diplomats, journalists, labor unions, religious groups, and even congressmen. Not long afterward, Senator Theodore Green, a liberal Democrat from Rhode Island, contended that the phones of government officials in his own state, as well as in Pennsylvania and Massachusetts, had been tapped by agents seeking political intelligence. Although Green didn't identify the offenders, he implied that they were FBI operatives. Green demanded an immediate inquiry by the administration.

The senator's charges were particularly explosive because wiretapping had been outlawed by Congress in 1934, with the Supreme Court upholding the ban five years later. Nonetheless, the FBI had continued the practice, rationalizing that the law did not mean to ban wiretapping itself but only disclosure of information collected as a result of such taps.

In mid-March, Robert Jackson announced that wiretapping would no longer be allowed under any circumstances unless and until Congress authorized it. Refusing to accept that ruling, Hoover struck back. As was his practice until the end of his career, he had collected considerable political dirt on the administration in power, and now he threatened to use it. He told Adolf Berle, who headed counterespionage activities at the State Department, that for the past few years the FBI had tapped phones at the request of the White House and various senior administration officials, including its most ardent supporter of civil liberties, Harold Ickes. Hoover also maintained that the FBI had actually "done far less actual wire tapping than the Treasury, the SEC, and several of these agencies." (A curious footnote to this account of Washington wiretapping run amok can be found in an entry from Ickes's diary in September 1939, in which he noted that FDR had warned cabinet members to "be careful about the telephone" because "some of our wires were being tapped." The interior secretary included no further details about what, on the surface at least, would appear to have been a startling announcement.)

As it turned out, Hoover had no need to resort to blackmail. He had passed on his concerns about Jackson's wiretapping ban to the columnists Walter Winchell and Drew Pearson, both of whom wrote pieces and delivered radio broadcasts about how the ban had hampered FBI investigations. According to Pearson, FBI agents had overheard German agents plotting to blow up a British ocean liner but, because of Jackson's order, were forced to stop listening in to the would-be saboteurs' phone conversations.

As Hoover was well aware, such stories, true or not, only served to heighten Roosevelt's worries about internal subversion. On May 21, the president sent Jackson a confidential memo acknowledging that wiretapping was "almost bound to lead to the abuse of civil rights."

Yet, he added, in times of national peril, the government could not sit back and allow foreign agents to work unhindered. Arguing that the Supreme Court surely never intended its decision to "apply to grave matters involving defense of the nation," FDR ordered Jackson to authorize wiretapping in cases of "suspected subversive activities . . . including suspected spies." He suggested that Jackson keep such activities to a minimum and "limit them insofar as possible to aliens."

Jackson knew that such imprecise and ambiguous instructions would give Hoover and the FBI enormous discretion to tap the phones of whomever they wanted to target, regardless of whether those persons did indeed pose a serious threat to national security. Nonetheless, the attorney general followed Roosevelt's orders. He was well aware that the president had been openly critical of what he called Jackson's inflexibility, telling the attorney general's predecessor, Frank Murphy, that Jackson "did not have the proper sense of balance between civil liberties and national security." Weary of fighting Roosevelt and knowing that he would not prevail in the argument, Jackson provided little further oversight of the FBI's surveillance activities.

Until the 1970s, FDR's directive on wiretapping and Jackson's compliance with it were used as the legal basis for the thousands of warrantless FBI wiretaps placed during that three-decade period on scores of targets, including embassies, civil rights leaders, political groups, journalists, and government officials. In 1976, a Senate Intelligence Committee report noted that "factors of political belief and association, group membership, and national affiliation became the criteria for intelligence investigations before the war." The purpose of such investigations, the report added, "was not to assist in the enforcement of criminal laws," but to provide top administration officials with political information. Such probes, the Senate committee observed, continued throughout World War II and well into the Cold War.

Having acceded to Hoover's request for wiretapping authority, Roosevelt had a request of his own. Two days after his May 16 address to Congress, Roosevelt handed to his press secretary a stack of more than a hundred telegrams, all of them critical of his speech. Their senders, the president said, were clearly opposed to a strong national defense, and he wanted Hoover "to go over these, noting the names and addresses" of the people who had dispatched them. Hoover did more than that, checking out each name in FBI files and reporting back to the White House on what he had found. If no information could be located on a critic, the FBI opened a new file.

Not long afterward, another sheaf of negative telegrams was sent to the FBI for investigation. By the end of May, Hoover had run background checks on dozens of critics of Roosevelt's policies, including Charles Lindbergh, Burton Wheeler, and Gerald Nye. As it turned out, Lindbergh already had a thick FBI file, begun in the mid-1930s after he irritated Hoover by crediting the Treasury Department, rather than the FBI, with solving the kidnapping and murder of his son.

In mid-June 1940, Roosevelt asked an aide to "prepare a nice letter to Edgar Hoover thanking him for all the reports on the investigations he has made and tell him I appreciate the fine job he is doing."

DURING THESE UNSETTLED, TENSION-FILLED days, the administration targeted yet another outspoken critic of FDR's policies—Colonel Truman Smith, Lindbergh's confidant and George Marshall's chief analyst on Germany. On May 27, Dwight Davis, secretary of war under President Calvin Coolidge, passed on to presidential press secretary Steve Early reports that Smith had helped prepare Lindbergh's anti-FDR speech the week before and that he was pro-Nazi. Two days later, Lindbergh received a phone call from Smith's wife, who told him that Marshall had been urged to court-martial her husband because of his antiadministration activities.

There was no question that Smith had been playing with fire for some time. Not only was he openly aligned with Lindbergh, but he also was the chief source on the Army General Staff for the German military attaché, General Friedrich von Boetticher, with whom he had been friends since Smith's first tour of duty in Germany in the 1920s. (After the war, von Boetticher told U.S. Army interrogators that Smith's "bitter opposition to Roosevelt and his friendship and admiration for Germany were well known.")

Repeating Dwight Davis's accusations, the White House charged Smith with being pro-Nazi, anti-American, and the ghostwriter for Lindbergh's speeches. The colonel denied all the allegations. About the last one, he would later write: "No human being, as I knew well, could influence Lindbergh on any matter, let alone write his speeches."

While committed to the subordination of the U.S. military to civilian authority, Marshall strenuously resisted what he saw as a White House attempt to meddle in Army personnel matters. He considered Smith to be an invaluable aide and refused to get rid of him. "Marshall protected Truman at all times," Albert Wedemeyer, a close friend and colleague of Smith's, later recalled. Another Marshall protégé, Wedemeyer, a West Point graduate, had recently returned to the United States after spending two years at Germany's prestigious war college, the Kriegsakademie, in Berlin.

Marshall told Roosevelt that a court-martial of Smith would surely end in an acquittal, not to mention an estrangement between the administration and the Army. Marshall also warned the president that any action taken against Smith would turn him into "an American Dreyfus," a reference to the French Army officer Alfred Dreyfus, whose trumped-up court-martial in the late 1800s caused an international furor.

Roosevelt backed down, but a flurry of press attacks on Smith prompted Marshall to order the colonel to leave Washington at once and to "stay away until the political heat had cooled." He also advised Smith to "avoid the appearance of a close relationship" with Lindbergh, at least for a while. For the next two weeks, the colonel and his wife took refuge with Wedemeyer, then a major, who was stationed at Fort Benning, Georgia. Before leaving for Georgia, Smith's wife warned Lindbergh, as he wrote in his journal, that "the Administration is out to 'get me.'" He noted laconically: "Well, it is not the first time, and it won't be the last."

In the midst of this tumult, the Lindberghs were coping with a new barrage of hate mail and crank phone messages. On a lovely evening in early June, Anne Lindbergh received a worried call from her mother. Elizabeth Morrow reported she had just gotten off the phone with an unknown woman, who had asked her: "Aren't you worried about your daughter?" When Mrs. Morrow asked which daughter the caller was referring to, she replied, "The famous one."

Anne's first thought was of her children. When she told Charles about the call, he dismissed it as inconsequential, yet both immediately went to check on their little boys, who were asleep in their bedrooms. Reassured that their sons were safe, the Lindberghs pulled down all the blinds and closed the curtains in their secluded Long Island house. "It's that awful feeling again," Anne wrote in her diary that night. "Someone might be watching."

CHAPTER 8

"THE ART OF MANIPULATION"

≡

Not long after Germany launched its blitzkrieg of Western Europe, a mysterious emissary from the British government arrived in New York. His name was William Stephenson, and his mission was the subject of considerable conjecture.

There were rumors that Stephenson, a forty-three-year-old multi-millionaire businessman from Canada, had come to set up a new press and propaganda operation for the British. But that seemed unlikely, since the current government press service, run by Aubrey Morgan and John Wheeler-Bennett and operating from the forty-fourth floor of the RCA building in Rockefeller Center, was, by all accounts, doing a brilliant job in getting the word out to American journalists about Britain's perilous state and its desperate need for American aid.

In fact, Stephenson had been sent by Winston Churchill to New York as the new head of British intelligence activities in America. On paper, his main job was to protect British munitions purchases from Axis sabotage and to gather information on other enemy operations aimed against Britain. Stephenson's real mission, however, turned out to be considerably broader. Over the next eighteen months, his operation would declare war on *all* of Britain's enemies in the United States—whether German, Italian, Vichy French, or American isolationists. More specifically, he and his colleagues would take whatever steps were necessary to silence those foes and bring America into the war. In doing so, they would pay no heed to questions of legality or morality. As one of Stephenson's colleagues later remarked, "In modern war . . . even those belligerents who are hampered by moral scruples must neglect no weapon that may be of service."

With Britain in such deadly peril, Churchill had no compunction about using what he called "ungentlemanly warfare" to save his country—a stand with which the buccaneering Stephenson fully agreed. Although a businessman, he was no novice in the art of spying.

The son of a poor laborer from western Canada, Stephenson, after completing only six years of school, had been forced to go to work in his early teens. During the Great War, he emigrated to England and ended up a much-decorated war hero, having shot down more than a dozen German planes as a Royal Flying Corps ace. A millionaire before he was thirty, he acquired a score of companies that manufactured everything from cement and aircraft to radio sets and auto bodies, which he ran from an office in central London. On his business travels to Germany in the 1930s, Stephenson discovered that practically all German steel production was being used for the manufacture of armaments and munitions, in violation of the Versailles Treaty. He passed that information on to the British intelligence service (MI6), as well as to Winston Churchill, then a backbencher member of Parliament fighting the appeasement policies of the British government.

Stephenson's reports greatly impressed Churchill. When he became prime minister in May 1940, he called on the Canadian to undertake this audacious, aggressive covert operation in America, which turned out to be, as the *Washington Post* columnist David Ignatius later wrote, "a virtual textbook in the art of manipulation." It was, said British historian Nicholas Cull, "one of the most diverse, extensive . . . undercover campaigns ever directed by one sovereign state at another."

With the knowledge of President Roosevelt and FBI chief J. Edgar Hoover, Stephenson's unconventional outfit planted propaganda in American newspapers, spied on isolationist groups, dug up political dirt on isolationists in Congress, and forged documents that, when brought to public attention, helped foment anti-Nazi sentiment. "If the isolationists had known the full extent" of the secret alliance between the United States and Britain, "their demands for the impeachment of the President would have been a great deal louder," noted Robert Sherwood, who, as a member of Roosevelt's staff, would later serve as a liaison between Stephenson and Roosevelt.

At its height, British Security Coordination, as the organization was blandly named, employed nearly one thousand people at its Rockefeller Center headquarters on Fifth Avenue, across the street from St. Patrick's Cathedral. Some two thousand additional staffers were stationed in Canada, Central and South America, and the Caribbean.

BSC employees in New York included linguists, cipher and cryptology experts, intelligence agents, propaganda officials, people knowledgeable about business and finance, and specialists in a host of other fields. Among them were the noted Oxford dons Alfred Ayer and Gilbert Highet; the advertising genius David Ogilvy; Eric Maschwitz, who wrote the lyrics for the hit song "A Nightingale Sang in Berkeley Square"; and Noel Langley, coauthor of the screenplay for *The Wizard of Oz*.

Although a fair number of positions were filled by Britons, the majority of BSC personnel were Canadians, who, because their accents and mannerisms were far closer to those of Americans, were thought to be less conspicuous than their British counterparts. Regardless of their national origin, employees were instructed to draw as little attention to themselves as possible. Female clerical staffers who worked irregular shifts were to tell their landlords and neighbors that they were nurses, which would explain their comings and goings at odd hours. Employees' apartments were vetted, as were doctors, dentists, and anybody else whose services they might need. They were not to talk about what they did at work, even to BSC colleagues. When they entered an elevator in their office building, they were under orders not to acknowledge any co-workers who might also be on the elevator, even if they had been chatting with each other just moments before.

Secrecy was William Stephenson's watchword in his personal as well as professional life. "An extremely private man. . . . An enigma all around," said the writer Roald Dahl, who worked as a BSC agent. According to another staffer, Stephenson "never told anybody about himself. Never." Only a handful of employees knew the small, slight BSC chief by sight. He moved "like a panther, a black panther," said a woman who worked in his private office. "He had that quality of blending into a crowd. You wouldn't see him. . . . He was so swift and so silent."

Adept at cultivating Americans who might be useful to him, Stephenson and his American wife gave frequent cocktail parties at their penthouse suite at the Dorset Hotel, just a couple of blocks from the BSC offices. "You'd meet almost anybody there," said a key aide of Stephenson's, from "admirals and generals to Henry Luce, Walter Winchell, and Robert Sherwood."

A suave and charming host, Stephenson was known for his potent martinis; another colleague, writer Ian Fleming, called them "the most powerful martinis in America." After a couple of them, the six-foot-seven-inch Sherwood was once heard to say: "If I have another cocktail, I'll just call timber and fall on my face." Fleming, who would model his famous fictional character James Bond in part on Stephenson, noted that the BSC chief was the source of Bond's martini recipe: "Booth's gin, high and dry, easy on the vermouth, shaken not stirred."

Sherwood's frequent presence at Stephenson's parties underscored the most remarkable aspect of the Canadian's organization: its presence was not only known to the White House and FBI, it was endorsed by both. In truth, the BSC's operations benefited Franklin Roosevelt as much as they did the British government, at least when it came to the effort to defeat his antiwar foes. In its covert work to discredit isolationists, the BSC was in effect an active partner of the president. Shortly after Stephenson arrived in the United States, FDR directed that "there should be the closest possible marriage between the FBI and British Intelligence." No other U.S. government agency, however, would be informed of the full extent of the BSC's operations. When Stephenson registered his outfit with the State Department, he said that its only purpose was to protect the security of munitions and other war material bound for Britain.

For Stephenson, J. Edgar Hoover's cooperation was especially crucial. The United States was still officially neutral, and Britain's campaign against German, Italian, and Vichy French activities in the country was a clear violation of U.S. law. The FBI chief not only closed his eyes to that fact, he provided valuable assistance to the British, which they returned in full measure.

Hoover, for example, allowed the BSC to use an FBI shortwave station to transmit top-secret coded messages to London. Through one of his agents, working undercover as a Nazi sympathizer, Hoover also passed along to the German embassy disinformation that the BSC wanted to plant with Hitler's government, such as rumors that the Soviet Union was preparing to invade Germany.

In return, British agents handed over to the FBI thousands of confidential reports dealing with their work in the United States. They also taught their American counterparts some of their many tricks of the counterintelligence trade, including their elaborate techniques for opening and resealing letters and packages without any trace of tampering. BSC personnel employed that skill at highly secret mail-opening centers in Bermuda and Trinidad, British islands through which virtually all correspondence between the Americas and Europe was routed, including supposedly inviolate diplomatic pouches from Axis and other embassies. In Bermuda, scores of British government employees toiled in the cellar of the luxurious colonial-style Princess Hotel, poring over letters and packages carried by the ships and aircraft that routinely stopped at that Atlantic island for refueling before heading for Europe. Photographs were taken of the contents of mail considered particularly significant, which then was resealed and sent on to its designated recipients.

Although the opening of others' mail was illegal under U.S. law, the FBI, following British instructions in the technique, instituted what it called the Z Coverage program, in which agents surreptitiously examined correspondence from, among other targets, the German, Italian, Japanese, and Vichy French embassies in Washington. The policy of opening mail for supposed national security purposes continued until 1966, during which time the FBI read and photographed more than 130,000 letters. According to a 1976 report by the Senate Intelligence Committee, "the mail of hundreds of American citizens was opened for every one communication that led to an illegal agent."

The FBI also bugged and tapped the phones of Axis embassies, as well as those of neutral foreign missions for such countries as Spain, Portugal, and Switzerland. The BSC followed suit, focusing especially on the Vichy French embassy, considered such a hotbed of pro-Nazi activity that both U.S. Navy and Army intelligence also had it under close surveillance.

Amy Elizabeth Pack, an American agent working for the BSC, was ordered to get whatever information she could from the Vichy French. Tall and slim, with honey-blond hair and green eyes, the thirty-year-old Pack was a well-traveled ex-Washington debutante who had gone to school in Switzerland, summered in Newport, and spoke fluent French and Spanish. The estranged wife of a British diplomat, she was known for her charm, strong will, passion for adventure, and sex appeal, which she put to good use in her work for British intelligence, becoming romantically involved with numerous foreign diplomats and military officers, including Charles Brousse, the Vichy French press attaché in Washington.

Soon after their affair began, the besotted Brousse raided the embassy safe to provide his lover with top-secret cables between France and the embassy, as well as France's naval cipher. Pack, whose code name was "Cynthia," passed the material on to Marion de Chastelain, an aide to William Stephenson, at surreptitious weekly meetings in New York and Washington. Of Pack, Chastelain would later note: "She was the type who reveled in espionage. She really loved it. . . . She did very well for us."* Pack herself told a journalist after the war: "I did my duty as I saw it. It involved me in situations from which respectable women draw back. But wars are not won by respectable methods."

Using the intelligence provided by Pack, together with the contents of tapped phone conversations, the BSC prepared a report charging the embassy and the Vichy government with working on Germany's behalf. The report was leaked, through an intermediary seemingly unconnected to the BSC, to the *New York Herald Tribune,* which published a series of articles linking the Vichy embassy to Nazi interests.

This was a common technique of Stephenson's—to uncover information damaging to the Axis or isolationist cause and pass it along, usually through cutouts, to American news organizations. "The greatest care had always to be exercised," noted a postwar BSC history, "for clearly if British Security Coordination had ever been uncovered or had the sources of its information been exposed, it would at once have been [identified as a] covert British propaganda organization, and as such would be considerably worse than useless."

Even though the recipients of this journalistic largesse might not have been fully aware of the material's source, they all were considered pro-British. According to the official BSC history, among those who "rendered services of particular value" were the columnists Dorothy Thompson, Walter Lippmann, Walter Winchell, and Drew Pearson. Also mentioned were a number of newspaper publishers, including

---

* After divorcing their spouses, Pack and Brousse married and lived in France following the war.

Arthur Sulzberger of *The New York Times,* Ralph Ingersoll of *PM,* and Helen Reid of the *New York Herald Tribune.* In the words of *The Washington Post*'s David Ignatius, "the British spymasters played this media network like a mighty Wurlitzer (organ)."

The *Herald Tribune,* which was noted for its outspoken, aggressive support of interventionism, was by far the biggest beneficiary. In addition to getting the Vichy embassy story, its reporters were tipped off by the British about one Gerhard Westrick, the commercial attaché at the German embassy, and his shady dealings with several American companies. Posing as a private citizen, Westrick had rented an expensive house in a New York suburb, where he entertained a number of representatives of U.S. firms, most of them in the oil business. Westrick's purpose was apparently to convince the executives that Germany was close to winning the war and that if they threw their support behind the isolationist movement, they would be provided abundant business opportunities in a Nazi-dominated Europe. He also had reportedly worked with a number of U.S. oil companies to break the British naval blockade of Germany and Italy and to supply the Axis with oil.

After undertaking an investigation of its own, the *Herald Tribune* ran a front-page series of articles about Westrick, which prompted a flood of abusive letters and phone calls to the unhappy attaché, as well as a demonstration by angry neighbors outside his house. At the instigation of the FBI (prompted by Stephenson), the State Department ordered Westrick's recall, and the *Herald Tribune* was widely congratulated for smoking out a dangerous emissary of Hitler. Its stories were reprinted in newspapers throughout the country and inspired numerous editorials on the dangers of the Nazi fifth column.

In a cable to Berlin, Hans Thomsen, the chargé d'affaires at the German embassy in Washington, complained about the "sensational and vicious attacks" on Westrick, apparently unaware that they had been prompted by British agents. "The deplorable part," Thomsen wrote, "is that as a result of this publicity, which was in no way provoked by Westrick, Americans who have still maintained business connections with Germany and social relations with the Embassy and Consular staffs, are so compromised before the public that they have found themselves compelled to sever these relations."

For Thomsen and his embassy colleagues, whose main goal was to

Hans Thomsen, Nazi Germany's chargé d'affaires in Washington, with his wife.

win over Americans to the isolationist cause, it was an extremely frustrating time. Instead of being in league with the FBI, as the British were, the Germans were spied on by both the FBI and the British. Even worse, from the Germans' perspective, most Americans, even though they had no desire to go to war with Germany, wanted nothing to do with the Reich or its government. At one point, Thomsen complained to Berlin about "the general anti-German mood and mistrust of all German efforts at enlightenment" in America. The isolationist movement, he added, was constantly being "shouted down by the press and terrorized by the Government." Ernst Weiszacker, a top German Foreign Ministry official, had the same complaint, writing to propaganda minister Joseph Goebbels: "The real friends of Germany in the United States are unfortunately so few and far between that they are hardly a political factor at the present time."

Because of U.S. antagonism, Hitler's government avoided giving overt support to American isolationists. The Germans even shied away from criticizing Roosevelt and his government, for fear such moves would increase the danger that America would enter the war. "The less we intervene spectacularly in this contest, and the more we skillfully let the Americans themselves carry on this fight . . . the better for us," Weiszacker noted. "On the other hand, any obvious intervention by Germany will only have the result that all Americans will unite against us."

But while the Germans did their best to lie low, the U.S. government and the British stepped up their efforts to persuade the American people of the dangers posed by a German fifth column. In a series of syndicated newspaper articles, the columnist Edgar Ansel Mowrer and the Wall Street lawyer William Donovan, an unofficial emissary for Roosevelt and a close friend of William Stephenson's, speculated that "a German-American colony of several million strong," including "thousands of domestic workers and waiters," was working undercover in the United States for the Reich. The most egregious example of such fifth-columnism, the authors wrote, was the German-American Bund.

Since the mid-1930s, oceans of ink had been spilled in press coverage of the Bund, the most notorious Fascist group in the United States. Openly referring to their organization as America's Nazi Party, Bundists wore Nazi-style uniforms, used the Hitler salute, held youth camps and drills, and attacked Jews wherever they could find them.

Members of the German–American Bund parade down a street in New York City. Note the Nazi flag preceding the American flags.

Two days before George Washington's birthday in 1939, the Bund captured front-page headlines across the country by staging a giant rally at New York's Madison Square Garden, attended by some twenty thousand Nazi sympathizers and picketed by thousands of protesters. Standing in front of giant portraits of Hitler and Washington, Bund leaders, swastikas adorning their uniforms, railed against "the invisible government of international Jewry" and the socialist plots of "President Franklin D. Rosenfeld."

For Germany, the event was a public relations disaster. It outraged Americans and made them think the Bund was considerably better organized and more dangerous to America's security than it actually was. Unquestionably hateful in its rhetoric and activities, the organization, for all the lurid publicity surrounding it, had never succeeded in rallying a sizable number of German Americans to the Nazi cause. At its peak in the late 1930s, it probably numbered no more than seventy-five hundred activists and another twenty thousand sympathizers.

By the summer of 1940, the Bund was virtually moribund, with fewer than two thousand members. After the Washington's birthday rally, the German government cut off all financial support and other ties. In late 1939, the Bund leader Fritz Kuhn was indicted and sent to prison for embezzling funds from the organization. Bund meetings were routinely broken up by protesters, and in several states, the group was investigated and in effect outlawed.

Although thoroughly discredited and defanged, the Bund, in the public mind, was still a dangerous presence in the United States— a belief that the U.S. government and the British were only too happy to encourage. "The best British ambassador we ever had in the U.S. was Adolf Hitler," declared Robert Bruce Lockhart, director general of Britain's wartime propaganda agency, the Political Warfare Executive. "The crass stupidity of Nazi propaganda, which reached the height of insolent absurdity in a pamphlet entitled *George Washington, the First Nazi,* did more than any British statement could have done" to underscore the chasm between Germany and America.

Lockhart's statement was a bit unfair to the German government, since the pamphlet in question was a product of the Bund. But there's no doubt that Hitler and his men were at times equally clueless in their understanding of the United States. Ernst Weiszacker underscored that point when he informed the German propaganda ministry in 1941 that it should rethink its name for the "Goebbels Hour," a new short-wave radio program beamed to America. Rather recklessly perhaps, Weiszacker wrote that there existed "in the U.S.A. such a misconception of the person of the Reich Minister of Propaganda that merely the announcement of a 'Goebbels Hour' would cause the American listeners to shut off their radios at once." The plan was reluctantly shelved.

In Washington, Hans Thomsen was having similar trouble with his own propaganda efforts. He confessed to Berlin that his attempts to place pro-isolationist articles in American newspapers had been, for the most part, an abject failure: "Influential journalists of high repute will not lend themselves, even for money, to publishing such material."

Having no luck with U.S. publications, Thomsen had to rely on Reich-supported organizations and institutions, such as the German Fellowship Forum and the German Information Library, to get the word out. Using German government funds, the chargé oversaw the creation of a publishing house in New Jersey that put out antiwar and anti-British books, which, he assured his superiors, would have "great results in regard to the enlightenment of American public opinion." Unfortunately for Thomsen, almost all the books went unsold.

CHAPTER 9

"IS THIS WAR OUR CONCERN?"

═══

On June 4, 1940, the new prime minister of Great Britain rose from his seat in the House of Commons to deliver one of the most magnificent speeches in British history.

"We shall fight on the beaches," Winston Churchill growled, "we shall fight on the landing grounds, we shall fight in the fields and in the streets, we shall fight in the hills." Pausing a moment, he proclaimed to his spellbound parliamentary colleagues: "We shall *never* surrender!"

At a time when the fall of France was imminent and a German invasion of Britain was expected soon afterward, Churchill's defiant jab in the eye of "Herr Hitler," as the prime minister sarcastically called the Führer, electrified not only his own country but the world. In that speech, as in a number of unforgettable addresses to come, Churchill made clear that Britain would resist, no matter the cost. When his foreign secretary, Lord Halifax, argued in late May that the country should consider peace negotiations with Germany, Churchill rejected the idea, vowing, "We shall fight it out." Years later, Sir Charles Portal, Britain's wartime chief of air staff, remarked, "They say there was no danger that we should have made peace with Hitler. I am not so sure. Without Winston we might have."

But what if Churchill were ousted from power? That was not an impossibility, as the prime minister made clear to Roosevelt in a series of desperate pleas for help immediately after he assumed office. Despite the miraculous rescue of more than two hundred thousand British soldiers from Dunkirk's beaches, the country's future verged on the calamitous. Many of the RAF's most experienced pilots—not to mention hundreds of planes and more than 68,000 ground troops—had been lost during Britain's attempt to come to the aid of Belgium and France during the German blitzkrieg. Britain now had only enough men to field twenty army divisions, less than a tenth of the forces mustered by Germany. And that small number had almost nothing to fight with, having left behind virtually all their tanks, armored cars, weapons, and other equipment in France. There were only a few hundred thousand rifles and five hundred cannon in all of Britain—and most of the cannon were antiques, appropriated from museums. Churchill was hardly exaggerating when he declared: "Never has a great nation been so naked before her foes."

Eleven days after delivering his "fight on the beaches" speech, Churchill sat down to compose his latest appeal to the president of the United States for aid. Gone was the tone of inspiration and defiance that he had used over and over to raise the morale of his countrymen and rally them to fight. This message contained only the bleakest of warnings. If France collapsed, as appeared increasingly likely, and his country received no help from America, Churchill warned, a "shattered, starving" Britain might well sweep his government out of power and install one willing to make peace with Germany.

Such a scenario would be almost as catastrophic for the United States as it would be for his own nation, he went on. America would be left to face "a United States of Europe under Nazi command far more numerous, far stronger, far better armed than the New World." To keep that from happening, the United States must waste no time in sending destroyers, planes, and weapons to the British. It was, the prime minister declared, "a matter of life or death."

Virtually from the day he replaced Neville Chamberlain, Churchill had been engaged in a battle of wits with the president. When he begged for destroyers, as he had done repeatedly, Roosevelt responded that he could not send them without the approval of Congress. At the same time, FDR urged Churchill to consider dispatching the British fleet to Canada or the United States in case of German invasion. The prime minister replied that Britain was hardly likely to entrust its navy, the very symbol of British power, to a neutral America. According to the British cabinet, Roosevelt "seemed to be taking the view that it would be nice of him to pick up the pieces of the British Empire if this country was overrun. . . . [H]e should realize that there was another aspect of the question."

Roosevelt certainly understood the importance of the British fleet to the defense of both Britain and America, and there's no question he wanted to do all he could to keep Britain fighting. Indeed, five days before receiving Churchill's warning of a defeatist government replacing his own, the president had pledged to use all "the material resources of this nation" to provide the British with the help they needed. "We will not slow down or detour," FDR declared during a June 10 commencement speech at the University of Virginia. "Signs and signals call for speed—full speed ahead."

John Wheeler-Bennett, the historian turned British propagandist, was present at the speech. He remembered "the shock of excitement which passed through me. . . . This was what we had been praying for—not only sympathy but pledges of support. If Britain could only hold on until these vast resources could be made available to her, we could yet survive and even win the war. It was the first gleam of hope." As *Time* saw it, the president's address marked the official end of American neutrality. "The U.S. has taken sides. . . . Ended is the utopian hope that [it] could remain an island of democracy in a totalitarian world."

Yet Roosevelt's prodigal promises were unlikely to be translated into action any time soon. Arguing that America lacked almost everything it needed for its own defense, George Marshall and most of his military colleagues, along with secretary of war Harry Woodring, were unalterably opposed to sending to the British any of the minuscule number of planes, tanks, ships, and weapons the country did have. They emphasized the necessity of building a strong armed force here before becoming entangled in Europe's struggle. "It is a drop in the bucket on the other side," Marshall told Treasury Secretary Henry Morgenthau, "and it is a very vital necessity on this side, and that is that."

When the president asked the Army and Navy in June to come up with ideas for utilizing U.S. naval and air power against German forces, the services' Joint Planning Board replied: "Our unreadiness to meet such aggression on its own scale is so great that, so long as the choice is

left to us, we should avoid the contest until we can be adequately prepared."

Complicating the situation for Churchill and the British was the
widespread belief in Washington, particularly among the military, that
Britain was already doomed and that any aid it received would be captured by Germany and used against the United States. If Britain were
vanquished after America sent supplies desperately needed at home,
Marshall declared, "the Army and the Administration could never justify to the American people the risk they had taken." In a tart letter to
the British ambassador in Washington, Churchill observed: "Up till
April, [U.S. officials] were so sure that the Allies would win that they
did not think help necessary. Now they are so sure we shall lose that
they do not think it possible."

On June 24, Marshall and his naval counterpart, Admiral Harold
Stark, urged Roosevelt to shut off all aid to Britain. The president rejected the idea out of hand, making clear to his service chiefs that
America would not renege on its commitment to help the last European country standing against Hitler. Nonetheless, the only equipment made available to the British over the next couple of months
was a few dozen planes and hundreds of thousands of World War I–era
rifles, machine guns, revolvers, mortars, and ammunition. While certainly important, such matériel could clearly do little in the long run to
stave off defeat by Germany. Indeed, as Marshall remembered, the rifles were sent with only ten rounds of ammunition per weapon.

Joining the military in opposing a transfer of arms was a majority
of members of Congress, who were as parsimonious toward Britain as
they had been generous in bolstering American defenses. Senator Key
Pittman, chairman of the Senate Foreign Relations Committee, went
so far as to urge the British government to surrender to Hitler. "It is no
secret that Great Britain is totally unprepared for defense," he said,
"and that nothing the United States has to give can do more than delay
the result." In early June, Pittman's committee blocked the sale of
modern warplanes and ships to the Allies, and later that month, Congress banned the sale of any further supplies unless U.S. military chiefs
declared them surplus to American national defense requirements.

Observing the events in Washington that fateful spring, the German chargé d'affaires assured his superiors in Berlin that America, to

the president's great chagrin, was unlikely to do much to help ward off British and French defeats. "Only the experienced observer," Hans Thomsen wrote, "can detect Roosevelt's tremendous fury at not seeing any possibility at the present of helping the allies in their fateful struggle."

THE ARGUMENTS RAGING IN Washington over aid to Britain were echoing throughout the country as well. "No newspaper was too small, no hamlet too remote, no group of citizens too insensitive to be untouched," *Time* wrote in late May. "The question under debate was, broadly: 'Is this war our concern?'" Americans from Maine to California began making their voices heard, with many enlisting in hastily organized and passionately waged campaigns to influence their government's actions. Advocates of aid, galvanized by the fall of France in late June, were the first to make their presence felt.

"If you could have asked millions of Americans what single moment made the war real to them, many would have answered that it was the day the Germans marched into Paris," the historian Richard Ketchum noted. Most people in the United States had little knowledge of the countries previously vanquished by Germany; for them, Hitler's earlier victims were, to paraphrase Neville Chamberlain's notorious remark about Czechoslovakia, faraway countries full of people about whom we knew nothing. But France—and its capital—was different. Even those who had never been to Paris could summon up mental images of the Eiffel Tower, the Arc de Triomphe, the lovely tree-lined boulevards, the bustling sidewalk cafés. Now Paris was gone. Would London be next?

If so, what would happen to the British fleet? If it, too, were swallowed up by Germany, the Reich would control the Atlantic sea-lanes, posing an agonizing dilemma for the United States. The main U.S. fleet was currently based in Hawaii as a deterrent to an increasingly aggressive Japan, now at war with China, while a considerably smaller, weaker naval force patrolled the Atlantic. If the fleet remained in the Pacific, Germany could send troop ships with impunity to South America or, in an equally nightmarish possibility, cut the United States off from its overseas sources of vital raw materials. If the ships were transferred to the Atlantic, the Pacific would be open to the Japanese fleet.

Supporters of aid to Britain used this troubling scenario as a key argument in their newly organized campaigns. One particularly influential advocate, the columnist Walter Lippmann, declared: "We have been deluding ourselves when we have looked upon a vast expanse of salt water as if it were a super Maginot Line. The ocean is a highway for those who control it. For that reason every war which involves the dominion of the seas is a world war in which America is inescapably involved."

The idea that America's security depended on Britain's continued independence was heavily promoted by the first major citizens' group to spring up. Headed by William Allen White, it was created in late May, just days after German troops began tearing through Western Europe. The organization's official title was the Committee to Defend America by Aiding the Allies, but virtually everyone referred to it as the White Committee.

After helping Roosevelt win congressional approval of "cash and carry" in the fall of 1939, the Kansas editor had grown increasingly alarmed by America's continuing apathy toward the war. A couple of days after the German juggernaut began, he sent a telegram to several hundred prominent Americans, many of them members of his former committee to lobby for neutrality law revisions, urging them to join him in championing the cause of "all aid short of war." Like Roosevelt, who had given his blessing to the new group, White argued that the main reason for aiding the Allies was to keep America out of the conflict. The future of Western civilization, White declared, was "being decided upon the battlefields of Europe." If Britain and France were allowed to fall, "war will inevitably come to the United States."

Serving in effect as an unofficial public relations agency for Roosevelt and his administration, the White Committee enlisted governors, mayors, college presidents, professors, newspaper editors, writers, businessmen, actors, and at least one prizefighter—Gene Tunney—to serve on its executive board. The board members, in turn, helped organize local groups throughout the country to generate widespread grassroots support. "Our idea," White wrote to a friend, "is to fill the radio and the newspapers and the Congressional mail with the voices of prominent citizens urging America to become the nonbelligerent ally of France and England."

With the fall of France, membership in the committee mushroomed. By July 1, it had three hundred local chapters across the nation; a month later, there were nearly seven hundred chapters in forty-seven states. Members sponsored rallies, radio broadcasts, and newspaper advertisements, while at the same time writing their congressmen and shipping pro-aid petitions bearing millions of signatures to Capitol Hill and the White House.

AMONG WHITE'S MOST PRIZED recruits was Elizabeth Morrow, then serving as acting president of Smith College. While Mrs. Morrow had long been involved in a wide range of charitable and philanthropic causes, her main value to the committee obviously lay in the fact that she was Charles Lindbergh's mother-in-law. An ardent advocate of aid to the Allies, she was already active in a number of organizations providing private help to European citizens caught up in the conflict. In her diary, Anne Lindbergh noted her mother's "terrible sense of shame and even guilt for Americans not helping more."

Mrs. Morrow had turned her New Jersey estate into a sort of informal headquarters for some of these private aid groups—a matter of considerable discomfort for Anne whenever she came to visit. On occasion, she would find old friends of hers helping her mother put together food and clothing parcels for refugees. When they asked her to pitch in, she declined. It would be a violation of her own personal neutrality to do so, she said; Charles and she weren't taking sides in this war, which, in Lindbergh's view, was a clash of rival imperialistic states, both undeserving of American support.

Until Lindbergh's May 19 broadcast, Elizabeth Morrow had held her tongue about his and Anne's stand on the war, at least when other people were around. But she was so upset by his speech that, in the presence of a close friend of Anne's, she suggested to her daughter that, at the very least, Lindbergh might in the future express some sympathy for Hitler's victims and revulsion toward Nazi methods. That was impossible, Anne replied: it was important to Charles that he be seen as an impartial observer, a kind of umpire, in the war in Europe. Her mother looked at her for a moment, then snapped, "I always understood that umpires have whistles and sometimes blow [them] when there's a foul."

Much of Mrs. Morrow's indignation stemmed from the obvious emotional toll that Lindbergh's activism was taking on Anne. She wrote to a friend: "I am in a difficult position just now between my two sons-in-law, but my chief worry is over Anne. She is torn in spirit, and it is telling on her health."

On the surface, Anne was her usual quiet, reserved self. Deep down, however, she was consumed by tension, pain, sadness, and regret. She felt so guilty about Charles's public repudiation of the British and French that when she and her sister Con had lunch in New York one afternoon, she insisted they go to an Italian rather than a French restaurant. "I can't bear to face French people," she wrote in her diary. A few days earlier, when an old French acquaintance—a military pilot on a mission to buy aircraft from the U.S. government—asked Lindbergh to lunch, Anne was amazed. "He has been there in the battle, he knows what France faces, and he can still meet and treat C. as a friend. It is incredible. I do not believe, placed in the same position, I could do it."

As the debate over the war grew more vitriolic, she found herself estranged from virtually all her old friends and acquaintances. Lindbergh, she mused, had become the "Anti-Christ" to a "certain class." She added: "I know the 'class' well. It is 'my' class. All the people I was brought up with. The East, the secure, the rich, the cultured, the sensitive, the academic, the good—those worthy intelligent people brought up in a hedged world so far from realities."

Her inner conflicts were further exacerbated by the escalating conflict between her mother and her husband. Despite her worries about Anne, Elizabeth Morrow, at the request of William Allen White and urged on by Aubrey Morgan, decided to go public with her opposition to Lindbergh's views. In early June, she made a national radio address on behalf of the White Committee, calling on the government to provide all-out support for the Allies: "I urge the sending of munitions and supplies, food, money, airplanes, ships, and everything that could help them in this struggle against Germany." Then, in what could easily be viewed as a rebuke to Lindbergh, Mrs. Morrow declared, "There are some things worse than war. There are some things supreme and noble that are worth fighting for."

Before the speech, she had insisted to Anne that it was not meant as an attack on Charles, but as her daughter noted, "Of course, it will be used and publicized in that light." After the broadcast, Mrs. Morrow returned to her New Jersey estate, where Con and Aubrey Morgan opened a bottle of champagne to toast her success. Anne, meanwhile, had listened to the speech by herself, glad that Charles was not at home to hear it. "It is a beautiful speech, a fighting speech, with much of her faith and spiritual force in it," she wrote in her diary. "But I cannot agree with its premises, and I feel only sad at not being able to, and [being] very much alone and separated from all these good people."

To her mother, she wrote: "How I wish, oh how I wish, I could feel wholehearted about this war, in any way. Either that I could feel it were necessary for our self-preservation, or that the war simply and purely was a struggle between evil and good. To so many people . . . it is clearly a case of the forces of evil vanquishing the forces of good. I cannot simplify it to that."

While Elizabeth Morrow's broadcast was clearly meant to counter Lindbergh's position on the war, it also was intended to challenge the widespread idea that women, because they were mothers, would be more inclined to oppose intervention. That view was pushed hard by the so-called "mothers' movement," a coalition of right-wing women's organizations that had sprung up in opposition to Roosevelt and his foreign policy, claiming that interventionism was both un-American and antifamily.

After her speech, Mrs. Morrow was bombarded by hate mail, with many of the letters using the rhetoric of motherhood in their assaults on her views. "Unless you recall your speech, it will not go well with you," one anonymous letter declared. "We, all the 'Mothers' of the United States, will see that you will be railroaded to England and France and put in the 'Front-line' where the likes of you belong. How dare you speak about war!! Have you sons to give? . . . Don't forget, We are coming for you. We are going to get you."

THE INCREASINGLY ACRIMONIOUS CLIMATE in the country also had a profound impact on another prominent member of William Allen White's committee. Robert Sherwood's friends knew him as a gentle, kind man, but when he received word in January 1940 that Senator

William Borah was dying, he wrote in his diary: "A bit of good news today. . . . Now—if only God will take [isolationist publisher William Randolph] Hearst." In a profile of Sherwood published later that year, *The New Yorker* described him as a "fiercely militant liberal" who "feels a burning indignation against those he considers callous and insensitive to the struggle in Europe."

Sherwood had accepted with alacrity White's invitation to join his group, and he threw himself into all its activities. But with his growing sense of urgency, he didn't feel that the committee—or any other organization or individual—was doing enough to convince Americans of the importance of saving Britain. So, with White's approval, Sherwood designed, wrote, and partially paid for a full-page newspaper advertisement that appeared on June 10 in more than one hundred newspapers across the country.

Topped by a headline proclaiming STOP HITLER NOW!, the ad warned that "if Hitler wins in Europe . . . the United States will find itself alone in a barbaric world—a world ruled by Nazis," in which "democracy will be wiped off the face of the earth." At the bottom was a dramatic appeal to readers to join the pro-aid cause: "In a dictatorship, the government tells the people what to do. But—this is a democracy—we can tell the government what to do. Exercise your right as citizens of a free nation. Tell your president—your senators—your congressmen—that you want them to help the allies to stop Hitler now!"

The day after the ad appeared, more than five hundred volunteers showed up at the White Committee's New York headquarters, and committee members delivered to the White House pro-aid petitions bearing the signatures of twenty-five thousand persons. At his news conference that day, Roosevelt commended Sherwood for the ad, calling it "a mighty good thing" and "a great piece of work, extremely educational for this country."

But William Allen White had quite a different view. He had been inundated by a flood of angry letters complaining about one sentence in the ad that claimed anyone who opposed its views was "either an imbecile or a traitor." Among his correspondents was Oswald Garrison Villard, a former editor of the liberal magazine *The Nation* and a good friend of White's. A lifelong pacifist, Villard protested to the Kansas editor that he and millions of others who opposed aid to the Allies were "just as loyal, just as sincere, and just as earnest as Sherwood or anybody else."

White agreed. In a letter to Sherwood, he wrote that the playwright's inflammatory statement "has aroused our opponents, and it seems to me quite unnecessary. Of course, there are millions of Americans who honestly believe in the isolationist theory. I don't; you don't. But when you call them imbeciles or traitors they rush to the nearest desk and write me letters which often are so intelligent that they have to be answered." So many complaints had descended on him, White added, that, even with the help of three stenographers, he had not been able to respond to them all.

An apologetic Sherwood replied that the "imbecile" line was meant to apply only "to those who give solemn assurances (specifically Lindbergh) that Hitler is not going to attack the Western Hemisphere." Years later, the playwright noted that White had scolded him "for having gone too far. But it was not long before such epithets as mine were commonplace."

TO WILLIAM ALLEN WHITE, it was clear that opinion in the country was shifting fast toward sending planes, ships, and weapons to Britain. Late that spring, a government study of the nation's newspapers showed that although most of them still opposed the idea of America's armed intervention in the war, the vast majority now backed "immediate and unstinted aid" to the British. In recent polls, more than 70 percent of the American people approved the dispatch of aid as well.

But the president ignored these positive signals from his countrymen and refrained from taking any bold new action to fulfill the pledges he had made at the University of Virginia. A frustrated White told a friend that his committee could be of no use unless it had something substantive to work on: "We are doing the best we can, but the trouble is there is nothing before Congress that we can get behind and boost." To Roosevelt, White cabled in early June: "My correspondence is heaping up unanimously behind the plan to aid the Allies by anything other than war. As an old friend, let me warn you that maybe you will not be able to lead the American people unless you catch up with them. They are going fast."

Still Roosevelt hesitated, his fear of the power of congressional isolationists overriding his faith in the public's support. The specter of Woodrow Wilson's 1919 humiliation by isolationist senators was always at the back of his mind. If he moved too quickly, he told the British ambassador, "you will get another 'battalion of death' in the Senate like Wilson did over the League of Nations—a group which will exploit the natural human reluctance to war, excite the women . . . and get the Senate so balled up as to produce complete paralysis of action in any direction." He explained to an aide that "it would have been too encouraging to the Axis, too disheartening to Britain, and too harmful to his own prestige to make this a matter of personal contest with Congress and be defeated."

But could the British hold out while the president and his administration temporized? On a beautiful spring afternoon in rural Virginia, a group of friends met over lunch to ponder that question. "The sense of impending doom was so strong," remembered Francis Pickens Miller, a noted foreign policy scholar, who hosted the lunch at his country home. "There was a desperate need in that hour for someone to speak for America. Why should not we? Perhaps if we did, others with more influence might take up the cry."

Two weeks after the lunch, newspapers across the country carried stories about the creation of a new citizens' lobbying group—one that spurned the middle ground championed by the White Committee and the administration, to provide all aid short of war. Instead it dared speak the unspeakable: it called on the U.S. government to declare immediate war against Germany. The thirty founding members of the group—"all men of high position," as one newspaper described them—included Miller, along with a former chief of the U.S. Navy, an Episcopal bishop, editors, publishers, writers, business executives, and lawyers.

Explaining the rationale for such a radical proposal, Herbert Agar, the editor of the Louisville *Courier-Journal* and another of the organization's founders, noted that, while Congress had voted billions of dollars for rearming America, no great economic or industrial mobilization was underway; instead, business as usual prevailed. "We who had asked for war on Germany . . . had foreseen that the U.S. would never rearm herself, let alone give decisive support to Great Britain, without an economic upheaval in which labor, capital and consumers all agreed to sacrifice for the nation," Agar wrote. "This does not happen among free people except in time of war."

In its founding statement, which it called "A Summons to Speak Out," the group urged "those citizens of the United States who share these views to express them publicly." But, as its members admitted, such an appeal for action was hardly likely to attract a groundswell of support. While most Americans supported giving aid to Britain and more than half the population felt that the United States probably would be dragged into the war eventually, fewer than 10 percent favored an immediate declaration of war against Germany. As Freda Kirchwey, editor of *The Nation,* rightly noted, "What a majority of the American people want is to be as unneutral as possible without getting into the war."

Of the more than 125 individuals who were asked to join the new group, only about 25 percent accepted. Several of those who were approached were violently opposed to the idea, warning that it would create even more friction in a country that desperately needed unity. After newspaper stories appeared about the group's creation, some of its members received threatening letters.

Unlike the White Committee, this band of radical interventionists would never become a mass-membership, grassroots organization. Nonetheless, despite its tiny core of true believers, it would end up having an extraordinary impact on the battle for America's future.

CHAPTER 10

"WHY DO WE NOT DEFEND HER?"

═══

Throughout the summer of 1940, a group of men came together for occasional dinners at a stately Italian Renaissance building just off Fifth Avenue in New York City. One by one they slipped through the door, crossed the entrance hall, and entered a small elevator that took them to a private meeting room on the fourth floor. As waiters circulated among them with drinks and food, they plotted ways to help Britain and get America into the war.

These well-dressed, well-bred revolutionaries were part of the new citizens' organization that had jolted the country with its call for immediate belligerency. In the weeks since its creation, it had attracted a small but glittering array of new members—about fifty in all. Movers and shakers in the East Coast's top journalistic, legal, financial, and intellectual circles, they were collectively known as the Century Group, after the private men's club where their dinner meetings were held and to which many of them belonged.

Their choice of meeting place was hardly surprising. One of the oldest and most exclusive clubs in New York, the Century Association was the very embodiment of the East Coast old boys' network. Seven Centurions (as the club's members called themselves) had occupied the White House, including the current occupant, Franklin D. Roosevelt.

Six more had sat on the Supreme Court, while more than thirty had served in the cabinet.

Such statistics were particularly impressive considering the club's small size and its criteria for membership, which had nothing to do with public service. Founded in 1847 by prominent American artists and writers, it limited its members to "authors, artists, and amateurs of letters and the fine arts." Unlike most New York men's clubs, it was regarded from its inception as a center of the city's intellectual and literary life, "a gracious place of conviviality and good talk in a smoky rumbling seaport."

The Century clubhouse, on Forty-third Street in midtown Manhattan, was designed by the eminent architect Stanford White, himself a Centurion, and boasted an extensive library and a distinguished American art collection including works by such noted painters as John LaFarge and Winslow Homer, both of whom were also members. The club's early membership list reads like an artistic and literary Who's Who: actor Edwin Booth; architects Richard Morris Hunt and James Renwick; landscape designer Frederick Law Olmsted; poet and editor William Cullen Bryant; sculptor Augustus Saint-Gaudens; writer Henry Adams; and book publishers Henry Holt, William Appleton, and Charles Scribner.

Century members liked to think of themselves as bohemians, but that was just a pleasant delusion; the poet Walt Whitman, a true bohemian, was never invited to become a Centurion because members did not regard him as a clubbable man. The Century, for all its artistic spirit, was very much a bastion of the Establishment, a fact that became increasingly obvious by the early twentieth century, when the club began adding more professional men—judges, Wall Street financiers, lawyers, and business executives—under the catchall category of "amateurs of letters and fine arts." Among them were such titans of industry and finance as Cornelius Vanderbilt, J. Pierpont Morgan, and Andrew Mellon.

Members in good standing of the East Coast's intellectual and business elite, Centurions prided themselves on their devotion to public service and disdain for the rancor of partisan politics. "When they thought of gentlemen in politics, they thought of each other, and though animated by no vulgar ambition for office, some of them were not unwilling, from time to time, to sacrifice themselves to the public good," the historian Henry Steele Commager, another Centurion, wryly noted. The writer David Halberstam once described former defense secretary Robert Lovett, also a Century member, as a man with "a sense of country rather than party"—an apt description of the Century ethos.

Within the Century Group, Democrats outnumbered Republicans. But the Republicans who did belong had far more in common with their Democratic counterparts than with their fellow party members in Congress, most of whom were conservative and isolationist. Like their idol, Theodore Roosevelt, many prominent East Coast Republicans favored fiscal prudence but leaned toward liberalism on social issues. While they opposed many of Franklin Roosevelt's economic policies, they supported a fair number of his New Deal reforms. Above all, they were internationalist and pro-British, many having close personal, social, and commercial ties with England.

A sizable percentage of the Century Group had attended Groton, St. Paul's, and other New England prep schools that were modeled after English public schools like Eton. (Some of the American schools were so Anglophile in outlook that they substituted cricket for baseball and encouraged students to use British rather than American spelling in their writing.)

After prep school, these young scions of the Eastern establishment went to Ivy League colleges, particularly Harvard and Yale. Once they'd graduated, many studied at British universities or traveled extensively in the British Isles or on the Continent. Following World War I, they did not retreat into isolationism like the majority of Americans; most supported U.S. participation in the League of Nations and World Court, and later opposed passage of the Neutrality acts. Those involved in business and finance, meanwhile, became immersed in the industrial and economic rebuilding of a devastated Europe.

Several men in the Century Group were members of the Council on Foreign Relations, the first American think tank to focus on international affairs. The New York–based council was the brainchild of a group of young advisers to the U.S. delegation at the 1919 Paris peace conference. During a series of informal meetings, the Americans and several of their British counterparts decided to form organizations in both countries for the study of international affairs and promotion of Anglo-American understanding and cooperation. The British equivalent of the U.S. group was—and is—the Royal Institute of International Affairs, also known as Chatham House.

In the interwar years, the Council on Foreign Relations was an island of internationalism in an isolationist sea, as it tried to awaken the United States to its world responsibilities. In addition to publishing the influential journal *Foreign Affairs* and sponsoring workshops and meetings for businessmen and foreign affairs professionals, it produced long-range planning papers for the State Department after the European war broke out in September 1939.

Ever since its creation, the council has been seen by its critics as an invisible government, secretly setting the parameters of U.S. foreign policy. But in the years before World War II, distrust of the council was also linked to an antipathy toward Europe—and internationalism in general—that had deep roots in the country. Unlike members of the Century Group, most Americans had never traveled in Britain or on the Continent, and a sizable percentage were not inclined to do so even if they could. There was considerable distrust of Europeans and their ideas, as well as of "rich, overeducated Easterners who still doted on Europe."

Underlying such suspicions was the enormous gulf of knowledge and understanding between America's heartland and the East Coast—and in particular the East's financial and cultural hub, New York City. These intense regional differences were wittily underscored in a play entitled *This Is New York,* written by Robert Sherwood (also a Century Group member) in the early thirties. Among its leading characters is a South Dakota senator who despises New York as "un-American" and declares that it should be kicked out of the United States and towed across the Atlantic to Europe, where it belongs.

Sherwood, who described the conflict between New York and the rest of the country as "a bloodless civil war," said he wrote the play because he was tired of "aggressive Americans of the West" who contended that "New York is not America." Sherwood viewed *This Is New York* as an homage to the city's energy and panache, as well as to its liberal atmosphere and the cultural and political stimulation it provided. In his view, New York was the "sole refuge from intolerance, from the Puritan inquisition," in addition to being "the American spirit in concentrate form."

Of course, other Americans, especially those living in the rural areas and small towns of Middle America, disagreed. They saw New York and other major American metropolises as corrupt, immoral, chaotic places, lacking in the community, religious, and family values they held dear. To some, big cities were full of dangerous alien influences—radicals, immigrants, labor organizers, and "transplanted Negroes," all of whom, one rural congressman claimed, "have introduced insidious influences into the New Deal."

Many in the country also resented the power and influence of members of the East Coast elite, who were seen as arrogant and condescending, intent on dominating mainstream America even though they were totally isolated from it. To some degree, the East's critics were correct in their suspicions. "New York, and to a lesser degree, Boston and Philadelphia felt a right—even a duty—to set a tone for the country," acknowledged Joseph Alsop, himself part of the Eastern establishment. "There was the feeling [among members of that establishment] that the country was really their country."

Believing themselves to be society's guardians, wellborn, well-connected Easterners were often as suspicious of and hostile to the rest of the nation as its inhabitants were to them. They devoured Sinclair Lewis's novels about the prejudices and closed-mindedness of small-town America and, in the words of the historian Frederick Lewis Allen, were "united in scorn of the great bourgeois majority, which they held responsible for prohibition, censorship, Fundamentalism and other repressions." *The New Yorker*, widely considered to be "the humor magazine of [the East's] ruling class," made clear what it thought of the American heartland when it announced upon its creation that it was "not for the old lady from Dubuque. It will not be concerned in what she is thinking about."

THE EDITOR OF *The New Yorker* was not a member of the Century Group, but many other major media figures were. And, as it turned out, they were extremely concerned about the old lady from Dubuque and what she thought of the question of America's involvement in the war.

While numerous members of the group ended up playing key roles in its pro-war campaign, those with the greatest impact on American public opinion would be the organization's columnists, editors, radio

Herbert Agar, editor of the Louisville Courier-Journal *and a leading member of the Century Group, with his wife.*

commentators, and publishers. Their involvement, which blossomed into an unapologetic advocacy for intervention, raised serious questions about journalistic objectivity and balance. With few exceptions, however, they had no second thoughts about what they were doing: this was not, in their view, a time for even-handedness.

The Century Group's most combative journalist-activist was Herbert Agar, who had taken an unofficial leave from the Louisville *Courier-Journal,* with the blessing of his publisher, to promote the cause of war. The son of a wealthy New York corporate lawyer, Agar had graduated from Columbia and received a Ph.D. in literature from Princeton. During the Great War, he served in the U.S. Navy as an ordinary seaman, and afterward he worked as the London correspondent for the *Courier-Journal,* then considered one of the best newspapers in the United States.

In the early 1930s, Agar settled in Louisville, becoming a columnist for the *Courier-Journal* and at the same time a noted poet and historian. At the age of thirty-seven, he won a Pulitzer Prize in history for *The People's Choice,* a survey of the U.S. presidency from George Washington to Warren G. Harding. He was also a member of the Fugitives, the famed group of southern poets that included Robert Penn Warren, John Crowe Ransom, and Allen Tate.

In early 1940, Agar was appointed editor of the *Courier-Journal.* As soon as he took charge, the newspaper became one of a tiny handful of papers in the country demanding that the United States go to war to save Britain. Its position "amounted to an incitement to riot" in militantly isolationist Louisville, which had a large German American population. Mary Bingham, the wife of *Courier-Journal* owner Barry Bingham, later described Agar as "the most outspoken and the most vile of all interventionists in the world." (She meant that as a compliment.)

Thanks to Agar's aggressively pro-war stance, the Binghams, staunch liberals who shared their editor's interventionist beliefs, were attacked verbally at dinners and cocktail parties and shunned by many acquaintances and friends. Years later, Mary Bingham would say that the months before Pearl Harbor were the worst time of the couple's lives.

As the Century Group's most outspoken firebrand, the darkly handsome Agar was openly contemptuous of William Allen White's more moderate committee. "I think the most unattractive title ever devised was 'The Committee to Defend America by Aiding the Allies,'" he later wrote. "If our country needed defending, why did we not defend her, instead of asking the French and British to do the job?"

At the same time, he took great pride in what the Century Group's opponents regarded as its extremism. "The isolationists called us warmongers as a term of abuse," he observed. "We made it a term of defiance. We wanted war with Germany and strove to promote it. We were not content with giving or selling arms to our friends in order that they might die in our defense."

Agar, said a Century Group colleague, "was our Old Testament prophet. Whenever our mental and spiritual batteries ran down, he recharged them, and whenever our vision grew dim, he restated and clarified our goals with passionate conviction."

Another Century Group member, Elmer Davis, was much less inflammatory in his interventionism than Agar, but as one of the most popular news commentators on CBS, he had a far greater influence on American public opinion. The only native midwesterner in the Century Group, Davis grew up in Indiana and went to college there. After attending Oxford on a Rhodes scholarship, he spent ten years at *The New York Times* as a reporter and editorial writer. When World War II began, he joined CBS as one of its top news analysts. Until the fall of France, Davis, like William Allen White and his committee, believed that America should do no more than provide aid to the Allies. Now, however, he was convinced that nothing short of active U.S. belligerency would save Britain and the rest of Western civilization.

Joining Davis at CBS was George Fielding Eliot, a retired Army major and the network's military analyst, and another diehard interventionist. Although an American, Eliot had been raised in Australia and had fought in World War I's bloody Gallipoli campaign as an officer in the Australian army. Later an intelligence officer in the U.S. Army, Eliot was the author of more than a dozen books on military and political matters. In addition to broadcasting for CBS, Eliot also wrote a column for the *New York Herald Tribune*.

Second only to *The New York Times* in prestige and influence, the *Herald Tribune* was known for its lively writing, excellent sports and books sections, extensive foreign coverage, and nationally known columnists, especially Dorothy Thompson and Walter Lippmann. As the voice of the East Coast Republican establishment, the *Herald Tribune* was a staunch defender of both American free enterprise and an internationalist foreign policy. After the German blitzkrieg in May 1940, its editorial page, as *Time* reported, "came out and said a thing which only a fortnight before no great paper would have said: '. . . The least costly solution in both life and welfare would be to declare war on Germany at once.'"

The author of that provocative statement was Geoffrey Parsons, the *Herald Tribune*'s editorial page editor and another key Century Group member. The grandson of a dean of the Harvard Law School, Parsons had been a lawyer himself before turning to journalism. A *Herald Tribune* reporter and editor for more than twenty years, he was credited with helping to steer the paper away from its once diehard conservatism toward a more progressive Republicanism.

Also on the Century Group's front lines was the *Herald Tribune* columnist Joseph Alsop, who, at thirty, was the group's youngest member. Based in Washington, the foppish Alsop was an object of amusement for some of his more hard-bitten journalistic colleagues. A product of Groton and Harvard, he wore expensive handmade suits, entertained lavishly at his Georgetown home, and spoke with an affected quasi-British accent. But, as one acquaintance wrote, "Those who underestimated him as sort of an American Bertie Wooster did so at their peril."

Blessed with a seemingly unassailable self-confidence and a biting wit, Alsop was a driven reporter and writer who was relentless in pursuit of a story. His close connections with Washington's top political and social circles were also a great help: his mother was the niece of Theodore Roosevelt and the first cousin and close friend of Eleanor Roosevelt, whom Alsop was brought up to call "Cousin Eleanor." When he first arrived in Washington, "Cousin Eleanor" invited him to the Roosevelt family's New Year's Eve celebration at the White House. In years to come, he was also, as a matter of course, summoned to join the Roosevelts for Christmas dinner and other social occasions.

Still, as influential as Alsop and the rest of the Century Group's journalists would turn out to be, none would have more of an impact on Americans' views of the war than the group's most self-conscious

Magazine publisher Henry Luce, a key Century Group member.

and uncomfortable member, the magazine publisher Henry Luce. Unlike the others, Luce was a seminal figure in U.S. journalism. Yet, with his rumpled suits and rough edges, he always felt like an outsider in this clubby, genteel collection of East Coast patricians.

On paper, Luce's establishment credentials were just as impressive as those of his colleagues. He had gone to Hotchkiss, another of the Northeast's top prep schools, and then to Yale, where he had been tapped by Skull and Bones, the school's most prestigious secret society. He'd even studied briefly at Oxford. But he hadn't felt at home at any of these institutions. The son of an American missionary, Luce had been born and raised in China, and he didn't know how to act around his much wealthier classmates, who laughed at his funny clothes and called him "Chink." Shy and awkward, he never developed the social graces that seemed to come naturally to those born to money.

What he did have was immense curiosity, driving energy, and a visionary spirit, which led him, at the age of twenty-three, to lay the foundation for a magazine empire that would transform American journalism. With his college classmate Briton Hadden, Luce launched *Time,* the country's first weekly newsmagazine, which aimed to explain current events and policy issues in lively, brief, understandable prose. Seven years later, in the midst of the Depression, Luce created the business magazine *Fortune.* In 1936, he founded *Life,* a publication devoted to photojournalism that quickly became the most popular magazine in the United States. In the days before television, *Life,* with its candid photos of newsmakers and events, offered a window on the country and the world that proved irresistible to millions of Americans. When it was first launched, people throughout the country lined up to buy copies, and at the height of its success, it could be found in virtually every middle-class home.

Luce's publications—in particular, *Life*—were far more in touch with the wide sweep of the country than were the outlets of the other media figures in the Century Group. Luce had long made it clear that he wanted nothing to do with the preciousness and exclusivity of Eastern publications like *The New Yorker.* "New York is not America," he wrote in 1938, contradicting Robert Sherwood. "Wall Street is not America. Broadway is not America . . . Park Avenue is not America. The intelligentsia are not America. . . . *Time* is edited for the gentleman of Indiana." Once, when he felt that *Time* was becoming too Eastern in outlook, Luce told his editorial staffers: "I want more corn in the magazine. Yes, I know you don't like it, you're too Ivy League and sophisticated, but I want more corn in it."

Even before World War II erupted, Luce had been an ardent advocate of U.S. intervention in the crisis in Europe. America, he said, was too powerful and her responsibilities too great to allow her to live "like an infinitely mightier Switzerland discreetly and dangerously in the midst of enemies." Increasingly frustrated by Roosevelt's slowness in moving the country to a war footing, he declared to a friend: "The American refusal to be 'drawn in' is a kind of failure to realize how deeply we *are* in, whatever we say or do."

By the end of 1939, both *Time* and *Life* were mobilizing their considerable resources for detailed coverage of the war. After the invasion of Poland, *Life* devoted a special issue to the burgeoning conflict, depicting in graphic photographs not only Poland's agony but also the massive strength of Germany's forces. Later, the magazine focused on Britain's determined fight to ward off defeat, paying special attention to the courage of its people and the inspiration of its leader, Winston Churchill. Interspersed with *Life's* dramatic photos were lengthy, dense essays by such pro-intervention writers as Walter Lippmann, who, in one five-page article, described in frightening detail a scenario in which Germany, after establishing control over all of Europe, was able to impose economic domination on the United States.

HENRY LUCE'S CONTRIBUTIONS TO the Century Group extended far beyond the enormous influence of his magazines. After putting up much of the money for Robert Sherwood's STOP HITLER NOW ad in early June, he helped finance the group's early efforts, including bankrolling the opening of a small office in a building on Forty-second Street. (The suite next door, as Francis Pickens Miller, the Century Group's executive director, soon discovered, was occupied by the German Fellowship Forum, a Nazi front that distributed pro-Hitler propaganda and was a meeting place for German agents. After keeping tabs on who went in and out of the Forum's office, Miller passed the information on to the FBI.)

While the Century Group's ultimate objective was American entry into the war, its members knew that the odds of that happening any

time soon were virtually nonexistent. During their first dinner meeting, they decided they would initially focus on pressuring Roosevelt
and his administration to grant Winston Churchill's repeated requests
for fifty old U.S. destroyers.

Britain's need for additional warships was undeniably desperate. In
its attempts to defend Norway, France, and the Low Countries from
Germany's lightning attacks in the spring of 1940, the Royal Navy had
lost almost half of its destroyers. It now had fewer than one hundred
ships in British waters and the Atlantic to carry out two monumental
tasks: guarding the country's coasts against an expected German invasion and protecting British merchant shipping from the growing dep-
redations of German submarines and surface raiders. In June, 140
merchant freighters had been sunk, more than double the tonnage lost
in May. The loss of more destroyers might well result in the complete
severing of British supply lines, which could lead in turn to starvation
and collapse.

When Luce and several other Century Group members met with
Roosevelt to urge him to transfer the over-age American ships, he told
them it was politically impossible, at least for the moment. The group
sent back word that "we were going to make it politically possible for
him to act," Herbert Agar remembered. "We felt he was unduly hesitant, but we realized that we had to accept his judgment on that point.
To prepare the country, and to reassure Roosevelt, several dramatic
steps had to be taken that would appeal to the nation as a whole."

To help put its plans into effect, the Century Group joined forces
with another key player in the Great Debate—Lord Lothian, the British ambassador to the United States. As it happened, he was a Centurion, too.

CHAPTER 11

"THE GREATEST OF ALL OUR AMBASSADORS"

═══

When John Wheeler-Bennett learned in mid-1939 who the next British ambassador to Washington was to be, his first reaction was shocked dismay. The new envoy, he was sure, "could have no possible appeal to the American public and would be suspect in official circles."

The black marks against Philip Kerr, the 11th marquess of Lothian, were many. A top member of the British aristocracy, he had had no diplomatic training. Even worse, he'd been a Neville Chamberlain ally, an outspoken appeaser of Germany, and a member of the notorious Cliveden Set, a group of prominent, pro-appeasement Britons who frequented the country estate of Nancy Astor, a Virginia-born member of Parliament with whom Lord Lothian was deeply, if platonically, in love.

In the view of Wheeler-Bennett and other British officials, Lothian was the worst possible candidate for the job, coming to America at the worst possible time. His mission seemed doomed to failure—to convince an isolationist America, already highly suspicious of British propaganda, that it was in the country's best interest to do all it could to aid Britain.

Yet, as Lothian's critics later admitted, they could not have been more wrong about him. Having recanted his pro-appeasement attitude six months before he arrived in Washington, he proved to be, in the

Lord Lothian,
British ambassador to
the United States.

words of one of his most outspoken detractors, Sir Robert Vansittart, "the greatest of all our Ambassadors." Employing his considerable charm and wit, he was assiduous in wooing the American people, managing to persuade many of them that the fates of his country and theirs were inextricably intertwined and that America might also be lost if Britain were defeated.

Americans liked Lothian, and he returned the favor. It's no exaggeration to say he understood this sprawling country and its people as well as or better than any other Briton. As secretary of the Rhodes Trust, the organization that administers the Rhodes Scholarships, he had made fourteen trips to the United States and visited forty-four states between 1924 and 1936. Unlike most British officials, whose knowledge of America was confined to the East Coast, Lothian, as one friend said, was familiar with "how Americans look at the world and what [they think] in the Middle West, South, and on the Pacific Coast, as well as in New York and Washington."

Unlike many of his countrymen, too, he was enamored by what he saw. He once told an American architect how exhilarated he felt while walking through the skyscraper-studded landscapes of New York, Chicago, and other major U.S. cities. Such architecture, Lothian said, "has caught the modern American spirit of boundless material enterprise, boundless confidence, and boundless energy." Shortly before he became ambassador, he remarked to reporters: "I always feel fifteen years younger when I land in New York." When he inherited his title in 1930, one of his biggest concerns was that it might "quite spoil the pleasure I used to have in traveling to the New World. One cannot fail to be unpleasantly conspicuous."

For Washington, Lothian's informality and down-to-earth attitude provided a refreshing change from Sir Ronald Lindsay, his chilly, stiff predecessor, who didn't know many Americans and didn't much like those he did. Lindsay, although a skilled, highly experienced diplomat, had been a public relations disaster: he was disdainful of Washington, which he considered a boring, provincial town, and when King George VI and Queen Elizabeth visited in 1938, he refused to invite members of Congress to an embassy reception for the royal couple.

From the day he presented his credentials to President Roosevelt, the fifty-seven-year-old Lothian made clear he shared none of Lindsay's elitist attitudes. With his horn-rimmed glasses, he looked more like a professor than a peer of the realm, and he reinforced that impression by appearing at the White House in a rumpled business suit instead of the traditional top hat, cutaway coat, and striped trousers. After the ceremony, the ambassador stopped to chat with reporters outside the White House, an act that undoubtedly would have appalled Sir Ronald. As he talked, a small black cat suddenly appeared and rubbed against his trousers. Picking it up, he perched it on his shoulder and continued the impromptu press conference. Not surprisingly, flashbulbs exploded, and captivating photos of the ambassador and kitten appeared the next day on newspaper front pages across the country. Describing the incident in a letter to Nancy Astor, Lothian wryly noted: "I am now voted human."

Throughout his tenure in Washington, he made himself accessible to reporters and talked to them freely. He knew how important the U.S. press was in forming public opinion, but he also genuinely enjoyed the company of journalists, many of whom belonged to his remarkably large and eclectic network of American friends and acquaintances. At British embassy social functions, "one would be as likely to meet the mayor of Kalamazoo as one of the famous dowagers of Washington, and the ambassador would display an evident and genuine interest in talking to either," recalled John Wheeler-Bennett, who became Lothian's personal assistant. Around his dining table could be found New Dealers, industrialists, Wall Street bankers, labor leaders, reporters, clergymen, and even isolationist members of Congress.

Lothian delighted in argument, and he enjoyed matching wits with anti-British senators like Hiram Johnson and Burton Wheeler. After dinner or lunch at the embassy, he was particularly fond of pointing out an oil painting of George III to Anglophobes and saying, "I hope you recognize the portrait of your last king." As Wheeler-Bennett observed, "These sallies met with a mixed reception."

PHILIP KERR FIRST CAME to public attention in the early 1900s, more than twenty-five years before he inherited his marquessate. At the age of twenty-three, he was a member of the famed "Milner Kindergarten," a group of recent Oxford graduates recruited by Sir Alfred Milner, the colonial governor of South Africa, to help rebuild a country divided and ravaged by the Boer War.

The prime aim of these young civil servants was to persuade the war's two antagonists—Boer and British settlers—that they must come together in mutual interest. The "kindergartners" helped draft a constitution that gave South Africa self-government within the British Commonwealth and restored the rights of the Boers. They worked to rebuild the country's infrastructure and economy, reviving its railroads and reopening mines, ports, and schools. As liberal imperialists, they earned praise for saving "South Africa for the [British] Empire as a self-governing dominion, and almost certainly from a further civil war, with the willing acquiescence of the Boers," the writer James Fox observed.

Less than a decade after this success, Kerr became personal secretary to Prime Minister David Lloyd George, acting as his principal foreign affairs adviser and, in Lloyd George's words, "my constant companion and collaborator" for the last two years of World War I. At the Paris peace conference in 1919, the thirty-seven-year-old Kerr, serving as "Lloyd George's other self," helped write the most controversial passage in the Versailles Treaty—the clause that put sole blame on Germany for causing the war. That clause was the Allies' justification for demanding huge reparations from Germany and became a flashpoint for German anger and resentment.

A high-minded idealist, Kerr became increasingly convinced that the Allies had made a terrible mistake, that the treaty had treated Germany unfairly and should be reversed. When Hitler came to power, he persuaded himself that the Führer, whom he described as "a visionary rather than a gangster," was simply trying to correct the injustices of the treaty. Failing to understand the essential nature of the Nazis, Kerr, who by then had inherited his title, naïvely told a friend: "If only we can get into a conference with the Germans on the fundamental problems of today . . . we could influence them, I think, to moderate the brutality of their practice."

Hitler and his associates skillfully exploited Lothian's sense of guilt. They invited him to Berlin and trumpeted his pro-appeasement views; the German foreign minister Joachim von Ribbentrop called him "the most influential Englishman outside the government." Jan Masaryk, the Czech minister to Britain, agreed, reporting to Prague in 1938 that Lothian was "the most dangerous" friend of Germany in England because he was "the most intelligent."

Lothian's pro-German attitude was reinforced by his intimate friendship with the equally appeasement-minded Nancy Astor, the wife of Viscount Astor and the first woman elected to the British House of Commons. The connection between the vivacious Nancy and the detached Philip was a perplexing one. "There isn't any question that they were in love—and also that it was never consummated in any way," one of Nancy's sons told James Fox, who wrote a biography of Nancy and her sisters. Nancy herself reported to her sister Phyllis that Lothian would have bolted had there been any hint of sex.

The grandson of the duke of Norfolk, the lay head of the Catholic Church in Britain, Lothian had had a strict Catholic upbringing, was "distinctly pious" as a boy, and at one point had even considered becoming a priest. For all his charm and gregariousness, there was an ascetic, monastic side to him that discouraged the attentions of women. Romantic love, he once said, was a sickness that "troubles the heart and soul."

While distinctly unconventional, the unmarried Lothian's relationship with Lady Astor seemed to give him the solace and support he could find nowhere else. Plagued by religious doubts for years, he abandoned his Catholicism and, under her influence, converted to Christian Science. Even after he had changed his mind about Hitler and Germany, she remained his closest friend.

Lothian's disillusionment with Germany was prompted by its seizure of Czechoslovakia in March 1939. Until then, he wrote an American friend, "it was possible to believe that Germany was only concerned with recovery of what might be called the normal rights of a great power, but it now seems clear that Hitler is in effect a fanatical gangster who will stop at nothing." He decided that the Führer could only be halted through resistance by a coalition of Western democracies, with Britain and the United States at its head.

This was not a new concept for Lothian: throughout most of his adult life, he had committed himself to furthering Anglo-American cooperation as the foundation for world security and peace. As one of the young British advisers at the Paris conference, he had worked with his American counterparts to create the Council on Foreign Relations and the Royal Institute of International Affairs. He had continued his mission of fostering closer U.S.-British ties while serving as secretary of the Rhodes Trust.

The summer before he became ambassador, Lothian toured America to judge public opinion for himself and to make contacts with people who might help Britain in its struggle against the European dictators. "America really holds the key to the whole future," he said at the time. In September 1939, soon after he arrived at the British embassy, he wrote to a friend in Britain: "Both winning the war and the prospects for a stable, free world afterwards depend ultimately on whether we win and keep the sympathy of 130 million Americans."

Lothian knew what a ticklish task that would be. From the beginning, he made clear to his government that it must be very careful in its approaches to the Roosevelt administration and the American people. "We have never listened to the advice of foreigners. Nor will the Americans," he wrote to Whitehall in early 1940. "They only differ in that we ignore such advice and the Americans get extremely angry when it is offered to them by any Briton."

Lothian also insisted that the British must try to put themselves in Americans' shoes, to make an effort to understand why they were so skittish about possible involvement in the war. In a memo to the Foreign Office, he argued that "there is generally as good a reason for Americans taking their view of international affairs as there is for our taking ours." And in a letter to Nancy Astor, he observed: "We really have no ground to abuse the U.S.A. She is simply doing exactly what we did" in trying to stay clear of war.

The British approach to America, Lothian was convinced, must focus not on Britain's desperate need for help but on the importance of his homeland's survival for U.S. national security. "The United States, like all other nations," he noted, "will only act when its own vital interests—which include its ideals—are menaced." He was sure that at some point, Americans would understand how essential Britain was to their safety. But would that realization come in time to counter isolationist arguments and ward off British defeat? The ambassador knew what a narrow tightrope he must walk, speeding up Americans' awareness of their country's potential danger while concealing from them the fact that that awareness was a product of British propaganda.

Without official sanction from his government, Lothian set out to mount a sophisticated, under-the-radar publicity campaign to appeal directly to the American people. This operation was kept separate from the covert activities of William Stephenson's British Security Coordination, which Lothian was informed of but with which he was not directly involved. In a cable to Lord Halifax, the British foreign secretary, the ambassador explained how important the views of ordinary Americans were: "To an extent unknown under the parliamentary system, it is public opinion as revealed in the press, the Gallup polls, the tornado of telegrams addressed to Congress" that proved to be the deciding factor in administration and congressional actions.

Throughout the early months of 1940, the ambassador made a series of speeches emphasizing the strategic interdependence of Britain and the United States, copies of which were widely distributed to U.S. opinion makers. Many major American newspapers ran front-page stories about his comments, which were also the subject of editorials and syndicated columns, most of them approving. Lothian's growing popularity in the United States prompted scathing comments in the German press about the turncoat aristocrat. "The same Lord Lothian who, not so long since, was so reasonable and understanding, appears to have lost his head completely," one paper snapped. "His utterances today appear simply unbelievable when compared with his past statements."

In addition, Lothian recruited John Wheeler-Bennett to travel throughout the country as his "eyes and ears"—to sample public opinion, set up a network of contacts, and speak to local groups about the importance of British survival to America. For more than two years, the tall, mustachioed Wheeler-Bennett crisscrossed the United States, visiting thirty-seven states and lecturing to a wide assortment of organizations—women's clubs, the Knights of Columbus, Lions, Kiwanis, Elks, Shriners, and Rotary. The elegant, erudite thirty-eight-year-old Briton often shared the program with other speakers, once finding himself "sandwiched between a dissertation on beekeeping and a fascinating discourse on how to deal with potato blight."

In making the British case, Wheeler-Bennett was faced with a daunting challenge. Although he encountered nothing but kindness and hospitality in his travels, he found in his audiences "an unqualified determination to keep out of war by all possible means, and woe betide those who might be foolhardy enough to try to make [America] do otherwise." Most Americans he met hated Hitler and his policies, but they were also wary of Britain and unsure it would survive. After the fall of France, Wheeler-Bennett recalled, "I found that it was I who had to sustain [Americans'] morale, for they had already written us off as defeated, albeit gallantly, and spoke to me in those hushed tones which are customarily used for the lately bereaved."

To help counter such beliefs, Lothian ordered a quiet expansion of British press and publicity operations in New York. He put Wheeler-Bennett and Aubrey Morgan in charge of a new organization called the British Press Service, whose job was to "create an American appetite for knowledge of Britain, her capacity to wage war, the determination of her people to see it through, her desire that a better world should emerge from the struggle."

The ambassador was adamant that in carrying out those objectives and in gathering intelligence about U.S. public opinion, British staffers must take extreme care to avoid attracting the attention of American isolationists and German operatives in the United States. He warned of "formidable, anti-British elements" which will "take every opportunity to misrepresent our motives and attack our methods."*

---

* Lothian's appeal for caution was not always heeded. In the summer of 1940, Sir George Paish, an elderly British economist, arrived in the United States for a lecture tour. During a conversation with Senator Burton Wheeler, Sir George declared: "I am responsible for getting the United States into the last war . . . and I am going to get this country into this war." That indiscreet comment prompted Wheeler and other isolationist members of Congress to demand Paish's immediate expulsion from the country and an inves-

To play to the sympathies and sentiment of the American people, Lothian urged his government to emphasize the heroic aspects of the rescue in late May 1940 of the British army at Dunkirk, particularly the hundreds of pleasure boats and other small craft owned by ordinary Britons that crossed the English Channel to help save British soldiers. British propaganda officials in London did so, and Americans were soon reading comments in their newspapers like this statement from *The New York Times*'s editorial page: "So long as the English tongue survives, the word Dunkirk will be spoken with reverence. For in that harbor . . . the rages and blemishes that have hidden the soul of democracy fell away. There, beaten but unconquered, in shining splendor [Britain] faced the enemy."

The ambassador also encouraged Winston Churchill to make it clear that whatever happened in France, Britain would continue the fight against Germany. The two men were hardly friends: they had clashed over the years on several major policy issues, prominently including appeasement. At one point, Lothian wrote to a friend: "I think that Winston has made a fool of himself. He is always doing these things." Churchill, in turn, considered Lothian to be a naïve, high-minded lightweight. But in the heat of war, each had come to appreciate the other. Lothian greatly admired Churchill's courage and resolution, while the prime minister observed how, under the stress of crisis, Lothian had transformed himself into "an earnest, deeply stirred man . . . primed with every aspect and detail of the American attitude."

Shortly after getting Lothian's request, Churchill gave his famed "fight on the beaches" speech, which captivated the American people just as the ambassador had hoped. As a result of that address, and others like it, Winston Churchill became a hero in the United States. When Drew Middleton, an Associated Press reporter based in London, returned in mid-1940 for a visit to his boyhood home in South Orange, New Jersey, he found his family totally under Churchill's spell. "What a great man!" an old uncle declared after listening to the prime minister's latest speech on the radio. "What a great people!" other family members chimed in.

---

tigation into British propaganda. When asked by *The Washington Post* for a reaction, a British embassy official tartly replied: "We wish someone would drop Sir George Paish over Germany as a pamphlet." At Lord Lothian's order, Paish was put on the next ship to Britain, and the furor died down.

The drama of Dunkirk and the eloquence of Churchill helped convince many Americans that their country must give Britain all possible support in its lonely struggle against Germany. In one poll taken after the rescue and speech, more than 80 percent of Americans now favored sending as many arms as possible to the British. But even this signal of overwhelming public backing for military aid failed to budge the administration. A frustrated Lord Lothian wrote to an acquaintance in July: "There is universal admiration here for Winston and the spirit of the country, but as you will say, admiration and sympathy are not much good when one is fighting Hitler at the gate."

The ambassador attempted to convince Roosevelt and Secretary of State Cordell Hull that they must take action *now*. With a German invasion of Britain apparently imminent, the situation was too perilous to indulge in further procrastination. By mid-July, the Luftwaffe had begun attacking British ship convoys in the Channel and targets on England's southern coast. The Battle of Britain was about to begin, and as Churchill noted, "the whole fury and might of the enemy must very soon be turned on us."

But Lothian's arguments left Roosevelt and Hull unmoved. After his talks with the president and secretary of state, the ambassador informed the Foreign Office that the U.S. government "has not yet faced the fact that the only way in which it can save itself from being confronted by totalitarian navies and air forces three or four times as powerful as its own in the near future is by setting the situation in all its stark brutality in front of Congress without delaying."

In his cable, however, Lothian chose to omit the political facts of life that had been explained to him by both Roosevelt and Hull. It was an election year, and although the president had not publicly announced it, he had recently decided to run for an unprecedented third term—a decision that he knew would be heavily criticized. Cautious at the best of times, he was determined not to give the Republican Party and his other isolationist foes any further ammunition for their charges that he was trying to lead the country into war.

With the president still on the sidelines, Lothian decided to go on the offensive himself. In a heavily publicized speech to Yale alumni, he warned the United States not to count on the British fleet's availability to defend North America in the event of a British defeat. "I hope you are not building on that expectation," he declared. "If you are . . . you have been building on an illusion." In any event, the ambassador added, the Royal Navy would be far more effective in preventing enemy ships from entering the Atlantic from European waters than in trying to help patrol the vast Canadian and U.S. eastern coastline.

A few weeks later, when asked in a broadcast interview whether it was in America's interest to help Britain, Lothian replied: "It is for you to decide what is in your own interest. But I should have thought that it was vital to you that Britain and the British Navy should stay in being until your own rearmament, your two-ocean navy, your fifty thousand airplanes and your big army were ready. Today we are your Maginot Line. If that goes, there is nothing left between Hitler and his allies and yourselves."

But while Lothian's voice was clearly being heard, he knew that his arguments would have far more impact if they were made by influential Americans. When a representative of the Century Group approached him in early July, he instantly recognized what a valuable resource these well-connected interventionists could be.

IN A TOUCH OF irony that Lothian couldn't resist pointing out, his first meeting with a Century Group member, arranged by Aubrey Morgan, took place on July 4. The group's emissary was the Reverend Henry Van Dusen, a prominent Protestant theologian who taught at New York's Union Theological Seminary. After explaining to the ambassador how the Century Group came into being, Van Dusen asked what he and his friends could do to help the British. The answer was simple, Lothian replied—put pressure on the administration to send the World War I–era destroyers requested by Churchill. To help in that effort, he promised to supply the group with the latest confidential data on Britain's defenses.

Not long afterward, he acquired a top-secret memo from Churchill stating that of the 176 destroyers with which Britain entered the war, only 68 were still fit for service in home waters—a point that underscored the gravity of Britain's danger. Lothian leaked the memo to several members of the Century Group, as well as to other prominent interventionists. He asked that in their use of the material, they not provide the exact number of available ships, to lessen the chances of Britain's foes discovering the source of the leak and also to reduce the strategic advantage that such information would give the Germans.

At about the same time, John Foster, the British embassy's legal adviser, leaked to Joseph Alsop the cables sent by Churchill to Roosevelt appealing for aid, as well as the president's discouraging responses. As the British intended, Alsop passed the information on to the rest of the Century Group, and, in his words, "the public agitation for transfer of the destroyers began." Stories, columns, and broadcasts pushing the importance of the destroyers for the survival of Britain—and thus America—began popping up in the American media, particularly in those outlets employing members of the Century Group. Alarmed at the sudden explosion of pro-British sentiment, the German chargé d'affaires in Washington complained to Berlin that American "public opinion is being systematically whipped into a state of panic."

Century Group members also decided to put direct pressure on key political and military figures in Washington, many of whom were their friends and acquaintances. In late July and early August, they fanned out across the capital, calling on the president, members of his cabinet, senators and congressmen, the top military brass, and other major players in the fight.

Joe Alsop paid a visit to Admiral Harold Stark, the chief of naval operations, who in the spring had testified before a congressional committee that America's old destroyers were too valuable to stay in drydock and should be refitted to help defend America's coastlines. Shortly after Stark's testimony, Congress approved a measure outlawing any transfer of surplus vessels unless the Navy chief expressly stated they were not needed for the defense of the United States.

Stark found himself in a difficult situation. Unlike many in his service, he was sympathetic to the plight of Britain, having spent time there as a young officer during World War I. He had also studied the cables from Captain Alan Kirk, the Anglophile U.S. naval attaché in London, who reported that "the situation in [British] home waters is growing desperate" and that, according to the Admiralty, "successful survival this year depends on the U.S. decision to release destroyers and aircraft." Yet Stark was on record as telling Congress his own navy needed the old destroyers. How could he now reverse himself and say they should be handed over to the British?

Aware of the admiral's dilemma, Alsop told him that the Century Group wanted to promote the destroyer transfer but would do so only with assurances of Navy approval. When Stark said he was unable to provide such a pledge, Alsop asked whether he would sanction the deal if problems over the congressional ban could be resolved. Yes, said Stark; in that case, he would be free to declare the transfer in the national interest.

Although Alsop had told Stark he was talking to him not as a journalist but as a member of the Century Group, he alluded to his interview with the admiral in a column he wrote several weeks later, declaring that U.S. destroyers were vital for holding the English Channel against Germany. "The highest naval officers join the President and virtually every other man in the government to whom the facts are known, in firmly believing that the needed destroyers ought to be made promptly available," Alsop claimed.

While obviously referring to Stark, the columnist was also misinterpreting his views—a fact that an angry Stark made clear when contacted by other journalists about his remarks. "A recheck" with the Navy chief "brought confirmation that his opposition still stands," the *New York Times* columnist Arthur Krock wrote.

Apart from the issue of misinterpretation, Alsop's actions raised other serious questions of journalistic integrity. He had concealed from his readers the fact that he was a member of a pressure group working for the destroyer transfer and had led Stark to believe the opposite—that he was acting as a political partisan and not as a journalist. "As an opinionated citizen, perhaps Joe could take satisfaction in what he had done; as newsman, he had brought discredit on himself," observed Robert Merry, Alsop's biographer.

While Alsop tried to tamp down the uproar caused by his column, Herbert Agar and two other Century Group members went to the White House to lobby FDR, who had won his party's presidential nomination just two weeks before. Like Stark, Roosevelt said his hands were tied by the congressional action on surplus ships. In his view, large-scale aid to Britain, notably the transfer of destroyers, would be possible only if Congress, with a minimum of opposition, passed special legislation approving such actions. And that, he indicated, was not going to happen—at least not in the immediate future.

Agar persisted. There must be *something* the Century Group could do, he said, to help the president in his effort to aid Britain. FDR thought for a moment, then nodded. It was a long shot, he made clear, but if the group's members could set certain events in motion, he might be able to do what they wanted.

First, Agar and the others must persuade General John Pershing, leader of the American Expeditionary Force in World War I and the country's most revered military figure, to give a national radio broadcast in favor of the destroyer deal. The president warned them, however, that if word leaked of their approach to Pershing "and you say the idea came from me, I shall call you a liar."

Although the Century Group representatives were disappointed by what they viewed as Roosevelt's lack of enthusiasm for the destroyer transfer, they set out to do what he asked. Agar was chosen as the emissary to the seventy-nine-year-old Pershing, then living in a suite at Walter Reed Hospital. The ailing general told Agar that he had wanted to speak out on the issue for months and had been waiting in vain for Roosevelt to call. Pershing shared Agar's belief that America should be a participant in the war rather than "equip other people to fight our battles." Nonetheless, he agreed to address the nation on the importance of the destroyer transfer, seeing it as "a necessary first step." He asked Agar to collaborate with Walter Lippmann in preparing a draft of the speech. While not a member of the Century Group, Lippmann was a close friend of both Pershing's and Lord Lothian's and had been a leading journalistic proponent of the idea that U.S. security ultimately depended on the British fleet.

In his August 1 broadcast, Pershing delivered an extremely blunt message to his listeners. "I am telling you tonight before it is too late," he said, "that the British Navy needs destroyers to convoy merchant ships, hunt submarines and repel invasion. We have an immense reserve of destroyers left over from the other war. . . . If there is anything we can do to save the British fleet, we shall be failing in our duty to America if we do not do it."

Pershing had avoided political controversy all his career and certainly had no partisan ax to grind in advocating the destroyer deal. When he said the British should have the destroyers, much of the public accepted his dictum as gospel. The general's broadcast, Agar later recalled, "was the turning point in our effort to create a public opinion favorable to the president's taking action."

Pershing's appeal was immediately seconded by several high-ranking retired naval officers, including Admiral William Standley, a former chief of naval operations and a Century Group member. A number of cabinet members, after being approached by Century Group representatives, also lobbied for the transfer. Among them was Harold Ickes, who wrote in his diary that he "spent a lot of time arguing with the President that, by hook or by crook, we ought to accede to England's request. . . . It seems to me so very foolish not to make it possible for England to put up the stiffest fight it can."

But the growing popular demand for the deal was outweighed, in Roosevelt's mind, by increasingly virulent opposition by isolationists. The *Chicago Tribune* declared that sending the destroyers to Britain would be an act of war. A reporter for the *St. Louis Post-Dispatch,* another isolationist newspaper, threatened Walter Lippmann with an investigation of the columnist's participation in what the reporter called "a plot to get America into the war." A shaken Lippmann persuaded the paper's publisher, Joseph Pulitzer, to squelch the proposed exposé.

The president was caught in the middle, pressured by public opinion to sanction the deal but aware that congressional isolationists would do their best to defeat any bill authorizing the transfer. Failing that, they could delay its passage for weeks. What he needed was a legally valid excuse to bypass Congress altogether.

Once again, the Century Group stepped in to help. On August 11, *The New York Times* published what was later called "one of the most important letters to the editor ever written." Signed by four of the most distinguished lawyers in the country, it was written by Dean Acheson, a former assistant secretary of the Treasury under Roosevelt and a Century Group member. The letter argued that congressional approval was not needed to transfer the destroyers, that the president already had the authority under the Constitution and existing legislation to do so by executive order.

There was a certain irony in Acheson's authorship of an opinion that said FDR could skirt procedure seen by many legal experts as necessary. Six years before, he had quit as assistant Treasury secretary after a violent argument with the president over a similar question. When Roosevelt had wanted to take steps to devalue the dollar in 1933, Acheson told him the law forbade him to do so. Roosevelt told Acheson that *his* job was to find a way to circumvent such laws, adding, "Don't you take my word for it that it will be all right?" Losing his temper, Acheson retorted that he was being asked to sign illegal documents. "That will do!" Roosevelt shouted. Not long afterward, Acheson resigned.

Many years later, Acheson noted that while he respected Roosevelt, he did not like him. He particularly disliked what he thought of as the patronizing informality with which the president treated his subordinates, himself included. "He condescended," Acheson wrote of FDR. "It is not gratifying to receive the easy greeting which milord might give a promising stable boy and pull one's forelock in return." Such casual treatment was especially maddening to a man who had more than a touch of patrician arrogance himself. The son of an Episcopal bishop, Acheson was a product of Groton, Yale, and Harvard Law School, where he led his class and was a protégé of one of the school's most eminent professors, Felix Frankfurter. The poet Archibald MacLeish, who was a Yale classmate of Acheson's, later described him as "gay, graceful, gallant," but also "socially snobby, with qualities of . . . arrogance and superciliousness."

Acheson's personal feelings about Roosevelt, however, were outweighed by his ardent interventionism. An early advocate of all-out U.S. support for Britain, he had declared in a 1939 speech: "To shrink from this decision, to be satisfied with anything short of it, is to risk . . . the death of everything which life in America holds for us."

In late July 1940, Roosevelt aide Benjamin Cohen asked Acheson, a partner at the Washington law firm of Covington and Burling, to work with him on a memo providing legal justification for the president to bypass Congress and send the destroyers to Britain by executive order. After considerable research, Acheson and Cohen concluded that under international law and current U.S. statutes, only the transfer of vessels built specifically for currently warring countries was prohibited. Since the old destroyers in question had not been constructed for such a purpose, it was therefore lawful to hand them over to Britain. The two men further agreed that such action was in America's national interest, as argued by General Pershing, who said that "the transfer . . . may be a vital factor in keeping war from our shores." If that were so, then the chief of naval operations could legitimately approve the transfer as essential for U.S. defense, and there would be no need to go to Congress for new legislation.

After refining his and Cohen's memo and putting it in the form of a letter, Acheson enlisted two prominent New York attorneys—Charles C. Burlingham and Thomas Thacher—to sign it, along with George Rublee, one of Acheson's Covington and Burling partners. Although not members of the Century Group, all three belonged to the Century Association. So did Charles Merz, the *New York Times* editorial page editor and a Yale classmate of Acheson's, who agreed to run the letter in full.

The lawyers' opinion, which took up three and a half columns in the *Times,* attracted tremendous attention, most of it favorable. It was, wrote Herbert Agar, "a fresh thought that changed everything." The president saw the opinion as the breakthrough he'd been seeking, and he quickly accepted and appropriated its contents. Admiral Stark did the same.

To make the deal even more palatable to the public, it was decided to link the destroyer transfer to American acquisition of military bases on British-held territory in the Caribbean and western Atlantic. Such a quid pro quo would mean an obvious increase in U.S. security, greatly strengthening the defenses of the Panama Canal and East Coast and helping to prevent Germany from establishing a bridgehead in Latin America. The idea had been floating around for years, even before Hitler's blitzkrieg in Western Europe. The U.S. military was in favor of it, as were many leading U.S. newspapers, notably the *Chicago Tribune,* which long had called for leasing such bases in return for cancellation of Britain's World War I debts to America.

The Century Group pressed the president to pursue such an exchange, as did several cabinet members. Agreeing, Roosevelt asked Lord Lothian in early August to take the matter up with his government. As it happened, Lothian had already done so. For months, he had been as assiduous in lobbying Churchill to allow the American acquisition of bases as he had been in pushing Roosevelt for the destroyers. The ambassador had repeatedly told the British government that such an offer would go far to encourage U.S. reciprocity in aid. Until August, Churchill and his cabinet rejected the idea, declaring they saw no reason for making such a handsome gesture when America had not yet provided any substantial aid for Britain. But with the country's situation growing increasingly desperate, the prime minister finally instructed his ambassador to "go full steam ahead" with the destroyers-bases swap.

The deal was clearly far more advantageous for the United States than for Britain, and Churchill, who feared being criticized at home for making a bad bargain, wanted the transaction to be seen as an exchange of gifts. Roosevelt, however, was adamant that it be presented to the American public as "a Yankee horse trade," a hardheaded business arrangement in which his country got the best of the deal. "There was an election coming," Herbert Agar sardonically observed, "and Roosevelt did not dare appear as merely generous and farsighted. . . . Hence, in all the discussions, the lectures, the letters to the press, there were discussions of . . . the wonderful benefits America was to receive for making a tiny gesture toward saving the world."*

To enlist public support for the deal, the Century Group joined William Allen White's committee and its six hundred local chapters in mounting a massive publicity campaign across the country. Although the two organizations differed radically in their approach to interventionism, they presented a united front throughout the late summer and early fall of 1940. "The committee was organized nationwide, while we were not as yet," Agar wrote. "The committee was respectable . . . whereas we were suspect because we always used the dread word 'war.' Thus the respectable and the outrageous joined hands on a program of broadcasting and newsletters and advertisements to tell the public that the destroyer deal would safeguard our shores."

Major U.S. newspapers carried full-page ads sponsored by the White Committee and bearing the headline BETWEEN US AND HITLER STANDS THE BRITISH FLEET! The ads urged readers to "write or telegraph your President—your Senators—your Congressmen—that you want the United States to sell over-age destroyers and give other material aid to Britain." Prominent backers of the destroyer deal, including Robert Sherwood and Elizabeth Morrow, spoke at rallies and signed public statements of support. Petitions were circulated, garnering millions of signatures.

Both pro-aid groups called on their journalist members and other media colleagues to write supportive editorials, columns, and radio commentaries. In one of his many columns on the subject, Joseph

---

* In the end, the two leaders compromised by dividing the bases into two groups. To appease Churchill, a few of the bases were given to the United States as a gift, while most of them were traded for the destroyers, which was what FDR wanted.

Alsop denounced Roosevelt for not acting faster on the destroyer transfer. When the president's press secretary, Steve Early, called him to "congratulate me on a useful and sensible contribution," Alsop was startled. But he soon realized that FDR didn't really mind public pressure, as long as it was meant to prod him into taking an action he already wanted to take. In fact, as Early's phone call revealed, the president actively encouraged such prodding.

Thanks in large part to the immense publicity effort, the American people's reaction to the proposed deal was overwhelmingly positive; polls taken throughout August consistently revealed approval ratings of more than 60 percent. But there was one more piece of the puzzle that had to be put in place before Roosevelt felt confident enough to sign off on the transaction. He told White and members of the Century Group that he needed the promise of Wendell Willkie, the Republican presidential nominee, not to make the destroyer deal a campaign issue. Knowing how formidable a candidate Willkie was likely to be, FDR was reluctant to give him and his party any more fuel to use against the Democrats.

It was an astonishing thing to ask of an opponent—to turn his back on a controversial issue that almost certainly would help him politically. The concept was almost as implausible as the idea, first bandied about the year before, that Wendell Willkie might actually capture the Republican nomination.

CHAPTER 12

"THE PEOPLE SAVED THE DAY"

In May 1940, just weeks before Wendell Willkie was anointed by the Republicans, polls showed him with the support of less than 3 percent of his party's membership. "I would crawl on my hands and knees from here to Washington if, by that act, I could bring about your nomination," a prominent midwestern newspaper publisher wrote him. Unfortunately, the publisher added, the GOP would never bestow its candidacy on a man who was everything party regulars despised: a registered Democrat virtually all his adult life and an outspoken advocate of U.S. aid to Britain and France.

Yet it was precisely Willkie's interventionism that made possible the stunning political coup staged by his supporters at the 1940 Republican convention in Philadelphia. "It wasn't the packing of the galleries or the flood of telegrams that nominated Willkie," one of his key advisers later said. "Adolf Hitler nominated Willkie. With the fall of France and the Low Countries, American public opinion shifted overnight—and that was responsible for Willkie's nomination." As *Life* saw it, "The people saved the day. They proved that when they are really aroused, they can push through the bicker and dicker of party politics and make their representatives pick the man they want."

For months, the Republican front-runners for the nomination—New York City district attorney Thomas Dewey and Senator Robert Taft—had contended that the war in Europe was of no concern to the United States. Willkie, by contrast, had been insistently warning his

Wendell Willkie.

countrymen about the dangers that a German-controlled Europe posed for America. He may have been a political amateur, but his passionate conviction appealed to a growing number of Americans, particularly those in his party who leaned toward liberalism and internationalism.

Before his meteoric rise in politics, Willkie had been president of one of the biggest power utilities in the country. But nothing in his appearance or manner suggested his close ties to big business. Tall, rumpled, and burly, he radiated warmth, magnetism, and an appealing homespun charm. He was, said novelist Booth Tarkington, a "man wholly natural in manner, with no pose and no condescension." David Halberstam would later describe him as "a Republican who did not look like a Republican—the rarest of things in those days, a Republican with sex appeal."

A native of Indiana, the forty-eight-year-old Willkie still spoke with a Hoosier twang. He retained other traces of his rural Midwest upbringing: having grown up in a community where people never locked their front doors, he did the same at his Fifth Avenue apartment in New York—a source of constant astonishment to his wealthy, more security-conscious neighbors. Underneath Willkie's unpretentiousness, however, was a tough, canny operator, who in 1933, at the age of forty-one, had become president of Commonwealth and Southern, a utility giant that held a monopoly on electric power generation in much of the South.

Within a few months of joining the company, Willkie clashed with the nascent Roosevelt administration over its proposal to establish the Tennessee Valley Authority, a bold federal program to provide electric power, flood control, soil conservation, and other benefits for the country's southeast region. Once completed, TVA would replace Commonwealth and Southern as the regional power monopoly— a prospect Willkie fought with vigor and tenacity.

Adept at public relations, he was masterful in portraying his company, an industry behemoth, as a powerless David "locked in combat with the Goliath of an oppressive government." To the bafflement of New Deal officials, Willkie's campaign to depict Commonwealth and Southern—and himself—as helpless victims of relentless government persecution struck a chord with the press and much of the public. Whenever he testified before congressional committees, one New Dealer drily recalled, the press tables were packed, with "eight or ten photographers snapping the great man." In his testimony, Willkie always positioned himself as "a plain American attacked by the 'interests'—a little, average, everyday man who stood up for his rights."

In the end, he lost his crusade. After protracted negotiations with the TVA, in which some administration officials thought he got the better of the deal, he turned over Commonwealth and Southern's facilities to the government for $78.6 million. Willkie himself emerged from the struggle as a winner. He had become a respected national figure, a voice for moderate, middle-class Americans, notably businessmen, who felt that the federal government had grown too big, too powerful, and too disdainful of private enterprise.

Yet he was also critical of big business's shortcomings and abuses, including those of his own industry. A registered Democrat until the fall of 1939, Willkie supported a number of the New Deal's reforms, including the minimum wage, a limit on workers' hours, Social Security, and collective bargaining—all of which were anathema to Republican conservatives. A strong champion of civil rights and liberties, he was noted for having led a successful fight, as a young lawyer practicing in Ohio, to break the influence of the Ku Klux Klan in local affairs.

WHILE WILLKIE CAME FROM America's heartland and had great appeal for those living there, his own attachment was to New York City and the urbane, sophisticated lifestyle he'd adopted. He was a frequent theatergoer and a member of several of the city's most exclusive clubs, including the Century. "I wouldn't live anywhere else!" he once exclaimed to a friend. "It is the most exciting, stimulating, satisfying spot in the world. I can't get enough of it."

Part of New York's allure had to do with his intimate relationship with a soft-spoken southerner named Irita Van Doren, with whom he fell in love and who, more than anyone else, was responsible for his becoming a major political force. The petite, curly-haired Van Doren was the book editor of the *New York Herald Tribune* and the former wife of the historian and critic Carl Van Doren. One of the country's most influential literary figures, she had transformed the *Herald Tribune*'s book pages into a worthy rival of *The New York Times*'s esteemed book section. She also was doyenne of an eclectic literary salon that included some of the most noted writers of the period, from Carl Sandburg and Sinclair Lewis to Rebecca West and André Maurois.

Shortly after they met, Van Doren and the married Willkie began an affair. She introduced him to her author friends and became his literary and intellectual mentor, singling out books and articles she thought he should read and helping him with his speeches and other writing. Under her tutelage, he began contributing articles and book reviews to such disparate publications as *The Atlantic Monthly*, *The New Republic*, *Life*, *The Saturday Evening Post*, *Forbes*, and *The New York Times*.

With Van Doren's encouragement, Willkie began thinking more and more about a political career. According to the journalist Joseph Barnes, a friend of the couple's, she was largely responsible for his "acceptance of himself as a potential leader with original and important ideas." That view of Willkie was also increasingly held by a number of other people in the high-level business and intellectual circles in which he and Van Doren moved. For the most part, these were moderate and liberal Republicans who had traveled frequently to Europe and had close financial and personal ties there. Some worked in Wall Street law firms and financial institutions, others in major media organizations.

Among those attracted to Willkie and his political potential were the *Herald Tribune*'s publisher, Ogden Reid, and his wife, Helen, who became two of his earliest supporters. Because of her husband's serious alcoholism, Helen Reid had emerged as the *Herald Tribune*'s driving force, playing an important role in its shift from rock-hard conservatism to a more progressive viewpoint. A stalwart feminist, Reid had promoted the career of Van Doren, who was a close friend and confidante.

On March 3, 1939, the *Herald Tribune* published a letter to the editor urging the nomination of Wendell Willkie for president in 1940. Its writer was G. Vernor Rogers, the former general manager of one of the paper's predecessors, the *New York Tribune*. He was also Helen Reid's brother. Rogers's letter was one of the first indications that some elements of the East Coast press might be looking for an alternative to the Republican candidates already in the presidential race.

The front-runner at that time—and until the convention—was Thomas Dewey, who had won national fame for his crackdown on organized crime and his relentless prosecution of some of the country's most notorious lawbreakers. By 1939, Dewey already had the makings of an impressive campaign staff—speechwriters, publicists, and two pollsters borrowed from George Gallup's organization. What he didn't have yet was his own opinions. Before he announced his positions on issues, his pollsters would take surveys to determine how popular such stands would be. If they got a negative response, changes were made. Not surprisingly, Dewey tilted toward isolationism.

His closest competitor was Senator Robert Taft of Ohio, the son of former president William Howard Taft. A former corporation lawyer, Taft was deeply conservative. After Hitler's blitzkrieg in May 1940, he remarked: "There is a good deal more danger of the infiltration of totalitarian ideas from the New Deal circles in Washington than there ever will be from the activities of the . . . Nazis." Taft was generally regarded as cold, aloof, and backward-looking. According to one English observer, he seemed to believe that "American life was at its best about 1910."

VERNOR ROGERS'S LETTER TOUTING Willkie was followed by a number of speculative pieces in other newspapers and magazines about the

Indianan's possible candidacy. But few people took the idea seriously: Willkie had almost no support or recognition and was not even a blip in the polls. Then, in the summer of 1939, he met Russell Davenport, the forty-year-old managing editor of *Fortune* magazine, and the tectonic plates of the political landscape began to shift.

The embodiment of WASPdom, Davenport, who resembled the actor Gregory Peck, was from the Main Line of Philadelphia and had gone to Yale, which had been founded by an ancestor of his. A would-be novelist and poet, he had lived in the mid-1920s in Paris, where he rubbed shoulders with Ernest Hemingway, Gertrude Stein, Janet Flanner, and other American literary expatriates. But he was unable to make a living as a writer and soon returned to America to join Henry Luce's expanding publishing empire. In 1929, he helped start *Fortune,* and eight years later, he became its managing editor.

Davenport and Willkie were kindred spirits, not only in their political outlook but in their attitude toward life. After their first encounter, Davenport came home and announced to his wife, Marcia, "I've met the man who ought to be the next President of the United States." Henry Luce later described the Willkie-Davenport meeting as a "chemical reaction [that] produced political history."

From the beginning, Davenport was the central figure in Willkie's improbable campaign, serving as his chief strategist, speechwriter, and confidant. Marcia Davenport, a novelist and former *New Yorker* writer, got involved, too. Through the fall of 1939 and winter of 1940, the Davenports hosted weekly dinners at their Manhattan apartment to introduce Willkie to a wide spectrum of prominent New Yorkers and other East Coast residents who might help him in his candidacy.

But they were fast running out of time. The Republican convention was only a few months away, and Willkie still had not established himself with the American people as a viable presidential contender. In April 1940, Davenport sought to remedy that by running two articles in *Fortune* aimed at sparking public interest in his friend. The first— a piece written by Willkie (with editorial help from Davenport and Irita Van Doren)—attacked Roosevelt for trying to grab too much power but also flayed congressional isolationists for blocking the sale of weapons to the Allies. "We are opposed to war," he wrote. "But we do not intend to relinquish our right to sell whatever we want to those defending themselves from aggression."

Accompanying Willkie's piece was a two-page editorial written by Davenport that praised Willkie's domestic and foreign policy views and implied that Americans should bypass the Republican party bosses and work to make him the presidential nominee. "The principles he stands for are American principles," the editorial declared. "Whether they will prevail in terms of his political candidacy is a question that depends upon the political sophistication of the American people."

The *Fortune* articles opened the floodgates for Willkie. Oren Root Jr., a young Princeton graduate working as an associate at a prominent Wall Street law firm, was so inspired by them that he and a friend immediately printed more than eight hundred Willkie-for-President petitions and mailed them to recent alumni of Princeton, Harvard, and Yale. At the same time, the *Herald Tribune* ran an ad in its public notices column calling on readers to "help Oren Root Jr. organize the people's demand for Willkie" and urging volunteers to get in touch with the twenty-eight-year-old Root at his law firm.

Within days, the firm's switchboard was so flooded with calls that its partners were unable to get an outside phone line. At the same time, large mail sacks bulging with petitions, letters, and contributions began to pile up in Root's office and the firm's lobby. After his exasperated superiors made it clear that this situation couldn't continue, Root took a leave of absence to devote full time to his quixotic one-man Willkie campaign. Within three weeks, he had gathered more than two hundred thousand signatures and had begun organizing Willkie-for-President clubs throughout the country. By the time of the convention, there were 750 such clubs, some fifty thousand volunteers, and more than three million signatures supporting Willkie's candidacy.

Root had done all this without Willkie's knowledge or support. In fact, he had never met him or Davenport. In a letter apologizing for not asking permission, Root told Willkie: "I have no illusions about your being nominated in Philadelphia. . . . [But] I am naïve enough to believe that even the Republican politicians may see the light if enough work of the right kind is done at once. I propose to contribute to that work with all the vigor and imagination at my command."

While Root reached out to Americans across the country, Davenport worked to enlist the support of influential columnists and editors in the East. To Raymond Clapper, who a few years before had been named America's "most significant, fair, and reliable" political columnist by his fellow Washington correspondents, Davenport wrote: "The one man in America with the ability and intellectual and oratorical power to rally progressive Republican forces is Wendell Willkie. You will, however . . . point out that Mr. Willkie is not a political reality. Check. But why in the hell don't we make him one?" The liberal Clapper, who once described himself as a "75 percent New Dealer," responded with several pro-Willkie columns.

Davenport's most prized conquest, however, was his boss, Henry Luce, who had met Willkie at one of the Davenports' dinners and was smitten by his charisma and interventionist views. The publisher was soon deeply committed to Willkie's candidacy, as were his two most influential magazines, *Time* and *Life*. In fact, both publications had been running favorable stories about Willkie for months. But after Luce pointedly made his own support clear, they moved from analysis with at least a hint of balance to all-out advocacy, showering lavish praise on Willkie while consistently debunking his opponents.

At about the same time, Willkie captured the backing of another publishing company, owned and run by two Harvard-educated brothers from the Midwest, John and Gardner Cowles. While smaller and less far-reaching than Luce's empire, the Cowles organization, based in Minneapolis, would also prove vitally important to Willkie. Among its properties were two influential newspapers—the *Minneapolis Star-Journal* and the *Des Moines Register*—and *Look*, a popular photojournalism magazine that was a serious competitor to *Life*.

But even more valuable than their publications' support was the political entrée that the Cowles brothers gave Willkie in the Midwest. They accompanied him in a small private plane all over the region, introducing him to local GOP leaders and arranging speeches before large crowds of Republican faithful. An "old-fashioned, hell-raising" speaker, as Marcia Davenport described him, Willkie wowed his audiences wherever he went. In St. Louis, he declared: "The curse of democracy today, in America as in Europe, is that everybody has been trying to please the public. Almost nobody ever gets up and says what he thinks." At each stop, he proceeded to do just that, demanding that the Roosevelt administration send more aid to France and Britain and saying he "trembled for the safety of the country" at the thought that one of his isolationist opponents might become president.

Until then, Americans had viewed Willkie through the filter of press stories and radio commentaries. Now, however, they were being given a chance to base their opinions on personal contact with him—and many liked what they saw. While old-line party regulars might reject his independence, ebullience, and fierce interventionism, a substantial number of moderate Republicans—small businessmen and entrepreneurs, teachers, lawyers, and other professionals—found those qualities appealing. "For Republicans like my father, whose affection for Teddy Roosevelt had never dimmed and whose loyalty to the party had been sorely tested by Harding and Coolidge, Wendell Willkie appeared as a gleaming banner of hope," the historian Richard Ketchum wrote. "On one hand, he represented business. . . . On the other, he was forward-looking on international issues."

In a poll taken in March 1940, Willkie had been the first choice of less than 1 percent of Republican voters. By the end of May, he had climbed to 17 percent, and in early June, he stood at 29 percent. During the week of the Republican convention, his face peered out from the covers of *Time, Life, The Saturday Evening Post,* and *Look,* all of which gave him ringing endorsements. "Republicans can nominate somebody who looks good in ephemeral straw votes, or some plodding politician," Raymond Clapper wrote in *Life.* "Or they can take a bold and audacious course, look at the job to be done, and select, regardless of tradition, the man best qualified to do it. They can leap over the 'keep off the grass' signs and nominate Wendell Willkie."

Still, few, including Clapper, believed that would happen. Rep. Joseph Martin, the House minority leader and chairman of the convention, arrived in Philadelphia with the conviction, as he later recalled, that "Willkie, despite his barrage of publicity, was not a serious contender."

WHEN THE CONVENTION BEGAN on Monday, June 24, no one was quite sure what to expect. France had capitulated to Germany the week before, and the specter of war hung over the convention as heavily as the crushing June heat. In one editorial cartoon, Hitler was shown standing in the middle of Philadelphia's Convention Hall, with the caption THE UNINVITED GUEST.

On the eve of the GOP gathering, Willkie had called for immediate U.S. aid for Britain, adding that he was "in accord with the national administration" on the issue—a clear thumb in the eye to Republican isolationists. Enraged by his remarks, some fifty Republican members of Congress signed a letter urging the convention to choose a "leader with a past record consistently supporting Republican policies . . . and whose recognized position and recent pronouncements are a guarantee to the American people that he will not lead the nation into a foreign war." They were reassured by the fact that most delegates were already committed to Taft or Dewey, who claimed he was within one hundred votes of clinching the nomination.

Willkie volunteers were frantically working to prevent that from happening. Among his most tireless campaign helpers in Philadelphia were the *Herald Tribune*'s Helen Reid, Dorothy Thompson, and Irita Van Doren, who, for fear of causing a political scandal, was keeping her distance from Willkie, at least in public. Dorothy Thompson was as vehement in her support of Willkie as she had been in her criticism of Charles Lindbergh. At dinner with Reid one night in Philadelphia, she pounded the table so hard that the dishes and glasses shook. "If the politicians won't nominate Wendell, believe me, Helen, we can elect him ourselves!" she exclaimed. "I'll go into the street and get the people to elect him!"

Yet despite the isolationists' "Stop Willkie" movement, the tousle-haired maverick continued to make impressive gains. In the middle of the convention, George Gallup announced a delay in the release of his latest poll, saying the results were not yet ready but acknowledging that "the Willkie trend has been sharply upward." Indeed it was. When the results were published shortly after the convention ended, they showed that Willkie had shot past Dewey, 44 to 29 percent. Gallup was widely regarded as a Dewey supporter, and some in Willkie's camp believed he had held up the poll results deliberately to help the New York district attorney.

Although Dewey and Taft had cornered the support of most GOP insiders, Willkie had collected a few party allies of his own, notably Samuel Pryor, the head of the party in Connecticut. As the official in charge of logistics for the convention, Pryor presided over the distribution of credentials for access to the hall, including tickets for spectators in the galleries. Unbeknownst to the Dewey and Taft camps, he had reduced the number of gallery tickets available for their supporters while greatly increasing those for Willkie backers. Among them were hundreds of members of Oren Root's Willkie clubs, who had poured into Philadelphia from all over the country.

On the night of June 26, Willkie's name was put into nomination by Charles Halleck, a young congressman from Indiana. When Dewey and Taft delegates disrupted Halleck's speech with boos, hisses, and catcalls, they were drowned out by a cacophony of cheers and applause from the galleries, accompanied by a chant of "We want Willkie!" As Halleck finished his address, the chant swelled in volume. Thousands of people in the galleries were on their feet, whooping, stamping, clapping, and shouting over and over at the top of their voices, "We want Willkie!" With the noise growing ever more deafening, the relatively few delegates pledged to Willkie grabbed state standards on the floor and marched around, holding them high, as Dewey and Taft delegates tried to snatch them back. Fistfights and other scuffles broke out in a number of delegations, several of which had to be broken up by police.

It was, political writers later said, the most rousing, raucous convention demonstration since the days of Teddy Roosevelt. It was also a dramatic display of the cultural and political chasm that divided not only the Republican Party but the entire country. As the writer Charles Peters has noted, "most of the people on the floor . . . represented conservative, isolationist, small-town America. Most of the people in the gallery were on the other side."

The following morning, the *New York Herald Tribune* carried a front-page editorial, the first in its history, urging the convention to nominate Willkie. In Philadelphia, tension and excitement mounted throughout the day as edgy delegates prepared to cast their ballots that evening. They were discomfited not only by the deafening Willkie demonstration the night before but by the blizzard of telegrams, letters, and postcards they had received throughout the week, demanding they choose Willkie. Later estimates put the number of such pro-Willkie missives at more than a million.

The 1940 Republican convention was the most suspenseful party gathering in years, and millions of Americans sat by their radios the night of June 27 to learn the outcome. The moment the balloting started, Willkie supporters in the galleries resumed their chanting. During the roll call, the heads of state delegations struggled to be heard above the din as Western Union messengers roamed the floor delivering last-minute telegrams. After the first ballot, Dewey led by 360 votes, followed by Taft with 189 and Willkie with 105.

After the second vote began, Rep. Joseph Martin tried to quell the furor by reminding those in the galleries they were there as guests of the convention. "Guests, hell, we *are* the convention," someone yelled back. Martin couldn't help but agree. "We professionals could not misread the lesson before us," he later wrote. "Willkie was becoming more inflammable by the moment."

As one ballot followed another in the sweltering hall, Willkie slowly but steadily gained support. "The suspense was so acute that I can feel it to this day," Marcia Davenport recalled. She remembered, too, "the bitterness of the Old Guard, the adamant resistance to [Willkie], the hatred of him and all of us who had worked for this moment. I looked at Russell, pale and sweating, with his green eyes glittering in the hot glare. He was watching the floor where delegations were roaring and cursing at one another," sometimes "almost at blows."

Finally, at 1:15 A.M., after more than eight hours of voting, Wendell Willkie was nominated as the Republican candidate for president of the United States. Sheer pandemonium reigned as Willkie supporters screamed, cried, cheered, hugged one another, and continued to chant "We want Willkie!" Later, journalists and others would dub the events of that night "the miracle of Philadelphia." H. L. Mencken was one of them. "I am thoroughly convinced that the nomination of Willkie was managed by the Holy Ghost in person," Mencken, who was present at the balloting, wrote to a friend. "At the moment the sixth ballot was being counted, I saw an angel in the gallery. It wore a Palm Beach suit and was smoking a five-cent cigar, but nevertheless it was palpably an angel."

In the weeks and months to come, Democratic party operatives would join Republican regulars in charging that Willkie's nomination had been engineered by East Coast businessmen, Wall Street bankers, and publishers, who allegedly packed the convention galleries and helped generate most of the telegrams and letters that rained down on the delegates.

Marcia Davenport and others close to the Republican candidate denied the allegations, declaring that while the Eastern media did indeed help to ignite the pro-Willkie wildfire, the enthusiasm of ordinary Americans was responsible for its spreading throughout the country. According to Editorial Research Reports, an independent organization that investigated the pro-Willkie telegrams, most of them were indeed dispatched by average voters. "I knew the Willkie people in my hometown," observed Charles Peters, a West Virginia–born writer and editor who wrote a book about Willkie's nomination. "They were independent souls who did not march to any drummer but their own. What had started among a small coterie of the elite had become a genuine people's movement."

Agreeing, *The New Yorker*'s Janet Flanner added a slightly different slant. "To millions of Americans sitting up after midnight over their radios, Willkie's sudden, distant nomination . . . brought more than the febrile thrill that goes with a winning dark horse," she wrote. "Because of the recent silencing of most European democracies, in the choice of Willkie that night there was, even to many cynical or Democratic ears, an exciting, stirring sound." It was, Flanner noted, the voice of the people.

When Willkie spoke to the delegates the night after his nomination, he declared that where the war was concerned, "we here are not Republicans alone, but Americans." His selection by the Republicans, in the words of Robert Sherwood, "guaranteed to the rest of the world— and particularly to the warring nations—a continuity of American foreign policy regardless of the outcome of the election." An elated Lord Lothian told Churchill and the Foreign Office that they would have a friend in Washington, no matter who won the election.

German officials, meanwhile, viewed the interventionist's victory as a major setback. "From the standpoint of foreign policy, Wendell Willkie's nomination is unfortunate for us," the German Foreign Ministry dourly acknowledged. The German embassy in Washington had spent thousands of dollars to send fifty isolationist Republican congressmen to the convention to work for the adoption of an isolationist platform. In a cable to Berlin, chargé d'affaires Hans Thomsen reported that the congressmen, who were not aware of the source of their travel funds, were to lobby platform committee members and other GOP delegates. At the same time, Thomsen said, full-page ads would run in several American newspapers with the headline STOP THE MARCH TO WAR!

In his message, Thomsen described the Philadelphia scheme as "a well-camouflaged lightning propaganda campaign." In reality, it was a total failure. Despite the congressmen's efforts, the GOP adopted a foreign policy plank that was an uneasy compromise between isolationist and interventionist points of view; it opposed the idea of America's going to war yet was willing to consider the idea of giving aid to "peoples whose liberty is threatened." As H. L. Mencken saw it, the platform was "so written that it will fit both the triumph of democracy and the collapse of democracy, and approve both sending arms to England or sending only flowers."

Yet even if the plank had been outspokenly isolationist, it still would have made little difference. What Thomsen and the Germans didn't seem to understand was that virtually no one in America, outside of Democratic and Republican regulars, paid attention to party platforms; Americans tended to vote for the candidate, not the platform. While German propagandists focused on influencing the content of the platform in Philadelphia, the party's delegates slipped their leash and nominated an outspoken interventionist for president.

For their part, Roosevelt and the Democrats, while relieved that the choice of Willkie had eased the way for providing aid to Britain, were greatly concerned about the Republican's popularity with voters. Acknowledging that Willkie would be the most formidable opponent he'd ever faced, the president told the columnist Walter Winchell: "His sincerity comes through with terrific impact. The people believe every word he says. We are going to have a heck of a fight on our hands with him."

CHAPTER 13

"CONGRESS IS GOING TO RAISE HELL"

===

Even before Wendell Willkie's selection, FDR knew he was in for an extremely tough election battle. According to a recent poll, more than half of those surveyed opposed the idea of the president's breaking the two-term precedent set by George Washington. He still was popular, of course, with millions of voters, particularly those who'd been aided by his economic and social policies. But an increasing number of Americans seemed to be tiring of him and the New Deal, which, although it had alleviated many of the problems of the Depression, had not come up with solutions for ending it. "The President's leadership in domestic affairs had accomplished everything that he could accomplish," Attorney General Robert Jackson later remarked. "I do not think there would have been any justification for a third term on the basis of his domestic program."

In the 1938 congressional elections, Republicans had picked up eight governorships, eight seats in the Senate, and more than eighty seats in the House. According to polls in the spring of 1940, the Republicans showed more strength than Democrats in a majority of states. "The shift toward the GOP is now so marked that nothing short of a Rooseveltian miracle . . . can save the election for the Democrats," *Time* concluded in April.

Hitler's invasion of Western Europe provided that miracle. In times of great crisis, Americans have traditionally turned to their president for leadership, and they did so with Roosevelt now. Within a week of the invasion, his popular support had shot up dramatically. It's not clear when he made up his mind to seek a third term—he confided in nobody, not even his wife—but several key aides believed he made his decision just before or at about the time of the fall of France.

For more than a year, Roosevelt had been telling associates that he intended to retire after his second term. He was tired, he said, and his health was not as good as it once was. He remarked to Harold Ickes that he was "slowing down," both physically and mentally. Eleanor Roosevelt confided to her husband's closest aide, Harry Hopkins, that he "has not the same zest for administrative detail that he had and is probably quite frankly bored."

While not ruling out the possibility of running again, he did nothing to discourage other Democrats from seeking the nomination. There was no shortage of prominent party figures who thought of themselves as Roosevelt's logical successor. Among them were Postmaster General James Farley; Vice President John Nance Garner, who had been estranged from the president since the Court-packing fiasco; and Senator Burton Wheeler, who in November 1939 approved the formation of a Wheeler for President committee.

Although he never fully explained his decision to seek reelection, Roosevelt likely concluded that only he had the ability and experience to deal with the European crisis. None of the other Democratic contenders was up to the task, he felt, nor was Wendell Willkie. Of the Republican nominee, Roosevelt later wrote to a friend: "I did not feel that he had much knowledge of the world and that he would have had to learn . . . in the school of hard experience. This would have been a rather dangerous experiment in 1940." Just as troublesome, in FDR's mind, was the fact that a GOP election sweep would result in staunch Republican isolationists taking over key chairmanships in Congress. Senator Hiram Johnson, for example, would become chairman of the Senate Foreign Relations Committee, while the House Foreign Affairs Committee would come under the control of Rep. Hamilton Fish, an ultraconservative who despised Roosevelt as much as the president loathed him.

Yet once Roosevelt's decision was made, he made clear to those around him that he would do nothing overt to capture the nomination.

Harold Ickes urged otherwise, pressing the president to go to the convention and say "frankly and clearly" why he believed it was important to seek a third term. Such a statement, Ickes declared, "would raise this political campaign to such a high plane [that it would be] an inspiration to the whole country."

Roosevelt ignored his advice. Keenly aware of the political touchiness of the third-term issue, he was determined to behave as if he were not actively seeking—and indeed had no interest in—another term. He also wanted a spontaneous demonstration of support from the delegates, "some show of affection, some semblance of genuine gratitude and loyalty from the party he led."

Nonetheless, a number of administration officials continued to believe that there was a grain of truth in Roosevelt's repeatedly stated lack of interest in another term. According to Solicitor General Francis Biddle, FDR was "bored and tired and stale. . . . He was not very much interested in his own nomination. It was as if he did not want to make the choice, and preferred to have someone make it for him. . . . He would not raise a finger."

THE PRESIDENT'S LISTLESSNESS SEEMED to have been transmitted to those participating in the Democratic convention, held in Chicago two weeks after the Republicans picked Willkie. The contrast between the two gatherings could not have been starker. Instead of the adrenaline-filled chaos of Philadelphia, a "dead, cold" feeling prevailed in Chicago, Ickes wrote. The columnist Marquis Childs called the convention "grim" and "grisly."

On the convention's second night, Senator Alben Barkley, the Senate majority leader and convention chairman, read a message from Roosevelt to the thousands of Democrats in the hall. In it, FDR declared that he had no desire to run for a third term and that the delegates were free to vote for any candidate they wished. For a moment, there was stunned silence. Not knowing how to react to the bombshell announcement, the delegates simply stared, first at Barkley and then at each other.

Then suddenly, a cry of "We Want Roosevelt!" reverberated throughout the cavernous space. Unlike the full-throated roar of the pro-Willkie crowds in Philadelphia, the call came from a single stentorian voice, amplified by loudspeakers, that chanted over and over: "We Want Roosevelt!" As a band played "Happy Days Are Here Again," spectators in the galleries poured onto the floor, while the delegates, many still in shock, rose to their feet and joined the demonstration.

The next day, reporters traced the mysterious voice to one Thomas McGarry, Chicago's superintendent of sewers, who, under orders from Mayor Edward J. Kelly, had sat in the basement of the convention hall and repeatedly shouted the "We Want Roosevelt" mantra into a microphone connected to the hall's loudspeakers. Kelly, a key Roosevelt backer, had also orchestrated the demonstration that followed.

"Of course, the delegates were free to vote for whom they wished," Ernest Cuneo, a Democratic Party troubleshooter, would later observe. "They were free to jump in Lake Michigan, too, if they felt like it, and for all the effect they had on the nomination, they might just as well have." In Richard Ketchum's view, "the affair had the unsavory odor of an assembly rigged by and for Roosevelt." Such suspicions were reinforced when Kelly and other party bosses made clear to the delegates that they were expected to nominate Roosevelt by acclamation. Farley, however, insisted on a roll call, with Roosevelt getting 946 votes, Farley 72, and Garner 61. Though resentful at being ordered about and angry at what they regarded as the president's deviousness, the delegates were somewhat mollified by the thought that they would at least be free to pick the vice presidential nominee. Several leading members of Congress, including House Speaker William Bankhead and Senator James Byrnes, were openly campaigning for the position, some with the belief that they had Roosevelt's blessing.

Once again, the president unveiled an unwelcome surprise: through Harry Hopkins, his emissary in Chicago, he made it clear that he alone would designate the man for the ticket's second spot. His choice was Agriculture Secretary Henry Wallace, an Iowa native who had revolutionized American farming through his key role in the development of hybrid corn and, even more important, through the revolutionary programs his department had introduced to save farmers from economic ruin. He was popular in the Midwest, a strong point in his favor as far as the president was concerned. But even more important to Roosevelt was the unwavering support of the staunchly liberal Wallace for the president and his domestic and foreign policies. "As Franklin noted the signs of eroding loyalty everywhere around him, it grew on him that Henry Wallace could be counted on to the limit," observed Rexford Tugwell, a leading Roosevelt adviser in the early days of his presidency.

In the eyes of a fair number of Democratic Party regulars, however, Wallace was an extremely poor choice. They saw him as a radical liberal, a poor administrator, an inarticulate campaigner, and a Democratic Johnny-come-lately, having only joined the party in 1936. He was, they believed, "a man more interested in the genetic properties of corn than in the precinct returns from Jersey City." A vegetarian and teetotaler, Wallace was also widely regarded as an eccentric who sought spiritual truth by dabbling in such phenomena as astrology, Native American religions, utopian communes, and Eastern mysticism.

In the late 1920s, Wallace had become close to a Russian-born guru and painter named Nicholas Roerich, who was as skilled in attracting wealthy American patrons as he was in teaching his own version of divine wisdom. In the mid-1930s, with Roosevelt's permission, Wallace sent Roerich on a government-funded expedition to Mongolia and Manchuria to find drought-resistant plants and grasses that might help fight soil erosion in the heat-seared plains of America's heartland. The sixteen-month mission, which cost $75,000 ($1.1 million in today's dollars), produced a total of twenty plants; instead of following his original mandate, Roerich, accompanied by his son and eight Cossack guards, spent much of his time riding around Mongolia and Manchuria and stirring up political trouble. Aghast at what it considered Roerich's mischief-making, the State Department pressured Wallace to end the expedition. He finally did so, cutting off all contact with Roerich and urging the Internal Revenue Service to investigate his finances.

Not surprisingly, this kind of activity did not exactly endear the agriculture secretary to Democratic Party regulars. Midway through the convention, Hopkins warned Roosevelt that Wallace's nomination would face "a hell of a lot of opposition"—a massive understatement, as it turned out. Both the delegates and those who had sought the nomination were outraged. Bankhead, for one, told Ickes he felt he'd been "manhandled." When Hopkins informed Roosevelt that a rebellion was brewing in Chicago, FDR snapped: "Well, damn it to hell, they will go for Wallace or I won't run, and you can jolly well tell them so."

Thanks to the vigorous intervention of Edward Kelly and other big-city party bosses, Wallace managed to eke out a slim victory in the roll call, winning 627 of the 1,100 votes cast. Bankhead had refused to withdraw his name from consideration, and the delegates showed their fury at the president by cheering wildly during the nominating speeches for the Speaker of the House while booing and hissing any mention of Wallace's name. The mood was so ugly and hostile that Hopkins would not allow Wallace to give an acceptance speech for fear of causing a riot. During the raucous balloting, Wallace's face was filled with "agony . . . just utter, blank suffering," recalled Labor Secretary Frances Perkins. "I have never lived through anything worse." Close to tears, Wallace's wife asked Eleanor Roosevelt, "Why are they booing my Henry?"

As the vote dragged on, a group of journalists, including Century Group members Herbert Agar and Joseph Alsop, passed a scathing note to Solicitor General Francis Biddle, who was sitting just above them in the gallery. "The President could have had anything on God's earth he wanted, if he had the guts to ask for it in the open," the message read. "The people . . . want to follow him [but] nobody can follow a man who will not lead, who will not stand up and be counted, who will not say openly what we all know he thinks privately, who thinks you can substitute tricks for morals, smartness for passion, cunning for a soul. . . . He'll get Wallace in the end. . . . But he'll get him out of the gutter, which is an insult to the President, to Mr. Wallace, to you, to us and to the American tradition of democracy."

In the days that followed, newspapers and magazines, many of them clearly pro-Willkie, portrayed the convention as a study in manipulation—by the White House, big-city bosses, and "the voice from the sewer." *Life* proclaimed: "No amount of rationalizing could disguise or demolish the solid fact that at Chicago last week, in a time of world democratic crisis, the greatest democracy treated the world to one of the shoddiest and most hypocritical spectacles in its history." Although not quite as hyperbolic in their criticism, a number of liberal, usually pro-Roosevelt publications agreed. *The New Republic,* for one, called the convention "a shambles" and described the White

House's performance as "fearful, panicky and weak." And the liberal columnist Raymond Clapper wrote: "Something has gone out of American life this week. At least I have lost something. It was faith in President Roosevelt."

Polls taken immediately after the conventions showed Willkie and the Republicans on the verge of overtaking FDR and his party. "If the President can retrieve this campaign after all the glaring blunders that he has made or been responsible for," Harold Ickes glumly mused in his diary, "then the god of elections is indeed on his side."

WITH THE FUROR OF the conventions finally over, the Century Group and William Allen White's committee could return to the task of trying to save Britain. At Roosevelt's request, White himself approached Willkie to see if he would support the destroyers-bases deal. A friend and strong backer of the Republican nominee, the Kansan, through his outspoken pro-Willkie editorials and his influence in the party, was believed to have sparked many of the telegrams and letters sent to the convention delegates. Another intermediary between the White House and Willkie was the Century Group's Lewis Douglas, a former head of the Bureau of the Budget who had defected from the New Deal and was now a key Willkie adviser.

Willkie made clear to both men that, for political reasons, he could not issue a public statement approving the destroyer transactions. He found himself in an intensely uncomfortable position: although he was an interventionist, most prominent Republicans, including members of the Senate and House, were not. As the GOP standard-bearer, he had to give the impression of unity within the party (false as that was), which a public avowal of support for the destroyer deal would undermine. Yet at the same time, Willkie gave his word he would not attack the deal once it was announced. He made the same pledge to Lord Lothian, who reported to Churchill that Willkie was "most insistent that this statement should not in any circumstances be allowed to leak out because it would certainly be used against him in the campaign."

With the winning of Willkie's tacit approval, the final obstacle to the destroyer transfer had been cleared away. On September 3, Roosevelt announced the deal, putting heavy emphasis on the importance of the bases acquired in exchange for the old ships: "The value to the Western Hemisphere of these outposts of security is beyond calculation."

Although Roosevelt seemed his usual ebullient self, he continued to be deeply worried about the deal's potential political fallout, telling a number of friends and advisers that he expected to lose the election over the issue. To his secretary, he declared: "Congress is going to raise hell about this."

Some legislators were indeed indignant—Gerald Nye called the president's circumvention of Congress "a dictatorial step"—and a few newspapers condemned the deal. But the storm of disapproval expected by the president never materialized. Thanks in large part to the publicity campaigns mounted by the White Committee and others, most Americans (70 percent in one survey) considered the destroyers-bases exchange to be highly beneficial for both the United States and Britain. "You can't attack a deal like that," one isolationist senator told the *New York Post*. "If you jump on the destroyer transfer, you're jumping on the acquisition of defense bases in the Western Hemisphere. And the voters wouldn't stand for that. Roosevelt outsmarted all of us when he tied up the two deals." Even the *Chicago Tribune* approved the exchange, noting that America would now have "naval and air bases in regions which must be brought within the American defense zone."

Later, Roosevelt would be rightly lauded for his courage in approving the politically risky transaction just two months before the election. He clearly had no idea beforehand that the response would be so favorable, yet he had gone ahead and done it. Credit, however, must also go to Wendell Willkie, who defied the urging of GOP leaders to issue a public condemnation of the deal and as a result was heavily criticized within his party. Lord Lothian played a major role, too, in bringing the deal to fruition, as did members of the Century Group and the White Committee, who acted as front men for the president, educating the public about the value of the exchange and making it politically possible for him to act.

THREE DAYS AFTER THE agreement was signed, eight destroyers slipped out of Boston Harbor, to the accompaniment of honking horns from cars crossing Charleston Bridge and cheers and applause from spectators standing along the shore. They were on their way to Halifax, Nova Scotia—the first batch of over-age ships to be transferred to the Royal Navy, which would immediately put them to work as escorts for merchant ship convoys across the Atlantic.

As the British would soon discover, the destroyers were hardly in the best of shape. "I thought they were the worst I had ever seen," one admiral fumed. "Poor seaboats with appalling armament and accommodation." Churchill was somewhat more tactful when he presented the U.S. naval attaché in London with a list of their problems: weak bridge structure, corroded superstructure, defective hatch covers, bad steering, and leaks everywhere.

For all their defects, however, the American ships played a key role in fighting the Battle of the Atlantic over the next nerve-racking year. Throughout the rest of 1940 and 1941, they comprised between 20 and 25 percent of the battleship escorts available for duty in the Atlantic; several were responsible for sinking German submarines. "Any destroyer that could steam, shoot, and drop depth charges was worth its weight in gold," noted Admiral of the Fleet Sir George Creasy, director of antisubmarine warfare at the British Admiralty. "Admittedly many of them were an appalling headache to keep running. But, taken by and large, they gave invaluable service at a time of really desperate need."

Yet even if the destroyers-bases deal had yielded no military value at all, it still would have been a significant milestone in America's reluctant march to war. For the first time, the United States had done something consequential to help Britain. In the process, it had served notice to Germany and the rest of the world that it would not stand idly by while the last bastion of democracy in Europe went down to defeat. As the Baltimore *Sun* noted, the destroyer transfer "makes our official neutrality, already highly diaphanous, a well-nigh transparent cover for nonbelligerent cooperation on the side of Great Britain." Hanson Baldwin, the military correspondent for *The New York Times,* went even further, declaring that the destroyers "sealed what in effect was an unofficial alliance between the English-speaking nations and brought the United States far closer than ever before to entry into the war." German officials agreed, calling the destroyers-bases exchange "an openly hostile act against Germany."

The U.S. public's enthusiastic support for a transaction that Roosevelt feared would cost him the election would later make it easier for him to propose a considerably more valuable aid program for Britain: Lend-Lease. The shift in Americans' views on Britain and the war was slow but unmistakable. During the German blitzkrieg in the spring of 1940, nearly two-thirds of the country thought it was more important for the United States to stay out of war than to risk getting involved in the conflict by helping Britain. By August, the country was evenly divided on the issue. By the end of the year, a majority of Americans would favor coming to the aid of Britain even if it meant entry into the war.

That change in attitude was especially crucial now. As Churchill had predicted, "the fury and might of the enemy" had finally descended upon his island nation.

SINCE THE MIDDLE OF August, German bombers had been wreaking havoc on airfields, aircraft factories, and radar installations in the south of England, trying to break the back of the Royal Air Force before launching a cross-Channel invasion. Then, on September 7, the day after the first American destroyers started steaming across the Atlantic, the Luftwaffe began a relentless reign of terror against London and other major British cities. For fifty-seven nights, German bombing raids would batter the British capital, killing tens of thousands of civilians and leaving millions homeless.

In this crucial showdown between Britain and Germany, both countries did their best to convince the United States that their forces were winning. General Raymond Lee, the American military attaché in London, provided Washington with British intelligence reports claiming the downing of huge numbers of German aircraft by the RAF. Similar messages came from the British embassy in Washington.

General Friedrich von Boetticher, in turn, passed along sheaves of top-secret cables and maps claiming the opposite to Colonel Truman Smith and the German attaché's other friends in U.S. Army intelligence. According to these detailed reports from Berlin, the Luftwaffe attacks were decimating British airpower and crippling the country's ports and industries. Army intelligence experts valued von Boetticher's information so highly that when he stopped by the War Department's headquarters on his daily rounds, he was exempted from the rigorous mandatory security search endured by other visitors. Summaries of the German reports, prepared by Truman Smith, were circulated throughout the War and State Departments. With their gloomy assessments of Britain's chances, they bolstered the arguments of those in both departments who opposed giving aid to Britain.

Most Americans, however, felt differently: their focus was not on Britain's losses but on the courage and toughness of its people in standing up to the German onslaught. Such admiration was stimulated by a flood of newspaper and magazine articles—and, above all, radio broadcasts—from American correspondents in London, who described the dogged determination of the capital's residents to live their lives while their world threatened to shatter around them. Virtually every issue of *Life* during that period featured dramatic photographs of the Blitz and its effect on ordinary British citizens. A particularly poignant photo—showing a cute, wide-eyed blond toddler in a hospital bed, her head swathed in bandages and clutching a teddy bear—appeared on *Life*'s cover and touched hearts everywhere. It soon became a poster for William Allen White's committee.

The journalist who did the most, however, to influence U.S. public opinion toward Britain was the CBS correspondent Edward R. Murrow, whose wartime broadcasts, with their famed "This is London" opening, were required listening for millions of Americans. In homes across the country, people gathered around their radios each evening to hear Murrow's vivid verbal portraits of the civilian heroes of the Blitz—the "little people . . . who have no uniforms, who get no decorations for bravery," but who were risking their lives night after night to aid the wounded, retrieve the dead, and bring their battered city back to life. Obsessed by the danger that Germany posed to the world and convinced of the vital importance of Britain's survival, Murrow was unapologetic in demanding that America must come to its rescue. "He was concerned, very concerned that his own country wasn't aware of the facts of life," said a British friend of his. "And that if Hitler & Co. were not stopped here, the next stop was Manhattan."

Thanks in large part to Murrow's reports and those of other American correspondents, Lord Halifax was able to inform the British war cabinet in late October of "an almost miraculous change of opinion" of Americans toward their country and the importance of saving it. As the historian Nicholas Cull later put it, "Hitler had given America something to hate; now Britain provided something for America to love."

In his travels throughout the United States that fall, John Wheeler-Bennett witnessed firsthand that rapidly changing sentiment. After he gave a speech to a midwestern group about the valor of the British people during the Blitz, a member of the audience rushed up to him, shaking his fist. "You're a scoundrel, sir, a damned dangerous insidious scoundrel!" the man exclaimed. "I've been an iron-bound isolationist all my life—and you've made me feel like a heel."

To his chagrin, Friedrich von Boetticher had also become aware of a distinct shift in the American mood. More and more, he was plagued by the uneasy feeling that some of his closest U.S. military contacts were losing their sympathy for Germany. One notable example was General George Strong, the head of the Army's War Plans Division, whom von Boetticher had known since the 1920s. Throughout the years of their friendship, Strong had been widely regarded as pro-German and hostile to Britain and France, so much so that a French officer once accused him of representing German interests.

In September 1940, Strong was one of several American officers sent to London to confer with their British counterparts and to judge for themselves the prospects for Britain's survival. When von Boetticher heard of Strong's presence in the delegation, he sent a gleeful cable to Berlin, noting that the U.S. general "has stood close to me for fifteen years and will report independently." Convinced that Strong would confirm the grievous British losses claimed by German reports, von Boetticher was appalled when his friend declared on his return that the Luftwaffe was nowhere close to vanquishing the RAF, that the damage done by air bombardment had been relatively small, and that British claims of German aircraft losses were "on the conservative side."

Groping for an explanation of Strong's stunning change in attitude, von Boetticher could only surmise that he had been ordered to make the remark "as an organ of Roosevelt, his superior." The idea that his own influence with the American military might soon be at an end was too awful for the German attaché to contemplate.

CHAPTER 14

"AN AMERICAN FIRST, AND A REPUBLICAN AFTERWARD"

═══

For America's interventionists, the summer of 1940 was an exceedingly busy time. Not only did they play crucial roles in crafting the destroyers-bases deal and nominating Wendell Willkie, they also were instrumental in engineering America's first peacetime draft. All three were daunting challenges, but none more so than what Robert Sherwood called the "supremely daring" and "seemingly hopeless" notion of requiring young Americans to take up arms for their country when it was not yet at war.

Conscription had been imposed on U.S. citizens only twice before—during the Civil War and World War I. In both conflicts, there was tremendous opposition to the draft. The concept of a standing army was anathema to many if not most Americans, as it had in fact been to America's Founding Fathers, who feared that such a force would engender an unwelcome spirit of military ardor. According to Thomas Jefferson, a standing army was nothing less than an "instrument . . . dangerous to the rights of the nation." As many Americans saw it, the idea of a draft smacked of state coercion, reminiscent of the militarism of Hitler's Germany and Mussolini's Italy. Compulsory military service during peacetime was especially unthinkable.

In 1940, isolationists claimed that conscription would be immediately followed by the dispatch of an American expeditionary force to fight in Europe. College students, who would be among the first drafted, were particularly vocal on the issue. In the early and mid-1930s, more than half a million American undergraduates signed a pledge refusing to serve in the armed forces in the event of another conflict. As war swept over Europe in 1939 and 1940, thousands of students across the country took part in antiwar demonstrations.

Ranged against these anticonscription forces were the private citizens who had come up with the concept—a group of influential men who strongly believed that a well-trained army was just as important to bolstering America's defenses as additional planes, ships, and weapons. General Hugh Drum, commander of the U.S. First Army, expressed their views when he said in late 1939: "Of what value are modern munitions without the manpower organized and trained to operate them?"

Compulsory military service would have been a hard sell at any time, but in a presidential election year, it was political dynamite. When the idea was first proposed in late May 1940, Roosevelt and most members of Congress immediately shied away from it, as did General George Marshall and the rest of the Army brass. So, on their own, its proponents wrote a bill and launched a publicity campaign to educate Americans about why it was necessary. Introduced in Congress two days before France's capitulation to Germany, the legislation, which would affect millions of Americans if passed, ignited a firestorm in Washington and the rest of the country.

THE MAN MOST RESPONSIBLE for the draft campaign was Grenville Clark, a square-jawed, broad-shouldered Manhattan attorney who looked as if he'd just stepped out of an Arrow shirt ad. The heir to a sizable banking and railroad fortune, the fifty-seven-year-old Clark was a founder and senior partner of the powerhouse Wall Street law firm of Root, Clark, Buckner and Ballantine. He was called Grenny by his friends and acquaintances, among them Franklin Roosevelt, whom Clark had known since childhood.

Like many members of the Century Group and others in the East Coast elite, Clark, a Centurion himself, had been raised to believe in the duty of private citizens to serve their country. He first put that belief into practice after the torpedoing of the British passenger liner

Lusitania by a German submarine in May 1915, less than a year after the outbreak of World War I. More than a thousand people, including 128 Americans, lost their lives.

Believing that America should take firm action against Germany, Clark and his law partner, Elihu Root Jr., were dismayed when President Woodrow Wilson did not declare war after the ship's sinking. The two young lawyers, who were sure that war was inevitable and that America must prepare for it, decided to set up a course of military training for university-educated professionals like themselves. Thanks to their efforts, more than two thousand lawyers, bankers, businessmen, politicians, and journalists devoted several weeks of their summer that year to learning the rudiments of soldiering, which included drills, maneuvers, and the use of artillery and other weapons. Among those who signed up for the training camp, located just outside Plattsburg in upstate New York, were New York City's mayor and police commissioner; the famed war correspondent Richard Harding Davis; and Frank Crowninshield, the future editor of *Vanity Fair*.

Because of the predominance of East Coast bluebloods among the first Plattsburg trainees, the endeavor was portrayed in some newspaper stories as a millionaires' summer lark. It was hardly that. The following year, as a result of the work of Clark and his fellow organizers, more than sixteen thousand university graduates throughout the country received the basics of military training in camps based on the Plattsburg model. When the United States finally declared war against Germany in April 1917, the camps were turned into officers' training schools, which Plattsburgers flocked to join. After ninety days of accelerated training, most of the new officers became instructors for the draftees now flooding into the Army. Many Plattsburg graduates went on to fight in France.

Years later, a French general would remark that America's most impressive military achievement in World War I was its ability to find and train enough skilled officers to lead an army of two million men in an amazingly short period of time. As the historians J. Garry Clifford and Samuel R. Spencer Jr. have observed, much of the credit for that accomplishment belongs to the Plattsburg movement.

After the war, the Plattsburg participants went back to their law firms, banks, newspapers, and other businesses, but many, particularly the early adherents, never lost their belief in the importance of military preparedness, as well as in the obligation of private citizens to get involved in their country's affairs. In May 1940, several dozen of these now middle-aged, prosperous, prominent men celebrated Plattsburg's twenty-fifth anniversary. In their view, the events of that month seemed like a reprise of the spring of 1915: a war raging in Europe, and a neutral America under increasing threat but too militarily weak to go to war or even to defend itself.

With Grenville Clark again serving as their leader, the group decided to launch a new campaign, this one considerably more dramatic and far-reaching than the Plattsburg camps. With the presidential election less than six months away, their plan—to work for the immediate enactment of compulsory military training—was breathtakingly audacious. But these movers and shakers, many at the top of their professions, had few qualms. They had not gotten where they were by agonizing over their beliefs and actions. They expected to be listened to—and heeded.

That was particularly true of Clark, whose aggressiveness and tenacity reminded his acquaintances of a well-bred, self-confident bulldog. Although polite and gentlemanly at all times, he was relentless in pursuing his objectives, disregarding or working to override those who disagreed with him.

In the middle of May, Clark sent a telegram to Roosevelt outlining what he and the other Plattsburgers had in mind and asking the president what he thought. The two men had been classmates at Harvard and, a few years later, had worked together as law clerks at an eminent Wall Street firm, where Roosevelt astonished Clark one lazy afternoon by outlining his intended career path—the New York State Assembly, assistant secretary of the Navy, governor of New York, and then the presidency.

Rather than laughing at his friend's audacity, Clark cheered him on as Roosevelt achieved each one of those posts. He supported FDR for president in 1932 and was one of the few denizens of Wall Street to back him again in 1936. Early in Roosevelt's first term, Clark helped the White House with the drafting of economic legislation; in return, Roosevelt offered him the chairmanship of the new National Labor Relations Board. Clark turned the job down, as he did all such offers. He was determined never to hold an official government position, fearing it would compromise his independence.

While generally admiring of Clark and his public service crusades, his friends in government felt he had no grasp of political reality. "Grenny Clark could not get elected to Congress in any district— North, South, East, or West," Roosevelt once grumbled to an aide. That lack of political acumen was particularly exasperating to the president in May 1940. The last thing he needed was another threat to his reelection, which the draft certainly would be. He sent back a polite, noncommittal reply.

Yet even if 1940 had not been an election year, Roosevelt probably would have shown little enthusiasm for Clark's proposal. In building up the defenses of the nation, the president had focused on the expansion of naval and, in particular, air power, which one observer described as his "Aladdin's lamp for instant and inexpensive national security." Throughout FDR's presidency, the Army had always been the neglected stepchild—and it remained so in the spring and summer of 1940. The president continued to resist the idea that the United States would have to send an army to Europe again, even if the country were forced at some point to go to war against Hitler.

Having been spurned by Roosevelt, Clark and Julius Ochs Adler, a top *New York Times* executive and fellow Plattsburger, flew to Washington on May 31 to try to convince the Army's chief to back their plan. Unlike the president, General George Marshall was keenly aware of the need to strengthen the Army. Indeed, he had been urging Roosevelt for months to correct its huge deficiencies, to little effect.

Yet Marshall, who had been Army chief of staff for only ten months, was also well aware how politically explosive the draft issue was likely to be. An intensely ambitious man whom one aide would later call "a consummate Army politician," he had quietly lobbied for the top Army job for more than a year, with the help of Harry Hopkins and other key presidential advisers. He knew Roosevelt had chosen him with great misgivings, in large part because of his lack of combat experience, and considered him "the best of a bad bargain."

Marshall's relationship with the president remained tentative and distant, and he had no desire to take the initiative on a controversial proposal that the White House and Capitol Hill had not approved, no matter how necessary it might be. "I thought," he said after the war, "that it was far more important in the long run that I be well established as a member of a team and try to do my convincing within that team than to take action publicly contrary to the desires of the President and certain members of Congress." If and when civilian leaders proposed legislation, he said, "I could take the floor and do all the urging that was required."

In his meeting with Clark and Adler, Marshall was courteous but blunt in vetoing their idea. The Army chief was fixated on the idea that the Germans were planning to take over one or more South American countries and then strike at the Panama Canal. He told his visitors that his primary focus was on the defense of the Americas, which required a steady, orderly buildup of troops. There were not enough instructors and weapons for the soldiers he had now, let alone for hundreds of thousands of draftees. A huge influx of untrained men would disrupt everything he was trying to accomplish.

Shocked by what they viewed as Marshall's misguided priorities and unwonted caution, Clark and Adler proceeded to tell the chief of staff how foolish he was to worry about South America when Britain and France were on the verge of collapse. The defeat of those two countries, the New Yorkers argued, would pose a far greater threat to America's security than any pro-Nazi coup in Uruguay or Argentina. Furthermore, Clark said, Marshall had a moral responsibility to make clear to Roosevelt the need for more trained manpower, especially when the Army chief clearly knew how great the need was.

A brusque, dignified, and distinctly formidable man, considered intimidating by even his closest associates, Marshall was not accustomed to being scolded, especially by a couple of overbearing civilians. "It was very hard to keep my temper," he later recalled. "I was being dictated to, and I mean dictated to . . . by this important New York fellow and this other important New York fellow. . . . I tried to listen politely but I couldn't do it." His face flushed, Marshall curtly told Clark and Adler that he did not think it his duty to give FDR advice that the president had not requested and that therefore he had no intention of doing so. With that, he terminated the meeting.

As upset with Marshall as Marshall was with him, Clark decided to try a different tack. Someone, preferably the secretary of war, must put pressure on the Army and president to back conscription. Since the current war secretary, Harry Woodring, was a diehard isolationist, he would have to be replaced by an equally committed interventionist.

Within hours of his confrontation with Marshall, Clark, self-confident as ever, set out to transform that pipe dream into reality.

IF A POLLSTER HAD asked Washington insiders to pick the worst member of Roosevelt's cabinet, Harry Woodring would have won in a landslide. Joseph Alsop called him "a sleazy third-rater" and "a peanut-sized politician distinguished only by the meanness of his nature." *The Kiplinger Letter,* an influential Washington-based financial newsletter, referred to him as "plainly incompetent."

A former governor of Kansas, Woodring was in fact never supposed to have been secretary of war. In 1933, he had been given the job of assistant war secretary in return for his support of Roosevelt in the previous year's presidential election. When his boss, George Dern, died in 1936, Woodring became acting secretary. Preoccupied by that year's election and then by the Court-packing controversy, FDR never got around to filling the cabinet position with someone more qualified, as he once planned. As a result, Woodring's appointment became permanent.

For years, members of the press and administration officials, including Woodring's fellow cabinet members, had urged the president to get rid of him. Not only did Woodring oppose aid for Britain, he was also at war with his own assistant secretary, Louis Johnson, who wanted his superior's job and openly intrigued to get it. The two men did not speak to each other, and unsurprisingly, chaos and confusion reigned in their department. Roosevelt declined to get involved and procrastinated about replacing Woodring, even though he had been promising to do so for months. The president found it difficult to fire anyone, and he had a habit of delaying that uncomfortable duty for as long as possible.

But that was before Grenville Clark entered the fray. Just hours after his contentious meeting with Marshall, Clark had lunch with his old friend Supreme Court Justice Felix Frankfurter, who served as an unofficial adviser to Roosevelt. An ardent interventionist and Anglophile, Frankfurter had long been urging FDR to dump Woodring.

During their lunch, Clark and Frankfurter discussed possible replacements, and within a minute or two, they came up with the same name: Henry Stimson. The country's most respected elder statesman and a pillar of the Republican Eastern establishment, the seventy-two-year-old Stimson had served as secretary of war under William Howard Taft and secretary of state under Herbert Hoover.

Even the cheeky young columnist Joseph Alsop was in awe of Stimson, describing him as "an impossibly grand figure" and "in matters of substance, as great a public servant as this country has ever seen." Alsop, who was used to dominating conversations, was uncharacteristically subdued whenever he encountered Stimson, who was known for his bluntness and integrity: "On the few impersonal occasions when we did meet, I could manage little more than a muted and respectful greeting."

A friend of both Clark and Frankfurter, Stimson had been a Plattsburger himself; four years after his stint as war secretary, he had participated in the 1916 summer camp. When the United States entered the war the following year, Stimson, then a forty-nine-year-old Wall Street lawyer, enlisted in the Army and was sent to France, where he commanded a field artillery battalion and attained the rank of colonel.

A forceful advocate of collective security all his adult life, Stimson had worked hard, if unsuccessfully, as secretary of state to encourage the creation of an international coalition to challenge Japan's seizure of Manchuria in 1931. Once out of office, he played the role of Cassandra, warning his countrymen about the perils of isolationism. In a series of hard-hitting speeches, broadcasts, and articles throughout the 1930s, he declared that the United States, "the world's most powerful nation today," must assume its responsibility to help maintain peace and justice in the world.

When America did nothing to help halt the aggression of Japan, Germany, and Italy, Stimson deplored its "passive and shameful acquiescence in the wrong that is now being done." The country, he charged, was putting "peace above righteousness. We have thereby gone far toward killing the influence of [the United States] in the progress of the world. . . . Such a policy of amoral drift by such a safe and powerful nation as our own . . . will not save us from entanglement. It will make entanglement more certain."

When World War II began and Roosevelt launched his campaign to help Britain and France, Stimson was one of his strongest supporters. But he was far bolder than the president. In a September 1939 radio broadcast advocating repeal of the embargo on arms sales to belligerent countries, Stimson refused to follow the administration line that selling munitions to the Allies was the best way to keep out of the war. Instead, he argued that the main reason for helping Britain and France was to make sure they were not defeated. He went even further, declaring that "a time might well come" when America would have to go to war itself.

Secretary of State Cordell Hull, who was given an advance copy of the radio speech, was so appalled by Stimson's forthrightness that he asked his predecessor to delete the offending language. Stimson refused, telling Hull that if he were not allowed to deliver it as written, he wouldn't speak at all. Hull gave in, and the speech turned out to be a huge success, so much so that William Allen White's pro-repeal committee printed and distributed tens of thousands of copies throughout the country.

ONCE CLARK AND FRANKFURTER decided on Stimson as Woodring's replacement, Clark called the former cabinet secretary to ask whether he would take the job if it were offered. At first Stimson said no, brusquely declaring it to be "a ridiculous idea." But Clark, in his typical bulldog fashion, continued to press him until, after an hour or so of argument, Stimson said he would accept the post—but with certain conditions. He must be allowed to choose his own subordinates and be free to lobby for policies he favored, which included all-out aid to Britain and France and compulsory military service.

With Stimson's agreement in hand, Frankfurter met with Roosevelt on June 3 to press his and Clark's case. Although Stimson had opposed much of the New Deal and had been an outspoken foe of FDR's Supreme Court legislation, the president had great admiration and respect for him; indeed, the two had exchanged friendly notes and letters for years. But while Roosevelt seemed to like the idea of Stimson at the War Department, he said nothing definite to Frankfurter. Knowing FDR's tendency to put off decisions, the Supreme Court justice wrote two long letters to him over the next few days, outlining again the need for Stimson's appointment.

Two weeks passed, and Frankfurter began to despair. Then, on June 18, Harry Woodring provided the president with the perfect excuse for his ouster when he refused to sign off on an FDR order to sell seventeen new U.S. bombers to Britain. The next morning, FDR requested and received Woodring's resignation. A few hours later, he called Stimson to offer him the job.

Before he accepted, Stimson said, he wanted to make sure the president was fully aware of his strong interventionist views. Just the night before, he had made another national broadcast, this one calling for conscription, repeal of the entire neutrality law, and the dispatch of massive numbers of planes and munitions to Britain—if necessary, in American ships and under American naval protection. "Short of a direct declaration of war, it would have been hard to frame a more complete program of resistance to the Nazis," noted McGeorge Bundy, the future aide to Presidents John F. Kennedy and Lyndon B. Johnson, who helped Stimson write his autobiography after the war. When FDR replied that he had read the speech and "was in full accord with it," Stimson took the job. He immediately phoned Grenville Clark to announce that "your ridiculous plot has succeeded."

Stimson, however, was not the only vigorous interventionist to join Roosevelt's cabinet that day. The president coupled the announcement of Stimson's appointment with that of another prominent Republican—Frank Knox, the publisher and owner of the *Chicago Daily News*—as secretary of the Navy. Knox was to replace the isolationist Charles Edison, whom administration officials had persuaded to run for governor of New Jersey.

A self-made multimillionaire, the short, stocky Knox was, if anything, even more of a hawk than Stimson. He had fought as a Rough Rider in Cuba with his mentor and idol, Teddy Roosevelt, who had inspired him to go into politics. Like Stimson, Knox had been in his forties when World War I erupted, and like Stimson, he had enlisted in the Army, beginning the war as a private and ending it as a major, in charge of an artillery unit in France. A fierce critic of the New Deal, Knox had been Alf Landon's vice presidential running mate in 1936. Since September 1939, however, he had unstintingly backed all Roosevelt's efforts to help the Allies.

For months, the president, urged on by his advisers, had been thinking about bringing more Republicans into his inner circle and thus creating a bipartisan coalition cabinet not unlike Winston Churchill's. When he announced the appointments of Stimson and Knox, Roosevelt declared that the selections had been made for no other reason than to encourage "national solidarity in a time of world crisis and on behalf of our national defense."

But that was hardly the entire truth, as Roosevelt—and everyone else in Washington—knew. The choice of Stimson and Knox, just days before the Republican convention, had been a masterful political move on the part of a masterful politician. It not only positioned FDR as a unifying, nonpartisan figure interested only in the public good, but also worked to weaken Republican election prospects by underscoring the split between the GOP's interventionist and isolationist wings.

Predictably, Republican leaders exploded. How dare two leading members of their party abandon it at a critical time to join the inner circle of its archenemy, Franklin D. Roosevelt? Both Stimson and Knox were read out of the GOP, but neither of them much cared. Stimson was hardly close to Republican isolationists, labeling their views as "hopelessly twisted." Knox, for his part, told friends: "I am an American first, and a Republican afterward."

This Washington Star *editorial cartoon depicts Republicans' fury over FDR's naming of two prominent Republicans, Frank Knox and Henry Stimson, to his cabinet in June 1940. Among those booing in the background are Thomas Dewey and Senators Burton Wheeler and Gerald Nye.*

One of the boldest steps taken by Roosevelt in the prewar years, the addition of Stimson and Knox to the cabinet was to have far greater consequences than simply providing two more voices in favor of conscription. Calling the appointments "a much-needed blood transfusion," Robert Sherwood would later write: "It is impossible to exaggerate the extent to which Stimson and Knox strengthened Roosevelt's hand in dealing with the immediate problems of 1940 and the longer-range problems of aid to Britain and the building up of our armed forces, as well as in the eventual fighting of the war."

Over the next eighteen months, the two men were relentless in urging the president to adopt more aggressive policies, joining Harold Ickes and Treasury Secretary Henry Morgenthau, the cabinet's other two ardent interventionists, in doing so. Both were outspoken advocates of the destroyers-bases deal; indeed, it was Knox, along with Lord Lothian, who was the earliest and strongest proponent of exchanging destroyers for bases.

Stimson and Knox also helped bring order and vigor to their departments, making it clear to the military and naval officers serving under them that they were in charge and expected to be obeyed. At the same time, Stimson forged a close relationship with Marshall, and, although the war secretary was well ahead of the Army chief of staff in his desire to help Britain, the two were in agreement on most other issues.

To serve as their top assistants, the two new cabinet secretaries brought to Washington an extraordinary crew of younger men, most of them from Wall Street law firms and banks. They included Robert Lovett, James Forrestal, John McCloy, and Robert Patterson, all of whom would have a major impact on American foreign policy during and after the war.

But that was in the future. Grenville Clark was worried about the present—and the fate of his conscription legislation. On the same day that Roosevelt announced the appointments of Stimson and Knox, the euphemistically named Selective Training and Service Act was introduced in Congress.

CLARK AND HIS ASSOCIATES knew they still faced extremely long odds in their quest for the draft. The appointment of Stimson was a vital

Grenville Clark, the main architect of the 1940 conscription bill,
testifies before a Senate committee.

first step, but they also needed the backing of Marshall, Roosevelt, and a majority of members of Congress, all of whom continued to treat them as if they had the plague. Following in the footsteps of William Allen White, they decided to launch a massive movement to enlist public support.

On June 3, the same day that Frankfurter and Roosevelt had their meeting, Clark and other leading proponents of conscription convened in the office of Julius Adler, *The New York Times*'s vice president and general manager, to plan their campaign. They formed what they called the National Emergency Committee, with Clark as chairman and Adler as one of four vice chairmen. That afternoon, two hundred men, most of them former Plattsburgers, joined the committee, and by the end of the week, the group had acquired more than a thousand members across the country, most of them influential figures in their communities. Some also belonged to the Century Group and the White Committee.

To direct a nationwide public relations campaign, the committee, having raised substantial funds from its members, hired Perley Boone, a former *New York Times* journalist who had been publicity director for the recently closed New York World's Fair. Boone in turn hired a staff of writers and photographers, who began churning out press releases and other material for newspapers, magazines, and radio stations throughout the United States.

Among the papers that ran stories and favorable editorials was *The New York Times,* which, unlike its crosstown rival, the *Herald Tribune,* had up to then been relatively neutral in the fight over America's involvement in the war. As the most influential paper in the nation, the *Times* had long emphasized its political objectivity, vowing in 1896 that it would "give the news impartially, without fear or favor, regardless of party, sect or interests involved."

Julius Adler, of course, was hardly impartial. A highly decorated veteran of World War I (in France, he had charged a German machine gun nest), the *Times* executive was a staunch interventionist. But he was scrupulous in not imposing his views on the paper's editorial staff.

It was the *Times*'s publisher, Arthur Hays Sulzberger, who played the central role in the paper's decision to support conscription. Sulzberger, who had been a pacifist until Hitler's blitzkrieg in Western Europe, told his editorial board in early June: "Gentlemen, we have got to do more than we are doing. I cannot live with myself much longer unless we do." A few days later, the *Times* ran an editorial advocating the immediate imposition of a draft, becoming the first major U.S. newspaper to do so. "In the interest of self-protection," the editorial said, "the American people should at once adopt a national system of universal compulsory military training. We say this as a newspaper which has never before believed in the wisdom of such a policy in time of peace. We say it because the logic of events drives us remorselessly to this conclusion."

On June 7, the day the editorial was published, Roosevelt mentioned it favorably at a news conference. But when a cascade of isolationist opposition followed (which included threatening letters and phone calls to Sulzberger and Adler), the president retreated, saying at his next press conference: "I did not . . . intend to imply that there should be compulsory military training for every boy in this country." With Roosevelt lying low, Democratic leaders in Congress would have nothing to do with the National Emergency Committee's bill. As Senator James Byrnes explained to Clark, the legislation would not have "a Chinaman's chance" without the president's backing.

Nonetheless, the bill was introduced in Congress, albeit by two highly improbable sponsors—a Republican congressman and an anti-Roosevelt Democratic senator. The House sponsor was Rep. James W. Wadsworth, a wealthy, highly respected gentleman farmer from upstate New York. A former senator, Wadsworth had once chaired the Senate Military Affairs Committee and was a strong supporter of military preparedness. About his decision to sponsor a bill considered political poison, Wadsworth would later note that Democratic leaders in the House were "perfectly willing to see an outsider stick his neck out . . . and I was perfectly willing to do it." In the Senate, the legislation's sponsor was Edward Burke of Nebraska, who, although a Democrat, was a bitter foe of the New Deal, had been a leader in the Supreme Court fight, and had been targeted by the president in the 1938 congressional purge.

Less than forty-eight hours after Grenville Clark approached the two members for their support, the Burke-Wadsworth bill was dropped into the House and Senate hoppers and distributed to Washington reporters. Perley Boone had already sent advance copies to several major newspapers, and once the legislation was introduced, its text was transmitted by the wire services to thousands of other papers around the country. Overnight, conscription had become a major national issue.

Boone was also on hand when congressional hearings began on July 3. As reporters filed into the House committee room, he handed out copies of a letter from General John Pershing endorsing the legislation. Grenville Clark had solicited the elderly general's support, and Pershing gave it in full measure. "If we had adopted compulsory military training in 1914," he declared, "it would not have been necessary for us to send partly trained boys into battle against the veteran troops of our adversary."

Belatedly, George Marshall had come to the same conclusion. A month after he had all but ejected Clark and Adler from his office, the Army chief of staff decided they were right about the need for conscription. The fall of France had helped change his mind, as had the determined arguments of the Army's new civilian chief, Henry Stimson. On July 9, just before the Senate confirmed his appointment, Stimson summoned Clark, Marshall, and other top Army leaders to his sprawling estate in Washington. While Roosevelt still wavered, Stimson emphasized that from then on, the War Department must give "strong and unequivocal support" to the draft legislation. Those who offered differing views were made to realize, in Marshall's words, that "they were in Dutch with the Secretary of War right from the start." Another Army officer at the meeting recalled: "We were given our marching orders."

Both Marshall and Stimson made repeated trips to Capitol Hill to testify on behalf of the conscription measure. On July 30, Marshall told the Senate Military Affairs Committee that there was "no conceivable way" to secure "trained, seasoned men in adequate numbers" to defend the country except through the draft. At an earlier House committee hearing, a congressman had asked the Army chief if he was not asking for more than was necessary to meet the current crisis. Dumbfounded by what he considered the stupidity of the question, Marshall snapped: "My relief of mind would be tremendous if we just had too much of something beside patriotism and spirit."

The testimony of Marshall and Stimson, coupled with the Clark committee's widespread publicity campaign and the stunning collapse

General George Marshall, Army chief of staff, and War Secretary Henry Stimson.

of France, prompted a significant change in public opinion about the draft. By the middle of June, 64 percent of Americans were in favor of compulsory military service; a month later, the number had reached 71 percent.

At the same time, however, congressional offices and the White House were being inundated with hundreds of thousands of letters, telegrams, postcards, and phone calls, most of them violently opposing the legislation. Senator Burton Wheeler, who, along with other congressional isolationists, helped orchestrate the antidraft campaign, declared that "Democrats who vote for [the draft] before the coming election . . . will be driving nails in their coffins."

Many of his congressional colleagues apparently agreed. In a cable to London, Aubrey Morgan's British press operation in New York noted: "Congressmen are frightened by their mail, which is overwhelmingly against the bill, and they don't trust the polls which indicate the country approves. They feel that even if not faked, they don't take into consideration the fact that a man sufficiently interested in a public question to write about it is a man prepared to turn out and vote, while a man who has to be hunted up and asked his opinion by a canvasser is likely to stay at home."

According to Lord Lothian, Roosevelt felt much the same way. Although American public opinion, by which Roosevelt set such great store, was overwhelmingly supportive of the draft, he remained mum on the subject, even though he, too, was increasingly convinced that conscription was necessary. In his own message to London, Lothian reported that FDR was "frightened of a die-hard bloc in Congress, has permitted no real trial of strength, and continues to encourage a seeping process . . . by letting facts, the Press, and his friends speak out" in favor of the bill.

By late July, tens of thousands of people, most of them opponents of conscription, had descended on Congress. Labor leaders lobbied against the legislation, as did representatives of a wide array of pacifist and other antiwar organizations. The crowds were dense on Capitol Hill, and feelings ran high. "I myself feared violence," said the head of one peace group. "The ugly, sinister atmosphere of war is already here." When several antidraft protesters held a prayer vigil on the Capitol steps after being denied permission to do so, the Capitol Hill police, brandishing nightsticks, broke up the demonstration.

A loose national coalition of right-wing women's groups, with names like the Congress of American Mothers and the American Mothers' Neutrality League, added to the furor. Thousands of supporters of this so-called "mothers' movement" traveled to Washington whenever Congress took up legislation they considered interventionist. Dressed in black, many with veils covering their faces, the women made life miserable for members of Congress who were not avowedly isolationist. They stalked their targets, screamed and spat at them, and held vigils outside their offices, keening and wailing.

One such group hanged an effigy of Senator Claude Pepper, a die-hard interventionist, from an oak tree in front of the Capitol. The dummy, with its coconut head, denim overalls, and straw-stuffed body, wore a sash inscribed with the words CLAUDE "BENEDICT ARNOLD"

Fist-Shaking Mothers Hang Pepper's Effigy On Capitol Maple While He Sits in Senate

An isolationist women's group, which called itself a "mothers' committee," hangs an effigy depicting interventionist Senator Claude Pepper on a tree outside the Capitol.

PEPPER. The women were disappointed when, instead of rising to the bait, the Florida Democrat professed himself delighted, declaring in the Senate that it was "a splendid demonstration of what we are all trying to preserve—freedom of speech and freedom of action."*

But the antidraft demonstrations and mail did succeed in cowing other legislators—so many, in fact, that the Burke-Wadsworth bill appeared likely to fail in committee. That was unacceptable to Stimson, who, along with Frank Knox, pressed Roosevelt hard at an August 2 cabinet meeting to support conscription. To the surprise of the two new secretaries and the rest of the cabinet, the president agreed. He told Stimson he would "call some of the [congressional] leaders in and tell them they must get busy on that bill," which he regarded as "one of the great fundamental pillars of national defense." The following day, FDR informed reporters he supported the draft legislation and considered it "essential to adequate national defense."

With that, the congressional battle was joined. It was a nasty, vitriolic fight, exacerbated by the hot, humid weather that had smothered Washington for weeks. "Whenever the Congress remains in session after August 1, you can look for trouble," said Senator James Byrnes. "The fellows begin to look like [the brawling prizefighter] Tony Galento and act like [the heavyweight champion] Joe Louis. They hit from any position, and the referee is in as much danger as the opposing fighters." Another senator remarked: "I shudder for the future of a country whose destiny must be decided in the dog days."

Byrnes's colleagues proved him prescient. In the Senate, Rush Holt, a thirty-year-old isolationist Democrat from West Virginia, accused Grenville Clark and his associates, whom he called "dollar patriots," of forming a cabal to lead America into war to protect their foreign investments. To accomplish their objective, he added, they were "willing to sacrifice American boys on European battlefields." The Senate visitors' gallery, packed with opponents of the draft, erupted in applause and cheers.

Jumping to his feet, Senator Sherman Minton, who supported the draft, declared that Clark and his friends were far more patriotic than Holt's own "slacker family." Holt's father, Minton contended, had

---

* Pepper kept the effigy as a memento. It is now on display at Florida State University's Claude Pepper Library in Jacksonville.

sent one of his sons to South America to dodge the draft during World War I and had opposed the dispatch of food to American troops fighting in Europe. "A malicious lie!" Holt shouted, then claimed that whenever the White House wanted filth thrown, it called on Minton. The Indiana Democrat shot back: "When Hitler wants it thrown, you throw it." At that point, Senator Alben Barkley, the majority leader, stepped in and put an end to the unseemly verbal duel.

In the House, the fight turned physical; once again, it involved two Democrats. After Rep. Martin Sweeney of Ohio delivered a scathing attack on the Roosevelt administration for allegedly using conscription as a way to get the United States into the war, Rep. Beverly Vincent of Kentucky, who was next to Sweeney, loudly muttered that he refused "to sit by a traitor." Sweeney swung at Vincent, who responded with a sharp right to the jaw that sent Sweeney staggering. It was, said the House doorkeeper, the best punch thrown by a member of Congress in fifty years.

Even without the punches, the debates in both House and Senate were noted for their flamboyant combativeness. Burton Wheeler was particularly melodramatic when he described his vision of America under the thrall of peacetime conscription: "[N]o longer will this be a free land—no longer will a citizen be able to say that he disagrees with a government edict. Hushed whispers will replace free speech—secret meetings in dark places will supplant free assemblage. . . . If this bill passes, it will slit the throat of the last great democracy still living—it will accord to Hitler his greatest and cheapest victory."

While public opinion remained overwhelmingly in favor of conscription, the bill's opponents stymied any attempt to bring it to a vote. They filibustered in the Senate and offered a series of amendments in both houses. Day after sweltering day, these delaying tactics continued, until Claude Pepper had had enough. In a speech to his Senate colleagues, he declared that their behavior reminded him of France's inept, incompetent Chamber of Deputies in the months before its country's defeat earlier that summer: "They debated; they haggled; they equivocated; they hesitated; they thought of the next election, and they lost France. . . . If we are not willing to make up our minds that we are facing a new kind of a war and a new kind of a world, then I venture to predict, sadly, that we are going to lose that kind of a war and our kind of a world."

After his declaration of support for the draft in early August, the president had done nothing to help push the bill along. He spent the next ten days out of Washington, giving his opponents the chance to dominate the discourse and the headlines. Stimson, Clark, and other conscription proponents feared that unless Roosevelt made his influence felt soon, Congress would approve a compromise Senate amendment to continue the Army's current volunteer system until after the election. Stimson urged FDR to speak up again for the legislation, but the president ignored the suggestion.

Then, on August 17, Wendell Willkie weighed in. The occasion was his speech formally accepting the Republican nomination. Coming two months after the Philadelphia convention, the address would finally spell out the GOP candidate's official stand on foreign and domestic issues.

For weeks, Willkie had been under enormous pressure to oppose conscription. He had received thousands of antidraft letters and telegrams, as well as phone calls and visits from Republican members of Congress. Rep. Joseph Martin, the House minority leader and Willkie's choice to head the Republican National Committee, told him: "These legislative issues are Roosevelt's responsibility, not yours. . . . You don't have to comment on every bill. The draft is a very unpopular issue. Naturally, people don't want their sons in uniform. Go slow on this thing."

Willkie knew that if he opposed the bill, Republicans would join isolationist Democrats in killing it. But if he backed it, the draft, like the destroyer deal, would no longer be a campaign issue, allowing nervous members of Congress to take much less of a political risk in voting for it.

The Republican nominee ended the suspense on a blazingly hot August day in his hometown of Elwood, Indiana. Speaking to a massive crowd of more than two hundred thousand people, he voiced support for "some form of selective service," saying it was "the only democratic way to secure the trained and competent manpower we need for national defense." At a press conference two days later, Willkie elaborated on his statement, declaring that conscription should be enacted immediately and that he would continue to support such a step, even if it meant his defeat in November. Soon afterward, Joseph Martin announced that the GOP would take no official stand on the draft measure. The Republican members of Congress were free to vote their conscience.

Roosevelt and Stimson had spent the day of Willkie's speech observing maneuvers by the First Army in upstate New York. Both were visibly relieved when they received news reports that night of the Republican's support. "The Willkie speech was a godsend," Stimson told an acquaintance the next day. In his diary, the war secretary wrote that Willkie "has gone far to hamstring the efforts of the little group of isolationists to play politics."

Willkie's acceptance of conscription, coupled with the lamentable performance of the troops during the New York maneuvers, finally convinced Roosevelt that he must make an unequivocal statement urging immediate passage of the bill. He suggested to Julius Adler that he get a *New York Times* reporter to pose a question about the draft at FDR's next press conference. On August 23, Charles Hurd of the *Times* did just that, asking Roosevelt if he would comment on the Senate amendment to postpone conscription. The president replied that he was "absolutely opposed" to any delay in enactment of the original bill. He described to reporters the poor training and physical condition of the soldiers he had seen the previous week, declaring that they "would have been licked by thoroughly trained forces of a similar size within a day or two." The army not only must be expanded as quickly as possible, he said, but must be given far better training and arms as well.

With the president's explicit endorsement, Democratic congressional leaders united behind the bill, and the momentum shifted dramatically. "While not a particularly courageous performance by the President, it was successful," noted J. Garry Clifford, who, with Samuel R. Spencer Jr., wrote an authoritative history of the draft legislation. "That it was so successful owed a great deal to Willkie." The measure's supporters were also aided by media stories and photos of Germany's aerial assaults on Britain and its capital. As one Army officer close to Marshall put it: "Every time Hitler bombed London, we got another couple of votes."

Nonetheless, the fight in both chambers was bitter to the end. After defeating a number of crippling amendments, the Senate and House on September 14 approved the Selective Service Act, instituting compulsory military service for one year and mandating the registration of all American men between the ages of twenty-one and thirty-five. Several GOP senators voted for the measure, as did a number of House Republicans, including minority leader Joseph Martin. Senator Hiram Johnson angrily complained that Willkie's speech "really broke the back of the opposition to the conscription law. He slapped every one of us . . . who were thinking American and acting American."

After he signed the bill, Roosevelt attempted to reassure his countrymen that its enactment did not mean the dispatch of young Americans to Europe. "We have started to train more men not because we expect to use them," he said, "but for the same reason [you put] your umbrellas . . . up—to keep from getting wet." Freda Kirchwey, editor of *The Nation,* called such talk foolish. "Openly and officially, we have identified ourselves with the nations fighting against Hitler," Kirchwey wrote. "The bill is a war measure, enacted on the assumption that active participation in the struggle cannot ultimately be avoided."

Roosevelt's caution also prompted him to seek a delay in the draft's actual implementation until after the election. Several aides, however, advised him not to do so. "To postpone [the draft lottery] until after the election would leave you open to the charge that it was postponed for political reasons," James Rowe, Roosevelt's administrative assistant, wrote him. Rowe also noted that a deferral would seriously disrupt the timetable for conscription that had just been set up.

FDR followed Rowe's advice. On October 29, less than a week before Americans went to the polls, he stood next to Henry Stimson on the stage of the War Department auditorium. Flashbulbs from news cameras popped as the blindfolded secretary reached into a huge glass fishbowl filled with thousands of bright blue capsules and retrieved one. He handed it to Roosevelt, who opened it and announced: "The first number is one-five-eight." A woman in the audience screamed. Her son and the more than six thousand other young Americans whose draft number was 158 would be the first ones called up to serve. For the next several hours, War Department officials drew the remainder of the numbers to determine the order in which more than a million men—of the more than sixteen million who had registered for the draft—would be inducted.

Stimson, who was generally sparing in his praise for the president, applauded FDR's courage and "good statesmanship" in launching conscription before the election. In his own analysis of the chief executive's behavior during the fight, the columnist Mark Sullivan described him as having a split personality—"Mr. Roosevelt the President and Mr. Roosevelt the candidate for a third term. . . . On this occasion, Mr. Roosevelt the President seems to have won."

Not surprisingly, the man most lauded for his role in the draft's enactment was Grenville Clark. "Without his tireless energy, unusual ability, influence in many areas, and perhaps most of all, dogged perseverance, the law would not have been enacted," declared General Lewis Hershey, who later became director of the Selective Service System. Stimson agreed. The day after Roosevelt signed the act, the war secretary wrote to Clark: "If it had not been for you, no such bill would have been enacted at this time. Of this, I am certain." In his own letter of thanks, Rep. James Wadsworth expressed his "admiration and gratitude" to Clark and his committee for their resolution in performing "a vital public service." Wadsworth added: "You paid me a high compliment in asking me to introduce the bill and what is more important, you gave me a chance to serve in a great cause."

In the view of J. Garry Clifford, the inception of conscription "was undoubtedly the most important of America's defense measures prior to Pearl Harbor." For the first time in U.S. history, the Army was given the authority to begin the training of massive numbers of troops, introduce modern weapons and tactics, and carry out large-scale maneuvers before war began. When America finally did enter the conflict in December 1941, the War Department had on its roster thirty-six divisions, numbering some 1.65 million men.

Without the million-plus troops made available by the draft, the U.S. military would not have been able to invade North Africa, the first in its series of offensives against Germany, less than a year after Pearl Harbor. According to Marshall's biographer, Forrest Pogue, "it was the Selective Service Act of 1940 . . . that made possible the huge United States Army and Air Force that fought World War II."

In addition, the national debate over the draft, drawn-out and contentious as it was, helped awaken the American people to the need to prepare themselves for a war that was drawing steadily closer. As Grenville Clark saw it, the passage of the measure, despite the initial foot-dragging by the White House, the Army, and Congress, proved the truth of Abraham Lincoln's maxim that "the people will save their government if the government itself will do its part only indifferently well."

CHAPTER 15

"THE YANKS ARE _NOT_ COMING"

In 1977, Kingman Brewster, the president of Yale University, was named U.S. ambassador to Britain. His appointment to the Court of St. James's was almost universally praised, with few people noting the irony of his selection. Thirty-seven years before, as a Yale undergraduate, Brewster had been one of the founders of the America First Committee, which, within months of its creation in the summer of 1940, emerged as the most powerful, vocal, and effective isolationist organization in the country. One of the group's chief goals was to stop America from going to war, even if that meant Britain's defeat by the Germans.

Although America First has usually been viewed as the embodiment of conservative midwestern isolationism, it was actually born on the Yale campus—the outgrowth of a nationwide student revolt against the very idea of another war. Brewster and most of his fellow student rebels had been born during or just after World War I, and the widespread disillusionment and bitterness over that bloodbath and its aftermath had helped shape their early years.

"The conduct of the war itself, with the years of stalemate, the slaughter of millions—all this chilled our marrow," recalled the CBS correspondent Eric Sevareid, who as a student at the University of Minnesota participated in a number of pacifist demonstrations in the mid-1930s. "We were young, and to those just beginning to taste the wonderful flavors of life, the idea of death was a stark tragedy of unutterable horror. . . . We began to detest the very word 'patriotism,' which we considered to be debased, a cheap medallion with which to decorate and justify a corpse."

On campus after campus, students demonstrated to keep America out of any future war, to "preserve at least one oasis of sanity in an insane world," as Sevareid put it. At the University of Chicago, marchers carried white crosses symbolic of "Flanders fields"; at the University of Missouri, students held up signs reading "The Yanks Are NOT Coming." Thousands of young Americans, including Sevareid, followed the lead of students at Britain's Oxford University in pledging not to "bear arms for flag or country."

Few people, however, expected such outbursts at Yale. Most of its students, after all, came from the upper-crust elite of the East Coast. Many of their fathers were Anglophiles and interventionists, a good number of whom had fought in the war themselves.

Several members of Kingman Brewster's own family were outspokenly pro-British. His first cousin, Janet Brewster, for one, was not only an ardent supporter of aid to Britain but was married to Edward R. Murrow, who championed the British cause in his CBS broadcasts from London. Products of an old New England family, Kingman and Janet were direct descendants of Elder William Brewster, who had come to America on the *Mayflower* and had been the chief religious leader of the Plymouth Colony.

But unlike Janet, Kingman Brewster, although sympathetic to Britain's plight, strongly believed that "we shouldn't be entrapped in war." He and other anti-interventionist students thought of themselves as smarter, more realistic, and less susceptible to propaganda than their fathers' generation had been. In their view, the values to which their Eastern establishment elders had clung had been smashed to bits by World War I and the Depression. McGeorge Bundy, a Yale classmate of Brewster's, wrote at the time that he and other young men his age felt "a deep-seated uncertainty about all ideals and every absolute. . . . About the things for which we are willing to die, we are confused and bewildered; we have played with many ideals, but we have generally given our devotion to none."

Anticipating the campus divisions of the 1960s, antiwar students in 1940 squared off against the presidents and professors of their schools, many of whom were interventionists. Indeed, Yale's president, Charles

Seymour, and Harvard's head, James Bryant Conant, were both members of the national committee of William Allen White's organization. When, after the fall of France, Conant made a national radio broadcast urging the Roosevelt administration to do everything possible to defeat Hitler, he was deluged with abusive letters, a fair number from Harvard students. The school's newspaper, *The Harvard Crimson*, ran a series of editorials urging a negotiated peace between Germany and Britain. "We are frankly determined to have peace at any price," declared one *Crimson* editorial. "We refuse to fight another balance of power war."

Antiwar students at Harvard also created an organization called the Committee for the Recognition of Classroom Generals. Its activities included sending tin soldiers and armchair citations to five interventionist professors and picketing an interventionist rally on campus with signs reading LET'S SEND 50 OVER-AGE PROFESSORS TO BRITAIN.

As was true on other campuses in 1940, Harvard's spring commencement ceremonies served as a backdrop for the increasingly contentious debate. A member of the Class of 1915 was greeted by boos and catcalls from younger graduates when he told an alumni convocation that "we were not too proud to fight [in World War I] and we are not too proud to fight now." Those who supported intervention responded with equal hostility when the 1940 class orator, in his commencement speech, denounced aid to Britain as "fantastic nonsense."

Two articles in *The Atlantic Monthly* underscored how wide the split between American college students and their elders had become. In the August 1940 issue, Arnold Whitridge, a Yale history professor and the grandson of the famed British poet Matthew Arnold, wrote what he called an "Open Letter to Undergraduates," under the headline WHERE DO YOU STAND? Whitridge, a World War I veteran, said he was bewildered and deeply troubled by the attitude of students at Yale, Harvard, Dartmouth, and other colleges who opposed aid to the Allies, said they would never take up arms for their country, and insisted that "there is no preponderance of good or evil on either side." Declaring those views myopic, Whitridge asserted: "I believe we shall have to do something besides hope for victory. . . . Much as we hate war, we shall have to fight, and the sooner we get ready for it, the better."

In the magazine's September issue, the nation's undergraduates—in the person of Brewster, who was chairman of the *Yale Daily News*, and

Spencer Klaw, president of *The Harvard Crimson*—delivered a scornful reply. Under the headline WE STAND HERE, Brewster and Klaw attacked what they saw as Whitridge's "casuistry and acrimony," which they labeled "unworthy" and "unjust." The two student editors argued that only by staying aloof from the war could the United States preserve its democratic way of life. Americans must "take our stand on this side of the Atlantic . . . because at least it offers a chance for the maintenance of all the things we care about in America."

As Brewster's biographer, Geoffrey Kabaservice, noted, the twenty-one-year-old Yale junior was fast becoming "one of the most controversial undergraduates of his day." In addition to coauthoring the *Atlantic Monthly* article, he gave frequent anti-interventionist speeches on campuses throughout the East and took part in a national radio debate on NBC's "America's Town Meeting of the Air." Several of his *Yale Daily News* editorials opposing intervention were picked up by the national press.

But Brewster was doing much more than writing and lecturing. He had emerged as a leading figure in a group of Yale undergraduates and law students who had come together in an effort to combat what they viewed as America's inexorable march toward war. Night after night, the students gathered to discuss ways to counter the growing strength of the interventionist movement, exemplified by the White Committee and the Century Group, which had been so successful in rousing public opinion to support the destroyer transfer and conscription.

The Yale students were convinced that isolationists were still a majority in America. Yet the movement was splintered, with no one group able to tap the country's strong isolationist mood and give it political cohesiveness. While Charles Lindbergh had attracted national attention with his antiwar views, he remained a loner, showing little interest in belonging to or heading any of the existing isolationist organizations.

In the students' view, the American people were being stampeded into war by the Roosevelt administration and the citizens' groups supporting the president. Since no one else was apparently able to provide a rallying point for resistance, they decided to take the lead themselves.

These Yalies could hardly be considered disaffected radicals. Like Kingman Brewster, virtually all of them were or had been top campus leaders. Also like Brewster, a number would go on to have celebrated careers. They included Potter Stewart, a future justice of the U.S. Supreme Court, and his close law school friend, Sargent Shriver, who two decades later would be appointed first head of the Peace Corps by his brother-in-law, President John F. Kennedy. Another participant was Gerald Ford, a former All-American football player at the University of Michigan and future president of the United States.

Their leaders were Brewster, who was considered "the idea man," and law student Robert Douglas Stuart, son of a Quaker Oats executive in Chicago, whose talents lay in organizing and administration. The group kicked off its campaign by circulating nonintervention petitions on campuses throughout the East and recruiting other students and recent graduates to lead opposition to American involvement in the war in their hometowns.

The response was extraordinary. Nearly half the undergraduates at Yale signed the petitions, with similar numbers reported at other colleges. Hundreds of students agreed to spend the summer of 1940 working to organize antiwar opposition, and many more sent money to help the effort. Among the donors was Harvard senior John F. Kennedy, whose $100 check was accompanied by a note that said, "What you are all doing is vital." Kennedy's older brother, Joe, meanwhile, helped organize a Harvard branch of the America First Committee, as the Yale-sponsored group was now called. Another student organizer was fifteen-year-old Gore Vidal, who established an America First chapter at Phillips Exeter, the prep school he attended in New Hampshire.

Brewster and Stuart then set out to make America First a nationwide crusade. Traveling throughout the country, they urged isolationist members of Congress and others to lend them support. But the man whose backing they wanted most was Charles Lindbergh. Not only was he the best-known isolationist in the country, he also had been the childhood hero of virtually every young American their age. These students had been little boys when Lindbergh flew the Atlantic in 1927, and he instantly became their role model. As a child, Robert Stuart used to daydream that Lindbergh would land his plane one day on the three acres behind the Stuarts' home and "I would get to meet him." Kingman Brewster would later note that he had been "a bug on flying" all his life, thanks to his hero worship of Lindbergh. But there was another reason why Stuart, Brewster, and their fellows were so drawn to

*Yale junior Kingman Brewster, a founder of the America First Committee
(on left) welcomes Charles Lindbergh to Yale in October 1940. On the right
is Richard Bissell Jr., a Yale economics instructor who went on to become
deputy director of the CIA after World War II.*

Lindbergh: he was a rebel who, with "his courage and straightforward-
ness," defied authority and could not be bought or intimidated. He
was, in other words, what they aspired to be.

When Stuart and Brewster invited Lindbergh to deliver a major address at Yale in the fall of 1940, he was inclined at first to turn the invitation down, believing that his reception at such a bastion of the East Coast
establishment would be hostile. But he was greatly impressed by the two
young men and their budding movement, and he finally accepted.

On a cool October night, more than three thousand Yale students
packed Woolsey Hall to hear Lindbergh speak. Instead of the heckling
he half expected, he was interrupted again and again by thunderous
cheers and applause. "Most of us were for the first time in the flesh-
and-blood presence of the most famous American of our childhood,
and you could feel the electricity because of that and because of
the sheer magnetism of his presence," recalled the historian Richard
Ketchum, one of the Yalies who attended the speech.

The month before, America First had made its official debut as a national organization. The principles it espoused were close to those of Lindbergh: an impregnable defense for America; preservation of democracy at home by staying out of foreign wars; no aid for Britain beyond "cash and carry." "When the peoples of Europe, Asia, and Africa, ravaged by all the horrors of modern war, turn to Peace at last, America's strength will help rebuild them and bring them back to health and hope," the group's founders declared. Until then, Americans must focus on maintaining their own freedoms and way of life.

With its emergence on the national stage, however, America First became a very different organization from the one created by the students at Yale. Of its initial founders, only Robert Stuart remained heavily involved on a day-to-day basis, emerging as America First's executive director. Its national headquarters was transferred to Chicago, Stuart's hometown, after his father agreed to provide rent-free space in the Quaker Oats executive offices there.

From then on, most of America First's leaders would be midwestern businessmen whose social and political views were considerably more conservative than those of the group's founders. Although most of the Yale students came from privileged backgrounds, they regarded themselves as moderates or liberals. Kingman Brewster, for one, applauded many of FDR's New Deal reforms in his *Yale Daily News* editorials and rejected membership in Skull and Bones, the school's most exclusive and revered secret society, because he considered it undemocratic.

In organizing America First, Brewster and Stuart had worked hard to make it a moderate, bipartisan group, whose ideas were "in agreement with the great majority of Americans of all ages." When it moved to Chicago, Brewster, who would remain as chairman of its Yale chapter, warned Stuart not to overload the organization with conservatives. Its leading members, he said, should be known and respected throughout the country—"substantial and prominent, but not stuffy and corporate. You need laborites and progressives. It would be awful if the committee turned out to be the instrument of one class."

Initially, America First lived up to Brewster's expectations, attracting people with widely varying social and economic views. The group encompassed conservatives and liberals; Republicans, Democrats, and independents; Protestants, Catholics, and Jews. Among the liberals who supported its aims were longtime pacifists such as the former *Nation* editor Oswald Garrison Villard and Norman Thomas, head of the American Socialist Party, who in 1938 formed an antiwar organization called Keep America Out of War Congress. Like other liberal pacifists, Villard and Thomas feared that going to war would greatly damage American democracy, giving rise to severe restrictions on civil liberties, destruction of New Deal social reforms, and a resurgence of right-wing sentiment.

Increasingly, however, the organization encountered difficulty in persuading prominent liberals, particularly intellectuals, to join. Robert Maynard Hutchins, the University of Chicago's outspokenly isolationist president, was one of many such figures whose views coincided with those of the group but who declined to become members.

As a result, within months of its founding, America First had become the conservative-dominated organization against which Kingman Brewster had warned.

NEITHER THE MIDWEST NOR the East was homogeneous in regard to their residents' attitudes toward America's involvement in the war. The country's heartland, with Chicago as its hub, contained a fair share of interventionists, just as isolationism maintained a strong presence in New York and on the rest of the Eastern Seaboard. Nonetheless, America First drew its greatest strength from the traditionally isolationist Midwest, while the White Committee and the Century Group continued to find their greatest support among the internationalist East Coast establishment. Of the nearly one million people who joined America First in the fourteen months of its existence, nearly two-thirds lived within a three-hundred-mile radius of Chicago, an area encompassing Illinois, Wisconsin, Indiana, Michigan, and parts of Ohio, Missouri, Minnesota, and Iowa.

The differences between Chicago and New York—and their outlook on the war—were evident in the two cities' disparate reactions to the release of a provocative British film, *Pastor Hall,* in the summer of 1940. Based on the true story of Martin Niemoller, a German Protestant minister who was sent to the Dachau concentration camp for speaking out against the Nazis, *Pastor Hall* featured graphic scenes of Nazi brutality—"an apocalyptic vision of horror seen through a barbed wire fence," as *The New York Times* put it.

Initially, no Hollywood studio would agree to distribute the controversial film. Through the intercession of FDR's son James, who fancied himself an independent producer, United Artists was finally persuaded to do so. The American print of the movie contained a short introduction written by Robert Sherwood and read by Eleanor Roosevelt, which called *Pastor Hall* "a story of the spirit of hatred, intolerance, suppression of liberty, which is now sweeping over the face of this earth."

When the movie opened in New York, it sparked not only critical acclaim but an anti-Nazi demonstration in Times Square. In Chicago, however, the city's film censorship board barred *Pastor Hall*'s release because it depicted Nazi Germany in an unfavorable light. German Americans made up a large percentage of Chicago's population, and, under considerable pressure from German American organizations, the censorship board issued its ban, citing a city ordinance that prohibited the "display of depravity, criminality or lack of virtue in a class of citizens of any race."

Pastor Hall was not the first anti-Nazi film to be barred by the board; in the previous two years, it had prohibited at least seven other such movies from being shown. At the same time, however, it allowed the release of *Feldzug in Polen,* a propaganda film produced by the German government that depicted the Wehrmacht's vanquishing of Poland in 1939 and portrayed Poland as the aggressor.

Noting this discrepancy, several Chicago organizations, including the local chapters of the American Civil Liberties Union and the American Jewish Congress, protested the banning of *Pastor Hall,* as did a number of women's clubs. Frank Knox's *Chicago Daily News* attacked what the paper called the "Nazi sensibilities" of the board. Faced with a barrage of unfavorable publicity, Chicago's mayor, Edward Kelly, ordered the censorship group to reconsider. Reluctantly, it reversed itself and cleared the film for showing.

Unquestionably, the sizable number of German Americans in Chicago, along with its significant (and generally anti-British) Irish American population, helped make the Windy City a center of isolationist sentiment. But other key factors, including geography, were also at work. Living in the middle of the country as they did, many if not most residents of Chicago (and other parts of the Midwest) had never had much to do with the rest of the world, nor did they worry about threats from abroad. In their view, the seemingly boundless spaces of America, protected by two oceans, offered a security available to no other country.

Also playing a role in the area's isolationist attitude was the resentment that many Chicagoans and other midwesterners felt toward what they viewed as the effete, snobbish East, with its close ties to the equally arrogant British. The second-largest city in the country and a stronghold of American industry, Chicago gloried in its bustle, swagger, and energy and considered itself, not New York, as America's dominant metropolis. It had nothing but contempt for critics such as British writer Rudyard Kipling, who, after a visit to Chicago, declared, "Having seen it, I urgently desire never to see it again. It is inhabited by savages."

In 1927, the city's mayor, "Big Bill" Thompson, whose informal alliance with the gangster Al Capone had helped produce an explosion of violent crime and government corruption, told his supporters that America's No. 1 enemy was George V. If the British king ever dared to set foot in Chicago, Thompson declared, he would punch him in the face.

Although sharply critical of Thompson's "moronic buffoonery" and "triumphant hoodlumism," Chicago's leading newspaper, the *Tribune,* and its flamboyant publisher, Robert McCormick, shared the mayor's implacable Anglophobia, as well as his belief that Chicago, rather than the hated East, was the center of the universe. Journalist John Gunther, a Chicago native, once described the *Tribune* as "aggressive, sensitive in the extreme, loaded with guts and braggadocio, expansionist, and medieval." It was an apt description of McCormick as well.

McCormick dubbed the *Tribune* "the World's Greatest Newspaper" and told his staff, "We are the most vital single force at the center of the world." Proudly provincial, he had nothing but contempt for anybody and anything east of the Mississippi. "The trouble with you people out there is that you can't see beyond Ohio," he remarked to a *New York Times* reporter. "And when you think of taking a trip farther west than Ohio, you think you're Buffalo Bill."

Chicago Tribune *publisher*
Robert McCormick.

To McCormick, New York was "a Sodom and Gomorrah of sin."
He described its youth as "immoral and its mature people burned out.
It is the reservoir of evil from which disintegrating revolutionary doctrine spreads over the country." In his view, Washington and the Roosevelt administration were equally wicked. He once urged that the
nation's capital be moved from Washington to a more representative
American city, like Grand Rapids, Michigan.

The archreactionary McCormick hated Roosevelt and the New
Deal with an unadulterated passion. The Democratic Congress, he declared, was "dominated and driven by Red members who are working
to destroy our government and civilization, and who in turn are supported by that group of scholastic morons calling themselves progressives and Liberals, whose principal concern is to make private enterprise
unprofitable." When Roosevelt ran for reelection in 1936, *Tribune* telephone operators were instructed to answer each call with the greeting:
"Did you know that there are only [X] more days to save the country?"

One of McCormick's great pleasures in life was to come up with
new ways to bait the president, who had been his classmate at Groton.
In 1937, the publisher learned that FDR was to make a speech in Chicago, directly opposite a *Tribune* warehouse on the north bank of the
Chicago River. McCormick dispatched several workers to the ware-

house, where, in letters ten feet high, they painted the single word UNDOMINATED over a sign reading CHICAGO TRIBUNE "THE WORLD'S GREATEST NEWSPAPER."

Along with William Randolph Hearst, McCormick and his two first cousins—Joseph Patterson, owner of the New York *Daily News,* and Eleanor "Cissy" Patterson, who ran the *Washington Times-Herald*— were the foremost isolationist publishers in the country. With its million-plus circulation and readership throughout five states, the *Tribune* in particular was a force to be reckoned with. Its huge staff included reporters in four domestic bureaus and a dozen bureaus in Europe and Asia. Among the paper's journalistic alumni were such distinguished foreign correspondents as William L. Shirer, Vincent Sheean, Floyd Gibbons, George Seldes, and Sigrid Schultz.

Inevitably, however, the high quality of these stars' reporting came into conflict with McCormick's insistence that *Tribune* stories reflect his own peeves and prejudices—particularly his hatred of Roosevelt, the East Coast, and the British, whose imperialism, he claimed, was no different from Nazi aggression. "The *Tribune* hammers away violently on the theme that the Roosevelt Administration is willfully ruining the country and purposely sabotaging democracy," a *Life* article noted in December 1941. "Just plain, common, ordinary hatred of Roosevelt is a factor in isolationism that, particularly in parts of Chicago, is a definite cult."

According to those who knew McCormick, his loathing of Britain and the East had roots in his childhood; as a boy, he had spent several unhappy years in both places. Early in his life, his father had been named U.S. ambassador to Britain, and young Robert, who was tall, shy, and awkward, was shipped off to a British boarding school, where his upper-class schoolmates looked down on him as an uncultured, bumbling American.

A few years later, McCormick attended Groton, where he received the same scornful treatment. "Condescension shot from his classmates like ink from a squid," McCormick's biographer, Richard Norton Smith, wrote. "It left [him] permanently embittered against New Englanders as latter-day colonials infatuated with their mother country."

Curiously, despite his antipathy toward Britain, McCormick as an adult adopted the lifestyle of an English country squire. He wore Savile Row suits, ordered his shoes from the eminent London firm of

John Lobb, spoke with a quasi-British accent, played polo, and rode to hounds. One can only speculate how different the future might have been for McCormick, the *Tribune,* and the fight over the war if the boys at his English school had been a little kinder to him.

As it was, he and his paper were, without doubt, the most strident journalistic voices in the isolationist movement, as well as strong backers of America First. Although McCormick never joined the organization, he gave it considerable money and favorable coverage and was a close friend of several of its leaders.

IN EARLY 1941, *Fortune* sent an investigative reporter to Chicago to look into America First. In a long memo that was passed along to the White House, the correspondent wrote that "the backbone of this committee are the vitriolic Roosevelt haters associated with 'big business.' It is they who supply most of its funds; they who shape its policy; and they, who with the support of the *Chicago Tribune,* have made it virtually impossible for any prominent Chicagoan to assume the leadership of the interventionist drive here."

Actually, the chairman of America First, General Robert Wood, had vigorously supported FDR and the New Deal in the first few years of the president's tenure, one of the few top business executives in the country to do so. Chief executive of the merchandising giant Sears, Roebuck, Wood was a graduate of West Point who had helped organize construction of the Panama Canal and served as quartermaster general of the Army during World War I. In the 1920s and 1930s, he had turned Sears into the country's leading retail store chain, shifting its emphasis from mail order sales to retail outlets.

In the late 1930s, Wood broke with FDR over his Court reform plan, as well as what he considered the administration's increasingly antagonistic attitude toward business. He also opposed Roosevelt's interventionist foreign policy, believing that American capitalism would collapse if the United States became involved in another war. Wood equated a U.S. alliance with Britain to "a well-organized, money-making business deciding to take a bankrupt firm in as partner." The British, he thought, should make a negotiated peace with Germany, leaving America free to go its own way.

At first, Wood had been reluctant to take the job as America First chairman, declaring that his work at Sears left him little time to do anything else. But Robert Stuart, who helped recruit Wood, convinced him that his participation was vital to the anti-interventionist effort. Wood's high standing in Chicago's business community lured other prominent corporate leaders—most of them Republican and anti–New Deal and several from Chicago's great industrial families—to the organization's fold. Among those joining its executive committee were Sterling Morton of Morton Salt and Jay Hormel, president of Hormel Meat Packing Co. The group's most significant financial backer was the textile manufacturer William Regnery, another early supporter of Roosevelt who abandoned him in the late 1930s. (Regnery's son, Henry, would go on to found the conservative publishing company that bears his family's name.)

For its advertising and publicity campaigns, America First could draw on the talents of three Madison Avenue legends, all of whom had helped transform the country's advertising industry into a corporate behemoth. Bruce Barton, a founder of the New York firm Batten, Barton, Durstine and Osborn, was a wizard at selling his ideas to the American people, among them the concept that Jesus Christ was in fact the founder of modern business. In his enormously popular book *The Man Nobody Knows,* Barton, who in 1936 was elected to Congress as a Republican, wrote that the parables of Jesus "were the most powerful advertisements of all time," and that if Jesus were alive today, he would be the head of a national advertising agency.

Joining Barton were William Benton and Chester Bowles, who, unlike the New York congressman, were liberal Democrats. Classmates at Yale, the two came together in 1929, five years after their graduation, to found Benton & Bowles, another powerhouse firm on Madison Avenue. Flourishing throughout the Depression, Benton & Bowles was the first advertising company to produce radio programs for networks, taking on the job of packaging casts, directors, scripts, and sponsors. By the mid-1930s, the firm was responsible for most of the top-rated shows on radio.

Benton had always vowed that once he made $10 million, he would abandon advertising for public service. At the age of thirty-six, he did so, becoming vice president of the University of Chicago and adviser to its president, Robert Maynard Hutchins. Benton was part of America First's intellectual brain trust, counseling the group on strategy and serving as an intermediary between it and Hutchins.

Bowles stayed on at Benton & Bowles, although, as he soon found out, it was not easy being a well-known supporter of America First in New York. "Several of our clients feel very emphatic against the stand that I have taken," he wrote an acquaintance. "Advertising is one helluva business—you can never call your soul your own. And whether you like it or not, you are usually more or less owned by the clients for whom you work."

Gerald Ford, as it happened, also discovered the hazards of espousing isolationism in the interventionist East. Just a few months after helping to found America First, Ford resigned from the committee, explaining he'd been warned by Yale officials that he might lose his part-time job as the school's assistant football coach because of his connection with the group. While no longer officially part of America First, Ford vowed to continue working on its behalf, adding, "As a matter of fact, I shall probably spend more time just as a bit of spite."*

Among the few other prominent easterners willing to take on leadership roles in the group were two children of Theodore Roosevelt—Alice Roosevelt Longworth and her brother Theodore Jr. A longtime isolationist, the wasp-tongued Alice had worked alongside her lover, Senator William Borah, to defeat Woodrow Wilson and the League of Nations in 1919. Indeed, Borah and the League's other senatorial opponents met at her Washington house to plot strategy.

Although ideology played an important part in the Roosevelt siblings' connection to America First, it was also fueled by a sharp personal animosity toward their distant cousin in the White House and his wife, Eleanor, their first cousin. Both Alice and Theodore Jr. thought of Franklin Roosevelt as a usurper who had no right to follow in their father's footsteps. "Alice has the outstanding Oedipus complex in American public life," noted a confidential report prepared by the White Committee on America First. "Having glorified Theodore and his service, [she feels] that any man in the White House since then has

---

* Interventionists in Chicago had similar problems. Adlai Stevenson, a well-known lawyer there, was told by his law partners that his chairmanship of the White Committee's Chicago chapter had antagonized many of the firm's clients and that he would have to choose between the firm and his interventionist activities. Stevenson solved the problem by taking a government position in Washington.

been, by definition, an impostor." At the 1940 Republican convention in Philadelphia, Alice spread the word that the initials "FDR" really stood for "Fuehrer, Duce, Roosevelt." Her brother, for his part, "always felt that Franklin was getting everything *he* was entitled to," a relative recalled. "Ted was always the instigator of anti-Franklin feeling."

As useful as the Roosevelts and others were in promoting the mission of America First, Robert Wood wanted one man above all— Charles Lindbergh—in the group's leadership. Over the next year, Wood tried repeatedly to step down as chairman, hoping that Lindbergh would succeed him, but was continually thwarted. Although Lindbergh admired and supported the work of the organization, he insisted, as usual, on going his own way. When asked to attend the 1940 Republican convention as a delegate, he declined, saying that to do so would compromise his nonpartisan position.

In the end, Robert Stuart thought it was just as well that Lindbergh kept his distance. Although the flier remained a hero of his, Stuart was uneasy about the extreme conservatism of some of Lindbergh's closest associates, particularly Truman Smith and former undersecretary of state William Castle. He also worried that if Lindbergh became too closely associated with America First, "the smear campaign which had been leveled against him throughout the country" would be directed at it as well. Another lightning rod was the last thing that the organization needed.

DESPITE EFFORTS BY ITS leaders to keep their distance from any groups or individuals likely to bring discredit on it, America First faced problems in maintaining an image of moderation and respectability almost as soon as it moved to Chicago. There was little doubt that most of its leadership and members were, as one historian wrote, "decent, honest, sincere citizens who passionately believed that foreign entanglements were bad for the United States and that, if menace to their safety came from overseas, they were better off meeting it alone." The group, which was described by a staffer as "American as the hot dog," officially banned anybody who belonged to Communist or pro-Fascist groups.

Nonetheless, it suffered from an insuperable handicap: its

objective—keeping America neutral—was also the goal of Hitler and those who supported him. "Because it was to Germany's advantage for the United States to stay out of war, it was inevitable that America First would be accused of pro-Nazism," acknowledged Ruth Sarles, the organization's Washington director. "Likewise, it was inevitable that real pro-Nazis would attempt to get on the America First bandwagon."

As the committee gained influence, a host of extremists, most of them right-wing, flocked to enlist under its banner. Initially, they were turned away. But many local chapters—there were more than four hundred by December 1941—were extremely relaxed in their membership standards and accepted people who, under the organization's guidelines, should have been rejected. The small, overworked national staff in Chicago found it impossible to provide proper supervision. As a result, the local committees varied widely: in some cities, as one observer noted, they were "a typical hodgepodge of sincere citizens, disillusioned supporters of Wendell Willkie, and inveterate joiners," while in other places, the chapters were dominated by "either a crust or core of bigots."

The organization, Ruth Sarles conceded, was particularly bedeviled by anti-Semitism. "There is no doubt," she wrote, "that there were anti-Semites among the rank-and-file members." Indeed, "there is evidence that some passionately anti-Semitic individuals deliberately sought to further anti-Semitism by working through the America First Committee."

In the beginning, at least, Robert Wood tried hard to avoid any hint of anti-Jewish prejudice. He had a personal reason for doing so: his company was owned by a Jewish family, the Rosenwalds, with whom he had a close relationship. At the same time, he and America First's other leaders created some of their own problems by appointing to the national committee two men who were regarded as flagrantly anti-Semitic.

The first was Avery Brundage, a wealthy Chicago construction executive who was also president of the U.S. Olympic Committee. In 1936, Brundage had created a national furor as a result of his actions at that year's summer Olympic games in Nazi Germany. Not only did he reject proposals from American Jewish organizations and other religious groups to boycott the Berlin Olympics, he gave in to German pressure to prevent Jewish athletes from participating in the games. At Brundage's insistence, the only two Jews on the U.S. teams—both of them track and field athletes—were replaced just before the 400-meter relay race.* Shortly after the Olympics were over, Hitler's government awarded Brundage's construction company a contract to build a new German embassy in Washington.

Embarrassing as it was, the uproar over Brundage's appointment to the America First Committee was minor compared to the fury aroused by the other choice: car manufacturer Henry Ford, whose blatant anti-Semitism had been praised by Hitler in *Mein Kampf*. In the early 1920s, the *Dearborn Independent,* a weekly newspaper published by Ford, ran dozens of virulently anti-Jewish articles, including the text of the notorious "Protocols of the Elders of Zion," a fraudulent document purporting to be the proceedings of an international Jewish conference plotting world domination. According to the historian Norman Cohn, the *Independent* "probably did more than any other work to make the Protocols famous."

The *Independent* and its publisher swiftly attracted the attention of Hitler, still a relatively unknown political agitator at that point, who displayed copies of the paper in his modest Munich office and hung a portrait of Ford on the wall. In the preface to *Mein Kampf,* Hitler praised Ford for the "great service" he had provided America and the world through his attacks on the Jews. In a 1923 interview with the *Chicago Tribune,* the future German leader declared: "We look to Heinrich Ford as the leader of the growing fascist movement in America."

Given Ford's decidedly unsavory background, it was astonishing that Wood could be so obtuse as to believe, as he apparently did, that the car maker's appointment might be accepted by the Jewish community if a prominent Jewish businessman—Sears director Lessing Rosenwald—was named to the committee at the same time. America First announced the two new members simultaneously, apparently hoping to demonstrate that people with widely varying views could put their differences aside to band together in the anti-intervention cause.

If that was the group's expectation, it failed spectacularly. The an-

* One of the substitutes was Jesse Owens, the black track and field superstar who won four gold medals in Berlin, including one for the 400-meter relay.

nouncement touched off a deluge of attacks on America First, culminating in Lessing Rosenwald's resignation from the organization and its executive board voting to drop Ford from the national committee. In what turned out to be a massive understatement, Robert Stuart wrote: "I am now convinced that we made a grave mistake." From then on, no prominent Jew would agree to be affiliated, at least publicly, with America First.

FOR A NUMBER OF anti-Semitic, isolationist fringe groups in America, Henry Ford was both an inspiration and a patron. His well-publicized, if brief, membership in America First helped bring many of their members into the committee's ranks.

This ragtag collection of extremists was united only by their tendency to blame the country's problems on those they considered threats to true Americanism, particularly Jews and Communists (usually conflated into one group), immigrants, the Eastern elite, and the Roosevelt administration. Such misplaced nativism had been fueled in large part by the massive social and economic upheaval that sent shock waves through America in the 1920s and 1930s. The Depression, the relaxed standards of conduct of the Roaring Twenties, and the collapse of Wilsonian idealism all produced tension, anxiety, and anger not only among the unemployed and dispossessed but in all social classes. The historian Richard Ketchum, who grew up in a middle-class home in Pittsburgh, recalled that "beneath the generally serene surface of life on my quiet street . . . was a layer of insecurity, a fear of the unknown and the unacceptable, an instinctive shying away from the alien. . . . A kind of thoughtless prejudice was the way of our carefully structured world."

The need to find scapegoats for the misery and uncertainty of modern life helped contribute to a growth in racial and religious intolerance that in many cases exploded into hatred. Groups with names like the Black Legion, Crusaders for America, and the Knights of the White Camellia sprang up like mushrooms after a rain. In the late 1930s, Eric Sevareid, then a reporter for a Minneapolis newspaper, was assigned to report on the activities of another such group, called the Silver Shirts, whose founder, William Dudley Pelley, was supposedly intent on marching on Washington to take over the country and rid it of Jews.

Sevareid's investigation of the Silver Shirts was "an unbelievably weird experience," he recalled, "like Alice going down the rabbit hole into the world of the Mad Hatter. I spent hair-raising evenings in the parlors of middle-class citizens who sang the praises of Adolf Hitler and longed for the day when Pelley would come to power as the Hitler of the U.S. . . . They were quite mad."

Another nativist group drawing considerable attention was the Vindicator Association, an anti-immigration movement fostered by Senator Robert Reynolds, who became chairman of the Senate Military Affairs Committee in 1941. A conservative Democrat from North Carolina, Reynolds was a passionate isolationist and Anglophobe, one of the few southerners in Congress holding those views. He had created the Vindicators, he said, to keep America out of war, stop all immigration for at least ten years, and "banish all isms but Americanism." Young people were encouraged to join the association's "border patrol" and catch "alien criminals," receiving ten dollars a head for each one they nabbed.

Reynolds's bill to impose a ten-year ban on immigration was one of more than sixty anti-alien and anti-immigration measures under consideration by Congress in the late 1930s and early 1940s. Rep. Martin Dies, chairman of the House Un-American Activities Committee, expressed the xenophobic attitude of many legislators when he thundered: "We must ignore the tears of sobbing sentimentalists and internationalists, and must permanently close, lock, and bar the gates of our country to new immigration waves and then throw the keys away."

Reynolds, for his part, bristled at any suggestion that his association was anti-Semitic. "We're just anti-alien," he told a reporter. "I want our own fine boys and lovely girls to have all the jobs in this wonderful country."

For all the attention paid to them, however, Reynolds's extremist group and most others like it had relatively small memberships and limited influence. The same could not be said for the mass movement begun by a rabble-rousing Catholic priest named Charles Coughlin, a close ally of Henry Ford, whose weekly radio broadcasts at their peak were heard by upwards of forty million listeners. Coughlin, who broadcast from church facilities in a Detroit suburb, thought of himself as a champion of the workingman and regularly delivered anti-government, anti–Wall Street diatribes. Deeply anti-Semitic, he also denounced the "anti-Christian conspiracy" of Jews, Communists, FDR, and the British. During the 1940 presidential campaign, Coughlin made a number of savage attacks on the president, during which he also spoke approvingly of Hitler and Mussolini, praised Nazi persecution of the Jews, and charged that Jewish bankers had financed the Russian Revolution. "When we get through with the Jews in America," he declared, "they'll think the treatment they received in Germany was nothing."

Much of Coughlin's support came from urban, blue-collar Catholics; he was particularly popular with working-class Irish American communities in Boston, New York, Chicago, and other cities. But his followers also included people such as Philip Johnson, a Harvard student from an eminent Ohio family who in later years would emerge as one of America's most celebrated and influential architects. Johnson became enamored with Nazism while traveling through Germany in the early 1930s. In 1939, he was sent to Berlin as a correspondent for Coughlin's anti-Semitic newspaper, *Social Justice*.

During the German invasion of Poland, Johnson visited the front with other foreign journalists at the invitation of Hitler's government. The CBS correspondent William L. Shirer, who was along on the trip, was forced by German propaganda officials to share a hotel room with Johnson in the Polish city of Sopot. "None of us can stand the fellow and suspect he is spying on us for the Nazis," Shirer grumbled in his diary. "For the last hour in our room, he has been posing as anti-Nazi and trying to pump me for my attitude."

Whatever Johnson was, he was, most assuredly, not anti-Nazi. In a letter home describing his tour of devastated Poland, he wrote: "The German green uniforms made the place look gay and happy. There were not many Jews to be seen. We saw Warsaw and Modlin being bombed. It was a stirring spectacle."*

Johnson's dispatches from Germany were published in *Social Justice*, a weekly tabloid that was mailed to subscribers and sold on city streets by youthful members of Coughlin's movement, who used their peddling as a way to pick fights with pedestrians who appeared to be Jewish. After denigrating such passersby and demanding they buy the

---

* In later years, Johnson would repent of his notorious past. "I have no excuse [for] such unbelievable stupidity," he said. "I don't know how you expiate guilt."

publication, Coughlin's bullyboys would often jump their targets and beat them up.

Throughout the early 1940s, the assaults on Jews in New York, Boston, and other cities grew in number and intensity. Bands of Coughlin supporters, many brandishing brass knuckles, attacked Jews on the street and in parks, desecrated Jewish cemeteries, and vandalized synagogues and Jewish-owned stores. *PM,* a New York liberal daily, called the violence an "organized campaign of terrorism."

To its chagrin, America First found itself increasingly linked with Father Coughlin and his followers. Vendors of *Social Justice* often gathered on the sidewalk outside America First rallies to sell their papers and harass those passing by. In a memo to local chapters, Ruth Sarles called the Coughlinites and other such organizations "a menace." She noted that they "wriggled like termites into various committee activities," causing many people to equate their point of view with that of America First. Although Sarles and committee leaders denounced such commingling, the fact remained that many local chapters happily accepted Coughlin supporters and other extremists as members, with Coughlin himself urging his followers to join the anti-interventionist group.

It was hardly surprising, then, that as the debate over the war intensified in late 1940 and early 1941, the interventionist critics of America First would feel no compunction in condemning the organization as "a Nazi transmission belt" and the "first fascist party in this nation's history."

CHAPTER 16

"THE BUBONIC PLAGUE AMONG WRITERS"

From the day she returned to the United States from Europe in the spring of 1939, Anne Lindbergh was determined to stay out of the spotlight: she wanted no involvement in the furor over the war. But the vitriolic criticism of her husband prompted her to rethink her position.

By the fall of 1940, it was open season on Charles Lindbergh. According to *Christian Century,* the flagship magazine of U.S. Protestantism, "the attack launched against Lindbergh has gone far beyond the ordinary canons of debate. It has pulsed with venom. If this man, who was once the nation's shining hero, had been proved another Benedict Arnold, he could not have been subjected to more defamation and calumny."

Lindbergh, dispassionate as always, revealed little or no emotion himself when he criticized the Roosevelt administration and his other interventionist opponents. As one newspaper noted, "he never 'gets personal,' is never abusive, indulges in no innuendoes or sly intimations, is severely factual and logical." Neither he nor Anne, who had grown up in a sheltered world where civility ruled, was able to understand why his critics could not keep their arguments on a similarly high plane.

In August 1940, Lindbergh showed Anne a couple of "very angry" telegrams from old friends. One read, "You have let America down"; the other, "You stand for all the atrocities of Hitler." Anne was stunned by their nastiness. "They had a right to criticize—but to throw mud, to leave issues and simply hurl names!" she wrote in her diary. "It shocks me, for they supposedly are the intelligent, the moderate, the tolerant."

When she reread her diary almost forty years later, Anne was appalled by her youthful, naïve "innocence of politics and the violence of my indignation." At the time, however, she felt compelled, "because of . . . my desperate feeling of the injustice [done] to C.," to explain and defend her husband and his position on the war, even though she still was unsure of her own feelings about it.

Although Anne had adopted Charles's views, she did not wholeheartedly believe in isolationism. Nor did she think much of others in the isolationist camp: "The arguments of the isolationists are so often narrow, materialistic, short-sighted, and wholly selfish—I am repelled by them."

She became even more conflicted after reading letters, shown to her by Con and Aubrey Morgan, from friends of the Morgans in Britain who were facing the Luftwaffe onslaught. "They are thrilling letters," Anne admitted, "infused with a kind of fire of sacrifice, gallantry, beauty of spirit, sureness of purpose, and courage heedless of danger, death, or discouragement. It is, as they say, truly Elizabethan." Later, she wrote: "When you hear this side, you feel the British are right to resist to the end, that there is no hope of dealing with the Germans."

In late August 1940, Anne sat down to compose what she called "a moral argument for isolationism," trying to reconcile "the terrible struggle that goes on eternally between [one's] heart, which is in Europe, and [one's] mind, which is trying to be American and determine what is the best course for this country." The result was an odd, muddled little book she called *The Wave of the Future.* The book's subtitle was *A Confession of Faith,* but Con Morgan thought a more apt subtitle would be *A Confession of Doubt,* to underscore the identity crisis its author was obviously experiencing, "torn as she was between being Anne Morrow and Mrs. Charles Lindbergh."

When one reads *The Wave of the Future,* it becomes clear that Anne had not resolved her doubts or cleared up her confusion in regard to the issues she wrote about. Her ideas are half-baked, her writing cloudy, imprecise, poetic, somewhat mystical, and illogical. Teasing out what she was trying to say is virtually impossible. According to *Life,* even her husband did "not fully understand" the book.

Its main point seemed to be that totalitarian ideologies like Fascism and Communism had been highly successful in using modern technological and scientific advances to instill energy, dynamism, and a sense of self-sacrifice and pride in the people under their control. Those ideologies were riding a revolutionary "wave of the future," a concept Anne did not really explain, except to say, "I keep feeling that it could be directed, it could be a force for good in the world, if only it could be looked at, acknowledged, turned in the right direction." She added that it "was not done right in Germany or Russia, but maybe could be done right" in America.

Anne labeled Nazism and other totalitarian beliefs "scum on the wave of the future." At the same time, she was severely critical of what she saw as the sins of the world's democracies—"blindness, selfishness, irresponsibility, smugness, lethargy, and resistance to change—sins which we 'Democracies,' all of us, are guilty of." To many if not most readers of her book, she seemed to be equating the inadequacies of free nations with the wanton aggression and brutal persecutions carried out by Germany and other dictatorships.

Instead of "climbing down into the maelstrom of war" and trying to combat what was in fact a revolution in Europe, Anne wrote, America must focus on reforming itself, on building a new society that would harness this amorphous "wave of the future" for the good of the country and the world. "There is no fighting the wave of the future, any more than as a child you could fight against the gigantic roller that loomed up ahead of you suddenly," she warned. "You learned then it was hopeless to stand against it or, even worse, to run away. All you could do was to dive into it or leap with it. Otherwise, it would surely overwhelm you."

From the moment she began writing *The Wave of the Future,* Anne had forebodings about the negative reaction she was sure it would receive. "It will be considered anti-British and 'tainted' with German propaganda (though I don't defend—and am outspoken in my dislike of the horrors in Germany—also of my admiration for the English)," she wrote. In reality, neither the dislike nor the admiration she mentions comes through clearly in the book.

Anne was also aware that her lack of credentials as an expert in the subjects she was writing about would draw fire from her critics. Among them was a friend to whom she showed the manuscript before publication. He "gave me back all my own doubts and fears on it and myself," she glumly noted. He called it "presumptuous—that I had no right to write it without more knowledge of history, economics, foreign affairs, etc. That it would be torn limb from limb. That it would be called—with some justification—'Fifth column.' That it would do C. no good and me, harm."

Her friend was right. Anne's book was published in October 1940 at the height of the Blitz, when the supposedly lethargic British, by her lights, were demonstrating the same pride, resolution, and self-sacrifice that she had attributed to Germany and other totalitarian states. Despite its ill-starred timing, *The Wave of the Future* swiftly became the No. 1 nonfiction bestseller in the country—fifty thousand copies were sold in the first two months—but most of the reaction, from critics and readers alike, was intensely unfavorable. One bookseller wrote Alfred Harcourt, Anne's publisher, that both Lindberghs "should be put behind barbed wire!"

Yet at least one reviewer—E. B. White, the noted essayist and children's book writer—was able to look beyond Anne's murky prose and hazy analysis to offer a balanced, judicious assessment of its author. "I couldn't make out what it is she believes in, and I did not think it a clear book or a good one," White wrote in *The New Yorker*. But he added that although he thought she was wrongheaded in her conclusions, "I do not believe that Mrs. Lindbergh is any more fascist-minded than I am, or that she wants a different sort of world, or that she is a defeatist; but I think instead she is a poetical and liberal and talented person troubled in her mind (as anybody is today) and trying to write her way into the clear."

Few other comments about the book were as perceptive or broadminded. Dorothy Thompson accused Anne of calling Communism, Fascism, and Nazism "the wave of the future" and implied that the book would be used as a handbook by Charles Lindbergh to create a Fascist movement in the United States. Echoing that view, Harold

Ickes labeled *The Wave of the Future* "the Bible of every American Nazi, fascist, Bundist and Appeaser." Half a decade later, Arthur Schlesinger Jr., in his autobiography, would refer to Anne's book as a "poisonous little bestseller" that saw totalitarianism as a "new and perhaps even ultimately good, conception of humanity trying to come to birth."

Anne was appalled by what she considered the critics' flagrant misquotation and misinterpretation of her work. "I never said Totalitarianism was the wave of the future," she wrote in her diary. "In fact, I said emphatically that it was *not*—and that I hoped we in America could be, in our way." In an article in *The Atlantic Monthly,* she attempted to set the record straight, reiterating that she regarded Fascism, Communism, and Nazism as "scum on the surface of the wave" of the future, not the wave itself. "To me, the wave of the future is . . . a movement of adjustment to a highly scientific, mechanized and material era of civilization . . . and it seems to me inevitable. I feel we must face this wave [but] do not say we must meet it in the same way as the dictator-governed nations. I oppose that way from the depths of my conviction."

Many years later, Anne would reveal how deeply she regretted writing the book. "It was a mistake," she said in a television interview. "It didn't help anybody . . . I didn't have the right to write it. I didn't know enough." At the time, she was shattered by the overwhelmingly negative reaction and furious at herself for not having had the literary skill to clearly explain her ideas to her readers. Not only had she failed in her mission to offer a persuasive defense of isolationism, she herself was now regarded by many as a leading proponent of Fascism. "Will I have to bear this lie through life?" she wondered in despair.

She was particularly upset by her estrangement from those she considered kindred spirits, notably writers; having created her own niche in that community, she now felt exiled from it. "My marriage," she observed sadly, "has stretched me out of my world, changed me so it is no longer possible to change back."

When a friend called to ask the Lindberghs to dinner with the novelist Robert Nathan and his wife, Anne asked her hostess if she was sure the Nathans wanted to see them. She was thrilled when the woman said yes. "Perhaps I am wrong," Anne thought, "perhaps people do not feel so bitterly, perhaps the two worlds can meet. Perhaps I myself have been raising a glass wall where one didn't exist." The next day, how-

French aviator and writer Antoine de Saint-Exupéry.

ever, her friend called back to say that the Nathans did in fact "feel bitterly." A dispirited Anne commented in her diary: "After all, it is just as I thought."

Her pain was compounded when she discovered that the French aviator and writer Antoine de Saint-Exupéry was in New York and that because he was "on the other side," she would not be able to see him. The year before, she had become emotionally involved with Saint-Exupéry after he wrote a highly laudatory preface to the French edition of her book *Listen! The Wind*. Even before they met, she felt a deep kinship with the French aristocrat turned mail pilot, whose best-selling books—*Wind, Sand and Stars* and *Night Flight*—described the exhilaration and dangers of flying and human relationships in lyrical, mystical language that Anne greatly admired. He, in turn, was so taken with *Listen! The Wind* that he insisted on writing a much longer preface than the publisher requested and regaled his fellow pilots with passages from the book.

In August 1939, the charming, voluble Saint-Exupéry spent a week-end with the Lindberghs at their house on the north shore of Long Island. He did not speak English, and Anne's French was somewhat halting. Nonetheless, the two were in each other's company for hours, pouring out their thoughts about writing and life. She was overwhelmed by his interest in her—"not because I was a woman to be polite to, to charm with superficials, not because I was my father's daughter or C.'s wife; no, simply because of my book, my mind, my *craft*."

In breathless, schoolgirl-like prose, Anne described in her diary that precious time with Saint-Exupéry, comparing their encounter to "summer lightning" and declaring, "My heavens, what a joy it was to talk, to compare, to throw things out, to be understood like that without an effort." She had finally found a soulmate, and for the rest of her life, she would look back on that weekend as one of the happiest, most exhilarating times she had ever spent. She missed Saint-Exupéry terribly when he left, and for years afterward, her diary was studded with references to him.

When France declared war against Germany, Saint-Exupéry joined the French air force, flying reconnaissance missions over enemy lines. After France capitulated ten months later, he returned to the United States. As Anne saw it, there was now an unbridgeable gulf between them—he, a passionate anti-Fascist, and she, a supposed apologist for Fascism, "the bubonic plague among writers." The idea of a rift between her and the man she had come to love was deeply painful.

Sequestered in their rambling white farmhouse, the Lindberghs led a lonely, reclusive life. A big black German shepherd patrolled the grounds, and local police set up a guard post on the road leading to the house. The family had almost nothing to do with their wealthy, mostly interventionist-minded neighbors, one of whom was Secretary of War Henry Stimson. Virtually all the East Coast establishment figures who had befriended Lindbergh after his flight had cut off contact with him.

When an acquaintance of Anne's told J. P. Morgan partner Thomas Lamont, a friend of the Morrow family who had befriended Lindbergh, that the Lindberghs were lonely and suggested he visit them, Lamont retorted icily: "I [will] have nothing to do with them." Henry Breckinridge, Lindbergh's longtime New York lawyer, not only rejected Lindbergh socially but spoke out against him, equating his former friend and client to such turncoats as Norway's Vidkun Quisling and France's Pierre Laval and declaring that "he who spreads the gospel of defeatism is an ally of Adolf Hitler." In Washington, Admiral Jerry Land, chairman of the U.S. Maritime Commission and Lindbergh's second cousin, erupted in anger when a friend mentioned the flier. "I just can't talk about him any more!" Land declared. "I think he's gotten into bad hands, and he's all wrong."

In her struggle to cope with this flood tide of rejection, Anne had one important solace: despite the intense strain on their relationships, her own family never abandoned her. Indeed, all the Morrows, including her mother, worked extraordinarily hard to maintain the closeness that was so important to them. When William Allen White made a speech boasting about the "really smart trick" he had played in persuading Elizabeth Morrow to deliver a radio broadcast countering Lindbergh's isolationist arguments, Elizabeth shot off a sharp letter to White, chiding him for the snideness of his comments. "Colonel Lindbergh and I differ about what our country's attitude toward the war should be," she wrote, "but each honors the sincerity of the other's opinions, and there is no misunderstanding between us."

Anne was particularly grateful that her close ties with her sister, Con Morgan, had not unraveled. After dinner with the Morgans one night, she expressed her delight that she and Con "can still talk. It was a good evening, a cementing one, keeping the bridges open." In 1943, Anne noted to an acquaintance that Con and Aubrey Morgan and their English colleagues in New York had been far kinder and more welcoming to her and Charles during that difficult time than any of Anne's old friends.

Aubrey Morgan, for his part, was determined not to give up his long-standing friendship with his brother-in-law, no matter how much they might disagree on a wide spectrum of issues. He and John Wheeler-Bennett, Morgan's colleague at the British Press Service, spent many evenings with Lindbergh, "arguing, debating, and fundamentally dissenting in the most amicable fashion," Wheeler-Bennett recalled. "We never lost our tempers nor jeopardized our friendship."

Wheeler-Bennett did not believe that Lindbergh was at heart anti-British—it was just that he felt that Britain could not win the war. "Nothing that Aubrey or I could say could compel his comprehension of Britain's genius for improvisation and her gift for inspired amateurism," Wheeler-Bennett wrote. "He had simply written Britain off as a bad bet. He disapproved of President Roosevelt's policies of 'all aid short of war' on the grounds there was no point in throwing good money after bad."

Years later, Morgan would tell Reeve Lindbergh, "Your father never really understood the British character." To reporters who could not believe that the brothers-in-law, with their wildly disparate views, could get along so well, Morgan laughingly said that their relationship stood as an "eternal refutation of the invincibility of British propaganda."

ANNE'S STEADFAST RELATIONSHIP WITH her family was one of the few bright spots in her life that fall. Her misbegotten defense of her husband's isolationist stance had certainly not helped diminish the attacks on him. If anything, it intensified them.

Everything that Lindbergh said or did continued to be front-page news. He had switched his focus from radio broadcasts to speaking at antiwar rallies throughout the country, which invariably drew huge, adoring crowds. Those who did not share his views deluged the White House and FBI with letters suggesting that he be silenced. "How can such an utterly disgusting yellow-bellied traitor as Charles A. Lindbergh be allowed to spew off at the mouth?" a Texas man wrote to President Roosevelt. "He should be tied with a long chain and dropped in the middle of the Atlantic, where his body will no longer contaminate the U.S.A." Other correspondents urged that Lindbergh be dispatched immediately to Germany.

Thousands of abusive letters were sent directly to the Lindberghs, many with such obscene, violent language that the U.S. Post Office began inspecting their mail. One letter, addressed to "Dear Nazi Lindbergh," demanded he stop his antiwar speeches "or else you will not see your other baby alive within three weeks from today."

What infuriated Lindbergh's critics was not just his opposition to the government's interventionist policy but his seeming lack of concern and sympathy for the suffering of the bomb-battered British and other victims of the Nazis. "There is nothing lovable about this Lindbergh," an Omaha newspaper declared. "It is impossible to warm up to him. . . . We turn from him amazed. Is it possible there is a human being whose feelings are not touched, if ever so little, by the spectacle of a world boiling in misery and fear?"

Even some of his fellow isolationists voiced concern about his refusal to condemn Nazi tactics and to express hope for the survival of

Britain. Norman Thomas advised Lindbergh to declare "your personal opposition to the cruelty, intolerance and tyranny of fascism. Make it clear that at the very least, a desirable peace would mean the continuance of Great Britain and her self-governing dominions as absolutely independent nations with real power, not as puppets to Hitler." The isolationist historian Charles Beard warned Lindbergh that he was "doing great damage to the cause of staying out of war by repeatedly saying in public that Britain has lost the war."

Lindbergh's archconservative friend William Castle was another who urged him to be more careful about what he said. "He does not care about his own reputation so long as he is saying what he believes to be true," Castle wrote in his diary. "I said that . . . I cared for his reputation only because it was an asset for those of us who believe in keeping out of the war [and] that he must not get the reputation of being pro-German." Castle offered to vet Lindbergh's speeches for overly inflammatory language—a proposition that Lindbergh politely declined. He spent hours on each speech, carefully choosing each word. He was going to say what he wanted to say, and he didn't care if it made him a pariah.

He had told his mother-in-law, among others, that he didn't want a German victory, that he opposed Nazi persecution of the Jews, and that he believed a British defeat would be "a tragedy to the whole world." At the same time, he continued to insist that Britain had already lost the war and should agree to a negotiated peace. Although he maintained repeatedly that he was neutral, the only combatant he criticized was Britain.

Even with the mushrooming growth of America First, Lindbergh remained isolationism's most potent weapon. His opinions, journalist Roger Butterfield observed, "have become as significant as bombs. . . . The magic of his legendary name, the appeal of his personality, the sincerity with which he comes before the microphone, have persuaded millions of Americans who were only half persuaded before that there is no reason for the U.S. to fight or fear Hitler."

Increasingly, President Roosevelt considered Lindbergh to be a major threat to his presidency and the survival of Britain. He and other interventionists would soon launch an all-out campaign to neutralize his influence. But first, FDR had to deal with another potent rival—Wendell Willkie.

CHAPTER 17

"A NATIONAL DISGRACE"

By any measure, the 1940 presidential campaign was one of the nastiest in modern American history. Henry Wallace called it "exceedingly dirty." Robert Sherwood labeled it "a national disgrace" and "a dreadful masquerade, in which the principal contestants felt compelled to wear false faces." Marcia Davenport, the wife of Wendell Willkie's campaign manager, described it as "a disgraceful slugging match in which neither candidate wholly kept his integrity."

Yet at its beginning, there was considerable optimism that the contest might be relatively civilized. No major differences existed between Willkie and Franklin Roosevelt on policy issues. Willkie had voiced his support for many of the New Deal's social programs and, despite the bitter opposition of GOP bosses, had done the same for the president's foreign policy. Indeed, he had been considerably bolder than FDR in his emphasis on the importance of sending aid to Britain as quickly as possible.

For Willkie, however, that similarity of views would swiftly become a serious problem—just one of a host of difficulties, many of them self-inflicted, that began almost immediately after the Republican convention. Instead of capitalizing on the nationwide excitement engendered at the convention and making appearances throughout the country, Willkie and his aides took a working vacation for five weeks in the Colorado mountains. Years later, an aide conceded, "We let what was the hottest thing in the world get cold."

Once his campaign did begin, it was, by all accounts, the most disorganized in memory—"a fountain of anarchy and confusion," according to Marcia Davenport. Raymond Clapper observed, "Seldom has there been more chaos in a presidential campaign," adding that "if the Willkie administration in the White House functioned with no more unity, coordination, and effectiveness than the Willkie administration in the campaign, then the Government would be almost paralyzed."

Willkie and Russell Davenport, who resigned as managing editor of *Fortune* to direct the campaign, made it abundantly clear from the start that they wanted little to do with Republican bosses, seemingly unaware that they needed the party's resources, in both money and manpower, to mount a full-fledged national contest. On the campaign train, a virtual state of war existed between Willkie's band of amateurs and the old-guard Republicans who occasionally traveled with the candidate.

But the most daunting challenge facing Willkie was how to convince Americans that, notwithstanding his agreement with Roosevelt on most major issues, there were important enough differences to warrant voting for a political neophyte over a seasoned veteran. The Republican decided on three lines of attack: Roosevelt's continuing inability to mend the economy and lower the high unemployment rate; his failure to mobilize industry and rearm the country swiftly enough in the face of a fast-growing German threat; and his alleged dictatorial instincts, as exemplified by his decision to run for a third term.

On all three counts, however, circumstances worked against Willkie. Although unemployment did remain unacceptably high and war mobilization was indeed in a state of disarray, enough defense money had been pumped into the economy over the previous few months to ignite a boom in jobs and spending. And even though voters remained wary about a third term, that concern, for many, was outweighed by their inclination to support the incumbent at a time of international crisis.

Frustrated by his inability to inflict much political damage on his opponent, Willkie was even more annoyed when, throughout September and into October, FDR acted as if he didn't even exist. The wily old pro was giving the amateur a master class in politics. Instead of engaging in traditional campaigning, he stayed above the fray, emphasizing his role as commander in chief by making heavily publicized inspection tours of booming shipyards and munitions and aircraft plants. Such visits were meant to underscore not only FDR's dedication to a strong national defense but also the steady increase in defense-related jobs.

While Roosevelt seemed oblivious to the fact that a presidential campaign was actually under way, his aides did their best to undermine the public's trust and confidence in the Republican nominee. They did so in part by skillfully playing on the divisions and contradictions in the GOP, attempting to tar the liberal, interventionist Willkie with the isolationism and extreme conservatism that dominated the Republican Party.

The word began to circulate that Willkie was nothing but a stalking horse for reactionary, big-business Republicans who planned a Fascist-style takeover of the government if he were elected. "The time has arrived to tell the American people bluntly of the plan to return this Government to Wall Street," declared an unsigned campaign memo found in Harry Hopkins's White House papers. "It will be a sorry day for labor and for other groups in this country who always have an uphill battle to fight if this sordid group is brought into this country in the dead of night."

There's no question that Roosevelt was still passionately hated by a substantial segment of the business community and that a number of prominent businessmen, fearing for their profits, had advocated a negotiated peace between the British and Hitler. But no evidence has ever come to light to support the idea that corporate leaders were planning a putsch or that Wendell Willkie was anything but a liberal who opposed the reactionaries in his own party as strongly as he did Roosevelt.

Nonetheless, FDR and many of those around him apparently convinced themselves that a Willkie victory would be followed almost immediately by a Fascist coup d'état. "Willkie is distinctly dangerous," Harold Ickes wrote in his diary. "With him in the White House, the monied interests would be in full control and we could expect an American brand of fascism as soon as he could set it up." Henry Wallace, meanwhile, noted in his diary that Roosevelt "was convinced that Willkie at heart was a totalitarian."

Because of the GOP's diehard isolationist image, Willkie was also vulnerable to the charge that his election would be welcomed, even advocated, by Nazi Germany and its adherents in the United States. In speech after speech, Wallace, the designated brawler on the Democratic ticket, came within an inch of saying that a vote for Willkie would be a vote for Hitler. "The Republican candidate is not an appeaser and not a friend of Hitler," the vice presidential nominee said in a speech in rural Nebraska. "But you can be sure that every Nazi, every Hitlerite, and every appeaser is a Republican." In another address, Wallace insisted that he did not mean to "imply that the Republican leaders are willfully and consciously giving aid to Hitler. But I wish to emphasize that the replacement of Roosevelt, even if it were by the most patriotic leadership that could be found, would cause Hitler to rejoice."

Disregarding the deliberate murkiness of Wallace's phrasing, newspaper headlines focused on the intent of his message. The New York *Daily News* trumpeted WILLKIE IS HITLER'S MAN, SAYS WALLACE, while the *Des Moines Register*'s wording was slightly more restrained: NAZIS PREFER GOP—WALLACE. In an editorial rebutting Wallace's contentions, *The New York Times,* which endorsed Willkie after having backed Roosevelt in the two previous presidential elections, declared: "We are under no illusion that Hitler and Mussolini like Mr. Roosevelt. We are also under no illusion that they will like Mr. Willkie any better . . . for Mr. Willkie is just as vigorously pro-America, and just as bitterly anti-Axis, as Mr. Roosevelt."

The fact that Willkie's parents were German immigrants was regarded by Democratic pols as another possible bit of political pay dirt. Acting on behalf of the president, Harold Ickes asked the FBI to run a background check on Willkie, but J. Edgar Hoover, who had been advised by one of his top agents that such a blatantly political investigation would be "a serious mistake," denied the request. Nonetheless, a whispering campaign about Willkie's German ancestry, including rumors that his last name was really Wulkje, was set in motion by Democratic regulars. Unsigned pamphlets were circulated asserting that Willkie approved of Hitler's theory of the Germans as a master race and charging that his sister was married to a Nazi naval officer. In fact, she was married to the U.S. naval attaché in Berlin.

Late in the campaign, the Democratic National Committee took aim at Willkie's attempt to lure black voters away from Roosevelt. The DNC's minorities division issued a statement alleging that Willkie's Indiana hometown sported signs warning, "Nigger, don't let the sun go down on you here." It also quoted a supposed frequent quip of Willkie's: "You can't do this to me. I'm a white man." Willkie, who had fought the Ku Klux Klan as a young lawyer and who in 1940 had won the endorsement of a number of black papers, angrily blasted the statement as "the most scurrilous and indecent" allegation of the entire political contest.

The attacks on Willkie were not merely verbal. According to Willkie biographer Steve Neal, the Republican "found himself the target of more violence than any presidential candidate in a generation." At many big-city campaign stops, particularly those in working-class districts, Willkie was pelted with everything from rotten eggs, fruits, vegetables, rocks, and lightbulbs to an office chair and wastebasket (the latter two hurled from office windows and landing close to the candidate). At one event, Willkie's wife was splattered by eggs. This rowdiness, which was usually accompanied by booing and heckling, occurred so frequently that *The New York Times* ran a daily box score of the number of items thrown and those that found their target.

Calling the attacks "reprehensible," Roosevelt urged local authorities to press charges against Willkie's assailants. But as it happened, much of the troublemaking had been orchestrated by big-city Democratic bosses, among them the same mayors and other local officials to whom the president had appealed for justice.

Enraged by such hooliganism, as well as by the Democrats' questioning of his patriotism and dedication to racial tolerance, Willkie began to rethink his determination to keep the campaign civil. He was encouraged in that effort by GOP leaders, who, no matter how much they disliked him personally, were desperate for a Republican victory over Roosevelt. They pointed out to the nominee that his reasonableness had earned him no political points, that in fact he had slipped dramatically in the polls despite weeks of frenetic campaigning all over the country. At the beginning of September, he and Roosevelt had been locked in a virtual tie; by the end of the month, the president had pulled ahead by at least ten points.

To regain the momentum, the Republican politicians counseled, Willkie had to give up this silly bipartisanship and attack Roosevelt where he was most vulnerable—on the war. They said in effect that Willkie must renounce everything he had stood for just a few weeks before and mount a scare campaign against the president, making an argument to voters that peace was the best policy for America and that a vote for FDR was a vote for war.

Willkie finally agreed, his anger at the Democrats and desire to beat Roosevelt winning out over his principles and conscience. Suddenly, the interventionist candidate was sounding like an apostle of isolationism, charging that the president had caused "a drift toward war." According to the political writer Richard Rovere, "By the time the campaign was over, Willkie was as much in opposition to the man he had been a few months earlier as he was to his opponent."

In a nationwide radio broadcast, Willkie declared that Roosevelt "had encouraged the European conflagration" and implied that his opponent had made a secret agreement with Britain to enter the war. "We can have peace," Willkie added, "but we must know how to preserve it. To begin with, we shall not undertake to fight anybody else's war. Our boys shall stay out of Europe." In another speech, he warned that under Roosevelt, young Americans were "already almost on the transports," but if they put *him* in the White House, "I shall not send one American boy into the shambles of another war."

Willkie's sudden metamorphosis upset many of his most prominent supporters, including a number of journalists who had championed his candidacy. Raymond Clapper deplored his "expediency" and "narrow-minded appeals," adding that such "bad judgment . . . had raised grave doubts, at least with me, about the kind of job he would do as president." Henry Luce, who had written drafts of campaign speeches for Willkie and showered Russell Davenport with political advice, lamented the Republican's handling of the war issue, later saying that he should have "told the truth and gone down [to defeat] with . . . honor."

Walter Lippmann, another influential journalist who supported and occasionally advised Willkie, urged him not to divide the country on the war issue. In the spring and summer of 1940, Lippmann had been intensely critical of Roosevelt for what he perceived as the president's timidity and lack of leadership and had applauded Willkie for his forthright advocacy of immediate, all-out aid to Britain. Now, appalled by Willkie's change of heart, Lippmann severed his connections with him.

Still, for all the disappointment felt by some Willkie backers over his strident fanning of war fears, the tactics began having their desired effect. By the middle of October, the president's comfortable lead in the polls had melted away; Willkie was leading FDR in most of the Midwest and showing signs of a surge in the Northeast.

Now it was the turn of Democratic politicians to panic. Phone calls and telegrams began pouring into the White House, urging the president to abandon his Olympian posture as commander in chief and get personally involved in the campaign. "The political leaders were learning in their own local districts that, as far as votes for a President are concerned, the American people just naturally refuse to be taken for granted," Samuel Rosenman, Roosevelt's principal speechwriter, noted. "They want to hear the campaign issues debated by the candidates. Fortunately for Roosevelt, the reports he was receiving made him realize this in time."

But before the president could enter the fight, he and his aides were forced to deal with an issue that could have greatly imperiled his reelection. The White House discovered that a Republican newspaper publisher named Paul Block had acquired a cache of letters between Henry Wallace and his onetime guru, Nicholas Roerich, and was thinking of publishing them.

Harry Hopkins, who somehow acquired copies of the letters, informed FDR that they were extremely damaging. Their extravagantly mystical, coded language, including Wallace's references to himself as "Galahad" and "Parsifal," could easily be employed to cast doubt on the mental stability of a man who, if elected, would be a heartbeat away from the presidency.

The president and his men, however, had a potent weapon of their own in reserve: Willkie's extramarital affair with the *New York Herald Tribune*'s Irita Van Doren—a relationship that he had done little to conceal. Before the campaign, the two had often been seen in public together, and Willkie had even held a press conference at Van Doren's apartment, explaining to friends, "Everybody knows about us—all the newspapermen in New York."

Willkie, as it turned out, was wrong: journalists may have known about the couple, but since they never wrote about the affair, the vast majority of Americans had no inkling of the candidate's complicated personal life. During the campaign, Willkie's wife dutifully accompanied him around the country, while he kept in touch with Van Doren through phone calls and telegrams.

At Roosevelt's instigation, top members of his campaign staff made clear to their Republican counterparts that if the Wallace-Roerich letters were published, the news of Willkie's affair would also be made public. "If people try to play dirty politics on me, I'm willing to try it on other people," FDR declared to a White House aide. He explained what the aide should do to get word of the affair out. "You can't have any of our principal speakers refer to it," the president said, adding that "people down the line," such as members of Congress and local officials, "can do it properly . . . so long as it's none of us people at the top."

Roosevelt's threat worked. In the end, neither side unleashed its secret weapon—a striking exception in a campaign known for dirty tricks and intemperate rhetoric.

WITH JUST SIX WEEKS to go before the election, FDR finally took his place in the thick of the battle. "I am an old campaigner, and I love a good fight," he proclaimed in his first political speech of the contest. Observing Roosevelt's "grim smile and set jaw" as he said those words, Samuel Rosenman knew "he was not exaggerating."

A new speechwriter—Robert Sherwood—had joined the president's campaign team for the final push. An unflagging Roosevelt supporter, Sherwood had been lobbying FDR and Harry Hopkins for a job for months; early in 1940, he had written the president, "I wish with all my heart to offer my services, for whatever they're worth, to you in this crucial year and to the cause which is yours, as surely as it was Lincoln's." From that point until Roosevelt's death, his three main speechwriters would be Rosenman, Hopkins, and Sherwood.

The playwright's appointment horrified his Republican family, particularly his mother, who "considered me a well-meaning but hopelessly befuddled renegade," Sherwood told a friend. Not long before, she had listened to a political broadcast, realizing after a few moments that the speaker, who was lavishing praise on Roosevelt, was none other than her beloved Bobby. "My poor boy," she moaned over and over, "my poor boy."

While never mentioning Willkie by name, Roosevelt's speeches followed Wallace's lead by indirectly associating the president's opponent with evil foreign and domestic influences. "There is something very ominous in this combination that has been forming within the Republican party between the extreme reactionary and extreme radical elements of this country," FDR declared in a Brooklyn speech. In Cleveland, he denounced "certain forces within our own national community, composed of men who call themselves American but who would destroy America." When New York governor Herbert Lehman, a Democrat, said that Hitler and Mussolini were working for Roosevelt's defeat and hence, by implication, for Willkie's election, the president said he agreed with that view.

All this mudslinging was going on at a time when hundreds of Britons were dying every night in Luftwaffe bombing raids and German submarines were choking off British supply lines. But Britain's peril was not mentioned much by the two presidential candidates. The main issue on which they focused was the necessity of preserving the peace and security of America. Forced on the defensive by Willkie, Roosevelt tried to outdo him in making sweeping pledges of peace, declaring in Philadelphia, "We will not participate in any foreign wars."

But the Republican was still gaining in the polls, and Democratic leaders pleaded for a stronger, more definitive statement from the president that he would not push the country into war. Just a few days before the election, Roosevelt gave it. In a speech in Boston, he assured American mothers and fathers: "I have said this before but I shall say it again and again and again—your boys are not going to be sent into any foreign wars."

Sherwood, who had come up with the catchphrase "again and again and again" and regretted it for the rest of his life, later called the speech "terrible." In his view, FDR made a mistake "in yielding to the hysterical demands for sweeping reassurance; but, unfortunately for my own conscience, I happened . . . to be one of those who urged him to go the limit on this."

At the time, a number of critics blasted both candidates for what they considered their reckless and irresponsible promises to the American people. Among them was Freda Kirchwey, editor of *The Nation,* who argued that Roosevelt and Willkie both had sacrificed their integrity as a result of their lack of honesty. In a column that appeared just days before the election, she addressed herself to the candidates, telling

them: "You should have refused to vie with your opponent in unqual-
ifiedly promising peace. Instead you should have bravely warned the
nation that war may be necessary. . . . You should have told the people
plainly that this country is already inextricably engaged in the struggle
against Hitlerism and that we shall not draw back from its uttermost
consequences."

Interestingly, despite Dorothy Thompson's earlier chastising of
Roosevelt for promising the American public "more security than it is
wise for them to think they can have," she did not ally herself now
with Kirchwey and the nominees' other detractors. As it happened, the
impetuous Thompson was now in the president's camp—so much so
that the last speech he delivered in the 1940 campaign was largely taken
from a draft she had written for him. Her transformation from ardent
Willkie admirer to zealous Roosevelt partisan was nothing short of
astonishing, even to those familiar with her mercurial nature.

Throughout Roosevelt's presidency, Thompson, a conservative on
domestic issues, had been an outspoken critic of the New Deal and of
what she considered FDR's lust for power, declaring at one point that
he was on the verge of becoming a dictator. But her main focus in
1940, as it had been for several years, was on the need to stop Hitler.
Having earlier vowed to support Willkie "to the hilt," she had second
thoughts when the Republican started spouting views that bordered
on isolationism. The president, of course, was also espousing decidedly
anti-interventionist beliefs, but Thompson decided that with his eight
years of experience, he was the better bet. Her abrupt change of heart
might also have had something to do with FDR's determined wooing:
he had invited Thompson to the White House for private meetings in
May and October, in an attempt to persuade her "to get this silly business of Wendell Willkie out of her head." Unlike her *Herald Tribune*
colleague Walter Lippmann, who refused to endorse either candidate,
Thompson, with her usual flair for the dramatic, announced to her
readers in late October that she had transferred her allegiance to the
president, adding that "Roosevelt must stay in office and see this thing
through."

With its early support of Willkie, the *Herald Tribune* had played a
crucial role in helping him get the Republican nomination, and not
surprisingly, its owners, Ogden and Helen Reid, were infuriated by
what they considered Thompson's betrayal. Helen Reid, who had been

instrumental in hiring Thompson and who considered her a close friend, was particularly irate.

When Thompson wrote another column, declaring that a Willkie victory would cause "Nazi jubilation in Germany and popular depression in Great Britain," the Reids ordered it suppressed. In its place, the *Herald Tribune* ran a sampling of the hundreds of negative letters it had received after Thompson's endorsement of FDR, along with the paper's formal disclaimer of her position.

The brouhaha over Thompson was a fitting coda to this extraordinarily bitter campaign. Sherwood, who later made clear how much he regretted his own role in adding to the vitriol, wrote that Roosevelt "despised" the 1940 contest, in large part because "it left a smear on his record which only the accomplishments of the next five years could remove."

ON THE NIGHT OF the election, Roosevelt, in the midst of studying early returns, called Mike Reilly, the head of his Secret Service detail, into a small room off the dining room of his home in Hyde Park. Reilly noticed that the president was sweating heavily and wore a grim expression. "Mike," Roosevelt told him, "I don't want to see anybody in here." Surprised by this unusual order from his normally gregarious boss, Reilly asked: "Including your family, Mr. President?" Roosevelt snapped back: "I said 'anybody.'"

It was the first and only time that Reilly would ever see Roosevelt in a state of nervous agitation. Later he speculated that the president had noticed something in the returns that led him to believe he was going to lose. FDR "always ran scared" prior to an election, one reporter noted, but this one was clearly going to be the closest he had ever experienced. Polls taken in the campaign's final days showed Willkie in the lead in six battleground states and closing the gap in several more.

Nonetheless, FDR did not remain sequestered for long that night. Later returns made clear he was on his way to an unprecedented third-term victory, and soon visitors were streaming into the room to congratulate the beaming president-elect. In the largest election turnout in American history, he had won by some five million votes—27.3 million cast for him, compared to 22.3 million for Willkie.

Roosevelt's pleasure in his triumph, however, was somewhat tempered by the knowledge that the 1940 election was the closest presidential contest in almost twenty-five years. His margin of victory was considerably reduced from his lopsided totals of 1932 and 1936; indeed, his 1936 plurality had been slashed by more than half. Willkie had received more popular votes than any previous Republican candidate—or, for that matter, *any* presidential candidate, with the exception of FDR. And, according to polls conducted after the election, the Republican likely would have won if it hadn't been for the war issue.

In Henry Luce's view, "the menace of Hitler helped to nominate [Willkie], and the menace of Hitler certainly defeated him for the Presidency." As much as many American voters apparently wanted a change in domestic policy, they were reluctant, with the world in flames, to take a chance on an untested novice. In the words of New York mayor Fiorello La Guardia, they preferred "Roosevelt with his known faults to Willkie with his unknown virtues."

Late on the night after the election, the doorbell rang at the Manhattan apartment of Russell Davenport, Willkie's campaign manager. Exhausted and in a state of near shock from the turbulence of the previous five months, Davenport's wife, Marcia, opened the door—and found an equally exhausted Harry Hopkins standing before her. Shuffling into the living room, Hopkins shook Russell Davenport's hand and sat down.

For the Willkie camp, the president's top aide had been a major villain, Marcia Davenport recalled, "a man on whom we had concentrated much mental and verbal opprobrium. . . . But his appearance at that moment was corroboration of the great crisis beyond domestic politics, which was the real concern of both Wendell Willkie and Franklin Roosevelt; of every man who . . . understood what our country was about to face."

Over beer and sandwiches, Davenport and Hopkins talked until early the next morning. Less than a week later, Willkie made clear that the time for political smears and partisan attacks was over. In a radio broadcast, he declared: "We have elected Franklin Roosevelt president. He is your president. He is my president. We all of us owe him the respect due to his high office. We give him that respect. We will support him."

CHAPTER 18

"WELL, BOYS, BRITAIN'S BROKE"

At the moment Roosevelt was celebrating his election victory at Hyde Park, Luftwaffe bombers were returning to their bases in France after their fiftieth night of bombing London. Since the Blitz began, more than thirty thousand Britons had been killed in German raids, at least half of them in the British capital. Millions of houses had been damaged or destroyed, along with a number of London's most famous landmarks. Ten Downing Street, the Colonial Office, the Treasury, and the Horse Guards Building all had been battered by bombs. Hardly a pane of glass was left in the War Office, and Buckingham Palace had been hit several times.

But the incessant bombing was far from the only peril facing Britain at the end of 1940. The country was encircled by a gauntlet of German submarines, ships, and aircraft, all waiting to feast on the merchant ships bringing vital supplies to the besieged island. "Not since the Spanish Armada swept north in 1588 has the maritime nation of Britain faced such a threat as now confronts it," *Life* reported. "Compared with its present situation, World War I was a pleasure cruise. Then Germany was bottled in the Baltic. Now it has naval and air bases scattered along the coast of Europe from Norway to Spain." In Washington, Admiral Harold Stark, the naval chief of staff, told Henry Stimson, Frank Knox, and General George Marshall that at its current rate of shipping losses, Britain could not hold out for more than six months.

Since June, the exigencies of the U.S. presidential campaign had taken precedence over the desperate needs of Britain; thus far, the only substantial aid it had received from America was several dozen bombers and the fifty old destroyers. Surely, with the election over, British officials thought, they could look to the White House for swift and decisive action.

Winston Churchill and many in his government had awaited the fifth of November like children anticipating Christmas; they had convinced themselves that if Roosevelt were reelected, he would finally fulfill his promises of aid and perhaps even enter the war. The day after the president's victory, an exultant Churchill sent a congratulatory cable, noting that during the campaign he had had to refrain from publicly supporting FDR's reelection but "now, I feel you will not mind my saying that I prayed for your success and that I am truly grateful for it."

Not only did Britain require considerably more assistance, it was in urgent need of a new way to finance it. Its purchases of armaments and other supplies from America—which, under the revised Neutrality Act, had to be paid for in dollars—had drained Britain of most of its dollar and gold reserves. To continue those shipments, the British Treasury had been forced to borrow from the gold reserves of the Belgian government in exile, now based in London.

Using sympathetic American correspondents in London as its conduits, the British government tried to convey to the American people how dire the country's situation really was. Drew Middleton of the Associated Press wrote a story outlining Britain's "staggering shipping losses" and noting that the nation was "reaching the end of her financial tether." According to *The New York Times,* "the British would like to convince the United States that its aid up to now has been insufficient and spasmodic. Negotiations, it is said here, have been mistaken for orders in the public mind, and orders have been mistaken for deliveries."

THE BRITISH, HOWEVER, WAITED in vain. Churchill received no answer from FDR to his exuberant cable—a silence that "rather chilled" the prime minister, he told his war cabinet. Roosevelt also kept mum about the possibility of new plans for aid. And there certainly was no sign that America was about to enter the war.

To those around him, the president's lassitude was extremely perplexing. Like the British, they, too, had expected him to come up with bold new measures to meet the crisis in the Atlantic now that he was free, in Admiral Stark's words, from "the political preoccupations which had necessarily influenced him" in the last few months. Lord Lothian reported to London that Roosevelt seemed unusually tired and depressed after the election, an assessment shared by a number of FDR's associates. What could the reason be? The relative closeness of his victory, compared to his two previous triumphs? Or was it his explicit promise that he would not send American boys to war? Did he feel that as a result of that pledge, he had no mandate to propose actions that might propel the country into the conflict?

Whatever the reason, FDR's lethargy was causing great frustration, not only in the British government but also among the American interventionist groups that had lobbied so hard for the destroyer transfer and other aid programs for Britain. "It really appalls me to think how little real leadership the country has had from the President from the beginning of the campaign right up to date," the Century Group's Geoffrey Parsons wrote to William Allen White in early December. In his reply, the usually genial White used unusually acerbic language that revealed his own exasperation. Calling Roosevelt "the Great White Bottleneck," the Kansas editor said that FDR was "taking this crisis too easily." Someone, White added, "should jolt him out of his complacence and make his hair stand on end."

Like the British, the interventionist organizations worried that as a result of the administration's silence, the American people had no idea of the seriousness of Britain's situation or what more they themselves could do to help. "Like a leaderless army, [Americans] waited, as they had been waiting for a full month since election day, to be given their marching orders, to be told clearly what the sacrifices are which all of them must make," *Life* observed.

In the meantime, Americans threw themselves with gusto into the approaching Christmas season, spending more lavishly than in any year since 1929. With the economy on the rebound, stores reported record holiday purchases. Big-ticket items like cars and refrigerators sold especially well; in November alone, more than four hundred thousand new cars found customers.

In all this consumer frenzy, there was a tip of the hat to patriotism and the distant war. Throughout the country, lavish benefit dances, parties, and concerts were staged to raise money for war victims in Britain and other nations attacked by Germany. At the Star-Spangled Ball, sponsored by the White Committee in New York, Gypsy Rose Lee stripped for Britain, allowing the guests, most of them from the city's affluent café society, to snip off the glittering stars covering strategic parts of her costume in return for significant donations. In Seattle, socialites hosted a gambling party to raise money for new British Spitfire fighter planes. "War relief has become a big business," one journalist noted. "But little by little it has assumed also the characteristics of show business, seeking support from those who care less for the quality of mercy than for self indulgence and personal fame. . . . Some people have begun to wonder how many dollars were left when all the bills for ballrooms and champagne had been paid."

Not all U.S. relief efforts were frivolous, however; many did in fact provide meaningful help for European war victims. A number of organizations raised enough money to send ambulances and other medical aid to Britain. Harvard University established a hospital there and financed its operation for the rest of the war. More than half a million American women—members of a nationwide group called Bundles for Britain—donated and raised money for clothing and other personal items to send to Britons who had lost their homes and belongings in bombing raids.

But as important as private assistance was, it was not the kind of help Britain needed in order to survive. That could only come from the deep pockets of the U.S. government. The British official who best understood the workings of that government—Lord Lothian—now stepped onto the stage to make the most important contribution of his diplomatic career.

UNLIKE HIS GOVERNMENT COLLEAGUES in London, the British ambassador never regarded November 5 as a "magic date"; in his opinion, neither Roosevelt nor the country was remotely ready to enter the war. The importance of America's election day, he believed, lay in the fact that Britain was now free to renew its pressure on both the Roosevelt administration and the public. And, he decided, he would be his country's agent in doing so.

As Lothian was well aware, what Britain needed from America was a comprehensive, far-reaching program of aid, rather than the patchwork of handouts—the old destroyers, planes, rifles, and other weapons—previously sent to Britain. Returning to London for a few weeks in late October, the ambassador devised a plan to put an end to American inertia and spark creation of such a program.

His first step was to persuade Churchill to write a letter to Roosevelt, outlining in the frankest terms possible the full extent of Britain's desperate situation, both strategically and financially. In his postwar memoirs, Churchill noted that this letter was "one of the most important I ever wrote," but at the time, he strongly resisted the idea of passing on to the president such "a ruthless exposé of the strategic dangers," as Lothian described it. The prime minister believed that the revelations, if they ever leaked, would cause harm to British morale and would be of great benefit to Germany. He preferred to wait, as he put it, on "the force of events" and on the response of "our best friend," Roosevelt.

Lothian strenuously disagreed, insisting that FDR would do nothing unless pushed to do so. He saw the letter as a kind of insurance policy for presidential action, believing that "its existence, and the knowledge that some day it might be published, would act as a continual spur in meeting our requirements for fear it should be said in years to come, 'He knew, he was warned, and he didn't take the necessary steps.'"

Lothian wrote a first draft of the letter for Churchill, but the prime minister continued to procrastinate. With the help of Lord Halifax and Alexander Cadogan, the Foreign Office permanent undersecretary, the ambassador kept the pressure on. He told Churchill that Roosevelt was about to embark on a Caribbean cruise and that it was vital that he have the letter to ponder during his trip. Though still reluctant, Churchill finally agreed.

Lothian returned to the United States in late November, with the letter still unfinished but with the prime minister's promise it soon would be on its way. On the ambassador's arrival in New York, he unveiled another important part of his plan. He knew from experience that Churchill's letter, vital as it was, probably would not be sufficient to goad Roosevelt into action; FDR would also require the force of

American public opinion behind him. From the moment he landed at La Guardia Airport, Lothian set out to mobilize that opinion.

He was met, as he knew he would be, by a horde of reporters and cameramen. There are varying reports of what he said in response to the cacophony of questions shouted at him. John Wheeler-Bennett, who was there to greet Lothian, wrote that the ambassador's statement to the newsmen, "one of the most momentous . . . in the history of war," was short and extremely blunt: "Well, boys, Britain's broke. It's your money we want."

Contemporary news reports of the press conference don't mention this colorful remark. But the articles made clear, in perhaps more elegant language, exactly what Lothian meant: if Britain was to survive and keep fighting, it would need massive amounts of American aid—and as swiftly as possible.

Lothian's frank message came as a bombshell. Wheeler-Bennett and Aubrey Morgan, who was also at the airport, "could scarcely believe our ears," Wheeler-Bennett recalled. Lothian's two colleagues asked him if he really meant what he said. "Oh, yes," he replied. "It's the truth, and they might as well know it." As Wheeler-Bennett noted, "Never was an indiscretion more calculated. It was Philip Lothian at his best."

Roosevelt and Churchill, however, didn't share that opinion. Furious at this obvious attempt to force his hand, the president also worried about the effect of Lothian's candid remarks on Congress. Churchill, for his part, feared that the ambassador's statement would so anger FDR that he would reject the contents of the prime minister's forthcoming letter. "I do not think it was wise to touch on very serious matters to reporters," Churchill gently chided Lothian. "It is safer to utter a few heartening generalities and leave graver matters to be raised formally with the President."

Yet it soon became clear, even to the prime minister, that Lothian's direct approach had produced exactly the reaction he sought. His decidedly undiplomatic remarks, featured on virtually every newspaper front page in the country, came as a shock to the American people and sparked an intense national debate about Britain's calamitous financial condition. "By revealing to Congress and the public another aspect of Britain's plight, hitherto known only to a few government officials," the historians William Langer and S. Everett Gleason wrote, "Lord Lothian was bringing the President to accept the conclusion which his own advisers had been urging on him—that he had no recourse but to go to Congress and the people for a fresh and unequivocal mandate on the program of assistance to Britain."

In fact, Roosevelt had already come to believe that Britain was indeed running out of money. But Lothian's statement jarred him into action, forcing him and Treasury Secretary Henry Morgenthau to "deal with the cash problem immediately," as Morgenthau put it. The ambassador's remarks also laid the groundwork for Churchill's letter to Roosevelt, which, after many drafts by the prime minister and Foreign Office, was finally sent to Lothian for review on December 2, just as the president left on his Caribbean trip. Following more consultations with 10 Downing Street and Whitehall, Lothian handed the letter in its final form to State Department officials on December 7, to be delivered to the president by seaplane.

Although exhilarated by the early success of his efforts, Lothian was also exhausted. He'd been working nonstop since his appointment as ambassador, and his associates had been worried for some time about his health. He had started to fall asleep at inopportune times—at luncheons and dinner parties, for example, or while dictating correspondence to his secretary. Wheeler-Bennett begged him to get more rest, but Lothian said he couldn't: there was far too much to do.

Once Churchill's letter was on its way to Roosevelt, Lothian began work on a major speech he was to deliver four days later in Baltimore. It was to be his first public address in nearly five months, and he reportedly considered it the most important of his career. After staying up virtually all night to finish it, he collapsed and was confined to bed.

Too weak to deliver the speech, he dispatched Nevile Butler, his second in command at the embassy, to Baltimore to read it for him. Lothian's "powerful statement," as *Time* described it, reviewed Britain's steadfast resistance and belief in ultimate victory and concluded with a heartfelt appeal to the American people. "It is for you to decide whether you share our hopes and what support you will give us in realizing them," he declared. "We are, I believe, doing all we can. Since May, there is no challenge we have evaded, no challenge we have refused. If you back us, you won't be backing a quitter. The issue now depends largely on what you decide to do."

It was, Wheeler-Bennett wrote, the ambassador's "valedictory to America, to Britain, and to the world." As Butler finished reading the speech that night, Philip Lothian, in the care of a Christian Science practitioner, died at the British embassy in Washington. His illness, which had caused his frequent bouts of drowsiness, was later diagnosed as uremia, a buildup of toxic waste products in the blood resulting from kidney failure.

Lothian's unexpected death came as a stunning blow to both America and Britain. Roosevelt, who was still at sea, conveyed to George VI his sorrow and shock "beyond measure" at the passing of a man he called "my old friend." Lothian's last public message to America—that Britain was confident of victory, but only if it received unstinted U.S. aid—echoed the theme of Churchill's letter, which Roosevelt was now studying.

After outlining his requests, which included more warships and other matériel, as well as U.S. protection of British merchant shipping, Churchill wrote to Roosevelt: "The moment approaches when we shall no longer be able to pay cash for shipping and other supplies. I believe you will agree that it would be wrong in principle and mutually disadvantageous if . . . after the victory was won with our blood, civilisation saved, and the time gained for the United States to be fully armed against all eventualities, we should stand stripped to the bone."

Freed from the daily stresses of the presidency during his two-week cruise, Roosevelt had plenty of time to reflect on Churchill's letter, Lothian's speech and death, and his own response. As it happened, he had been thinking for some time about new policy initiatives to help the British. Two months earlier, he had mused to an acquaintance: "Might it not be possible for the United States to build cargo vessels and lease them to Great Britain?" Near the end of the voyage, FDR outlined to Harry Hopkins the ingeniously bold and groundbreaking scheme he had devised—a comprehensive program that would allow the government to lend or lease war matériel to any nation the president considered vital to the defense of the United States.

As FDR worked on his plan, the British peer who had helped spark the creation of Lend-Lease was mourned in Washington and throughout the country he considered his second home. "He had arrived in the United States five days before the war began, at a moment when the U.S. was doubly suspicious of all foreign—especially all British—

propaganda," *Time* wrote. "At his death a major U.S. concern was how aid to Britain could be increased. Though no historian would credit that great shift wholly to the Ambassador, there is no doubt that he had been an integral part of it."

In New York, a taxi driver told a passenger: "I didn't think Americans would ever be keen about an Englishman, but I swear every customer I have had today feels terribly bad about that Lord Lothian's death." About the ambassador, one radio commentator noted: "He was a marquess, but he made you forget it. He was a Britisher, but he made you forget that, too."

In Washington, bystanders silently lined Massachusetts Avenue as horse-mounted U.S. cavalry troops accompanied a caisson bearing Lothian's flag-draped coffin from the British embassy to the National Cathedral, where his funeral was held. Thousands of mourners, including Supreme Court justices, cabinet members, and congressional leaders, attended the services, which included a special prayer commending to God's "loving care and protection the people of Great Britain. In this hour of their need, guard and save them from the violence of their enemies."

The following morning, Lothian's ashes were taken to Arlington National Cemetery, where they were interred, with full military honors, at the base of the mast of the USS *Maine,* the battleship whose sinking in Cuba in 1898 helped precipitate the Spanish-American War. "Very softly and reverently, the urn was placed on a folded British flag and carried into the vault to rest with the men of the *Maine,*" Eleanor Shepardson, an American friend of Lothian's, wrote to the marquess's two sisters in Scotland. "He now rests in a country which loved him and believed in him."*

In Britain, meanwhile, Lothian's death was regarded as an incalculable loss. "When the news was brought to me, I felt stunned, as if a bomb had exploded at my feet," former prime minister David Lloyd George remarked. *The New York Times* noted: "It is no exaggeration to say that Lord Lothian's death struck government circles [in London] first as a major disaster and secondly as a personal deprivation." One radio commentator equated the impact of his death to the sinking of a battleship; a government official said it was worse than losing two

---

* In December 1945, Lord Lothian's ashes were transported to Scotland aboard an American warship.

army corps. The only "graver blow to Britain's cause" would have been the death of Churchill, another official declared.

In the draft of a cable to Roosevelt about Lothian's death, Churchill initially referred to the peer as "one of our greatest Ambassadors to the United States." Then he struck out "one" and changed the sentence to read "our greatest Ambassador to the United States."

Like Churchill, Lothian had achieved his greatest triumph in the climactic years of 1940 and 1941. In his eloquent, wistful House of Commons eulogy to the ambassador, the British leader alluded to that when he said: "I cannot help feeling that to die at the height of a man's career, universally honoured and admired, to die while great issues are still commanding the whole of his interest, to be taken from us at the moment when he could already see ultimate success in view—is not the most unenviable of fates." A number of those present thought Churchill was talking about himself, as well as the man to whom he was paying tribute.

TWO WEEKS AFTER LORD Lothian's death, FDR wheeled himself into the Diplomatic Dining Room of the White House and took his place behind a large desk covered with microphones. He was about to deliver another of his famed fireside chats to the American people, one of the most significant of his presidency.

In the simple, informal language of which he was a master, he sketched for his radio listeners an outline of the revolutionary new aid program he had conceived, and then he told them why it was vital for the safety of America as well as Britain. "Never before since Jamestown and Plymouth Rock has our American civilization been in such danger as now," he said. If the British were defeated, the Axis powers would "control the continents of Europe, Asia, Africa, Australasia, and the high seas." They would be "in a position to bring enormous military and naval resources against this hemisphere. It is no exaggeration to say that all of us, in all the Americas, would be living at the point of a gun—a gun loaded with explosive bullets, economic as well as military."

To avert such a horrific future, the United States "must become the great arsenal of democracy," supplying Britain and other nations fighting the enemy with everything they needed. "We must apply ourselves to our task with the same resolution, the same sense of urgency, the same spirit of patriotism and sacrifice as we would show were we at war."

A genius at explaining difficult and complex issues to his countrymen in terms they could relate to, Roosevelt had paved the way for his announcement of Lend-Lease when, at a White House press conference a few days earlier, he presented the analogy of the neighbor and the garden hose. The new aid program, he said, was akin to lending a hose to a neighbor whose house was on fire. Once the fire was put out, the hose would be returned. Similarly, military supplies would be of considerably more benefit to the United States if employed by the British to defeat Germany and Italy than remaining unused here. When the war was over, Roosevelt implied, they would be sent back to America. (The improbability of this actually happening was left unmentioned.)

But there was a problem with Roosevelt's garden hose analogy, as the historian Richard Snow has pointed out: "If your neighbor's house is on fire, you not only lend him your garden hose, you help him use it." In his fireside chat, the president took pains to emphasize, as he had done repeatedly since the beginning of the war, that the main purpose of this initiative, like the others before it, was to keep America out of the conflict. "There is far less chance of the United States getting into the war if we do all we can now to support the nations defending themselves against attack by the Axis," he said. "You can nail any talk about sending armies to Europe as a deliberate untruth."

In his effort to rally the American people behind Lend-Lease, Roosevelt failed to address the disquieting question in the minds of many in both isolationist and interventionist camps. Even with supplies from the United States, how could Britain's forces vanquish an enemy whose army was ten times bigger? And if they couldn't, what action, if any, would America take? FDR himself had said that the preservation of American democracy demanded the destruction of Hitler and Nazism. How could that be accomplished unless the United States entered the war as a full belligerent?

Accusing Roosevelt of duplicity, isolationist leaders contended that Lend-Lease was just another of his furtive, indirect means to get the country into the war. "If it is our war," Senator Burton Wheeler declared, "how can we justify lending [the British] stuff and asking them to pay us back? If it *is* our war, we ought to have the courage to go over and fight it. But it is not our war."

Herbert Agar was as ardent an interventionist as Wheeler was an isolationist, yet he agreed with the senator that the idea of Lend-Lease as a guarantee of peace for America was "bunk." When Wheeler asked Agar during the Lend-Lease debate if he was not, in fact, working for an undeclared war against Germany, Agar retorted: "Certainly not. I am working for a declared war against Germany. Today, Lend-Lease is the best we can get." Later, the *Courier-Journal* editor would write: "The opponents of the bill and the warmongers were the only ones free to say what they thought. When Roosevelt said the bill would make us the arsenal of democracy, we said this was wishful thinking: we could never be the arsenal of anything until we went to war."

Four key figures in the administration's fight for Lend-Lease— Henry Stimson, Frank Knox, General George Marshall, and Admiral Harold Stark—agreed. At a meeting shortly before Roosevelt's fireside chat, they came to the conclusion, as Stimson noted in his diary, "that this emergency could hardly be passed over without this country being drawn into war." Several months earlier, Knox had written to his wife: "The sooner we declare war, the sooner we will get ready."

Roosevelt, however, made clear to the civilian and military chiefs that they were not to voice that opinion in public. Unlike the conscription legislation, Lend-Lease was a White House initiative, and its advocates in the administration were told they must follow the president's lead and use his arguments when they testified on Capitol Hill. For Stimson and Knox, especially, the strictures posed a painful dilemma. Convinced that war was drawing ever closer, they had to insist to skeptical members of Congress that with the passage of Lend-Lease, peace would continue to reign in America.

THE CONGRESSIONAL FIGHT OVER Lend-Lease was in several respects reminiscent of the battle over the administration's proposal to expand the Supreme Court four years earlier. The leader of the opposition in both cases was Burton Wheeler, and a key issue—the unprecedented amount of power the legislation would grant to Roosevelt—was also the same.

In addition to putting a clear end to U.S. neutrality, Lend-Lease would give the president sole authority to decide which countries should get U.S. military aid, how much they would receive, and whether—and how—that help would be repaid. Once again, Roosevelt's opponents raised the charge of incipient dictatorship. Describing the Lend-Lease measure as "monstrous," Senator Hiram Johnson declared: "I decline to change the whole form of my government on the specious plea of assisting one belligerent. . . . It is up to Congress now to determine whether our government shall be as ordained or become a member of the totalitarian states." Echoing Johnson's allegations, Philip LaFollette, an isolationist former governor of Wisconsin, contended that the administration's "only answer to the menace of Hitlerism in Europe is to create Hitlerism step by step in the United States."

As inflammatory as these assertions were, none approached the stridency of Burton Wheeler's invective. The Montana Democrat despised Roosevelt—a sentiment that FDR cordially reciprocated—and was determined to curb what he saw as the president's insatiable appetite for power. In a dispatch to his superiors in Berlin about the Lend-Lease struggle, Hans Dieckhoff, the Reich's former ambassador to the United States, reported: "Wheeler fights more out of personal hatred of Roosevelt than out of objective conviction."

In a radio broadcast blasting Lend-Lease in January 1941, Wheeler snapped: "Never before has the U.S. given to one man the power to strip this nation of its defenses." Then, in a reference to the administration's controversial farm program to plow under crops and kill livestock to raise prices, he declared: "The lend-lease-give program is the New Deal's triple-A foreign policy; it will plow under every fourth American boy."

That incendiary comment ignited a political firestorm, as Wheeler realized it would. "I must confess," he said years later, "that it did sound somewhat harsh." An enraged Roosevelt told reporters that the remark was "the most untruthful, the most dastardly, unpatriotic thing that has ever been said." He added icily: "Quote me on that."*

---

* The Almanac Singers, an antiwar folksinging group whose members included Pete Seeger and Woody Guthrie, introduced a song called "Plow Under" soon after Wheeler made his remark. It began:

Instead of hogs it's men today
Plow the fourth one under.

Wheeler's statement set the tone for a two-month nationwide battle over Lend-Lease and America's growing involvement in the war—a debate that the 1940 presidential candidates had declined to have and one whose vehemence and venom would surpass the passions unleashed by the clash over conscription. The isolationists knew that this was their last major chance to stop the United States from becoming a fully committed partner, at least economically, in Britain's fight against Hitler. In their view, H.R. 1776—the deliberately patriotic number assigned the Lend-Lease bill by its House authors—meant a renewed subservience to Great Britain, rather than the declaration of independence signified by its title.

An extraordinarily high number of Americans—91 percent, in one poll—were aware of Lend-Lease, and, unfortunately for the isolationists, most thought it was a good idea. According to a Gallup poll taken shortly after Roosevelt's fireside chat, 61 percent approved of the plan while only 24 percent opposed it. A survey taken more than a month later showed that 68 percent of Americans favored aid to Britain even at the risk of war for the United States.

But, as both sides knew from their fight over conscription, favorable public opinion did not necessarily translate into congressional support. Aware that they must defeat Lend-Lease to have any realistic chance of keeping the country out of war, the isolationists marshaled their forces for an all-out attack. The America First Committee was in the vanguard.

For the first four months of its existence, America First had done relatively little. Lend-Lease was the catalyst it needed to spark a huge increase in its membership and establish it as the country's leading anti-intervention organization. Within weeks, hundreds of new chapters sprang up, and tens of thousands of America First volunteers circulated anti-Lend-Lease petitions, put up posters, staged rallies, and showered Capitol Hill and the White House with letters and telegrams. In Washington, America First staff members became unofficial staffers for isolationist senators and congressmen, providing them with research and writing speeches opposing the legislation.

As with conscription, congressional mail on Lend-Lease was solidly opposed, bearing no resemblance to American public opinion as measured by the polls; indeed, some congressmen reported receiving up to twenty times more letters against the bill than for it. "The opposition has us on the run here," Adlai Stevenson, head of the pro-Lend-Lease effort in Chicago, admitted to Frank Knox.

Alarmed by the intensity of the isolationists' lobbying campaign, Roosevelt reached out to the White Committee and the Century Group for help. During the campaign, the president had shied away from contact with both. He was irritated by their pressure on him and feared that their increasingly outspoken interventionism would hurt him politically. But now, using Robert Sherwood as his intermediary, he appealed to them to "use all our efforts," as Herbert Agar recalled, on behalf of Lend-Lease.

The two organizations immediately responded. While the Century Group worked behind the scenes, soliciting favorable newspaper editorials and radio commentaries, the White Committee vied with America First in turning out huge numbers of leaflets, bumper stickers, buttons, posters, and petitions. Throughout the country, both sides went door to door collecting signatures and passing out material. They also staged community debates and forums. As Roosevelt noted, the "great debate" over Lend-Lease "was argued in every newspaper, on every wave length, over every cracker barrel in all the land."

The historian Wayne Cole has referred to the nationwide discussion as "democracy in action." That it certainly was, albeit with a high degree of acrimony. Contending that the purpose of the legislation was "the destruction of the American Republic," the *Chicago Tribune* refused to use the term "Lend-Lease" and instead referred to "the war dictatorship bill" in all its editorials, columns, and news stories. The *Tribune*'s crosstown rival, Frank Knox's *Chicago Daily News,* accused Robert McCormick and other isolationists of "playing Hitler's game." The interventionist Louisville *Courier-Journal,* meanwhile, compared congressional opponents of Lend-Lease to German submarine commanders, declaring that both were intent on preventing aid from reaching Britain.

As the debate raged throughout the nation, thousands of activists poured into Washington to buttonhole members of Congress and argue their positions. Lend-Lease foes paraded down Pennsylvania Avenue, waving American flags and banners reading "Kill Bill 1776, Not Our Boys." An organization called American Peace Mobilization picketed day and night outside the White House, its members carrying signs denouncing Roosevelt as a warmonger. One of the ubiquitous right-wing mothers' groups also appeared outside the White House bearing a parchment scroll quoting Roosevelt's numerous pledges to keep the country out of war. As news photographers aimed their cameras, the women burned the scroll and placed the blackened pieces in an undertaker's urn labeled "Ashes of FDR's Promises."

On Capitol Hill, women in black dresses, with veils covering their faces, sat day after day outside the Senate chamber, weeping and moaning. Others kept a so-called "death watch" in the Senate and House galleries; during one House discussion, a woman wearing a black robe and skull mask jumped up and shouted "Death is the final victor!"

Members of yet another mothers' group, chanting "Down with the Union Jack," staged a sit-down strike in the corridor outside the office of Senator Carter Glass, a staunch interventionist. The group's leader called the Virginia Democrat "a traitor to the republic," while he blasted her and her followers for creating "a noisy disorder of which any self-respecting fishwife would be ashamed." Later, Glass asked the FBI to investigate whether the "mothers" had links to Germany or any other foreign country. "I likewise believe it would be pertinent to inquire whether they really are mothers," he added tartly. "For the sake of America, I devoutly hope not."*

WHEN CONGRESSIONAL HEARINGS ON Lend-Lease began in mid-January 1941, huge crowds packed each session. The atmosphere in the House and Senate committee rooms resembled a sporting event, with highly partisan spectators cheering the champions of their point of view and booing opponents.

There were two unmistakable stars on the committees' long lists of witnesses: Charles Lindbergh, the country's most prominent isolationist, and his interventionist counterpart, Wendell Willkie. Hours before Lindbergh appeared before the House Foreign Affairs Committee on January 15, long lines of people hoping for admittance snaked down

---

* In response to the mothers' organizations "who are giving Congress the idea that all women are against war and help to Britain," the Century Group formed its own women's unit. Called the Women's Committee for Action, the group organized informal networks of women throughout the country to put pressure on members of Congress and rally public opinion.

the sidewalk outside the Longworth Office Building. When he entered the cavernous committee room, he was greeted by raucous cheers and applause from the hundreds of onlookers jammed into the room.

The applause continued throughout his testimony, along with boos and hisses for one congressman who asked him which side he preferred to win the war. "I want neither side to win," Lindbergh responded, touching off another round of frenzied clapping. He added that he favored a negotiated peace to a British or German triumph, contending that "complete victory on either side would result in prostration in Europe such as we have never seen."

As notable as Lindbergh's appearance was, however, it did not come close to the drama and controversy of Wendell Willkie's February 11 testimony before the Senate Foreign Relations Committee. Well before dawn that day, throngs of people were already milling outside the Senate Office Building, even though Willkie was not scheduled to testify until that afternoon. When he finally arrived, the high-ceilinged, marble-walled Senate Caucus Room was jammed to overflowing with some twelve hundred spectators, more than double the room's supposed capacity and the largest crowd ever to gather there.

The testimony of the man who took his seat at the witness table bore little resemblance to the speeches of Willkie the presidential candidate. By all accounts, he deeply regretted his surrender to expediency and divisiveness during the campaign, and he vowed it would never happen again. After the election, in addition to offering his own personal support for Roosevelt as president, Willkie called on his backers to become "a vigorous, public-spirited loyal opposition which would not oppose for the sake of opposition." Underscoring the importance of putting aside political differences and antagonisms at this time of great crisis, he pledged "to work for the unity of our people in the completion of the defense effort [and] in sending aid to Britain."

Willkie's avowal of bipartisanship infuriated Republican leaders. Most prominent Republicans in Congress and the party hierarchy strongly opposed Lend-Lease, and they hoped that Willkie, as titular head of the GOP, would do the same. Nothwithstanding his defeat, he was still extremely popular with a significant segment of the American people.

But the Republicans' desire for a solid anti-Lend-Lease front had come to naught when Willkie declared his support for the program in January. "Under such dire circumstances," he said, "extraordinary powers must be granted to the elected executive. Democracy cannot hope to defend itself in any other way." What's more, he attacked those in the GOP who opposed Lend-Lease, asserting that "if the Republican party allows itself to be presented to the American people as the isolationist party, it will never again gain control of the American government."

Making matters still worse, as the Republican old guard saw it, Willkie announced that he was going to Britain, as Roosevelt's personal representative, to see for himself how that beleaguered country was faring. Rep. Joseph Martin, whom Willkie had appointed head of the Republican National Committee, begged him not to go. "Roosevelt is just trying to win you over," he argued, pointing out that "this won't be well received by Republicans."

That was putting it mildly. Willkie was immediately denounced as a turncoat and traitor by members of his party; Robert McCormick called him the "Republican Quisling." Roy Howard, the isolationist publisher of the Scripps-Howard newspaper chain, invited Willkie to dinner to tell him that "all the time and effort I have spent on helping you has been wasted" and that his newspapers were now going to "tear your reputation to shreds." Willkie later told friends he managed to keep his temper during this diatribe, "though if Howard wasn't such a little pipsqueak, I'd have felt like knocking him down."

According to the columnist Raymond Clapper, most of the GOP's most influential members were "conspiring to get rid of [Willkie]. They hate him more than they hate Mr. Roosevelt." One of them, former RNC chairman John Hamilton, snapped: "Out of the 190-odd Republican members of the House and Senate, Willkie couldn't dig up ten friends if his life depended on it."

On January 19, 1941, the night before FDR's third-term inauguration, the president met with the man who, three months before, had been his bitter foe and was now his most important foreign policy ally. While Roosevelt "took an immediate liking to Willkie," in the words of Labor Secretary Frances Perkins, the former Republican nominee apparently didn't return the favor. Although the meeting was cordial, Willkie failed to succumb to Roosevelt's fabled charm, according to the *Christian Science Monitor* columnist Roscoe Drummond. The Republican's "incalculable services to the government," Drummond observed, were performed out of a sense of duty rather than any feeling of kinship with the president.

Other occupants of the White House apparently were as interested in Willkie as FDR was. In her memoirs, Eleanor Roosevelt recalled that members of Roosevelt's professional and household staffs were so anxious to catch a glimpse of Willkie that they pretended to have errands taking them into the room where he waited for the president. She added, "I would have gone myself" if other urgent tasks hadn't prevented it.

Willkie's warmth and magnetism had much the same effect on the British people. He made a whirlwind tour of the country in the last week of January, buying a round of drinks and playing darts at a London pub, clambering through the ruins of bombed-out buildings, dropping in on an aircraft factory, and visiting underground shelters during Luftwaffe raids. When Churchill discovered that Willkie had been striding around London without a steel helmet, he immediately sent the former presidential candidate six helmets and three gas masks. British newspapers waxed rhapsodic about his visit; one glowing editorial bore the headline VENI, VIDI, WILLKIE.

Americans were also avidly following Willkie's mission to Britain; according to one Washington columnist, his tour had "been more stirring to national interest than any journey ever taken by another American in public life." In early February, with the Lend-Lease debate nearing its climax and its outcome still uncertain, the administration was in urgent need of Willkie's star power. Secretary of State Cordell Hull sent him a cable asking him to cut his trip short and return to Washington to appear before the Senate Foreign Relations Committee.

Agreeing, Willkie arrived in Washington just hours before he was scheduled to testify. While clearly exhausted from his strenuous travels, he was ebullient and forceful in his assurances to the committee that Lend-Lease offered "the last best chance for us to avoid war" and that Britain would stand "firm and strong" against Hitler as long as it received the aid promised under the legislation. "The people of Britain are united almost beyond belief," he added. "Millions of them will die before they give up that island."

The isolationists on the Senate Foreign Relations Committee pelted

Willkie with hostile questions. One senator grilled him about his campaign accusation that the president was secretly planning to dispatch American boys to war. Shifting uncomfortably in his chair and running his fingers through his hair, Willkie finally said with a sheepish grin: "I struggled as hard as I could to defeat Franklin Roosevelt. And I tried not to pull my punches. But he was elected president. And he is my president now."

Willkie's remarks drew loud applause and cheers, as well as a spate of approving newspaper editorials, many of which endorsed Lend-Lease. "Whatever influence he has lost among professional Republicans," wrote the *Washington Post* columnist Ernest Lindley, "has been more than offset by his increased prestige among those who voted against him." The day after he testified, the Senate Foreign Relations Committee, by a vote of 15–8, voted in favor of the bill.

Although Willkie's resolute support of the legislation had clearly influenced a number of legislators, the battle for passage in both houses of Congress was still difficult. In the House, it became clear that in order to win approval for the measure, the president would have to agree to a number of restrictive amendments, including a two-year limit to the program. Roosevelt agreed, and on February 9 the House passed the bill, 260–165.

The opponents of Lend-Lease in the Senate still hoped to stymie the measure. They thought that what had happened in the 1937 Court-packing battle might happen again: that the debate could be extended long enough to give isolationists a chance to turn public opinion against Lend-Lease. For more than two weeks, Burton Wheeler, Gerald Nye, Hiram Johnson, and a score of others rose on the Senate floor to deliver lengthy diatribes (some lasting up to nine hours) against the bill and the undeserving "British plutocrats" who they claimed would be the recipients of its largesse.

The CBS correspondent Eric Sevareid, who covered the prolonged, tedious debate, was appalled by the scene playing out before him. Three months earlier, he had been in London, dodging bombs while covering the Blitz; he knew firsthand how desperately Britain needed the aid being debated on the Senate floor. A pacifist in his college days, Sevareid had been transformed by his experiences reporting on the German aerial assault on Britain and, before that, on the fall of France. Now committed to the idea that America must "fight the war with every means available," he was stunned that so few of his country-men, especially in "leafy, dreaming" Washington, shared his convic-tion. Watching the isolationist senators ramble on, he later wrote, filled him with "physical revulsion." He described the orators as "tobacco-chewing, gravy-stained, overstuffed gila monsters who, nestled in their bed of chins, would doze through other speeches, then haul up their torpid bodies and mouth the old, evil shibboleths about King George III, the war debts, Uncle Sap, and decadent France." They were, he added, "very dangerous men."

Clearly, the Roosevelt administration thought so, too. Worried that the American public might be swayed by senatorial arguments that the British were trying to fleece the United States, the White House demanded that Britain liquidate its most valuable industrial holding in America—a textile company called American Viscose—to prove that it had exhausted all financial options before receiving U.S. aid. Ameri-can Viscose was sold to a group of American bankers, who promptly resold it for a much higher price.

Infuriated by what he regarded as high-handed coercion, Churchill wrote to Roosevelt, in a cable never sent, that the administration's de-mands "wear the aspect of a sheriff collecting the last assets of a help-less debtor. You will not, I am sure, mind my saying that if you are not able to stand by us in all measures apart from war, we cannot guarantee to beat the Nazi tyranny and gain you the time you require for your rearmament." To one of his cabinet ministers, the prime minister raged: "As far as I can make out, we are not only to be skinned but flayed to the bone." (Henry Stimson agreed with Churchill, writing in his diary, "We were not paying the money to Great Britain because we were investing but . . . to secure a certain military advantage which she gave us by keeping up her defense.")

In retrospect, it is doubtful that the forced sale of American Viscose had much of an impact on American public opinion, which, through-out congressional consideration of Lend-Lease, never wavered in its strong support of the measure. The Senate isolationists never received the break they were hoping for, and their colleagues, along with an increasingly large segment of the American people, began to show their displeasure at the opponents' delaying tactics. Groans, hoots, and shouts of "Vote! Vote!" were now heard on the Senate floor every time one of the bill's foes stood up to speak. After the White House agreed to yet more amendments, a weary Senate on March 8 finally approved the legislation, by a vote of 60 to 31.

Despite the compromises, the passage of Lend-Lease was considered, quite rightly, to be an enormous triumph for Roosevelt; indeed, it was one of the greatest successes of his presidency. He not only devised this revolutionary plan, which would end up playing a crucial role in the Allies' ultimate victory, but also conducted a brilliant campaign to sell it to the public.

Yet Lord Lothian and Wendell Willkie deserve much credit as well. If not for the British ambassador's pressure, it's uncertain that the president would have come up with Lend-Lease when he did. And Willkie's backing, as demonstrated in his congressional testimony, played a major role in guaranteeing the public's support of the program, as well as the votes of many members of Congress, both Democrats and Republicans.

Roosevelt, for his part, was well aware of how much he owed his former opponent. When Harry Hopkins, in the presence of the president and Robert Sherwood, made a wisecrack about Willkie later in the war, FDR "slapped him with as sharp a reproof as I ever heard him utter," Sherwood wrote. He quoted Roosevelt as saying to Hopkins: "Don't ever say anything like that around here again. Don't even *think* it. You of all people ought to know that we might not have had Lend-Lease or Selective Service or a lot of other things if it hadn't been for Wendell Willkie. He was a godsend to this country when we needed him most."

THE PRESIDENT'S SIGNING OF the Lend-Lease measure marked an extraordinary shift in America's role in the war, as well as in its ties to Britain. A stroke of a pen had erased all pretense of U.S. neutrality; there was no question that America was now an ally of Britain, albeit a noncombatant ally. The two countries were linked in an unprecedented economic relationship, requiring them to work together to plan and implement defense production and allocations of matériel. In a very real sense, the "special relationship" had begun.

Uncomfortably aware of how much the landscape had changed,

some isolationists began to rethink their position. Among them was Senator Arthur Vandenberg, a Republican from Michigan, who wrote in his diary: "We have taken the first step upon a course from which we can never hereafter retreat. . . . We have said to Britain, 'We will see you through to victory'—and it would be unbelievably dishonorable for us to stop short of full participation in the war if that be necessary." Although Vandenberg had fought Lend-Lease "from start to finish," as he told a friend, he decided he must now support the program: "It is now the law of the land [and] we have no alternative except to go along."

Sharing that view was Kingman Brewster, who had testified against Lend-Lease before the Senate Foreign Relations Committee. Immediately after passage of the legislation, however, Brewster resigned from America First. Explaining his reasoning to Robert Stuart, he wrote: "Whether we like it or not, America has decided what its ends are. . . . A national pressure group therefore is not aiming to determine policy, it is seeking to obstruct it. I cannot be a part of that effort."

Another prominent young isolationist had also rethought his position. John F. Kennedy had come to the conclusion that Britain must be saved and that the United States must be the savior. "The danger of our not giving Britain enough aid, of not getting Congress and the country stirred up sufficiently . . . is to me just as great as the danger of our getting into war now," he wrote. "We should see that our immediate menace is that England may fall . . . America must get going."

In Chicago, one of America First's most prominent members—Sterling Morton—posed several questions to his colleagues on the group's national committee: With national policy now set, was it possible for loyal Americans to continue to oppose their government? Wasn't it time to swallow all misgivings and close ranks behind the president?

America First's chairman, Robert Wood, answered Morton's questions with an unequivocal *no*. Wood, who himself was under increasing pressure from Sears, Roebuck to resign from America First, wrote his troubled friend: "True, in a sense we are in the war now, but there is a vast difference in the position of being a friendly nonbelligerent and in the position of an active belligerent." America First had suffered a devastating defeat, Wood acknowledged, but it had not yet lost the war over intervention. The organization would fight on.

IN THE MIDST OF this angst and rejoicing over Lend-Lease, little attention was paid to the fact that America had an agonizingly long way to go before it could actually become the "arsenal of democracy." As General Friedrich von Boetticher noted in a cable to Berlin, American industry was not prepared to meet British needs and would not be for many months to come. U.S. officials "want to arouse the impression in the world that American aid will immediately begin with the greatest impetus," von Boetticher wrote. "With this propaganda measure they conceal the simple fact that the United States is today not yet capable of giving help that could decisively influence the course of the war."

In Britain, Winston Churchill was plagued by similar thoughts. To members of Parliament, Churchill praised Lend-Lease, calling it "the most unsordid action in history of any nation." Privately, though, he was not that impressed. Instead of expressing his appreciation to Roosevelt, he wrote a sharp note to the president questioning details of the plan and noting that it would not go into effect for several months. Appalled by the toughness of Churchill's draft, the British embassy in Washington urged him to tone it down and to offer unequivocal thanks for the new offer of aid. The prime minister reluctantly agreed to an expression of gratitude but retained his skepticism and anxiety. "Remember, Mr. President," he wrote, "we do not know what you have in mind, or exactly what the United States is going to do, and we are fighting for our lives."

Had Churchill known about the inertia that would settle over Washington as soon as Lend-Lease became law, he might have sent the cable as originally worded.

CHAPTER 19

"A RACE AGAINST TIME"

$\equiv$

Four days after signing Lend-Lease into law, Franklin Roosevelt went before the White House Correspondents Association to declare, "Our democracy has gone into action. . . . Every plane, every instrument of war that we can spare now, we will send overseas." Those listening to him were struck by the president's fervor and sense of urgency as he underscored the vital importance of this new effort to save Britain and help defeat Hitler. "Here in Washington," he continued, "we are thinking in terms of speed, and speed now. And I hope that that watchword—'speed, and speed now'—will find its way into every home in the nation."

Roosevelt's energy and combativeness that night reminded some in the audience of a warrior donning his armor for battle. To Raymond Clapper, FDR's address "was a fighting speech without the troops, a speech that a President might make after war had been declared."

But then . . . nothing happened. As was true following a number of other rousing speeches by Roosevelt, little was done afterward to transform his rhetoric into reality. Despite the president's optimistic prediction, neither Washington nor the rest of the country had yet discovered the virtue of speed. There were delays at every turn—snags in setting up the agency implementing Lend-Lease, holdups in producing planes, tanks, ships, and other matériel. While war-related production was indeed on the rise, it was infinitesimal compared to the massive combined needs of the British and American military. To meet those needs, new defense plants had to be built immediately, the labor force greatly expanded, and ways found to resolve the problem of critical shortages of certain raw materials.

But none of that could be done without attacking the root of the problem, which one administration official described as the "fiction that we can perform a miracle of industrial transformation without hurting anyone." With a reviving economy, private industry was hardly eager to deny consumers the new cars and other items they were demanding—or to give up the profits that resulted. And no federal agency could force it to do so. The Office of Production Management, set up by Roosevelt in January 1941 to oversee industrial mobilization, was not given the authority to compel companies to convert to war work or ensure that raw materials be used for defense needs rather than the production of civilian goods. With no presidential call for urgency and sacrifice, the all-out war effort that FDR wanted was nothing but a chimera.

During the crucial weeks and months following Lend-Lease's passage, Roosevelt seemed disinclined to do much about the problem. According to FDR biographer Kenneth S. Davis, "a strange, prolonged, exceedingly dangerous pause in presidential leadership" set in. That malaise was due in part to a series of illnesses that afflicted Roosevelt throughout the spring of 1941 and into early summer. Shortly before the approval of Lend-Lease, he was hit hard by the flu, which he was unable to shake completely for several months. He also was reportedly suffering from bleeding hemorrhoids, as well as increasingly high blood pressure.

Having endured the crushing pressures of the presidency for more than eight difficult years, FDR was, by all accounts, "an exceedingly tired man." During dinner with several close aides the year before, he had suddenly become pale and limp, then briefly lost consciousness. His doctor told worried staff members that the president had suffered "a very slight heart attack."

But while Roosevelt's physical problems almost certainly contributed to his lethargy, it may also have been attributable to his frustration at being caught between the fierce conflicting pressures of isolationists and interventionists. In late spring, he spent two weeks in bed, isolated from almost everybody, with what he claimed was a persistent cold. Robert Sherwood, who briefly consulted with FDR during this period, remarked to the president's secretary, Missy LeHand, that he had neither sneezed nor coughed while Sherwood was with him. With a smile, LeHand observed: "What he's suffering from most of all is a case of pure exasperation."

Whatever the reasons for the president's torpor, it was causing restiveness and unease in Washington and throughout the country. A government report on current public opinion noted considerable dissatisfaction with FDR's handling of both domestic and international matters. "The one course more disastrous than having no policy at all is to decide upon a policy and then fail to fulfill it," a *New York Herald Tribune* editorial warned. "The United States has decided upon its policy—all aid to Britain short of war. The time has come to implement it."

Years later, the columnist Marquis Childs remembered that "a fog of confusion lay as thick as a blanket over everything. No one seemed to have the power or the will to bring form and substance out of the void." In early April, Henry Stimson wrote in his diary: "I feel very keenly that something must be done in the way of leadership here at the center, and I am beginning to feel very troubled about the lack of it. . . . There isn't any strong leadership to catch the minds of the people and show them what is right."

For the British, this inertia couldn't have come at a worse time. Not only were they losing the Battle of the Atlantic in the spring of 1941, they were close to losing the war.

AFTER ALMOST A YEAR of standing alone against the mightiest military power in the world, Britain was in mortal peril. Financially, emotionally, and physically exhausted, its people "were hanging on only by our eyelids," recalled Field Marshal Lord Alanbrooke, who headed the wartime British army.

As the spring days lengthened, the shipping losses in the Atlantic rose to astronomical proportions. The new German battle cruisers *Gneisenau* and *Scharnhorst* joined the U-boat wolf packs in picking off British merchant ships. The amount of matériel sunk in April—nearly 700,000 tons—was more than twice the losses of two months earlier. On a single night that month, a swarm of German submarines sank ten out of twenty-two ships in a British convoy. To the German navy, this period was known as "the happy time."

Shortly before the passage of Lend-Lease, one of Winston Churchill's private secretaries passed on to the prime minister the latest in a series of reports of merchant ship sinkings. When the secretary remarked how "very distressing" the news was, Churchill glared at him. "Distressing?" he exclaimed. "It is terrifying! If it goes on, it will be the end of us." Top German officials agreed. Foreign Minister Joachim von Ribbentrop told the Japanese ambassador in Berlin that "even now England was experiencing serious trouble in keeping up her food supply. . . . The important thing now [is] to sink enough ships to reduce England's imports to below the absolute minimum necessary for existence."

In that period, Britain was as close to starvation as it ever would be during the war. Rationing of many food items was now draconian; individuals were limited, for example, to one ounce of cheese and a minimal amount of meat a week and eight ounces of jam and margarine a month. Some foods, like tomatoes, onions, eggs, and oranges, had disappeared almost completely from store shelves. Clothes rationing had also begun, and most consumer goods, from saucepans to matches, were almost impossible to find.

The British army, meanwhile, suffered one disaster after another. In April, Germany swept through the Balkans, overpowering Greece and, after inflicting heavy casualties, routing British forces there. The British retreated to Crete, where in May they again were driven out by the Germans.

In the Middle East, a string of early British triumphs over the Italians in Libya turned to dust when Field Marshal Erwin Rommel and his Afrika Korps rushed to the Italians' rescue. In only ten days the Germans regained almost all the ground that the British had captured in three months and threw the Tommies back to Egypt. Rommel's victory, which Churchill termed "a disaster of the first magnitude," was a strategic calamity for Britain, threatening its access to Middle Eastern oil as well as its control of the Suez Canal, a vital conduit to India and the rest of the Far East.

During this bitter time, Churchill acknowledged a sense of "discouragement and disheartenment" in the country. He told the House:

"I feel that we are fighting for life and survival from day to day and hour to hour." Painfully aware that his country's only hope was U.S. intervention, Churchill lobbied John Gilbert Winant, America's new ambassador in London, and Averell Harriman, the U.S. administrator of Lend-Lease for Britain, with an intensity bordering on obsession. He wanted more aid, he wanted the U.S. Navy to protect merchant ship convoys. But, above all, he wanted America to enter the war.

THE MEN CLOSEST TO the president, including the U.S. chiefs of staff and most of the cabinet, shared Churchill's alarm. At the very least, they felt, protection must be given to British convoys to stanch the hemorrhaging shipping losses. "The situation is obviously critical in the Atlantic," Admiral Harold Stark wrote to a colleague. "In my opinion, it is hopeless [unless] we take strong measures to save it." Since the war began in September 1939, Stark had been preparing the Navy for combat, including the start of antisubmarine training for U.S. ships. The chief of naval operations firmly believed that American security required the survival of Britain and was willing to do whatever was necessary, even a declaration of war, to accomplish that.

As forceful as Stark was in urging the president to begin escort duty, however, it was the seventy-three-year-old secretary of war, Henry Stimson, who proved to be the idea's most relentless advocate. Throughout his long career in government and on Wall Street, Stimson had never hesitated to speak his mind about a course of action once he was convinced it was the right thing to do. In his memoirs, Francis Biddle, who succeeded Robert Jackson as attorney general in the summer of 1941, noted that Stimson was the cabinet colleague he admired most. "He was loyal to the President . . . but he stood up to him," Biddle wrote. "To me, he was a heroic figure of sincerity and strength."

From the day Stimson joined the administration, he acted as a spur to Roosevelt, prodding him to lead rather than follow public opinion. But on the issue of convoy protection, the president stubbornly resisted Stimson's attempts at persuasion, as he did all other efforts on the subject. FDR had earlier told reporters that convoy duty would almost inevitably involve shooting, and shooting "comes awfully close to war, doesn't it? That is about the last thing we have in our minds." Having sold Lend-Lease to the American people as a way to defeat Hitler without the United States' having to go to war, he was not about to risk getting into the conflict now, especially with the isolationists again on the attack.

Thanks in large part to the string of German victories in the Balkans and Middle East, the anti-interventionists, still trying to recoup from their defeat over Lend-Lease, found themselves suddenly in the resurgence. Americans were expressing increasing doubt about the British armed forces' ability to resist Germany, as well as Britain's overall chances for survival. In public opinion polls, the percentage of people who believed it more important to help England than stay out of the war dipped to just above 50 percent (although it began to rise again soon thereafter).

Buoyed by the uptick in antiwar feeling, Burton Wheeler, Gerald Nye, and other isolationist members of Congress toured the country, speaking out, mostly at rallies organized by America First, against the use of U.S. naval forces to escort British shipping. Joining them was Charles Lindbergh, who in late April overcame his scruples against allying himself with organizations and joined America First. He immediately became the group's star.

In a widely discussed article in London's *Sunday Express,* an influential American radio commentator, Raymond Gram Swing, declared that he believed Roosevelt could "get convoying now if he asked for it" from Congress, but only by a very narrow margin. Swing, who was known to be a confidant of the president's, went on to say that a close vote wasn't good enough, that the support of at least two-thirds of Congress was needed for this "life or death issue." He added that Roosevelt stood aloof from the convoying issue because any intervention on his part would "compromise fatally his position at the center of national unity; he would destroy himself as the symbolic figure around whom a solid national opinion could cohere." Others inside and outside his administration would have to take the initiative.

Swing's reasoning, which was thought to be Roosevelt's as well, failed to convince Stimson and the others to whom the commentator referred. There simply wasn't time, in their opinion, for such a leisurely, politically safe method of gaining public support. The administration's activists believed that Roosevelt had greatly overestimated the strength of isolationism in the country and Congress, that much of the power of his opponents stemmed from his "obviously fearful respect" of them.

Reinforcing that belief were reports from around the nation of increasing public concern over the lack of presidential guidance and direction. Vice President Henry Wallace wrote that the farmers in his native Iowa were ready for "more forceful and definite leadership." At a national governors' conference in Washington, several governors commented to Stimson and Frank Knox that "their constituents were ahead of the president and their Representatives in Congress and were ready to do more to help Great Britain." In a conversation with Stimson, Rep. James Wadsworth, the House sponsor of the conscription legislation, said he thought "the people were getting a little impatient" with Roosevelt. House Speaker Sam Rayburn and other congressional colleagues, Wadsworth added, felt much the same way.

Dismissing all such reports, Roosevelt made clear to his old friend former ambassador William Bullitt, who was also pressuring him, that he had no plans for direct, forceful action against Germany. The president told Bullitt he was waiting for Hitler to provoke an incident that would bring Americans together, no matter how unlikely such a provocation might be.

After a talk with Harry Hopkins, Treasury Secretary Henry Morgenthau noted in his diary that both Roosevelt and Hopkins "are groping as to what to do. They feel that something has to be done but don't know just what. Hopkins said . . . he thinks the President is loath to get into the war and would rather follow public opinion than lead it." In mid-May, Roosevelt told Morgenthau: "I am waiting to be pushed in."

ADOLF HITLER, HOWEVER, WAS determined not to do the pushing. He and Roosevelt were like cautious players in an extremely high-stakes game of chess. Their advisers were pressing both men to be more aggressive in the Battle of the Atlantic, but neither wanted to provoke an incident that might lead to war between their countries.

Throughout 1939 and well into 1940, Hitler had professed indifference to any action the United States might take regarding the war. "America," he sneered, "is not important to us." Convinced that his forces would vanquish Britain as easily as they had France and the Low Countries, he discounted, not without reason, any possibility of U.S. involvement. But when British resistance dashed his hopes for a short conflict, the Führer emphasized to his subordinates the crucial importance of not rousing the country he saw as a sleeping tiger. The German navy was ordered to avoid any incident in the Atlantic that might propel America into the war.

In September 1939, after Roosevelt had announced that U.S. forces would patrol a neutrality zone extending three hundred miles off America's east coast, Hitler—to the fury of Admiral Erich Raeder, his naval chief of staff—forbade German ships to attack vessels in the area. Even worse, in Raeder's eyes, was Hitler's uncompromising ban against any assaults on American ships, regardless of where they were found in the Atlantic.

Throughout the summer and fall of 1940, Raeder argued that the United States, as a result of its increasing commitment to Britain's survival, had shed all pretense of neutrality and that its ships should be fair game. Although Hitler continued to resist the admiral's appeals, even he could not ignore Lend-Lease and the important shift it signified in America's role in the conflict. The German army's high command viewed Lend-Lease as nothing less than "a declaration of war on Germany."

On March 25, 1941, the German government announced a significant expansion of Germany's naval combat zone around Britain, extending it several hundred miles westward into the Atlantic, past Iceland and approaching Greenland. In this enormous expanse of sea, German submarines, ships, and aircraft were now allowed full and unrestricted use of their weapons against merchant vessels and any neutral (i.e. American) warships that might try to protect them. Yet at the same time, Hitler rejected Raeder's request for permission to attack American ships that were not guarding convoys.

Roosevelt studied the new German move for the next several days, engaging in a spirited debate with his advisers about how to respond. Stimson and the other interventionists in his administration urged him to order immediate convoy protection by the Navy.

While making up his mind on the issue, the president answered Hitler's provocation with one of his own, announcing on April 10 that the Army and Navy would immediately establish bases on Greenland, to prevent any future German occupation of that huge snow-covered Danish colony. American officials argued that Greenland was in fact part of the Western Hemisphere and, as such, was subject to the Monroe Doctrine's prohibition against intervention by foreign powers. That claim went largely unchallenged by Germany.

Perhaps that was because Roosevelt, in the end, decided against the even more provocative step of ordering U.S. naval vessels to escort British convoys. He settled instead for extending the three-hundred-mile U.S. neutrality zone to a demarcation line more than halfway across the Atlantic, encompassing virtually all of Greenland and over-lapping a sizable part of Hitler's new naval combat zone. American ships and planes were ordered to patrol this vast area and warn the British if they spotted any German submarines or surface raiders.

While clearly upping the ante, both Roosevelt and Hitler remained determined to minimize the risk of confrontation with each other's forces. The president made clear that U.S. ships and planes were not to fire on German vessels unless they were attacked first. And in late April, Hitler repeated his order to Raeder to avoid any clashes with U.S. ships.

The increased American surveillance was certainly useful to the British, but it did little to stop the U-boat rampage. Since U.S. patrols were prohibited from engaging German vessels, the British remained solely responsible for protecting their convoys, and the losses continued to mount. In the first three weeks of May, German submarines sank twenty British merchant ships in the extended U.S. area.

Roosevelt's announcement of the Greenland bases and increased U.S. patrolling failed to quell the calls in his own country for stronger action. In early May, a resident of Los Angeles sent an irate letter to the White House pointing out what he saw as the contradictory and pusil-lanimous attitudes of FDR and America toward the war: "The American people, according to Gallup, believe that the country should risk war, but that it should not actually wage it. We are not at war with Germany, but Germany is our enemy. We will use the Navy for 'pa-trolling,' but not for 'convoying.' There is a terrible danger of Germany winning, but Lindbergh is a traitor for saying so."

GREATLY DISAPPOINTED BY THE president's decision not to utilize naval escorts, Henry Stimson considered it vital that someone speak out on the issue. That someone, he decided, would be he. On May 6, the war secretary, in a nationwide radio broadcast approved by Roosevelt (in keeping with his predilection for letting others take the initiative), called for U.S. naval protection of cargo headed for Britain, pointing out that Lend-Lease would have no meaning unless such supplies actually reached their destination. But Stimson went even further. He warned Americans that war might lie ahead for their own nation and that they must understand the responsibilities they would then have to assume. "I am not one of those who think that the priceless freedom of our country can be saved without sacrifice," he said. "It cannot. Unless we on our side are ready to sacrifice and, if need be, die for the conviction that the freedom of America must be saved, it will not be saved."

Other key figures in the administration followed Stimson's lead. Frank Knox proclaimed in a speech: "We are in the fight to stay. . . . We have declared that the aggressor nations must not be permitted to win. We have irrevocably committed ourselves to see that this is prevented. . . . This is our fight." Even Agriculture Secretary Claude Wickard got into the act, stating, "It is a cruel and bitter mockery to let the English people believe we are going to make our help effective if we have only halfway measures in mind." In New York, Wendell Willkie won a standing ovation from the huge crowd listening to him when he dramatically proclaimed in slow and measured words: "We . . . want . . . those . . . cargoes . . . protected."

Willkie's ovation and the torrent of letters that Stimson received applauding his broadcast revealed, as the war secretary told Harry Hopkins, that "people are asking for leadership and not more talk." In a meeting with Knox, Harold Ickes, and Robert Jackson, Stimson discussed the need to get the president to stop dithering and take action. "I do know that in every direction I find a growing discontent with the President's lack of leadership," Ickes wrote in his diary. "He still has the country if he will take it and lead it. But he won't have it very much longer unless he does something."

In early May, Ickes, unbeknownst to Roosevelt, traveled to New York to attend a dinner meeting of key interventionists, most of them members of the Century Group. He told them that the administration had been "absolutely hopeless" in educating the public about the need for action and that "since the government was failing the country in this important matter, it was up to the people themselves either to make the government act or act in its default." Later that month, Ickes told a friend that "if I could have looked this far ahead and seen an inactive and uninspiring President, I would not have supported Roosevelt for a third term."

Stimson was the only cabinet member with the moral and political stature to tell the president to his face that he was failing in his responsibility to lead. In a tête-à-tête with Roosevelt in late April, he did exactly that. Instead of relying on public opinion to decide what to do, FDR must guide that opinion. "I cautioned him," Stimson later wrote in his diary, "that without a lead on his part, it was useless to expect that people would voluntarily take the initiative in letting him know whether or not they would follow him."

Roosevelt accepted Stimson's admonition with good humor but paid little or no attention to it. Determined to keep his position "at the center of national unity," as Raymond Gram Swing had put it, the president was happy to let Stimson and others advocate more forceful interventionism. But he was not yet willing to do so himself.

And so the paralysis continued.

WHILE THE WAR SECRETARY and several of his colleagues urged the president to become more aggressive, other major figures in the administration believed Roosevelt had already gone too far in helping the British and risking the threat of war. Among those counseling caution was Cordell Hull, who possessed what one observer called a "constitutional aversion to strong or decisive action." After a particularly dispiriting meeting with Hull in late May, Stimson noted in his diary that the secretary of state "does nothing but emit sentiments of defeatism. . . . 'Everything is going hellward' was the expression he kept using again and again." Other key figures in the State Department, including assistant secretaries of state Adolf Berle and Breckinridge Long, were noted for their Anglophobia and antiwar attitudes. Indeed, Long, who did his best to prevent Jewish refugees from entering the United States in the late 1930s and early 1940s, was labeled a "fascist" by Eleanor Roosevelt.

Even more disturbing to Stimson was the active resistance of many high-level Army and Navy officers to an all-out effort to save the British. General George Marshall, who was rapidly becoming the country's most respected military leader, played a complex role in the internecine bureaucratic battles waged over the issue. Marshall had testified in favor of Lend-Lease and supported the idea of U.S. protection for British convoys, but his rationale in both cases was to help the American defense effort rather than to aid Britain. In the case of Lend-Lease, he told Congress that the vast increases in war production mandated under the plan would be of great benefit to the U.S. military as well; if Britain were defeated, expanded U.S. industrial capacity would provide additional weapons and munitions for the defense of the United States and the rest of the Western Hemisphere. As for convoying, Marshall believed that providing naval escorts would help strengthen hemispheric defense, in addition to keeping Britain in the fight long enough to allow America to adequately arm itself.

At the same time, the Army chief resisted the notion that the United States should enter the war. Testifying before a congressional committee, he remarked: "I do not believe there is a group of people in the United States who are more unanimous in their earnest desire to avoid involvement in this ghastly war than the officers of the War Department." Marshall opposed even more strongly Roosevelt's plan for an equal division of weapons and other supplies between the British and U.S. armed forces, an idea FDR had come up with shortly after the 1940 election. "It would be stretching the point too far to call Marshall an isolationist," the historians J. Garry Clifford and Samuel R. Spencer Jr. have written. "But his concern for hemispheric defense and his desire to place American rearmament needs ahead of military assistance to the Allies were compatible with the Gibraltar America ideas of the America First Committee." In his memoirs, General Albert Wedemeyer, who mounted a stout defense of his own isolationist beliefs and activities before America entered the war, wrote that Marshall "realized that American interests were being jeopardized by President Roosevelt's policy of extending all possible aid to any nation fighting" the Axis.

Marshall and his advisers were convinced that if, despite their best efforts, the United States was pulled into the war, the only hope for defeating the Germans would be the dispatch of a large American land force to Europe, numbering well over a million men. But in the spring of 1941, the U.S. Army had only enough weapons and equipment for less than a tenth of that number of troops. The Army brass were horrified by the idea that half the war supplies emerging from U.S. factories, scant in number as they were, would automatically go to the British.

Marshall and his air chief, Hap Arnold, also felt that if America were forced to turn over much of its modern aircraft to others, the Army Air Corps would be powerless to help defend the country or participate meaningfully in any future overseas conflict. Arnold, with Marshall's support, had repeatedly and vociferously protested the transfer of U.S.-made aircraft to Britain. The two generals were particularly upset about FDR's plan to send to the British 50 percent of America's new heavy bombers, the powerful B-17s, which were still being produced in relatively small numbers. At one point, Marshall ordered Arnold to "see if there is anything more we dare do" to prevent implementation of Roosevelt's "even-stephen directive."

Grenville Clark, recalling his own disagreements with Marshall over conscription, had the Army chief of staff in mind when he wrote to Stimson about his fear of "a too narrow approach by our military people—too much emphasis on 'home' and 'hemisphere' defense; undue emphasis on so-called 'American interests' and a defensive attitude against British views. . . . If it prevailed, this approach would be the best way to lose the war. It must be resisted and broken down."

Throughout 1941, Marshall received much of his military intelligence from staffers who were both anti-British and antiwar. Early in the year, he brought to Washington arguably the most isolationist-minded officer in the entire U.S. Army. A close friend of Marshall's, General Stanley Embick was a former deputy chief of staff and ex-head of the Army's War Plans Division. He was also a fierce Anglophobe who believed that America should arm itself only for defense. While serving as deputy chief, Embick had openly aligned himself with a prominent pacifist organization, the National Council for Prevention of War. In 1938, he circulated copies of an antiwar speech by the council's president among his colleagues in the War Department that, among other things, advocated passage of a constitutional amendment requiring a national plebiscite before the country could go to war. Now commander of the Third Army, the sixty-four-year-old Embick had recently declared that America's interventionists showed "less historical sense than the average European peasant."

In March 1941, a few weeks before Embick was to retire, Marshall summoned him to the War Department to participate in secret Anglo-American talks about possible joint action when and if the United States ever entered the war. Embick was an interesting choice for the assignment, considering his isolationism and his well-known dislike of the British and their leader, Winston Churchill.

During the meetings, the U.S. and British delegations agreed that if their countries did indeed find themselves fighting together, their main effort would be against Germany rather than Japan. They also decided that a large detachment of the American navy would be deployed to guard British merchant ships, while up to thirty U.S. submarines would operate against enemy shipping. The British were pleased with the plans, but they went no further, since Roosevelt showed little interest in implementing them.

A month later, Marshall called Embick back to Washington. This time, Marshall wanted his friend to participate in high-level strategy discussions at the War Department about what advice the Army should give the president as he pondered possible responses to Hitler's March 25 expansion of the German combat zone around Britain.

Under heavy pressure from Stimson, Knox, Admiral Stark, Henry Morgenthau, and other top administration officials, Roosevelt was leaning at that point toward ordering convoy protection by the U.S. Navy as far as Iceland and even, perhaps, all the way to Britain. He also had decided to transfer a sizable number of warships from Pearl Harbor to the Atlantic. If both those actions were taken, the possibility of war with Germany, as everyone knew, would increase dramatically.

At the request of Harry Hopkins, Marshall asked his top strategists in the War Plans Division to come up with answers to two key questions: Was it a sound strategic move to propel the country into war at that moment? Or was it possible to put off such a momentous step?

The war planners' response was a qualified yes for active U.S. participation in the war effort. Acknowledging that the Navy initially would have to bear the brunt of the fighting since the Army was so weak, Marshall's strategists still thought it "highly desirable" that the United States enter the war "sufficiently soon" to ensure the survival of Britain. A state of war, they said, would awaken the American people "to the gravity of the current situation" and bring them together "in a cohesive effort that does not today prevail. Production of equipment and preparation in general would be materially speeded up," and "the Churchill Government would be strengthened."

In a meeting with Marshall to discuss the report, one of the planners, Colonel Joseph McNarney, was even more outspoken about the need for belligerency. "It is important," he argued, "that we start reducing the war-making ability of Germany. We do have a Navy in being that can do something. If we wait, we will end up standing alone . . . I may be called a fire-eater, but something must be done."

In the course of the discussion, Embick walked into the room. Asked his views, he replied that he agreed with none of the planners' conclusions. Not only was he strongly opposed to America's entry into the war (which he said would be "wrong from military and naval viewpoints" and "wrong to the American people"), he was against providing any military or economic aid to Britain. Unlike members of the War Plans Division, Embick did not see Britain's situation as perilous. Even if it were, he said, "if the current crisis led to the fall of the Churchill government, so much the better for the British." (Embick's disdain for Churchill was well known; he had once referred to the prime minister as "a vainglorious fool who ought to be thrown out of office for not making peace with the Nazis.")

After the meeting, Marshall took Embick with him to the White House, where Embick repeated to the president his remarks about America's unreadiness for war and the inadvisability of entering this one—or, for that matter, doing anything at all to provoke the Germans. Following the session, Roosevelt decided against the idea of Navy convoy escorts and settled instead for expanded patrols in the Atlantic. He also canceled his order transferring warships from the Pacific. According to several accounts, Embick's advice, which bolstered FDR's natural inclination toward caution, played a major role in his decisions.

Not long afterward, Marshall made Embick, in effect, his senior military adviser—a decision that would have profound consequences for American military policy, especially with regard to Britain, throughout the war.

EMBICK WAS HARDLY THE only key member of Marshall's staff known for his anti-British, isolationist bent. Lindbergh's confidant, Colonel

Truman Smith, also remained close to the Army chief, despite his run-ins with the White House the previous year. Like most of his colleagues in Army intelligence, Smith made no secret of his belief that Germany would soon overpower Britain and that America should abandon what Smith saw as its hopeless attempt to save the country.

Although Marshall had urged Smith to stay away from Lindbergh, he disregarded the warning, continuing to meet regularly with the country's top isolationist to plot antiwar strategy while at the same time serving as the Army chief of staff's main expert on Germany. Smith also remained close to General Friedrich von Boetticher, Germany's military attaché in Washington, who told his superiors in Berlin that the colonel was "in a choice position to know what the administration was planning and could be relied upon to do his best through his influential friends to thwart the President's plans."

Throughout 1941, Smith passed on military information to Lindbergh and other prominent isolationists, including former president Herbert Hoover. At a meeting with Hoover, Smith said that no one in Army intelligence "could see any point of our going to war," adding that "no member of the General Staff wants to go to war but they can bring no great influence to bear on the situation." The political "pressures on General Marshall were so great," Smith told Hoover, that if questioned publicly about its attitudes toward war, the General Staff "would be compelled to issue some kind of equivocation."

For months, Smith had been circulating throughout the government pessimistic intelligence reports about the chances for British survival. In mid-April 1941, according to Henry Stimson, Smith "made it about as bad as it could be in the Mediterranean," predicting Britain's imminent defeat in Greece and the Middle East and charging the Churchill government with "disastrous interference" in British military affairs. An infuriated Stimson ordered Marshall to warn Smith and others in Army intelligence never to make such "a dangerous statement" again. The war secretary declared to Marshall that "the success of the United States depends on the safety of the British fleet; the safety of the British fleet and its preservation depends on the preservation of the Churchill government. Therefore, in circulating such rumors or comments, [Smith and the others] are attacking the vital safety of the United States, and I won't have it."

Marshall later reported to Stimson that he had followed his order.

Nonetheless, Stimson soon afterward received another gloomy report from Smith about Britain's chances that included more scathing comments about Churchill and his government. Stimson exploded, shouting to Marshall that he "couldn't stand it any more" and demanding that the Army chief do something to stop the "pro-German influence" pervading his intelligence division. After Marshall shouted back, defending his men, the two calmed down; Marshall said he would think about what Stimson had said and discuss it with Smith again. Whether the promised conversation actually took place is unclear. If it did, it had scant results, since Army intelligence reports denigrating Britain and its leaders continued.

Truman Smith and several of his Army intelligence colleagues also gave strong if tacit support to the America First Committee, as did a fair number of other high-ranking officers. Former undersecretary of state William Castle, a close associate of Lindbergh's and the head of America First's Washington chapter, noted in his diary that many active-duty military men sought him out to offer their enthusiastic endorsement for the committee's work. Among them was General Levin Campbell, assistant chief of Army ordnance, who supervised the planning and construction of new munitions factories throughout the country. Campbell's supportive remarks were indicative of "the attitude, seldom expressed because to do so would be dangerous, of a large part of the higher officers of the Army and Navy," Castle wrote. "They don't want to get into this war, and they don't like the way things are run." An admiral told Castle that "practically all the Navy is with me. But they cannot say anything in public. . . . He gave me a list of Admirals who agree and are worth talking to."

The admiral was probably overstating the pervasiveness of Navy antiwar sentiment, but there was no question that it was widespread in the service's upper ranks. (Admiral Stark was a prominent exception.) A White House adviser told Roosevelt that many top naval officers viewed the zealous interventionism of their civilian chief, Frank Knox, with "great alarm. They think he is off base." Knox, for his part, acknowledged to an associate that he "was very much disturbed at finding officers of the United States Navy very defeatist in their point of view." The Navy secretary described to Stimson "how he had to fight against the timidity of his own admirals on any aggressive movement . . . how all their estimates and advice were predicated on the failure of the British."

As difficult as he found many officers in his own department, Stimson agreed that Knox's situation was far worse. "Some of the Naval Officers are a good deal more stubborn and verging on insubordination than anything that I have," Stimson wrote in his diary.

TRY AS HE MIGHT, however, the president was unable to ignore mounting pressure from the public and from interventionist officials within his administration to take bolder action on behalf of Britain. A government survey of the press informed the White House in early May that a sizable percentage of the country's newspapers were now openly critical of the president's failure to shape public opinion. According to the newspapers' editorial writers, there was considerable "apathy, confusion, and timidity" among the American people, thanks to Roosevelt's apparent lack of confidence in their ability to understand and respond to what needed to be done to save Britain and defeat Hitler.

According to the survey, a majority of the public had come to believe that U.S. naval protection of British merchant shipping was essential for Britain's survival. The report urged the president to clarify the issue for his fellow citizens—a recommendation vigorously seconded by several of his advisers.

In response, Roosevelt decided to give another speech, his first major policy address since his Lend-Lease fireside chat five months earlier. The speech, to be broadcast nationwide, was scheduled for May 14 and then delayed until May 27, adding to the already high level of tension and suspense. Rumors about its contents circulated around Washington. The president was going to announce the beginning of convoying, some said. No, others responded, he was planning to ask Congress to repeal the neutrality law. Still others said he would call for a congressional declaration of war.

FDR was deluged by advice from all over the country on what he should say; more than twelve thousand letters were delivered to the White House in a period of three days. Among those weighing in was Henry Stimson, who, in an exceedingly blunt note, did his best to stiffen the president's resolve. The American people, Stimson wrote, are "looking to you to lead and guide them . . . and it would be disastrous for you to disappoint them." The war secretary added that "expedients and halfway measures" were no longer enough, that Americans should not be asked to go to war because of "an accident or mistake" in the Atlantic. "They must be brought to that momentous resolution by your leadership."

For several weeks, the militant interventionists in Roosevelt's circle had been urging him to proclaim an unlimited state of emergency, an executive decision that would allow him to exercise a number of broad war powers. While working on the speech with his two main speechwriters, Robert Sherwood and Sam Rosenman, FDR did not mention the emergency declaration; after several drafts, the speechwriters, on their own initiative, put it in. When Roosevelt spied it in the text, he asked with a faint smile: "Hasn't somebody been taking some liberties?" Rosenman and Sherwood admitted that they had but that they thought it was what he really wanted to say. The president was silent for a moment. Then he mused: "You know, there is only a small number of rounds of ammunition left to use unless the Congress is willing to give me more. This declaration of an unlimited emergency is one of those few rounds, and a very important one. Is this the right time to use it, or should we wait until things get worse—as they surely will?" The speechwriters made no reply, and the declaration stayed in the speech.

On the evening of May 27, Roosevelt spoke to the nation from the East Room of the White House. An estimated eighty-five million Americans, more than 65 percent of the nation's population and the largest radio audience in history up until then, had tuned in to listen.

In highly graphic terms, Roosevelt outlined the great peril that would face the United States if Britain were defeated. The Nazis would "strangle" the country economically; American workers "would have to compete with slave labor in the rest of the world. . . . The American farmer would get for his products exactly what Hitler wanted to give. . . . We would be permanently pouring out our resources into armaments."

But, he declared, he and his administration would never allow that to happen. The president proclaimed a state of unlimited national emergency and vowed full-scale support for Britain. "The delivery of necessary supplies to Britain is imperative," he said, and "all additional measures necessary to deliver the goods will be taken." With great emphasis, he added: "This can be done. It must be done. It will be done."

These were passionate and galvanizing words, and to many in Roosevelt's audience, they sounded "almost like a call to arms." Telegrams began pouring into the White House even before the president finished speaking, and, to his delight and relief, they were, as he told Sherwood, "ninety-five percent favorable!" (Whenever he gave a major policy address or announced a new initiative, such as Lend-Lease or the destroyers-bases deal, Roosevelt seemed surprised when the public responded positively. As those around him saw it, he always believed he was taking a far bigger political risk than he actually was.)

Sherwood would later write that the American press and public interpreted the president's May 27 speech as "a solemn commitment. The entry of the United States in the war against Germany was now considered inevitable and even imminent." In an editorial, *The New York Times* praised FDR for striking "a mighty blow for freedom," adding that the course to which the president "had pledged the country . . . will have the endorsement of the vast majority of our people." But in all the favorable comment, there was little mention of FDR's failure to commit to any future action.

The day after the broadcast, more than two hundred reporters crowded into Roosevelt's office, eager to learn the specifics of what he was going to do now. They were doomed to disappointment. As had happened so often before, the president, having talked tough, backed away from all notions of belligerency. There would be no convoying, at least for the present; no repeal of the neutrality law; and no fighting. In addition, Roosevelt said, he had no plans "at the present time" to issue the executive orders necessary for putting into effect the unlimited emergency he had just proclaimed.

Throughout the country, there was a sense of deflation. The president's speech, *Life* wrote, had clearly seemed to promise action: "On your marks, he had said to the nation, for a race with destiny. . . . Get set for the greatest effort of our history. Then, while the people waited poised and tense, he tucked the starter's gun back in his pocket and went off to a Hyde Park weekend."

The British, meanwhile, were fast running out of patience. A London newspaper, the *News Chronicle,* pulled no punches in the first paragraph of an editorial directed at the United States: "We want you in this war on our side. Fighting. Now." About Americans' indecision, London's *Daily Mirror* noted with exasperation: "They seem to have taken up permanent residence on the brink of a precipice. . . . Don't miss the next tense installment of this gripping drama next week . . . next month . . . sometime . . . never."

In late May, a quasiofficial British publication, *Jane's All the World's Aircraft,* carried a statement by its editor that the United States had decided to support the war "to the last Englishman." Embarrassed officials of the Ministry of Aircraft Production disavowed any connection with the book, and its publishers said the insult would be deleted.

For U.S. officials in London, Washington—in its unwillingness to come to grips with the possible defeat of Britain—seemed like another planet. "It is impossible for me to understand the ostrich-like attitude of America," Averell Harriman fumed to a friend. "Either we have an interest in the outcome of this war or we have not. . . . If we have, why do we not realize that every day we delay direct participation . . . we are taking an extreme risk that the war will be lost?"

"The whole thing is going to be a race against time," General Raymond Lee, the U.S. military attaché in London, wrote in his journal. "It is a question whether our support will arrive soon enough to bolster up what is a gradually failing cause."

CHAPTER 20

"A TRAITOROUS POINT OF VIEW"

The president's lethargy clearly did not extend to his feelings about his political enemies—a fact that Robert Sherwood discovered when he helped Roosevelt write a speech just days after congressional approval of Lend-Lease. In Sherwood's view, the address should have been used as an occasion to celebrate the administration's triumph. That, however, was not how the president saw it.

Announcing that he was going "to get really tough in this one," Roosevelt, looking gray and tired, unleashed what Sherwood later described as a "scathing and vindictive" attack against those who opposed his efforts to help the British, referring angrily to "a certain columnist" and "a certain Senator" as well as "certain Republican orators." Sherwood was stunned. He had never seen the president in such a vile mood, had never observed him "lose his temper . . . or be the least bit jittery, or be anything but scrupulously cautious to subordinates."

After about an hour of dictating this "dossier of grudges" to a stenographer, FDR abruptly stopped and, without a word, left the room. An appalled Sherwood immediately tracked down Harry Hopkins to let him know what had happened. Hopkins airily told the speechwriter not to worry: he was sure that the president was simply getting all "the irritable stuff" off his chest and that he had no intention of using it in the speech.

Hopkins was right, but only in regard to that one address. Roosevelt was furious at his isolationist foes, and from early 1941 on, he threw his energy into a no-holds-barred effort to destroy their credibility and influence. "If 1940 was like the start of a rough chariot race, 1941 was its brutal climax," Ernest Cuneo, a Democratic Party operative, recalled. "Once having cleared the election barrier, FDR threw off his wraps, strapped on his helmet, and went in."

Initially, the president had hoped that the passage of Lend-Lease would mark the end of isolationism's influence, that Americans would now come together to support their country's new role as a nonbelligerent ally of Britain. Many did. But while the interventionist movement had unquestionably gained ground by the spring of 1941, isolationism, although considerably diminished, remained an unmistakable force, and its diehard proponents vowed to fight Roosevelt to the end.

Again and again, Roosevelt and his allies stressed the need for national unity—on their terms. In one post-Lend-Lease speech, the president insisted that the time for questioning and dissent was over: "Your government has the right to expect of all citizens that they take part in the common work of our common defense—take loyal part from this moment forward." Those who continued to dissent were criticized as narrow, self-serving, partisan, and unpatriotic. According to Roosevelt, they were aiding, "unwittingly in most cases," the work of Axis agents in this country, who sought "to divide our people into hostile groups and destroy our unity and shatter our will to defend ourselves." FDR went on: "I do not charge these American citizens with being foreign agents. But I do charge them with doing exactly the kind of work that the dictators want done in the United States."

About Roosevelt's tactics, historian Richard Steele would later observe: "What the president battled . . . was not disloyalty but the doubt of a minority of Americans concerning the origins and purposes of the war. Instead of tackling those misgivings head on, admittedly a difficult task of education, FDR chose to discredit and dismiss them." Roosevelt's strategem—to question his critics' patriotism and accuse them of giving aid and comfort to the enemy—would be used by a number of later presidents, including Lyndon Johnson, Ronald Reagan, and George W. Bush, when faced with opposition to their own foreign policy.

The historian Wayne Cole, a scholar of the isolationist movement, wrote about this period: "Theoretically, freedom of speech prevailed on foreign policy issues, but in practice, by 1941, any individual who spoke out on the noninterventionist side was suspect and had to be prepared to have his reputation besmirched and his wisdom and even his loyalty questioned."

Not surprisingly, the main targets in the anti-isolationist campaign were America First and its most famous member, Charles Lindbergh. Lindbergh's decision to join the organization in April 1941 was an enormous boon to America First, which had seen its membership and fund-raising plummet following its defeat over Lend-Lease. Both shot up as soon as General Robert Wood announced the aviator's appointment to America First's national board. Speaking of Lindbergh, Wood declared: "He has emerged as the real leader of our point of view, with a tremendous following amongst the people of this country." The journalist H. R. Knickerbocker noted that Lindbergh's reputation might have been tarnished over the previous year, but "because he had something that appealed so profoundly to America that he has not lost it all yet . . . he towers in influence above our other isolationists. . . . Lindbergh is, I am convinced, mainly responsible for the long hesitation of this country to go to war to defend its life."

Roosevelt clearly believed that, too. According to the historian Kenneth S. Davis, the president was convinced that Lindbergh controlled the balance of power in the isolationist movement: "By holding together a hard core, which would otherwise disintegrate from obvious stresses, and by confusing and dividing a significant minority of people . . . he was able to prevent truly effective action by the administration. Ergo, Lindbergh should be muzzled."

Within a few weeks of Lindbergh's joining America First, the reenergized group had signed up hundreds of thousands of new members. Wherever he spoke at America First rallies, enormous overflow crowds showed up to cheer him on. He was so popular with the organization's rank and file that he was used as a sort of door prize: America First announced that the chapter showing the largest increase in membership would win the privilege of hosting Lindbergh's next speech.

All this was greatly worrying to the president and his men. They were particularly concerned about Lindbergh's continuing appeal to young people, such as the Yale students who founded America First. Dorothy Thompson, who remained a stalwart supporter of the president after the 1940 election, went so far as to equate U.S. college students' interest in Lindbergh and his views with the Hitler youth movement's adoration of the Führer.

Yet while America First reached the peak of its strength after Lindbergh joined its ranks, it also was subjected to considerably more criticism because of him. Ironically, one of Lindbergh's most outspoken antagonists during this time was Robert Sherwood, who had been so aghast at Roosevelt's bitter criticism of his opponents. Shortly before beginning work at the White House, Sherwood, in a radio speech to Canadian listeners, referred to the man he had once considered a hero as "a bootlicker of Adolph Hitler" who had "a traitorous point of view" and "devoted himself to pleading Hitler's cause." Having all but called Lindbergh a Nazi, Sherwood did, in fact, do so in a later speech to a White Committee gathering, in which he labeled Lindbergh as "simply a Nazi with a Nazi's Olympian contempt for all democratic processes."

The White House recruited a long list of members of Congress and administration officials to join Sherwood in its vilification of Lind-

Interior Secretary Harold Ickes shakes hands in Washington with Anthony Eden, former—and future—British foreign secretary.

bergh. The main presidential surrogate was Interior Secretary Harold Ickes, who clearly relished the job, repeatedly reminding his audiences that he had been the first man of prominence to attack the flier, for his acceptance of a German medal in 1938. A man with "a genius for . . . hitting the jugular," as Francis Biddle noted, Ickes was so obsessed with Lindbergh that he maintained an indexed, annotated file of all his speeches and articles.

In a 1940 speech, Ickes blasted Lindbergh as a "native fascist" and "peripatetic appeaser who would abjectly surrender his sword even before it is demanded." In February 1941, the interior secretary said Lindbergh and his allies were "the quislings who, in pretended patriotism, would cravenly spike our guns and ground our planes in order that Hitlerism might more easily overcome us." Two months later, in his most slashing attack yet, Ickes accused Lindbergh of being the "No. 1 Nazi fellow traveler" in the United States and "the first American to raise aloft the standard of pro-Nazism." In that same April speech, he referred to Anne Lindbergh's notorious *The Wave of the Future* as "the bible of every American Nazi, Fascist, Bundist and appeaser."

A few days after Ickes's address, FDR himself decided to take on Lindbergh. Until then, he had made only oblique derogatory references to the aviator and his wife. Encouraged by Sherwood, he had, for example, disparagingly taken note of Anne Lindbergh's book in his third inaugural address, declaring: "There are men who believe that . . . tyranny and slavery have become the surging wave of the future—and that freedom is an ebbing tide. We Americans know that this is not true."

But by the early spring of 1941, Roosevelt was convinced that what Ickes repeatedly told him was true—that Lindbergh was "a ruthless and conscious fascist," motivated by his hatred for the president and determined to "obtain ultimate power for himself." Toward the end of April, the president summoned to his office a man named John Franklin Carter, the head of a small, secret White House research and intelligence unit that FDR had created. A Yale graduate and syndicated newspaper columnist, Carter, together with his staff of researchers, collected information on a wide variety of subjects for Roosevelt, from public opinion to the president's political opponents. On this occasion, the president asked Carter to provide him with material on Civil War Copperheads, northerners with pro-southern sympathies who had been critical of President Lincoln and the war.

Once Carter completed his research, Roosevelt's press secretary, Steve Early, told White House reporters that if, at the next presidential press conference, they brought up the question of why Lindbergh, unlike so many other reserve officers, hadn't yet been called into active military service, they might get an interesting answer.

On April 25, a reporter did ask the question, and Roosevelt's ready response took the form of a history lesson. During the Civil War, he said, some men were deliberately barred from serving in the U.S. Army because of their defeatist attitudes. Prominent among them were the antiwar Copperheads, led by an Ohio senator named Clement Vallandigham, who made "violent speeches" against the Lincoln administration and declared that the North could never win a conflict with the South. Arrested and banished to the Confederacy, Vallandigham made his way to Canada, then returned to the North, where he continued agitating. Pressured to try him for treason, Lincoln decided not to do so.

When reporters asked Roosevelt if he was equating Lindbergh with Vallandigham, the president said yes. In that same context, he mentioned Revolutionary War appeasers who tried to persuade George Washington to quit at Valley Forge, arguing that the British could not be defeated. No journalist at the press conference apparently thought to mention that the analogy between Lindbergh and the earlier defeatists was faulty in at least one respect: in April 1941, the United States was not yet at war.

Roosevelt's denunciation of Lindbergh made front-page headlines across the country, with many of the headlines and stories noting that the president had all but called Lindbergh a traitor. FDR's statements unleashed a new flood of public attacks on the flier. In Charleston, West Virginia, a federal judge, while swearing in a grand jury, went off topic to condemn Lindbergh for criticizing Roosevelt's foreign policy. "You say that we have freedom of speech in this country," the judge declared, "but I'll tell you that no man should be allowed to attack our government, especially in these days." He added that "Lindbergh's type destroys America." In a letter to the editor of The New York Times in early June, a reader called Lindbergh "a maggot" and demanded that he be arrested on charges of treason and incitement of revolution.

Roosevelt's anti-Lindbergh statement and the reaction to it received considerable criticism, even from a number of prominent interventionists. While Lindbergh's foreign policy views were similar to those advocated by Nazi propaganda, he had never favored Nazism for Germany or any other country, including the United States. Indeed, he opposed the idea of any foreign government or party influencing America. As *Life* pointed out, "There is nothing on record or available as evidence to show that Lindbergh deliberately follows the Nazi Party line or has any contacts today with German leaders or agents. Perhaps Lindbergh appears pro-Nazi because practically everyone else is so anti-Nazi."

According to a government report sent to FDR, "There has been rather unfavorable press reaction to the President's verbal castigation of [Lindbergh]. . . . It is argued that presidential indulgence in personalities diminishes national unity." Wendell Willkie said he hoped that "the administration will discontinue these constant and bitter attacks. . . . Democracy should function through orderly and thoughtful discussion and not through adolescent name-calling. Nothing can contribute more to disunity than such attacks." Speaking days later at an interventionist rally in New York, Willkie chided the audience for booing and catcalling when Lindbergh's name was mentioned. "Let's not boo any American citizen," he said. "We come here tonight, men and women of all faiths and parties, not to slander our fellow citizens. We want all of them. Let's save all our boos for Hitler."

Lindbergh, for his part, was uncharacteristically shaken by the president's attack. He had long been noted for what his wife called "his immobile, tolerant unconcern" regarding criticism, once telling a reporter that he only cared about "the future welfare of my country, my family, my friends, and my fellow citizens. In relation to these things, the names one is called makes very little difference."

But this was not just a political attack, he thought: the president of the United States had directly questioned his loyalty and impugned his honor. "What luck it is to find myself opposing my country's entrance into a war I *don't* believe in, when I would so much rather be fighting for my country in a war I *do* believe in," Lindbergh bitterly observed in his journal. "If only the United States could be on the *right* side of an intelligent war! There *are* wars worth fighting, but if we get into this one, we will bring disaster to the country."

After brooding for several days about what to do, Lindbergh wrote a letter to Roosevelt resigning his commission. "I take this action with the utmost regret," he told the president, "for my relationship with the Air Corps is one of the things which has meant most to me in my life. I place it second only to my right as a citizen to speak freely to my fellow countrymen, and to discuss with them the issues of war and peace which confront our nation in this crisis."

In what the columnist Doris Fleeson called "this new and crackling chapter of the Roosevelt-Lindbergh feud," Steve Early sharply criticized Lindbergh for releasing to the press his letter to FDR at the same time it was sent to the White House. It was a tactic, Early noted, that Lindbergh had used in 1934 when he dispatched a letter to Roosevelt criticizing his cancellation of airmail contracts. Then, in another dig at Lindbergh, Early wondered aloud whether he was also "returning his decoration by Mr. Hitler." According to one newspaper account of Early's comments, he "had just left the President, and none doubted that the Hitlerian wisecrack was of Rooseveltian authorship."

Many in the press charged both Lindbergh and Roosevelt with unseemly, petulant behavior. "No evidence existed to justify the President's comparison of Mr. Lindbergh with Senator Vallandigham," *The New York Times* editorialized. "Nor is any American, from private to general officer, in service or on reserve, big enough to take the position that he will not serve his country because he has been, as he believes, unjustly reprimanded by his commander in chief or any other superior." The incident, said *Life*, had "left a bad taste in America's mouth. The President had delivered an unnecessary insult. The Lone Eagle had resigned in an unnecessary tantrum."

UP TO THAT POINT, Lindbergh's speeches had been relatively measured and objective, refraining, for the most part, from personal attacks. That changed, however, after the White House assault. His addresses became much more contentious, bitter, and demagogic, with frequent, strident criticisms of Roosevelt and other administration officials. Specifically, he charged the president with undermining democracy and representative government.

Democracy, Lindbergh told an America First rally in Minneapolis, "doesn't exist today, even in our own country." He denounced what he called "government by subterfuge" and charged that Roosevelt had denied Americans "freedom of information—the right of a free people

Charles Lindbergh addresses a jammed America First rally in Fort Wayne, Indiana.

to know where they are being led by their government." At New York's Madison Square Garden, he declared that during the 1940 presidential campaign, voters were given "just about as much chance" to express their views on foreign policy "as the Germans would have been given if Hitler had run against Goering."

When, in one speech, he urged "new policies and new leadership" for the country, his critics charged him with calling for the overthrow of the Roosevelt administration. Lindbergh vigorously denied the charge and, for the first and only time in his antiwar campaign, issued a statement clarifying what he had meant. In a telegram to the Baltimore *Sun,* which had requested the clarification, he said: "Neither I nor anyone else on the America First Committee advocate proceeding by anything but constitutional methods." In a rather strained additional explanation, he insisted that his call for a change in leadership had actually been aimed at the interventionist movement—"the leadership of the opposition which we (the Nation) have been following in recent months."

With Roosevelt and Lindbergh setting the tone, the debate over

America's involvement in the war grew ever more poisonous. "Individuals on both sides found it increasingly difficult to see their opponents as honest people who happened to hold different opinions," the historian Wayne Cole observed. "Attacks on both sides became more personal, vicious, and destructive. It became easier to see one's adversaries not just as mistaken but as evil, and possibly motivated by selfish, antidemocratic, or even subversive considerations."

The wife of the journalist Raymond Clapper learned firsthand how brutal the debate had become when her husband began receiving hundreds of "filthy, profane" letters, threatening his life and those of his two children, for merely advocating in his syndicated column the dispatch of more aid to Britain. One day, Olive Clapper received a gift-wrapped package in the mail. She opened it to find a miniature black coffin with a paper skeleton inside, labeled "Your husband."

Interventionist newspapers and magazines easily matched their isolationist counterparts—the *Chicago Tribune,* the Hearst press, and Scripps-Howard papers—in venomous assaults on their opponents. While the *San Francisco Chronicle* ran a cartoon showing Senator Gerald Nye waving an America First banner aboard a caboose labeled "Nazi," Robert McCormick's *Tribune* referred to Roosevelt and his men as "fat old men, senile hysterics . . . who devote their every energy to stirring up wars for other men to fight." *Time,* meanwhile, called America First a collection of "Jew-haters, Roosevelt-haters, England-haters, Coughlinites, politicians, and demagogues." In an editorial, the *Chicago Daily News* implied that the stands taken by America First had given aid and comfort to the enemy, which, the paper said, constituted treason.

Also taking part in the blame game was a man who would soon emerge as one of America's most beloved authors of children's books—the incomparable Dr. Seuss. Theodor Geisel—Dr. Seuss's real name—was then working as an editorial cartoonist for *PM,* a left-leaning, interventionist New York daily newspaper. According to Ralph Ingersoll, *PM*'s editor and publisher, isolationists were "enemies of Democracy," and thus his paper had "a special obligation—and privilege—to expose them."

A Dartmouth graduate, Geisel had already published two children's books—*King's Stilts* and *Horton Hatches the Egg*—when he began work at *PM* in 1941. Employing the knife-sharp wit and whimsical surrealistic animals that became the trademarks of his books, Geisel's cartoons skewered both Axis leaders and American isolationists. Next to Hitler, his favorite subject was Charles Lindbergh.

In one cartoon, Lindbergh is shown patting a Nazi dragon on the head. In another, a group of ostriches (the ostrich was Geisel's symbol for isolationism) march down a street carrying a sign reading LINDBERGH FOR PRESIDENT IN 1944! while several sinister black-hooded figures, labeled "U.S. fascists," follow with their own sign: YEAH, BUT WHY WAIT UNTIL 1944? In yet another, a smiling whale cavorts on a mountaintop, singing: "I'm saving my scalp / Living high on an Alp / Dear Lindy! He gave me the notion!"

America First was also a frequent target of Geisel's satiric pen. One of his 1941 cartoons featured a mother, labeled "America First," reading a book called *Adolf the Wolf* to her frightened children. The caption reads: ". . . and the wolf chewed up the children and spit out their bones. . . . But those were Foreign Children, and it really didn't matter."

Thanks to the withering criticism aimed at America First by Geisel and others, a sizable number of the organization's more moderate members resigned, and in several chapters, there was a significant shift to the extreme right. Members of fringe groups like Father Coughlin's National Union of Social Justice made up an increasingly large part of America First audiences, loudly booing any mention of Roosevelt, Winston Churchill, or Wendell Willkie and cheering speakers' gibes at the British and "international bankers," as well as assertions that Britain was losing the war.

To underscore his point that Britain should negotiate with Germany, Lindbergh told one rally that the British were in danger of starvation and that their cities were being "devastated by bombing." The cavernous hall promptly erupted in riotous applause. At another rally at which he spoke, several members of the audience chanted "Hang Roosevelt!" and "Impeach the president!" Like other America First leaders, Lindbergh denounced such outpourings of hate, but his scolding had little or no effect. According to the historian Geoffrey Perret, "Lindbergh became, against his will, the darling of the worst elements of isolationism."

DURING THIS TIME, THE interventionist movement was also roiled by a rancorous struggle between moderation and radicalism. It, too, ended with the moderates' defeat, as well as the abrupt resignation of their leader, William Allen White, as head of the committee he had founded in the spring of 1940.

For months, White had been at odds with the more extreme interventionists in his organization, many of whom were also members of the Century Group. Although he had fought hard for all-out aid to Britain, the seventy-two-year-old editor remained steadfast in his belief that America must stay out of the war. "What right has an old man to tell youth to go out and lose its life?" White wrote to Robert Sherwood. "Always I have been restrained by an old man's fear and doubt when it comes to lifting my voice for war. Of such seeds, unhappiness grows and tragedy comes to fruit."

But with Britain edging closer to the brink of disaster, a growing number of people in White's committee lost patience with such personal doubts and scruples. The Century Group was even more outspoken in its disdain for White's desire for moderation and civility. In a letter to *New York Times* publisher Arthur Sulzberger, White complained that the "radical" Century Group "has given me more headaches and has kept me awake at night longer than any other part of my job."

By late 1940, the interventionist split had become a chasm, as seen in a nasty dispute between White and a majority of members in the group's New York chapter over what role the organization should take in the 1940 congressional elections. Most people in the chapter believed the White Committee should support candidates who backed aid to Britain and work to defeat those who did not. White, on the other hand, argued for nonpartisanship. A staunch Republican, he knew that most isolationist members of Congress were members of his own party, and he was determined not to do anything that would hurt their chances for victory.

The issue came to a head when the New York militants formed a group to oppose the election of Hamilton Fish, the archisolationist Republican congressman from their state. The anti-Fish organization used the office of the committee's New York chapter as its headquarters, leading outsiders to conclude that the committee was behind the effort to stop Fish.

Dashing off a letter to the congressman, White disavowed any connection with the campaign against him, adding: "However you and I may disagree about some issues of the campaign, I hope as Republicans we are united in our support of the Republican ticket from top to bottom in every district and every state." He made clear to Fish, an old friend of his, that he could use the letter in any way he wished. Fish immediately made the letter public—and won reelection. Stunned by White's public support for this diehard opponent of his committee's cause, many in his group angrily questioned where their leader's loyalties lay: to his fellow Republicans or to the survival of Britain and the defeat of Nazi Germany.

This fracas was soon followed by a controversy over the committee's future direction. Against White's better judgment, the group's executive board issued a statement in December 1940 urging Roosevelt to step up war mobilization and to assume responsibility for maintaining "the lifeline between Great Britain and the United States," which "under no circumstances" must be cut. In effect, the board was calling for the use of U.S. naval escorts for British merchant shipping if all other measures failed. White, who opposed convoying, worried that the committee was "getting out too far in front" of public opinion and the president. From his home in Kansas, he informed other committee leaders of his deep concerns.

A few days later, White learned that the publisher Roy Howard was planning to run an article in his Scripps-Howard newspapers attacking him and his group as advocates of war. Worn out from his work on the committee, exasperated by those he called "radical warmongers," and worried about his wife's poor health, White had had enough. He notified Howard that the premise for his story was completely false: "The only reason in God's world I am in this organization is to keep this country out of war. . . . The story is floating around that I and our outfit are in favor of sending convoys [which is] a silly thing, for convoys, unless you shoot, are confetti, and it's not time to shoot now— or ever." White added this parting shot: "If I was making a motto for the Committee to Defend America by Aiding the Allies, it would be 'The Yanks Are Not Coming.'" He gave Howard permission to print the letter.

Its publication stunned White's colleagues on the executive board, as well as the group's rank and file. Their leader had, in effect, committed them to a policy that many were adamantly against: opposition to U.S. participation in the war, regardless of Britain's fate. "The mis-

understanding over your Howard interview is having national reper-
cussions, and unless we can agree quickly on a statement, our movement
is threatened with disaster," the committee's executive director, Clark
Eichelberger, told White in an urgent telegram.

But there was no misunderstanding, and isolationist leaders quickly
moved to capitalize on this obvious deep split in the interventionist
movement. "Mr. White has rendered a great service to this country by
clarifying his position and the position of his committee," Charles
Lindbergh said. "It seems to me advisable to accept his statement at its
face value and to welcome him to the camp of the 'isolationists.'"

The isolationists' glee over White's letter was matched by an out-
pouring of interventionist fury. Fiorello La Guardia, New York City's
mayor, accused White of "doing a typical Laval," referring to the pro-
German foreign minister of Vichy France. In a letter he made public,
La Guardia suggested to White that he "continue as Chairman of the
Committee to Defend America by Aiding the Allies with Words and
the rest of us would join a Committee to Defend America by Aiding
the Allies with Deeds."

The White Committee's New York chapter promptly invited La
Guardia to be its honorary chairman. "If anybody had been looking
for the best possible way to kick Mr. White out," J. P. Morgan partner
Thomas Lamont wrote to Roosevelt, "nothing could have been so
perfect as to have the New York chapter applaud Mayor La Guardia's
insulting letter."

White took the hint. On January 1, 1941, he resigned as the committee's national chairman. Six months before, his presence as its head
had helped win wide national support for the idea of giving aid to the
Allies, but his moderation now was considered passé. He complained
to a friend that the committee was under the control of diehard interventionists, "and there is no way to oust them . . . I just can't remain the
head of an organization which is being used to ghost dance for war."

With White's resignation, Lewis Douglas, a firebrand member of
the Century Group, became the committee's most influential figure.
"Whatever is needed to insure the defeat of the Axis," he wrote, "will
be the policy of the Committee." That, he made clear, included the
possibility—even the probability—of war.

Members of the Century Group, meanwhile, dissolved their organization in early 1941, believing that its effectiveness had been limited

by its lack of a grassroots structure and broad-based financial support. Several of the group's members immediately formed a new, more hawkish entity called Fight for Freedom. Among the organization's founders were Herbert Agar and his Louisville *Courier-Journal* colleague Ulric Bell, who became the group's executive director.

Fight for Freedom, which advocated outright U.S. military intervention, was much more aggressive in its demands and inflammatory in its attacks on opponents than the Century Group had been. Its chairman—Henry Hobson, the Episcopal bishop of Cincinnati—introduced the group on April 19, 1941, by declaring that the United States was "in the immoral and craven position of asking others to make the supreme sacrifice for this victory which we recognize as essential to us. Once the U.S. accepts the fact that we are at war, we shall at last find peace within ourselves." In an open letter to General Robert Wood a few months later, Hobson accused America First of becoming "the first fascist party in this nation's history" and told Wood that it was "time for you to disband your organ of Nazi terror and hate."

When the chairman of a Connecticut chapter of America First challenged his Fight for Freedom counterpart to a public debate on foreign affairs, the FFF representative replied that "instead of spending money hiring a hall," America First should hire "an airplane and a few parachutes and [send] Messrs. Lindbergh, Wheeler, Taft and some others . . . into Hitler's Germany, which they are aiding so much by their present activities. . . . In our first fight for freedom, we got rid of Benedict Arnold. In this fight for freedom, let us get rid of all of the Benedict Arnolds."

A Who's Who of the East Coast's business, academic, and cultural elites, Fight for Freedom's membership included Wendell Willkie, Grenville Clark, Lewis Douglas, members of the Rockefeller family, and the presidents of Harvard, Mount Holyoke, and Smith. Also in the group were the writers Maxwell Anderson, Edna Ferber, George S. Kaufman, Moss Hart, Edna St. Vincent Millay, and Dorothy Parker. The organization's main watering hole was the exclusive Manhattan restaurant "21," one of whose owners, Mac Kriendler, was on FFF's national board.

Kriendler made clear where his sympathies lay. Donors to the organization were assured of good tables at "21," while known isolationists were barred from the restaurant. Hamilton Fish once managed to slip past the net but was spotted and confronted by Kriendler's brother and co-owner, Jack, as he was leaving. "Mr. Fish, I'm afraid that I don't like either you or your politics," Jack Kriendler said. "I personally would appreciate your not coming in here again."

Fight for Freedom followed the White Committee's lead in organizing an extensive network of chapters throughout the country which circulated petitions, recruited local newspaper editors to support their cause, and sponsored rallies and letter-writing campaigns to Congress. The new group maintained close ties with the White House; its top leaders were in daily touch with Robert Sherwood, whose wife worked as a volunteer in Fight for Freedom's headquarters, and other members of FDR's staff. At the request of Ulric Bell, press secretary Steve Early authorized White House typists to compile mailing lists for the organization from names and addresses of interventionist letters sent to the president.

Fight for Freedom also collaborated closely with an organization called Friends of Democracy, which proved to be even more militant than FFF. Organized by the Reverend Leon Birkhead, a Unitarian minister from Kansas City, Friends of Democracy hired freelance journalists and investigators to infiltrate right-wing extremist groups and antiwar organizations and observe and publicize their activities.

Early in 1941, Birkhead's organization published an expensively produced pamphlet about America First entitled "The Nazi Transmission Belt," which dubbed the group "a Nazi front . . . by means of which the apostles of Nazism are spreading their antidemocratic ideas into millions of homes." Tens of thousands of copies of the brochure, which received widespread publicity, were distributed by Fight for Freedom chapters across the country.

Soon afterward, Birkhead sought contributions from FFF members for "a publicity campaign branding Charles Lindbergh as a Nazi." The fruit of that campaign was another elaborate pamphlet, this one charging Lindbergh with being "a very real threat to our democratic way of life" and a future "American Hitler." When Lindbergh addressed an overflow America First rally in New York in April 1941, more than a hundred members of Friends of Democracy distributed anti-Lindbergh handbills and picketed outside. Dozens of policemen, many on horseback, spent the evening breaking up scuffles between the interventionists and thousands of America First supporters milling about on nearby streets.

In the country's savage political climate, such scenes were becoming common. Street-corner rallies were staged by both sides in New York and other urban areas. They were supposed to enlighten passersby on the issues but often degenerated into verbal clashes and physical brawls. "A new hysterical note shrills in the oratory," one journalist reported. "Organized hecklers at these meetings frequently precipitate fights. Partisans taunt each other as 'Jews' and 'Nazis.'"

In the early summer of 1941, a Fight for Freedom rally on the steps of St. Thomas Episcopal Church, on Fifth Avenue in Manhattan, dissolved into a nasty fight. A few blocks away, hordes of people leaving an America First rally at Carnegie Hall ran into crowds listening to an interventionist orator on a nearby street corner. Several people were injured in the melee that followed.

As 1941 wore on, the growing intolerance took a particularly heavy toll on the operations of America First and other antiwar groups. In Miami, Atlanta, Pittsburgh, Los Angeles, Seattle, and other major cities, America First was denied permission to hold rallies in public places such as parks and city auditoriums. In Brooklyn, the president of the Dodgers baseball team refused to allow the group to use Ebbets Field. In Oklahoma City, the city council unanimously voted to revoke America First's lease with the municipal auditorium for a rally at which Lindbergh was to speak. (It was held instead at a ballpark outside the city limits.)

Opposition to Lindbergh had become so vocal and threats to his safety so frequent that policemen guarded him in every city where he made an appearance. They searched the rooms where he was to stay and posted guards along his travel routes and in the halls where he spoke. He kept his public exposure to a minimum, appearing only long enough to make his speeches and then quickly making an exit.

In several cities, libraries banned books about him, streets named after him were renamed, and monuments and plaques removed. In New York, the Lafayette Hotel—once owned by Raymond Orteig, the rich businessman whose $25,000 prize spawned Lindbergh's historic flight to Paris—took down from its restaurant wall a flag that Lindbergh had carried on his transatlantic journey. When a reporter asked Orteig's son, who now owned the hotel, why it had disappeared, the son responded with a shrug. "Too many pros and cons," he said. "When we hung it there in 1927, everyone was proud of him. But now he's talking politics, and lately, when people notice the flag, they start getting into arguments. So it seemed best simply to remove it."

Even at home on Long Island, Lindbergh and his family were sur-rounded, as his wife put it, by "bitterness, suspicion, and hate." In her journal, Anne Lindbergh wrote: "I am sick of this place. We no longer have any privacy here; people telephone all day long—they know where we are. They even come out without calling up beforehand and look for us through the house and garden. The beach is so crowded with (chilly to us) people that I no longer can bear to go down there. I feel trapped—on weekends I don't want to walk for fear of meeting people."

In midsummer 1941, Charles and Anne Lindbergh moved again, this time to a small rented house on an isolated, windswept part of Martha's Vineyard, an island off Massachusetts. The family's move prompted an immediate avalanche of letters to the FBI warning of the potential dangers. Declaring that Martha's Vineyard was "a perfect base for German invasion," one letter writer demanded to know: "What is being done to guard this island? Who is watching this man who so loves the Germans and the New Order?" Another correspon-dent wrote: "Most of us would appreciate knowing that 'enemy Americans' are being controlled as well as German and Japanese sus-pects. . . . Martha's Vineyard, being a place easily accessible from a boat off the coast, would of course be an ideal location for a person whose sympathies lay with Germany."

AS IT HAPPENED, THE FBI already had Lindbergh under close observa-tion. Shortly before he and Anne moved to Martha's Vineyard, he dis-covered from an America First acquaintance that the FBI had been tapping the Lindberghs' phone for several months. The agents who passed on the information were "friendly" to Lindbergh, the acquain-tance said, but were obliged to follow orders.

According to William Sullivan, a top FBI official for more than thirty years, Roosevelt had asked J. Edgar Hoover in early 1941 to launch new investigations into the activities of prominent Lend-Lease opponents. The president "also had us look into the activities of others who opposed our entrance into World War II," Sullivan wrote in his memoirs, "just as later administrations had the FBI look into those opposing the conflict in Vietnam."

While Robert Jackson and his successor as attorney general, Francis Biddle, looked the other way, the FBI placed taps on the phones of nearly one hundred individuals and organizations in 1941. Not all administration officials, however, went along with the operation. When Hoover asked James Fly, chairman of the Federal Communications Commission, to monitor all long-distance phone calls between the United States and Axis countries, Fly flatly refused, citing congressional and Supreme Court bans on wiretapping. Fly also strongly opposed administration efforts to introduce legislation that would legalize wiretapping in certain instances.

The FCC chairman's defiance angered Hoover as well as the president, who curtly dismissed his objections that tapping phones was a clear violation of privacy. "I do not think," FDR wrote to Fly, "that any of us should be in a position of hampering legislation . . . by going too much into technicalities." Hoover, for his part, accused Fly of hindering the FBI in its efforts to protect the country from subversion. He passed along such allegations to his close friend, the columnist Walter Winchell, who promptly printed them.

IN THESE TUMULTUOUS pre–Pearl Harbor years, the FBI was not the only government entity whose investigations were raising troubling questions about the violation of civil liberties. The House Committee on Un-American Activities had embarked on similar probes. But instead of going after isolationist groups and native Fascist organizations, its main quarry were liberals, leftists, and the Roosevelt administration.

HUAC had been set up in 1934 as a special committee to investigate pro-Nazi and other right-wing extremist groups in the United States. After ending its operations a year later, it was revived by Congress in 1938 under the chairmanship of Rep. Martin Dies, a right-wing, anti–New Deal Democrat from Texas who, in addition to being addicted to publicity, was opposed to immigration, organized labor, intellectuals, and social change of almost any kind.

Although the committee's mandate was to investigate both Fascist and Communist activities in the United States, Dies focused instead on what he claimed was an extensive Communist presence in organized labor and the federal government. From his first hearings in 1938, the Texas congressman worked to portray the New Deal as part of a vast Communist conspiracy.

That same year, Dies called for the resignation of Harry Hopkins, Harold Ickes, Labor Secretary Frances Perkins, and their "many radical associates" who "range in political insanity from Socialist to Communist." His committee conducted a widely publicized investigation into the Federal Theatre Project, which funded nationwide theater and other live artistic performances during the Depression—a probe that ended in the Project's cancellation. In 1940, Dies published a book called *The Trojan Horse in America,* which declared that Eleanor Roosevelt "has been one of the most valuable assets which the Trojan Horse organizations of the Communist Party possesses."

Although the president took a dim view of Dies's smears of his wife and associates, he nonetheless tried to appease the congressman, whose red-baiting and anti-immigration activities had won a great deal of support on Capitol Hill and, according to polls, among a majority of Americans as well. In an attempt to keep Dies quiet, FDR agreed in early 1939 to supply him with confidential details from tax returns of witnesses called before the committee and to order the FBI to investigate several organizations on Dies's hit list.

But Roosevelt's efforts at conciliation failed to stifle Dies. In 1939, he began publishing the names of alleged Communists and fellow travelers in the administration—more than five hundred in all—with no evidence to back up the charges. According to the historian Robert Griffith, "Martin Dies named more names in one single year than [Senator Joseph] McCarthy did in a lifetime." Griffith, who has written extensively about McCarthy's investigation of purported Communists in the early 1950s, noted: "The Dies Committee pioneered the whole spectrum of slogans, techniques, and political mythologies that would be later called 'McCarthyism.'"

Liberals, many of whom had applauded earlier efforts to quiet those who attacked the president and opposed his foreign policy, now found themselves under assault. Background checks were ordered for applicants for federal government positions, and the Justice Department created a list of subversive organizations, membership in any of which was grounds for dismissal from federal employment.

A number of state and city governments followed suit. In New York, the legislature ordered the firing of more than sixty professors from Brooklyn, Hunter, and City Colleges after they had been denounced as Communists. Several secondary schools in New York were also purged of suspected Communist teachers.

Perhaps the most striking example of obeisance to the repressive temper of the times was the American Civil Liberties Union's decision in 1940 to bar from its staff and leadership any person belonging to a "political organization which supports totalitarian dictatorship in any country." As a result of its new dictum, the ACLU, which had long opposed the idea of guilt by association, sought the resignation of a member of its board of directors who was a Communist. When the member refused to resign, she was expelled from the organization.

CHAPTER 21

"DER FÜHRER THANKS YOU FOR YOUR LOYALTY"

═══

By the middle of 1941, a onetime poet named George Sylvester Viereck had become one of the most closely watched men in America. A naturalized U.S. citizen, Viereck was now Nazi Germany's chief publicist in the United States. For years he had advised the German Foreign Ministry on the state of American public opinion and the mood on Capitol Hill regarding the Reich. In the course of his work, he had cultivated a number of isolationist members of Congress, including Rep. Hamilton Fish and Senator Ernest Lundeen, a Republican from Minnesota. In late 1939, with German money, Viereck organized an anti-British group called the Make Europe Pay Its War Debts Committee. Lundeen was named its chairman.

For more than a year, Viereck, who worked closely with the German chargé d'affaires, Hans Thomsen, had been under heavy surveillance by British intelligence and the FBI, both of which were also keeping a watchful eye on the America First Committee and Capitol Hill isolationists. Joining in that effort were Fight for Freedom and other interventionist groups, as well as the Anti-Defamation League, a Jewish organization organized to fight anti-Semitism and other bigotry and discrimination.

Through American intermediaries, British Security Coordination had established close ties with several interventionist organizations, giving them information its agents had uncovered and in some cases reportedly helping to subsidize them. According to the BSC official history, the British allied themselves with Fight for Freedom, whose offices were in the same Rockefeller Center building as BSC's, to disrupt America First rallies and discredit their speakers. When Senator Gerald Nye spoke at one such gathering in Boston in September 1941, Fight for Freedom members booed and heckled him and passed out thousands of handbills attacking him as an appeaser and Nazi-lover. They also placed anti-Nye ads in Boston newspapers. When Hamilton Fish appeared at an America First rally in Milwaukee, a Fight for Freedom member approached him as he was giving his speech and handed him a card on which was written, "Der Führer thanks you for your loyalty." Tipped off beforehand, newspaper photographers were on hand to capture pictures of the flustered congressman, which were then featured in papers throughout the country.

Another tactic used by the FBI, BSC, and private interventionist groups was to place agents inside America First and other isolationist organizations. By all accounts, the Anti-Defamation League, under the direction of its New York counsel, Arnold Forster, was particularly skilled at such work. "When it came to the radical right," one historian noted, "Forster had one of the best intelligence gathering operations in the country, with spies everywhere."

During the 1930s and early 1940s, the Anti-Defamation League penetrated such organizations as the German-American Bund, America First, the so-called mothers' organizations, and the offices of a number of isolationist members of Congress. The purpose of the surveillance, Forster said, was to find out whether the groups and individuals "were giving aid and comfort, wittingly or otherwise, to the anti-Jewish, pro-Nazi cabal within our borders."

One of ADL's most successful operatives was a New Yorker named Marjorie Lane, who, like most of the organization's agents, was not Jewish. For several years, Lane worked undercover as a volunteer for a number of extremist women's groups, with names like "Women for the USA" and "We the Mothers Mobilize for America." During the day, she would type, answer phones, and welcome visitors at these organizations' offices; at night, using a miniature state-of-the art camera, she would photograph incriminating letters and documents. Forster passed all such material along to the FBI and BSC, as well as to friendly columnists like Drew Pearson and Walter Winchell. Indeed, Forster was so close to Winchell that he frequently ghostwrote columns for him about the anti-Semitic right.

In their investigations of America First, none of the group's adversaries turned up clear-cut evidence of direct links between its leaders and Germany. Nonetheless, in other ways, the organization proved susceptible to the charge by interventionist organizations that it was "a Nazi transmission belt." Several of its most active speakers were found to have ties with the German government, prominently including Laura Ingalls, a record-breaking aviator second only to Amelia Earhart in celebrity. The daughter of a wealthy New York businessman, Ingalls in 1935 became the first woman to fly nonstop between the two U.S. coasts. The year before, she won the Harmon Trophy as the most distinguished woman pilot of the year.

Ingalls's fame, however, turned to notoriety when she flew over the White House in September 1939 and showered it with antiwar pamphlets. An ardent isolationist, she was a frequent speaker at America First meetings and rallies; it was later revealed that she received money from the German embassy in Washington to do so. Her main contact at the embassy—a Nazi operative named Baron Ulrich von Gienanth— was said to have told her: "The best thing you can do for our cause is to continue to support the America First Committee." In 1942, she was arrested by the FBI for failing to register as a German agent and sentenced to two years in prison. Although America First leaders argued that the pro-German activities of Ingalls and a few other members "should not be magnified out of their proper proportion," there's no question that the organization helped create its own problems in this regard by its less than rigorous attempts to weed out such people.

A number of isolationist legislators proved to be equally easy targets. In 1940 the British uncovered a scheme, masterminded by George Sylvester Viereck, to arrange free mass mailings of antiwar and anti-British speeches and other material, using the franking privilege of congressional isolationists.

According to Congress's franking rules, members were permitted to send out their own speeches and other excerpts from the *Congressional Record,* the official account of Capitol Hill debates and other proceedings, without paying postage. They also were allowed to send bulk packages of franked articles to a third party, who then could address them and mail them for free.

As BSC told the story, Viereck had befriended George Hill, a low-level staffer working for Rep. Hamilton Fish, who arranged for isolationist speeches given by congressmen and senators to be inserted into the *Congressional Record* and then reprinted. Thousands of those reprints were bought by the Committee to Make Europe Pay Its War Debts and other German-backed groups, which then bundled and sent them to other parts of the country. There they were mailed out to hundreds of thousands of Americans on a wide variety of mailing lists. In the words of BSC's official history, "It almost seemed as if Congress were being converted into a distributing house for German propaganda."

In early 1941, the British used American surrogates to bring the franking operation to public attention. Fight for Freedom also joined the campaign, accusing Burton Wheeler, Gerald Nye, Hamilton Fish, and other members of Congress of knowingly allowing their franking privileges to be used by pro-German and anti-Semitic groups. A few months later, Viereck was arrested, convicted, and sent to prison for failing to give sufficient information about his activities when he registered as a foreign agent with the State Department. George Hill, meanwhile, was indicted for perjury by a federal grand jury for lying when asked about his relationship with Viereck.

The government, however, took no legal action against any of the congressmen and senators whose franks were used. In a Justice Department report issued after the war, John Rogge, a government attorney investigating the case, cited four legislators, including Fish and Senator Ernest Lundeen, as having actively collaborated with Viereck in the franking operation.* Rogge listed twenty other members of Congress, including Nye and Wheeler, as having been "used" by Viereck. There was no evidence, he said, that any of the twenty knew that Viereck was behind the scheme or that German funding was involved.

---

* On August 31, 1940, Lundeen was killed, along with twenty-four other passengers, in a commercial airliner crash near the Blue Ridge Mountains of Virginia. Two weeks after Lundeen's death, columnist Drew Pearson reported that the senator, whom he called "a rabid pro-German isolationist," had been under investigation by the FBI at the time of the crash for collaboration with the Reich. Pearson also raised the possibility of the plane's sabotage. Neither allegation was ever proven.

Fish, Wheeler, Nye, and others took to the floor of Congress to defend themselves; all said they were innocent of wrongdoing and defended their use of the frank. "Members of Congress, who are in opposition to the administration's views, would have very little if any opportunity to get their views before a large segment of the population" if it were not for their ability to send out franked material, Wheeler declared. Fish, for his part, said the furor was an effort to "smear" those trying to keep America out of the war.

However innocent the legislators may have been in legal terms, the franking scandal cast a shadow over their integrity and patriotism from which they never fully recovered.

LIFE WAS ALSO BECOMING considerably more difficult for Hans Thomsen and his German colleagues in the United States. Embassy staffers were now under close surveillance by the FBI, as were the Reich's employees in New York and other U.S. cities. In Washington, German diplomats were frequently ostracized at embassy and other social functions. In a message to the German Foreign Ministry, Thomsen complained of an "ever-widening hate campaign against Germany," adding that "the government of the Reich and its official representatives [are being presented] as Public Enemy No. 1 to American public opinion."

Even Friedrich von Boetticher was having problems. The German military attaché had long believed that the anti-British, antiwar viewpoint of his circle of friends in the War Department would eventually emerge as administration policy. But it was increasingly apparent, much to his dismay, that he had miscalculated. Some of his American friends were now shying away from public association with von Boetticher; it was too impolitic to be seen with him. At the order of General George Marshall, von Boetticher's practice of turning over Luftwaffe telegrams and other reports, with their inflated estimates of German capabilities, to Army intelligence was also discontinued.

On June 16, 1941, the Roosevelt administration ordered the expulsion of all German consular officials in the United States, along with the staffs of several German news, propaganda, and commercial agencies, claiming they were involved in "activities incompatible with their legitimate functions"—i.e., espionage. Thomsen, however, attributed the expulsions to the "dilemma in which the American Government finds itself regarding the urgent calls for assistance from England. Inasmuch as they are not ready, for the time being, to produce more concrete war aid . . . they proceed with strong words and deeds against the Axis Powers."

Berlin retaliated by ordering the expulsion of all personnel in U.S. consulates in Germany. Yet Hitler did not break off diplomatic relations with America: the German embassy in Washington remained open, as did the U.S. embassy in Berlin. "Despite these new aggressive measures," the Ministry of Propaganda declared, "the Reich government is not going to yield to provocations."

Then, one month after the expulsion of the German government employees, the FBI arrested more than two dozen people, most of them German-born U.S. citizens, on charges of spying and sabotage. This was Thomsen's worst nightmare. He had repeatedly begged Berlin not to send spies or saboteurs to the United States, writing that "I cannot warn too urgently against this method" and that "these activities are the surest way of bringing America into action on the side of our enemies and destroying the last vestiges of sympathy for Germany."

While the Foreign Ministry sympathized with Thomsen, it informed him that the German army's intelligence division, the Abwehr, had "compelling military reasons" for collecting information in the United States and would continue to do so. In fact, it had been doing so for most of the 1930s, with considerable help from American companies, which had no compunction, at least until 1940, about selling to the Germans such vital military devices as automatic pilots, gyro compasses, and even control systems for antiaircraft guns.

Thomsen had good reason to complain about the Abwehr agents and those from other German intelligence agencies operating in America. For the most part, they were terrible at their jobs. Their operations, Thomsen wrote his superiors, were "marked by naivete and irresponsible carelessness, and on top of that, lacked any kind of coordination."

In all their years of prewar spying, German agents could boast of only one notable success: acquisition of the plans for the Norden bombsight, a revolutionary technological development that made it possible for bombardiers to hit industrial targets with surgical precision. In 1937, Hermann Lang, a German immigrant working at the

Norden plant in Manhattan, turned over blueprints he had copied to Nikolaus Ritter, an Abwehr major based in the United States. The plans were smuggled aboard a German ocean liner and taken to the Reich, where engineers used them to construct their own version of the bombsight. In the end, however, the device proved to be of no value to Germany. The Luftwaffe decided not to use it, much preferring its own bombsight, which was already in production and was familiar to its bombardiers.

Two years after Lang approached him, Ritter acquired another promising recruit—a German-born U.S. citizen named William G. Sebold, who was traveling to visit his mother in the Ruhr when the Gestapo coerced him into working as a spy. Taken on by Ritter, Sebold was sent to an Abwehr spy school in Hamburg. At the end of his training, he was given a false name and forged passport, then was dispatched to New York as a radio operator, responsible for sending back to Hamburg the reports of several Abwehr agents living in the area.

Sebold, whose German code name was "Tramp," proved to be so good at his job that the Abwehr asked him to transmit messages from a number of other agents, including Hermann Lang. He did so, setting up an office in the Knickerbocker Building in downtown Manhattan as a meeting place for the twenty or so spies whose intelligence he was to relay back to Germany.

Unbeknownst to the German operatives, their conversations with Sebold about their past feats and future plans were being recorded by FBI bugs and cameras. Sebold, the ace radio operator, was, as it turned out, a double agent, who had approached American officials in Germany as soon as the Gestapo suborned him and had worked with the FBI from the moment he arrived back in America. His messages to Germany had actually been transmitted by FBI agents, who eliminated any material that might have been damaging to U.S. interests and who also passed along disinformation to the Abwehr. The incoming messages from Germany alerted the FBI to future Abwehr intelligence targets and the recruitment of new operatives.

Among the spies swept up in the July 1941 arrests was Hermann Lang, who, together with his cohorts, was found guilty of espionage and sentenced to a long term in prison. William Sebold was the chief government witness at their trial.

The spy sweep was a debacle for Germany, a point underscored by an exasperated Hans Thomsen in an "I-told-you-so" cable to Berlin: "Most, and probably all, of the persons involved in this affair were totally unqualified for operations of this kind. . . . It can be assumed that the American authorities had long known all about the network, which certainly would not have been any great feat, considering the naïve and sometimes downright stupid behavior of these people."

Yet the ineptness of the German agents and their lack of success went largely unmentioned by the FBI when it trumpeted to the American public its success in breaking up the spy network. At one point, Hoover noted privately that Germany "today relies far more on propaganda than on espionage." According to Attorney General Robert Jackson, "the Nazis never had an extensively organized espionage or sabotage ring in this country."

Indeed, the United States never faced any serious threat of internal subversion before or during the war. But the American people never knew that; in fact, they were told the opposite. According to the FBI and the White House, the roundup of the German spies was incontrovertible proof that swarms of fifth columnists and enemy agents were busily at work throughout the country.

AS IT HAPPENED, THE Germans were not the only targets on J. Edgar Hoover's hit list in the summer of 1941: he was also gunning for his erstwhile allies, William Stephenson and the BSC. Despite all the help that the British had given the FBI, including providing some of the evidence that convicted the German spy ring, the relationship between Hoover and Stephenson had begun to unravel. The FBI chief became increasingly concerned that the British were getting involved in activities that, by rights, should be carried out by the bureau. He was, for example, greatly displeased by the espionage activities of the BSC operative Amy Pack, keeping her under constant surveillance and tapping her phone. Hoover also was upset by Stephenson's role in helping to set up the Office of Strategic Services, America's first centralized intelligence agency, which Hoover regarded as a rival to the FBI.

Virtually from the day he arrived in the United States, Stephenson had championed the creation of an American entity similar to the BSC, with which he and other British intelligence officials could collaborate in planning covert activities against the Axis throughout the world.

OSS director William Donovan decorates spymaster William Stephenson,
head of the wartime British Security Coordination, with the Medal of Merit,
America's highest civilian award at the time, in a postwar ceremony.

His American partner in the venture was William Donovan, a multimillionaire Wall Street lawyer who had been assistant attorney general in the Coolidge administration and, before that, a much-decorated
hero in the Great War. An officer in the Army's famed "Fighting 69th"
regiment, Donovan, who acquired the nickname "Wild Bill" for his
wartime exploits, had been awarded the nation's three highest medals
for valor, including the Medal of Honor. He was a close friend and
political ally of Frank Knox, who prevailed on Roosevelt in 1940 to
send Donovan on several secret missions to Europe and the Middle
East, including one to Britain to determine if that nation would continue to survive. Donovan, who was a member of the Century Group,
reported back to FDR in the affirmative and urged the immediate dispatch of all possible aid to the British.

Having met Donovan during the Great War, Stephenson contacted
him as soon as he arrived in America, and the two quickly formed a
close personal and professional relationship. To their mutual associates,

the tall, husky Donovan became known as "Big Bill," while the short, slender Stephenson was "Little Bill."

Until 1941, America's intelligence-gathering functions had been scattered among several government agencies, including the FBI and the War, Navy, and State Departments. With Stephenson's help, Donovan persuaded Roosevelt in July of that year to establish a new organization called the Office of Coordinator of Information (COI) and to make him its head. The forerunner of the Office of Strategic Services (OSS), the COI was created not only to collect intelligence against U.S. foes, real and potential, but also to carry out subversive propaganda and sabotage operations, thus acting as the American counterpart of BSC.

From the day of its inception, Stephenson served as the COI's god-father, helping to set up its headquarters and field operations, providing training facilities and instructors for its agents, and passing on to Donovan "a regular flow of secret information . . . including highly confidential material not normally circulated outside the British government." As Donovan himself later acknowledged, "Bill Stephenson taught us all we ever knew about foreign intelligence."

In London, Desmond Morton, Churchill's liaison officer with British intelligence, wrote: "A most secret fact of which the Prime Minister is aware but not all other persons concerned, is that to all intents and purposes U.S. Security is being run for them at the President's request by the British. . . . It is of course essential that this fact should not be known in view of the furious uproar it would cause if known to the isolationists."

The close relationship between Stephenson's and Donovan's operations was, of course, no secret to J. Edgar Hoover, who was as enraged as any isolationist might have been. He not only deeply resented the establishment of a rival intelligence organization, he also despised Donovan, who felt much the same about him. The two had clashed repeatedly in the early 1920s, when Donovan served as assistant attorney general. At one point, Donovan urged Attorney General Harlan Stone to fire Hoover. Stone ignored the recommendation, and Donovan acquired a powerful lifelong enemy.

In his battle against BSC (and, in effect, Donovan), Hoover enlisted the aid of a potent ally—Assistant Secretary of State Adolf Berle, the State Department's intelligence liaison with the White House, FBI, and other information-gathering units within the government. One of Roosevelt's original brain trusters, Berle, a former law professor at Columbia University, was both antiwar and anti-British, denouncing what he called the British record of "half truths, broken faith, and intrigue behind the back of the State Department and even the President."

In the early spring of 1941, Hoover informed Berle that the British, as Berle later explained to Undersecretary of State Sumner Welles, had set up in the United States "a full size secret police and intelligence service [which] enters into the whole field of political, financial, industrial and probably military intelligence. . . . I have reason to believe that a good many things being done are probably in violation of our espionage acts."

With Hoover's assistance, Berle began a strenuous campaign to shut down most or all of Stephenson's operation. Both officials supported a bill by Senator Kenneth McKellar, a Tennessee Democrat, to impose severe restrictions on the work of all foreign agents, friendly or otherwise, in the United States, including the requirement that they open their records to the FBI.

BSC fought back, assigning an agent to "get the dirt" on Berle and reportedly tapping his phones. When Hoover discovered the surveillance, he told Stephenson he wanted the agent out of the country by six o'clock that night. Although Stephenson professed "surprise and horror that any of his men should do such a thing," he did as the FBI chief demanded.

Shortly after Pearl Harbor, the McKellar bill was passed by Congress and sent to the president for his signature; Donovan, on behalf of Stephenson, persuaded FDR to veto it. A later amended version, which specifically exempted BSC from its restrictions, was approved by Roosevelt and enacted into law.

As Hoover and Berle probably should have known, the president would never have agreed to emasculate an organization that had proved so useful in his battle against those he considered his and his country's enemies, both foreign and domestic.

CHAPTER 22

"WHERE IS THIS CRISIS?"

By the summer of 1941, morale in the U.S. Army had sunk to rock bottom. Young men drafted the previous year talked of going AWOL; some even raised the possibility of mutiny. In a camp in Mississippi, soldiers watching a newsreel booed loudly when images of President Roosevelt and General George Marshall flashed on the screen.

Here the draftees were, digging latrines, peeling potatoes, and endlessly drilling, all for a measly thirty dollars a month, while friends back home were earning six and seven times that much in defense factory jobs. And for what? There was no war, and despite what the president said in his May 27 speech, there didn't appear to be a national emergency, either. Anyone with eyes could see that life was proceeding as usual outside the training camps. "Where is this crisis?" one draftee grumbled. "All I see are people with more dough than they had before and more dough for the guys who've already got it." Why should he and the others have to make sacrifices when no one else had to? In fact, why the hell were they there?

No one seemed to know. "As far as the men can see," *Life* noted, "the Army has no goal. It does not know whether it is going to fight, or when or where. If the U.S. political leaders have set any military objective, they have not made it clear to the Army. This is reflected in the training, which is not geared to any real military situation."

The country's faltering defense mobilization program revealed the same lack of direction. Roosevelt continued to refuse to appoint a czar of war production, and administration of the effort remained chaotic. Bitter conflict had erupted everywhere. Defense industries were plagued by strikes and shortages. Government bureaucrats clashed with businessmen brought to Washington to help direct the mobilization effort. Army, Navy, and Air Corps officials fought with one another to get a bigger slice of the procurement pie. As Attorney General Francis Biddle observed, the bickering "gave the country a sense of disunity and a feeling that the administration did not know where it was going."

In August, the editors of *Fortune* reported that America was "not merely falling short" in becoming the arsenal of democracy that Roosevelt had envisaged; it was "failing spectacularly, in nine different ways and nine different places." Among the problems, the magazine said, was the fact that Americans had "not yet been asked to do what is necessary to win."

The key question was, as it had been for months: What was the country's key objective in this fight? Was it solely a defense of the Americas and aid for Britain—or was it active participation in the war? Whatever it was, "the people at the top better damn quick give us something we can sink our teeth in, believe in—before it's too late," one soldier declared.

An anxious Henry Stimson had begun to wonder if it wasn't already too late. "Tonight I feel more up against it than ever before," he wrote in his diary in early July. "It is not clear whether this country has it in itself to meet such an emergency. Whether we are really powerful enough and sincere enough and devoted enough to meet the Germans is getting to be more and more of a real problem."

According to polls, a majority of Americans continued to hold what seemed, at first glance, diametrically opposite views of what their country's role should be. In one Gallup survey, three-quarters of those questioned said yes when asked whether they favored going to war if there was no other way to defeat the Axis. Eighty percent said they thought the United States would have to go to war eventually. Yet, when asked if the country should enter the conflict now, an identical 80 percent said no.

These opinions, however, were not as contradictory as they appeared. Understandably, Americans were reluctant to plunge into war unless and until they felt it was necessary. And so far, they were not convinced it was. According to Stimson and other interventionists, it was the president's obligation to connect the dots for the American people, to persuade them that in order to defeat Hitler, the United States must take bold action *now*. If only he would lead, they said, the people would follow. Among those who argued this position was Hadley Cantril, a social psychologist who had become, in effect, Roosevelt's private pollster.

In 1940, Cantril had created the Office of Public Opinion Research at Princeton University to study public attitudes on political and social issues. He worked closely with George Gallup's polling organization, also based in Princeton, New Jersey, which did the actual canvassing of the public. Cantril's group helped design questions for the Gallup pollsters and conducted its own analyses of Gallup data. A strong liberal and FDR loyalist, Cantril offered his services to the White House, making it clear he would do everything he could to make the polls on which he worked serve the president's needs: "We can get confidential information on questions you suggest, follow up any hunches you may care to see tested regarding the determinants of opinion, and provide you with the answers to any questions asked."

For the next year, Cantril used the Gallup operation to get responses to specific questions posed by the White House, which in turn were used to formulate the administration's political strategy. Cantril repeatedly stressed to presidential aides the need for confidentiality regarding Roosevelt's privileged access to the survey results and his involvement in their design. "Since all of these questions were on the most recent Gallup poll," he wrote to FDR adviser Anna Rosenberg in May 1941, "I am trusting you and your friend [the president] not to let others in Washington know about them. The old problem of property rights—plus the fact that if certain Senators know about this, they would raise hell with Gallup, and his faith in me would be shaken."

A couple of weeks after FDR's speech declaring an unlimited national emergency, a puzzled Roosevelt asked Cantril why the public, in the most recent polls, no longer seemed as enthusiastic about what he had said as they had immediately after the speech. The main reason, Cantril replied, was that Roosevelt had "failed to indicate any new, overt policy that people could readily conceptualize, and that 'national emergency' meant little when it required no change whatever in daily life." He went on: "Any increase in interventionist action resulting from a Presidential radio address will not be maintained unless the address announces or is shortly followed by action."

Each time the president had proposed a bold move, such as Lend-Lease or the destroyers-bases deal, a large majority of Americans had supported him, Cantril pointed out. And he was sure that a similar majority would back FDR now if he called for convoying or other more extreme measures to help Britain, even if it involved considerable sacrifice on the public's part. "I have tried to make this point dozens of times," Cantril told Anna Rosenberg in a memo, "but somehow there seems little connection between the information all of us gather and policy formation." Echoing Cantril's view, George Gallup had earlier noted that "the best way to influence public opinion" on an issue was "to get Mr. Roosevelt to talk about it and favor it."

In Cantril's opinion, Roosevelt faced a greater political risk by *not* acting than by calling for new initiatives to aid the British. He predicted large Republican gains in the next congressional election, stemming, he said, from the public's dissatisfaction with the absence of strong presidential leadership. Using capital letters to make his point, Cantril wrote to Rosenberg: "WHAT THE PEOPLE WANT IS TO BE TOLD WHAT TO DO."

Roosevelt, however, refused to accept Cantril's argument. The more favorable the poll results were for him and his policies, the less he seemed to believe them. He was clearly more influenced by his own more pessimistic assessment of public opinion, which he saw reflected in the words and actions of the diminished but still potent isolationist bloc in Congress.

Insisting that a majority of Americans had not yet grasped "the facts of life" about the war, despite considerable evidence to the contrary, he was reluctant to test his leadership in a showdown with his opponents. Although Robert Jackson and others around Roosevelt believed that he, in Jackson's words, "could have gone much farther in disregarding Congress . . . as far as public sentiment was concerned," FDR disagreed. He felt, said his speechwriter Samuel Rosenman, that "this was no time to get out too far in advance of the American people. Nor was it a time to meet a defeat in Congress at the hands of isolationists."

In a letter to Winston Churchill, Lord Halifax, who had succeeded Lord Lothian as British ambassador, explained Roosevelt's dilemma as the president saw it: "His perpetual problem is to steer a course be-tween (1) the wish of 70% of Americans to keep out of war; (2) the wish of 70% of Americans to do everything to break Hitler, even if it means war. He said that if he asked for a declaration of war he wouldn't get it, and opinion would swing against him."

AMONG THOSE CONFOUNDED BY Roosevelt's months-long inertia was the German government. Less than two weeks after the president's fire-eating speech on May 27, word came that a German submarine had sunk the American freighter *Robin Moor* in the south Atlantic, well outside Germany's declared war zone. Violating international conven-tions, the submarine captain had put the *Robin Moor*'s crew in lifeboats with scant food and water and without radioing their position to ships that might be nearby. The crewmen drifted in the Atlantic for nineteen days before their rescue on June 9.

Hitler and his men worried that the sinking, which was in direct violation of the Führer's orders to stay away from U.S. ships, would bring America into the war—or, at the very least, result in U.S. naval protection for convoys. American interventionists, including those in the president's circle, pressed him to retaliate by ordering the Navy to begin escort duty immediately. But to Germany's relief, Roosevelt re-sponded with considerably more moderation, ordering the closing of German consulates in the United States and freezing all Axis-owned assets.

Once the crisis was over, Hitler made it clear to Admiral Erich Raeder that for the next few months, his navy must avoid any more incidents of this kind. They must not attack any ships, inside or outside the combat zone, unless they were clearly marked enemy vessels. And under no circumstances were American ships to be targeted.

The reason for Hitler's caution became obvious on June 22, 1941, when two million German troops launched a lightning attack on the Soviet Union. Almost no one believed that the Russians could hold out for much longer than six or seven weeks. But in the eyes of Amer-ican interventionists, that period, however short it might be, provided the perfect opportunity for dramatic new steps to aid the British. "For the first time since Hitler loosed the dogs of war on this world, we are provided with a God-given chance to determine the outcome of this worldwide struggle," Frank Knox declared in a nationwide radio broadcast. "While his back is turned, we must answer his obvious contempt with a smashing blow that can and will change the entire world perspective."

Knox, Henry Stimson, and Admiral Stark pressured Roosevelt to order immediate naval protection for all merchant shipping crossing the Atlantic. Stark acknowledged to FDR that such action "would almost certainly involve us in war" but added that "much more delay might be fatal to Britain's survival." On July 2, the president, to the delight of Stark and the others, ordered plans drawn up for U.S. ships to begin escort duty the following week. But a few days later, he had second thoughts and canceled the order.

A man who liked to keep his options open for as long as possible, Roosevelt decided to wait and see how events developed. Unlike his advisers, he still wasn't convinced that the situation was urgent. As he viewed it, Hitler had relieved the pressure on Britain by invading Russia, giving his administration a little more time to assess the situation and decide what to do. He cautiously followed Churchill's lead in promising aid to the Russians but, while the British prime minister pledged immediate, all-out support, Roosevelt was initially vague about the extent of American help and when it would begin.

Such reluctance was hardly surprising. He faced strong opposition from isolationists, many of whom, like Charles Lindbergh, were ferociously anti-Soviet. At an America First rally in San Francisco, Lindbergh declared that while he opposed U.S. alliances with foreign countries, he "would a hundred times rather see my country ally herself with England, or even with Germany with all her faults, than with the cruelty, the godlessness, and the barbarism that exist in Soviet Russia." Unsurprisingly, this inflammatory remark touched off another round of bitter attacks against him.

But antagonism to the idea of aid for Russia was not confined solely to the isolationists. A substantial number of Americans, including some who supported the president's policies, opposed helping Joseph Stalin's Communist dictatorship. Senator Harry Truman of Missouri spoke for many when he said: "If we see that Germany is winning, we ought to help Russia, and if Russia is winning, we ought to help Germany, and that way let them kill as many as possible."

Senior officers in the Army were among the most outspoken opponents of aid to Stalin and his country. Many shared Lindbergh's passionate antipathy toward the Soviet Union and Communism, and they strongly resisted sending any munitions so urgently needed by their own service to a country they considered their enemy.

Nonetheless, when Roosevelt finally joined Churchill in August in pledging to send planes, tanks, trucks, and other aid to Stalin, most Americans, seeing Germany as a far greater immediate danger to the United States than Russia, supported the president's decision.

WHILE STILL RESISTING THE idea of convoying, Roosevelt did take advantage of Hitler's preoccupation with Russia that summer to make another move in the Atlantic chess game. For months, Churchill had been urging him to send U.S. troops to Iceland, a former Danish territory in the North Atlantic strategically located near the convoy route between Canada and Britain. Britain had occupied the island shortly after Denmark was seized by Germany in 1940, and Churchill was anxious to transfer the British forces there to battlefields in the Middle East.

On July 8, four thousand U.S. Marines landed in Iceland. In a statement to the American public, Roosevelt explained his decision as purely a defensive measure, taken to prevent the Germans from using the subarctic island as "a naval or air base for eventual attack against the Western Hemisphere." Since Iceland lay 3,900 miles east of New York, it's understandable that some considered that rationale a bit outlandish.

Still, public reaction was largely favorable. That came as a surprise to Roosevelt, who, as so often before, had prepared himself for a "vitriolic outburst." In its August 4 issue, *Life* sardonically noted: "The people voting 70% to 80% against war in the polls still were not ready to lead the President. But a resounding 61% approval of the occupation of Iceland seemed to show that they were ready to follow where the President led."

FDR's action in Iceland was seen by many as an attempt to placate American interventionists and to bolster the morale of the British, rather than as a deliberate step toward war. Hans Thomsen assured his superiors in Berlin that the president was not interested "in carrying on a full war with all its consequences." As Thomsen saw it, Roosevelt probably would continue taking interim actions, like closing the German consulates and occupying Iceland, "which basically obligate America to very little and do not involve any immediate dangers."

Yet no one could deny that the U.S. takeover of Iceland was a direct challenge to Germany, considerably raising the ante in the Atlantic war of nerves. On July 8, the head of the German submarine force requested permission to attack American ships off the coast of Iceland. Hitler, however, reiterated his order that no U.S. vessel was to be sunk, even inside the combat zone. "It is absolutely essential that all incidents with the United States should be avoided," the German navy was told. "Germany's attitude to America is therefore to remain as before: not to let herself be provoked, and to avoid all discussion."

When Admiral Raeder protested to Hitler that the U.S. presence in Iceland should be regarded as an act of war, the Führer replied that he was "most anxious to postpone the United States's entry into war" until German forces had vanquished Russia, which he said should only take another month or two. Once that was accomplished, he "reserved the right to take severe action against the United States as well."

ALTHOUGH PLEASED WITH FDR's decision to station troops in Iceland, Henry Stimson, Frank Knox, and the other interventionists in the administration were deeply disappointed by what they considered his dithering on the use of naval convoy escorts. Yet as it turned out, landing troops on Iceland provided a back door to the introduction of limited convoy protection in the Atlantic.

The American forces on Iceland would clearly have to be supplied with food, weapons, and other necessities ferried from the United States by American and Icelandic merchant ships. These ships, in turn, would need U.S. naval escorts, which would be authorized to destroy any "hostile forces which threaten such shipping." As it happened, the American convoys supplying bases in Iceland and the convoys heading to Britain left from the same ports in Canada and used the same route—a coincidence on which Admiral Stark capitalized. With Roosevelt's permission, the chief of naval operations arranged the schedule of American convoys so that some would leave Canada at the same time as British or Canadian convoys heading for the United Kingdom. By sailing together, they all would come under the protection of the U.S. Navy.

As of mid-July, all friendly ships sailing to and from Iceland were accompanied by American naval escorts. Stark told his subordinates and the British that "the whole thing must be kept as quiet as possible." Yet, as the Navy chief knew, that situation likely would not last for long. In weeks if not days, U.S. and German naval forces were bound to clash.

THE STEEPLY ESCALATING RISK of war, however, was not matched by an equally dramatic growth in defense mobilization. While industrial production had risen about 30 percent in the past year, with aircraft manufacturing climbing 158 percent and shipbuilding 120 percent, these were paltry figures compared to the vast demands and needs of the American military, the British, and now the Russians. As the columnist Raymond Clapper noted, "Ours is still a popgun arsenal."

Of the $7 billion allocated for Lend-Lease assistance to Britain, only about 2 percent of that amount had actually reached the British in the form of supplies, most of it dried eggs, canned meat, beans, and other food. So dismal was the situation that in July 1941, William Whitney, an American Lend-Lease official in London, quit in protest over America's failure to do more. "We are deceiving the people on both sides of the Atlantic by allowing them to think that there is today a stream of lease-lend war materiels crossing the Atlantic, when in fact there is little or none," Whitney wrote in his letter of resignation. "My view is that the Administration . . . should show Congress and the people that, while we are boasting that we are at enmity with Hitler alongside Britain, we are doing a disgracefully small share of the job."

America's booming economy was still largely devoted to satisfying civilian needs; the sales of cars and other big-ticket items were at an all-time high, and most Americans were living better than they ever had in their lives. Antoine de Saint-Exupéry neatly summed up the problem when asked at a New York dinner party what America could do for the war effort. "As things stand," the French writer responded, "your country devotes 90 percent of its industrial potential to making consumer goods that Americans want—in other words cars and chewing gum—and 10 percent to stopping Hitler. Only when those figures are reversed—10 percent to cars and chewing gum and 90 percent to stopping Hitler—will there be any hope."

Saint-Exupéry was exaggerating—but not by much. Reluctant to give up their high profits from consumer goods, many companies continued to resist converting their factories and other facilities to defense production. While eager to make more money for themselves, they declined to share the bounty with their workers in the form of better wages and other benefits, which resulted in widespread walkouts in key industries such as aircraft manufacturing. Shortages of machine tools and essential materials like aluminum and steel rose sharply; in some places, shipyards lay idle for lack of steel.

In March 1941, Harry Truman launched a Senate investigation that revealed extensive bungling of the defense program, including fraud, overcharging, and shoddy workmanship by private business and industry. "We are advertising to the world . . . that we are in a mess," Senator Tom Connally, a member of Truman's investigating committee, said in disgust. Unless the United States intensified its mobilization, a government report warned, its war production would be outstripped by Britain and Canada within the year.

In the view of many, the only way to straighten out the mess would be the appointment of a single government official with the authority to set priorities and prices and to coerce obedience from manufacturers. But the president was having none of that. Loath as always to yield power, he insisted on retaining administrative control of the defense effort, even though he was too busy with other pressing matters to provide any real leadership or direction.

Pushed hard by Stimson and others, FDR finally agreed in July 1941 to replace the faltering Office of Production Management with yet another new agency, the Supply Priorities and Allocation Board (SPAB). Although Roosevelt retained ultimate authority over the defense program, SPAB was given the power to set priorities and allocations of raw materials in regard to defense and civilian production. In short order, the agency announced plans to ration rubber and to cut the production of cars, refrigerators, and washing machines by 50 percent.

Very gradually, defense production began to improve. Tanks were rolling off assembly lines at a greater rate, and shipbuilding and aircraft manufacturing were picking up speed. Yet, as SPAB chairman Donald Nelson acknowledged years later, "1941 will go down in history as the year we almost lost the war before we finally got into it."

Contributing to that nightmarish scenario was the distinct possibility that the U.S. Army might soon collapse.

WHEN CONGRESS PASSED CONSCRIPTION legislation in September 1940, it limited the draftees' tour of duty to twelve months—a compromise to which General Marshall had reluctantly agreed. As a result, his 1.4-million-man service was set to lose about 70 percent of its soldiers in the early fall of 1941. With war drawing ever closer to the United States, the Army would all but disintegrate at a time when the country needed it most.

The legislation, however, did contain an escape clause: the term of service could be extended if Congress found that the national interest was imperiled. In July, Marshall declared bluntly that "such an emergency now exists." For members of Congress, it was the worst possible news. For weeks, they had been deluged by letters and telegrams from angry, resentful draftees and their parents, who insisted that the young men, at great financial and other personal sacrifice, had lived up to the terms of their yearlong contract and now must be allowed to return to their homes and jobs.

After interviewing draftees in one camp, a *Life* journalist reported in August 1941 that 50 percent had threatened to desert if they were not discharged when their year was up. Wherever he looked, the correspondent noted, he saw the chalked letters OHIO, standing for "Over the Hill in October." As the *Life* article put it, the men "do not want to fight because they do not see any reason for fighting. Accordingly they see little point in their being in an Army camp at all. There is a very strong anti-Roosevelt feeling."

Bored and restless, draftees complained about rudimentary or non-existent combat training, as well as the lack of modern weapons. In training exercises, trucks with the word TANK painted on their sides took the place of real tanks, pieces of drainpipe substituted for anti-tank guns, and wooden tripods acted as 60 mm mortars. "The boys here hate the Army," noted one private. "They have no fighting spirit, except among themselves when they get stinking drunk." Another private snarled, "To hell with Roosevelt and Marshall and the Army and especially this goddamn hole!"

Life's study of crumbling Army morale caused a considerable stir in

Washington and across the country. War Department officials claimed it was greatly exaggerated—a belief shared by *New York Times* publisher Arthur Sulzberger, who ordered his own investigation into the situation. For two months, Hilton Howell Railey, an experienced military correspondent and close friend of Sulzberger's, interviewed more than a thousand soldiers at seven Army forts and camps. When he started the probe, Railey, like Sulzberger, was sure the *Life* piece was grossly overblown. When he finished, he thought it had greatly underestimated the problem.

Appalled by the conduct of soldiers on weekend passes outside Louisiana's Camp Polk, Railey described them as "an undisciplined mob," adding that if he had been a military policeman, "I might have arrested 5,000 men, including many of their officers . . . for flagrant violations of the articles of war." Virtually all the soldiers he interviewed expressed great hostility to their officers and the Roosevelt administration, with "more than 90 percent having lost faith in the government's word." One soldier told Railey that "the government isn't fooling us. . . . We are being jockeyed into a war that we ought to damned well keep out of."

Instead of publishing Railey's alarming report, Sulzberger ordered that it be kept quiet—a decision that, when later revealed, prompted a cascade of criticism about what many saw as the *Times*'s self-censoring, cozy relationship with the government. The publisher was unrepentant, declaring that he had acted "in the public interest." He personally delivered copies of Railey's findings to Roosevelt and Marshall, assuring them that "I, for one, did not propose to make Hitler a present of the fact that there was bad morale in the armed forces." After reading the *Times* report, Henry Stimson noted in his diary that the cause of the morale problem was clear: "We have been trying to train an army for war without a declaration of war by Congress and with the country not facing the dangers before it."

Exacerbating the situation was the widespread feeling that the administration was reneging on its commitment to send draftees home after their year of service. In the congressional debate preceding passage of the conscription bill, advocates of the legislation had placed little emphasis on the provision allowing for an extension of service. In any case, members of Congress, already focusing on the 1942 elections, clearly wanted nothing to do with it now. House Speaker Sam Rayburn and majority leader John McCormack told Stimson that a bill extending the draft would never pass their chamber. Even the administration's staunchest supporters in Congress, they said, viewed such legislation as breaching a moral contract between the government and draftees. In the words of Rep. James Wadsworth, the New York Republican who sponsored the original conscription measure and supported its extension, "The whole thing was portrayed as an outrage, a breaking of faith. Everyone said there was no necessity for it, we were still at peace."

When Marshall and Stimson first urged Roosevelt in the early spring of 1941 to propose a draft extension bill, the president, aware of the passionate public outcry that would ensue, hesitated. Finally, in late June, he reluctantly signed off on the measure but did not publicly endorse it. It was left to Marshall to shoulder the burden of pushing it through Congress.

As the administration's point man, the Army chief of staff made frequent trips to Capitol Hill to sell the extension to lawmakers. Insisting that the danger to the country was real and imminent, he bluntly remarked to one committee: "I cannot for the life of me see how anyone can read what has happened . . . and not agree that we have to take such measures as I have recommended." Privately, he told aides that if the draft were not extended, it "would be the greatest of tragedies. . . . We [are] in a very desperate situation." When legislators brought up draftees' complaints of discomforts and inconveniences, Marshall snapped back that these men were soldiers and could not expect to be treated as if they were at home. "We cannot have a political club and call it an army," he said.

Although Marshall's arguments swayed some members of Congress, many still resisted. One veteran congressional aide told the Army chief that never in his forty years on Capitol Hill had he seen such fear of a bill. Pressured by Marshall and Stimson, Roosevelt finally agreed to explain to the public and Congress why the legislation was so desperately needed.

In a forceful radio broadcast on July 21, the president declared that the danger to the country was "infinitely greater today" than it had been a year before, when the conscription measure was passed. "We Americans cannot afford to speculate with the security of America," he said. While he realized that extending the term of service involved "personal sacrifices," he flatly warned that the consequences of not doing so would be the disintegration of the U.S. armed forces.

As had happened frequently in the past, the public responded positively to the president's call for action. According to public opinion polls conducted shortly after FDR's speech, slightly more than 50 percent of Americans now favored lengthening the term of service for draftees. Word came that some congressmen were rethinking their opposition. "The current," Stimson crowed, "is running strongly in our favor."

The administration's isolationist opponents, meanwhile, were working feverishly to resist that current. Although America First did not take an official position on extending the draft—as a West Point graduate and retired general, Robert Wood was conflicted about the issue—other officials and staffers in the organization privately advised their members to fight it. "I suggest personally that you push every single effort to stop passage of this extension of service proposal," one staff member wrote to local America First chapters. "I think we can win this fight, and if we do, it will be a terrific blow against the administration forces."

As both houses of Congress prepared to debate the bill, the ubiquitous mothers' groups descended on Washington once more. Women in black dresses and veils did their customary weeping and moaning on benches in a reception room just off the Senate chamber, making life uncomfortable for any senators who happened by. At night, holding lighted candles, they continued their crying outside the homes of the extension's congressional supporters. Such tactics had little effect. On August 7, the Senate, by a vote of 45 to 30, passed the legislation.

In the House, thanks to Marshall's arguments, both Sam Rayburn and John McCormack had finally thrown their support behind the extension measure, but many of their Democratic colleagues failed to join them. In early August, McCormack reported that of the 267 Democrats in the House, about 60 were opposed to the bill, while several dozen more were undecided.

On both sides of the aisle, there was growing enthusiasm for a Republican amendment that would place all draftees on reserve status at the end of the year and give Roosevelt the authority to call them back to duty if he believed it was necessary. As Stimson noted, the amendment's aim was obvious—to shift the responsibility of an unpopular action from Congress to FDR and then, if he should indeed take action, "to be the first ones to jump on him." In his diary, Stimson denounced the amendment's sponsors as "cowards," an accusation with which it is hard to argue. For years, Roosevelt's congressional critics had denounced him as dictatorial. But when given the opportunity to exert their own authority, they shrank from taking it.

Rayburn, who had been Speaker of the House for less than a year, assumed responsibility for shepherding the bill through the lower chamber. Short and bald with a broad, powerful frame, the fifty-nine-year-old bachelor had served twenty-nine years in the House, four of them as majority leader. The House was the love of his life, and he knew its workings far better than any other member. As White House aide James Landis noted, Rayburn "was an expert in procedure—and sizing up the motives of what made human beings tick." With his fierce integrity and hot temper, the Speaker was an intimidating figure to many of his colleagues—according to the House sergeant-at-arms, some congressmen were "literally afraid to start talking to him"—but he also evoked deep respect and, in some members, great affection.

As chairman of the House Interstate and Foreign Commerce Committee in the early and mid 1930s, he had played a major role in the passage of New Deal legislation, sponsoring five key administration measures, including the Securities Exchange Act and Public Utilities Act, and ramrodding them through the House. Yet for all the president's reliance on him, the two men had long had a problematic relationship. Like other congressional leaders, Rayburn had never been included in FDR's inner circle of advisers and was allowed little input in the formation of administration policy. A product of rural Texas, he was scorned by the young, Ivy League–educated intellectuals of the New Deal as not "one of us." To Henry Wallace, Rayburn complained that "the President didn't take him sufficiently into his confidence." He felt, said White House aide Jonathan Daniels, that "his advice was not wanted."

Nonetheless, he remained intensely loyal to Roosevelt—an allegiance that extended to FDR's foreign policy. Although he had left the United States only twice in his life, for short trips to the Panama Canal and Mexico, Rayburn had always been a stalwart internationalist, convinced that America's fate was inextricably entwined with those of other nations. Now, having been convinced by Marshall that an extension of the draft was vitally important to U.S. security, he devoted all his formidable talents to the job of getting it passed.

During three days of bitter House debate, Rayburn relinquished his Speaker's chair to others. He strolled through Capitol meeting rooms and corridors, buttonholing colleagues to tell them: "I need your vote. I wish you'd stand by me because it means a lot to me." It was a request that many heeded, in large part because they owed Rayburn a great deal; as majority leader, he had showered Democratic lawmakers with a cornucopia of favors, including good committee assignments and favorable treatment of legislation. Now, they understood, it was payback time.

When the legislation was brought to the House floor for a vote on August 12, the chamber's galleries were packed with uniformed soldiers and black-clad members of mothers' groups. The atmosphere was extremely tense. As Rayburn took the Speaker's chair, he had no idea whether he and James Wadsworth had rounded up enough support to pass the bill. To win, it would have to attract twenty or more Republican votes, which Wadsworth had frantically been working to get. Although the GOP had formally opposed the legislation, minority leader Joseph Martin, who personally felt that the extension was necessary, had told his Republican colleagues to "follow your own preferences on this." But House isolationists predicted that no more than a dozen Republicans would vote for it, and Democratic whip Pat Boland told Rayburn he had no clue how many Republican votes they could count on.

As the clerk called the roll, the vote seesawed back and forth. In the press gallery, reporters compared notes: some had tallies showing the extension winning, others had it losing. The only thing they could agree on was that the final margin would be razor-thin.

After reading all the members' names, the clerk went back through the list a second time, repeating the names of those who had not yet voted. When he was finished, he wrote the numbers on a piece of paper and handed it to Rayburn. But before the Speaker could announce the results, a Democratic member rose, asking to be recognized. When Rayburn called on him, the congressman changed his vote from aye to nay—a step that is permitted until the final tally is announced. Rayburn looked down at the paper; with this change, the vote stood at 203 for the bill and 202 against. Just then, another member jumped up.

Realizing that the measure's fate was in the balance, Rayburn ignored the man, who was now frantically waving his arm, and recognized instead a Republican deputy whip, who asked for a recapitulation of the vote (a routine motion to determine that each member's tally had been recorded correctly).

The motion was Rayburn's lifeline, and he grabbed it. He quickly announced the tally, declared "the bill is passed," and ordered the recapitulation. Only then did the legislation's opponents realize that they had been outsmarted. Under House rules, once the vote is announced and recapitulation is under way, no member may change his or her vote. The recapitulation showed no errors, and pandemonium reigned in the chamber. Angry Republicans rushed to the well of the House, demanding that Rayburn order a reconsideration. The bill's advocates erupted in cheers and applause, while, in the galleries, the "mothers" screamed in fury. In the midst of the cacophony, the Speaker serenely banged his gavel and called for order. Thanks to Rayburn's mastery of arcane House procedure, the 1.4-million-man army had been preserved. Four months later, the Japanese bombed Pearl Harbor.

Of the 203 House members voting for the extension, 21 were Republicans, who, thanks to the intense lobbying of James Wadsworth, had helped provide the critical one-vote margin for victory. Wadsworth, for his part, attributed the closeness of the tally to "cowardice" on the part of members facing reelection. As if to prove Wadsworth's point, one congressman had written to colleagues shortly before the vote: "If you don't watch your step, your political hide, which is very near and dear to you, will be tanning on the barn door."

While the narrowness of the House vote was a shock to Washington and much of the rest of the nation, it was hardly an accurate reflection of the overall mood of the American people. Public opinion polls still showed a majority in favor of the extension. Indeed, a fair number of the 65 Democrats who voted against the measure personally favored its passage but, as Wadsworth noted, were too craven to take a political risk. Reportedly, some believed that the measure would pass handily without their support and were surprised by the closeness of the tally.

Among those severely jarred by the hairbreadth victory were Winston Churchill and British military leaders, who at the time of the House vote were meeting with Roosevelt and his military chiefs in Placentia Bay, off the coast of Newfoundland. The British tended to equate their parliamentary form of government with America's very different system of separation of powers. If such a vote had taken place in the House of Commons, the Churchill government, harnessed to Parliament as it was, might well have fallen.

Roosevelt was in no such danger, but the news from Washington certainly did not inspire him to take any new, dramatic action to help the British. He rejected Churchill's appeals to enter the war, although he promised the prime minister that he "would become more and more provocative" in the Battle of Atlantic. As a first step in this direction, he agreed to formalize the unofficial U.S. naval protection being provided to British as well as American convoys as far as Iceland.

After returning home, Churchill wrote glumly to his son: "The President, for all his warm heart and good intentions, is thought by many of his admirers to move with public opinion rather than to lead and form it." When FDR held a press conference to assure the American people that the Newfoundland meeting had brought the United States no closer to war, Churchill dashed off a telegram to Harry Hopkins about the disheartening effect of the president's statement on the British public and government, which he said were experiencing "a wave of depression." The prime minister closed with this veiled warning: "If 1942 opens with Russia knocked out and Britain left again alone, all kinds of dangers may arise."

Back in Washington, Roosevelt complained to reporters about what he saw as the public's apathy toward the U.S. war effort. The trouble with the country, he said, is that "too many Americans have not yet made up their minds that we have a war to win, and that it will take a hard fight to win it." In the view of many in Roosevelt's circle, the president failed to realize that a major cause of the American people's inertia was his failure to educate and lead them.

Shortly after the extension vote, General Marshall wrote FDR: "The public has been so confused as to the facts and logic of the situation . . . that something must be done to bring them to an understanding of the national emergency and of the necessity for a highly trained Army. Within the War Department organization, we are doing our best to counteract this weakness on the home front, but as it relates to the civil population . . . prompt action is necessary."

Roosevelt replied: "Got any ideas?"

CHAPTER 23

"PROPAGANDA . . . WITH A VERY THICK COATING OF SUGAR"

≡

Burton Wheeler was tired of losing.

Since the war began, he and his fellow isolationists had been defeated in every legislative battle they had waged over America's role in the conflict. A major reason for those failures, he believed, was a media bias against him and his allies that prevented their message from getting through to the public. For months, Wheeler had complained about how difficult it was for antiwar activists to get fair and equal coverage; the media, in his view, were allowing the Roosevelt administration free rein to frame the discussion. The Montana Democrat was particularly critical of newsreels and movies, which he accused of a fixation on pro-British and pro-war themes.

After Roosevelt's speech announcing Lend-Lease in December 1940, Wheeler had responded with a passionate, detailed denunciation of the plan. The newsreels ignored his response while paying considerable attention to the president's address. "Will you kindly inform me when, if at all, you intend to carry my answer?" he demanded of Paramount News, one of the country's largest newsreel production companies. "And what, if anything, you are going to do about carrying both sides of the controversy on pending legislation which directly involves the question of war and peace?" Charging the film industry with fomenting war propaganda, Wheeler raised the possibility of restrictive legislation unless moviemakers started displaying "a more impartial attitude."

As the country's most powerful creator of mass culture, Hollywood was considered an especially potent threat by Wheeler and other isolationist leaders. There was little doubt about the influence of movies: more than half of the American people saw at least one movie a week in the late 1930s and early 1940s. "We really have two education systems in America," *Christian Century* noted, "the public school system and the movies."

In August 1941, Senator Gerald Nye fanned the flames that his Senate colleague had ignited. Calling movie studios "the most gigantic engines of war propaganda in existence," Nye demanded an immediate Senate investigation of Hollywood and what he saw as its collusion with the Roosevelt administration. "The silver screen has been flooded with picture after picture designed to rouse us to a state of war hysteria," the South Dakota Republican declared at an America First rally in St. Louis. "The truth is that in twenty thousand theaters in the United States tonight, they are holding mass war meetings."

As overheated as Nye's remarks were, they didn't come close to the incendiary quality of his comments about the movie studio heads he held most responsible for this state of affairs—men who had emigrated from "Russia, Hungary, Germany, and the Balkan countries" and as a result were "naturally susceptible" to "racial emotions." The senator was clearly referring to Louis B. Mayer, Samuel Goldwyn, the Warner brothers, and other Jewish film moguls, who, according to Nye, "came to our land and took citizenship here" while "entertaining violent animosities toward certain causes abroad." In the frustration he shared with Wheeler and other isolationists over the media's negative reaction to their cause, Nye was not only declaring war on Hollywood, he was also raising the specter of anti-Semitism.

A few hours before his St. Louis speech, Nye joined Senator Bennett Champ Clark of Missouri in introducing a Senate resolution that called for a formal investigation into film and radio propaganda. Burton Wheeler, as chairman of the Senate Interstate Commerce Committee, referred the resolution to a subcommittee headed by another prominent isolationist, Senator D. Worth Clark of Idaho, who, in turn, immediately scheduled hearings.

It was now Hollywood's turn to take center stage in the isolationist-interventionist struggle.

AS IT HAPPENED, THE senators' allegations about the film industry's pro-British and interventionist bent were largely true. Several dozen films depicting the evils of Nazi Germany, lauding Britain's resistance to the German onslaught, and even suggesting the possibility of U.S. involvement in the war made their debuts between September 1939 and December 1941.

In mid-1941, Lord Halifax wrote to a colleague in London that movies in America "are doing a very good job of work in our cause." The enthusiastic response of U.S. moviegoers to American-made feature films like *A Yank in the RAF* and *International Squadron* and British documentaries like *London Can Take It!* and *This Is England* proved Halifax's point. In close cooperation with the administration, the studios were also producing short films promoting the current defense buildup and urging young Americans to enlist in the armed forces.

What's more, a substantial number of prominent Hollywood figures had given their personal endorsement to the interventionist crusade. Walter Wanger, a noted independent producer and president of the Academy of Motion Picture Arts and Sciences, was an active member of the Century Group and its successor, Fight for Freedom. Also belonging to Fight for Freedom were directors Howard Hawks and William Wyler and actors Douglas Fairbanks Jr., Humphrey Bogart, Helen Hayes, Burgess Meredith, Melvyn Douglas, and Edward G. Robinson. Studio tycoons Darryl Zanuck and Harry and Jack Warner made substantial donations to the organization.

By 1941, many in Hollywood were already old hands at political activism. Five years before, energized by the growing threat of Nazi Germany, hundreds of screenwriters, directors, actors, and producers had come together to form the Hollywood Anti-Nazi League, which became the focal point of liberal, interventionist activity in the film community. Intent on raising the industry's political consciousness, the league sponsored rallies, mass meetings, and letter-writing campaigns for a wide array of causes, from support of the Loyalist forces in the Spanish Civil War to backing the beleaguered Federal Theatre

Project in its fight against Martin Dies's House Un-American Activities Committee.

America First, by contrast, found it virtually impossible to recruit members in the film capital. One of the few prominent Hollywood figures who did enlist in the isolationist cause was actress Lillian Gish, who became a member of America First's national committee. In August 1941, however, Gish resigned from the organization after informing Robert Wood that producers had made clear they wouldn't hire her as long as she belonged to his group.

Still, the question of Hollywood's interventionist sentiment was far more complex than Gerald Nye and other isolationist critics made it out to be. While much of Hollywood's creative community had indeed become politically energized by the late 1930s, those with the actual power to make movies—the studio heads—were, until very late in the game, reluctant to use their products to promote any cause, political or otherwise. The first explicitly anti-Nazi film—Warner Bros.' *Confessions of a Nazi Spy*—did not appear until May 1939, several years after American newsreels, radio, newspapers, and magazines had begun paying attention to the evils of Hitler's regime. Other studios waited until mid-1940 to join the anti-Fascist parade; even when they did, the number of such films was a small percentage of the studios' total yearly output.

Throughout the film industry's relatively brief existence, moviemakers—protective of their profits and worried about private pressure groups and government censorship—had done their best to avoid controversy. They were particularly concerned about not offending important foreign markets, which accounted for at least half their annual revenues. In the 1930s, Germany and Italy were key outlets for American movies, and studio heads were reluctant to do anything that might anger those countries' totalitarian leaders.

Robert Sherwood was made aware of that fact when his Pulitzer Prize–winning play, *Idiot's Delight,* was optioned by Metro-Goldwyn-Mayer in 1936. Both antiwar and anti-Fascist, *Idiot's Delight,* set in a small Italian hotel on the Swiss border, focuses on a disparate group of international travelers who are stranded when Italy launches a surprise air raid on Paris. To avoid annoying Italy, the head of MGM, Louis B. Mayer, ordered the story's setting changed to an unnamed country whose inhabitants spoke Esperanto instead of Italian. There also was to be no mention of Fascism. The Italian consul in Los Angeles was given final script approval, and MGM previewed the film for representatives of the Italian government.

When Sherwood, who wrote the screenplay, was asked if he had had any collaborators, he ruefully replied, "Yes—Mussolini." Expurgated and defanged, *Idiot's Delight* was roundly panned by the critics when it was finally released in early 1939. And despite all MGM's efforts to placate Italian sensibilities, Italy ended up banning it, as did Spain, France, Switzerland, and Estonia.

Hollywood's self-censorship system, embodied by the Hays Office and its production code, also played a major role in keeping social and political issues out of films. Hired by studio heads in 1922 to clean up their industry after a series of Hollywood sex scandals, Will Hays, Warren Harding's postmaster general, greatly restricted the depiction of sex, violence, and America's social ills on the screen. "The question of public order, of public good, of avoiding the inflammatory, the prejudicial or the subversive," Hays primly wrote, "is a problem of social responsibility everlastingly imposed upon those who would produce, distribute and exhibit pictures."

When war began in September 1939, Hays urged studio heads to observe strict neutrality in the conflict, warning that war-related movies might prompt federal regulation and a warlike spirit in the nation. "The primary purpose . . . of motion pictures," he reminded the moguls, "is entertainment." The equally conservative Joseph Breen, who was in charge of the production code's enforcement, informed the studios that they must respect "the just rights, history, and feelings of any nation," including Germany and Italy.

At that point, most studio heads were not inclined to argue. Louis B. Mayer, for one, "believed movies should be an escape from the ugliness of the world," Edward G. Robinson observed, "and should contain no messages except that love and fieldstone houses and gorgeous women and manly men were, in sum, God's true purpose." In the words of screenwriter-producer Jesse Lasky Jr., "we were always expert at closing our eyes to reality, near or far."

But there was another factor at work—one that everyone recognized but few openly acknowledged. As Nye nastily noted, a majority of studio chiefs were Jews of Central or Eastern European descent. But instead of being susceptible to "racial emotions," as he claimed, most had done their best to shed their Jewish pasts and blend in with mainstream American society. That was not especially easy, considering the strong streak of anti-Semitism then prevailing in the United States. Studio bosses feared that the production of anti-Nazi films, particularly those focusing on Jewish persecution, might set off a backlash against "Jewish warmongers," which in turn would call unwanted attention to their own backgrounds and identities.

According to a poll in the late 1930s, 60 percent of Americans agreed with statements describing Jews as avaricious and dishonest, and 72 percent opposed allowing more Jewish refugees to enter the United States. "The Jews are to some extent still foreigners," the novelist Raymond Chandler, a Los Angeles resident who had more than a passing acquaintance with Hollywood, wrote to his English publisher. "I've lived in a Jewish neighborhood, and I've watched one become Jewish, and it was pretty awful."

THANKS TO THE MAJOR studios' timidity toward war-related subjects, American moviegoers' only glimpse of what was happening overseas for most of the 1930s was through the newsreels that preceded the feature films they came to see. For half a decade, the major newsreel companies, which were not subject to the feature films' self-censorship system, had increasingly featured stories on Hitler and Mussolini and the threat they posed to peace in Europe.

Of all the newsreel services, *March of Time,* a product of Henry Luce's empire, was by far the most anti-Nazi and pro-British. Unlike its competitors, it added staged dramatizations to its narration and documentary footage, creating a new and powerful form of film journalism that its detractors called biased and inflammatory.

In 1938, *March of Time* ignited a storm of controversy with a short film called "Inside Nazi Germany," which showed, among other things, police rounding up Jews and bullyboys painting anti-Semitic slogans on buildings. "From the time the German child is old enough to understand anything, he ceases to be an individual and is taught that he was born to die for the fatherland," the film's announcer declared in stentorian tones. While German officials protested its showing and the city of Chicago banned it, millions of Americans flocked to more than five thousand theaters around the country to see the film.

For the next three years, most of the newsreels produced by *March of Time* touched on the European crisis. Outspokenly anti-Fascist, they also openly championed a more prominent American involvement in the conflict.

BY 1939, HITLER AND Mussolini had pulled the plug on Hollywood, severely restricting the showing of American films in their countries and, in the process, cutting off much of the studios' foreign revenue. With Great Britain as the only lucrative film market left in Europe, the way was now clear for the major studios to join the newsreels in depicting the Nazi threat. But the only studio to do so in 1939 was Warner Bros., which long had specialized in movies with explicitly political and social themes. In May of that year, Warner Bros. released *Confessions of a Nazi Spy,* which depicted German American agents, in league with Joseph Goebbels, trying to win power for the Nazis in the United States. Discovered in the nick of time, the conspiracy is broken up by the FBI and New York police. In the final scene, the district attorney, at the agents' trial, lectures the jury—i.e., the American public—about the dangers of isolationism.

In Washington, German chargé d'affaires Hans Thomsen lodged a sharp complaint with the State Department over *Confessions'* anti-German themes. He did the same after the 1940 release of MGM's *The Mortal Storm,* a powerful if melodramatic account of the rise of Nazism in Germany and its horrific effects on a Jewish professor and his family. Shown in June 1940, just before the fall of France, *The Mortal Storm* was the first in a flood of major anti-Nazi Hollywood releases that came after the German blitzkrieg in Western Europe. As *Life* sardonically noted, "So fast are the studios filming diatribes against Adolf Hitler . . . that no Hollywood visitor can sit down in a studio commissary without finding a plug-ugly in Nazi uniform beside him."

Two months later, just as German bombs began raining down on London, Americans flocked to theaters to see a spine-tingling spy thriller whose story, like that of *The Mortal Storm,* was unsettlingly close to real life. The film, entitled *Foreign Correspondent* and directed by Alfred Hitchcock, focuses on Johnny Jones, a newspaper reporter in New York who at the beginning cares little or nothing about the growing crisis in Europe. After being transferred to London, however,

Jones, played by Joel McCrea, is pitchforked into a surreal world of assassinations, fifth columnists, and murderous Nazi spies. No longer apathetic about Germany's danger to the world, he becomes a fierce champion of the anti-Nazi cause.

In the movie's last scene, Jones, in the midst of a Luftwaffe air raid on London, makes an impassioned radio broadcast to listeners back home, in effect urging them to shed their isolationism and come to the aid of an imperiled Europe. With lights flickering and an air raid siren wailing in the background, he declares: "All that noise you hear . . . is death coming to London. You can hear the bombs falling on the streets and the homes. Don't tune me out—this is a big story and you're part of it. . . . The lights are all out everywhere, except in America. Keep those lights burning. . . . Hang on to your lights, they're the only lights left in the world."

Foreign Correspondent was produced by Walter Wanger, Hollywood's most outspoken interventionist. The son of well-to-do German Jewish immigrants and a product of Dartmouth, Wanger was one of the film industry's few successful independent producers. He was unapologetic about using his movies as ideological weapons, making it clear that his goal with *Foreign Correspondent* was "to shake the U.S. into awareness of what must threaten her if she turned her back on Europe."

Alfred Hitchcock was another unabashed advocate of using films for political ends. In his case, the aim was to further the cause of his native Britain. Hitchcock was just one of many prominent British citizens in Hollywood who worked closely with their government to promote Britain and its war effort. When the war began in 1939, Lord Lothian had advised members of the large British film colony, among them actors Cary Grant, Ronald Colman, and Cedric Hardwicke, to stay where they were instead of returning home. "The maintenance of a powerful British nucleus of actors in Hollywood is of great importance to our interests," Lothian wrote Lord Halifax, "partly because they are continually championing the British cause in a very volatile community which would otherwise be left to the mercies of German propagandists, and because the production of films with strong British themes is one of the best and subtlest forms of British propaganda."

While some younger actors, including David Niven, ignored Lothian's advice and went back to Britain to enlist, most stayed in America. They were joined by an influx of British directors and writers, many of them recruited by their government to go to Hollywood. In 1940, Alexander Korda, a Hungarian émigré who had emerged as one of Britain's foremost producers and directors, arrived to make *That Hamilton Woman,* a costume drama about the love affair between Emma Hamilton and Lord Nelson, the British admiral who defeated Napoleon's forces at the Battle of Trafalgar.

Starring Laurence Olivier and Vivien Leigh, the movie, as Korda freely acknowledged, was "propaganda . . . with a very thick coating of sugar," meant to underline the parallels between Britain's struggle against Napoleon's crusade for world domination and its current fight against another European conqueror. In one speech, Nelson declares to his fellow admirals: "You cannot make peace with dictators. You have to destroy them. Wipe them out!" In New York and other cities with strong interventionist sympathies, those stirring lines invariably drew loud applause from moviegoers.

Winston Churchill, who loved *That Hamilton Woman* and saw it many times, reportedly recruited Korda to do more than make pro-British movies. According to Korda, he worked closely with William Stephenson, a close friend of his, at the prime minister's behest, setting up an office in Rockefeller Center and acting as an intermediary between the British government and British Security Coordination operatives. Although there's no official proof of this, Churchill did, without explanation, confer a knighthood on Korda in 1942.

Also doing their bit for Britain were some of its best-known novelists and playwrights. Two of the screenwriters who worked on *Foreign Correspondent,* for example, were R. C. Sherriff, whose poignant play about World War I, *Journey's End,* became a classic, and James Hilton, who wrote the bestselling novels *Goodbye, Mr. Chips* and *Lost Horizon* (both of which became popular movies, too).

Sherriff and Hilton, who was particularly adept at evoking the image of an idealized, inspiring Britain, also helped write *Mrs. Miniver,* about the experiences of an upper-middle-class family in the London suburbs at the time of Dunkirk and the Blitz. An enormous hit, *Mrs. Miniver,* with its story of British resolution and courage in the midst of catastrophe, touched the hearts of millions of Americans. Churchill called it "propaganda worth a hundred battleships." But as *Mrs. Miniver*'s director, William Wyler, noted, his film, like *That Hamilton Woman,* was hardly a realistic portrait of the conflict. Wyler, who called himself "a warmonger" and said he made *Mrs. Miniver* because "I was concerned about Americans being isolationists," nonetheless acknowledged that the movie "only scratched the surface of war."

Yet even hard-boiled films like *Confessions of a Nazi Spy* and *The Mortal Storm* tiptoed around the war's grim reality. With one prominent exception, no Hollywood film in the late 1930s and early 1940s ever made clear, for example, that Jews were the main targets of Nazi persecution. In Hollywood movies, it was acceptable to condemn Nazism but unacceptable to make specific mention of its savage anti-Semitism. In *The Mortal Storm,* which is clearly about the destruction of a Jewish family in Germany, the word "Jew" is never mentioned.

The decision to sidestep the issue was made by the studio heads, who feared that raising it in films would stir up an even greater wave of anti-Semitism in the United States. Their concern was fueled by a visit paid to Hollywood in late 1940 by Joseph P. Kennedy, the isolationist American ambassador to Britain and a former movie mogul himself. At a lunch with fifty top film executives, most of them Jewish, Kennedy warned his former colleagues of the danger to themselves and their fellow Jews if they continued "using the film medium to promote or show sympathy to the cause of democracies versus the dictators." Such movies, he said, only served to highlight Jewish control of the film industry, which in turn could lead to an anti-Semitic backlash against Hollywood.

The only major industry figure to thumb his nose at such fears was Charlie Chaplin, whose 1940 movie *The Great Dictator* was the sole Hollywood product in that period to single out anti-Semitism as a core tenet of Hitler's ideology. Remembered today mostly for its satiric depiction of Hitler and Mussolini as blowhard buffoons, *The Great Dictator* also takes an unsparing look at the Nazis' savagery toward Jews.

Chaplin, who was not Jewish and who produced and directed his own films, was under ceaseless pressure to cancel the project from the day it was first announced. Hate mail poured in, and even the White House, which encouraged him to make the movie, warned Chaplin that it probably would be an enormous failure. In fact, it was a major box-office hit and, as it turned out, Chaplin's most commercially successful film, which today is regarded as a classic.

INTERESTINGLY, THE MOVIE WITH the greatest impact on Americans prior to Pearl Harbor had nothing to do with anti-Semitism, Nazis, the British, or World War II. Instead, it dealt with the true story of a Tennessee farmer named Alvin York, who in 1917 was forced to reconcile his strong pacifism with what others told him was his patriotic duty to fight for his country in World War I.

Drafted into the Army, York, an excellent marksman, briefly considered becoming a conscientious objector before finally—and reluctantly—agreeing to serve. During the Meuse-Argonne offensive in France, he led an attack on an enemy machine gun nest, disregarding heavy fire to capture 132 Germans and kill 28 others. For that, York was awarded the Medal of Honor and, when he returned home, was honored as one of America's greatest wartime heroes.

For years, York had resisted the idea of a film about his exploits, but in 1940, he finally yielded to the persistence of producer Jesse Lasky Jr. With the help of screenwriters Howard Koch and John Huston, Lasky set out to make York's story a parable for modern times, depicting the dilemma between America's antipathy toward war and the need to fight to preserve the country's cherished freedoms and principles. In the process of making the film, the real-life York, who had retained his pacifism after the Great War and had spoken out in the 1930s against getting involved in another conflict, became a convert to interventionism.

Released in the summer of 1941, *Sergeant York,* starring Gary Cooper, was given a lavish premiere in New York City. Among those in the audience were York, General John Pershing, Eleanor Roosevelt, Wendell Willkie, Henry Luce, and General Lewis B. Hershey, the director of the Selective Service System. Four weeks later, Washington staged its own premiere, lending *Sergeant York* the distinct aura of a government-sanctioned film. Troops accompanied York from Union Station to the White House, where Roosevelt told him—and reporters—that he was "thrilled" with the picture. The morning after its screening, which was attended by members of Congress, military leaders, and other government officials, York was invited to deliver the daily invocation in the Senate.

The film more than lived up to the administration's hopes, striking a deep chord with millions of Americans struggling with the same dilemma faced by York more than twenty years earlier. The movie's message, as the historian David Welky put it, was that "men must fight for . . . freedom, liberty, democracy—and implied that the time was right to fight for them again." For young male moviegoers who might be inspired by York's onscreen actions to enlist, the Army had prepared an eight-page recruitment brochure detailing the hero's life.

A huge hit, *Sergeant York* was the highest-grossing U.S. film in 1941. It was nominated for eleven Academy Awards and won two, including the best-actor honor for Gary Cooper.

ON SEPTEMBER 9, 1941, Senator D. Worth Clark banged down a glass ashtray in lieu of a gavel to begin Senate hearings into charges that the film industry was, in Senator Gerald Nye's words, "trying to make America punch drunk with propaganda to push her into war." The hearings were widely publicized, and nearly five hundred spectators crowded into the Senate caucus room that morning, some standing on chairs to get a better view of the action. They had come not only to witness the expected verbal fireworks between studio executives and subcommittee members, all but one of whom were staunch isolationists, but also to catch a glimpse of the film industry's famed legal counsel—Wendell Willkie.

Willkie, who had joined a New York law firm shortly after his 1940 defeat by FDR, reportedly was paid $100,000 (about $1.5 million in today's dollars) for his services. Steep as his fee was, there was no denying that the studios received full value for their money. A genius at public relations, Willkie was extraordinarily adept at using congressional hearings to further his own cause, as he had demonstrated in his early-1930s battle against the Roosevelt administration over the Tennessee Valley Authority.

Assisted by a battery of studio lawyers and coordinating his strategy with the White House, Willkie advised movie executives to go on the attack. He gave them a master class in doing so, issuing a blistering prehearing press release denouncing the subcommittee's assault on the film industry as un-American and anti-Semitic and accusing it of trying to extinguish basic human freedoms.

According to Willkie, Hollywood made no apologies for its opposition to Hitler and the Nazis. Alluding to Nye's comments about the moguls' Jewish roots, Willkie maintained that the movie executives were deep-dyed Americans and that only a traitor could doubt their loyalty. He argued that the isolationists were trying to intimidate Hollywood into making films reflecting their own perspective, which would be a gross violation of American civil liberties. "It is just a small step to the newspapers, magazines, and other periodicals," Willkie declared. "And from the freedom of the press, it is just a small step to the freedom of the individual to say what he believes."

Thanks to Willkie's arguments, the subcommittee had been placed squarely on the defensive even before the hearings started. In questioning the senators' purpose for launching the investigation, the former presidential candidate had managed to "put his clients on the side of God and country and their enemies at the other extreme," David Welky has written. "To oppose Hollywood was to oppose the United States. To question its motives was to embrace Nazism."

On the first day of the hearings, Willkie sat at a table off to the side of the room, strategically close to the large press contingent covering the proceedings. Initially, D. Worth Clark had told him he would be allowed to cross-examine witnesses and ask questions of the subcommittee, but the Idaho Republican changed his mind after the release of Willkie's inflammatory press statement. If Clark thought he had silenced the voluble counsel for the film industry, however, he soon realized his error.

To his chagrin, Clark also discovered that one of his panel's five members, Senator Ernest McFarland, was in fact a Willkie ally. A freshman Democrat from Arizona, McFarland was known as an interventionist, but he had never been particularly vocal on the issue and had maintained friendly relations with Nye, Clark, Wheeler, and other isolationist Westerners. Considering McFarland a tame supporter of Roosevelt, Clark had chosen him as the subcommittee's token interventionist. As it turned out, the burly Arizonan despised the isolationist views of his Senate colleagues and wasted no time in making that clear. His first target was the hearing's first witness, Gerald Nye.

During his testimony, the senator from South Dakota did nothing to help himself. Stung by Willkie's accusations of anti-Semitism, he read a forty-one-page statement denying that "bigotry, race, and religious prejudice played any role in the hearings" and declaring that he was opposed to "the injection of anti-Semitism . . . in American thinking and acting." But then he negated everything he'd said by fulminating against film executives who, "born abroad and animated by the hatreds of the Old World," were "injecting into U.S. films the most vicious propaganda I've ever seen." According to Nye, many Americans believed "that our Jewish citizenry would willingly have our country and its sons taken into this foreign war." By encouraging such an attitude, the senator argued, American Jews were contributing to the growth of anti-Semitism in the United States.

In his questioning of Nye, McFarland demanded to know what the senator and his colleagues hoped to accomplish by their investigation of the film industry. Nye could not come up with an answer. Nor was he able to respond to McFarland's question about which war films Nye had found most objectionable, actually admitting, "It is a terrible weakness of mine to go to a picture tonight and not be able to state the title of it tomorrow morning."

Seeing an opening, McFarland exploited it for all it was worth. "Have you seen *Flight Command*?" he asked his Republican colleague.

"I do not believe I did, Senator."

"*That Hamilton Woman*?"

"I did not see that."

"*Man Hunt*?"

"I think not."

"*Sergeant York*?"

"I think not."

"*Escape*?"

"Would you tell me a part of the story so I could try to remember?"

"*Confessions of a Nazi Spy*?"

Nye might have seen that one, he said, but he had it confused with *I Married a Nazi*: "For the life of me I could not tell you which was which."

It soon became embarrassingly clear that Nye had not seen or could not remember any of the films he and his isolationist colleagues found so objectionable, with the sole exception of *The Great Dictator*. McFarland had skewered Nye, the *Hollywood Reporter* later wrote, "like a censor working on *Lady Chatterley's Lover*."

The one-sided verbal duel between McFarland and Nye set the tone for the rest of the hearings. The isolationist senators clearly had not done their homework and, as a result, were made to look ridiculous. Unprepared to discuss the movies they had targeted, they also were vague about their objectives for the investigation. Their ineptness worked to fuel the suspicion that the only reason for the hearings was to gain publicity for the isolationist cause.

Willkie, for his part, circumvented Clark's attempt to silence him by making frequent whispered comments to reporters, who wrote down everything he said and then put the remarks in their stories. He also grabbed a microphone several times to make off-the-cuff remarks to the subcommittee. On the hearing's third day, he pointed out that it had not produced any legislation thus far, which was, after all, the ostensible reason that the probe was being conducted.

Unsurprisingly, the hearings were doomed to failure. Willkie's talk of attempted censorship resonated with newspapers across the country, many of which condemned what they dubbed a witch hunt. According to the *Buffalo Courier-Express,* the hearings were "a frontal attack on the constitutional guarantee of freedom of expression." In exasperation, the *Milwaukee Journal* asked of the senators: "Do they want some pro-Hitler films produced? Do they want some anti-defense films shown? Just what is it they want?"

Even America First thought the hearings were a disaster. "Certain aspects of the investigation are so unsavory that I question the advisability of publicizing it any further," Ruth Sarles, the group's Washington director, wrote to a colleague.

Faced with a firestorm of ridicule and criticism, the subcommittee abruptly adjourned after the first week. The hearings were never reopened.

HOLLYWOOD'S VICTORY OVER THE isolationists emboldened those working there to remain in the forefront of national debates over contentious political issues. As David Welky has noted, the industry's activism against the dictators in the prewar years was its "political coming out party." From then on, leading Hollywood figures would have no qualms about making their voices heard on major national and international matters.

Having helped nudge public opinion toward the view that America must enter the war, the movie industry worked closely with the Roosevelt administration for the conflict's duration. Many of its members actively campaigned for the president's reelection in 1944, and studio heads produced movies that the administration encouraged them to make, such as *Mission to Moscow,* which sang the praises of America's crucial wartime ally, the Soviet Union.

For years, the film community had been everything that conservatives in Congress and elsewhere despised—predominantly to the left in its political orientation and unabashedly pro-FDR and pro–New Deal. It's not surprising, then, that after conservatism made a comeback following the war and FDR's death, one of its first targets would be the film industry.

With the Soviet Union shifting from ally to antagonist and the first chill of the Cold War sweeping over the country, the FBI and the House Un-American Activities Committee would launch an investigation of Communist influence in Hollywood. The probe would result in the jailing and blacklisting of writers, directors, actors, and producers, most of whom had cut their political teeth in Hollywood's prewar campaigns against the dictators. Anyone who had ever marched against Hitler or Mussolini was at risk of losing his or her livelihood. This ice age would last more than a dozen years, damaging and ruining hundreds if not thousands of lives.

CHAPTER 24

"SETTING THE GROUND FOR ANTI-SEMITISM"

Soon after the Senate movie hearings began, Charles Lindbergh handed his wife a copy of a speech he was about to give at an America First rally in Des Moines. As Anne Lindbergh read it, her anxiety mounted with every page. She knew, however, that any concern she expressed would probably have little effect. Although she was the only person Lindbergh trusted enough to read and comment on drafts of his speeches and articles, he often did not follow her advice. "There were many times when I wanted him to change his speeches," she later recalled. "There were many things I wish Charles had not said."

She had, for example, urged him in May not to call for "new policies and new leadership" for the country, arguing that such language would be interpreted as advocating insurrection. He ignored her counsel, and, as she predicted, his speech was roundly condemned. Similarly, after the German invasion of the Soviet Union, she advised him not to make his inflammatory remarks about preferring a U.S. alliance with Britain or Germany to one with the Soviets. Again, he disregarded her plea. He didn't care what other people thought. *He* believed his case was sound, and that's all that mattered.

This new speech, in Anne's view, surpassed all the others in its provocation. This one, she told him, would ignite a whirlwind. But nothing she said made a difference. Increasingly sensitive and suspicious, Lindbergh was convinced that the Roosevelt administration was trying to silence him. He was also sure that America was about to get into the war, and he was determined to fire one last salvo before Washington shut him up for good.

Feeding Lindbergh's persecution complex were Harold Ickes's unrelenting attacks on him, each new assault more blistering than the one before. The interior secretary was obsessed with the idea that Lindbergh was plotting to take over the country. Of his bête noire, Ickes wrote Roosevelt: "His actions have been coldly calculated with a view to obtaining ultimate power for himself—what he calls 'new leadership.'"

Having studied Lindbergh closely, Ickes decided he was most likely to touch a nerve by hammering away at the flier's 1938 acceptance of a medal from Hermann Goering. In speech after speech, he referred to Lindbergh not by name but as "the Knight of the German Eagle." On July 14, 1941, Ickes delivered his most brutal assault yet, accusing "ex-Colonel Lindbergh" of visiting prewar Germany because of his affinity for Nazism and of lying when he said he had traveled there at the request of the U.S. military. Lindbergh, Ickes declared, was devoted to the Hitler regime and the medal it gave him: "He preferred to keep the German Eagle. The colonelcy in our Army he returned to the President of the United States." Lindbergh, Ickes added, was "a menace to this country and its free institutions."

Both Charles and Anne Lindbergh were deeply angered by Ickes's attack, which Anne called "full of lies and calumny and false insinuations from beginning to end." In the past, Lindbergh had not responded to Ickes's sallies, but he finally had had enough. Convinced that Roosevelt was behind them, he decided to complain to the president. "Nothing is to be gained by my entering a controversy with a man of Ickes's type," he wrote in his journal. "But if I can pin Ickes's actions on Roosevelt, it will have the utmost effect."

In a letter to FDR, which he also released to the press, Lindbergh outlined the circumstances of his trips to Germany and Goering's presentation of the medal. The U.S. military, he said, had asked him to assess German aircraft developments, and the U.S. ambassador had urged him to come to the stag dinner at which the Luftwaffe chief had surprised him with the decoration. "Mr. President," Lindbergh declared, "I give you my word that I have no connection with any foreign Government . . . I will willingly open my files to your investigation. . . . If there is a question in your mind, I ask that you give me the opportunity of answering any charges." He added that he thought Ickes owed him an apology.

He failed to get one. The only response from the administration was a note from press secretary Steve Early dismissing his letter, which had been featured on newspaper front pages across the country, as a cheap publicity stunt. Ickes, for his part, was delighted that his goading had made Lindbergh "squeal," underscoring the flier's vulnerability and political naïveté. "For the first time, he has allowed himself to be put on the defensive," Ickes exulted in his diary.

At the same time, the secretary's slash-and-burn tactics received heavy criticism of their own. "Free speech is no longer free speech if character assassination from the highest places is to be the penalty for its exercise," an Omaha, Nebraska, newspaper editorialized after Ickes's July 14 address. "If the Ickes manner of settling a dispute were to be adopted, then we should all be out fighting each other with hatchets."

The interior secretary was deluged with letters, many of them denouncing his vitriol. Among them was a long, passionate missive from Miles Hart, a Democrat from Oswego, Kansas, who said he opposed Lindbergh's isolationism and believed that America must go to war. Nonetheless, Hart wrote, Lindbergh had every right to say what he believed, and "we have a right to listen to him without being bothered by the outbursts of those who would have us shun his opinions for extraneous reasons. . . . You do not answer his arguments by calling him a fool. . . . You've plenty of good arguments to refute his assertions. Why not use them?"

Hart went on to say that he resented "this business of questioning the motives of every man who happens to disagree with the administration. . . . The American people are faced with great problems. We cannot solve them in an atmosphere of hysteria and personal vituperation. We must have all the facts given to us and then be permitted calmly and reasonably to decide what we should do. . . . You and your associates, including Mr. Roosevelt, have fiddled long enough. The city burns, and it's time you cast away your entertaining diversions and went to work to put out the fire."

LINDBERGH HAD BEEN PLANNING his September speech for six months before he delivered it. In several previous addresses, he had mentioned what he called "powerful elements" that were trying to propel America into the war but refrained from naming them. Convinced now that U.S. involvement was "practically inevitable" and that "an incident to involve us might arise on any day," Lindbergh decided he must identify those "powerful elements" in a last-ditch step to alert Americans to the danger they posed.

The three groups he singled out as "war agitators" were the Roosevelt administration, the British, and American Jews. He reserved his sharpest criticism for the president and his men, and in a long speech, he devoted only three paragraphs to Jewish influence. But, as Anne knew, these were the comments that would set off the storm.

Lindbergh began his remarks about the Jews by saying he understood why they wanted America to get into the war and defeat Germany. Nazi persecution "would be sufficient to make bitter enemies of any race. No person with a sense of the dignity of mankind could condone" what was happening to the Jews in Europe.

Nonetheless, Lindbergh said, American Jews must realize that if the country did enter the conflict, they would be among the first to feel the consequences, which, he indicated, would include a violent outbreak of anti-Semitism in the country. "Tolerance is a virtue that depends upon peace and strength," he said. "History shows that it cannot survive war and devastation."

Insisting he was attacking neither the Jews nor the British, Lindbergh said he admired both groups. His objection lay in the fact that leaders of "both races . . . for reasons . . . which are not American, wish to involve us in the war. We cannot blame them for looking out for what they believe to be their own interests, but we must also look out for ours. We cannot allow the natural passions and prejudices of other peoples to lead our country to destruction." Jews, Lindbergh went on, posed a particular "danger to this country" because of "their large ownership and influence in our motion pictures, our press, our radio, and our government."

After reading the speech, Anne, sunk in "black gloom," pleaded with him not to give it. It was perfectly acceptable to criticize the

Roosevelt administration and the British, she said, but didn't he realize that his remarks about the Jews were "segregating them as a group," thereby "setting the ground for anti-Semitism"? Just as the Nazis had done in Germany, he was branding Jews as a separate race, whose own agenda was antithetical to the interests of their country. According to Lindbergh's rhetoric, they were Jews first, Americans second. In short, they were "the other."

When Anne told Lindbergh that his remarks would be interpreted as "Jew-baiting," he argued that he didn't mean to do that and that he certainly was not anti-Semitic. With both comments, Anne agreed. "I have never heard my husband tell a Jewish joke," she wrote a friend. "I have never heard him say anything derogatory about a Jew." Nonetheless, she asserted, his speech was "at best unconsciously a bid for anti-Semitism" and that "the anti-Semitic forces will rally to him, exultant." She declared that she would rather see America at war than "shaken by violent anti-Semitism."

Baffled by Anne's outburst, Lindbergh rejected all her arguments. The only reason he was making the speech, he told her, was to identify for the American people the forces behind the propaganda leading the country into war, with the hope of inoculating the public against war fever. Instead of trying to rouse passions, he wanted Americans to look at the situation dispassionately.

Years later, Anne described to an interviewer "the terrible row" she had had with Lindbergh over the Des Moines speech. "He just didn't believe me," she said. "He simply couldn't see" what she was saying. Tone-deaf to nuance and the sensitivities of others, he felt that the views he held were invariably correct and that he had a right—indeed an obligation—to express them, no matter the consequences to himself or others. Lindbergh regarded such stubbornness as courage, not hubris. Explaining once why he had no desire to enter politics, he declared: "I would rather say what I believe when I want to say it than to measure every statement I make by its probable popularity."

There's no question that Lindbergh's own dark view of America colored his belief that U.S. Jews would face an upsurge of persecution in wartime. Tolerance and individual freedom, he told friends, were fast disappearing in the country; he predicted "a bloody revolution" if war broke out, with "upheavals of great violence in the nation."

At the same time, his anti-Semitism, however unconscious it may have been, was clear. He firmly believed that Jews had a disproportionate and unhealthy influence on American life, particularly in the press, radio, and movies. "A few Jews add strength and character to a country, but too many create chaos," he wrote in his journal in April 1939. "And we are getting too many." In July 1941, he told an acquaintance that Jewish influence in the media would "end with their undoing. Instead of acting in the interests of their country and of the majority of their audience, they are acting in the interest—or presumed interest—of their race."

Such views were hardly uncommon in America at the time. William L. Langer, a Harvard historian who later co-wrote a two-volume history of American foreign policy in the four years leading up to Pearl Harbor, made much the same point in a 1939 lecture at the U.S. War College. "You have to face the fact that some of our most important American newspapers are Jewish-controlled, and I suppose if I were a Jew, I would feel about Nazi Germany as most Jews feel, and it would be most inevitable that the coloring of the news takes on that tinge," Langer said. Singling out *The New York Times,* whose owners were Jewish, Langer declared that the paper gave "a great deal of prominence" to "every little upset that occurs in Germany (and after all many upsets occur in a country of 70 million people). . . . The other part of it is soft-pedaled or put off with a sneer. So that in a rather subtle way, the picture you get is that there is no good in the Germans whatever."

In the 1930s and early 1940s, overt anti-Semitism was a distinctive feature of life in the United States, as it was in a great many countries. Not until after World War II and the revelations of the Holocaust did most elements of U.S. society consider open anti-Jewish prejudice to be unacceptable.

The influx of millions of Jewish immigrants from Eastern Europe had contributed heavily to the spread of anti-Semitism in America at the beginning of the twentieth century. Since bigotry traditionally flourishes in times of economic instability and unsettling social change, it's not surprising that the Great Depression and its accompanying turmoil provided another fertile seedbed for intolerance toward Jews. "Economic hardship was taking its toll," noted the Anti-Defamation League's Arnold Forster. "People needed a scapegoat for their Depression miseries."

No social class in America was immune to the virus of anti-Semitism. It infected Wall Street lawyers along with rednecks, well-regarded statesmen as well as populist extremists. At a 1939 lunch in Washington attended by prominent State Department officials and members of Congress, the discussion turned to the Jewish refugee issue. One of the guests—a former Baptist minister turned congressman—jocularly said: "I don't often criticize the Lord, but I do feel that he drowned the wrong lot in the Red Sea."

Most major U.S. colleges and universities, including virtually all the Ivy League schools, had strict quota systems for the acceptance of Jews. The relatively few Jews who were admitted often found what Kingman Brewster called a climate of "subliminal anti-Semitism." As Yale students, Brewster, McGeorge Bundy, and a few others sponsored a campaign in 1938 to help German Jews immigrate to the United States. The response from fellow Yalies was disheartening. As Bundy wrote in the *Yale Daily News,* "An all-too-large group has said: 'We don't like Jews. There are too many at Yale already. Why bring more over?' This is not an argument. It is an expression of intolerance and prejudice."

The American Jews who did attend college found still more doors closed to them after graduation. Most were barred from attending prestigious graduate schools, including those in medicine and law. Many if not most major companies and law firms refused to hire them. They were not permitted to live in certain residential areas; were prevented from joining private clubs, including country clubs; and could not stay at many hotels and resorts.

A number of federal government agencies, particularly the State and War Departments, were rife with anti-Semitism. The upper echelons of the State Department were dominated by wealthy Ivy League Brahmins who resisted the hiring of Jews and made life difficult for the few who slipped through the net. They also consistently denigrated Jews in their daily conversations, as the diary of former undersecretary of state William Castle makes clear.

Anti-Semitic himself, Castle wrote about frequent gatherings of senior State Department officials in which the maligning of Jews made up a large part of the talk. Describing one dinner party in early 1940, Castle observed: "I am afraid that many unpleasant things were said about the Jews, so it was as well that the company was small." Among the guests that night was Hugh Wilson, the former U.S. ambassador to Germany, whose own prejudice against Jews was well known.

Although not a career diplomat, Assistant Secretary of State Adolf Berle was also noted for his antipathy toward Jews. After the fall of France, Berle inveighed in his diary against the attempts by Supreme Court Justice Felix Frankfurter, who was Jewish, to persuade Roosevelt to provide more aid for the British. "The Jewish group, wherever you find it," Berle wrote, "is not only pro-English, but will sacrifice American interests to English interests—often without knowing it."

Many high-level U.S. military officers exhibited a similar prejudice. In 1938, General George van Horn Moseley, a former Army deputy chief of staff and one of the country's most decorated soldiers, advocated mandatory sterilization of Jewish refugees from Nazi Germany before they could be admitted to the United States. "Only in that way can we properly protect our future," Moseley declared.

Also espousing anti-Semitic views were the two Army officers considered the War Department's foremost experts on Germany—Colonel Truman Smith and his friend Major Albert Wedemeyer, who had been assigned to the Army War Plans Division shortly after spending two years at the German war college in Berlin. As Wedemeyer saw it, Jews were inherently abrasive, scheming, and selfish, which made them "suspect or distasteful and incompatible" with other groups. Wedemeyer developed his dislike for Jews during his stay in Berlin, where he first realized, he wrote, how strongly Roosevelt was influenced by Jewish interests. After World War II, Wedemeyer, who was by then the deputy Army chief of staff, asserted that the president's Jewish advisers—among them Samuel Rosenman, Felix Frankfurter, and Henry Morgenthau—"did everything possible to spread venom and hatred against the Nazis and to arouse Roosevelt against the Germans." Motivated by selfish interests, those Jews and others, he said, helped make America's entry into the war inevitable.

Wedemeyer was reiterating a common charge of the prewar years— that FDR had brought to Washington a swarm of radical Jews to run the government. Some opponents of FDR even contended that the president himself was a Jew. Both contentions were false. Although Jewish lawyers, economists, and other professionals certainly were an important source of talent and expertise for the administration, Jews made up less than 15 percent of Roosevelt's top-level appointees.

Yet that number, small as it was, was considerably larger than the number of Jews hired in high-level positions in private business and industry. In the 1930s, the federal government—particularly agencies dealing with economic and social reform—provided one of the few employment bright spots for college-educated Jews, who tended to be strong New Deal supporters.

Nonetheless, as unflinching and steady as the president was in providing vital job and other opportunities for Jews, he, along with his family and gentile advisers, were not free themselves from what FDR biographer Geoffrey Ward called the "open and almost universal" anti-Semitism of the Eastern establishment. T. H. Watkins, Harold Ickes's biographer, wrote that the president "had a way of using the word 'Hebrew' with such a tone of arch superiority that across all the decades it still has the effect of fingernails on a blackboard."

On at least one occasion, FDR voiced the same sentiment expressed by Lindbergh—that Jews were outsiders in American society and needed to watch their behavior. At a lunch with Leo Crowley, a Catholic economist who had just been given an important job in the administration, FDR remarked: "Leo, you know this is a Protestant country, and the Catholics and Jews are here under sufferance. It is up to you to go along with anything that I want." The president may well have meant his comment as a joke, but the underlying point was clear.

Even Harold Ickes, known as the administration's most forceful critic of anti-Semitism, warned American Jews to watch their step. In the November 1938 speech in which he made his first attack on Lindbergh, Ickes admonished affluent Jews "to exercise extreme caution in the acquisition of their wealth and great scrupulousness in their social behavior. A mistake made by a non-Jewish millionaire reflects upon him alone, but a false step made by a Jewish man of wealth reflects upon his whole race. This is harsh and unjust but it is a fact that must be faced."

Many if not most American Jews were inclined to go along with the idea of keeping a low profile, especially with regard to the war. "Jews in the U.S. remain quiescent and hope for the best," Isaiah Berlin, an Oxford don working for the British government in New York, wrote to his Russian Jewish parents in July 1941. "They are, above all things, terrified of being thought warmongers and to be acting in their own, rather than general, American interests."

For the most part, American Jews kept quiet when confronted with one of the most agonizing issues facing the Jewish community during that period: the controversy over whether to allow more European Jews to immigrate to the United States. According to Arnold Forster, "even leading Jewish organizations in New York, fearful of the outbreak of anti-Semitism, were largely silent on the refugee crisis."

In the late 1930s and early 1940s, thousands of desperate Jews lined up each day in front of U.S. consulates in Germany, Austria, and other Nazi-controlled countries to apply for visas. However, with little sentiment in America for providing them with a means of escape, almost all were turned away.

Most Americans, including a majority in Congress and the State Department, were adamantly opposed to admitting more refugees. More than two-thirds of those surveyed in a *Fortune* poll agreed with the statement that "with conditions as they are, we should try to keep [immigrants] out." As *Time* put it in March 1940, "The American people have so far shown no inclination to do anything for the world's refugees except read about them."

The U.S. public feared that a new influx of refugees would mean fewer jobs for native-born Americans. Americans also worried that Nazi agents might be planted among the immigrants—an idea emphasized by Roosevelt and J. Edgar Hoover in their warnings about fifth columnists. Unquestionably, anti-Semitism was also an important factor in fostering the anti-immigrant mood. When a proposal was floated after the 1938 Kristallnacht pogrom to take in ten thousand Jewish children from Germany, more than two out of three Americans were against the idea. Britain eventually accepted nine thousand, while the United States took only 240. That meager response stood in stark contrast to Americans' reaction in 1940 to the idea of providing a haven for British children escaping the dangers of the Battle of Britain and the Blitz. A Gallup poll estimated that five to seven million U.S. families were willing to house young British evacuees for the duration of the war.

Although Roosevelt was sympathetic to the plight of Jewish refugees, he did little of a concrete nature to help them before and during the war. As Arnold Forster saw it, "FDR failed Jews in their darkest hour. . . . The sorry truth [was] that throughout the Holocaust, Roosevelt kept the Jewish catastrophe low on his roster of priorities." In his inertia, however, he was no different from a majority of Americans.

As it happened, Lindbergh was undoubtedly correct in believing that most American Jews championed Britain's cause and that many wanted the United States to get into the war. But he was woefully mistaken in alleging that Jewish organizations and individuals were key "war agitators" among the American people. While prominent Jews did indeed belong to such interventionist organizations as the Century Group and Fight for Freedom, they comprised only a small minority of those groups' members, most of whom were upper-class East Coast Protestants. In July 1941, the German chargé d'affaires, Hans Thomsen, noted to his country's foreign ministry that because of fears of scapegoating, "far-sighted Jewish circles are avoiding taking an active part in warmongering and leave this to radical warmongers in the Roosevelt cabinet and to English propaganda."

Lindbergh's claim that Jews dominated the media also turned out to be erroneous. Fewer than 3 percent of U.S. newspaper publishers were Jewish, and those who were tended to be extremely cautious in their handling of the question of U.S. involvement in the war. A case in point was Arthur Sulzberger, publisher of *The New York Times,* who, while inclined toward interventionism, was far less outspoken than the publishers of the *Herald Tribune, PM,* the *Post,* and other New York newspapers. In September 1941, Sulzberger told Valentine Williams, a British propaganda official working for William Stephenson, that "for the first time in his life he regretted being a Jew because, with the tide of anti-Semitism rising, he was unable to champion the anti-Hitler policy of the administration as vigorously and as universally as he would like." The *Times* publisher added that "his sponsorship would be attributed to Jewish influence by isolationists and thus lose something of its force."

ANNE LINDBERGH OFTEN ACCOMPANIED her husband on his travels for America First, but she did not go with him to Des Moines, which was shaping up to be one of the most unfriendly places in which he had spoken. An anomaly in the largely isolationist Midwest, Iowa—the home state of Vice President Henry Wallace—had large pockets of interventionist sentiment, fostered by the Cowles brothers' *Des Moines Register,* the state's leading newspaper. Shortly before Lindbergh's speech, the editor of the *Register,* who was also chairman of the Des Moines chapter of Fight for Freedom, called Lindbergh "public enemy No. 1 in the United States," adding that if he "were a paid agent of the German government he could not serve the cause of Hitler so well." On the day of the speech, the *Register* ran an editorial cartoon on its front page showing Lindbergh speaking in front of several microphones, while Hitler and Mussolini sat before him, applauding enthusiastically. The caption over the cartoon read: HIS MOST APPRECIATIVE AUDIENCE.

Unsmiling and visibly tense when he stepped onto the stage of the Des Moines Coliseum, Lindbergh was greeted by a mixture of cheers, applause, and boos, along with scattered heckling, from the crowd of more than eight thousand. In his speech, which was broadcast nationwide, he preceded his attacks on the "war agitators" with a denunciation of the way he and other isolationists, along with their cause, had been treated in the media. "Newsreels," he said, had "lost all semblance of objectivity. . . . A smear campaign was instituted against individuals who opposed intervention. The terms fifth columnist, traitor, Nazi, anti-Semitic were thrown ceaselessly at anyone who dared to suggest that it was not in the best interests of the United States to enter the war."

When Lindbergh reached the heart of his address, the applause clearly outweighed the jeering. His mention of the British, the Roosevelt administration, and Jews as the main instigators of war fever brought most of the crowd to its feet, and, as he later wrote in his journal, "whatever opposition existed was completely drowned out by our support."

He told his audience that all three groups had been working for months to involve the country in the war "without our realization" and now were trying to create "a series of incidents which would force us into the actual conflict." Still, though America stood on the brink of war, it was "not yet too late to stay out." Lindbergh urged those listening, in the auditorium and on the radio, to contact members of Congress, "the last stronghold of democracy and representative government in this country."

He reserved his most scathing attacks for Roosevelt and his advisers, whom he charged with "using war to justify restriction of congressional power and assumption of dictatorial procedures." But as Anne feared, his comments about Jews were the only part of the speech that received any attention. A few days after the address, she wrote in her diary that "the storm is beginning to blow up hard," which was, by any measure, a massive understatement. Lindbergh's remarks had spawned a hurricane of fury that swept the country and dealt the isolationist movement a near-lethal blow. "Rarely has any public address in American history caused more of an uproar or brought more criticism on any speaker, than did Lindbergh's Des Moines speech," wrote the historian Wayne Cole.

Virtually every newspaper and magazine in the nation denounced him. The *New York Herald Tribune* called his speech an appeal to "the dark forces of prejudice and intolerance." In a *PM* cartoon entitled "Spreading the Lovely Goebbels Stuff," Theodor Geisel drew Lindbergh sitting atop "a Nazi Anti-Semite Stink Wagon." *Liberty* magazine called him "the most dangerous man in America." Before Lindbergh, the magazine wrote, "leaders of anti-Semitism were shoddy little crooks and fanatics sending scurrilous circulars through the mails. . . . But now all that is changed. . . . He, the famous one, has stood up in public and given brazen tongue to what obscure malcontents have only whispered."

Among Lindbergh's critics were the country's leading isolationist newspapers, which only days before had showered him with praise. The Hearst press assailed his "intemperate and intolerant address," while the *Chicago Tribune* inveighed against the "impropriety" of his comments about the Jews.

In New York, Wendell Willkie, who earlier had upheld Lindbergh's right to speak out against the administration's policies, called his speech "the most un-American talk made in my time by any person of national reputation." Willkie added: "If the American people permit race prejudice to arise at this crucial moment, they little deserve to preserve democracy."

For interventionists, the Lindbergh speech was a godsend. Neither Roosevelt nor Harold Ickes made a public comment, but then they didn't need to: the national reaction was already one of outrage. The only White House official to make note of the speech was Steve Early, who merely said he thought there was "a striking similarity" between Lindbergh's remarks and the "outpourings of Berlin in the last few days."

Isolationists, for their part, were painfully aware of the enormous damage done to their cause. The executive director of the Keep America Out of War Congress, whose members were largely liberal pacifists, wrote that the Des Moines speech had "done more to fan the flames of Anti-Semitism and push 'on-the-fence' Jews into the war camp than Mr. Lindbergh can possibly imagine." The congress's governing board made clear its "deep disagreement" with Lindbergh's "implication that American citizens of Jewish extraction or religion are a separate group, apart from the rest of the American people, or that they react as a separate group, or that they are unanimously for our entrance into the European war."

The Socialist leader Norman Thomas, one of the congress's founders, was so infuriated by the speech that he severed all ties with America First and Lindbergh, to whom he once had been close. "Didn't our friend Lindbergh do us a lot of harm?" Thomas wrote to a friend. "I honestly don't think Lindbergh is an anti-Semite, but I think he is a great idiot. . . . Not all Jews are for war, and Jews have a right to agitate for war if we have a right to agitate against it. . . . It is an enormous pity that . . . the Colonel will not take the advice on public relations which he would expect an amateur in aviation to take from an expert."

Thrown into turmoil by the speech, America First was bitterly divided about how to respond. In a letter to Robert Wood, executive committee member Sterling Morton condemned Lindbergh's inflammatory remarks, saying, "There are no people who have more right than the Jewish people to oppose Hitler and all he has done, and they have a perfect right to use their influence in favor of war if they so wish."

Robert Stuart and John T. Flynn, head of America First's New York chapter, strongly urged the organization to issue a vehement denunciation of anti-Semitism. Flynn, who did not disagree with Lindbergh's statements about Jews, nonetheless called the speech "stupid" and said it "has given us all a terrible kick in the pants. This just pins the anti-Semitic label on the whole isolationist fight [and] lays us wide open to this charge of racial persecution."

Other America First leaders, however, supported what Lindbergh had said, and Lindbergh himself refused to repudiate or modify any of his statements. Loath to excoriate the most popular isolationist in America—"the heart of our fight," as one America First official described him—and faced with a lack of consensus on what to do, America First settled for a vague statement denying that either it or Lindbergh was guilty of anti-Semitism. The document satisfied no one and added fuel to interventionists' charges against the group. Lessing Rosenwald, whose family owned Sears, Roebuck and who once had been a member of America First's national committee, demanded that Robert Wood publicly disavow Lindbergh's speech. When Wood failed to do so, Rosenwald ended his close friendship with the Sears chairman. The breach was never healed.

For all the recrimination heaped on Lindbergh, there were a few people who spoke up in his defense. One was a nineteen-year-old Cornell University student named Kurt Vonnegut, who wrote a passionate pro-Lindbergh column in the school newspaper attacking "the mud-slingers" for stirring up hate against "a loyal and sincere patriot." Vonnegut, whose 1945 experiences as an American prisoner of war in the firebombed German city of Dresden would lead him to write his iconic novel *Slaughterhouse-Five,* was in 1941 a committed isolationist who believed America should stay as far away from war as possible. "The United States is a democracy, that's what they say we'll be fighting for," he wrote. "What a prize monument to that ideal—a cry to smother Lindy. . . . Lindy, you're a rat. We read that somewhere, so it must be so. They say you should be deported. In that event, leave room in the boat for us."

Others, while not defending Lindbergh's comments, charged those who attacked him with hypocrisy. Even as he disparaged Lindbergh's remarks, Norman Thomas declared that the aviator "was not as anti-Semitic as some who seize the opportunity to criticize him." In an editorial, *Christian Century* noted sardonically that "one hundred clubs and hotel foyers rang with a denouncement of Lindbergh on the morning after his Des Moines speech—clubs and hotels barring their doors to Jews."

Dr. Gregory Mason, chairman of the America First chapter in the affluent Connecticut towns of Greenwich and Stamford, made the same point in a letter to his White Committee counterpart in southern Connecticut. According to Mason, a number of the White Committee and Fight for Freedom's most prominent members in the area belonged to "exclusive social clubs from which Jews are strictly barred. Pick at random any local newspaper report of the attendance at a Bundles for Britain party or a rummage sale for the RAF, and you'll find a very high percentage of names of wealthy snobs who would shun a Jew socially as they would shun a leper."

Yet while there was much truth in Mason's allegations, they did not alter the fact that Lindbergh's remarks in Des Moines were unmistakably anti-Semitic and that they did incalculable harm to the cause of isolationism. They diverted attention from the main issue of America's involvement in the war and, as Anne Lindbergh feared, encouraged the country's anti-Semites to become even more outspoken.

America First had always had a problem with anti-Semitism, but in the days and weeks following the Des Moines speech, the problem became a full-blown crisis. Thousands of letters, many of them flagrantly anti-Semitic, flooded the group's headquarters. One correspondent wrote: "We need thousands of fearless men and women to rid this country of the JEWS, who have already taken it over."

America First's weak reaction to the Lindbergh speech and its failure to condemn anti-Semitism left no doubt that, by the fall of 1941, the organization had strayed far from the path that its idealistic young founders at Yale had envisioned for it just the year before.

WHILE LINDBERGH SEEMED IMPERVIOUS, at least outwardly, to the allegations of anti-Semitism, the specter of the Des Moines speech would haunt his wife and children for decades. "Isn't it strange," Anne wrote to a friend at the time, "there is no hate in him, no hate at all, and yet he rouses it and spreads it." Years later, she told an interviewer: "I cannot blame people for misinterpreting [what he said]. I can understand why the Jews dislike him."

Reeve Lindbergh, the only child of Charles and Anne's to write and speak publicly about her family, struggled to come to grips with her father's explosive words for much of her adult life. She first learned of the speech while attending Radcliffe in the early 1960s, after the parents of several friends acted oddly toward her, and the roommate of a boy she was dating told him that he wouldn't mind meeting Reeve but he would never shake hands with her father.

When she expressed puzzlement at such antagonism, her closest friend at college advised her to read Lindbergh's Des Moines speech. She was devastated when she did. "I can still feel the sick dizziness that I felt then," she wrote years later, "bending over the page, reading his words." As a child, Reeve had read Anne Frank's diary and knew the horrific dimensions of the Holocaust. She understood the implications that her father's remarks would have for "so many people."

Stunned and bewildered, she kept thinking that this was not the father she knew—a man who had never made an anti-Semitic comment in her presence, who never told a racial joke or uttered an ethnic slur like those she had heard in the homes of her friends, who taught his children that such words were "repellent and unspeakable."

Reeve's confusion swiftly turned to shame and fury. She wrestled with the question of what her father had intended to say—and, in doing so, grappled with the issue of what constitutes anti-Semitism. "Did he really believe that he was simply, dispassionately 'stating the facts,' as he later persistently claimed, without understanding that the very framework of the statement reverberated with anti-Semitic resonance? And if he really believed [it], was that in itself not a form, however innocent he might think it, of anti-Semitism? Was there, in fact, such a thing as innocent, unconscious anti-Semitism? . . . [D]id the Holocaust forever criminalize an attitude that was previously acceptable and widespread among the non-Jewish population of this country and others? . . . Or was I simply playing with semantics and denying the obvious?"

She concluded that her father was doing what he always did: "identifying a situation as he saw it . . . and then clarifying it, in his logical way, and then proceeding with his argument in an orderly fashion. . . . He talked to the American people about isolationism, about the pros and cons of war, about persecution of Jews in Germany, the way he talked to his children about Independence and Responsibility, or the Seven Signs of Frostbite or Punk Design. What was he thinking? How could he have been so insensitive?"

When Reeve asked her mother about the infamous speech, Anne said that Lindbergh had refused to believe her when she warned him he would be labeled an anti-Semite if he gave it. Reeve was astonished: in her experience, her father had always listened to her mother. That was not the case when he was younger, Anne replied. He had grown up listening only to himself and relying on his own judgment: his survival as a pilot had depended on following his own instincts. "If he had listened to others," Anne told her daughter, "he never would have gotten to Paris."

AS LINDBERGH'S CRITICS RUSHED to heap opprobrium on him in the aftermath of the Des Moines speech, there was one prominent exception—his mother-in-law.

Elizabeth Morrow's silence had nothing to do with a lessening of commitment on her part to the interventionist cause; in fact, the opposite was true. Now a diehard believer that America must go to war to save Britain and the rest of the world from Germany, she was honorary chairwoman of the women's division of Fight for Freedom, the most extreme of the interventionist organizations.

On November 21, 1941, Mrs. Morrow made a nationwide radio broadcast explaining the rationale for her pro-war views: "I consider the consequences of a German victory so disastrous for us that I think this country should, if necessary, enter an all-out war to prevent that victory." But toward the end of her broadcast, she abruptly shifted her focus to an issue that obviously was causing her intense worry—the mudslinging and increasingly vicious name-calling that was tearing apart not only her own family but the country as a whole.

In an appeal to her interventionist allies, Mrs. Morrow said she hoped "desperately that we can all be not only good fighters but fair fighters. There are honest, conscientious and honorable citizens who hold that involvement in the European war will not help our national defense and will not preserve the American way of life so precious to us all. We must respect the sincerity of their opinions while differing with them."

With considerable emotion in her voice, she went on: " 'War Monger' is an unpleasant name, but 'Unpatriotic' and 'Un-American' are equally disagreeable adjectives. When it comes to motives, let us leave the role of omniscience to God."

CHAPTER 25

"HE WAS NOT GOING TO LEAD THE COUNTRY INTO WAR"

═══

By the fall of 1941, a new superhero had captured the imagination of young comic book readers across the country. The debut issue of *Captain America,* whose cover showed its red-white-and-blue-clad protagonist knocking Adolf Hitler silly with a right to the jaw, sold nearly one million copies. Dedicated to saving the United States from Nazis and other threats, Captain America quickly took his place in the superhero pantheon.

Years later, Joe Simon, a cocreator of Captain America, readily admitted that he and his colleague Jack Kirby were making a political statement with their new comic book character: both believed that the United States must enter the war to end Nazi Germany's reign of terror. "The opponents to the war were all quite organized," Simon said. "We wanted to have our say too."

The popular new comic book was hardly alone in its strong interventionist bent. By that time, many newspaper comic strips had also sent their main characters into action against the Axis. In Al Capp's *Li'l Abner,* the villains invading Dogpatch were obvious caricatures of German leaders. *Joe Palooka,* which once had portrayed Britons as effete monocle-wearing appeasers, now showed them in heroic Nazi-fighting mode.

Newspaper readers who glanced at more than the comics found reminders of the war on virtually every page. According to a government analysis of the press, most U.S. newspapers now backed Roosevelt's interventionist policy, with an increasing number endorsing immediate American participation in the conflict. More than three hundred papers had done so, including the *New York Post, New York Herald Tribune, San Francisco Chronicle,* Cleveland *Plain Dealer, The Atlanta Constitution,* and Louisville *Courier-Journal.*

Many of the bestselling books in 1941 also had war-related themes. William Shirer's *Berlin Diary* was high on the nonfiction list, as were a collection of Winston Churchill's speeches and *This Is London,* a compilation of Edward R. Murrow's London broadcasts. In fiction, *Mrs. Miniver,* a collection of stories on which the wildly popular film was based, and James Hilton's *Random Harvest* were atop the list.

There was no question that war had left a distinct imprint on the national consciousness. A *Vogue* fashion layout featured models posing in front of a London-bound plane loaded with Bundles for Britain parcels. The Elizabeth Arden cosmetics company began featuring V for Victory lipsticks. In Newark, San Francisco, and other major cities, practice blackouts were staged, with volunteer wardens bustling around their neighborhoods demanding that people turn out their lights. In New York City, more than 62,000 residents volunteered as wardens in Mayor Fiorello La Guardia's new civil defense program.

Congressmen returning from their summer recess reported that many of their constituents had shifted their views toward war, with some isolationist districts becoming "middle of the road, and middle of the roaders now interventionists." At its annual convention, the American Legion, once fervently isolationist, called for a repeal of the neutrality law and for a plan "to carry the war to the enemy."

A *Life* reporter traveled to Neosho, Missouri, a small town on the edge of the Ozarks, to sample opinion there. After interviewing several dozen Neosho residents, he came to the conclusion that the majority of townspeople, although Republican and "conservative about almost everything," had decided that their country must enter the war.

"I would hate to see our boys sent over there to fight, and I've got one nineteen years old," said C. W. Crawford, a flour miller, "but if England can't win without it, we've got to send them . . . we've got to chip in and do it." Glen Woods, a grocer and the Neosho mayor, remarked: "I can't see how we can help getting in it actively, and I can't see how we could live with ourselves if we don't." Glenn Wolfender, editor of the town's weekly paper, told the *Life* reporter that he and other Neosho residents had become interventionists out of a moral conviction that America must put an end to Hitler. "When you got [such a conviction], you can't get anything stronger in this world," Wolfender added. "Maybe it's something you city people could use, and I don't intend no offense, you understand."

A poll taken in the fall of 1941 showed that 75 percent of those identifying themselves as Republicans now supported FDR's foreign policy. Fewer than 20 percent of the American people would admit to being an isolationist, and 72 percent regarded "defeating Nazism" as "the biggest job facing their country." The pollster Elmo Roper reported: "The willingness to use our armed forces has increased even more than our nominal tendency toward intervention. . . . Now you have big majorities for using all branches of the armed forces—if necessary." From Chicago, Graham Hutton, a British propaganda official, wrote: "The Isolationists are fighting a vocal and stubborn but hopeless rear-guard action."

By virtually all standards, then, it seemed that Americans were prepared for war. And yet they were still afraid to take the leap into full-fledged hostilities. According to polls, 75 to 80 percent of the public continued to oppose an immediate declaration of war against Germany.

News from the war fronts, meanwhile, grew steadily bleaker. Having swept across much of Russia, the Germans were now threatening Moscow and laying siege to Leningrad. Fearful that the Soviets might soon collapse and that Germany would once again turn its full fury against Britain, Winston Churchill was desperate for unequivocal American involvement.

As the historian Geoffrey Perret noted, a strange scenario was playing itself out in Washington and the rest of America that fall: "grown men jostling and nudging, daring and egging one another on, talking tough yet trembling on the brink." It was "an unhappy sight," Perret added, "—people adrift for the lack of sure purpose on which to attach their will."

And then came the strange case of the *Greer*.

———

ON SEPTEMBER 4, THE American destroyer *Greer* was steaming toward Reykjavik, the capital of Iceland, when it received word from a British patrol plane that a German submarine had been spotted about ten miles ahead. Just two weeks before, the U.S. Navy had authorized its Atlantic-based ships to begin escorting all friendly merchant shipping, including cargoes bound for Britain and Russia, as far as Iceland. There, the British navy would take over as protector. U.S. naval vessels were also given authority to destroy any German submarines or surface raiders that threatened the merchant convoys.

Because the *Greer* was not escorting merchant shipping when it was notified of the submarine, it was not permitted to open fire. Its only option was to trail the U-boat and report its location to the British, which it did for more than three hours. At one point, the British patrol plane dropped several depth charges, but to no evident effect.

Finally, the German submarine commander had had enough. Apparently believing that the depth charges had come from the *Greer,* he fired two torpedoes at the U.S. ship. The *Greer* evaded them and, having been attacked, dropped its own depth charges in response. In the confrontation, neither vessel suffered damage or casualties.

A week later, FDR used the episode as the rationale for broadening the rules of engagement to allow U.S. Navy ships to shoot on sight any Axis vessels they encountered, regardless of whether they posed threats to merchant shipping. In a September 11 radio broadcast, the president charged that the German submarine had "fired first upon this American destroyer without warning, and with deliberate design to sink her." (True enough, but the president did not mention the incident's other details: the British depth charges dropped on the U-boat and the *Greer*'s three-hour surveillance preceding the attack.)

Describing the assault on the *Greer* as "piracy," Roosevelt, using some of his toughest language yet, blasted German submarines and surface ships as "rattlesnakes of the Atlantic" that posed a "menace to the free pathways of the high seas" and "a challenge to our sovereignty." He insisted that his "shoot on sight" order was not meant as an act of war but as a defensive measure taken in waters vital to American security: "When you see a rattlesnake poised to strike, you do not wait until he has struck before you crush him. . . . The time for active defense is now." In his broadcast, the president also slipped in an announcement of his earlier decision to provide U.S. naval escorts for all merchant shipping as far as Iceland.

Over the next month, American destroyers operating under battle conditions shepherded fourteen convoys, numbering 675 ships, across the stormy North Atlantic. The U.S. Navy had thus become the country's first armed service to go to war, albeit one that was still undeclared.

Most junior naval officers and crew did not share the isolationism and Anglophobia of their high-ranking superiors. When the fifty overage destroyers were handed to the Royal Navy the year before, British seamen, to their delight, found that their American counterparts had stocked the ships with luxuries unheard of in their service, including cigarettes, blankets, sheets, steaks, and bacon. American naval officers were "forthright in saying how much they wished they could bring the ships over themselves and join us in the fight against the Hun," said British vice admiral Sir Guy Sayer.

In late September 1941, the first British convoy officially escorted by American ships was handed off to the Royal Navy south of Iceland. The convoy's commodore, British rear admiral E. Manners, and the escort group leader, Captain Morton Deyo of the U.S. Navy, exchanged messages of mutual gratitude and good wishes as they bade each other farewell. "Please accept my best congratulations," Manners signaled, ". . . for looking after us so very well, and my grateful thanks for all your kindly advice and help. Wish you success, with best of luck and good hunting." Deyo signaled back: "This being our first escort job, your message is doubly appreciated. As in the last war I know our people afloat will see eye to eye. . . . I hope we shall meet again."

AS THE DEBATE ABOUT U.S. involvement in the war raged on, the Navy's Atlantic force joined an estimated ten thousand Americans who were already engaged in the fighting. At least two dozen U.S. citizens, volunteers in the Royal Navy, were serving as officers aboard British ships escorting convoys from Iceland to Britain. They came from a variety of backgrounds and occupations—doctor, yacht broker, theater advertising, and real estate among them—but most had grown up as avid sailors. One of the Royal Navy's Americans—Edwin Russell, a

Princeton graduate whose father owned New Jersey's largest paper, the Newark *Star-Ledger*—ended up marrying Lady Sarah Spencer Churchill, daughter of the Duke of Marlborough and a cousin of Winston Churchill.

Several hundred more Americans had gone to Britain to enlist in the Royal Air Force, seven of them flying in the Battle of Britain. So many U.S. citizens, in fact, had become RAF pilots that they were given their own units, called the Eagle Squadrons. More than five thousand Americans, meanwhile, were serving with the Canadian army and air force in Britain, while several dozen had joined the British army.

Among the British army volunteers were five young Ivy Leaguers who had left their Dartmouth and Harvard classrooms to enlist in Britain's cause. They included Charles Bolté, a Dartmouth student leader, who in the course of a year had moved from ardent pacifism to an equally fierce belief in interventionism. In April 1941, Bolté had published an open letter to President Roosevelt on the front page of the Dartmouth daily newspaper. "[W]e have waited long enough," he wrote. "We hear that Greece has fallen, and on the same radio broadcast we hear that the United States is sending Britain some ships— 'small ships, 20 torpedo boats.' It is travesty in the midst of tragedy. . . . We have not produced enough guns, tanks, airplanes, bombs. We have not supplied the ships. . . . We have not supplied the men. . . . Now we ask you to send American pilots, mechanics, sailors and soldiers to fight wherever they are needed. . . . We ask you to make us our best selves by waging war."*

The British government quickly realized the propaganda value of young Americans fighting and dying for Britain while their own country remained aloof. As one official wrote, "Every American enlisting in the armed forces of the crown is worth his weight in gold to us." Newspapers in Britain and the United States ran glowing stories about the American volunteers, and the BBC featured them in a number of their broadcasts, as did Ed Murrow at CBS.

There were few stories, however, about the thousands of other

---

* Bolté would later lose a leg while fighting with the British at El Alamein, and two of his Ivy League comrades would die in combat shortly before the 1943 Allied victory in North Africa.

Americans on the front line—the sailors of the Merchant Marine and U.S. Navy who were now engaged in the Battle of the Atlantic, waged across twenty-five hundred miles of frigid, treacherous seas. On any given day, four or five convoys were heading for Britain or returning to America, guarded by long lines of gray U.S. destroyers. It was the greatest cargo lift operation in history.

Setting off from ports in Nova Scotia and Halifax, the makeshift, motley armadas were usually composed of thirty to forty tankers and freighters—some gleaming and new, others aging, rusting wrecks. For their escorts, it was a nail-biting task to ride herd on these widely disparate ships, so unequal in size, speed, and maneuverability, and to keep them in as tight a formation as possible.

In the ocean's vast, rolling, gray wastes, finding enemy surface ships was difficult enough, but locating submerged submarines with primitive sonar was far trickier—more art than science. Much of the time, the sudden, blinding glare of an exploding merchant ship was the first and only sign that German U-boats were on the prowl.

The weather proved to be an equally formidable enemy. The convoys followed a route in the North Atlantic noted for its treacherous weather, particularly in winter. And as it turned out, the fall and winter that year were among the worst in memory. The ships and their crews were pummeled almost daily by bitter cold, howling, razor-sharp winds, and towering waves that broke over the decks and poured down any open hatches, making life perpetually miserable for those aboard. Not infrequently, ships were cloaked in ice and blinded by snow. Thick fogs were always a hazard, greatly increasing the risk of collisions.

In the fall of 1941, most Americans still had no personal stake in the war. That, however, was not the case for the wives and families of the American naval personnel on convoy duty. Hundreds of women and children moved to Portland, Maine, a key base for the U.S. Atlantic Fleet, to be with their men when they returned from their hazardous journeys. In Portland, one journalist noted, "the people speak of America's war in the present tense." Filled with "waiting women," it was "the U.S. city nearest the war."

Not surprisingly, Portland was rife with rumors and worry. In this perilous cat-and-mouse game in the North Atlantic, who would be the first American casualties?

THE ANSWER CAME ON the night of October 16, in freezing waters southeast of Iceland. A convoy guarded by the Royal Navy and steaming toward Britain was attacked by a U-boat wolf pack. After receiving an urgent SOS from the convoy, five U.S. destroyers based in Iceland raced to its aid. In the confused fighting that ensued, one of the destroyers, the *Kearney,* was struck by a German torpedo. Eleven sailors were killed in the blast, and twenty-two were wounded.

News of the first American deaths in official action reached Washington just as Congress was debating a proposal by Roosevelt to allow the arming of American merchant ships and to permit them to carry their cargoes through German war zones and into British and other belligerent ports. The legislation was, in effect, a repeal of several key provisions of the neutrality law.

On October 27, the president delivered one of his strongest speeches yet, condemning the attack on the *Kearney* and declaring that "in the face of this newest and greatest challenge, we Americans have cleared our decks and taken our battle stations." But no new action followed his belligerent words.

During the Atlantic Conference, Roosevelt had told Churchill he planned to "look for an incident which would justify him in opening hostilities." He had made similar statements to several of those in his inner circle. To Churchill and the others, it seemed that the attack on the *Kearney* was just what FDR had been waiting for. The president, however, obviously did not agree.

There was no question that a majority of Americans supported FDR in his avowed toughness. In one poll, nearly two-thirds of the public said they favored his "shoot on sight" policy. According to other surveys, more than 70 percent of the public approved of U.S. escorts for convoying. Clearly prepared to fight if necessary, Roosevelt's countrymen had, as he noted, taken their battle stations. Now, as one historian put it, they "waited for battle orders [that] their commander-in-chief refrained from issuing. . . . They had been told by him again and again in fervent words that American survival required Hitler's defeat. But the Executive action logically implied by Executive words had not been taken."

The people wanted FDR to lead them, while he seemed to expect them to lead *him.* The result, once again, was stasis.

DURING THESE TENSION-FILLED DAYS and weeks, the president focused his efforts on winning congressional approval of the Neutrality Act revisions, another interim step toward war. He had in fact been under considerable pressure to take even more aggressive measures. A number of interventionist newspapers had called for outright appeal of the Neutrality Act, as did the American Legion at its September convention.

For months, Wendell Willkie had also urged him to seek repeal of the act, which Willkie termed "a piece of hypocrisy and deliberate self-deception." Complaining about the administration's lassitude, Willkie accused it of "pursuing its usual course at critical moments—consulting polls, putting up trial balloons, having some of its members make statements that others can deny—the same course that has led to so much of people's confusion and misunderstanding." After the attack on the *Kearney,* the former Republican presidential candidate bluntly told reporters that "the United States already is in the war and has been for some time," adding that the American people should "abandon the hope of peace."

After Roosevelt sent his message to Congress seeking the Neutrality Act changes, Willkie persuaded three Republican senators to offer an amendment that would scrap the entire law. At his urging, more than a hundred prominent Republicans from forty states signed a letter calling on GOP lawmakers to support the amendment. Millions of Republicans, the letter declared, are determined "to wipe the ugly smudge of obstructive isolationism from the face of their party." Two Democratic senators, Carter Glass and Claude Pepper, joined their three Republican colleagues in urging outright abolition of the law. But Democratic congressional leaders, following the lead of the White House, opted only for repeal of the provisions banning the arming of merchant ships and the delivery of cargo to belligerent ports.

Once again, most of the country was clearly behind the president's proposal. According to a Gallup poll, 81 percent of Americans favored arming the ships and 61 percent backed the idea of allowing them to transport supplies all the way to Britain. But Roosevelt again paid more attention to the opposition of the dwindling but determinedly vocal isolationist minority in Congress. He insisted that the legislation be seen not as a direct challenge to Germany but as a simple defense of American rights.

His opponents, by now stripped down to isolationism's hard core, rejected that argument. In what turned out to be its final lobbying campaign, America First, although badly weakened by Lindbergh's Des Moines speech, ferociously fought the White House proposals. On the day the bill was sent to Congress, Robert Wood condemned the measure as the equivalent of "an engraved drowning license for American seamen." He and his organization contended that revising the Neutrality Act would immediately plunge the country into war.

In a letter headed "The Crisis Is Here," the America First leadership urged its local chapters to flood Capitol Hill with letters and telegrams against the bill. "We will fight it," the letter declared, "as we would fight a declaration of war." Every member of Congress should be told, the message said, that a vote for the measure would be considered a vote "to send American seamen to their deaths. They must be reminded that the American people will hold them responsible for doing, by subterfuge, what they dare not do directly."

Fighting back, the president in his October 27 speech made an announcement that jolted the country. He had in his possession, he said, a secret German map showing how the Reich planned to carve South America and much of Central America into five vassal states. He also spoke of a detailed Nazi plan to abolish all existing religions in the world, replacing them with an International Nazi Church.

The map mentioned by Roosevelt was in fact an outline of air traffic routes in South and Central America that featured a realignment of the area into four states and one colony, all under German rule. On the map, the proposed German airline network had lines leading to Natal, a port on the east coast of Brazil, and to Panama.

General George Marshall and others in the U.S. military were still greatly worried that a German force might one day be transported from the west coast of Africa to Brazil's east coast and then northward to the Panama Canal. Indeed, as recently as the week of the president's speech, the Army's War Plans Division had warned that the German threat to Brazil remained extremely serious.

Not surprisingly, then, Roosevelt's revelation set off alarms in his administration and the nation. Reporters clamored for further information from the White House and asked to see the map. The president refused, saying that making it public would jeopardize its source, which he described as "undoubtedly reliable."

German officials, however, begged to differ. Four days after Roosevelt's speech, Foreign Minister Joachim von Ribbentrop flatly denied the existence of such a map, declaring that both it and the document referring to the extermination of the world's religions were "forgeries of the crudest and most brazen kind." Ribbentrop's statement had been preceded by a frantic search by the German government to find out if any such documents had actually been produced. None was discovered.

For once the Reich was telling the truth; the map, as it turned out, was the creation of William Stephenson's British Security Coordination. In its official history, BSC claimed that agents from its extensive South American network had intercepted a German courier and discovered the map in his dispatch case. In fact, it was a forgery, the product of a clandestine BSC unit in downtown Toronto called Station M, which had been assigned the task of fabricating letters and other documents.

Sent to New York, the map had been given to William Donovan, who in turn passed it on to Roosevelt. According to Donovan's executive assistant, who actually delivered the document to the White House, neither his boss nor the president knew it was counterfeit. While that may well have been true, it was also the case that other senior officials in the administration had been warning for some time of the possibility that the British would try to transmit fake documents to the government for their own purposes. In early September, Assistant Secretary of State Adolf Berle informed Undersecretary Sumner Welles that "British intelligence has been very active in making things appear dangerous" in South America, adding that "we have to be a little on our guard against false scares." As an example, he mentioned "the manufacturing of documents detailing Nazi conspiracies in South America."

It's not clear how much influence FDR's announcement of the map had on the vote in Congress. Quite possibly, news of the *Kearney* had more of an impact on those inclined to vote for the Neutrality Act revisions. Lawmakers leaning against the measure, meanwhile, were influenced not only by the thousands of anti-revision letters and telegrams pouring into their offices but also by their own sense of outrage at Roosevelt for not doing enough to stem continuing labor unrest at aircraft and other defense manufacturing plants.

On Capitol Hill and throughout the country, there were growing demands for legislation banning strikes during a time of national emergency—demands that the pro-labor Roosevelt administration was loath to meet. In early November 1941, Henry Stimson noted in his diary: "The feeling that the President has been too soft with Labor has made many in Congress very angry and reluctant to do anything he wants until he takes a sterner hand with Labor."

As they had done in fighting every previous interventionist measure, isolationists in the Senate held out for as long as possible, delivering seemingly endless speeches against the Neutrality Act changes. In an eight-hour address delivered over two days, Burton Wheeler issued a blistering warning to his pro-administration colleagues: "You men who follow blindly the administration's policy, you men who, under the whip and lash, are going to take this country to war—you are going to take it to hell!" One of those whom Wheeler was addressing, Senator Claude Pepper, wearily noted in his diary: "Tragic indifference still apparent in Congress. Democracy will just be saved, if at all."

Early in November, the Senate finally passed the measure by a relatively narrow 50–37 margin. Despite Wendell Willkie's best efforts, only six Republicans voted for it. A few days later, the House followed the Senate's lead, approving the revisions in another close vote, 212–194.

The fact that Congress's antilabor mood was a significant factor in the narrowness of the vote did not seem to make much of a difference to Roosevelt. His sole focus was on the fact that once again an interventionist proposal by the administration had barely squeaked through Congress. The vote certainly did nothing to lessen his profound sense of caution.

In the midst of the continuing Sturm und Drang in Washington came word of another attack on an American destroyer in the Atlantic—this one far more calamitous than the assault on the *Kearney*. On October 31, off the west coast of Iceland, the *Reuben James* was sunk and 115 of its crew killed. The World War I–era destroyer thus earned the melancholy distinction of being the first U.S. naval ship lost in combat in World War II.

A FEW WEEKS BEFORE the sinking, Wallace Lee Sowers, a seaman aboard the *Reuben James,* had written to his parents about his harrowing experiences thus far in protecting convoys. He described how a submarine had attacked his ship late one freezing night, how the *Reuben James,* which Sowers fondly called "this old tin can," had evaded the torpedoes and gone on to search for survivors from British merchant ships that had not been so lucky. "We did not find any," the young sailor wrote. He told his parents he hoped to be home for Christmas.

The *Reuben James* was indeed a "tin can," an aging wreck with ancient, misfiring guns. Before being sent to a boatyard for a thorough refit, however, it had been ordered to make one final convoy run to Iceland. On October 23, it and four other destroyers left Halifax with their armada of merchant ships in tow. En route, the naval escorts received several reports of U-boat sightings. On the night of October 31, the submarines finally struck. One of them fired a single torpedo into the *Reuben James,* smashing it amidships and breaking it in two. As orange flames lit up the sky, the destroyer sank in a matter of minutes.

Wallace Lee Sowers and the other young men who died represented a cross-section of America, hailing from tiny towns in Louisiana and Alabama as well as from big cities like New York and Chicago. The father of one of them—Lloyd LaFleur, a pharmacist's mate from Texas—told reporters after being notified of his son's death: "I think the U.S. should go into the war and wipe the German submarines forever from the sea. If I were young enough I would like to help do this job."

German officials awaited the U.S. response to the sinking with great trepidation, convinced that Roosevelt would use it as a pretext for breaking off relations with Germany and declaring war. But FDR did nothing. To the consternation of his aides, he did not even issue a condemnatory statement. The torpedoing of the *Reuben James,* they were sure, was the incident he had been waiting for. Why didn't he act?

Harold Ickes presented the president with a letter from an old friend who pointed out that while only Congress had the power to declare war, Roosevelt as commander in chief had the authority to wage war defensively. An interesting point, FDR said, but what Ickes's friend didn't understand was that "it was simply a question of timing." The interior secretary glumly wrote in his diary: "Apparently the president is going to wait. . . . God knows for how long and for what." Admiral Stark, meanwhile, complained to a friend: "The Navy is already in the war in the Atlantic, but the country doesn't seem to realize it." Instead of a popular outcry in the United States, demanding that Roosevelt avenge "our boys," the predominant reaction seemed to be one of apathy. Yet, in its mood of fatalistic resignation, the American public seems simply to have been following the lead of its president.

Upset that no one seemed to care about the hundred-plus young sailors who had lost their lives, the folksinger Woody Guthrie wrote a song called "The Sinking of the Reuben James" and recorded it with Pete Seeger. The song became a folk classic, and millions of Americans came to know its stirring refrain:

> *Tell me what were their names, tell me what were their names,*
> *Did you have a friend on the good Reuben James?*

IN LONDON, WINSTON CHURCHILL was near the end of his emotional tether. He railed to his subordinates about America's paralysis and Roosevelt's unwillingness to do anything about it. In a speech to the House of Commons, he declared: "Nothing is more dangerous in wartime than to live in the temperamental atmosphere of Gallup polls or of feeling one's pulse or taking one's temperature. . . . There is only one duty, only one safe course, and that is to be right and not to fear to do or say what you believe to be right."

Roosevelt, who once described himself as a "juggler," had always taken great pride in his mastery of improvisation and manipulation. But, as Robert Sherwood later wrote, "he had no more tricks left. The bag from which he had pulled so many rabbits was empty." In America's quietude, Sherwood observed, was seen "the awful picture of a great nation which had surrendered all powers of initiative and therefore must wait in a state of flabby impotence for its potential enemies to decide where, when and how action would be taken."

Like several others close to the president, Sherwood had long suspected that Roosevelt's failure to take the initiative was largely due to his resolve that "whatever the peril, he was not going to lead the country into war." Echoing that view, Samuel Rosenman later wrote that "the last thing [FDR] wanted then, or any time before Pearl Harbor, was a formal declaration of war either against, or by, Hitler or the Japanese." Former attorney general Robert Jackson, who had known Roosevelt since he was governor of New York, told an interviewer that FDR had always had "a great confidence that something would happen to bring things out right. He felt that by some stroke of diplomacy, or some other stroke, it will come out all right." According to Herbert Agar, "the historians who insist that Roosevelt always knew where he was heading . . . were either not present during those dark months or they have forgotten the ambiguities of democratic politics."

For the previous two years, Roosevelt had been juggling threats from both Japan and Germany, trying to avert a showdown with the two for as long as possible. With his attention focused on the German offensive, particularly in the Atlantic, Roosevelt intended, he told his advisers, to "baby the Japs along." As he saw it, a fight with Japan would be "the wrong war in the wrong ocean at the wrong time."

What Roosevelt apparently didn't bargain for was that the Japanese, unlike their German allies, were quite open to the idea of confrontation with the United States—on their own terms and as soon as possible.

CHAPTER 26

"THE GREATEST SCOOP
IN HISTORY"

E ver since the Japanese takeover of Manchuria in 1931, tensions between Japan and the United States had been ratcheting up. The Japanese, determined to expand their empire, had launched a full-scale invasion of China in 1937, bombing cities, massacring hundreds of thousands of civilians, and seizing control of Shanghai and other major ports along the coast. Clearly on a mission to establish hegemony over the Far East, Japan now posed a direct threat to vital American, British, and Dutch interests in the area.

From the beginning, the United States had condemned Japan's aggression but, like other Western powers, did nothing to stop it. The Roosevelt administration was caught in a dilemma. While recognizing the mounting danger posed by the Japanese to the United States, Washington concluded that the peril of Nazi Germany was far greater and more immediate. Because America at that point was incapable of defending both the Atlantic and the Pacific, it was thought best to keep Japan at bay while helping Britain fend off Germany.

Japan depended on the United States for many of its most important strategic materials, so the administration turned to economic sanctions as its primary tool for restraining Tokyo and pressuring it to modify or renounce its expansionist program. The Japanese, however, had no intention of yielding on issues they considered vital for their country's future.

It was clear that the two countries were headed for a confrontation. In the spring of 1940, Washington allowed its fifty-year-old trade agreement with Japan to expire—for Tokyo, an ominous portent. A few months later, the administration declared an embargo on all shipments of premium-grade scrap iron and steel, as well as high-octane aviation gas, to the Japanese.

Japan responded by signing a Tripartite Pact with Germany and Italy in September 1940, all the signatories agreeing that if any one of them were attacked, the others would come to its aid. Washington reacted to that provocation by barring the export of all scrap metals to Japan. Three months later, it stopped the shipment of additional exports, including machine tools.

Oil—the most essential of all strategic materials for the Japanese—was the only major export left untouched. More than 80 percent of Japan's fuel supplies came from America, and an embargo would be devastating to the country's military operations as well as its economy. For months, the Roosevelt administration had kept its final and most potent economic weapon in reserve, not only for leverage but also because both the president and Cordell Hull feared that a ban on oil would prompt the Japanese to seize oil-rich territories in Asia, including the Dutch East Indies, the string of islands in the Pacific that is now Indonesia.

Yet in trying to "baby the Japs along," as FDR put it, he and his government ran into opposition from the American people, a growing number of whom wanted the administration to put the screws once and for all to the Japanese. "There seems to be no fierce emotional resistance to war in the Pacific as there is among many people to war in Europe," *Life* noted in early 1941. A conflict with the vaunted German army was something to be feared because, in the minds of many Americans, it would mean millions of U.S. casualties. War with Japan, on the other hand, was seen as a tidier conflict, likely to be confined to the seas, and one that the U.S. Navy would easily win.

Such confidence—quite misplaced, as it turned out—stemmed in large part from the racist idea that the Japanese "yellow peril" could easily be vanquished by the morally and physically superior white race.

Among those who favored a tougher U.S. policy against Japan were the country's leading isolationists, including Charles Lindbergh and Senator Burton Wheeler. Americans made their assumptions about Japan with little or no knowledge of the country and its people. They were given scant help by the U.S. press, which, focused as it was on the war in Europe, had all but ignored developments in Asia and the Pacific over the previous two years.

The American government, particularly the military, also underestimated the Japanese, discounting the strength of their navy and belittling the ability of their army, which in four years of undeclared war had not been able to take complete control of China. Administration officials persuaded themselves that the U.S. Pacific fleet, based at Pearl Harbor, would have no trouble denying the western Pacific to Japan.

For Tokyo, the implicit threat of a U.S. oil embargo was a sword of Damocles suspended over its head. Japan's oil reserves would last barely two more years; by then, the United States would be close to its goal of building a two-ocean navy. Japan saw only two choices: imminent war or reversing its foreign and military policy. The latter option was, for the country's leaders, unacceptable.

In the summer of 1941, Japanese forces occupied Indochina, a major source of rubber, and demanded army bases from strategically situated Siam (now Thailand). There was no doubt in anyone's mind that British and Dutch possessions in the Far East—Malaya, Burma, Singapore, Hong Kong, and the Dutch East Indies—were all in peril. In response, Roosevelt announced an immediate freeze on all Japanese assets in the United States. Under the order, further Japanese purchases of American goods, including oil, had to be cleared by a government committee. Although the freeze did not involve a direct embargo on oil, its dire implications for Japan were clear.

Having lobbied hard for an oil embargo, many U.S. newspapers applauded what they saw as the end of the administration's "appeasement" of Tokyo. "Let there be no mistake," the *New York Post* declared. "The United States must relentlessly apply its crushing strength." *PM*, meanwhile, rejoiced that "the noose is around Japan's neck at last. . . . For a time it may bluster and retaliate, but in the end it can only whimper and capitulate."

The president, however, had not intended his order to signal an automatic cutoff of oil. He wanted to keep his options open and the

Japanese at the negotiating table. Nonetheless, State Department officials applied the freeze in such a way that no further exports of any consequence, including oil, were released to Japan. U.S.-Japanese trade was brought to an abrupt halt, and the crisis that Roosevelt hoped to put off for as long as possible was now on his doorstep.

By the end of November 1941, both the U.S. and British governments expected a major Japanese attack at any moment, with the betting on Siam or Malaya as the probable targets. At their meeting in Newfoundland, Churchill had appealed to Roosevelt to join him in warning Japan that any future incursions in Asia would be met with British and American force. But Roosevelt declined to issue such a blunt ultimatum. If the blow fell on non-U.S. territory, as most observers expected it would, the British prime minister feared that the American president and people would refrain from entering the conflict, leaving Britain alone to face two mighty enemies, Germany *and* Japan.

The American public, meanwhile, seemed blasé about the entire situation. "No one worried," one journalist wrote. "Nobody talked about the Japanese or the Pacific. All this indicated just one thing: that Americans were not frightened by the Japanese." That may have been true. But Americans' lack of concentration could also be explained by the fact that another major news event had, at least momentarily, captured their attention.

ON DECEMBER 4, ROBERT McCormick's *Chicago Tribune* and the *Washington Times-Herald,* published by McCormick's cousin, Cissy Patterson, sent shock waves of seismic proportions throughout official Washington. Under an enormous headline screaming FDR'S SECRET WAR PLANS REVEALED!, the *Tribune's* front page, like that of the *Times-Herald,* was devoted to an exposé of an alleged government "blueprint for total war"—a top-secret administration document outlining plans for an all-out confrontation with Germany.

According to the story, written by the *Tribune's* Capitol Hill correspondent, Chesly Manly, the plans called for an American expeditionary force of some five million men to launch, in the "final supreme effort," a full-scale invasion of German-occupied Europe by July 1943. Eventually, the article said, U.S. armed forces would total more than ten million men. Manly wrote that the report on which he based his story "represents decisions and commitments affecting the destinies of peoples throughout the civilized world." If accurate, it also showed the president of the United States to be a liar.

Washington was in a frenzy. The *Times-Herald* sold out all its copies that day within an hour or two, and work in many government departments came to a standstill. Reporters flocked to the White House clamoring for an explanation and were immediately shunted over to the War Department. There, a livid Henry Stimson declared that while the document leaked to Manly was genuine, the reporter had completely and perhaps deliberately misinterpreted its purpose. It was, Stimson said, a set of unfinished staff studies that had "never been constituted and authorized as a program of government." In short, it was a contingency plan, evaluating the state of U.S. military preparedness and the various options open to America in the event of its involvement in the war.

The war secretary, as angry as anyone had ever seen him, railed against McCormick and his cousin for publishing such extraordinarily sensitive material. "What do you think of the patriotism of a man or a newspaper," he snapped, "which would take these confidential studies and make them public to the enemies of the country?"

What Stimson did not disclose was that the plans had been drawn up only a couple of months before. That fact—that there was no detailed assessment of what the United States needed to do to defeat the Axis until just before Pearl Harbor—was, in a sense, just as stunning as the contents of the document itself.

For more than a year, Stimson, Frank Knox, George Marshall, Harold Stark, and other government officials involved in defense mobilization had been pressing the president to set clear, specific policy guidelines for America's objectives in the war. What role was the country to have in the conflict? Should it plan simply for the defense of its own borders and those of its Latin American neighbors? Or should it come up with a blueprint for all-out intervention, including the buildup of a massive expeditionary force?

Over the years, the U.S. military had devised a series of contingency plans for possible future conflicts. In early 1940, Admiral Stark had formulated a blueprint of his own, known as Plan Dog, which focused on the possibility of a two-front war in Europe and the Pacific.

Stark's plan advocated fighting a limited defensive war against Japan while giving first priority to defeating Germany and Italy. It formed the basis for the U.S.-British military discussions held in Washington in March of that year. Roosevelt, however, declined to commit himself to Plan Dog, just as he refused to sign off on any other comprehensive, long-term proposal. "This is a period of flux," he told Frank Knox. "I want no authorization for what may happen beyond July 1, 1941."

FDR's reluctance to issue clear-cut directives, along with his habit of changing his mind about production priorities, drove his service chiefs crazy. "First the President wants 500 bombers a month and that dislocates the program," Marshall grumbled. "Then he says he wants so many tanks and that dislocates the program. The President will never sit down and talk about a complete program and have the whole thing move forward at the same time."

With no concrete plan to meet, U.S. defense production remained slow and erratic; the flow of munitions to Britain was still a relative trickle, and the delivery of arms to the Soviet Union not much more than a promise. In a toughly worded memo to Stimson, Undersecretary of War Robert Patterson, who was in charge of military mobilization, asked how on earth the United States could hope to arm itself and fulfill its commitments to other nations without a detailed, well-thought-out plan for doing so.

Armed with Patterson's memo, Stimson finally persuaded the president to act. On July 9, Roosevelt instructed Stimson and Knox to come up with a plan for the "overall production requirements required to defeat our potential enemies." Finally, very late in the game, the Army and Navy were given the authority to draw up comprehensive estimates of likely enemies and battle theaters, the size and composition of U.S. armed forces, and the financial and industrial means required to meet the defense needs of America and its potential allies.

In a supreme irony, the man chosen to direct this extraordinarily complex study, dubbed the Victory Program, was none other than Major Albert Wedemeyer, one of the most isolationist officers in the Army. Recently assigned to the War Plans Division by Marshall, Wedemeyer thus became, as he wrote in his memoirs, "the planner of a war I did not want." In the late 1930s, he had spent two years at the German war college in Berlin and acknowledged he had "come to

General Albert
Wedemeyer after
World War II.

see Germany in a different light from most of my contemporaries." He
fully accepted the Third Reich's view that a "worldwide Communist
conspiracy centered in Moscow" was the major cause of world tensions and conflict and that "the German search for *Lebensraum* did not
menace the Western World to anything like the same degree" as Communism. Dismissing the Nazis' brutal treatment of the countries they
vanquished, he described *Lebensraum* as simply "a national movement
to win living space [from] more backward peoples."

Wedemeyer's pro-German views were considered extreme even in
an environment that was decidedly uncritical of the German military.
He wrote years later that "some of my fellow officers and friends [at
the War Department] considered me sympathetic to Nazism. . . . I had
perhaps at times been too outspoken or indiscreet in expressing my
conviction that we should not become involved in the war."

Despite all this, he undertook the planning assignment. As a professional soldier, he noted, he had no right to make decisions regarding
war and peace. "It was my job to anticipate developments and con-
tinuously make plans so that my country would be prepared for any
contingency which fate, politicians, or power-drunk leaders [i.e.,
Roosevelt] might precipitate." It was also his job, he said, to come up

with a plan "calculated to bring our enemies to their knees in the short-est possible time."

For almost three months, Wedemeyer and his small staff worked virtually around the clock on their gigantic task. They sifted through a multitude of priorities and requirements, including the smallest de-tails involving training, equipment, armaments, ships, planes, trucks, and thousands of other items needed for defense. The result was a stunningly prescient analysis that ended up serving as the basic blue-print for U.S. military planning and mobilization throughout the war. Years later, Robert Sherwood would call the Victory Program "one of the most remarkable documents of American history, for it set down the basic strategy of a global war before this country was involved in it."

In the study, Wedemeyer and his team declared that Britain was not capable of defeating Germany on its own and that if the Axis were to be beaten, the United States would have to enter the war. Once it did, its first major objective must be the "complete military defeat of Ger-many . . . while holding Japan in check pending future developments." Noting that "by themselves, naval and air forces seldom if ever win important wars," the authors of the Victory Program made it clear that vanquishing Germany and Japan would require a massive U.S. land force. The date that Chesly Manly claimed was fixed for the start of a U.S. invasion of Europe—July 1, 1943—was actually the first date on which, according to Wedemeyer's estimates, America would be fully prepared for action.

The Victory Program study served as a rude wake-up call for the country's lackadaisical mobilization program. It estimated that defense production would have to double, at a cost of at least $150 billion, to meet the needs of the United States and its Lend-Lease partners. "Ul-timate victory over the Axis powers," the analysis observed, "will place a demand upon industry few have yet conceived."

Thanks to the Victory Program, the White House and the rest of the administration were finally confronted with the stark reality that business as usual was no longer an option. In the words of Donald Nel-son, a key defense mobilization official, the plan "revolutionized our production and may well have been a decisive turning point."

In mid-September, copies of the lengthy top-secret report were handed out to Stimson, Knox, Marshall, Stark, and a few other top officials, all of whom understood they were to disclose the contents to no one. On September 25, Stimson hand-delivered a copy to the president. After hearing a summary of the program, FDR indicated disagreement with one of its conclusions. "He was afraid of any assumption of the position that we must invade . . . and crush Germany," Stimson wrote in his diary. "He thought that would [lead to] a very bad reaction." The war secretary replied that he believed U.S. entry into the war "would help production very much and would help the psychology of the people." On that point, Stimson noted, the president "fully agreed."

Yet Roosevelt never formally signed off on the plan. He apparently still clung to the hope that the United States might be able to participate in the war without having to send an army to Europe. Indeed, at about the time he received the Victory Program report, he suggested to Stimson and Marshall that the size of the army actually be cut in order to help pay for more resources for Britain and Russia.

Nonetheless, the president did send to Capitol Hill a request for $8 billion in additional military appropriations to push defense production into high gear. Congress had just begun considering the legislation when the *Chicago Tribune* and *Washington Times-Herald* dropped their Victory Program bombshell.

WHILE WEDEMEYER AND HIS team were working on their report in the late summer and early fall of 1941, Robert McCormick was trying to figure out a way to ruin the debut of a new morning newspaper in Chicago, created specifically as an interventionist rival to the *Tribune*.

The Chicago *Sun* was the brainchild of Marshall Field III, a grandson and heir of the department store magnate Marshall Field. The year before, Field had bankrolled the launching of *PM,* the interventionist New York daily. Now he wanted to replicate the feat in his family's hometown.

Field was encouraged in the effort by two of McCormick's fiercest enemies: the president of the United States and Navy Secretary Frank Knox, who owned Chicago's main afternoon paper, the *Daily News*. Knox, who leased the top three floors of the *Daily News* building to Field and allowed him to use his paper's presses, boasted to members of the Chicago Club: "Well, we have got the *Tribune* fixed now. Marshall Field is going to start a morning paper with the backing of every-one from the President down." According to the London *Daily Mail,* the founding of the *Sun* represented "the last great drive to torpedo isolationism" in America.

Members of the Chicago chapter of Fight for Freedom distributed buttons emblazoned with the slogan "Chicago Needs a Morning Newspaper," along with leaflets showing a swastika atop the *Tribune* building and reading "Billions for defense, but not 2 cents for the Tri-bune." An anti-*Tribune* rally on South Michigan Avenue turned into a raucous street brawl, with McCormick opponents smashing *Tribune* vending boxes and setting copies of the paper afire.

McCormick, for his part, was determined to do everything he could to spoil the *Sun's* first day and take vengeance on FDR and Knox. Months before the paper's December 4 launch date, the *Tribune* publisher ordered his managing editor and Washington bureau to find a scoop sensational enough to take attention away from the *Sun's* birth.

Chesly Manly, the correspondent who came up with the story, was a diehard conservative who believed that the Roosevelt administration was riddled with "Godless Communists." On Capitol Hill, Manly's best sources were lawmakers, many of them isolationists, who were as implacably opposed as he was to the president and his policies. When Manly produced his account of the Victory Program, leaked by an anonymous source, red flags went up in the *Tribune* hierarchy. Managing editor J. Loy Maloney was troubled by the idea of revealing vital, highly sensitive military secrets that clearly would be of great value to potential enemies of the United States. Sharing Maloney's concern was Walter Trohan, the *Tribune's* White House correspondent. Although anti–New Deal himself, Trohan believed that Manly was deliberately deceiving his readers by referring to the Victory Program, clearly a contingency plan, as a cast-in-iron program for war.

His underlings' doubts, however, had no impact on the jubilant McCormick, who called the Victory Program leak "the greatest scoop in history." The story not only completely overshadowed the *Sun's* debut, as he had hoped, it also, in his view, dealt a potentially devastating blow to the credibility and prestige of Roosevelt and his administration.

On December 5, a front-page *Times-Herald* headline blared: WAR PLAN EXPOSÉ ROCKS CAPITAL, PERILS ARMY APPROPRIATION BILL;

CONGRESS IN UPROAR. In the Senate, Burton Wheeler declared that the story proved what he and other isolationists had been saying all along—that the president was trying to trick the country into war and that his promises to keep the country out of the conflict were nothing but lies. The Montana Democrat said he would introduce a resolution calling for an investigation into the origins of the secret plan.

Ruth Sarles, the Washington director of America First, wrote to a colleague that although the Victory Program was clearly "the sort of plan any War Department would have ready if it were on their toes," nonetheless "we can take advantage of this break if we make it stick. . . . If Senator Wheeler introduces a resolution of inquiry . . . as he has said he would do, we ought to give it tremendous support."

Stimson and Knox, meanwhile, insisted that McCormick and other *Tribune* and *Times-Herald* executives should be prosecuted and punished, along with the still unknown government leaker or leakers. "Nothing more unpatriotic or damaging to our plans for defense could very well be conceived of," Stimson fumed. He told War Department associates that every effort must be made to "get rid of this infernal disloyalty which we now have working in America First and in these McCormick family papers." At a December 4 cabinet meeting, Attorney General Francis Biddle said he believed the newspaper executives could be indicted under the Espionage Act of 1917.

Initially, the president approved the idea of prosecuting McCormick and others, but he soon had second thoughts, instructing his press secretary, Steve Early, to release a statement declaring that the administration would not challenge the right of newspapers "to print the news," no matter how inaccurate it might be. FDR did, however, authorize investigations by the FBI and Army into the source of the leak.

Tribune reporters and editors were questioned, and their home and office phones were tapped. Walter Trohan asked a Washington police lieutenant, who was a friend of his, to check his home phone for monitoring devices. After doing so, the lieutenant told Trohan that he "had never seen such a setup, that I had taps on taps." According to the *Tribune* correspondent, his phone conversations were being recorded by the FBI, Army and Navy intelligence, and even, somehow, the Anti-Defamation League. For all their digging into *Tribune* affairs, however, FBI investigators failed to turn up the leak's origins. Despite vigorous questioning, Chesly Manly refused to divulge any information about how he acquired the government report.

Unsurprisingly, given his well-known isolationist leanings, the main suspect in the case was Albert Wedemeyer, the Victory Program's architect. When Wedemeyer arrived at the War Plans Division office early on the morning of December 4, all conversation abruptly stopped. His secretary, who clearly had been crying, handed him a copy of the *Times-Herald*. He knew he was in deep trouble as soon as he saw the front-page headline. "I could not have been more appalled and astounded if a bomb had been dropped on Washington," he later recalled.

The strikes against Wedemeyer were many: his intense opposition to U.S. involvement in the war; his intimate knowledge of the secret plan; his training in Germany; his marriage to the daughter of another noted isolationist, General Stanley Embick; and his close relationships with Truman Smith, America First, and Charles Lindbergh, whom he had first met during one of the aviator's trips to Germany. Stimson received an anonymous letter accusing both Wedemeyer and his father-in-law of being the guilty parties. Several of Wedemeyer's Army colleagues told FBI investigators that they believed he was the leaker. The FBI, said Wedemeyer, "descended upon me like vultures upon a prostrate antelope."

In its report on Wedemeyer, the FBI noted: "He is reported to be most pro-German in his feelings, his utterances, and his sympathies. . . . He engaged in rather heated discussions with fellow officers at the War Department concerning his lack of sympathy with the Administration's international program. . . . He personally traveled through Germany with Colonel Lindbergh. He has entertained Lindbergh in Washington and has been entertained by Lindbergh." The report added that Wedemeyer had taken four days' leave in September 1941 to attend an America First event in New York at which Lindbergh spoke.

Wedemeyer did not deny any of that. He acknowledged his closeness to Lindbergh: "I respect him and agree with many of his ideas concerning our entrance into the war." He also said he agreed with many of America First's views and had often attended meetings of the group, although never in uniform. Nonetheless his FBI questioners were unable to find anything that directly tied the leak to Wedemeyer, who stoutly proclaimed his innocence. Later, the FBI publicly exonerated him.

Hiding in plain sight, meanwhile, was the middleman who had been given a copy of the Victory Program and passed it along to Manly—none other than Burton Wheeler, who had indignantly called for an investigation on the floor of the Senate. No one implicated him at the time, and it was not until he published his autobiography in 1962 that Wheeler himself disclosed he had been the intermediary.

According to the senator, the report had been handed to him by the same Army Air Forces captain who had been passing him confidential information for more than a year.* During the Lend-Lease debate in early 1941, the captain had given Wheeler statistics showing that the country's air force was still seriously lacking in modern aircraft—information that Wheeler used in a speech to protest Roosevelt's plan to hand over planes and other armaments to Britain. In September 1941, the captain told Wheeler that the armed forces, at Roosevelt's behest, had drawn up a master plan for a "gigantic American Expeditionary Force." When the senator asked to see the plan, the captain said he would see what he could do.

Less than two months later, he appeared at Wheeler's house with a "document as thick as an average novel, wrapped in brown paper and labeled 'Victory Program.'" When Wheeler asked him if he was afraid of "delivering the most closely guarded secret in Washington" to a senator, the officer replied: "Congress is a branch of government. I think it has a right to know what's really going on in the executive branch when it concerns human lives."

Wheeler, who had been one of Chesly Manly's key sources for years, invited the *Chicago Tribune* reporter to his home, where the two men skimmed the report, marked the most important sections, and had them copied in shorthand by one of Wheeler's secretaries. Late that night, Wheeler gave the document back to the captain so he could return it to the War Department early the next morning.

The Montana senator rationalized his unauthorized disclosure of military secrets by claiming that the public had a right to know "what was in store for them if we entered the war—and the fact that we probably would." But if he felt so strongly about sharing the information,

---

* The U.S. Army Air Corps changed its name to the U.S. Army Air Forces in June 1941.

why didn't he do so on the floor of the Senate, rather than turning it over to a reporter? In his autobiography, Wheeler claimed he had considered giving the report to the Senate Foreign Relations Committee but had decided against it because he feared the interventionists on the committee would bury it.

It was a weak excuse. Wheeler clearly had no intention of taking responsibility for his actions, and neither did the high military officer who was behind the leak. According to Wheeler, Walter Trohan, and FBI officials, that officer was General Henry "Hap" Arnold, chief of the U.S. Army Air Forces.

In his book, Wheeler did not name Arnold—or anyone else—as the leaker. But he did tell Wedemeyer after the war that the Air Forces chief had "made available" the study to him through "one of his boys low down." According to Wedemeyer, the senator added that Arnold "did not approve of this business of going to war until he had raised an Air Force, and he would do all he could to retard it."

Arnold already had developed a reputation as a skilled leaker— "second only to Roosevelt," Walter Trohan said—and an adept bureaucratic infighter. Earlier in his career, he had repeatedly rebelled against superiors' actions and decisions; after one such revolt, he was exiled to Panama for a time. In March 1940, FDR threatened to send him to Guam if he did not stop his rearguard actions.

The Air Forces chief lowered his profile after his confrontation with Roosevelt but continued his impassioned lobbying for more and better aircraft. He was particularly opposed to the Lend-Lease program, accusing its creators of leaving the Air Forces' cupboard bare and making clear he was against going to war until that cupboard was fully stocked. In the fall of 1941, he pointed out that only two bomber squadrons and three fighter groups were ready for combat.

According to several accounts, Arnold and others in his service were also incensed by what they viewed as the failure of the War Department to recognize the vital role of airpower, citing as an example the Victory Program's alleged shortchanging of the Air Forces in its suggested allocation of resources.

The Air Forces brass vigorously opposed the report's emphasis on a large ground army and objected to what they considered an overly generous allocation of funds to the Navy for building more destroyers, aircraft carriers, submarines, and other vessels. "There was a strong conflict right away," Wedemeyer acknowledged, "not only as to the industrial side, but also as to the strategic implications. The Navy was going to usurp a lot of the missions." Echoing that view, Stimson noted after the war that the Navy's "whole effort was to . . . put everything of ours [i.e., the Army and Air Forces] behind everything of theirs." To stop that, Wedemeyer said, Arnold "would fight, and he would fight well." By leaking the report, he would take his case to Congress and the American people, hoping to halt the Victory Program—and the kind of war it proposed—in their tracks.

Officially, the case remained unsolved. But in 1963, Frank Waldrop, who had been the managing editor of the *Washington Times-Herald* at the time of the leak, said he had been told by a top FBI official after the war that his agency had uncovered the guilty party in ten days. According to Waldrop, the official—Louis Nichols, an assistant director of the bureau—described the culprit as "a general of high renown and invaluable importance to the war," whose motive was to reveal the plan's "deficiencies in regard to air power." In a later interview with the historian Thomas Fleming, Waldrop quoted Nichols as saying, "When we got to Arnold, we quit."

Throughout the years, there has been speculation on the part of Fleming and others that the president himself leaked the Victory Program to goad Hitler into declaring war on the United States. Those espousing that view have stressed that FDR seemed loath to pursue the culprit and that, if in fact it *was* Arnold, the president and Marshall took no action against him. Yet even without Burton Wheeler's and Louis Nichols's identification of Arnold as the guilty party, the scenario of FDR as leaker seems highly improbable. At the time, Japan was clearly on the verge of entering the war, and the idea that the president, so cautious in the past, would suddenly encourage a two-front conflict is far-fetched. In the words of Frank Waldrop, it was hard to believe that Roosevelt would have "thrown gasoline on a fire."

It is also important to note that the FBI's identification of Arnold was reportedly made just a few days after the United States entered the war. For the administration, creating a sense of national unity was the paramount goal. If that meant covering up an act by the chief of the Air Forces that many saw as unpatriotic and disloyal, then so be it.

——————

ON DECEMBER 5, THE day after Chesly Manly's story appeared, Roosevelt was handed an intercepted message from the Japanese government to their embassy in Washington. After reading the belligerent dispatch, which had been deciphered by U.S. codebreakers, the president soberly remarked, "This means war."

The Japanese clearly were on the move. Two large convoys of ships had been sighted off China's coast, but no one knew where they were headed. Such intelligence as there was pointed to Siam, Malaya, Singapore, or the Dutch East Indies.

The idea that Hawaii might be a target was discounted by virtually everyone in the Roosevelt administration and, indeed, in the country. There was some speculation that the Philippines might be in danger, but the idea that Pearl Harbor lay in harm's way was widely regarded as ridiculous, largely because of Hawaii's distance from Japan. This despite a number of warnings from Navy intelligence officers that the Japanese might precipitate war with the United States by a sneak attack on Pearl Harbor. Indeed, Frank Knox in early 1941 issued a memo declaring that "the inherent possibilities of a major disaster to the fleet or naval base [at Pearl Harbor] warrant taking every step, as rapidly as can be done, that will increase the joint readiness of the Army and Navy to withstand [such a] raid." Little attention, however, was paid to Knox's memo or, for that matter, to any other warning, several of which were issued in early December.

As it turned out, another Japanese naval task force, unbeknownst to nervous American and British officials, was also on the high seas. On the early morning of Wednesday, November 26, the clamorous sounds of anchors being hauled up and ships' engines throbbing to life had filled the air at a closely guarded harbor in the Japanese-controlled Kurile Islands. Shrouded by heavy cloud cover and swirling snow, a mighty armada of battleships, aircraft carriers, destroyers, submarines, and tankers set sail, bound for Pearl Harbor.

"LET'S LICK HELL OUT OF THEM"

≡

For many Americans, it began as a typical Sunday. Church in the morning, followed by a big Sunday dinner at midday. Then maybe a nap, reading the paper, taking a leisurely drive, or listening to the weekly CBS broadcast of the New York Philharmonic Orchestra.

Like other New Yorkers on December 7, 1941, Aubrey and Con Morgan, along with their houseguest, John Wheeler-Bennett, tuned in to the popular Philharmonic broadcast at 3:00 P.M. to hear Brahms's Second Piano Concerto, performed by Arthur Rubinstein. In Boston, Arthur Schlesinger Jr., a graduate fellow at Harvard, did the same. During the intermission, the Philharmonic radio audience heard CBS announcer John Charles Daly break in with a stunning news bulletin—the Japanese had bombed Pearl Harbor. At that moment, Schlesinger later wrote, "an era came to an end."

It was also the end of the debate over America's involvement in the war. And, as it happened, the Pearl Harbor attack gave the lie to the arguments of many who had taken part in that discussion. As the columnist Marquis Childs put it, "the boldest interventionists had pitifully underestimated Japan's striking power. Isolationists had their chief argument—that no foreign power wanted to assail us in our own sphere—completely knocked out from under them."

President Roosevelt, in the midst of a conversation with Harry Hopkins at the White House, was given the news by Frank Knox over the phone. "No!" FDR exclaimed. He sat still, staring straight ahead, for several minutes. Finally rousing himself, he called Cordell Hull, then dictated the first news bulletin about the attack. Throughout the afternoon and evening, the president received a flood of new dispatches updating the losses at Pearl Harbor and detailing other Japanese assaults in Asia and the Pacific.

Struggling to come to grips with the disaster, Roosevelt looked "very strained and tired," his wife later wrote. "But he was completely calm. His reaction to any great event was always to be calm. If it was something that was bad, he just became almost like an iceberg, and there was never the slightest emotion that was allowed to show." Others, however, had slightly different memories of FDR that day. His secretary, Grace Tully, remembered him as angry, tense, and excited, while Attorney General Francis Biddle described Roosevelt as "deeply shaken, graver than I had ever seen him."

Early in the evening, he summoned cabinet members and congressional leaders to the White House. In a reflection of the bitterness of the pre–Pearl Harbor debate, FDR refused to allow Rep. Hamilton Fish, the ranking Republican on the House Foreign Affairs Committee, to take part. Another congressional isolationist, Senator Hiram Johnson, was included only at the last minute. Tempers ran high at the meeting. Jumping to his feet, a red-faced Senator Tom Connally, the new chairman of the Senate Foreign Relations Committee, banged a table with his fist and exclaimed: "How did they catch us with our pants down, Mr. President?" His head bowed, Roosevelt said softly, "I don't know, Tom. I just don't know."

Henry Stimson posed the same question: How could the U.S. military, "who had been warned long ago and were standing on the alert, have been taken so completely by surprise?" But the postmortems, the explanations and excuses, would have to wait for later. The task now at hand was to draft a declaration of war against Japan. For that, Stimson summoned Grenville Clark, the architect of conscription, who was working for him as an unpaid adviser. Clark immediately set to work drawing up the document.

The White House guard was doubled, blackout curtains were hastily installed to cover the Executive Mansion's windows, and antiaircraft guns were set up on the roof of the old State, War, and Navy building next door. Motorists returning from their Sunday drives spotted soldiers guarding Washington bridges. Those who were especially sharp-eyed might have noticed that one of the famed Japanese cherry trees surrounding the Tidal Basin was lying on the ground, apparently chopped down by an angry citizen.

Large crowds milled outside the White House until late that night. Many bystanders huddled together in Lafayette Park across the street while others pressed against the tall iron fence in front. Throughout the misty evening, the silence was broken periodically by the spontaneous singing of patriotic songs, with "God Bless America" a particular favorite.

Near midnight, FDR invited the CBS newsman Edward R. Murrow, who was on home leave from London, to join him in his office. Also there was William Donovan, the head of the U.S. government's new intelligence agency. Over beer and sandwiches, Roosevelt told his visitors of the staggering losses at Pearl Harbor—the eight battleships sunk or badly damaged, the hundreds of planes destroyed, the thousands of men dead, wounded, and missing. The president kept his rage under control until he started talking about the aircraft. "Destroyed on the ground, by God!" he shouted, pounding his fist on his desk. "On the ground!" As Murrow later recalled, "the idea seemed to hurt him."

At one point, the president asked Murrow and Donovan what both considered a rather curious question. Did they believe that, given the Japanese attack on U.S. soil, the American people would now support a declaration of war? The two men were firm in their assurances that their countrymen would indeed rally around the president.

CHARLES AND ANNE LINDBERGH were on Martha's Vineyard, spending a quiet day with their children, when they heard the news. Since Lindbergh's notorious Des Moines address, he had not done much public speaking. In the few appearances he did make, he seemed unfazed by the almost universal denunciation of his remarks in Iowa. In an October speech in Fort Wayne, Indiana, for example, he again claimed that free speech was dead in America and suggested that Roosevelt might well call off the 1942 congressional elections.

None of that kind of talk was evident in the statement Lindbergh released shortly after learning of the Japanese attack. "We have been stepping closer to war for many months," he said. "Now it has come and we must meet it as united Americans, regardless of our attitude in the past. . . . Whether or not that policy has been wise, our country has been attacked by force of arms, and by force of arms we must retaliate." He went on: "We must now turn every effort to building the greatest and most efficient Army, Navy and Air Force in the world."

With that, Lindbergh fell silent. He refused to answer his constantly ringing phone, reply to a deluge of telegrams from former supporters and detractors, or give interviews to reporters. After two tumultuous years, the most famous isolationist in America was suddenly gone from the public arena.

Other prominent isolationists echoed Lindbergh's call for national unity. At lunch with, of all people, a journalist from London and a British propaganda official, Robert McCormick excused himself when he heard news of the attack. "The Japanese have bombed Pearl Harbor," he declared. "I must leave my guests and write an editorial that will rally the nation against aggression." In the next day's *Tribune,* McCormick's front-page editorial began: "All of us, from this day forth, have only one task. That is to strike with all our might to protect and preserve the American freedom that we all hold dear." Alongside the editorial was a cartoon showing Uncle Sam standing next to John Bull (the stocky, blimpish figure used by cartoonists to portray Britain) as they watched a monster labeled WORLD WAR II rising from its grave. "This time, John," Uncle Sam said, "we must bury the monster deeper!"

Senator Burton Wheeler's reaction to the attack was short and succinct: "Let's lick hell out of them." Rep. Hamilton Fish told his fellow isolationists: "The time for debate is past. The time for action has come. . . . There is only one answer to the treacherous attack by Japan— war to victory." America First, meanwhile, issued a statement urging its members to unite behind the war effort and pledging to support Roosevelt as commander in chief. The organization then closed its doors for good. "I just remember feeling sick," Robert Stuart said years later. "Not only over the loss of Pearl Harbor but what it meant. The game was over."

Senator Gerald Nye was the only isolationist leader to offer a graceless response to Pearl Harbor. He was waiting offstage to make a speech at an America First rally in Pittsburgh when someone told him the news. Rather than seek confirmation, he went on with his antiwar address until a reporter walked onto the stage and handed him a note saying that the Japanese had just declared war on the United States. Glancing at the paper, Nye announced to the audience "the worst news that I have had in twenty years to report," then, unbelievably, finished his speech as written, adding only the comment, "This was just what Great Britain planned for us. . . . We have been maneuvered into this by the President." As reporters crowded around him afterward, the senator grumbled, "It sounds terribly fishy to me."

THE BRITISH, MEANWHILE, WERE overjoyed. Marion de Chastelain, who worked for William Stephenson in New York, rushed from her apartment to the British Security Coordination office as soon as she heard the news. She arrived just as officials from the Japanese consulate in New York, whose office was in the same Rockefeller Center building as BSC's, were being escorted away by U.S. authorities. For the rest of the afternoon and into the evening, Chastelain and other BSC staffers toasted the new Anglo-American alliance with champagne.

In Britain, Winston Churchill learned of the attack while at dinner with U.S. ambassador John Gilbert Winant and Lend-Lease administrator Averell Harriman at Chequers, the prime minister's country house. Earlier in the day, Churchill, haunted by the fear of an imminent Japanese offensive, had asked Winant, "If they declare war on us, will you declare war on them?" The ambassador replied: "I can't answer that, Prime Minister. Only the Congress has the right to declare war under the United States Constitution." Churchill was silent for a moment, and Winant knew what he was thinking: a Japanese attack on British territory in Asia would force British forces into a two-front war, with the possibility of no lifeline from the United States.

That night, the prime minister—tired, moody, and obviously depressed—uncharacteristically had little to say to anyone. A little before nine o'clock, Churchill's valet brought a flip-top portable radio into the dining room so that the British leader and his guests could listen to the BBC news. It seemed a routine broadcast at first: war communiqués at the beginning, followed by a few tidbits of domestic news. Then, at the end, one brief, unemotional sentence: "The news has just been given that Japanese aircraft have raided Pearl Harbor, the American naval base in Hawaii."

With that, Churchill headed toward the door, exclaiming, "We shall declare war on Japan!" Winant jumped up and ran after him. "Good God," he said, "you can't declare war on a radio announcement!" Churchill stopped and, looking at him quizzically, asked, "What shall I do?" When Winant said he would call Roosevelt at once, Churchill replied, "And I shall talk to him too."

A few minutes later, FDR was on the phone. "Mr. President, what's this about Japan?" Churchill asked. Roosevelt replied: "They've attacked us at Pearl Harbor. We are all in the same boat now." That night, Churchill later wrote, he "slept the sleep of the saved and thankful," quite convinced now that "we had won the war. England would live."

ACTUALLY, CHURCHILL, IN HIS conviction that all would be well, had gotten a little ahead of himself. The following day, Roosevelt would ask Congress for a declaration of war against Japan alone, without even mentioning Germany or Italy. Most of his closest advisers had urged war against all the Axis powers, with Stimson arguing correctly that Germany had pushed Japan to attack the United States. But the president held out, detecting, he said, "a lingering distinction in some quarters of the public between war with Japan and war with Germany."

Early in the afternoon of December 8, Roosevelt, enveloped in a dark naval cape, was driven to Capitol Hill. Guarded by dozens of Marines holding fixed bayonets, the Capitol looked like an armed camp. Steel cables, strung between posts outside the building, kept back the hundreds of people who had gathered in the chill air to be part of the historic event.

Braced on the arm of his son James, FDR, his face drawn and grim, slowly mounted the steps of the rostrum in the House chamber. The cavernous room—filled with members of Congress and the Supreme Court, along with foreign diplomats, the cabinet, and other key administration officials—erupted in applause and cheers. In the gallery, Eleanor Roosevelt and Edith Wilson, the widow of the only other president to preside over U.S. involvement in a world war, looked on.

Roosevelt's call for a declaration of war lasted barely six minutes, but it made an indelible impression on those listening in the House chamber, as well as on the millions of Americans gathered around their radios that afternoon. From his first sentence, describing December 7 as a "date which will live in infamy," the president, whose voice burned with barely restrained anger, underscored the outrage felt by himself and his countrymen at the "dastardly" attack, and he left no doubt about the nation's resolve to take vengeance. At the speech's conclusion, lawmakers of both parties jumped to their feet in a standing ovation.

Half an hour after Roosevelt spoke, the Senate voted unanimously for war against Japan. The scene in the House was somewhat more turbulent. One member—Jeannette Rankin, a Montana Republican and the first woman to serve in Congress—had made it clear to colleagues before the tally that she would vote no, just as she had in 1917, when America entered World War I. House Republicans tried to dissuade her, but the sixty-one-year-old Rankin, a lifelong pacifist who had spoken at several America First rallies, held firm. As House majority leader John McCormack read the war resolution, she rose from her seat and cried out, "Mr. Speaker, I object." Sam Rayburn icily cut her short. "There can be no objection," he declared, gesturing to McCormack to continue.

Cheering and stamping their feet, congressmen from both parties yelled, "Vote! Vote!" Banging his gavel, Rayburn called for order, and McCormack urged the House to cast a unanimous vote for the resolution. Rankin jumped to her feet again and sought recognition from Rayburn. "Sit down!" one congressman shouted, as Rankin declared, "I rise to a point of order." Rayburn ignored her, and the clerk, his voice booming out over repeated appeals by Rankin for recognition, called the roll. The final vote was 388–1.

Columnist Marquis Childs, watching the chaotic scene from the House press gallery, later wrote: "It seemed to me that those who tried to coerce [Rankin] into voting aye were foolish. A solitary no was a demonstration to the world that even in the critical moment of attack, we do not compel the false *Ja* vote of dictatorship."

The resolution was signed by Rayburn at 3:15 P.M.; by Vice President Henry Wallace, on behalf of the Senate, ten minutes later; and, at 4:10 P.M., by President Roosevelt. The United States was now officially at war.

The following night, the light atop the Capitol was extinguished. It would remain dark until the end of the conflict.

———

FOR THREE LONG DAYS, Britain faced the horrifying prospect of war in both Europe and Asia with the United States committed only to the latter. Nothing was heard from Berlin. Hitler had gone out of his way for well over a year to avoid war with America. What if he continued to do so? Would the president finally seize the initiative? If not, how could the British possibly hold out?

According to the terms of the Tripartite Pact, the Japanese attack on Pearl Harbor did not obligate Germany and Italy to go to war against the United States: the treaty applied only to situations in which its signatories were victims of attack. Over the course of those days in early December, arguments raged in the highest ranks of the German government over whether to add America to Germany's list of enemies. A number of Hitler's advisers advised him not to do so. Ranged against them were Foreign Minister Joachim von Ribbentrop and others, who pointed out that Germany had long sought Japan's involvement in the war by dangling the promise that if the Japanese engaged in war with the United States, "Germany, of course, would join the war immediately."

In the end, Hitler resolved the issue. For months, he had counseled patience, despite what he saw as repeated provocations by the United States. Inwardly, he seethed with anger and hatred toward Roosevelt and his country. The Japanese aggression at Pearl Harbor, which he hailed as "the turning point," freed him to do what he had wanted to do all along.

On December 11, Hitler appeared before the Reichstag to declare war against the United States. In response, Roosevelt sent a resolution to Congress calling for war against Germany and Italy. This time, Jeannette Rankin decided to abstain, and both chambers voted unanimously in favor.

FOR NEARLY A YEAR, many officials in the German government had been convinced that Roosevelt was poised to enter the war at any moment. Postponing a declaration of war against America at the time of Pearl Harbor, they felt, would simply be putting off the inevitable.

President Roosevelt signs the U.S. declaration of war against Germany on December 11, 1941.

But was that true? What would have happened if Hitler had not declared war on the United States, or if the Japanese had not attacked American soil?

When one considers that even after Pearl Harbor, Roosevelt apparently was unsure of the public's support for a declaration of war, it's hard to believe that a Japanese assault on British or Dutch possessions in the Pacific would have prompted the administration to push for such a declaration, at least at that point. At a White House meeting before Pearl Harbor, FDR said he doubted that the United States would go to war even if Japan ended up attacking the Philippines, a U.S. territory with a major Army presence. In that situation, Winston Churchill's fears of facing a two-front war alone might well have been realized.

And had Hitler not decided, in a fit of anger, to go to war against the United States, the odds are high that Congress and the American people would have pressured the president to turn away from an undeclared war against Germany in the Atlantic and focus instead on defeating Japan, the only country that had actually attacked the United States. In that case, American shipment of arms to Britain and Russia might have been cut dramatically or even halted, and Germany would have had a clear shot at defeating both countries.

Happily for the Allies, none of those scenarios became reality. As Dean Acheson aptly put it, "At last our enemies, with unparalleled stupidity, resolved our dilemmas, clarified our doubts and uncertainties, and united our people for the long, hard course that the national interest required." FDR need not have been concerned about the national mood after Pearl Harbor. Instead of demoralizing America, as the Japanese government hoped, the attack did the opposite: it brought the country together. "The war came as a great relief, like a reverse earthquake that in one terrible jerk, shook everything disjointed and distorted back into place," *Time* wrote in its first issue after Pearl Harbor. "Japanese bombs had finally brought national unity to the United States."

With Congress and the American people now solidly behind him, President Roosevelt cast off his pre–Pearl Harbor caution, shedding his deference to Capitol Hill and emerging again as the bold leader he had been in the early days of the New Deal. Demonstrating calm and a reborn sense of confidence, he told a December 9 press conference: "We are now in this war. We are all in it—all the way. Every single man, woman, and child is a partner in the most tremendous undertaking of our American history."

On that day, and for many days afterward, thousands of young Americans flocked to their local recruiting offices to enlist. Soldiers on leave reported back to their posts and began drilling with new urgency. In Washington, all officers were ordered to switch from civilian clothes to full military uniforms. As one amused observer noted, the corridors of the Munitions Building "were filled with officers [wearing] uniforms and parts of uniforms dating back to 1918. . . . Majors were in outfits they had bought when second lieutenants. . . . It was a rummage sale called to war."

After months of dithering, U.S. industry shifted into high gear, working twenty-four hours a day, seven days a week, to turn out the planes, guns, ships, tanks, and other armaments and supplies that would end up playing such a key role in winning the war. Americans were told they must do without new cars, refrigerators, and other big-ticket items for the duration. Defense workers, for their part, displayed a new intensity. An employee at a bomber manufacturing plant in California observed that before Pearl Harbor, "most of the men worked no harder to turn out planes than they would have worked manufacturing ashtrays—just hard enough to satisfy the boss." Afterward, he said, production skyrocketed.

THROUGHOUT THE THREE AND a half years of U.S. participation in the war, only one of the isolationists' dire predictions about the country's fate in wartime was actually realized. That was the concern, voiced chiefly by liberals, that entering the conflict would result in restrictions on civil rights and liberties, a curbing of New Deal reforms, and a resurgence of conservative sentiment.

To the dismay of liberals, the administration now paid far more attention to encouraging the defense effort than to advancing social and economic change. As Roosevelt himself said, "Dr. New Deal" had given way to "Dr. Win the War." The government showed a new willingness to give business what it wanted, allowing defense contractors to earn huge profits. The country itself began edging to the right, sweeping progressives out of Congress in the 1942 elections and giving de facto control to conservatives. Republicans gained seven seats in the Senate and forty-four in the House. "Ordinary people were more conservative now," noted one historian, "because they finally had something to conserve."

Civil liberties also took a beating. Although the vast majority of Americans lived through World War II with few strictures on their constitutional freedoms, more than a hundred thousand Japanese Americans on the West Coast were abruptly removed from their homes, businesses, and farms in early 1942 and confined to bleak internment camps for the duration. It was, the ACLU declared, "the worst single wholesale violation of civil rights of American citizens in our history."

A few months later, Attorney General Francis Biddle, succumbing to pressure from the president, indicted twenty-eight American Fascists on charges of sedition. The defendants, who included Silver Shirts' leader William Dudley Pelley and Gerald L. K. Smith, a pro-Nazi political organizer, had, even after Pearl Harbor, continued to express antiwar, antiadministration, and anti-Semitic views in hate-filled newspapers and newsletters.

In early 1942, Biddle told Roosevelt that while the ideas expressed by the publications were indeed loathsome, they and those who espoused them posed no immediate danger to America and the war effort. Biddle added that it would be extremely difficult under current law to prove the native Fascists guilty of sedition. None of them, he said, was guilty of advocating the overthrow of the government by force. Roosevelt, however, wanted them stopped, and Biddle finally gave in. The Justice Department accused the defendants of conspiring with Germany to establish a Fascist government in the United States by undermining the loyalty and morale of the armed forces.

The case was a fiasco from the beginning. Except for their hate-filled outpourings, the defendants had little in common. Indeed, most did not even know each other—an inconvenient fact when one is trying to prove conspiracy. Struggling to come up with evidence, the Justice Department did not bring the case to trial until April 1944. It dragged on for eight months—until the presiding judge died and a mistrial was declared. The government reindicted the defendants in 1945, just as the war was drawing to a close. The following year, an appeals court threw the charges out, calling them a travesty of justice.

Although the number of Americans whose civil rights were breached during the war was relatively small, such violations remain a haunting reminder of the fragility of constitutional freedoms in the face of national insecurity and fear. "The test of the protection of fundamental rights is not how they are served in times of calm but how vigilantly they are defended in times of danger," the historian Geoffrey Perret observed. "By that test the wartime experience may be fairly described as a disaster for tens of thousands of Americans."

MOST OF THE REST of the nation, however, had a far more positive wartime experience. "No war is 'good,'" British historian David

Reynolds has written, "but America's war was about as good as one could get."

Before Pearl Harbor, Charles Lindbergh, Burton Wheeler, and other leading isolationists had predicted the deaths of millions of young Americans in the event of U.S. involvement. The actual death toll was 417,000—a large and tragic number, to be sure, but by far the lowest casualty rate of any of the major combatant countries. Alone among the major belligerents, the U.S. civilian population was spared widespread devastation and suffering. There was no bombing of the U.S. mainland, no civilian casualties, no destruction of millions of homes.

Contrary to the fears of Robert Wood and other isolationist businessmen that war would mean the collapse of the U.S. economy and capitalism, it brought instead the end of the Depression and an infusion of real economic growth. Thanks to the defense boom, the unemployment rate dropped from 14 percent to less than 2 percent over the three and a half years of the war. The annual income of Americans rose by more than 50 percent, and many in the country were now earning wages beyond their wildest dreams. After spending time in one thriving town, a journalist reported: "If the war ended today with a victory for us, the mass of folks here could truthfully say that the war was the best thing to ever happen in their lives."

The predictions of Lindbergh and others that U.S. entry into the war would trigger mass riots and a violent outbreak of anti-Semitism were also unfounded. While there were indeed instances of domestic unrest—the 1943 race riot in Detroit, in which thirty-four people were killed, is a prime example—they were relatively rare. And while Father Coughlin's bullyboys continued to attack Jews in New York, Boston, and other major cities, there was no widespread upsurge in anti-Semitism. Indeed, with the revelations toward the end of the conflict of the deaths of millions of Jews in Nazi death camps, overt anti-Semitism in America began to recede.

The news of the Holocaust exposed, once and for all, the speciousness of Lindbergh's argument that the war was a clash of rival imperialistic states, with both sides undeserving of U.S. support. But even before the Holocaust's full extent was known, the American people found common cause in the belief they were fighting a just and necessary conflict to save Western civilization. In doing so, they coalesced as never before in history. "It was a precious thing," Geoffrey Perret wrote, "a strong sense of genuine community."

Much of the credit for that feeling of unity must be given to the two-year public debate over the war, which, despite its unseemly acrimony, helped educate Americans about the need to ready themselves for entry into the conflict. The pros and cons of U.S. involvement—not to mention the significance of each important step, from the destroyers-bases deal to conscription to Lend-Lease—were thoroughly explored and weighed in government offices, in the halls of Congress, on radio and in the press, and in homes and businesses across the country. Equally important were the key roles played by private citizens—from college undergraduates to housewives to denizens of Wall Street—in working to help influence their countrymen. It was a robust, if tumultuous, example of democracy in action.

The result, as *The Army and Navy Journal* noted in November 1945, was that "when the Japanese attacked us, and when their Axis Allies in Europe declared war on us, this nation was better prepared, spiritually as well as militarily, than it had ever been for any war in our history."

CHAPTER 28

AFTERMATH

In the days following Pearl Harbor, Charles Lindbergh, hoping all would be forgiven, did his best to return to active duty in the Army Air Forces. Naïvely, as it turned out, he believed that his earlier opposition to Roosevelt might make him "of more value [to the administration] rather than less. It seems to me that the unity necessary for a successful war demands that all viewpoints be presented in Washington."

Lindbergh asked Hap Arnold, with whom he had remained in close contact, what he thought of the idea. Arnold referred it to the White House. Instead of making a public comment himself, Roosevelt and his aides put Arnold at the center of the controversy that soon erupted over the question of Lindbergh's reinstatement.

Despite his apparent culpability in leaking the Victory Program, Arnold had managed to keep his job. The Pearl Harbor disaster and America's entry into the war brought an end to the FBI investigation into the leak, and although investigators believed Arnold to be the culprit, no further action was taken. Revealing his role would have exposed fundamental differences within the administration—a situation that the White House, determined to demonstrate wartime unity, was anxious to avoid.

U.S. officials did not learn until after the war that disclosure of the Victory Program had prompted Germany's military high command to urge Hitler to pull back from Russia. Instead of focusing on the Eastern front, the military chiefs argued in early December 1941, Germany should establish a strong defensive line there and shift more than a hundred divisions to the tasks of conquering Britain and taking control of the entire Mediterranean area, including the Suez Canal, before an expected American invasion of Europe in mid-1943. If the high command's recommendation had been implemented, there likely would have been no Allied landings in North Africa in 1942 and, quite possibly, no Allied victory in Europe.

Initially, Hitler had agreed to this radical shift in strategy, but after Pearl Harbor, he decided against it. A major withdrawal from Russia was unnecessary and out of the question, he declared. Tied down by Japanese forces in the Pacific, the United States, the Führer predicted, would now pose a far less significant threat to German positions in the West.

Unaware of the potentially fateful consequences of the leak, General George Marshall, in Albert Wedemeyer's view, served as a key defender and protector of Arnold in the brouhaha that followed. Asked by Arnold biographer Murray Green if he believed Marshall would have allowed Arnold to stay in his job if proven guilty, Wedemeyer replied: "I think he would. I think he would have subordinated anything to win the war." He added: "Many people in uniform felt that George Marshall knew who [the culprit] was and that he should have been more forthright, no matter whom it involved. And I incline that way."

As for FDR, although he agreed to retain Arnold, he was not averse to making life uncomfortable for him from time to time. He did that now by having his aides leak to the press the news of Lindbergh's request for reinstatement in the Air Forces and urging them to contact Arnold for comment. When they did, the startled Air Forces chief made it clear he thought Lindbergh's offer should be accepted. It "indicates a definite change from his isolationist stand," Arnold said, "and expresses his deep desire to help the country along the lines in which he trained himself for many years."

Arnold's statement garnered some support, including that of *The New York Times*. "There cannot be the slightest doubt that Mr. Lindbergh's offer should be and will be accepted," the *Times* editorialized. "It will be accepted not only as a symbol of our newfound unity and an effective means of burying the dead past [but] also because Mr. Lindbergh can be useful to his country. . . . There can be no question of his great knowledge of aircraft and his immense experience as a flier. Nor have we any doubt that he will serve in the line of duty with credit to himself and to his country."

But many others disagreed, as FDR undoubtedly knew when he made the offer public. A torrent of anti-Lindbergh mail was delivered to the White House—and was immediately rerouted to Arnold's office. The Air Forces chief was shocked at how venomous most of it was. A typical letter read: "Our son is in the service, and we want no Quislings behind his back."

It became increasingly obvious that the administration had no intention of granting Lindbergh's request. Not surprisingly, the chief naysayer turned out to be Harold Ickes, who, rather like Inspector Javert in Victor Hugo's *Les Misérables*, continued a relentless pursuit of his quarry. Shortly before Pearl Harbor, Ickes had signed a contract with a New York publisher to write a savagely critical book, tentatively entitled *Why Hitler Sounds Like Lindbergh,* about the aviator. After the United States entered the war, Ickes reluctantly agreed to the publisher's request to put the book aside for the sake of national unity. But three years later, the interior secretary again urged its publication, declaring, "I am strongly of the opinion that Lindbergh ought not to be allowed to get off practically scot-free." (The book was never published.)

Ickes was, if anything, even more vengeful in the immediate post–Pearl Harbor period. In a memo to Roosevelt in early 1942, he insisted that Lindbergh was intent on overthrowing the government and that if he were allowed to become a war hero, "this loyal friend of Hitler's" would emerge as a rallying point for all of Roosevelt's opponents. "It would be a tragic disservice to American democracy," Ickes argued, "to give one of its bitterest and most ruthless enemies a chance to gain a military record. . . . He should be buried in merciful oblivion." In his response, the president said he agreed "wholeheartedly" with "what you say about Lindbergh and the potential danger of the man."

Henry Stimson was handed the assignment of giving Lindbergh the bad news. In a tense meeting in Stimson's office, the secretary of war informed Lindbergh that he was loath to bestow a position of command on someone "who has shown . . . no faith in the righteousness of our cause," adding that he didn't believe such a person could "carry on the war with sufficient aggressiveness." In reply, Lindbergh said he would not retract his view that entering the war was a mistake. But, he added, now that the decision for war had been made, he supported it and was eager to help in any way he could. Stimson, however, remained adamant. Nothing could or would be offered to a man whose loyalty, in the eyes of many, was still in question.

Having thus been banned from serving in the armed forces, Lindbergh talked to several old friends in the aircraft business about working for them as a civilian consultant for the development and testing of new bombers and fighters. Initially, the executives were enthusiastic—after all, Lindbergh had been involved in the design and production of aircraft since before his historic flight to Paris—but, one by one, they turned thumbs down on the idea. Juan Trippe, the head of Pan American Airways and an old friend of Lindbergh's, told him that "obstacles had been put in the way." The White House, Trippe explained, "was angry with him for even bringing up the subject" and told him it did not want Lindbergh "to be connected with Pan American in any capacity." With billions of dollars in defense contracts at stake, no aircraft manufacturer could afford to offend the administration by taking Lindbergh on.

No one, that is, but Henry Ford. For years one of the most ardent isolationists in the country, Ford now presided over a thriving defense manufacturing empire, turning out engines, tanks, jeeps, staff cars, and aircraft, above all, B-24 bombers, which were built at Willow Run, Ford's mile-long aircraft assembly plant outside Detroit. The government needed Ford as much as he needed the government's business, and he made it clear he didn't care what administration officials had to say about his hiring Lindbergh as a technical consultant.

For more than a year, Lindbergh worked to improve the design and performance of Ford-manufactured planes, including the B-24 and the P-47 fighter, known as the Thunderbolt. Making dozens of test flights, he operated the P-47 at extremely high altitudes to test the effect of such heights on both pilots and planes. As a result of his study, Ford modified the Thunderbolt's design and oxygen equipment, which, according to the Air Forces, bettered the craft's performance and helped save many pilots' lives. Later in the conflict, Lindbergh worked as a consultant to United Aircraft Corp., where he played a major role in the development and design of the Corsair, a new Navy and Marine fighter that could take off from aircraft carriers as well as from land bases.

Throughout the next three and a half years of war, Lindbergh belied the predictions of his critics that his goal was to topple the president. He resolutely stayed out of politics and the public eye, avoiding comment on the war's progress and uttering no criticism of FDR and his policies. He had "purposely entered technical fields," he told friends, so that he could give his "utmost support" to the country's war effort and not be swept up again in political controversy.

Ever since his return from Europe in the spring of 1939, conventional wisdom had had it that Lindbergh would eventually run for public office. "Among most of Lindbergh's friends," *Life* wrote in August 1941, "it is an accepted fact that he will take a more active part in politics, in or out of war. They say he will be 'forced into it,' to prove that he has been right; that consciously or unconsciously he knows he must remain 'in the forefront.'" In November 1941, Dorothy Thompson said she was "absolutely certain" that Lindbergh would form a new party and do everything in his power to become president. As it happened, a host of politicians, including Burton Wheeler and William Borah, had urged him to do just that.

Each time the idea came up, however, Lindbergh rejected it. "I do not feel that I am suited, either by temperament or desire, to the field of active politics," he wrote to Robert Wood in late 1941. "I have entered this field during the last two years, only because of the extreme wartime emergency which confronts my country." Entering the political arena, he said, would force him to give up the independence he so prized—the ability to say and do exactly what he thought. Then, in a statement that is key to understanding him, he noted: "Personally, I prefer the adventure and freedom of going as far from the center as my thoughts, ideals, and convictions lead me. I do not like to be held back by the question of influencing the mass of people or by the desire for the utmost security. I must admit, and I have no apology to make for the fact, that I prefer adventure to security, freedom to popularity, and conviction to influence." Anne later told a reporter: "I don't think Charles . . . ever wanted to be a leader in the sense of attracting followers, influence, popularity, and a movement behind him. Charles never really went after any of these things. He had causes he advanced, but usually he advanced them alone."

While Lindbergh remained persona non grata in the upper reaches of the Roosevelt administration throughout the war, his military friends stayed loyal. In early 1944, some of them encouraged him to travel as a civilian consultant to the Pacific theater, where he could test fighters under combat conditions, show pilots how to get the best out of their aircraft, and make recommendations for design improvements. When he said the White House would never allow it, they replied, "Why does the White House have to know?"

A few weeks later, wearing a naval officer's uniform without insignia, Lindbergh was on his way to the Pacific, without the knowledge of Roosevelt, Frank Knox, or Henry Stimson. For the next five months, the forty-two-year-old civilian flew some fifty combat missions against the Japanese in Navy, Marine, and Air Forces planes while squadron leaders and higher-ranking officers looked the other way. During those missions, which included patrol, escort, strafing, and dive-bombing runs, he shot down at least one Japanese Zero and came close to being shot down himself. As had been true back home, Lindbergh's suggestions for changes improved the effectiveness of the planes he flew; in the case of the P-38 Lightning, his recommendations increased its range by five hundred miles.

By all accounts, he was supremely happy during those perilous, exciting months. In photographs taken of him during that period, he almost always had a wide smile on his face. Flying with the military, Anne wrote, "had made a new man of him—made him boyish again." He developed close relationships with some of the young pilots with whom he flew, a number of whom were at least twenty years his junior. One morning, when he was a little slow retracting his landing gear while taking off on a mission, one of his youthful compatriots laughingly radioed him: "Lindbergh! . . . Get your wheels up! You ain't flying the *Spirit of St. Louis!*" According to his daughter Reeve, Lindbergh was in his element: "Everything was very well ordered, and there was a kind of camaraderie, and there wasn't the confusion and tension of the rest of the world."

After the war, even some of Lindbergh's harshest critics acknowledged that he had acquitted himself well. Robert Sherwood, for one, conceded in his Pulitzer Prize–winning book *Hopkins and Roosevelt* that the man he had once denounced as a "Nazi" and "Hitler bootlicker" had in fact "rendered valuable wartime service as a civilian flyer."

For Lindbergh's wife, though, there was little good about the war. With her husband gone for most of it, Anne was left to raise four small children (a daughter, Anne, had been born in 1940, and a son, Scott, in 1943) by herself in a rented house in a Detroit suburb. In the South Pacific, Lindbergh had managed to escape the odium surrounding his isolationism. In the isolation of Detroit, Anne remained haunted by the past.

When Harcourt, Brace published a short novel she had written, called *The Steep Ascent,* in the summer of 1943, the Book-of-the-Month Club refused to consider it as a possible selection, explaining that many readers had threatened to cancel their membership if the book was chosen. Reluctantly concluding that a large portion of the reading public would not buy any book by the author of *The Wave of the Future,* Harcourt, Brace limited *The Steep Ascent*'s print run to twenty-five thousand copies, far fewer than any of her previous books.

Already disheartened by the perpetual cloud she seemed to be under, Anne was devastated to learn in August 1944 of the death of Antoine de Saint-Exupéry, who had joined the Free French forces in 1943 and disappeared a year later on a reconnaissance flight over southern France to map the terrain for an upcoming Allied landing.[*] Although she had spent only three days with Saint-Exupéry in 1939, their encounter had transformed her life. She had written *The Steep Ascent* as "a letter to him," she noted, adding that he "spoke 'my language' better than anyone I have ever met, before or since." She added: "Of what use to write if he were not there to read it—perhaps—sometime—somewhere?"

For weeks, she was benumbed by grief, frequently giving way to gusts of tears. Saint-Exupéry's death, she wrote, was as painful to her as the losses of her son and sister. At the time, she reproached herself for feeling so strongly about a man with whom she had spent so short a time. She was not his wife or mistress, she acknowledged, nor even a close friend. But after rereading her diary entries about that fateful

---

[*] During his eighteen-month stay in the United States, Saint-Exupéry wrote two books, *Flight to Arras* and his masterpiece, *The Little Prince.*

weekend, she concluded that her memories about the intimate connection she had formed with Saint-Exupéry were indeed accurate.

Pouring out her sorrow in her diary, she wrote: "I am sad we never met again. I am sad he never tried to see us, though I understand it; I am sad that politics and the fierceness of the anti-war fight and the glare of publicity and the calumny and mixed-up pain and hurt and wrong of my book kept us from meeting again. I am sad that I never had the luxury of knowing whether or not he forgave us for our stand, forgave me for my book."

Earlier in her life, she had described Lindbergh as her "sun." Saint-Exupéry seemed to have replaced him. For Anne, Charles was now "earth," while Saint-Exupéry was "a sun or a moon or stars which light the earth, which make the whole world and life more beautiful. Now the earth is unlit and it is no longer so beautiful. I go ahead in it stumbling and without joy."

CHARLES LINDBERGH WAS NOT the only leading former isolationist to be given the brush-off by the White House after America entered the war. Robert Wood, the chairman of America First, also failed in his bid for active military duty. Hap Arnold, a good friend of Wood's, interceded for him with Roosevelt, saying he needed the help of the former Army quartermaster general in improving the Air Forces' supply system. The president was unmoved. "I do not think that General Wood should be put into uniform," he told Arnold. "He is too old and has, in the past, shown far too great approval of Nazi methods." But if Arnold wanted to use Wood as a civilian adviser, FDR added, he would have no objection. Arnold promptly put Wood to work, dispatching him to Air Forces bases in Europe, the Middle East, and the Pacific to check on their supply operations and make recommendations for their improvement. At the end of the war, the Sears, Roebuck chairman was awarded the Legion of Merit, a military decoration for exceptional service.

The young founders of America First, however, did not encounter the same hostility experienced by their more prominent elders. Robert Stuart, who held a ROTC commission in the Army Reserve, went on active duty shortly after Pearl Harbor and rose to the rank of major, serving on General Dwight D. Eisenhower's staff in London. He saw combat in France immediately after D-Day. Kingman Brewster, Gerald Ford, Sargent Shriver, and Potter Stewart all joined the Navy. Brewster became an aviator, while Stewart served on ships in the Atlantic and Mediterranean and Ford and Shriver were assigned to sea duty in the Pacific. Shriver was injured in the battle for Guadalcanal.

Even before Pearl Harbor, the mood on most college campuses had largely swung toward interventionism. Former antiwar activists enlisted in droves when war broke out, among them Neal Anderson Scott, whose 1940 commencement speech at Davidson College, like so many other graduation speeches that year, proclaimed that "the Yanks are *not* coming." Scott, a Navy ensign, was killed in 1942 during the Battle of Santa Cruz in the South Pacific.

MEANWHILE, THE SENIOR MILITARY officers who had worked against the president's interventionist policies before Pearl Harbor suffered no retribution, and in some cases, thanks to General George Marshall, they were given influential wartime positions.

In September 1941, an Army board ordered the mandatory retirement of Colonel Truman Smith because of his diabetes. Marshall, who had been cleaning out the Army's officer corps—getting rid of many older officers for health reasons—regretfully told Smith he could no longer protect him. Shortly after his retirement, Smith emerged as an outspoken supporter of America First, openly associating with Lindbergh and other leaders of the group. Nonetheless, as soon as the United States entered the war, Marshall reinstated Smith as the Army chief's top adviser on Germany. If Marshall had been appointed commander of the Allied forces invading Europe, as he hoped, he planned to take Smith to London as a key aide. (General Dwight D. Eisenhower got the nod as commander instead.) Although Marshall failed to get a promotion for Smith to brigadier general, he saw to it that his trusted adviser was awarded the Distinguished Service Medal at the end of the war for "his contribution to the war effort of the nation," which was described as "of major significance."

While Smith, by all accounts, served his country loyally during the conflict, he and his wife remained ardent Roosevelt haters. When they heard in April 1945 that FDR had died, the Smiths "burst into roars of laughter" and embraced each other and a friend, who threw "his arms high in the air in exultation," Katharine Smith wrote in an unpublished memoir. "The evil man was dead! I know how right we were to hate him so bitterly. There is no ill, foreign or domestic, that cannot be traced back directly to his policies. Our decline, our degeneracy stems from that man and his socialist, blinded, greedy wife."

Meanwhile, General Stanley Embick, who had opposed aid to Britain and U.S. participation in the war until Pearl Harbor, emerged as arguably the most influential and powerful Army strategist of World War II. In the fall of 1942, Marshall named Embick as the Army's representative to the Joint Strategic Survey Committee, a group of senior officers who advised the Joint Chiefs of Staff on strategic and political decisions related to the war. According to one historian, the committee was at times "equal in influence" to the Joint Chiefs themselves. Embick was widely regarded as the committee's dominant force.

Embick strongly opposed a key British strategy—to stage the first Allied offensives against Germany in North Africa and other areas on the perimeter of Europe rather than aim for an invasion of France across the English Channel. The strategic survey committee, under Embick's direction, described the British strategy as a scheme to protect their empire and to preserve the balance of power in Europe.

Heavily influenced by Embick's views, Marshall made clear to Roosevelt his own opposition to the 1942 Allied invasion of North Africa—a position that the president eventually overruled. For the Army chief of staff, "suspicion of British imperial designs under Churchill underlay every wartime scheme," the historian Stanley Weintraub has written. Marshall himself acknowledged after the war that "too much anti-British feeling [existed] on our side, more than we should have had. Our people were always ready to find Albion perfidious."

Another of Albion's critics was Lieutenant Colonel Albert Wedemeyer, Embick's son-in-law and the architect of the Victory Program, who, as one of the Army's chief planners, also vociferously opposed Allied operations in the Mediterranean. After playing a major role in the initial planning of the Normandy invasion, Wedemeyer, whom the historian John Keegan called "one of the most intellectual and farsighted military minds America has ever produced," was reassigned in 1943 to the Far East, where he became chief of staff to Lord Louis Mountbatten, the supreme allied commander of the Southeast Asia Command. In 1944, Wedemeyer was named U.S. commander in

China. He was convinced that his assignment to Asia came at the behest of Winston Churchill and the British, who resented his incessant criticism of them and their strategy and prevailed on Roosevelt to transfer him.

And then there was Hap Arnold, who, having survived the leak of the Victory Program, succeeded in doing what he had set out to accomplish: build the most powerful air force in the world. In just four years, his service mushroomed from several thousand men and a few hundred obsolescent aircraft to a 2.4-million-man force and eighty thousand modern planes. Convinced that strategic bombing could win the conflict virtually by itself, Arnold hoped to prove what he had long believed: that airpower was far superior to any other armed force. He was wrong on both counts.

As Marshall had long argued and Wedemeyer noted in the Victory Program, the war in Europe could not have been won without the fighting of massive numbers of ground troops. Although Arnold's Air Forces did play an important role in the victory, the human cost, both on the ground and in the air, was huge and bloody. By the end of the war, U.S. air operations in Europe suffered more casualties than the entire Marine Corps in its protracted campaigns in the Pacific.

THE MAN WHO, MORE than any other private citizen, helped unite the country behind the idea of aiding Britain and opposing Germany spent the war promoting the importance of international cooperation after the conflict. Although he rejected an attempt by FDR to bring him into his administration, Wendell Willkie, whom one newspaper labeled "a vocal and patriotic alarm clock," became a sort of ambassador-at-large for Roosevelt, traveling around the globe to meet with Allied heads of state, soldiers, and ordinary citizens. Wherever he went, he talked about the importance of a united, democratic world, free from the taints of totalitarianism, imperialism, and colonialism.

In 1943, Willkie published a book called *One World,* setting forth his internationalist views. It became a runaway bestseller, helping to nudge public opinion toward the idea of a postwar United Nations but also making him even more of a controversial figure within the Republican Party. Dubbing Willkie a "stooge for Roosevelt," the GOP's conservative old guard never forgave him for his liberalism, which included strong protests against racial discrimination in the country. When a violent race riot erupted in Detroit in June 1943, Willkie blasted both Republicans and Democrats for ignoring what he called "the Negro question." In his view, "the desire to deprive some of our citizens of their rights—economic, civic or political—has the same basic motivation as actuates the Fascist mind when it seeks to dominate whole peoples and nations. It is essential that we eliminate it at home as well as abroad."

Willkie had dreams of winning the Republican presidential nomination in 1944, but the party regulars thwarted his efforts. They didn't even invite him to the convention in Chicago, even though he had won more votes in 1940 than any previous Republican candidate in history. Willkie's influence was felt in Chicago all the same: the GOP adopted an internationalist platform that called for "responsible participation by the United States in a postwar cooperative organization among sovereign nations to prevent military aggression and to attain permanent peace."

In late September 1944, Willkie told an acquaintance, "If I could write my own epitaph and if I had to choose between saying, 'Here lies an unimportant President,' or 'Here lies one who contributed to saving freedom at a moment of great peril,' I would prefer the latter." A few days later, Willkie, whose appetites for smoking, drinking, and eating were as prodigal as his idealism, died of a heart attack. He was fifty-two.

According to The New York Times, Willkie's death plunged the country "into deep mourning." In an editorial, the Times declared: "His party and his country owe this man a debt which the years will not discharge. . . . Sorrow that his work is done will be felt wherever people cherish freedom. We salute a great American." Roosevelt lauded Willkie for his "tremendous courage—his dominating trait." Echoing that view, a young black leader named Channing Tobias declared: "As a Negro, I grieve the loss of the most courageously outspoken champion of the rights of my people since Lincoln." According to Harry Bridges, the leftist head of the West Coast longshoremen's union, "Wendell Willkie was the only man in America who has proved that he would rather be right than president."

WHILE WILLKIE HAD STAYED clear of government employment, carving out, as always, a path of his own, many of his interventionist colleagues did join the administration. The Century Group's Elmer Davis became head of the Office of War Information, the propaganda arm of America's war effort. Robert Sherwood was named director of the OWI's overseas branch, where he helped create the Voice of America, a U.S. government radio network that to this day broadcasts international news to countries around the world. Herbert Agar, meanwhile, joined the staff of U.S. ambassador John Gilbert Winant in London, then moved on to head the OWI's London office. Agar divorced his wife to marry an Englishwoman and remained in Britain for the rest of his life.

In 1941, Henry Luce, who forswore government service to remain firmly in charge of his magazine empire, designated the twentieth century as the "American Century," in which the United States would finally fulfill its destiny as leader of the world. His was a sentiment that combined internationalism with ardent nationalism and even imperialism that would increasingly resonate with ordinary Americans, as well as those fashioning U.S. foreign policy.

The architects of America's overarching role in the postwar world would include the Century Group's Dean Acheson and advisers to Henry Stimson and Frank Knox before and during the war—John McCloy, Robert Lovett, James Forrestal, and Robert Patterson. These "Wise Men," as they came to be known, were determined to create a Pax Americana, a vision of their country's future that, in the words of their biographers Walter Isaacson and Even Thomas, demanded "the reshaping of America's traditional role . . . and a restructuring of the global balance of power." It was a reshaping that would lead to the Vietnam and Iraq wars, among other future conflicts.

WHILE THEIR PREWAR FOES worked to extend America's influence after World War II, the country's most prominent isolationists were engaged in a far different struggle. They were fighting to rebuild their reputations, an effort that many would lose. As Geoffrey Perret has noted of the isolationists, "Collectively, they would generally be regarded for years to come as stupid, vicious, pro-Nazi reactionaries, or at least as people blind to the realities of a new day and a menace to their country's safety."

In 1944, Senators Gerald Nye and Bennett Champ Clark, along with FDR nemesis Rep. Hamilton Fish, lost their bids for reelection. Two years later, Senator Burton Wheeler was also defeated. Senator Robert Taft would make two more attempts to capture the Republican presidential nomination; his failure was attributed in large part to his isolationism.

Yet some prewar isolationists, such as the advertising genius Chester Bowles, did manage to put their pasts behind them. Despite his active participation in America First, Bowles, a liberal Democrat, became, in short order, wartime head of the Office of Price Administration, governor of Connecticut, a member of the House of Representatives, U.S. ambassador to India and Nepal, and finally undersecretary of state in the Kennedy administration. Where America First was concerned, Bowles seemed to have suffered a kind of amnesia. He did not mention his membership in his memoirs, nor was it brought up during his confirmation hearings. None of the many letters he exchanged with Robert Wood, Robert Stuart, and other America First leaders are in his papers at Yale.

In his autobiography, Gerald Ford, while acknowledging a flirtation with isolationism at Yale, also failed to note his involvement with America First; it never became an issue in his subsequent political career. Likewise, Kingman Brewster didn't suffer any long-term consequences from his role as a founder of America First—a role that went unmentioned in his 1988 New York Times obituary.

Sargent Shriver was one of the few people associated with America First who had no qualms about publicly discussing his prewar isolationism. "Yes, I did belong to America First," he replied to a letter writer demanding to know the extent of his involvement. "I joined it because I believed at the time we could better help to secure a just settlement of the war in Europe by staying out of it. History proved that my judgment was wrong, neither for the first time nor the last. None of the people I knew in the organization expressed any views within my hearing that were either pro-German or anti-Semitic. I can see how people with such views might have supported America First, just as people with pro-Russian or Communist views might have supported an interventionist organization at that time." Later, Shriver would tell a journalist: "I wanted to spare American lives. If that's an ignoble motive, then I'm perfectly willing to be convicted."

Robert Stuart, who after the war rose through the ranks of the Quaker Oats Company to become chief executive officer and chairman of the board, was once asked if he had ever organized a reunion of those participating in America First. "No," he replied. "We may be a little sensitive to the fact that the world still thinks we're the bad guys."

LESS THAN A MONTH before the end of the war in Europe, Franklin D. Roosevelt died of a cerebral hemorrhage in Warm Springs, Georgia. The president's death, Lindbergh biographer A. Scott Berg noted, "did not affect Washington's official attitude toward Lindbergh overnight. It took a week."

In late April 1945, Charles Lindbergh officially emerged from political purdah. Summoned to Washington, he was asked to join a Navy-sponsored mission to Europe to study German developments in high-speed aircraft. With Roosevelt's passing, he observed, "the vindictiveness in Washington practically disappeared as far as I was concerned." He would later tell an interviewer that it was like the sun finally emerging from behind the clouds.

Throughout the late 1940s and into the 1950s, Lindbergh served as a special adviser to the U.S. Air Force (as the U.S. Army Air Forces was rechristened in 1947) and the Joint Chiefs of Staff, working on a multitude of projects, several of them focusing on rocketry, missiles, and the space program. As a consultant and director of Pan American Airways, he also made frequent business trips to Europe, Asia, and South America.

In 1954, President Dwight D. Eisenhower reinstated Lindbergh in the Air Force Reserve, with the rank of brigadier general. Eisenhower's successor as president, John F. Kennedy, was another Lindbergh admirer. Like Kingman Brewster and Robert Stuart, Kennedy had idolized the flier since childhood; an isolationist himself in college, he also had admired Lindbergh's antiwar stand. In addition, he and Lindbergh shared a high literary distinction. They both had been awarded the Pulitzer Prize for biography—Lindbergh in 1954 for *Spirit of St. Louis,* an autobiographical account of his flight to Paris, and Kennedy in 1957 for *Profiles in Courage.*

So it was not surprising that when Jacqueline Kennedy began planning one of the most glittering state dinners ever staged at the White House—a dinner in honor of French cultural minister André Malraux in April 1962—her husband insisted that Charles and Anne Lindbergh be the first ones invited. Lindbergh was the guest whom "President Kennedy was most anxious to have attend the dinner," his wife later said, "because of his lifelong admiration for him and for Mrs. Lindbergh." Knowing that the reclusive Lindberghs were loath to attend public functions, the Kennedys invited them to spend the night at the White House so that they would not be bothered by journalists. In a thank-you note to Kennedy after the event, Lindbergh wrote: "We left with a deep feeling of gratitude and—even more—encouragement."

Yet for all the honors and feting of Lindbergh, he never was entirely able to put his problematic prewar past behind him. He told friends, for example, that he felt "very constrained" whenever he visited Britain. "Even after all these years," said one Englishman who had met him, "he fears someone will attack him . . . over his behavior toward England in World War II."

Unquestionably, Lindbergh himself was responsible for much of the controversy that arose in the postwar years over his isolationism. To the end of his life, he never admitted he was wrong about anything he had said or done. Unlike Anne, who acknowledged that "we were both very blind, especially in the beginning, to the worst evils of the Nazi system," he uttered no word of remorse or apology for his uncritical attitude toward the horrors of Hitler's regime. When his wartime journals were published in 1970, Lindbergh defiantly equated the Nazis' wholesale murder of Jews with other war crimes, including the brutality of some American troops toward Japanese prisoners of war. He still insisted that the United States had made a mistake in entering the war.

"Like many civilized people in this country and abroad, he could not comprehend the radical evil of Nazism," *The New York Times* wrote about Lindbergh and his journals. "Even in the retrospect of a quarter-century, he is unable to grasp it. . . . [T]here is simply no comparison between individual misdeeds of American soldiers toward dead or captured Japanese and the coldly planned, systematically executed

German government policy of murdering or enslaving Jews, Slavs, and other 'inferior' people. . . . The world is admittedly not what Americans—or anyone else—would like, but it is decidedly better than it would have been if the United States had not helped to defeat German and Japanese militarism. . . . If any war can be said to be worth fighting and winning, it was World War II."

Yet although Lindbergh shared the views of anti-Communist conservatives that "in order to defeat Germany and Japan, we supported the still greater menaces of Russia and China," he never became involved in Senator Joseph McCarthy's crusade against Communists in government, as did Burton Wheeler, Robert Wood, Albert Wedemeyer, and Truman Smith. All of them, with the exception of Lindbergh, were also prominent in other right-wing causes in the 1950s and 1960s; Wedemeyer, for example, served as an adviser to the editors of a magazine published by the John Birch Society. In contrast, at the height of McCarthyism in 1952, Lindbergh, stubbornly independent and unpredictable as usual, voted for a liberal Democrat, Adlai Stevenson, for president.

As Lindbergh aged, he shed many of his previous interests, including his focus on modern technology, especially as it related to aviation. In 1928, when he had first begun courting Anne, he told her that his most cherished dream was to "break up the prejudices between nations by linking them up through aviation." In later years, even though aircraft had indeed brought the peoples of the world closer together in a technical sense, "they have more than counteracted this accomplishment through their ruthless bombardments in war," he would write. Both militarily and ecologically, he added, "I have seen the science I worshiped and the aircraft I loved destroying the civilization I expected them to serve."

In the last decade of his life, he committed himself to the cause of halting man's despoliation of nature, throwing himself into campaigns to save whales, water buffalo, eagles, and other endangered species. "If I had to choose," he said shortly before he died, "I'd rather have birds than airplanes."

WHEN LINDBERGH CAME BACK from his wartime adventures in the Pacific, he, like many returning servicemen, found his wife very much changed. Forced to cope on her own during the long separations of the previous three years, Anne Lindbergh had become stronger and considerably more self-reliant.

In Detroit, she had managed to carve out, for the first time in years, a satisfying life for herself. She took painting and sculpting lessons at the Cranbrook Academy of Art, an artists' colony just outside the city, and became close to many of its members, among them the Finnish architect Eero Saarinen and the Swedish sculptor Carl Milles. Virtually all her new friends, she noted, were Europeans, with whom she identified, emotionally and intellectually, far more than she did with most Americans.

Finally emerging from Lindbergh's shadow, Anne had found a community of her own, one to which she could "give my true self," she observed in her diary, "as I have never done to a group of people before. . . . Certainly not in my marriage, because the groups we have entered have never been *my* people. In political groups, aviation groups, quite naturally everyone looked to C. But here I am perpetually my own self—and they like me!"

Less than a year before the end of the war, the Lindberghs moved back east, to a rented house in Westport, Connecticut, where they began to lead increasingly divergent lives. Occupied with her five children (Reeve, the youngest, was born in October 1945), Anne no longer took part in Lindbergh's nomadic wanderings. Just as in Detroit, she built her own circle of friends—"artists, writers, dancers, sometimes psychologists or teachers," Reeve remembered, "but not so often businesspeople or aviators."

Lindbergh, for his part, traveled incessantly. While on the road, he rarely communicated with his family, often not letting them know where he was or when he would return. "He liked to be mysterious," one of his children recalled. In a letter to a friend after the war, Anne wrote: "Charles only touches base now and then. He is, I think, on his fourth or fifth trip around the world this year." He frequently missed Christmas and other family celebrations; after one holiday season, Anne wrote to him that on New Year's Day, she and the children "played a game [in which] we all guessed where you were."

When he did return home, he brought a sense of excitement and energy but also, his mother-in-law observed, a "terrible" tension. In her diary, Elizabeth Morrow noted, "He must control everything, every act in the house." A loving but demanding father, Lindbergh spent considerable time with his children, playing with them but also lecturing and disciplining them. Annoyed by Anne's blossoming independence, he found fault with her as well. When the time came for him to leave again on his travels, Reeve Lindbergh wrote, there was "a sense of release, an exhalation of long-held family breath, and a noticeable relaxation in discipline."

Struggling with the disappointments and conflicts of her marriage, Anne began seeing a psychotherapist. She also became close to her New York internist, who encouraged her to talk about the depression, anger, and grief she had bottled up for so many years. During this period of self-examination, she spent considerable time mulling over the battle she had waged most of her life—how to maintain her own identity while fulfilling her duties as a daughter, wife, and mother.

In the late 1940s, Anne had begun taking an annual sabbatical from family duties, renting a rustic cottage on Captiva Island, off the west Florida coast, where she strolled the beaches for hours searching for shells. In the course of her wanderings, the outlines of a book took shape in her mind. She had stayed away from book writing since her traumatic wartime experiences with *The Wave of the Future* and *The Steep Ascent*. "I was very upset," she later acknowledged. "So upset that I did not want to go on writing. I can understand why [*The Wave of the Future*] was misinterpreted. . . . But my reaction was that if I expressed myself so poorly, I should not continue writing."

But the book she now had in mind had nothing to do with the war or isolationism. It would focus on the issues facing her and the many other women like her who, in the midst of juggling their various roles, were trying to figure out "how to remain whole in the midst of the distractions of life; how to remain balanced, no matter what centrifugal forces tend to pull one off center; how to remain strong."

A series of lyrical meditations about youth, age, love, marriage, friendship, and the need to take care of oneself, *Gift from the Sea* was published in 1955 and quickly became one of the biggest successes in U.S. publishing history. It was on the *New York Times* bestseller list for two years, the first year as No. 1. It sold more than five million copies in its first twenty years in print; today, more than fifty years after it was first published, it is still selling well.

In *Gift from the Sea*, Anne argued that women must periodically take time away from their myriad responsibilities—"the circus act we women perform every day of our lives"—to seek solitude in order to recharge their creative energies and nourish themselves spiritually. "If it is woman's function to give, she must be replenished too."

Emphasizing the importance of women developing mutually nurturing relationships with others, she provided an example of one such relationship in her own life—not with her husband, but with her sister Con. During one stay in Florida, Anne noted in her book, her sister came to stay with her for a week. In describing the way she and Con undertook daily household chores together, Anne underscored the strength and comfort of their bond: "We work easily and instinctively together, not bumping into each other as we go back and forth about our task. We talk as we sweep, as we dry, as we put away, discussing a person or a poem or a memory. . . . We have moved through our day like dancers, not needing to touch more than lightly because we were instinctively moving to the same rhythm."

The extraordinary success of her book, however, did not seem to bring Anne much enjoyment or satisfaction. She felt uncomfortable in the spotlight that once again shone on her; fame, she wrote in her diary, "makes it very cumbersome to live one's life." What bothered her most, though, was the feeling that she had "outgrown" the sentiments she had expressed in the book. While *Gift from the Sea* aided countless women in reevaluating their needs, desires, and relationships, its author had considerable trouble following her own advice. One day in the summer of 1956, after Charles abruptly announced he was leaving again on another lengthy trip, Anne observed in her diary that she was feeling "rather sad [and] let down." Then came this ironic observation: "How it would startle all the readers of my *Gift from the Sea*! What? Not like to be alone?!"

A year and a half later, she wrote to her husband from a New York hospital, where she was recovering from knee surgery: "Where are you? I have been expecting you every day for the past two weeks. I know I made light of the operation, but I did hope you'd get here in time to take me home."

With her marriage becoming increasingly problematic, Anne noted the "agonies of mind & emotions" and the "banked bitterness" she felt toward Charles for his long and frequent absences and his "un-understanding and hostility" toward her when he was at home. As A.

Scott Berg put it, "the Lindbergh marriage had become a one-sided affair, at Charles's disposal whenever he chose to partake. When together, he expected [Anne's] attention to be focused on him."

On the twentieth anniversary of their marriage, she poured out her feelings in a diary essay she called "Marriage Vows Annotated After Twenty Years." Before she wed Lindbergh, the starstruck Anne had described him as "the last of the gods" and "a knight in shining armor." Her amended vows made clear that she had long since given up on that romantic, fairy-tale image. The essay included these statements: "Since I know you are not perfect, I do not worship you . . . I do not promise to obey you . . . I do not look on marriage as a solution to any of my problems."

In her anger and frustration, she turned to her internist and adviser, Dr. Dana Atchley, for solace. "Dana pulled me through . . . kept me alive," she noted. The close relationship between doctor and patient blossomed into an intense affair. In 1956, Anne rented a small apartment in New York to which she could retreat to write, see friends, and spend time with Atchley. At one point, she considered the possibility of a divorce, but in the end she decided against it. As "badly mated" as she and Charles were and as "abandoned and put upon" as she felt, she couldn't bring herself to break the ties that bound them.

Lindbergh apparently never knew about Anne's involvement with Atchley; as it happened, he, too, had developed private interests during his incessant travels. His footloose postwar existence, away from family responsibilities, seemed to have infused him with a new vigor. Anne's psychotherapist told her he believed that Lindbergh, now in his mid-fifties, "was running away from old age."

While probably correct, that premise was just one piece of a very complicated reality. From 1957 until his death in 1974, Lindbergh led a secret life that was breathtaking in its audacity. In those seventeen years, he fathered no fewer than seven children by three different women, all of them German, and made frequent visits to his children and mistresses at the homes he provided for them in Germany and Switzerland.

His first inamorata was Brigitte Hesshaimer, a hatmaker he met in Munich in 1957. He later took up with Brigitte's sister Marietta, who, like Brigitte, was more than twenty years younger than Lindbergh. His third relationship was with Valeska, a German secretary whose last name was never revealed and who helped him with his business affairs in Germany. Lindbergh's European children—three by Brigitte, two by Marietta, and two by Valeska—were born between 1958 and 1967.

His clandestine existence did not come to light until 2003, almost thirty years after his death and two years after Anne's. The news came as a total shock to his family and acquaintances, although a close friend of Anne's told Reeve that her mother apparently had had an inkling that something was amiss. "She knew," the friend said, "but she didn't know *what* she knew."

Lindbergh took great care to ensure that his covert life remained just that during his lifetime. His mistresses told their children that their father was a famous American writer named Careu Kent who was on a secret mission and that they must never talk about him to anyone. When the women wrote to Lindbergh, their letters were sent to post office boxes, which he changed regularly.

Brigitte's children, who discovered their father's true identity and made it public after their mother's death, were the only German offspring of Lindbergh's to speak openly about his visits to them and their mother, which occurred about four times a year. He made them pancakes, they recalled, and took them to the park. "We were always very happy when he came," one son said. "He really gave us the feeling he was there for us."

Hit with yet another bombshell about their father's past, Reeve Lindbergh and her siblings struggled to make sense of the incomprehensible. How could Lindbergh—"the stern arbiter of moral and ethical conduct in our family," Reeve noted—have, for decades, violated virtually every standard he had demanded they follow?

One possible explanation lay in Lindbergh's oft-expressed desire for at least a dozen children, perhaps to make up for his own loneliness and solitude as an only child. Anne was forty when she gave birth to Reeve, their sixth child, and would have no more. The seven additional children Charles sired with his mistresses fulfilled his wish for a brood of twelve. (The slain Charles Jr. would have made thirteen.)

Still a believer in the pseudoscience of eugenics, which advocated selective breeding to ensure the dominance of Northern and Western "European blood," Lindbergh apparently was also interested in further perpetuating his own Northern European gene pool. (Reeve Lindbergh recalled how her father used to lecture his children about the importance of choosing mates with good genes.) If he was inclined to have children out of wedlock, as he obviously was, what better mates could there be, from his Nordic point of view, than Germans, the ultimate Aryans? Yet there was one major problem with that hypothesis: both Brigitte and her sister suffered from tuberculosis of the spine, making them less than perfect physical specimens.

In making families with these three other women, Lindbergh may also have been tempted by the opportunity to create a parallel universe of a life, where he could shed his identity as one of the most famous people on the planet and come and go as he liked, staying just a few days at a time with each, with no lasting commitments. Reeve Lindbergh offered another take on the situation: "One of my first thoughts was that this arrangement made a certain kind of sense. No one woman could possibly have lived with him all the time."

At first, Reeve was consumed with rage over Lindbergh's duplicity and hypocrisy. Shortly after learning about her half-siblings, she wrote in her journal: "These children did not even know who he was! He used a pseudonym with them. (To protect them, perhaps? To protect himself, absolutely!)" But in the ensuing years, during which she visited all seven of her newfound brothers and sisters, she made a sort of peace with her impenetrable father, whom she realized she had never really known. "Being in my family is like a melodrama sometimes," she noted, "with a story line that is simultaneously powerfully compelling and utterly baffling."

Reeve once had a dream in which she told Lindbergh that all of his children—in Europe and America—had been hurt by what he had done. In the dream, her father made no response to her complaint. "He just didn't get it," she observed. "At that moment, I thought I knew the truth about my father. . . . With all his gifts and his abilities, he had come into the world without one very specific piece of listening equipment, and whatever it was, it was critical to a complete understanding of the sufferings of other people."

In learning more about Lindbergh's secret life, Reeve was struck by the fact that "every intimate human connection my father had during his later years was fractured by secrecy. He could not be completely open with anybody who loved him anywhere on earth. . . . [W]hat remains with me is a sense of his unutterable loneliness."

There was one place, however, where Lindbergh could escape from that loneliness, where he could forget, for at least a few moments, the complications and demands of his strange, conflicted life. A place where he could turn back the clock and experience again the adventure—the sheer, simple joy—of his youth, skimming low over waves, touching a cloud, climbing high above a mountain.

Several times a year until he died, Lindbergh traveled to Washington to visit the Smithsonian Arts and Industries Building. With his lined face and white, thinning hair, he was no longer recognizable to most tourists. Yet he always took the same precaution, inconspicuously stationing himself behind a showcase. From there, he gazed up at the *Spirit of St. Louis,* riding high in the air above him.

ACKNOWLEDGMENTS

In all my books, I've worked hard to bring to life the people and historical periods I write about. Obviously, to do that, an author has to find good resource material, and in researching *Those Angry Days,* I was fortunate enough to turn up a real wealth of information. Contemporary newspaper and magazine accounts were invaluable in yielding colorful, revealing details about the country's mood in the two tumultuous years before America's entry into World War II. Even more important was the information, often surprising and provocative, gleaned from the letters, journals, diaries, and other personal papers of the book's major and minor characters.

My deep appreciation goes to the librarians and archivists who were so helpful to me in my search. They are the true preservers of history, and their enthusiastic, selfless work is nothing short of heroic. Chief among them are Bob Clark, the head archivist at the Franklin D. Roosevelt Library, and his staff, who are simply the best at what they do. I also owe a great debt of gratitude to the staff of the Library of Congress Manuscript Division, as well as to the archivists at the Hoover Institution, Harvard's Houghton and Baker Libraries, and Smith College's Sophia Smith Collection. Special thanks, too, to Dr. Edward Scott and Dr. Mary Elizabeth Ruwell for granting me access to the Air Force Academy archives, and to Dr. Russell Flinchum, archivist at the Century Association Archives Foundation, for his generous sharing of materials about the Century Group.

A word of thanks as well to the writers and scholars whose ground-breaking work assisted me immeasurably in writing this book. I'd like to single out A. Scott Berg, whose magisterial biography of Charles Lindbergh is an essential resource for anyone writing about Lindbergh; Dr. J. Garry Clifford, for his impressive scholarship on Grenville Clark and the peacetime draft; Dr. Wayne S. Cole, unquestionably the premier authority on America's prewar isolationist movement; and Richard Ketchum, whose history/memoir of the years 1938–1941 was an invaluable font of information.

Thanks, too, to Elizabeth M. Pendleton, Rachel Cox, Fisher Howe, Margaret Shannon, Dr. Raymond Callahan, and Roger Cirillo.

I am also grateful to everyone at Random House, particularly my superb editor, Susanna Porter, for their unflagging support and guidance and for creating such a welcoming, collegial environment for authors. Gail Ross, my agent for almost twenty years, has been outstanding as always in her advice, representation, and friendship.

Above all, my deep love and thanks to Carly, my daughter and nonpareil adviser on social media, and to my husband, Stan Cloud, whose editing of *Those Angry Days* helped make it a better book and whose partnership with me, both professional and personal, has been the greatest joy of my life.

NOTES

INTRODUCTION

xiv "*mano a mano*": Gore Vidal, *The Last Empire: Essays 1992–2000* (New York: Doubleday, 2001), p. 138.

"a loveless quality": Geoffrey C. Ward, *A First-Class Temperament: The Emergence of Franklin Roosevelt* (New York: Harper & Row, 1989), p. 315.

"The people he called": Walter S. Ross, *The Last Hero: Charles A. Lindbergh* (Harper & Row, 1976), p. 212.

xv "untold humiliation": Thomas M. Coffey, *Hap: The Story of the U.S. Air Force and the Man Who Built It* (New York: Viking, 1982), p. 157.

"the fight dented": Arthur M. Schlesinger Jr., *The Coming of the New Deal, 1933–1935* (Boston: Houghton Mifflin, 2003), p. 455.

"Roosevelt judges": Charles A. Lindbergh, *The Wartime Journals of Charles A. Lindbergh* (New York: Harcourt Brace Jovanovich, 1970), p. 187.

xvii "The war was": Arthur M. Schlesinger Jr., *A Life in the Twentieth Century: Innocent Beginnings, 1917–1950* (New York: Houghton Mifflin, 2000), p. 249.

xviii "bitter": Eric Sevareid, *Not So Wild a Dream* (New York: Atheneum, 1976), p. 195.

"the most savage": Arthur M. Schlesinger Jr. interview, "Lindbergh," *American Experience*, PBS.

"The intense feelings": Anne Morrow Lindbergh, *War Within and Without: Diaries and Letters of Anne Morrow Lindbergh, 1939–1944* (New York: Harcourt Brace, 1980), p. xvii.

"Though historians": Schlesinger, *A Life in the Twentieth Century*, p. 241.

"People have forgotten": George Marshall interview with Forrest Pogue, George C. Marshall Foundation, Lexington, Va., www.marshallfoundation.org/library/pogue.html.

xix "to take open": Ibid.

xix **"a dirty fight"**: Adolf Berle diary, Sept. 22, 1939, Berle papers, FDRPL.

xx **"doesn't exist"**: Roger Butterfield, "Lindbergh," *Life,* Aug. 11, 1941.

"recoiled from the prospect": William S. Langer and S. Everett Gleason, *The Challenge to Isolation: 1937–1940* (New York: Harper, 1952), p. 203.

"I hadn't thought": Forrest C. Pogue, *George C. Marshall: Ordeal and Hope, 1939–1942* (New York: Viking, 1966), p. 23.

xxi **"move gingerly"**: Herbert Agar, *The Darkest Year: Britain Alone, June 1940–June 1941* (Garden City, N.Y.: Doubleday, 1973), p. 56.

"godsend": Robert Sherwood, *Roosevelt and Hopkins: An Intimate History* (New York: Harper, 1948), p. 355.

xxii **"defeating Nazism"**: Nicholas John Cull, *Selling War: The British Propaganda Campaign Against American "Neutrality" in World War II* (New York: Oxford University Press, 1995), p. 185.

CHAPTER 1: "A MODERN GALAHAD"

4 **"like a god"**: Charles Lindbergh, *Wartime Journals,* p. 222.

"I rather envied": Ibid., p. 319.

"Fame—Opportunity": A. Scott Berg, *Lindbergh* (New York: Berkley Books, 1999), p. 5.

"Sometimes . . . I wonder": Reeve Lindbergh, "The Flyer—Charles Lindbergh," *Time,* June 14, 1999.

5 **"the greatest feat"**: Frederick Lewis Allen, *Only Yesterday: An Informal History of the 1920's* (New York: Perennial, 2000), p. 189.

6 **"a modern Galahad"**: Ibid., p. 191.

7 **"The underwriters"**: Kenneth S. Davis, *The Hero: Charles A. Lindbergh and the American Dream* (Garden City, N.Y.: Doubleday, 1959), p. 192.

"No attempt at jokes": Berg, *Lindbergh,* p. 121.

"We measure heroes": Ibid., p. 159.

"demigod": Ibid., p. 170.

8 **"In his flight"**: Davis, *The Hero,* p. 244.

"Like criminals": Anne Morrow Lindbergh, *Hour of Gold, Hour of Lead: Diaries and Letters of Anne Morrow Lindbergh, 1929–1932* (New York: Harcourt Brace Jovanovich, 1973), p. 5.

9 **"into waters"**: Frederic Sondern Jr., "Lindbergh Walks Alone," *Life,* April 3, 1939.

10 **"Because he kept"**: "Press v. Lindbergh," *Time,* June 19, 1939.

"since the Resurrection": Berg, *Lindbergh,* p. 308.

"If it were not": Anne Lindbergh, *Hour of Gold,* p. 249.

"a personification": "Press v. Lindbergh," *Time,* June 19, 1939.

11 **"Between the . . . tabloid"**: Berg, *Lindbergh,* p. 340.

"we Americans": Roger Butterfield, "Lindbergh," *Life,* Aug. 11, 1941.

"I can imagine": Reeve Lindbergh, *Under a Wing: A Memoir* (New York: Simon & Schuster, 1998), p. 79.

"You should have": Leonard Mosley, *Lindbergh* (New York: Dell, 1977), p. 184.

"the man who": *New York Times,* Dec. 23, 1935.

12 **"a wonderful feeling"**: Anne Morrow Lindbergh, *The Flower and the Nettle:*

Diaries and Letters of Anne Morrow Lindbergh, 1936–1939 (New York: Harcourt Brace Jovanovich, 1976), p. 17.

12 **"I have never"**: Charles Lindbergh, *Wartime Journals,* p. 10.

13 **"It would be murder"**: Lynne Olson, *Troublesome Young Men: The Rebels Who Brought Churchill to Power and Helped Save England* (New York: Farrar, Straus & Giroux, 2007), p. 127.
"the grossest act": Ibid., p. 139.

14 **"had never adjusted"**: Wayne S. Cole, *Charles A. Lindbergh and the Battle Against American Intervention in World War II* (New York: Harcourt Brace Jovanovich, 1974), p. 28.
"I cannot see": Charles Lindbergh, *Wartime Journals,* p. 11.
"Aviation has largely": Ibid., p. 147.
"The whole idea": Ibid., p. 9.
"It is necessary": Ibid., p. 22.
"The British have always": Lynne Olson and Stanley Cloud, *A Question of Honor: The Kosciuszko Squadron: Forgotten Heroes of World War II* (New York: Knopf, 2003), p. 92.

15 **"fanatical"**: Truman Smith, *Berlin Alert: The Memoirs of Truman Smith* (Stanford: Hoover Institution Press, 1984), p. 60.
"already a potential": Ibid., p. 68.

16 **"the strictest censorship"**: Ibid., p. 89.
"There is no doubt": Anne Lindbergh, *Flower and the Nettle,* p. xxi.

17 **"Germany now has"**: Truman Smith, *Berlin Alert,* pp. 154–55.
"operate meaningfully": Berg, *Lindbergh,* p. 375.
"the bomber will": Olson, *Troublesome Young Men,* p. 64.
"French cities": Cole, *Lindbergh,* p. 53.

18 **"The Fuhrer has found"**: Ibid.
"extremely likable": Davis, *Hero,* pp. 378–79.
"All his life": Sir John Wheeler-Bennett, *Special Relationships: America in Peace and War* (London: Macmillan, 1975), p. 131.
"I cannot help": Charles Lindbergh, *Wartime Journals,* p. 5.
"refusal to admit": Cole, *Lindbergh,* p. 29.
"a sense of festivity": Anne Lindbergh, *Flower and the Nettle,* p. 83.
"For twelve years": Charles Lindbergh, *Wartime Journals,* p. 166.

19 **"the ice-cold evil"**: Ronald Steel, *Walter Lippmann and the American Century* (New York: Vintage, 1981), p. 331.
"I shared the repulsion": Berg, *Lindbergh,* p. 382.
"undoubtedly a great man": Ibid., p. 361.
"hypersensitive man": Lloyd Shearer, *Parade,* March 13, 1977.
"I do not understand": Charles Lindbergh, *Wartime Journals,* p. 115.

20 **"Perhaps it is because"**: Dorothy Herrmann, *Anne Morrow Lindbergh: A Gift for Life* (New York: Ticknor & Fields, 1993), p. 236.
"If England and Germany": Charles Lindbergh, *Wartime Journals,* p. 136.
"has, if any man": "The Talk of the Town," *New Yorker,* Nov. 26, 1938.
"flabbergasted": Murray Green interview with Gen. Arthur W. Vanaman, Green papers, AFA.
"the albatross": Truman Smith, *Berlin Alert,* p. 134.
"A hurricane": Cooper C. Graham, " 'Olympia' in America, 1938: Leni Rief-

enstahl, Hollywood and the Kristallnacht," *Historical Journal of Film, Radio and Television,* 1993.

21   **"We know Charles":** Berg, *Lindbergh,* p. 380.

   "His refusal": Roger Butterfield, "Lindbergh," *Life,* Aug. 11, 1941.

   "the fuss about it": Truman Smith, *Berlin Alert,* p. 134.

   "I cannot be tolerant": Robert Sherwood interview with Harold Ickes, Sherwood papers, HL.

   "a world without": T. H. Watkins, *Righteous Pilgrim: The Life and Times of Harold L. Ickes, 1874–1952* (New York: Henry Holt, 1990), p. 163.

   "a common scold": *Life,* Sept. 2, 1940.

22   **"Washington's tough guy":** Watkins, *Righteous Pilgrim,* p. 337.

   "fundamentally": Adolf Berle diary, Sept. 11, 1940, Berle papers, FDRPL.

   "a decoration": *New York Times,* Dec. 19, 1938.

   "the first man": Harold Ickes to John Wheeler, May 9, 1941, Ickes papers, LC.

   "convenient channel": Berg, *Lindbergh,* p. 380.

   "his immobile": Anne Morrow Lindbergh, *Bring Me a Unicorn: Diaries and Letters of Anne Morrow Lindbergh, 1922–1928* (New York: Harcourt Brace Jovanovich, 1971), p. 216.

   "Their scorn": Anne Lindbergh, *Flower and the Nettle,* p. 470.

23   **"I felt I could":** Berg, *Lindbergh,* p. 383.

CHAPTER 2: "WE WERE FOOLS"

24   **"There must have been":** Charles Lindbergh, *Wartime Journals,* pp. 182–83.

   "walking on eggshells": Murray Green interview with Gen. Arthur A. Vanaman, Green papers, AFA.

25   **"seemed to seek":** Coffey, *Hap,* p. 10.

   "as a great personal": Richard M. Ketchum, *The Borrowed Years, 1938–1941: America on the Way to War* (New York: Random House, 1989), p. 103.

26   **"practically nonexistent":** Henry H. Arnold, *Global Mission* (New York: Harper, 1949), p. 165.

   "we damned airmen": Ibid., p. 151.

   "for the first time": Ketchum, *Borrowed Years,* pp. 86–87.

   "would cost less": John Lamberton Harper, *American Visions of Europe: Franklin D. Roosevelt, George F. Kennan and Dean Acheson* (Cambridge: Cambridge University Press, 1994), p. 68.

27   **"tremendous":** Berg, *Lindbergh,* p. 388.

28   **"Americans, having once":** Langer and Gleason, *Challenge to Isolation,* p. 14.

   "Of the hell broth": Lynne Olson, *Citizens of London: The Americans Who Stood with Britain in Its Darkest, Finest Hour* (New York: Random House, 2010), p. 67.

   "the smallest": Ketchum, *Borrowed Years,* p. 540.

29   **"repel raids":** Olson, *Citizens of London,* p. 19.

   "Although Roosevelt": Milton Goldin, " 'The Jewish Threat:' Anti-Semitic Politics of the U.S. Army," *H-Antisemitism,* February 2001.

   "gross injustice": Alfred M. Beck, *Hitler's Ambivalent Attaché: Friedrich von Boetticher in America, 1933–1941* (Washington, D.C.: Potomac Books, 2005), p. 66.

30 **"an incubator"**: Pogue, *Ordeal and Hope,* pp. 120–21.
    "would mean": Joseph Bendersky, *The "Jewish Threat": The Anti-Semitic Politics of the U.S. Army* (New York: Basic Books, 2000), p. 275.
31 **"there was not"**: Beck, *Hitler's Ambivalent Attaché,* p. 132.
32 **"We shun political"**: Philip Goodhart, *Fifty Ships That Saved the World: The Foundation of the Anglo-American Alliance* (Garden City, N.Y.: Doubleday, 1965), p. 15.
33 **"its almost pathological"**: Ketchum, *Borrowed Years,* p. 128.
    "armed banditry": James MacGregor Burns, *Roosevelt: The Lion and the Fox* (New York: Harcourt, Brace & World, 1956), p. 352.
    "It is always best": Ibid., p. 354.
    "He hoped": Ibid., p. 262.
34 **"anxious to do"**: Wayne S. Cole, *Roosevelt and the Isolationists, 1932–1945* (Lincoln: University of Nebraska Press, 1983), p. 311.
    "repeal or emasculate": Kenneth S. Davis, *FDR: Into the Storm, 1937–1940* (New York: Random House, 1993), p. 415.
    "the situation in Europe": Ibid., pp. 450–51.

CHAPTER 3: "WHERE IS MY WORLD?"

35 **"nothing solid"**: Anne Lindbergh, *War Within and Without,* p. 4.
    "the sense of": Ibid.
    "very near": Anne Lindbergh, *Flower and the Nettle,* p. 47.
36 **"a half-mad"**: Anne Lindbergh, *Hour of Gold,* p. 311.
    "a long period": Anne Lindbergh, *Flower and the Nettle,* p. 462.
    "I see no place": Anne Lindbergh, *War Within and Without,* p. 38.
    "the sleeping princesses": Anne Lindbergh, *Bring Me a Unicorn,* p. xviii.
    "haze of insulation": Ibid.
37 **"the belle of the ball"**: Berg, *Lindbergh,* p. 182.
    "the complete loss": Anne Lindbergh, *Bring Me a Unicorn,* p. 114.
    "She carries action": Anne Morrow Lindbergh, *Locked Rooms and Open Doors: Diaries and Letters of Anne Morrow Lindbergh, 1933–1935* (New York: Harcourt Brace Jovanovich, 1974), p. 285.
38 **"The chain"**: Berg, *Lindbergh,* p. 184.
    "a brown-haired": Davis, *Hero,* p. 274.
39 **"this shy, cool"**: Anne Lindbergh, *Bring Me a Unicorn,* p. 82.
    "as though it": Ibid., p. 178.
    "I want to marry": Julie Nixon Eisenhower, *Special People* (New York: Simon & Schuster, 1977), p. 127.
    "Colonel L . . .": Anne Lindbergh, *Bring Me a Unicorn,* p. 135.
    "I discovered": Ibid., p. 194.
40 **"was given confidence"**: Anne Lindbergh, *Hour of Gold,* p. 3.
    "The sheer fact": Ibid.
    "He doesn't seem": Anne Lindbergh, *Bring Me a Unicorn,* p. 219.
    "I have more": Ibid., p. 139.
    "speculative parasites": Berg, *Lindbergh,* p. 35.
    "You like to": Anne Morrow Lindbergh, *Against Wind and Tide: Letters and Journals, 1947–1986* (New York: Pantheon, 2012), p. 85.

40   **"He is terribly"**: Anne Lindbergh, *Bring Me a Unicorn*, p. 219.
"**this amazing**": Ibid., p. 224.
"**if you write**": Ibid., p. 228.

41   **"The worst problem"**: Anne Lindbergh, *Hour of Gold*, p. 59.
"**Oh, it is brutal**": Ibid., p. 106.
"**They seemed to**": Lauren D. Lyman, "The Lindbergh I Knew," *Saturday Evening Post*, April 4, 1953.
"**a knight**": Anne Lindbergh, *Hour of Gold*, p. 4.

42   **"Damn, damn, damn!"**: Anne Lindbergh, *Locked Rooms*, p. 107.
"**gay, lordly**": Anne Lindbergh, *Hour of Gold*, p. 252.
"**a failure**": Berg, *Lindbergh*, p. 330.
"**I feel completely**": Anne Lindbergh, *Locked Rooms*, pp. 240–41.
"**She didn't know**": Anne Morrow Lindbergh, *Dearly Beloved* (New York: Harcourt Brace & World, 1962), p. 33.
"**There were**": Berg, *Lindbergh*, p. 480.
"**the most infuriatingly**": Reeve Lindbergh, *Forward from Here: Leaving Middle Age—and Other Unexpected Adventures* (New York: Simon & Schuster, 2008), p. 204.

43   **"shy and retreating"**: Harold Nicolson, *Diaries and Letters, 1930–1939* (London: Collins, 1969), p. 132.
"**something inside me**": Anne Lindbergh, *Locked Rooms*, p. 210.
"**having been brought**": Anne Lindbergh, *Against Wind and Tide*, p. 188.
"**Who am I**": Anne Lindbergh, *Flower and the Nettle*, p. 44.
"**to go by**": Anne Lindbergh, *Locked Rooms*, p. 331.
"**all my life**": Ibid.

44   **"a small work"**: *New Yorker*, Oct. 15, 1938.
"**is a very great**": Berg, *Lindbergh*, p. 362.
"**The talk I heard**": Anne Lindbergh, *Flower and the Nettle*, p. xxv.
"**converted to**": Ibid., p. 421.
"**their treatment of the Jews**": Ibid., p. 101.
"**This time**": Ibid., p. 554.

45   **"how wrapped up"**: Anne Lindbergh, *War Within and Without*, p. 48.
"**Lindbergh is really**": Nigel Nicolson, ed., *Vita and Harold: The Letters of Vita Sackville-West and Harold Nicolson* (New York: Putman, 1992), p. 255.
"**Charles isn't capable**": Berg, *Lindbergh*, p. 330.

46   **"eternal struggle"**: Anne Lindbergh, *Locked Rooms*, p. 221.

47   **"She rags him"**: Mosley, *Lindbergh*, p. 196.
"**We understand**": Anne Lindbergh, *Locked Rooms*, p. 223.
"**Do you feel**": Anne Lindbergh, *Hour of Gold*, p. 37.
"**yes, it is**": Anne Lindbergh, *Flower and the Nettle*, p. 11.
"**warm, fearless**": Wheeler-Bennett, *Special Relationships*, p. 75.
"**Although many**": Reeve Lindbergh, *Under a Wing*, p. 143.

48   **"How wonderful"**: Anne Lindbergh, *Flower and the Nettle*, p. 154.

49   **"Anglo-American"**: Robert Calder, *Beware the British Serpent: The Role of Writers in British Propaganda in the United States, 1939–1945* (Montreal: Queen's University Press, 2004), p. 24.
"**No colonist**": Burton K. Wheeler, *Yankee from the West* (Garden City, N.Y.: Doubleday, 1962), p. 43.

49   **"America for Americans"**: John E. Moser, "The Decline of American An-
glophobia," Lecture at Université de Rouen, November 2002.
      "the innocent pastoral": Mark Lincoln Chadwin, *The War Hawks: American
Interventionists Before Pearl Harbor* (Chapel Hill: University of North Carolina
Press, 1968), p. 7.

50   **"Paint me a picture"**: Calder, *Beware the British Serpent,* pp. 24–25.
      "God save America": Anthony Cave Brown, *"C": The Secret Life of Sir Stew-
art Graham Menzies* (New York: Macmillan, 1987), p. 328.
      "lose American sympathy": Olson, *Troublesome Young Men,* p. 157.
      "the melodramatic": Sir Robert Bruce Lockhart, *Comes the Reckoning* (Lon-
don: Putnam, 1947), p. 23.

51   **"criticism of the British"**: Ibid.
      BEWARE THE BRITISH: Calder, *Beware the British Serpent,* p. 43.
      "There were times": Ibid., p. 42.

52   **"the spirit of lethargy"**: Wheeler-Bennett, *Special Relationships,* p. 76.
      "a river of intelligence": Cull, *Selling War,* p. 60.

CHAPTER 4: "YOU HAVEN'T GOT THE VOTES"

53   **"impartial in thought"**: Davis, *FDR: Into the Storm,* p. 490.

54   **"This nation"**: Ketchum, *Borrowed Years,* p. 212.
      "I hope": Ibid.
      "were probably": Sherwood, *Roosevelt and Hopkins,* p. 134.
      "This country is literally": Peter Kurth, *American Cassandra: The Life of Doro-
thy Thompson* (Boston: Little, Brown, 1990), p. 311.

55   **"There is not"**: Davis, *FDR: Into the Storm,* p. 457.
      "would come": Ibid.
      "inconceivable arrogance": Joseph W. Alsop, *"I've Seen the Best of It": Mem-
oirs* (New York: Norton, 1992), p. 141.
      "Well, captain": Davis, *FDR: Into the Storm,* p. 458.

56   **"Congress has done"**: *Life,* Feb. 27, 1939.

58   **"filled with unbounded"**: Samuel and Dorothy Rosenman, *Presidential Style:
Some Giants and a Pygmy in the White House* (New York: Harper & Row, 1976),
p. 268.
      "overconfidence": Ibid., p. 350.
      "The people": Robert A. Caro, *The Years of Lyndon Johnson: Master of the Senate*
(New York: Vintage, 2003), p. 58.
      "[M]any Congressmen": Ibid., p. 79.
      "news was scarce": Alsop, *"I've Seen the Best of It,"* p. 109.

59   **"men rush in"**: Olson, *Citizens of London,* p. 20.
      "expert staffs": Caro, *Master of the Senate,* p. 65.
      "They didn't want": Ibid., p. 67.
      "It's no fun": *Life,* Jan. 1, 1940.
      "a target": Robert H. Jackson, *That Man: An Insider's Portrait of Franklin D.
Roosevelt* (Oxford: Oxford University Press, 2003), p. 46.
      "Boys, here's": Frederick Lewis Allen, *Since Yesterday: The 1930s in America*
(New York: Perennial, 1986), p. 296.

60   **"the signal that"**: Marquis W. Childs, *I Write from Washington* (New York: Harper, 1942), p. 127.

"one of the wiliest": "Boss Isolationist," *Life,* May 19, 1941.

"cool and deadly": Jeff Shesol, *Supreme Power: Franklin Roosevelt vs. the Supreme Court* (New York: Norton, 2010), p. 318.

"If I don't": "Boss Isolationist," *Life,* May 19, 1941.

61   **"Anything the Company"**: Childs, *I Write from Washington,* p. 186.

62   **"I've been watching"**: Watkins, *Righteous Pilgrim,* p. 621.

"greatest national debate": Alsop, *"I've Seen the Best of It,"* pp. 114–15.

63   **"the chances of congressional"**: Davis, *FDR: Into the Storm,* p. 100.

"I must confess": Wheeler, *Yankee from the West,* p. 425.

"an Old Testament": Francis Biddle, *In Brief Authority* (Garden City, N.Y.: Doubleday, 1962), p. 5.

"had made up": Robert A. Caro, *The Years of Lyndon Johnson: The Path to Power* (New York: Knopf, 1982), p. 562.

64   **"Punch drunk"**: Davis, *FDR: Into the Storm,* p. 107.

65   **"sons of the wild"**: Wheeler, *Yankee from the West,* p. 278.

"wants to knock": Ketchum, *Borrowed Years,* p. 174.

66   **"snug, over-safe"**: Rachel Maddow, *Drift: The Unmooring of American Military Power* (New York: Crown, 2012), p. 43.

"unscrupulous": Cole, *Roosevelt and the Isolationists,* p. 309.

"had no principles": Alsop, *"I've Seen the Best of It,"* p. 97.

67   **"a falsification"**: Steel, *Walter Lippmann,* p. 382.

CHAPTER 5: "THIS WAR HAS COME HOME TO ME"

69   **"I do not intend"**: Charles Lindbergh, *Wartime Journals,* p. 252.

"had something": Roger Butterfield, "Lindbergh," *Life,* Aug. 11, 1941.

"I don't believe": Ibid.

70   **"fully within"**: Charles Lindbergh, *Wartime Journals,* p. 254.

"He is just": *New York Times Magazine,* April 30, 1939.

71   **"You see"**: Charles Lindbergh, *Wartime Journals,* p. 257.

"take part": *New York Times,* Sept. 16, 1939.

"a quarrel": "Hero Speaks," *Time,* Sept. 25, 1939.

72   **"This is the test"**: *New York Times,* Sept. 16, 1939.

"Asiatic intruder": Cole, *Lindbergh,* p. 78.

"the exemplar": Bendersky, *"Jewish Threat,"* p. 28.

"racial characteristics": Ibid., p. 29.

73   **"the leading part"**: Ibid., p. 26.

"all the things": Anne Lindbergh, *War Within and Without,* p. 48.

"That is the nightmare": Ibid., pp. 38–39.

74   **"all kinds"**: Berg, *Lindbergh,* p. 397.

"very well worded": Murray Green, unpublished manuscript, Green papers, AFA.

"Lindbergh": Walter Isaacson, *Einstein: His Life and Universe* (New York: Simon & Schuster, 2007), p. 475.

75   **"offered a hand"**: *New York Times,* Oct. 14, 1939.

"Racial strength": Davis, *Hero,* p. 391.

75 **"To many"**: "Hounds in Cry," *Time,* Oct. 30, 1939.

  "pro-Ally": Thomas Lamont to *New York Times,* Oct. 14, 1935, Lamont papers, BL.

  "obviously, my": Charles Lindbergh, *Wartime Journals,* p. 269.

76 **"almost pathological"**: *New York Times,* Oct. 21, 1939.

  "rather silly": Charles Lindbergh, *Wartime Journals,* p. 279.

  "that biting": Anne Lindbergh, *War Within and Without,* p. 65.

77 **"People who"**: Vincent Sheean, *Dorothy and Red* (Boston: Houghton Mifflin, 1963), p. 255.

78 **"a very good"**: Ibid., p. 173.

  "is a complete": Kurth, *American Cassandra,* p. 163.

  "The spectacle": Ibid., p. 281.

  "civilized world": Ibid, p. 241.

  "If I ever": Ibid., p. 167.

79 **"She plainly feels"**: "The It Girl," *New Yorker,* April 27, 1940.

  "Believe it": Kurth, *American Cassandra,* p. 242.

  "a somber cretin": Ibid., p. 312.

  "Colonel Lindbergh's": "The It Girl," *New Yorker,* April 27, 1940.

  "She sensed": "Hounds in Cry," *Time,* Oct. 30, 1939.

  "heartily approved": Harold Ickes, *The Secret Diary of Harold L. Ickes,* Vol. 3, *The Lowering Clouds, 1939–1941* (New York: Simon & Schuster, 1955), p. 20.

  "that terrible": Anne Lindbergh, *War Within and Without,* p. 104.

  "We are thrown": Ibid., p. 64.

80 **"I feel"**: Charles Lindbergh, *Wartime Journals,* p. 282.

  "I pray": Kurth, *American Cassandra,* p. 313.

  "Why not": Ibid.

81 **"represented Nobody"**: John Mason Brown, *The Ordeal of a Playwright: Robert E. Sherwood and the Challenge of War* (New York: Harper & Row, 1970), p. 96.

  "Sherwood remains": S. N. Behrman, "Old Monotonous," *New Yorker,* June 8, 1940.

82 **"my bit"**: John Mason Brown, *The Worlds of Robert E. Sherwood: Mirror to His Times, 1896–1939* (New York: Harper & Row, 1965), p. 209.

83 **"crap games"**: Ibid., p. 210.

  "The best thing": Ibid., p. 211.

84 **"a hymn of hate"**: Harriet Hyman Alonso, *Robert E. Sherwood: The Playwright in Peace and War* (Amherst: University of Massachusetts Press, 2007), p. 100.

  "Oh God": Ibid., p. 189.

  "practically every word": Ibid., pp. 203–4.

  "I feel that I": Ibid., p. 190.

85 **"leave its neighbors"**: Ibid., p. 194.

  "the finest piece": Ibid., p. 200.

  "in a frenzy": Brown, *Ordeal of a Playwright,* p. 45.

  "the most sordid": Brown, *Worlds of Robert E. Sherwood,* p. 235.

  "It makes me": Brown, *Ordeal of a Playwright,* p. 96.

86 **"rather sick"**: Sherwood diary, Sept. 15, 1939, Sherwood papers, HL.

  "Hitlerism was already": Brown, *Ordeal of a Playwright,* p. 48.

  "Will Lindbergh": Sherwood diary, Sept. 18, 1939, Sherwood papers, HL.

86 **"give all the"**: Sherwood to William Allen White, Oct. 4, 1939, Sherwood papers, HL.
    "the terrible": Sherwood to William Allen White, Dec. 11, 1939, Sherwood papers, HL.

CHAPTER 6: "I AM ALMOST LITERALLY WALKING ON EGGS"

87 **"as close to"**: Ketchum, *Borrowed Years*, p. 470.
88 **"three and a half"**: John DeWitt McKee, *William Allen White: Maverick on Main Street* (Westport, Conn.: Greenwood Press, 1975), p. 180.
89 **"If America really"**: Langer and Gleason, *Challenge to Isolation*, p. 220.
90 **"I am almost"**: Ketchum, *Borrowed Years*, p. 227.
    "could charm snakes": *Time*, Sept. 25, 1939.
91 **"tired and worn"**: Vincent Sheean, "Reporter at Large," *New Yorker*, Oct. 7, 1939.
    "I regret": Burns, *Roosevelt: The Lion and the Fox*, p. 396.
    "We're mothers!": *Time*, Oct. 2, 1939.
    "nerves were strung": *Time*, Oct. 16, 1939.
92 **"One might have"**: Agar, *Darkest Year*, p. 136.
    "from hell to": *Life*, Oct. 2, 1939.
    "If you believe": Ketchum, *Borrowed Years*, p. 228.
    "the elaborate pretense": Davis, *FDR: Into the Storm*, p. 500.
    "We have won": Ketchum, *Borrowed Years*, p. 228.
93 **"We have forced"**: Cole, *Roosevelt and the Isolationists*, p. 330.
    "more security": Margaret Paton-Walsh, *Our War Too: American Women Against the Axis* (Lawrence: University Press of Kansas, 2002), p. 53.
    "Why don't you": Burns, *Roosevelt: The Lion and the Fox*, pp. 397–98.
    "Say I was": Ibid., p. 398.
    "with an uneasy": Ketchum, *Borrowed Years*, p. 229.

CHAPTER 7: "PARANOIA CAN BE CATCHING"

94 **"a queer sort"**: *Life*, Sept. 18, 1939.
    "the smallest domestic": James C. Schneider, *Should America Go to War? The Debate Over Foreign Policy in Chicago, 1939–1941* (Chapel Hill: University of North Carolina Press, 1989), p. 35.
    "it is not good": Ketchum, *Borrowed Years*, p. 299.
95 **"would be tantamount"**: Langer and Gleason, *Challenge to Isolation*, p. 339.
    "not engage in": Goodhart, *Fifty Ships*, p. 56.
    "How long can": Alonso, *Robert E. Sherwood*, p. 206.
    "the hysterical escapism": Ibid., p. 207.
    "Warmongers Capture": Ibid., p. 211.
    "rank and inflammatory": "The Great Debate," *Time*, May 13, 1940.
96 **"American foreign policy"**: Davis, *FDR: Into the Storm*, p. 513.
    "an international danger": Ibid., p. 526.
    "considered repeal": Langer and Gleason, *Challenge to Isolation*, p. 272.
    "shortened the war": Pogue, *Ordeal and Hope*, p. 5.
97 **"chaotic world conditions"**: Davis, *FDR: Into the Storm*, p. 538.

97   **"hurricane of events"**: Burns, *Roosevelt: The Lion and the Fox*, p. 419.
    "would be left": *Life,* May 27, 1940.
98   **"There is no"**: Ickes, *Secret Diary*, p. 188.
    "near hysteria": J. Garry Clifford and Samuel R. Spencer Jr., *The First Peace-time Draft* (Lawrence: University Press of Kansas, 1986), p. 10.
99   **"Dollars cannot"**: Agar, *Darkest Year,* p. 169.
100   **"a victorious Fascist Army"**: *Life,* June 24, 1940.
    "so graphic": Berle diary, June 26, 1940, Berle papers, FDRPL.
    "paranoia can be": Berle diary, Aug. 28, 1940, Berle papers, FDRPL.
    "President Roosevelt": Gen. Albert C. Wedemeyer, *Wedemeyer Reports!* (New York, Henry Holt, 1958), pp. 17–18.
    "with diabolical cleverness": Clifford and Spencer, *First Peacetime Draft,* p. 11.
101   **"The man at"**: Wheeler, *Yankee from the West,* p. 18.
    "apparently were going": Murray Green interview with Mrs. Henry Arnold, Green papers, AFA.
102   **"it is doubtful"**: Murray Green unpublished manuscript, Green papers, AFA.
    "Are you going": Wheeler, *Yankee from the West,* p. 21.
    "The press is hysterical": Charles Lindbergh, *Wartime Journals,* p. 348.
    "childish": Castle diary, May 19, 1940, Castle papers, HL.
    "furious at the": Ibid.
    "must stop this": *New York Times,* May 20, 1940.
103   **"This will raise"**: Anne Lindbergh, *War Within and Without,* p. 84.
    "The 'hysterical chatter' ": Herrmann, *Anne Morrow Lindbergh,* p. 238.
    "If I should die": Cole, *Lindbergh,* p. 128.
    "When I read": FDR to Henry Stimson, May 21, 1940, President's Secretary File, FDRPL.
104   **"fifth-column activities"**: *New York Times,* May 23, 1940.
    "Fifth columns": Ibid.
    "weakening a nation": *New York Times,* May 27, 1940.
    "its friends in": Richard W. Steele, *Propaganda in an Open Society: The Roosevelt Administration and the Media, 1939–1941* (Westport, Conn.: Greenwood Press, 1985), p. 70.
    "apologists to foreign": Ibid.
105   **"treacherous use"**: Ibid., p. 72.
    "did not view": Ibid., p. 69.
    "a wholesome political": *New York Times,* May 27, 1940.
    "a hysteria was": Ickes, *Secret Diary,* p. 211.
106   **"morbid fears"**: "Under Strain," *Time,* June 3, 1940.
    "was hunting down": Harold Ickes diary, May 26, 1940, Ickes papers, LC.
    "America isn't going": Ibid.
    "Some of our": Ibid., June 2, 1940.
    "our own excitement": Richard W. Steele, *Free Speech in the Good War* (New York: St. Martin's, 1999), p. 79.
107   **"patriotic judges"**: Ibid., p. 111.
    "an orgy of": Ibid., p. 4.
    "a clear and present": Ibid., p. 10.
108   **"the Holy War"**: Geoffrey Perret, *Days of Sadness, Years of Triumph: The American People, 1939–1945* (New York: Coward, McCann & Geoghegan, 1973), p. 95.

108   "**more and more**": Steele, *Free Speech,* p. 85.
      "**Why shouldn't Lindbergh**": Ibid., p. 121.
      "**had a tendency**": Jackson, *That Man,* p. 74.
      "**It was all**": Biddle, *In Brief Authority,* p. 108.
109   "**the Nazi movement**": Steele, *Free Speech,* p. 30.
110   "**the general [Communist]**": Ibid.
      "**identifying data**": Ibid., p.32.
      "**in the event**": Ibid., p. 34.
111   "**done far less**": Berle diary, March 21, 1940, Berle papers, FDRPL.
      "**be careful about**": Ickes, *Secret Diary,* p. 10.
      "**almost bound to**": Steele, *Free Speech,* p. 90.
112   "**apply to grave**": Ibid., p. 91.
      "**did not have**": Ibid., p. 112.
      "**factors of political**": Robert Justin Goldstein, *Political Repression in Modern America: From 1870 to the Present* (Cambridge, Mass.: Schenkman, 1978), p. 253.
      "**to go over these**": Curt Gentry, *J. Edgar Hoover: The Man and the Secrets* (New York: Norton, 1991), p. 225.
113   "**prepare a nice**": Ibid., p. 226.
      "**bitter opposition**": Mosley, *Lindbergh,* p. 417.
      "**No human being**": Truman Smith, *Berlin Alert,* p. 33.
114   "**Marshall protected**": Wedemeyer biographical sketch of Marshall, Wedemeyer papers, HI.
      "**an American Dreyfus**": Truman Smith, *Berlin Alert,* p. 33.
      "**stay away**": Ibid., p. 34.
      "**the Administration**": Charles Lindbergh, *Wartime Journals,* p. 352.
      "**Aren't you worried**": Anne Lindbergh, *War Within and Without,* p. 104.
      "**It's that awful**": Ibid.

CHAPTER 8: "THE ART OF MANIPULATION"

116   "**In modern war**": Cull, *Selling War,* p. 80.
      "**a virtual textbook**": David Ignatius, "Britain's War in America," *Washington Post,* Sept. 17, 1989.
      "**one of the**": Cull, *Selling War,* p. 4.
      "**If the isolationists**": Sherwood, *Roosevelt and Hopkins,* p. 270.
117   "**An extremely private**": Bill Macdonald, *The True Intrepid: Sir William Stephenson and the Unknown Agents* (Vancouver, B.C.: Raincoast Books, 2001), p. 239.
      "**never told anybody**": Ibid., p. 225.
      "**like a panther**": Ibid., pp. 273–74.
118   "**You'd meet**": Ibid., p. 326.
      "**the most powerful**": H. Montgomery Hyde, *Room 3603: The Story of the British Intelligence Center in New York During World War II* (New York: Farrar, Straus, 1963), p. xi.
      "**If I have**": Macdonald, *True Intrepid,* p. 327.
      "**Booth's gin**": William Stevenson, *Spymistress: The True Story of the Greatest Female Secret Agent of World War II* (New York: Arcade, 2007), p. 155.
      "**there should be**": British Security Coordination, *The Secret History of British*

Intelligence in the Americas, 1940–1945 (New York: Fromm International, 1999), p. xxv.

119   **"the mail of"**: Gentry, *J. Edgar Hoover,* p. 282.

120   **"She was the"**: Macdonald, *True Intrepid,* p. 175.
      "The greatest care": British Security Coordination, pp. 19–20.
      "rendered services": Ibid., p. 20.

121   **"sensational and vicious"**: *Documents on German Foreign Policy 1918–45,* Series D, Vol. 10 (Washington, D.C.: U.S. Government Printing Office), p. 413.

122   **"the general"**: *Documents on German Foreign Policy 1918–45,* Series D, Vol. 9 (Washington, D.C.: U.S. Government Printing Office), p. 626.
      "shouted down": *Documents on German Foreign Policy 1918–45,* Series D, Vol. 12 (Washington, D.C.: U.S. Government Printing Office), p. 60.
      "The real friends": Ibid., p. 906.
      "The less we": Ibid.

123   **"a German-American"**: F. Bradley Smith, *The Shadow Warriors: O.S.S. and the Origins of the C.I.A.* (New York: Basic, 1983), p. 39.

124   **"the invisible government"**: Ketchum, *Borrowed Years,* p. 187.
      "The best British": Lockhart, *Comes the Reckoning,* p. 29.

125   **"in the U.S.A."**: *Documents on German Foreign Policy 1918–45,* Series D, Vol. 12 (Washington, D.C.: U.S. Government Printing Office), p. 907.
      "Influential journalists": *Documents on German Foreign Policy 1918–45,* Series D, Vol. 9 (Washington, D.C.: U.S. Government Printing Office), p. 43.
      "great results": Ibid., p. 559.

CHAPTER 9: "IS THIS WAR OUR CONCERN?"

126   **"We shall fight"**: Ketchum, *Borrowed Years,* p. 351.
      "We shall fight": Olson, *Troublesome Young Men,* p. 316.
      "They say there": Ketchum, *Borrowed Years,* p. 319.

127   **"Never has a"**: Olson and Cloud, *A Question of Honor,* p. 93.
      "shattered, starving": Davis, *FDR: Into the Storm,* p. 558.
      "seemed to be": David Reynolds, *Lord Lothian and Anglo-American Relations, 1939–1940* (Philadelphia: American Philosophical Society, 1983), p. 19.

128   **"the material resources"**: Ketchum, *Borrowed Years,* p. 358.
      "the shock of excitement": Wheeler-Bennett, *Special Relationships,* p. 97.
      "The U.S. has": Ketchum, *Borrowed Years,* p. 358.
      "It is a drop": David Kennedy, *Freedom from Fear: The American People in Depression and War, 1929–1945* (Oxford: Oxford University Press, 1990), p. 448.
      "Our unreadiness": Clifford and Spencer, *First Peacetime Draft,* p. 45.

129   **"the Army"**: Langer and Gleason, *Challenge to Isolation,* p. 569.
      "Up till April": James R. M. Butler, *Lord Lothian: Philip Kerr, 1882–1940* (New York: St. Martin's, 1960), p. 120.
      "It is no": "Lord Lothian's Job," *Time,* July 8, 1940.

130   **"Only the experienced"**: *Documents on German Foreign Policy 1918–45,* Series D, Vol. 9 (Washington, D.C.: U.S. Government Printing Office), p. 339.
      "No newspaper was": "The Great Debate," *Time,* May 13, 1940.
      "If you could": Ketchum, *Borrowed Years,* p. 375.

131   **"We have been"**: *Life,* June 3, 1940.

131   **"being decided upon"**: William Allen White, "Is Our Way of Life Doomed?,"
New York Times, Sept. 9, 1940.
"Our idea": Langer and Gleason, *Challenge to Isolation,* p. 487.

132   **"terrible sense"**: Paton-Walsh, *Our War Too,* p. 82.
"I always understood": Mosley, *Lindbergh,* p. 263.

133   **"I am in"**: Elizabeth Morrow to Thomas Lamont, May 25, 1940, Lamont papers, BL.
"I can't bear": Anne Lindbergh, *War Within and Without,* p. 99.
"He has been": Ibid., p. 96.
"Anti-Christ": Ibid.
"I urge the": Herrmann, *Anne Morrow Lindbergh,* p. 232.

134   **"Of course"**: Anne Lindbergh, *War Within and Without,* p. 97.
"How I wish": Ibid., p. 100.
"Unless you recall": Paton-Walsh, *Our War Too,* p. 5.

135   **"A bit of"**: Sherwood diary, Jan. 18, 1940, Sherwood papers, HL.
"fiercely militant liberal": "Old Monotonous," *New Yorker,* June 8, 1940.
"if Hitler wins": Alonso, *Robert E. Sherwood,* p. 214.
"a mighty good thing": Brown, *Ordeal of a Playwright,* pp. 85–86.
"either an imbecile": Ibid., p. 87.

136   **"just as loyal"**: Oswald Garrison Villard to William Allen White, undated, White papers, LC.
"has aroused": William Allen White to Sherwood, June 14, 1940, Sherwood papers, HL.
"to those who": Sherwood to William Allen White, June 17, 1940, Sherwood papers, HL.
"for having gone": Sherwood, *Roosevelt and Hopkins,* p. 167.
"immediate and unstinted": Steele, *Propaganda,* p. 100.
"We are doing": William Allen White to Herbert Bayard Swope, May 31, 1940, White papers, LC.
"My correspondence is": William Allen White telegram to FDR, June 10, 1940, White papers, LC.

137   **"you will get"**: Ketchum, *Borrowed Years,* p. 355.
"it would have": Clifford and Spencer, *First Peacetime Draft,* p. 55.
"The sense of": Francis Pickens Miller, *Man from the Valley: Memoirs of a 20th-Century Virginian* (Chapel Hill: University of North Carolina Press, 1971), p. 89.
"We who": Agar, *Darkest Year,* p. 145.

138   **"those citizens"**: Ibid., p. 56.
"What a majority": *Life,* Oct. 9, 1939.

CHAPTER 10: "WHY DO WE NOT DEFEND HER?"

140   **"authors, artists"**: The Century Association, *The Century 1847–1946* (New York: The Century Association, 1947), p. 5.
"a gracious place": Ibid., p. 103.
"When they thought": Ibid., p. 62.

141   **"a sense of country"**: Frederic S. Nathan, *Centurions in Public Service* (New York: The Century Association, 2010), p. 54.

142   **"rich, overeducated"**: William Manchester, *The Glory and the Dream: A Narrative History of America, 1932–1972* (Boston: Little, Brown, 1973), p. 175.
      "a bloodless": Robert Sherwood, *This Is New York* (New York: Scribner's, 1931), p. ix.
      "aggressive Americans": Ibid.
      "sole refuge": Ibid., p. xiii.
      "the American spirit": Ibid., p. xii.

143   **"transplanted Negroes"**: Manchester, *Glory and the Dream*, p. 167.
      "New York": Alsop, *"I've Seen the Best of It,"* p. 35.
      "united in scorn": Allen, *Only Yesterday*, p. 203.
      "the humor magazine": Alan Brinkley, *The Publisher: Henry Luce and His American Century* (New York: Knopf, 2010), p. 197.
      "not for the": Ibid., p. 196.

145   **"amounted to"**: Susan E. Tifft and Alex S. Jones, *The Patriarch: The Rise and Fall of the Bingham Dynasty* (New York: Summit, 1991), p. 162.
      "the most outspoken": Ibid.
      "I think the": Agar, *Darkest Year*, p. 144.
      "The isolationists": Ibid., p. 1.
      "was our Old": Chadwin, *War Hawks*, p. 53.

146   **"came out"**: "Reaction," *Time*, May 27, 1940.

148   **"New York is"**: Robert T. Elson, *Time, Inc.: The Intimate History of a Publishing Enterprise, 1923–1941* (New York: Atheneum, 1968), pp. 373–74.

149   **"I want more"**: David Halberstam, *The Powers That Be* (Urbana: University of Illinois Press, 2000), p. 48.
      "like an infinitely": Chadwin, *War Hawks*, p. 63.
      "The American refusal": Alan Brinkley, *Publisher*, p. 141.

150   **"we were going"**: Miller, *Man from the Valley*, p. 98.

CHAPTER 11: "THE GREATEST OF ALL OUR AMBASSADORS"

151   **"could have no"**: Wheeler-Bennett, *Special Relationships*, p. 66.

152   **"the greatest"**: Ibid.
      "how Americans look": Butler, *Lord Lothian*, p. 260.
      "has caught": Priscilla Roberts, "Lord Lothian and the Atlantic World," *The Historian*, March 2004, p. 105.

153   **"I always feel"**: Ibid.
      "quite spoil": Butler, *Lord Lothian*, p. 144.
      "I am now": Ibid., p. 261.
      "one would be": Wheeler-Bennett, *Special Relationships*, p. 72.

154   **"I hope you"**: Ibid., p. 73.
      "South Africa for": James Fox, *Five Sisters: The Langhornes of Virginia* (New York: Simon & Schuster, 2000), p. 156.
      "my constant companion": *New York Times*, Dec. 13, 1940.
      "Lloyd George's other": Ibid.

155   **"a visionary"**: Butler, *Lord Lothian*, p. 236.
      "If only": Ibid., p. 206.
      "the most influential": Fox, *Five Sisters*, p. 435.
      "the most dangerous": Ibid.

155   **"There isn't any"**: Ibid., p. 204.

    "distinctly pious": Butler, *Lord Lothian*, p. 3.

    "troubles the heart": Fox, *Five Sisters*, p. 169.

156   **"it was possible"**: Butler, *Lord Lothian*, p. 227.

    "America really holds": Cull, *Selling War*, p. 20.

    "Both winning the": Ibid., p. 33.

    "We have never": Butler, *Lord Lothian*, p. 277.

    "there is generally": Ibid., p. 258.

    "We really have": Ibid., p. 277.

157   **"The United States"**: Cull, *Selling War*, pp. 63–64.

    "To an extent": Ibid., p. 34.

    "The same Lord": *New York Times*, Jan. 16, 1940.

158   **"sandwiched between"**: Wheeler-Bennett, *Special Relationships*, p. 81.

    "an unqualified determination": Ibid.

    "I found that": Ibid., p. 82.

    "create an American": Ibid., p. 93.

    "formidable, anti-British": Cull, *Selling War*, p. 61.

159   **"So long as"**: Ketchum, *Borrowed Years*, p. 352.

    "I think that": Butler, *Lord Lothian*, p. 281.

    "an earnest": Winston S. Churchill, *Their Finest Hour* (Boston: Houghton Mifflin, 1949), p. 555.

    "What a great": Cull, *Selling War*, p. 109.

160   **"There is universal"**: Ibid., p. 73.

    "the whole fury": Ketchum, *Borrowed Years*, p. 377.

    "has not yet": Reynolds, *Lord Lothian*, p. 20.

    "I hope you": "Lord Lothian's Job," *Time*, July 8, 1940.

161   **"It is for you"**: Butler, *Lord Lothian*, p. 291.

162   **"the public agitation"**: Joseph W. Alsop, *FDR: 1882–1945: A Centenary Remembrance* (New York: Viking, 1982), p. 203.

    "public opinion is": Cull, *Selling War*, p. 78.

    "the situation in": Goodhart, *Fifty Ships*, p. 75.

163   **"The highest naval"**: Robert W. Merry, *Taking On the World: Joseph and Stewart Alsop—Guardians of the American Century* (New York: Viking, 1996), p. 84.

    "A recheck": Ibid.

    "As an opinionated": Ibid., p. 85.

164   **"and you say"**: Agar, *Darkest Year*, p. 147.

    "equip other people": Ibid., pp. 148–49.

    "I am telling": Goodhart, *Fifty Ships*, p. 160.

    "was the turning": Agar, *Darkest Year*, p. 149.

165   **"spent a lot"**: Ickes, *Secret Diary*, p. 233.

    "a plot to": Steel, *Walter Lippmann*, p. 385.

    "one of the": Agar, *Darkest Year*, p. 153.

    "Don't you take": Walter Isaacson and Evan Thomas, *The Wise Men: Six Friends and the World They Made* (New York: Touchstone, 1988), p. 135.

166   **"He condescended"**: Dean Acheson, *Morning and Noon* (Boston: Houghton Mifflin, 1965), p. 165.

    "gay, graceful": Isaacson and Thomas, *The Wise Men*, p. 85.

    "To shrink": Acheson, *Morning and Noon*, p. 221.

166   **"the transfer"**: Ketchum, *Borrowed Years,* p. 478.
167   **"a fresh thought"**: Agar, *Darkest Year,* p. 154.
        "go full steam": Butler, *Lord Lothian,* p. 295.
168   **"a Yankee horse"**: Agar, *Darkest Year,* p. 153.
        "There was an": Ibid., pp. 152–53.
        "The committee was": Ibid., p. 150.
        BETWEEN US AND HITLER: Chadwin, *War Hawks,* p. 79.
169   **"congratulate me"**: Alsop, *FDR: 1882–1945,* p. 203.

CHAPTER 12: "THE PEOPLE SAVED THE DAY"

170   **"I would crawl"**: Steve Neal, *Dark Horse: A Biography of Wendell Willkie* (Garden City, N.Y.: Doubleday, 1984), p. 69.
        "It wasn't": Ibid., p. 120.
        "The people saved": *Life,* July 8, 1940.
        "man wholly": Charles Peters, *Five Days in Philadelphia: The Amazing "We Want Willkie" Convention of 1940 and How It Freed FDR to Save the Western World* (New York: Public Affairs, 2005), p. 23.
171   **"a Republican who"**: Halberstam, *Powers That Be,* p. 60.
172   **"locked in combat"**: Kurth, *American Cassandra,* p. 320.
        "eight or ten photographers": Biddle, *In Brief Authority,* p. 69.
        "a plain American": Ibid.
173   **"I wouldn't live"**: Neal, *Dark Horse,* p. 25.
        "acceptance of himself": Peters, *Five Days in Philadelphia,* p. 35.
174   **"There is a"**: Ibid., p. 21.
        "American life was": Goodhart, *Fifty Ships,* p. 106.
175   **"I've met the"**: Marcia Davenport, *Too Strong for Fantasy* (New York: Pocket, 1969), p. 216.
        "chemical reaction": Elson, *Time, Inc.,* p. 417.
        "We are opposed": Neal, *Dark Horse,* p. 68.
176   **"The principles he"**: Elson, *Time, Inc.,* p. 417.
        "help Oren Root": "President-Maker," *New Yorker,* June 8, 1940.
        "I have no": Neal, *Dark Horse,* p. 69.
        "most significant": Donald A. Ritchie, *Reporting from Washington: The History of the Washington Press Corps* (Oxford: Oxford University Press, 2005), p. 135.
177   **"The one man"**: Neal, *Dark Horse,* p. 71.
        "75 percent": Shesol, *Supreme Power,* p. 283.
        "old-fashioned": Davenport, *Too Strong for Fantasy,* pp. 216–17.
        "The curse of": Ketchum, *Borrowed Years,* p. 415.
        "trembled for": Neal, *Dark Horse,* p. 75.
178   **"For Republicans like"**: Ketchum, *Borrowed Years,* p. 424.
        "Republicans can": Raymond Clapper, "GOP's Chance," *Life,* June 24, 1940.
        "Willkie, despite": Goodhart, *Fifty Ships,* pp. 106–7.
        THE UNINVITED GUEST: Neal, *Dark Horse,* p. 108.
        "in accord with": Langer and Gleason, *Challenge to Isolation,* p. 670.
179   **"leader with a"**: Neal, *Dark Horse,* pp. 97–98.
        "If the politicians": Sheean, *Dorothy and Red,* p. 312.

179   **"the Willkie trend"**: Peters, *Five Days in Philadelphia,* p. 99.
180   **"We want Willkie!"**: Neal, *Dark Horse,* p. 106.
      "most of the": Peters, *Five Days in Philadelphia,* p. 95.
181   **"Guests, hell"**: Goodhart, *Fifty Ships,* p. 108.
      "We professionals": Ibid., p. 107.
      "The suspense was": Davenport, *Too Strong for Fantasy,* p. 228.
      "the miracle of Philadelphia": Neal, *Dark Horse,* p. 122.
      "I am thoroughly": Ibid., p. 116.
182   **"I knew the"**: Peters, *Five Days in Philadelphia,* p. 115.
      "To millions of": Janet Flanner, "Rushville's Renowned Son-in-Law," *New Yorker,* Oct. 12, 1940.
      "we here are": Neal, *Dark Horse,* p. 121.
      "guaranteed to the": Sherwood, *Roosevelt and Hopkins,* p. 174.
      "From the standpoint": *Documents on German Foreign Policy 1918–45,* Series D, Vol. 9 (Washington, D.C.: U.S. Government Printing Office), p. 49.
183   **"a well-camouflaged"**: Ibid., p. 551.
      "peoples whose": Langer and Gleason, *Challenge to Isolation,* p. 669.
      "so written": Ketchum, *Borrowed Years,* p. 426.
      "His sincerity comes": Neal, *Dark Horse,* p. 122.

CHAPTER 13: "CONGRESS IS GOING TO RAISE HELL"

184   **"The President's"**: Jackson, *That Man,* p. 42.
      "The shift toward": Neal, *Dark Horse,* pp. 56–57.
185   **"slowing down"**: Davis, *FDR: Into the Storm,* p. 533.
      "has not the": Ibid.
      "I did not": Jackson, *That Man,* p. 45.
186   **"frankly and clearly"**: Ickes, *Secret Diary,* p. 250.
      "some show of": Perret, *Days of Sadness,* p. 48.
      "bored and tired": Biddle, *In Brief Authority,* pp. 140–41.
      "dead, cold": Ickes, *Secret Diary,* p. 243.
      "grim": Childs, *I Write from Washington,* p. 196.
      "We Want Roosevelt!": Perret, *Days of Sadness,* p. 49.
187   **"Of course"**: Ernest Cuneo unpublished autobiography, Cuneo papers, FDRPL.
      "the affair had": Ketchum, *Borrowed Years,* p. 463.
      "As Franklin noted": Rexford G. Tugwell, *The Democratic Roosevelt* (Garden City, N.Y.: Doubleday, 1957), p. 462.
188   **"a man more"**: John C. Culver and John Hyde, *American Dreamer: The Life and Times of Henry A. Wallace* (New York: Norton, 2000), p. 209.
      "a hell of": Davis, *FDR: Into the Storm,* p. 599.
      "manhandled": Ickes, *Secret Diary,* p. 272.
      "Well, damn it": Ketchum, *Borrowed Years,* p. 464.
189   **"agony . . . just utter"**: Culver and Hyde, *American Dreamer,* p. 221.
      "Why are they": Ibid.
      "The President could": Biddle, *In Brief Authority,* p. 142.
      "No amount of": *Life,* July 29, 1940.
      "a shambles": Peters, *Five Days in Philadelphia,* p. 152.

189   "Something has gone": Ibid.
190   "If the President": Ickes, *Secret Diary*, p. 266.
       "most insistent": Cole, *Roosevelt and the Isolationists*, p. 395.
191   "The value to": Goodhart, *Fifty Ships*, p. 182.
       "Congress is going": Burns, *Roosevelt: The Lion and the Fox*, p. 441.
       "a dictatorial step": Chadwin, *War Hawks*, p. 106.
       "You can't attack": Goodhart, *Fifty Ships*, p. 187.
       "naval and air": Ketchum, *Borrowed Years*, pp. 479–80.
192   "I thought they": Olson, *Citizens of London*, p. 7.
       "Any destroyer that": Goodhart, *Fifty Ships*, p. 237.
       "makes our official": Langer and Gleason, *Challenge to Isolation*, pp. 773–74.
       "sealed what in": Goodhart, *Fifty Ships*, p. 187.
       "an openly hostile": Langer and Gleason, *Challenge to Isolation*, p. 775.
194   "little people": Olson, *Citizens of London*, p. 46.
       "He was concerned": Ibid., p. 33.
       "an almost miraculous": Cull, *Selling War*, p. 109.
       "Hitler had given": Ibid., p. 110.
195   "You're a scoundrel": Wheeler-Bennett, *Special Relationships*, p. 84.
       "has stood close": Beck, *Hitler's Ambivalent Attaché*, p. 168.
       "on the conservative": Ibid.
       "as an organ": Ibid.

CHAPTER 14: "AN AMERICAN FIRST, AND A
             REPUBLICAN AFTERWARD"

196   "supremely daring": Sherwood, *Roosevelt and Hopkins*, p. 157.
197   "Of what value": *Life*, Aug. 28, 1939.
200   "Grenny Clark": Clifford and Spencer, *First Peacetime Draft*, pp. 21–22.
       "Aladdin's lamp": Ibid., p. 41.
       "a consummate Army": Ed Cray, *General of the Army: George Marshall, Soldier and Statesman* (New York: Norton, 1990), p. 195.
       "the best of": Ibid., p. 7.
       "I thought": Pogue, *Ordeal and Hope*, p. 24.
201   "It was very": Ibid.
202   "a sleazy third-rater": Alsop, *"I've Seen the Best of It,"* p. 139.
       "plainly incompetent": Clifford and Spencer, *First Peacetime Draft*, p. 56.
203   "an impossibly grand": Alsop, *"I've Seen the Best of It,"* p. 143.
       "the world's most": Henry L. Stimson and McGeorge Bundy, *On Active Service in Peace and War* (New York: Harper, 1948), p. 308.
       "passive and shameful": Ibid., p. 311.
       "peace above righteousness": Ibid., p. 312.
204   "a time might": Ibid., p. 317.
       "a ridiculous idea": Clifford and Spencer, *First Peacetime Draft*, p. 64.
205   "Short of a direct": Stimson and Bundy, *On Active Service*, p. 320.
       "was in full": Ketchum, *Borrowed Years*, p. 564.
       "your ridiculous plot": Clifford and Spencer, *First Peacetime Draft*, p. 89.
206   "national solidarity": Ibid.
       "hopelessly twisted": Stimson and Bundy, *On Active Service*, p. 330.

206   **"I am an American first"**: Biddle, *In Brief Authority,* p. 175.

207   **"a much-needed blood transfusion"**: Sherwood, *Roosevelt and Hopkins,* p. 164.

209   **"give the news"**: Susan E. Tifft and Alex S. Jones, *The Trust: The Private and Powerful Family Behind* The New York Times (Boston: Little, Brown, 1999), p. xix.

       "Gentlemen, we have": Meyer Berger, *The New York Times: 1851–1951* (New York: Simon & Schuster, 1951), p. 439.

       "In the interest": Ibid., pp. 439–40.

       "I did not": Davis, *FDR: Into the Storm,* p. 605.

210   **"a Chinaman's chance"**: Clifford and Spencer, *First Peacetime Draft,* p. 84.

       "perfectly willing": James Wadsworth, Oral History Collection, Columbia University.

       "If we had": Clifford and Spencer, *First Peacetime Draft,* p. 103.

211   **"strong and unequivocal"**: Ibid., p. 110.

       "they were in": Ibid.

       "We were given": Ibid.

       "no conceivable way": Pogue, *Ordeal and Hope,* p. 60.

       "My relief of": Cray, *General of the Army,* p. 170.

212   **"Democrats who vote"**: "Conscription," *Time,* Aug. 12, 1940.

       "Congressmen are": Clifford and Spencer, *First Peacetime Draft,* p. 284.

       "frightened of a": Ibid., p. 97.

       "I myself feared": Ibid., p. 217.

214   **"a splendid demonstration"**: *Life,* Sept. 2, 1940.

       "call some of": Clifford and Spencer, *First Peacetime Draft,* p. 170.

       "essential to adequate": Ibid., p. 171.

       "Whenever the Congress": Ibid., p. 174.

       "I shudder for": Ibid., p. 175.

       "dollar patriots": John G. Clifford, "Grenville Clark and the Origins of the Selective Service," *The Review of Politics,* January 1973.

       "slacker family": William E. Coffey, "Isolationism and Pacifism: Senator Rush D. Holt and American Foreign Policy," *West Virginia History,* 1992.

215   **"to sit by"**: Clifford and Spencer, *First Peacetime Draft,* p. 214.

       "[N]o longer will": Langer and Gleason, *Challenge to Isolation,* p. 682.

216   **"These legislative"**: Clifford and Spencer, *First Peacetime Draft,* p. 193.

       "some form of": Ibid., p. 194.

217   **"The Willkie speech"**: Ibid., p. 201.

       "absolutely opposed": Ibid., p. 203.

       "While not a": John G. Clifford, "Grenville Clark and the Origins of the Selective Service," *The Review of Politics,* January 1973.

       "Every time Hitler": Ibid.

218   **"really broke the"**: Clifford and Spencer, *First Peacetime Draft,* p. 196.

       "We have started": Ketchum, *Borrowed Years,* p. 515.

       "Openly and officially": Paton-Walsh, *Our War Too,* pp. 115–16.

       "To postpone": James Rowe memo to FDR, Oct. 14, 1940, President's Secretary's File, FDRPL.

       "The first number": Clifford and Spencer, *First Peacetime Draft,* p. 2.

       "good statesmanship": Stimson diary, Oct. 29, 1940, FDRPL.

219   **"Mr. Roosevelt the"**: Clifford and Spencer, *First Peacetime Draft,* p. 203.
      "Without his": Lewis B. Hershey, "Grenville Clark and Selective Service," in *Memoirs of a Man: Grenville Clark,* Norman Cousins and J. Garry Clifford, eds. (New York: Norton, 1975), p. 209.
      "If it had": Clifford and Spencer, *First Peacetime Draft,* pp. 224–25.
      "admiration and gratitude": Ibid., p. 225.
      "was undoubtedly the": John G. Clifford, "Grenville Clark and the Origins of the Selective Service," *The Review of Politics,* January 1973.
      "it was the": Pogue, *Ordeal and Hope,* p. 62.
      "the people will": Clifford and Spencer, *First Peacetime Draft,* p. 5.

CHAPTER 15: "THE YANKS ARE *NOT* COMING"

220   **"The conduct of"**: Sevareid, *Not So Wild,* pp. 62–63.
221   **"preserve at least"**: Ibid., p. 64.
      "Flanders fields": Chadwin, *War Hawks,* p. 9.
      "The Yanks Are": Ibid.
      "bear arms": Sevareid, *Not So Wild,* p. 60.
      "we shouldn't be": Ruth Sarles, *A Story of America First: The Men and Women Who Opposed U.S. Intervention in World War II* (Westport, Conn.: Praeger, 2003), p. 250.
      "a deep-seated": Geoffrey Kabaservice, *The Guardians: Kingman Brewster, His Circle, and the Rise of the Liberal Establishment* (New York: Henry Holt, 2004), p. 80.
222   **"We are frankly"**: Schlesinger, *A Life in the Twentieth Century,* p. 231.
      LET'S SEND 50: Eileen Eagan, *Class, Culture, and the Classroom: The Student Peace Movement of the 1930s* (Philadelphia: Temple University Press, 1981), p. 214.
      "we were not": Schlesinger, *A Life in the Twentieth Century,* p. 245.
      "fantastic nonsense": Ibid.
      "Open Letter": Ketchum, *Borrowed Years,* pp. 507–8.
223   **WE STAND HERE**: Ibid., pp. 508–9.
      "one of the": Kabaservice, *Guardians,* p. 70.
224   **"the idea man"**: Ibid., p. 74.
      "What you are": Sarles, *Story of America First,* p. xxii.
      "I would get": Ibid., p. 213.
      "a bug on": Kabaservice, *Guardians,* p. 77.
225   **"his courage and"**: Ketchum, *Borrowed Years,* p. 513.
      "Most of us": Ibid.
226   **"When the peoples"**: America First flyer, Sherwood papers, HL.
      "in agreement with": Kabaservice, *Guardians,* p. 75.
      "substantial and prominent": Ibid., p. 74.
228   **"an apocalyptic"**: *New York Times,* Sept. 21, 1940.
      "a story of": Sherwood introduction to *Pastor Hall,* Sherwood papers, HL.
      "display of depravity": Cull, *Selling War,* p. 50.
      "Nazi sensibilities": Schneider, *Should America Go to War?,* p. 93.
229   **"Having seen it"**: Richard Norton Smith, *The Colonel: The Life and Legend of Robert R. McCormick, 1880–1955* (Boston: Houghton Mifflin, 1997), p. 42.

229   **"moronic buffoonery"**: Ibid., p. 181.
       "aggressive, sensitive": Ibid., p. xvi.
       "the World's Greatest Newspaper": Ibid.
       "We are the": Ibid., p. 263.
       "The trouble with": Ibid., p. xvi.
230   **"a Sodom and"**: Ibid.
       "dominated and driven": Ibid., p. 312.
       "Did you know": Ibid., p. xx.
231   **"The *Tribune* hammers"**: *Life,* Dec. 1, 1941.
       "Condescension shot": Richard Norton Smith, *Colonel,* p. 53.
232   **"the backbone"**: *Fortune* memo, July 22, 1941, President's Secretary's File,
       FDRPL.
       "a well-organized": "Follow What Leader?," *Time,* Oct. 6, 1941.
233   **"were the most"**: Allen, *Only Yesterday,* p. 156.
234   **"Several of our"**: Howard B. Schaffer, *Chester Bowles: New Dealer in the Cold
       War* (Cambridge, Mass.: Harvard University Press, 1993), p. 28.
       "As a matter": Gerald Ford to Robert Douglas Stuart, June 1940, America
       First Committee papers, HI.
       "Alice has": White Committee report on America First, William Allen White
       papers, LC.
235   **"Fuehrer, Duce, Roosevelt"**: Stacy A. Cordery, *Alice: Alice Roosevelt Long-
       worth: From White House Princess to Washington Power Broker* (New York: Viking,
       2007), p. 394.
       "always felt that": Ward, *A First-Class Temperament,* p. 532.
       "the smear campaign": Cole, *Lindbergh,* p. 120.
       "decent, honest": Mosley, *Lindbergh,* p. 278.
       "American as": Sarles, *Story of America First,* p. 1.
236   **"Because it was"**: Ibid., p. 40.
       "a typical hodgepodge": *Life,* Dec. 1, 1941.
       "There is no": Sarles, *Story of America First,* pp. 50–51.
237   **"probably did more"**: Neil Baldwin, *Henry Ford and the Jews: The Mass Pro-
       duction of Hate* (New York: Public Affairs, 2001), p. 145.
       "great service": Ibid.
       "We look to": Ibid.
238   **"I am now"**: Sarles, *Story of America First,* p. 50.
       "beneath the generally": Ketchum, *Borrowed Years,* p. 108.
239   **"an unbelievably"**: Sevareid, *Not So Wild,* pp. 69–70.
       "banish all isms": *Life,* Sept. 8, 1941.
       "We must ignore": Ketchum, *Borrowed Years,* p. 113.
       "We're just": *Life,* Sept. 8, 1941.
240   **"anti-Christian conspiracy"**: Ibid.
       "When we get through": Ketchum, *Borrowed Years,* p. 124.
       "None of us": William L. Shirer, *Berlin Diary: The Journal of a Foreign Corre-
       spondent, 1931–1941* (New York: Knopf, 1941), p. 213.
       "The German green": Mark Stevens, "Form Follows Fascism," *New York
       Times,* Jan. 31, 2005.
241   **"organized campaign"**: "Marauding Youth and the Christian Front: Anti-

Semitic Violence in Boston and New York During World War II," *American Jewish History*, June 1, 2003.

241   "a menace": Sarles, *Story of America First*, p. 43.
"wriggled": Ibid., p. 39.
"a Nazi transmission belt": Kabaservice, *Guardians*, p. 81.
"first fascist party": Ibid.

CHAPTER 16: "THE BUBONIC PLAGUE AMONG WRITERS"

242   "the attack launched": Berg, *Lindbergh*, p. 409.
"he never 'gets personal'": *Omaha Morning World Herald* editorial, Friday, July 18, 1941, President's Official File, FDRPL.
"very angry": Anne Lindbergh, *War Within and Without*, p. 136.
243   "innocence of politics": Ibid., p. xxi.
"because of . . . my": Ibid., p. 143.
"The arguments of": Ibid.
"They are": Ibid., p. 131.
"When you hear": Ibid.
"a moral argument": Ibid., p. 143.
"torn as she": Berg, *Lindbergh*, p. 406.
244   "not fully": Roger Butterfield, "Lindbergh," *Life*, Aug. 11, 1941.
"wave of the": Anne Morrow Lindbergh, *The Wave of the Future: A Confession of Faith* (New York: Harcourt Brace, 1940), p. 34.
"I keep feeling": Anne Lindbergh, *Flower and the Nettle*, p. 101.
"scum on the wave": Anne Lindbergh, *Wave of the Future*, p. 19.
"blindness, selfishness": Ibid., pp. 11–12.
"climbing down": Ibid., p. 29.
"There is no": Ibid., p. 34.
"It will be": Anne Lindbergh, *War Within and Without*, p. 143.
245   "gave me back": Ibid., p. 145.
"should be put": Berg, *Lindbergh*, p. 406.
"I couldn't make": Herrmann, *Anne Morrow Lindbergh*, pp. 243–44.
246   "the Bible": Berg, *Lindbergh*, p. 407.
"poisonous little": Schlesinger, *A Life in the Twentieth Century*, p. 242.
"I never said": Anne Lindbergh, *War Within and Without*, p. 170.
"scum on the": Anne Morrow Lindbergh, "Reaffirmation," *The Atlantic Monthly*, June 1941.
"Will I have": Anne Lindbergh, *War Within and Without*, p. 359.
"My marriage": Ibid., p. 148.
"Perhaps I am": Ibid., p. 171.
247   "After all": Ibid., p. 172.
248   "not because I": Ibid., p. 23.
"summer lightning": Berg, *Lindbergh*, p. 392.
"the bubonic plague": Anne Lindbergh, *War Within and Without*, p. 161.
"I [will] have": Roger Butterfield, "Lindbergh," *Life*, Aug. 11, 1941.
"he who spreads": *New York Times*, April 27, 1941.
249   "I just can't": Roger Butterfield, "Lindbergh," *Life*, Aug. 11, 1941.

249 **"really smart"**: *New York Times,* Nov. 29, 1940.

"Colonel Lindbergh": Berg, *Lindbergh,* p. 407.

"can still talk": Anne Lindbergh, *War Within and Without,* p. 105.

"arguing, debating": Wheeler-Bennett, *Special Relationships,* p. 130.

"Nothing that Aubrey": Ibid., p. 131.

250 **"Your father never"**: Reeve Lindbergh, *Under a Wing,* p. 146.

"eternal refutation": Roger Butterfield, "Lindbergh," *Life,* Aug. 11, 1941.

"How can such": Mosley, *Lindbergh,* pp. 280–81.

"Dear Nazi Lindbergh": Cole, *Lindbergh,* p. 147.

"There is nothing": *Omaha Morning World Herald* editorial, Friday, July 18, 1941, President's Official File, FDRPL.

251 **"your personal opposition"**: Cole, *Lindbergh,* p. 145.

"doing great damage": Ibid.

"He does not": Castle diary, Aug. 12, 1940, Castle papers, HL.

"a tragedy to": Cole, *Lindbergh,* p. 85.

"have become as": Roger Butterfield, "Lindbergh," *Life,* Aug. 11, 1941.

CHAPTER 17: "A NATIONAL DISGRACE"

252 **"exceedingly dirty"**: Culver and Hyde, *American Dreamer,* p. 242.

"a national disgrace": Sherwood, *Roosevelt and Hopkins,* p. 187.

"a disgraceful slugging": Davenport, *Too Strong for Fantasy,* p. 235.

"We let what": Neal, *Dark Horse,* p. 132.

253 **"a fountain of"**: Davenport, *Too Strong for Fantasy,* p. 230.

"Seldom has there": Raymond Clapper, *Watching the World: 1934–1944* (New York: McGraw Hill, 1944), p. 160.

254 **"The time has"**: Unsigned memo, Harry Hopkins papers, FDRPL.

"Willkie is distinctly": Ickes, *Secret Diary,* p. 212.

"was convinced that": Culver and Hyde, *American Dreamer,* p. 213.

255 **"The Republican candidate"**: Ibid., p. 237.

"imply that the": Ibid., p. 235.

WILLKIE IS: *Life,* Nov. 11, 1940.

NAZIS PREFER: Culver and Hyde, *American Dreamer,* p. 235.

"We are under": Neal, *Dark Horse,* p. 162.

"a serious mistake": Gentry, *J. Edgar Hoover,* p. 227.

256 **"Nigger, don't"**: Neal, *Dark Horse,* p. 163.

"You can't do": Ibid.

"the most scurrilous": Ibid.

"found himself": Ibid.

"reprehensible": Ibid., p. 164.

257 **"a drift toward"**: Ibid., p. 159.

"By the time": Ibid., p. 160.

"had encouraged the": Culver and Hyde, *American Dreamer,* p. 237.

"We can have": Neal, *Dark Horse,* p. 159.

"already almost on": Ibid.

"expediency": Raymond Clapper, *Watching the World,* p. 161.

"told the truth": Neal, *Dark Horse,* p. 160.

258   **"The political leaders"**: Samuel I. Rosenman, *Working with Roosevelt* (New York: Harper, 1952), p. 222.
      "Galahad": Culver and Hyde, *American Dreamer,* p. 135.
      "Everybody knows about": Neal, *Dark Horse,* p. 43.

259   **"If people try"**: Joseph E. Persico, *Roosevelt's Secret War: FDR and World War II Espionage* (New York: Random House, 2001), p. 41.
      "I am an": Rosenman, *Working with Roosevelt,* p. 238.
      "grim smile": Ibid.
      "I wish with": Robert Sherwood to FDR, Jan. 25, 1940, Sherwood papers, HL.
      "considered me": Robert Sherwood to Felix Frankfurter, Jan. 24, 1948, Sherwood papers, HL.
      "My poor boy": Alonso, *Robert E. Sherwood,* p. 221.

260   **"There is something"**: Davis, *FDR: Into the Storm,* p. 623.
      "certain forces": Cole, *Roosevelt and the Isolationists,* p. 401.
      "We will not": Neal, *Dark Horse,* p. 167.
      "I have said": Ibid.
      "terrible": Sherwood, *Roosevelt and Hopkins,* p. 191.
      "in yielding": Ibid., p. 201.

261   **"You should have"**: Paton-Walsh, *Our War Too,* pp. 117–18.
      "to the hilt": Kurth, *American Cassandra,* p. 321.
      "to get this": Ibid.
      "Roosevelt must stay": Ibid., p. 322.

262   **"Nazi jubilation"**: Paton-Walsh, *Our War Too,* p. 116.
      "despised": Sherwood, *Roosevelt and Hopkins,* p. 201.
      "Mike": Michael F. Reilly, *Reilly of the White House* (New York: Simon & Schuster, 1947), p. 66.
      "always ran scared": Walter Trohan, *Political Animals: Memoirs of a Sentimental Cynic* (Garden City, N.Y.: Doubleday, 1975), p. 83.

263   **"the menace of Hitler"**: Elson, *Time, Inc.,* pp. 444–45.
      "Roosevelt with his": Perret, *Days of Sadness,* p. 53.
      "a man on": Ibid., p. 237.
      "We have elected": Neal, *Dark Horse,* pp. 181–82.

CHAPTER 18: "WELL, BOYS, BRITAIN'S BROKE"

264   **"Not since"**: *Life,* March 24, 1941.

265   **"now, I feel"**: Churchill, *Their Finest Hour,* p. 553.
      "staggering shipping": Peters, *Five Days in Philadelphia,* p. 179.
      "the British would": *New York Times,* Dec. 12, 1940.
      "rather chilled": Reynolds, *Lord Lothian,* p. 43.

266   **"the political preoccupations"**: William S. Langer and S. Everett Gleason, *The Undeclared War: 1940–1941* (New York: Harper, 1953), p. 215.
      "It really": Geoffrey Parsons to William Allen White, Dec. 2, 1940, White papers, LC.
      "the Great White": William Allen White to Geoffrey Parsons, Dec. 5, 1940, White papers, LC.

266   **"Like a leaderless"**: *Life,* Dec. 16, 1940.

267   **"War relief"**: *Life,* Jan. 6, 1941.
"magic date": Reynolds, *Lord Lothian,* p. 43.

268   **"one of"**: Churchill, *Their Finest Hour,* p. 558.
"a ruthless": Reynolds, *Lord Lothian,* p. 45.
"the force of": Ibid., p. 58.
"its existence": Ibid., p. 47.

269   **"one of the most"**: Wheeler-Bennett, *Special Relationships,* p. 112.
"Well, boys": Ibid.
"could scarcely": Ibid.
"Oh, yes": Ibid.
"Never was": Ibid., p. 113.
"I do not think": Reynolds, *Lord Lothian,* p. 50.
"By revealing": Langer and Gleason, *Undeclared War,* p. 225.

270   **"deal with the"**: Reynolds, *Lord Lothian,* p. 55.
"powerful statement": "Death of Lothian," *Time,* Dec. 23, 1940.
"It is for you": Wheeler-Bennett, *Special Relationships,* p. 114.

271   **"valedictory to America"**: Ibid.
"beyond measure": Cable from Roosevelt to George VI, President's Personal File, FDRPL.
"The moment approaches": Churchill, *Their Finest Hour,* p. 566.
"Might it not": Kenneth S. Davis, *FDR: The War President, 1940–1943* (New York: Random House, 2000), p. 48.
"He had arrived": "Death of Lothian," *Time,* Dec. 23, 1940.

272   **"I didn't think"**: Butler, *Lord Lothian,* p. 314.
"He was a": Ibid., p. 316.
"loving care and": "Death of Lothian," *Time,* Dec. 23, 1940.
"Very softly and": Eleanor Shepardson to Lothian sisters, Whitney Shepardson papers, FDRPL.
"When the news": *New York Times,* Dec.13, 1940.
"It is no": Ibid.

273   **"graver blow to"**: Ibid.
"one of our": Butler, *Lord Lothian,* p. 318.
"I cannot help": Reynolds, *Lord Lothian,* p. 60.
"Never before since": Davis, *FDR: The War President,* pp. 82–83.

274   **"If your neighbor's"**: Richard Snow, *A Measureless Peril: America in the Fight for the Atlantic, The Longest Battle of World War II* (New York: Scribner, 2010), p. 115.
"There is far": Agar, *Darkest Year,* p. 164.
"If it is": Wheeler, *Yankee from the West,* pp. 26–27.

275   **"bunk"**: Agar, *Darkest Year,* p. 156.
"Certainly not": Ibid., p. 165.
"The opponents of": Ibid.
"that this emergency": Stimson diary, Dec. 14, 1940, FDRPL.
"The sooner we": Agar, *Darkest Year,* p. 156.

276   **"monstrous"**: Paton-Walsh, *Our War Too,* p. 134.
"only answer to": Wayne S. Cole, *America First: The Battle Against Intervention, 1940–1941* (Madison: University of Wisconsin Press, 1953), p. 55.

276   **"Wheeler fights"**: *Documents on German Foreign Policy 1918–45,* Series D, Vol. 12 (Washington, D.C.: U.S. Government Printing Office), p. 258.

"Never before has": Davis, *FDR: The War President,* p. 98.

"I must confess": Wheeler, *Yankee from the West,* p. 27.

"the most untruthful": Sherwood, *Roosevelt and Hopkins,* p. 229.

278   **"The opposition has"**: Schneider, *Should America Go to War?,* p. 84.

"use all our": Agar, *Darkest Year,* p. 165.

"great debate": Andrew Johnstone, "Private Interest Groups and the Lend-Lease Debate," *49th Parallel,* Summer 2001.

"democracy in action": Cole, *Lindbergh,* p. 103.

"the destruction of": Davis, *FDR: The War President,* p. 99.

"the war dictatorship bill": Ibid.

"playing Hitler's game": Schneider, *Should America Go to War?,* p. 85.

279   **"Ashes of"**: David Brinkley, *Washington Goes to War* (New York: Knopf, 1988), p. 30.

"Death is": Paton-Walsh, *Our War Too,* p. 148.

"Down with the": Ibid.

"a traitor to": Ibid.

"a noisy disorder": Ibid.

"I likewise believe": Ibid.

280   **"I want neither"**: Davis, *Hero,* p. 398.

"complete victory": Davis, *FDR: The War President,* p. 110.

"a vigorous": Ketchum, *Borrowed Years,* pp. 527–28.

"to work for": Chadwin, *War Hawks,* p. 133.

281   **"Under such dire"**: Neal, *Dark Horse,* p. 187.

"if the Republican": Davis, *FDR: The War President,* p. 100.

"Roosevelt is just": Neal, *Dark Horse,* p. 189.

"Republican Quisling": Richard Norton Smith, *Colonel,* p. 403.

"all the time": Unsigned memo, President's Secretary's File, FDRPL.

"though if Howard": Ibid.

"conspiring to get": Raymond Clapper, *Watching the World,* p. 166.

"Out of the": Neal, *Dark Horse,* p. 189.

"took an immediate": Ibid., p. 191.

282   **"incalculable services"**: Ketchum, *Borrowed Years,* p. 579.

"I would have": Neal, *Dark Horse,* p. 193.

VENI, VIDI, WILLKIE: *Life,* Feb. 17, 1941.

"been more stirring": Neal, *Dark Horse,* p. 201.

"the last best": Davis, *FDR: The War President,* p. 117.

"The people of": Ketchum, *Borrowed Years,* p. 580.

283   **"I struggled as"**: Davis, *FDR: The War President,* p. 118.

"Whatever influence": Neal, *Dark Horse,* p. 206.

"fight the war": Sevareid, *Not So Wild,* p. 193.

284   **"leafy, dreaming"**: Ibid.

"physical revulsion": Ibid., pp. 196–97.

"tobacco-chewing": Ibid., p. 197.

"wear the aspect": Olson, *Citizens of London,* p. 73.

"As far as": Ibid., pp. 73–74.

"We were not": Langer and Gleason, *The Undeclared War,* p. 261.

284   **"Vote!"**: Davis, *FDR: The War President,* p. 135.
285   **"slapped him"**: Sherwood, *Roosevelt and Hopkins,* p. 355.
286   **"We have taken"**: Ketchum, *Borrowed Years,* p. 582.
       "It is now": Ibid.
       "Whether we": Kabaservice, *Guardians,* p. 83.
       "The danger of": Nigel Hamilton, *JFK: Reckless Youth* (New York: Random House, 1992), p. 392.
       "True, in a sense": Schneider, *Should America Go to War?,* p. 130.
287   **"want to arouse"**: *Documents on German Foreign Policy 1918–45,* Series D, Vol. 12 (Washington, D.C.: U.S. Government Printing Office), p. 365.
       "the most unsordid action": Olson, *Citizens of London,* p. 11.
       "Remember, Mr. President": Ibid.

CHAPTER 19: "A RACE AGAINST TIME"

288   **"Our democracy"**: James MacGregor Burns, *Roosevelt: The Soldier of Freedom, 1940–1945* (New York: Harcourt Brace Jovanovich, 1970), p. 51.
       "was a fighting speech": Raymond Clapper, *Watching the World,* p. 269.
289   **"fiction that we can perform"**: Langer and Gleason, *Undeclared War,* p. 437.
       "a strange, prolonged": Davis, *FDR: The War President,* p. 152.
       "an exceedingly tired": Ickes, *Secret Diary,* p. 459.
       "a very slight": Davis, *FDR: Into the Storm,* p. 584.
290   **"What he's suffering"**: Sherwood, *Roosevelt and Hopkins,* p. 293.
       "The one course": Langer and Gleason, *Undeclared War,* p. 223.
       "a fog of": Childs, *I Write from Washington,* p. 217.
       "I feel very": Stimson diary, April 9, 1941, FDRPL.
       "were hanging on": Olson, *Citizens of London,* p. xiv.
291   **"the happy time"**: Snow, *Measureless Peril,* p. 105.
       "very distressing": Olson, *Citizens of London,* p. 5.
       "even now": Ibid., p. 6.
       "a disaster of": Ibid., p. 85.
       "discouragement and": Ibid., p. 86.
292   **"I feel that"**: Ibid.
       "The situation is": Steele, *Propaganda,* p. 114.
       "He was loyal": Biddle, *In Brief Authority,* pp. 184–85.
       "comes awfully close": Burns, *Soldier of Freedom,* p. 89.
293   **"get convoying now"**: Davis, *FDR: The War President,* p. 173.
294   **"obviously fearful"**: Ibid., p. 172.
       "more forceful": Burns, *Soldier of Freedom,* p. 91.
       "their constituents": Stimson diary, Jan. 19, 1941, FDRPL.
       "the people were": Stimson diary, April 25, 1941, FDRPL.
       "are groping": Langer and Gleason, *Undeclared War,* p. 456.
       "I am waiting": Ketchum, *Borrowed Years,* p. 589.
       "America": Kennedy, *Freedom from Fear,* p. 368.
295   **"a declaration of"**: Saul Friedlander, *Prelude to Downfall: Hitler and the United States, 1939–1941* (New York: Knopf, 1967), p. 175.
296   **"The American people"**: Perret, *Days of Sadness,* p. 79.
297   **"I am not"**: Stimson and Bundy, *On Active Service,* p. 370.

297   **"We are in"**: *Life,* May 5, 1941.
      "It is a": *Life,* May 19, 1941.
      "We . . . want": Ibid.
      "people are asking": Stimson diary, May 9, 1941, FDRPL.
      "I do know": Ickes, *Secret Diary,* p. 511.
      "absolutely hopeless": Ibid., p. 497.

298   **"if I could"**: Ibid., p. 511.
      "I cautioned him": Stimson diary, April 22, 1941, FDRPL.
      "constitutional aversion": Langer and Gleason, *Undeclared War,* p. 696.
      "does nothing": Stimson diary, May 27, 1941, FDRPL.
      "fascist": Doris Kearns Goodwin, *No Ordinary Time: Franklin and Eleanor Roosevelt: The Home Front in World War II* (New York: Simon & Schuster, 1994), p. 174.

299   **"I do not"**: Cray, *General of the Army,* p. 153.
      "It would be": Clifford and Spencer, *First Peacetime Draft,* p. 246.
      "realized that American": Wedemeyer, *Wedemeyer Reports!,* p. 69.

300   **"see if there"**: Murray Green unpublished manuscript, Green papers, AFA.
      "a too narrow": Grenville Clark to Henry Stimson, Dec. 23, 1940, Sherwood papers, HL.
      "less historical sense": Ronald Schaffer, "General Stanley D. Embick: Military Dissenter," *Military Affairs,* 1973.

301   **"highly desirable"**: Mark Watson, *Chief of Staff: Prewar Plans and Preparations* (Washington, D.C.: Center of Military History, 1991), p. 389.

302   **"It is important"**: Ibid., p. 390.
      "wrong from": Ibid.
      "if the current": Ronald Schaffer, "General Stanley D. Embick: Military Dissenter," *Military Affairs,* 1973.
      "a vainglorious fool": Leonard Mosley, *Marshall: Hero For Our Time* (New York: Hearst, 1982), p. 153.

303   **"in a choice position"**: Mosley, *Lindbergh,* p. 417.
      "could see any": Bendersky, *"Jewish Threat,"* p. 284.
      "made it about": Stimson diary, April 14, 1941, FDRPL.
      "a dangerous statement": Ibid.
      "the success of": Ibid.

304   **"couldn't stand it"**: Stimson diary, April 17, 1941, FDRPL.
      "the attitude": Castle diary, Sept. 20, 1941, Castle papers, HL.
      "practically all the": Castle diary, Dec. 18, 1940, Castle papers, HL.
      "great alarm": John Franklin Carter report to FDR, July 11, 1941, President's Secretary's File, FDRPL.
      "was very much disturbed": Olson, *Citizens of London,* p. 68.
      "how he had": Stimson diary, June 20, 1941, FDRPL.

305   **"Some of the"**: Stimson diary, Dec. 17, 1940, FDRPL.
      "apathy, confusion": Steele, *Propaganda,* p. 116.

306   **"looking to you"**: Stimson to FDR, May 24, 1941, FDRPL.
      "Hasn't somebody": Samuel and Dorothy Rosenman, *Presidential Style,* p. 384.
      "You know": Ibid.
      "strangle": Davis, *FDR: The War President,* p. 186.

307   **"almost like"**: Sherwood, *Roosevelt and Hopkins*, p. 298.
    "ninety-five": Ibid.
    "a solemn commitment": Ibid.
    "a mighty blow": Davis, *FDR: The War President*, p. 188.
    "at the present": Ibid.
    "On your marks": *Life,* June 16, 1941.
    "We want you": *Life,* June 2, 1941.
308   **"They seem to"**: Ibid.
    "to the last": *Life,* April 14, 1941.
    "It is impossible": Olson, *Citizens of London*, p. 91.
    "The whole thing": Ibid., p. 87.

CHAPTER 20: "A TRAITOROUS POINT OF VIEW"

309   **"to get really"**: Sherwood, *Roosevelt and Hopkins,* p. 265.
    "scathing and vindictive": Ibid., p. 266.
310   **"If 1940 was"**: Cuneo unpublished autobiography, Cuneo papers, FDRPL.
    "Your government has": Steele, *Propaganda*, p. 117.
    "unwittingly in most": Davis, *FDR: The War President*, p. 83.
    "What the president": Richard W. Steele, "Franklin D. Roosevelt and His Foreign Policy Critics," *Political Science Quarterly,* Spring 1979.
    "Theoretically, freedom": Cole, *Roosevelt and the Isolationists*, p. 418.
311   **"He has emerged"**: Cole, *Lindbergh*, p. 120.
    "because he had": Davis, *Hero*, p. 400.
    "By holding": Ibid., p. 403.
312   **"a bootlicker of"**: Brown, *Ordeal of a Playwright*, p. 97.
    "simply a Nazi": Cole, *Lindbergh*, p. 147.
313   **"a genius for"**: Biddle, *In Brief Authority*, p. 179.
    "native fascist": Ickes speech, Dec. 17, 1940, Ickes papers, LC.
    "the quislings": Ickes speech, Feb. 25, 1941, Ickes papers, LC.
    "No. 1 Nazi": Cole, *Lindbergh*, p. 130.
    "There are men": Berg, *Lindbergh*, p. 407.
    "a ruthless and conscious fascist": Ickes to FDR, Steve Early papers, FDRPL.
314   **"violent speeches"**: Davis, *Hero*, p. 403.
    "You say that": *Charleston Evening Post,* May 26, 1941.
    "a maggot": Charles Wolfert, letters to the editor, *New York Times,* June 5, 1940.
315   **"There is nothing"**: Roger Butterfield, "Lindbergh," *Life,* Aug. 11, 1941.
    "There has been": Steele, *Propaganda*, p. 191.
    "the administration will": Neal, *Dark Horse*, p. 212.
    "Let's not boo": Ibid.
    "the future welfare": Ross, *Last Hero*, p. 319.
    "What luck": Charles Lindbergh, *Wartime Journals*, p. 478.
    "I take this": Davis, *Hero*, p. 404.
316   **"this new"**: *Washington Times-Herald,* April 30, 1941.
    "returning his": *New York Times,* April 30, 1941.
    "had just left the": *Washington Times-Herald,* April 30, 1941.
    "No evidence existed": *New York Times,* April 29, 1941.

316   **"left a bad"**: *Life,* May 12, 1941.

      "doesn't exist today": Roger Butterfield, "Lindbergh," *Life,* Aug. 11, 1941.

      "government by subterfuge": Cole, *Lindbergh,* p. 189.

317   **"just about as"**: Ibid.

      "new policies": Ibid.

      "Neither I nor": Ibid., p. 190.

318   **"Individuals on both"**: Cole, *Lindbergh,* pp. 140–41.

      "filthy, profane": Olive Clapper, *Washington Tapestry* (New York: McGraw Hill, 1946), p. 250.

      "fat old men": Joseph Gies, *The Colonel of Chicago* (New York: Dutton, 1979), p. 170.

      "Jew-haters": Kabaservice, *Guardians,* pp. 80–81.

      "enemies of Democracy": Richard H. Minear, *Dr. Seuss Goes to War: The World War II Editorial Cartoons of Theodor Seuss Geisel* (New York: New Press, 1999), p. 14.

319   **LINDBERGH FOR**: Ibid., p. 20.

      "I'm saving my": Ibid., p. 21.

      ". . . and the wolf": Ibid.

      "devastated by bombing": Perret, *Days of Sadness,* p. 159.

      "Hang Roosevelt!": Isabel Leighton, *The Aspirin Age: 1919–1941* (New York: Simon & Schuster, 1949), p. 211.

      "Lindbergh became": Perret, *Days of Sadness,* p. 159.

320   **"What right has"**: Brown, *Ordeal of a Playwright,* pp. 32–33.

      "has given me": White to Arthur Sulzberger, Dec. 10, 1941, White papers, LC.

      "However you and": Davis, *FDR: The War President,* p. 87.

321   **"the lifeline between"**: Ibid.

      "getting out": Ibid.

      "The only reason": Ibid., p. 88.

      "The misunderstanding": Clark Eichelberger to White, Dec. 26, 1940, White papers, LC.

322   **"Mr. White has"**: Cole, *Lindbergh,* pp. 137–38.

      "doing a typical": Ibid., p. 138.

      "continue as": Ibid.

      "If anybody had": Thomas Lamont to FDR, Jan. 3, 1941, President's Official File, FDRPL.

      "and there is": Perret, *Days of Sadness,* p. 155.

      "Whatever is needed": William M. Tuttle Jr., "Aid-to-the-Allies Short-of-War vs. American Intervention, 1940: A Reappraisal of William Allen White's Leadership," *Journal of American History,* March 1970.

323   **"in the immoral"**: Paton-Walsh, *Our War Too,* pp. 154–55.

      "the first fascist": Justus Doenecke, *In Danger Undaunted: The Anti-Interventionist Movement of 1940–1941 as Revealed in the Papers of the America First Committee* (Stanford: Hoover Institution Press, 1990), p. 389.

      "instead of": Cole, *Lindbergh,* p. 150.

324   **"Mr. Fish"**: Marilyn Kaytor, *"21": The Life and Times of New York's Favorite Club* (New York: Viking, 1975), p. 96.

      "a Nazi front": Cole, *Lindbergh,* p. 140.

      "a publicity campaign": Ibid., p. 151.

324   **"a very real"**: Ibid.

325   **"A new hysterical"**: *Life,* Sept. 29, 1941.

326   **"Too many pros"**: Mosley, *Lindbergh,* p. 306.

      "bitterness, suspicion": Berg, *Lindbergh,* pp. 424–25.

      "I am sick": Anne Lindbergh, *War Within and Without,* p. 210.

      "a perfect base": Herrmann, *Anne Morrow Lindbergh,* p. 259.

      "Most of us": Ibid.

      "friendly": Charles Lindbergh, *Wartime Journals,* p. 515.

327   **"also had us"**: William C. Sullivan, *The Bureau: My Thirty Years in Hoover's FBI* (New York: Norton, 1979), p. 37.

      "I do not": Steele, *Free Speech in the Good War,* p. 93.

328   **"many radical"**: Goldstein, *Political Repression,* p. 243.

      "has been one": Ibid.

      "Martin Dies": Ibid., pp. 243–44.

      "The Dies Committee": Robert Griffith, *The Politics of Fear: Joseph R. McCarthy and the Senate* (Amherst: University of Massachusetts Press, 1970), p. 32.

329   **"political organization"**: Goldstein, *Political Repression,* p. 262.

CHAPTER 21: "DER FÜHRER THANKS YOU FOR YOUR LOYALTY"

331   **"Der Führer"**: British Security Coordination, p. 71.

      "When it came": Neal Gabler, *Winchell: Gossip, Power, and the Culture of Celebrity* (New York: Knopf, 1995), p. 295.

      "were giving aid": Arnold Forster, *Square One: A Memoir* (New York: Donald I. Fine, 1988), p. 57.

332   **"The best thing"**: Cole, *America First,* p. 121.

      "should not be": Ibid.

333   **"It almost seemed"**: British Security Coordination, p. 76.

      "used": Cole, *Roosevelt and the Isolationists,* p. 473.

334   **"Members of Congress"**: Ibid.

      "smear": Ibid.

      "ever-widening": *Documents on German Foreign Policy 1918–45,* Series D, Vol. 11 (Washington, D.C.: U.S. Government Printing Office), p. 337.

      "the government of": Ibid., pp. 409–10.

      "activities incompatible": Friedlander, *Prelude to Downfall,* p. 243.

      "dilemma in which": *Documents on German Foreign Policy 1918–45,* Series D, Vol. 12 (Washington, D.C.: U.S. Government Printing Office), pp. 1035–36.

335   **"Despite these new"**: Friedlander, *Prelude to Downfall,* p. 244.

      "I cannot warn": *Documents on German Foreign Policy 1918–45,* Series D, Vol. 9 (Washington, D.C.: U.S. Government Printing Office), p. 399.

      "these activities": Ibid., p. 411.

      "compelling military": Friedlander, *Prelude to Downfall,* p. 103.

      "marked by naivete": *Documents on German Foreign Policy 1918–45,* Series D, Vol. 13 (Washington, D.C.: U.S. Government Printing Office), p. 99.

336   **"Most, and probably"**: Ibid., p. 98.

337   **"today relies"**: Persico, *Roosevelt's Secret War,* p. 43.

337   **"the Nazis never"**: Jackson, *That Man,* p. 73.
339   **"a regular flow"**: Macdonald, *True Intrepid,* p. 78.
      "Bill Stephenson": Ibid., p. 82.
      "A most secret": Ibid., p. 68.
340   **"half truths"**: Berle diary, Sept. 13, 1939, Berle papers, FDRPL.
      "a full size": Cull, *Selling War,* p. 145.
      "get the dirt": Macdonald, *True Intrepid,* p. 93.
      "surprise and horror": Gentry, *J. Edgar Hoover,* p. 268.

CHAPTER 22: "WHERE IS THIS CRISIS?"

341   **"Where is this"**: Maj. Stephen D. Wesbrook, "The Railey Report and Army Morale 1941," *Military Review,* June 1980.
      "As far as": *Life,* Aug. 18, 1941.
342   **"gave the country"**: Biddle, *In Brief Authority,* p. 186.
      "not merely falling": Pogue, *Ordeal and Hope,* p. 157.
      "the people at": Maj. Stephen D. Wesbrook, "The Railey Report and Army Morale 1941," *Military Review,* June 1980.
      "Tonight I feel": Stimson diary, July 2, 1941, FDRPL.
343   **"We can"**: Michael Leigh, *Mobilizing Consent: Public Opinion and American Foreign Policy, 1937–1947* (Westport, Conn.: Greenwood Press, 1976), p. 73.
      "Since all of": Hadley Cantril to Anna Rosenberg, May 1941, President's Secretary's File, FDRPL.
      "failed to indicate": Hadley Cantril to Anna Rosenberg, July 3, 1941, President's Secretary's File, FDRPL.
344   **"I have tried"**: Leigh, *Mobilizing Consent,* p. 72.
      "the best way": J. Garry Clifford, "Both Ends of the Telescope: New Perspectives on FDR and American Entry into World War II," *Diplomatic History,* Spring 1989.
      "WHAT THE PEOPLE": Leigh, *Mobilizing Consent,* p. 73.
      "the facts of life": Langer and Gleason, *Undeclared War,* p. 444.
      "could have gone": Jackson, *That Man,* p. 41.
      "this was no": Rosenman, *Working with Roosevelt,* p. 280.
345   **"His perpetual"**: Ketchum, *Borrowed Years,* p. 603.
      "For the first": Langer and Gleason, *Undeclared War,* p. 539.
346   **"would almost"**: Ibid., p. 538.
      "would a hundred": Cole, *Roosevelt and the Isolationists,* p. 435.
      "If we see": David McCullough, *Truman* (New York: Simon & Schuster, 1992), p. 262.
347   **"a naval or"**: Langer and Gleason, *Undeclared War,* p. 557.
      "vitriolic outburst": Ibid., p. 578.
      "The people voting": *Life,* Aug. 4, 1941.
      "in carrying on": *Documents on German Foreign Policy 1918–45,* Series D, Vol. 13 (Washington, D.C.: U.S. Government Printing Office), p. 103.
348   **"which basically obligate"**: Ibid.
      "It is absolutely essential": Friedlander, *Prelude to Downfall,* p. 258.
      "most anxious to": Ibid.

348 **"hostile forces"**: Langer and Gleason, *Undeclared War,* p. 579.

349 **"the whole thing"**: B. Mitchell Simpson, *Admiral Harold R. Stark: Architect of Victory* (Columbia: University of South Carolina Press, 1989), p. 89.
"Ours is still": *Life,* Sept. 29, 1941.
"We are deceiving": Olson, *Citizens of London,* p. 115.
"As things stand": Stacy Schiff, *Saint-Exupéry: A Biography* (New York: Knopf, 1995), p. 358.

350 **"We are advertising"**: Burns, *Soldier of Freedom,* p. 119.
"1941 will go": Ketchum, *Borrowed Years,* p. 626.

351 **"such an emergency"**: *Life,* July 28, 1941.
"do not want": *Life,* Aug. 18, 1941.
"The boys here": Ibid.
"To hell with": Ibid.

352 **"an undisciplined mob"**: Maj. Stephen D. Wesbrook, "The Railey Report and Army Morale 1941," *Military Review,* June 1980.
"more than 90": Ibid.
"the government isn't": Ibid.
"in the public": Ibid.
"I, for one": Ibid.
"We have been": Stimson diary, Sept. 15, 1941, FDRPL.

353 **"The whole thing"**: James Wadsworth, Oral History Collection, CU.
"I cannot for": Pogue, *Ordeal and Hope,* p. 151.
"would be the": Marshall interview with Forrest Pogue, Marshall papers, Marshall Foundation, www.marshallfoundation.org/library/pogue.html.
"We cannot have": Ketchum, *Borrowed Years,* p. 645.
"infinitely greater today": Davis, *FDR, The War President,* p. 252.

354 **"The current"**: Stimson diary, July 21, 1941, FDRPL.
"I suggest personally": Cole, *Roosevelt and the Isolationists,* p. 437.

355 **"to be the"**: Stimson diary, Aug. 7, 1941, FDRPL.
"cowards": Ibid.
"was an expert": Caro, *Path to Power,* p. 323.
"literally afraid": Ibid, p. 330.
"one of us": D. B. Hardeman and Donald C. Bacon, *Rayburn: A Biography* (Austin: Texas Monthly Press, 1987), p. 233.
"the President didn't": Caro, *Path to Power,* p. 596.
"his advice was": Ibid.

356 **"I need your"**: Hardeman and Bacon, *Rayburn,* p. 264.
"follow your own": Ibid., p. 265.

357 **"the bill is"**: Ibid., p. 267.
"cowardice": Pogue, *Ordeal and Hope,* p. 152.
"If you don't": Langer and Gleason, *Undeclared War,* p. 574.

358 **"would become more"**: Olson, *Citizens of London,* p. 122.
"The President": Ibid., pp. 122–23.
"a wave of depression": Langer and Gleason, *Undeclared War,* p. 734.
"too many Americans": *Life,* Sept. 1, 1941.
"The public has been": Maj. Stephen D. Wesbrook, "The Railey Report and Army Morale 1941," *Military Review,* June 1980.
"Got any ideas?": Ibid.

CHAPTER 23: "PROPAGANDA . . . WITH A VERY
THICK COATING OF SUGAR"

359   **"Will you kindly"**: John E. Moser, " 'Gigantic Engines of Propaganda': The 1941 Senate Investigation of Hollywood," *Historian,* Summer 2001.

360   **"a more impartial"**: David Welky, *The Moguls and the Dictators: Hollywood and the Coming of World War II* (Baltimore: Johns Hopkins University Press, 2008), p. 251.

      "We really have": Ibid., p. 4.

      "the most gigantic": Calder, *Beware the British Serpent,* p. 239.

      "The silver screen": Welky, *Moguls and the Dictators,* p. 293.

      "Russia, Hungary": Neal Gabler, *An Empire of Their Own: How the Jews Invented Hollywood* (New York: Crown, 1988), p. 345.

361   **"are doing a"**: Welky, *Moguls and the Dictators,* p. 274.

363   **"Yes—Mussolini"**: *Life,* Feb. 13, 1939.

      "The question of": Welky, *Moguls and the Dictators,* p. 29.

      "The primary purpose": Ibid., p. 159.

      "the just rights": Ibid., p. 60.

      "believed movies": Ibid., p. 59.

      "we were always": Ibid., p. 3.

364   **"The Jews are"**: Otto Friedrich, *City of Nets: A Portrait of Hollywood in the 1940's* (New York: Harper & Row, 1986), p. 47.

      "From the time": Alan Brinkley, *Publisher,* p. 187.

365   **"So fast are"**: *Life,* June 17, 1940.

366   **"All that noise"**: Cull, *Selling War,* p. 112.

      "to shake the": Calder, *Beware the British Serpent,* p. 248.

      "The maintenance of": Cull, *Selling War,* p. 50.

367   **"propaganda . . ."**: Calder, *Beware the British Serpent,* p. 251.

      "You cannot": Ibid.

      "propaganda worth": Olson, *Citizens of London,* p. 236.

368   **"I was concerned"**: Ibid.

      "using the film": Welky, *Moguls and the Dictators,* p. 244.

369   **"thrilled"**: Ibid., p. 295.

370   **"men must fight"**: Ibid., p. 286.

      "trying to": Neal, *Dark Horse,* p. 213.

371   **"It is just"**: Welky, *Moguls and the Dictators,* p. 299.

      "put his clients": Ibid., p. 300.

      "bigotry, race": Ibid., p. 302.

372   **"It is a"**: Ibid., p. 303.

      "Have you seen": Ibid.

      "like a censor": Clayton R. Koppes and Gregory D. Black, *Hollywood Goes to War: How Politics, Profits and Propaganda Shaped World War II Movies* (London: Tauris, 1988), p. 44.

373   **"a frontal attack"**: Welky, *Moguls and the Dictators,* p. 298.

      "Do they want": Ibid., p. 308.

      "Certain aspects": Ibid., p. 309.

      "political coming": Ibid., p. 329.

CHAPTER 24: "SETTING THE GROUND FOR ANTI-SEMITISM"

375   **"There were many"**: Eisenhower, *Special People,* p. 136.
376   **"His actions"**: Undated Ickes memo to FDR, Stephen Early papers, FDRPL.
"the Knight of": Mosley, *Lindbergh,* p. 294.
"ex-Colonel": *New York Times,* July 15, 1941.
"full of lies": Anne Lindbergh, *War Within and Without,* p. 210.
"Nothing is to": Charles Lindbergh, *Wartime Journals,* p. 518.
"Mr. President": Mosley, *Lindbergh,* p. 295.
377   **"squeal"**: Ickes, *Secret Diary,* p. 581.
"For the first": Ibid., p. 582.
"Free speech": *Omaha Morning World Herald* editorial, Friday, July 18, 1941,
President's Official File, FDRPL.
"we have a": Miles Hart letter to Ickes, July 5, 1941, Ickes papers, LC.
378   **"powerful elements"**: Cole, *Lindbergh,* p. 158.
"practically inevitable": Ibid.
"war agitators": Ibid., p. 160.
"would be": Ibid., p. 171.
"Tolerance is": Ibid.
"both races": Ibid., p. 172.
"black gloom": Anne Lindbergh, *War Within and Without,* p. 220.
379   **"segregating them"**: Ibid., p. 223.
"Jew-baiting": Ibid., p. 224.
"I have never": Ibid., p. 227.
"at best unconsciously": Ibid., p. 221.
"shaken by": Ibid., p. 224.
"the terrible row": Herrmann, *Anne Morrow Lindbergh,* p. 322.
"I would rather": Ketchum, *Borrowed Years,* p. 642.
"a bloody revolution": William Castle diary, Aug. 11, 1941, HL.
380   **"A few Jews"**: Berg, *Lindbergh,* p. 386.
"end with their": Herrmann, *Anne Morrow Lindbergh,* p. 235.
"You have to": Bendersky, *"Jewish Threat,"* p. 273.
"Economic hardship": Forster, *Square One,* p. 38.
381   **"I don't often"**: Castle diary, Jan. 29, 1939, Castle papers, HL.
"subliminal anti-Semitism": Kabaservice, *Guardians,* p. 66.
"An all-too-large group": Ibid.
"I am afraid": Castle diary, Jan. 30, 1940, Castle papers, HL.
382   **"The Jewish group"**: Berle diary, Oct. 11, 1940, Berle papers, FDRPL.
"Only in that": Bendersky, *"Jewish Threat,"* p. 250.
"suspect or distasteful": Ibid., p. 238.
"did everything": Ibid., p. 274.
383   **"open and almost"**: Ward, *First-Class Temperament,* p. 59.
"had a way": Watkins, *Righteous Pilgrim,* p. 661.
"Leo, you know": Ward, *First-Class Temperament,* p. 255.
"to exercise": *New York Times,* Dec. 13, 1938.
"Jews in the": Henry Hardy, ed., *Isaiah Berlin: Letters 1928–1946* (Cambridge:
Cambridge University Press, 2004), p. 375.

384   **"even leading"**: Forster, *Square One,* p. 52.

"**with conditions"**: Kennedy, *Freedom from Fear,* p. 415.

"**The American"**: Perret, *Days of Sadness,* p. 97.

385   **"FDR failed Jews"**: Forster, *Square One,* p. 51.

"**far-sighted"**: *Documents on German Foreign Policy 1918–45,* Series D, Vol. 13 (Washington, D.C.: U.S. Government Printing Office), p. 213.

"**for the first"**: Thomas E. Mahl, *Desperate Deception: British Covert Operations in the United States, 1939–1944* (Washington, D.C.: Brassey's, 1998), p. 53.

386   **"public enemy"**: Cole, *Lindbergh,* p. 160.

HIS MOST APPRECIATIVE AUDIENCE: *Des Moines Register* cartoon, Sept. 11, 1941, America First papers, HI.

"**Newsreels"**: Sarles, *Story of America First,* p. 67.

"**whatever opposition"**: Charles Lindbergh, *Wartime Journals,* p. 538.

"**without our"**: Cole, *Lindbergh,* p. 162.

387   **"using war"**: Ibid., p. 187.

"**the storm is"**: Anne Lindbergh, *War Within and Without,* p. 225.

"**Rarely has"**: Cole, *Lindbergh,* p. 173.

"**the dark forces"**: Ibid., p. 174.

"**Spreading the Lovely"**: Minear, *Dr. Seuss Goes to War,* p. 21.

"**the most dangerous"**: Berg, *Lindbergh,* p. 428.

"**intemperate and"**: Cole, *Lindbergh,* p. 177.

"**impropriety"**: Ibid.

"**the most un-American"**: Berg, *Lindbergh,* p. 428.

388   **"a striking similarity"**: Cole, *Lindbergh,* p. 175.

"**done more to"**: Ibid., p. 178.

"**deep disagreement"**: Ibid.

"**Didn't our friend"**: Herrmann, *Anne Morrow Lindbergh,* pp. 262–63.

"**There are no"**: Sarles, *Story of America First,* p. xxxiii.

"**stupid"**: Welky, *Moguls and the Dictators,* p. 307.

389   **"the heart of"**: Unsigned memo, Sept. 19, 1941, America First papers, HI.

"**the mud-slingers"**: Sarles, *Story of America First,* p. xxxiii.

"**was not as"**: Ibid.

"**one hundred"**: Ibid., p. 58.

390   **"exclusive social"**: Cole, *Lindbergh,* pp. 181–82.

"**We need thousands"**: Ibid., p. 176.

"**Isn't it strange"**: Ketchum, *Borrowed Years,* p. 642.

"**I cannot blame"**: Eisenhower, *Special People,* p. 136.

391   **"I can still"**: Reeve Lindbergh, *Under a Wing,* p. 214.

"**so many"**: Ibid.

"**repellent and"**: Ibid., p. 203.

"**Did he really"**: Ibid., p. 202.

"**identifying a situation"**: Ibid., p. 215.

392   **"If he had"**: Ibid., p. 216.

"**I consider the"**: Paton-Walsh, *Our War Too,* p. 186.

"**desperately that we"**: Ibid., p. 187.

"**'War Monger'"**: Ibid.

CHAPTER 25: "HE WAS NOT GOING TO LEAD THE
             COUNTRY INTO WAR"

393   **"The opponents to"**: Bradford W. Wright, *Comic Book Nation: The Transformation of Youth Culture in America* (Baltimore: Johns Hopkins University Press,
2003), p. 36.

394   **"middle of the"**: Ketchum, *Borrowed Years*, p. 622.
"to carry the war": Ibid.
"conservative about": *Life*, May 26, 1941.
"I would hate": Ibid.

395   **"defeating Nazism"**: Cull, *Selling War*, p. 185.
"The Isolationists": Ibid.
"grown men": Perret, *Days of Sadness*, p. 191.

396   **"fired first upon"**: Langer and Gleason, *Undeclared War*, p. 745.
"piracy": Ibid.

397   **"forthright in saying"**: Goodhart, *Fifty Ships*, p. 198.
"Please accept": David Fairbank White, *Bitter Ocean: The Battle of the Atlantic,
1939–1945* (New York: Simon & Schuster, 2006), p. 134.

398   **"[W]e have waited"**: Rachel S. Cox, *Into Dust and Fire: Five Young Americans
Who Went First to Fight the Nazi Army* (New York: New American Library,
2012), p. 9.
"Every American": Olson, *Citizens of London*, p. 132.

399   **"the people speak"**: *Life*, Nov. 24, 1941.

400   **"in the face"**: Perret, *Days of Sadness*, p. 171.
"look for": Davis, *FDR: The War President*, p. 274.
"waited for": Ibid., p. 324.

401   **"a piece of"**: Neal, *Dark Horse*, p. 213.
"pursuing its usual": Ibid., p. 214.
"the United States": Ibid., p. 215.
"to wipe the": *Life*, Nov. 3, 1941.

402   **"an engraved"**: Cole, *America First*, p. 163.
"The Crisis Is": Cole, *Roosevelt and the Isolationists*, p. 451.

403   **"undoubtedly reliable"**: Persico, *Roosevelt's Secret War*, p. 127.
"forgeries of": *Documents on German Foreign Policy 1918–45*, Series D, Vol. 13
(Washington, D.C.: U.S. Government Printing Office), p. 724.
"British intelligence": Cull, *Selling War*, p. 173.

404   **"The feeling that"**: Stimson diary, Nov. 13, 1941, FDRPL.
"You men who": Cole, *Roosevelt and the Isolationists*, p. 452.
"Tragic indifference": Claude Denson Pepper, *Pepper: Eyewitness to a Century*
(New York: Harcourt Brace Jovanovich, 1987), p. 107.

405   **"this old tin can"**: *Life*, Nov. 17, 1941.
"I think the": *Life*, Nov. 10, 1941.

406   **"it was simply"**: Ickes, *Secret Diary*, p. 650.
"The Navy is": Ketchum, *Borrowed Years*, p. 606.
"Tell me": Snow, *Measureless Peril*, p. 141.
"Nothing is more": Olson, *Citizens of London*, p. 140.
"juggler": Goodwin, *No Ordinary Time*, p. 137.

406 **"he had no"**: Sherwood, *Roosevelt and Hopkins,* p. 383.
    "the awful picture": Ibid., p. 429.
407 **"whatever the peril"**: Ibid., p. 299.
    "the last thing": Samuel and Dorothy Rosenman, *Presidential Style,* p. 384.
    "a great confidence": Jackson, *That Man,* p. 106.
    "the historians who": Agar, *Darkest Year,* p. 168.
    "baby the Japs": Olson, *Citizens of London,* p. 138.

CHAPTER 26: "THE GREATEST SCOOP IN HISTORY"

409 **"There seems to"**: *Life,* March 3, 1941.
410 **"Let there be"**: Langer and Gleason, *Undeclared War,* p. 652.
    "the noose is": Ibid.
411 **"No one worried"**: *Life,* Dec. 8, 1941.
    FDR'S SECRET WAR PLANS: Pogue, *Ordeal and Hope,* p. 160.
    "final supreme effort": Ibid., p. 161.
412 **"represents decisions"**: Gies, *Colonel of Chicago,* p. 189.
    "never been constituted": Wheeler, *Yankee from the West,* p. 35.
    "What do you": Pogue, *Ordeal and Hope,* p. 161.
413 **"This is a"**: Burns, *Soldier of Freedom,* p. 84.
    "First the President": Pogue, *Ordeal and Hope,* pp. 156–57.
    "overall production": FDR to Stimson, July 9, 1941, President's Secretary's File, FDRPL.
    "the planner of": Wedemeyer, *Wedemeyer Reports!,* p. 14.
    "come to see Germany": Ibid., p. 10.
414 **"worldwide Communist conspiracy"**: Ibid.
    "the German search": Ibid.
    "a national movement": Bendersky, *"Jewish Threat,"* p. 232.
    "some of my fellow": Wedemeyer, *Wedemeyer Reports!,* p. 41.
    "It was my": Ibid.
415 **"one of the most"**: Eric Larrabee, *Commander in Chief: Franklin D. Roosevelt, His Lieutenants, and Their War* (New York: Harper & Row, 1987), p. 121.
    "complete military": Langer and Gleason, *Undeclared War,* p. 739.
    "Ultimate victory": Kennedy, *Freedom from Fear,* p. 487.
    "revolutionized our": Ketchum, *Borrowed Years,* p. 629.
416 **"He was afraid"**: Stimson diary, Sept. 25, 1941, FDRPL.
    "Well, we": Richard Norton Smith, *Colonel,* p. 410.
417 **"the last great"**: Ibid., p. 414.
    "Chicago Needs": Schneider, *Should America Go to War?,* p. 168.
    "Billions for defense": Ibid.
    "Godless Communists": Ritchie, *Reporting from Washington,* p. 10.
    "the greatest scoop": Richard Norton Smith, *Colonel,* p. xxi.
418 **"the sort of"**: Doenecke, *In Danger Undaunted,* p. 36.
    "Nothing more": Stimson diary, Dec. 4 1941, FDRPL.
    "get rid of": Ibid.
    "to print the": Gies, *Colonel of Chicago,* p. 192.
    "had never seen": Trohan, *Political Animals,* p. 171.

419   **"I could not"**: Wedemeyer, *Wedemeyer Reports!*, p. 16.
      "descended upon me": Wedemeyer to Chesly Manly, Aug. 22, 1957, Wedemeyer papers, HI.

419   **"He is reported"**: FBI report on Victory Program leak, Wedemeyer papers, HI.
      "I respect him": Wedemeyer, *Wedemeyer Reports!*, p. 40.

420   **"gigantic American"**: Wheeler, *Yankee from the West,* p. 32.
      "document": Ibid.
      "what was in": Ibid.

421   **"made available"**: Murray Green interview with Wedemeyer, Green papers, AFA.
      "second only": Richard Norton Smith, *Colonel,* p. 415.
      "There was a": Murray Green interview with Wedemeyer, Green papers, AFA.

422   **"whole effort was"**: Stimson, *On Active Service,* p. 355.
      "would fight": Murray Green interview with Wedemeyer, Green papers, AFA.
      "a general of": Thomas Fleming, *The New Dealers' War: FDR and the War Within World War II* (New York: Basic, 2001), p. 27.
      "When we got": Ibid., p. 28.
      "thrown gasoline": Ibid.

423   **"This means"**: Olson, *Citizens of London,* p. 143.
      "the inherent possibilities": Berg, *Lindbergh,* pp. 555–56.

CHAPTER 27: "LET'S LICK HELL OUT OF THEM"

424   **"an era came"**: Schlesinger, *A Life in the Twentieth Century,* p. 261.
      "the boldest interventionists": Childs, *I Write from Washington,* p. 242.

425   **"very strained"**: Ward, *First-Class Temperament,* p. 591.
      "deeply shaken": Biddle, *In Brief Authority,* p. 206.
      "How did they": Ibid.
      "who had been": Stimson diary, Dec. 7, 1941, FDRPL.

426   **"Destroyed on"**: Olson, *Citizens of London,* p. 146.
      "We have been": Davis, *Hero,* p. 555.

427   **"The Japanese"**: Cull, *Selling War,* p. 187.
      "All of us": Gies, *Colonel of Chicago,* p. 194.
      "This time": Ibid.
      "Let's lick": Wheeler, *Yankee from the West,* p. 36.
      "The time for": Cole, *Roosevelt and the Isolationists,* p. 504.
      "I just remember": Sarles, *Story of America First,* p. 215.

428   **"the worst news"**: Ketchum, *Borrowed Years,* p. 783.
      "If they": Olson, *Citizens of London,* p. 143.
      "The news has": Ibid., p. 144.
      "We shall": Ibid.

429   **"a lingering distinction"**: Robert Dallek, *Franklin D. Roosevelt and American Foreign Policy, 1932–1945* (New York: Oxford University Press, 1995), p. 312.

430   **"date which will"**: Burns, *Soldier of Freedom,* p. 165.
      "Mr. Speaker": Hardeman and Bacon, *Rayburn,* p. 276.
      "It seemed": Childs, *I Write from Washington,* p. 244.

431   **"Germany, of course"**: Langer and Gleason, *Undeclared War,* p. 910.

431   **"the turning point"**: Ketchum, *Borrowed Years*, p. 791.
433   **"At last"**: Manchester, *Glory and the Dream*, p. 260.
      "The war came": Perret, *Days of Sadness*, p. 203.
      "We are now": Burns, *Soldier of Freedom*, p. 172.
      "were filled": David Brinkley, *Washington Goes to War*, p. 91.
434   **"most of the men"**: Perret, *Days of Sadness*, p. 255.
      "Ordinary people": Ibid., p. 213.
      "the worst single": Biddle, *In Brief Authority*, p. 213.
435   **"The test of"**: Perret, *Days of Sadness*, p. 367.
      "No war": Olson, *Citizens of London*, p. 229.
436   **"If the war"**: Perret, *Days of Sadness*, p. 213.
437   **"It was a"**: Ibid., p. 215.
      "when the Japanese": "U.S. at War," *Army and Navy Journal*, Nov. 2, 1945.

CHAPTER 28: AFTERMATH

438   **"of more value"**: Berg, *Lindbergh*, p. 437.
439   **"I think he"**: Murray Green interview with Wedemeyer, Green papers, AFA.
      "indicates a": Davis, *Hero*, p. 416.
      "There cannot be": Berg, *Lindbergh*, p. 434.
440   **"Our son is"**: Cole, *Lindbergh*, p. 213.
      "I am strongly": Ickes to James Henle, Aug. 28, 1944, Ickes papers, LC.
      "this loyal friend": Ickes to FDR, Stephen Early papers, FDRPL.
      "It would be": Ibid.
      "wholeheartedly": Ibid.
      "who has shown": Murray Green unpublished manuscript, Green papers, AFA.
441   **"obstacles had been"**: Berg, *Lindbergh*, p. 437.
      "was angry": Ibid.
442   **"purposely entered"**: Cole, *Lindbergh*, p. 222.
      "Among most": Roger Butterfield, "Lindbergh," *Life*, Aug. 11, 1941.
      "absolutely certain": Davis, *Hero*, p. 414.
      "I do not": Sarles, *Story of America First*, p. 118.
      "Personally": Charles Lindbergh, *Wartime Journals*, p. 452.
      "I don't think": Alden Whitman, "Life with Lindy," *New York Times Magazine*, May 8, 1977.
443   **"Why does the"**: Mosley, *Lindbergh*, p. 320.
      "Lindbergh!": Lauren D. Lyman, "The Lindbergh I Knew," *Saturday Evening Post*, April 4, 1953.
      "Everything was": Herrmann, *Anne Morrow Lindbergh*, p. 284.
444   **"rendered valuable"**: Sherwood, *Roosevelt and Hopkins*, p. 155.
      "a letter to him": Anne Lindbergh, *War Within and Without*, p. 447.
445   **"I am sad"**: Ibid., pp. 449–50.
      "sun": Joyce Milton, *Loss of Eden: A Biography of Charles and Anne Morrow Lindbergh* (New York: HarperCollins, 1993), p. 474.
      "earth": Ibid., p. 447.
      "a sun": Ibid.
      "I do not": Cole, *Roosevelt and the Isolationists*, p. 509.

446   **"his contribution"**: Truman Smith, *Berlin Alert,* p. 42.
"burst into roars": Katharine Smith unpublished autobiography, Truman Smith papers, HI.

447   **"equal in influence"**: Mark A. Stoler, "From Continentalism to Globalism: Gen. Stanley D. Embick, the Joint Strategic Survey Committee and the Military View of American National Policy During the Second World War," *Diplomatic History,* July 1982.
"suspicion of British": Olson, *Citizens of London,* p. 152.
"too much": Ibid.
"one of the most": Wedemeyer obituary, *New York Times,* Dec. 20, 1989.

448   **"a vocal"**: *Life,* Aug. 11, 1941.
"stooge for Roosevelt": *Life,* Nov. 3, 1941.

449   **"the Negro question"**: Neal, *Dark Horse,* p. 275.
"the desire to": Ibid.
"responsible participation": Cole, *Roosevelt and the Isolationists,* p. 522.
"If I could": Peters, *Five Days in Philadelphia,* p. 195.
"into deep mourning": *New York Times,* Oct. 9, 1941.
"His party": Ibid.
"tremendous courage": Ibid.
"As a Negro": Ibid.
"Wendell Willkie": Ibid.

450   **"American Century"**: Henry Luce, "American Century," *Life,* Feb. 17, 1941.
"the reshaping": Isaacson and Thomas, *Wise Men,* p. 407.
"Collectively, they": Perret, *Days of Sadness,* p. 160.

451   **"Yes, I did"**: Scott Stossel, *Sarge: The Life and Times of Sargent Shriver* (Washington, D.C.: Smithsonian Books, 2004), p. 58.

452   **"I wanted"**: Ibid.
"No": Sarles, *Story of America First,* p. 219.
"did not affect": Berg, *Lindbergh,* p. 463.
"the vindictiveness": Ibid.

453   **"President Kennedy"**: Herrmann, *Anne Morrow Lindbergh,* p. 299.
"We left with": Berg, *Lindbergh,* p. 517.
"very constrained": Mosley, *Lindbergh,* p. xii.
"Even after": Ibid.
"we were both": Anne Morrow Lindbergh obituary, *New York Times,* Feb. 8, 2001.
"Like many": Mosley, *Lindbergh,* pp. 378–79.

454   **"break up"**: Anne Lindbergh, *Bring Me a Unicorn,* pp. 204–5.
"they have more": Berg, *Lindbergh,* p. 520.
"I have seen": "Lindbergh: The Way of a Hero," *Time,* May 26, 1967.
"If I had": Alden Whitman, "Lindbergh Speaks Out," *New York Times Magazine,* May 8, 1977.

455   **"give my true"**: Anne Lindbergh, *War Within and Without,* p. 427.
"artists, writers": Reeve Lindbergh, *Under a Wing,* p. 57.
"He liked to": Ross, *Last Hero,* p. 335.
"Charles only touches": Mosley, *Lindbergh,* p. xvii.
"terrible": Berg, *Lindbergh,* p. 480.
"He must control": Ibid.

456   **"a sense of"**: Reeve Lindbergh, *Under a Wing,* p. 61.
"**I was very**": Eisenhower, *Special People,* p. 140.
"**how to remain**": Anne Morrow Lindbergh, *Gift from the Sea* (New York: Pantheon, 2005), p. 23.
457   "**the circus act**": Ibid., p. 20.
"**We work easily**": Ibid., p. 92.
"**makes it very**": Anne Lindbergh, *Against Wind and Tide,* p. 144.
"**outgrown**": Ibid.
"**rather sad**": Ibid, p. 155.
"**Where are you?**": Ibid., p. 173.
"**agonies of mind**": Berg, *Lindbergh,* p. 497.
458   "**the Lindbergh marriage**": Ibid., pp. 547–48.
"**Since I know**": Anne Lindbergh, *Against Wind and Tide,* pp. 54–55.
"**Dana pulled me**": Berg, *Lindbergh,* p. 497.
"**badly mated**": Ibid., p. 509.
"**abandoned and put upon**": Anne Lindbergh, *Against Wind and Tide,* p. 169.
"**was running**": Berg, *Lindbergh,* p. 510.
459   "**She knew**": Reeve Lindbergh, *Forward from Here,* p. 210.
"**We were always**": "Lindbergh's Double Life," *Deutsche Welle,* June 20, 2005.
"**the stern arbiter**": Reeve Lindbergh, *Forward from Here,* p. 201.
460   "**One of my**": Ibid., p. 204.
"**These children**": Ibid., p. 203.
"**Being in my**": Ibid., p. 217.
"**He just didn't**": Ibid., pp. 217–18.
"**every intimate**": Ibid., p. 218.

BIBLIOGRAPHY

ARCHIVAL MATERIAL

Franklin D. Roosevelt Presidential Library
Adolf A. Berle Papers
Francis Biddle Papers
Ernest Cuneo Papers
Stephen T. Early Papers
Harry Hopkins Papers
Franklin D. Roosevelt Papers
Whitney Shepardson Papers
Henry L. Stimson Diaries (microfilm)

Library of Congress
John Balderston Papers
Harold L. Ickes Papers
William Allen White Papers

Hoover Institution, Stanford University
America First Committee Papers
Truman Smith Papers
Albert Wedemeyer Papers

Oral History Collection, Columbia University
William Benton
Samuel Rosenman
James Wadsworth

Houghton Library, Harvard University
William Castle Papers
Robert E. Sherwood Papers

Baker Library, Harvard University Business School
Thomas Lamont Papers

Sophia Smith Collection, Smith College
Anne Morrow Lindbergh Papers
Charles Lindbergh Papers
Elizabeth C. Morrow Papers

Air Force Academy
Murray Green Papers

PUBLISHED MATERIAL

Acheson, Dean. *Morning and Noon*. Boston: Houghton Mifflin, 1965.

Agar, Herbert. *The Darkest Year: Britain Alone, June 1940–June 1941*. Garden City, N.Y.: Doubleday, 1973.

Allen, Frederick Lewis. *Only Yesterday: An Informal History of the 1920's*. New York: Perennial, 2000.

———. *Since Yesterday: The 1930s in America*. New York: Perennial, 1986.

Alonso, Harriet Hyman. *Robert E. Sherwood: The Playwright in Peace and War*. Amherst: University of Massachusetts Press, 2007.

Alsop, Joseph W. *FDR: 1882–1945: A Centenary Remembrance*. New York: Viking, 1982.

———. *"I've Seen the Best of It": Memoirs*. New York: Norton, 1992.

Arnold, Henry H. *Global Mission*. New York: Harper, 1949.

Baldwin, Neil. *Henry Ford and the Jews: The Mass Production of Hate*. New York: Public Affairs, 2001.

Beck, Alfred M. *Hitler's Ambivalent Attaché: Friedrich von Boetticher in America, 1933–1941*. Washington, D.C.: Potomac Books, 2005.

Bendersky, Joseph. *The "Jewish Threat": The Anti-Semitic Politics of the U.S. Army*. New York: Basic Books, 2000.

Berg, A. Scott. *Lindbergh*. New York: Berkley Books, 1999.

Berger, Meyer. *The New York Times: 1851–1951*. New York: Simon & Schuster, 1951.

Biddle, Francis. *In Brief Authority*. Garden City, N.Y.: Doubleday, 1962.

Brinkley, Alan. *The Publisher: Henry Luce and His American Century*. New York: Knopf, 2010.

Brinkley, David. *Washington Goes to War*. New York: Knopf, 1988.

Brinkley, Douglas. *Gerald R. Ford*. New York: Times Books, 2007.

British Security Coordination. *The Secret History of British Intelligence in the Americas, 1940–1945*. New York: Fromm International, 1999.

Brown, Anthony Cave. *"C": The Secret Life of Sir Stewart Graham Menzies*. New York: Macmillan, 1987.

Brown, John Mason. *The Ordeal of a Playwright: Robert E. Sherwood and the Challenge of War*. New York: Harper & Row, 1970.

————. *The Worlds of Robert E. Sherwood: Mirror to His Times, 1896–1939*. New York: Harper & Row, 1965.

Bryce, Ivar. *You Only Live Once: Memories of Ian Fleming*. Frederick, Md.: University Publications of America, 1984.

Burns, James MacGregor. *Roosevelt: The Lion and the Fox*. New York: Harcourt, Brace & World, 1956.

————. *Roosevelt: The Soldier of Freedom, 1940–1945*. New York: Harcourt Brace Jovanovich, 1970.

Butler, James R. M. *Lord Lothian: Philip Kerr, 1882–1940*. New York: St. Martin's, 1960.

Calder, Robert. *Beware the British Serpent: The Role of Writers in British Propaganda in the United States, 1939–1945*. Montreal: Queen's University Press, 2004.

Cantril, Hadley. *The Human Dimension: Experiences in Policy Research*. New Brunswick, N.J.: Rutgers University Press, 1967.

Carlson, John Roy. *Under Cover: My Four Years in the Nazi Underworld of America*. New York: Dutton, 1943.

Caro, Robert A. *The Years of Lyndon Johnson: The Path to Power*. New York: Knopf, 1982.

————. *The Years of Lyndon Johnson: Master of the Senate*. New York: Vintage, 2003.

The Century Association. *The Century 1847–1946*. New York: The Century Association, 1947.

Chadwin, Mark Lincoln. *The War Hawks: American Interventionists Before Pearl Harbor*. Chapel Hill: University of North Carolina Press, 1968.

Chernow, Ron. *The House of Morgan: An American Banking Dynasty and the Rise of Modern Finance*. New York: Grove Press, 2010.

Childs, Marquis W. *I Write from Washington*. New York: Harper, 1942.

Churchill, Winston S. *Their Finest Hour*. Boston: Houghton Mifflin, 1949.

Clapper, Olive. *Washington Tapestry*. New York: McGraw Hill, 1946.

Clapper, Raymond. *Watching the World: 1934–1944*. New York: McGraw Hill, 1944.

Clifford, J. Garry. *The Citizen Soldiers: The Plattsburg Training Camp Movement, 1913–1920*. Lexington: University Press of Kentucky, 1972.

————, and Samuel R. Spencer Jr. *The First Peacetime Draft*. Lawrence: University Press of Kansas, 1986.

Cloud, Stanley, and Lynne Olson. *The Murrow Boys: Pioneers on the Front Lines of American Journalism*. Boston: Houghton Mifflin, 1996.

Coffey, Thomas M. *Hap: The Story of the U.S. Air Force and the Man Who Built It*. New York: Viking, 1982.

Cole, Wayne S. *America First: The Battle Against Intervention, 1940–1941*. Madison: University of Wisconsin Press, 1953.

————. *Charles A. Lindbergh and the Battle Against American Intervention in World War II*. New York: Harcourt Brace Jovanovich, 1974.

————. *Roosevelt and the Isolationists, 1932–1945*. Lincoln: University of Nebraska Press, 1983.

————. *Senator Gerald P. Nye and American Foreign Relations*. Minneapolis: University of Minnesota Press, 1962.

Conant, Jennet. *The Irregulars: Roald Dahl and the British Spy Ring in Wartime Washington*. New York: Simon & Schuster, 2008.

Cordery, Stacy A. *Alice: Alice Roosevelt Longworth: From White House Princess to Washington Power Broker*. New York: Viking, 2007.

Cousins, Norman, and J. Garry Clifford, eds. *Memoirs of a Man: Grenville Clark*. New York: Norton, 1975.

Cox, Rachel S. *Into Dust and Fire: Five Young Americans Who Went First to Fight the Nazi Army*. New York: New American Library, 2012.

Cray, Ed. *General of the Army: George Marshall, Soldier and Statesman*. New York: Norton, 1990.

Cull, Nicholas John. *Selling War: The British Propaganda Campaign Against American "Neutrality" in World War II*. New York: Oxford University Press, 1995.

Culver, John C., and John Hyde. *American Dreamer: The Life and Times of Henry A. Wallace*. New York: Norton, 2000.

Dallek, Robert. *Franklin D. Roosevelt and American Foreign Policy, 1932–1945*. New York: Oxford University Press, 1995.

Daso, Dik Alan. *Hap Arnold and the Evolution of American Air Power*. Washington, D.C.: Smithsonian Institution Press, 2000.

Davenport, Marcia. *Too Strong for Fantasy*. New York: Pocket, 1969.

Davis, Kenneth S. *FDR: Into the Storm, 1937–1940*. New York: Random House, 1993.

———. *FDR: The New Deal Years, 1933–1937*. New York: Random House, 1986.

———. *FDR: The War President, 1940–1943*. New York: Random House, 2000.

———. *The Hero: Charles A. Lindbergh and the American Dream*. Garden City, N.Y.: Doubleday, 1959.

Dietrich-Berryman, Eric, Charlotte Hammond, and R. E. White. *Passport Not Required: U.S. Volunteers in the Royal Navy, 1939–1941*. Annapolis, Md.: Naval Institute Press, 2010.

Doenecke, Justus. *In Danger Undaunted: The Anti-Interventionist Movement of 1940–1941 as Revealed in the Papers of the America First Committee*. Stanford: Hoover Institution Press, 1990.

Dunne, Gerald T. *Grenville Clark: Public Citizen*. New York: Farrar, Straus & Giroux, 1986.

Eagan, Eileen. *Class, Culture, and the Classroom: The Student Peace Movement of the 1930s*. Philadelphia: Temple University Press, 1981.

Eisenhower, Julie Nixon. *Special People*. New York: Simon & Schuster, 1977.

Elson, Robert T. *Time, Inc.: The Intimate History of a Publishing Enterprise, 1923–1941*. New York: Atheneum, 1968.

Feldman, Noah. *Scorpions: The Battles and Triumphs of FDR's Great Supreme Court Justices*. New York: Twelve, 2010.

Ferber, Edna. *A Peculiar Treasure*. New York: Doubleday, Doran & Co., 1939.

Fleming, Thomas. *The New Dealers' War: FDR and the War Within World War II*. New York: Basic, 2001.

Forster, Arnold. *Square One: A Memoir*. New York: Donald I. Fine, 1988.

Fox, James. *Five Sisters: The Langhornes of Virginia*. New York: Simon & Schuster, 2000.

Friedlander, Saul. *Prelude to Downfall: Hitler and the United States, 1939–1941*. New York: Knopf, 1967.

Friedrich, Otto. *City of Nets: A Portrait of Hollywood in the 1940's*. New York: Harper & Row, 1986.

Gabler, Neal. *An Empire of Their Own: How the Jews Invented Hollywood*. New York: Crown, 1988.

————. *Winchell: Gossip, Power, and the Culture of Celebrity*. New York: Knopf, 1995.

Gaines, James R. *Wit's End: Days and Nights of the Algonquin Round Table*. New York: Harcourt, 1977.

Gentry, Curt. *J. Edgar Hoover: The Man and the Secrets*. New York: Norton, 1991.

German Auswärtiges Amt. *Documents on German Foreign Policy 1918–45,* Series D, Vols. 9–13. Washington, D.C.: U.S. Government Printing Office, 1949.

Gies, Joseph. *The Colonel of Chicago*. New York: Dutton, 1979.

Ginsberg, Benjamin. *The Fatal Embrace: Jews and the State*. Chicago: University of Chicago Press, 1993.

Goldstein, Robert Justin. *Political Repression in Modern America: From 1870 to the Present*. Cambridge, Mass.: Schenkman, 1978.

Goodhart, Philip. *Fifty Ships That Saved the World: The Foundation of the Anglo-American Alliance*. Garden City, N.Y.: Doubleday, 1965.

Goodwin, Doris Kearns. *No Ordinary Time: Franklin and Eleanor Roosevelt: The Home Front in World War II*. New York: Simon & Schuster, 1994.

Griffith, Robert. *The Politics of Fear: Joseph R. McCarthy and the Senate*. Amherst: University of Massachusetts Press, 1970.

Gunther, John. *Roosevelt in Retrospect*. New York: Harper, 1950.

Halberstam, David. *The Powers That Be*. Urbana: University of Illinois Press, 2000.

Hamilton, Nigel. *JFK: Reckless Youth*. New York: Random House, 1992.

Hardeman, D. B., and Donald C. Bacon. *Rayburn: A Biography*. Austin: Texas Monthly Press, 1987.

Hardy, Henry, ed. *Isaiah Berlin: Letters 1928–1946*. Cambridge: Cambridge University Press, 2004.

Harper, John Lamberton. *American Visions of Europe: Franklin D. Roosevelt, George F. Kennan and Dean Acheson*. Cambridge: Cambridge University Press, 1994.

Herrmann, Dorothy. *Anne Morrow Lindbergh: A Gift for Life*. New York: Ticknor & Fields, 1993.

Hertog, Susan. *Anne Morrow Lindbergh: Her Life*. New York: Anchor, 1999.

Higham, Charles. *American Swastika*. Garden City, N.Y.: Doubleday, 1985.

Hogan, Michael J., and Thomas G. Paterson, eds. *Explaining the History of American Foreign Relations*. Cambridge: Cambridge University Press, 1991.

Hyde, H. Montgomery. *Room 3603: The Story of the British Intelligence Center in New York During World War II*. New York: Farrar, Straus, 1963.

Ickes, Harold. *The Secret Diary of Harold L. Ickes,* Vol. 3, *The Lowering Clouds, 1939–1941*. New York: Simon & Schuster, 1955.

Isaacson, Walter. *Einstein: His Life and Universe*. New York: Simon & Schuster, 2007.

————, and Evan Thomas. *The Wise Men: Six Friends and the World They Made*. New York: Touchstone, 1988.

Jackson, Robert H. *That Man: An Insider's Portrait of Franklin D. Roosevelt*. Oxford: Oxford University Press, 2003.

Jeansonne, Glen. *Women of the Far Right: The Mothers' Movement and World War II*. Chicago: University of Chicago Press, 1996.

Kabaservice, Geoffrey. *The Guardians: Kingman Brewster, His Circle, and the Rise of the Liberal Establishment*. New York: Henry Holt, 2004.

Kahn, David. *Hitler's Spies: German Military Intelligence in World War II.* New York: Collier Books, 1985.

Kaytor, Marilyn. *"21": The Life and Times of New York's Favorite Club.* New York: Viking, 1975.

Kennedy, David. *Freedom from Fear: The American People in Depression and War, 1929–1945.* Oxford: Oxford University Press, 1990.

Ketchum, Richard M. *The Borrowed Years, 1938–1941: America on the Way to War.* New York: Random House, 1989.

Kimball, Warren F. *The Most Unsordid Act: Lend-Lease, 1939–1941.* Baltimore: Johns Hopkins University Press, 1969.

Kluger, Richard. *The Paper: The Life and Death of the New York Herald Tribune.* New York: Knopf, 1986.

Koppes, Clayton R., and Gregory D. Black. *Hollywood Goes to War: How Politics, Profits and Propaganda Shaped World War II Movies.* London: Tauris, 1988.

Kurth, Peter. *American Cassandra: The Life of Dorothy Thompson.* Boston: Little, Brown, 1990.

Langer, William S., and S. Everett Gleason. *The Challenge to Isolation: 1937–1940.* New York: Harper, 1952.

———. *The Undeclared War: 1940–1941.* New York: Harper, 1953.

Larrabee, Eric. *Commander in Chief: Franklin D. Roosevelt, His Lieutenants, and Their War.* New York: Harper & Row, 1987.

Leaming, Barbara. *Jack Kennedy: The Education of a Statesman.* New York: Norton, 2006.

Lees-Milne, James. *Harold Nicolson: A Biography.* London: Chatto & Windus, 1980.

Leigh, Michael. *Mobilizing Consent: Public Opinion and American Foreign Policy, 1937–1947.* Westport, Conn.: Greenwood Press, 1976.

Leighton, Isabel. *The Aspirin Age: 1919–1941.* New York: Simon & Schuster, 1949.

Lindbergh, Anne Morrow. *Against Wind and Tide: Letters and Journals, 1947–1986.* New York: Pantheon, 2012.

———. *Bring Me a Unicorn: Diaries and Letters of Anne Morrow Lindbergh, 1922–1928.* New York: Harcourt Brace Jovanovich, 1971.

———. *Dearly Beloved.* New York: Harcourt Brace & World, 1962.

———. *The Flower and the Nettle: Diaries and Letters of Anne Morrow Lindbergh, 1936–1939.* New York: Harcourt Brace Jovanovich, 1976.

———. *Gift from the Sea.* New York: Pantheon, 2005.

———. *Hour of Gold, Hour of Lead: Diaries and Letters of Anne Morrow Lindbergh, 1929–1932.* New York: Harcourt Brace Jovanovich, 1973.

———. *Locked Rooms and Open Doors: Diaries and Letters of Anne Morrow Lindbergh, 1933–1935.* New York: Harcourt Brace Jovanovich, 1974.

———. *North to the Orient.* New York: Harcourt, Brace, 1935.

———. *War Within and Without: Diaries and Letters of Anne Morrow Lindbergh, 1939–1944.* New York: Harcourt Brace, 1980.

———. *The Wave of the Future: A Confession of Faith.* New York: Harcourt Brace, 1940.

Lindbergh, Charles A. *The Wartime Journals of Charles A. Lindbergh.* New York: Harcourt Brace Jovanovich, 1970.

Lindbergh, Reeve. *Forward from Here: Leaving Middle Age—and Other Unexpected Adventures.* New York: Simon & Schuster, 2008.

————. *Under a Wing: A Memoir.* New York: Simon & Schuster, 1998.

Lockhart, Sir Robert Bruce. *Comes the Reckoning.* London: Putnam, 1947.

————. *Giants Cast Long Shadows.* London: Putnam, 1960.

Lovell, Mary S. *Cast No Shadow: The Life of the American Spy Who Changed the Course of World War II.* New York: Pantheon, 1992.

Macdonald, Bill. *The True Intrepid: Sir William Stephenson and the Unknown Agents.* Vancouver, B.C.: Raincoast Books, 2001.

Maddow, Rachel. *Drift: The Unmooring of American Military Power.* New York: Crown, 2012.

Mahl, Thomas E. *Desperate Deception: British Covert Operations in the United States, 1939–1944.* Washington, D.C.: Brassey's, 1998.

Manchester, William. *The Glory and the Dream: A Narrative History of America, 1932–1972.* Boston: Little, Brown, 1973.

McCullough, David. *Truman.* New York: Simon & Schuster, 1992.

McKee, John DeWitt. *William Allen White: Maverick on Main Street.* Westport, Conn.: Greenwood Press, 1975.

Merry, Robert W. *Taking On the World: Joseph and Stewart Alsop—Guardians of the American Century.* New York: Viking, 1996.

Miller, Francis Pickens. *Man from the Valley: Memoirs of a 20th-Century Virginian.* Chapel Hill: University of North Carolina Press, 1971.

Milton, Joyce. *Loss of Eden: A Biography of Charles and Anne Morrow Lindbergh.* New York: HarperCollins, 1993.

Minear, Richard H. *Dr. Seuss Goes to War: The World War II Editorial Cartoons of Theodor Seuss Geisel.* New York: New Press, 1999.

Mosley, Leonard. *Lindbergh.* New York: Dell, 1977.

————. *Marshall: Hero for Our Time.* New York: Hearst, 1982.

Nathan, Frederic S. *Centurions in Public Service.* New York: The Century Association, 2010.

Neal, Steve. *Dark Horse: A Biography of Wendell Willkie.* Garden City, N.Y.: Doubleday, 1984.

Nicolson, Harold. *Diaries and Letters, 1930–1939.* London: Collins, 1969.

Nicolson, Nigel, ed. *Vita and Harold: The Letters of Vita Sackville-West and Harold Nicolson.* New York: Putman, 1992.

Olson, Lynne. *Citizens of London: The Americans Who Stood with Britain in Its Darkest, Finest Hour.* New York: Random House, 2010.

————. *Troublesome Young Men: The Rebels Who Brought Churchill to Power and Helped Save England.* New York: Farrar, Straus & Giroux, 2007.

————, and Stanley Cloud. *A Question of Honor: The Kosciuszko Squadron: Forgotten Heroes of World War II.* New York: Knopf, 2003.

Paton-Walsh, Margaret. *Our War Too: American Women Against the Axis.* Lawrence: University Press of Kansas, 2002.

Pepper, Claude Denson. *Pepper: Eyewitness to a Century.* New York: Harcourt Brace Jovanovich, 1987.

Perret, Geoffrey. *Days of Sadness, Years of Triumph: The American People, 1939–1945.* New York: Coward, McCann & Geoghegan, 1973.

Perry, Mark. *Partners in Command: George Marshall and Dwight Eisenhower in War and Peace.* New York: Penguin, 2007.

Persico, Joseph E. *Roosevelt's Secret War: FDR and World War II Espionage*. New York: Random House, 2001.

Peters, Charles. *Five Days in Philadelphia: The Amazing "We Want Willkie" Convention of 1940 and How It Freed FDR to Save the Western World*. New York: Public Affairs, 2005.

Pitt, Barrie. *The Battle of the Atlantic*. Alexandria, Va.: Time-Life Books, 1977.

Pogue, Forrest C. *George C. Marshall: Education of a General, 1880–1939*. New York: Viking, 1963.

———. *George C. Marshall: Ordeal and Hope, 1939–1942*. New York: Viking, 1966.

Reilly, Michael F. *Reilly of the White House*. New York: Simon & Schuster, 1947.

Reynolds, David. *Lord Lothian and Anglo-American Relations, 1939–1940*. Philadelphia: American Philosophical Society, 1983.

Ritchie, Donald A. *Reporting from Washington: The History of the Washington Press Corps*. Oxford: Oxford University Press, 2005.

Root, Oren. *Persons and Persuasions*. New York: Norton, 1974.

Rosenman, Samuel I. *Working with Roosevelt*. New York: Harper, 1952.

———, and Dorothy Rosenman. *Presidential Style: Some Giants and a Pygmy in the White House*. New York: Harper & Row, 1976.

Ross, Walter S. *The Last Hero: Charles A. Lindbergh*. New York: Harper & Row, 1976.

Roth, Philip. *The Plot Against America*. Boston: Houghton Mifflin, 2004.

Sarles, Ruth. *A Story of America First: The Men and Women Who Opposed U.S. Intervention in World War II*. Westport, Conn.: Praeger, 2003.

Schaffer, Howard B. *Chester Bowles: New Dealer in the Cold War*. Cambridge, Mass.: Harvard University Press, 1993.

Schiff, Stacy. *Saint-Exupéry: A Biography*. New York: Knopf, 1995.

Schlesinger, Arthur M., Jr. *The Coming of the New Deal, 1933–1935*. Boston: Houghton Mifflin, 2003.

———. *A Life in the Twentieth Century: Innocent Beginnings, 1917–1950*. New York: Houghton Mifflin, 2000.

———. *The Politics of Upheaval, 1935–1936*. Boston: Houghton Mifflin, 2003.

Schneider, James C. *Should America Go to War? The Debate Over Foreign Policy in Chicago, 1939–1941*. Chapel Hill: University of North Carolina Press, 1989.

Sevareid, Eric. *Not So Wild a Dream*. New York: Atheneum, 1976.

Sheean, Vincent. *Dorothy and Red*. Boston: Houghton Mifflin, 1963.

Sherwood, Robert. *Roosevelt and Hopkins: An Intimate History*. New York: Harper, 1948.

———. *There Shall Be No Night*. New York: Scribner's, 1940.

———. *This Is New York*. New York: Scribner's, 1931.

Shesol, Jeff. *Supreme Power: Franklin Roosevelt vs. the Supreme Court*. New York: Norton, 2010.

Shirer, William L. *Berlin Diary: The Journal of a Foreign Correspondent, 1931–1941*. New York: Knopf, 1941.

———. *The Rise and Fall of the Third Reich: A History of Nazi Germany*. New York: Simon & Schuster, 1960.

Simpson, B. Mitchell. *Admiral Harold R. Stark: Architect of Victory*. Columbia: University of South Carolina Press, 1989.

Smith, F. Bradley. *The Shadow Warriors: O.S.S. and the Origins of the C.I.A.* New York: Basic, 1983.

Smith, Jean Edward. *FDR*. New York: Random House, 2007.

Smith, Richard Norton. *The Colonel: The Life and Legend of Robert R. McCormick, 1880–1955*. Boston: Houghton Mifflin, 1997.

Smith, Truman. *Berlin Alert: The Memoirs of Truman Smith*. Stanford: Hoover Institution Press, 1984.

Snow, Richard. *A Measureless Peril: America in the Fight for the Atlantic, the Longest Battle of World War II*. New York: Scribner, 2010.

Steel, Ronald. *Walter Lippmann and the American Century*. New York: Vintage, 1981.

Steele, Richard W. *Free Speech in the Good War*. New York: St. Martin's, 1999.

————. *Propaganda in an Open Society: The Roosevelt Administration and the Media, 1939–1941*. Westport, Conn.: Greenwood Press, 1985.

Stevenson, William. *Spymistress: The True Story of the Greatest Female Secret Agent of World War II*. New York: Arcade, 2007.

Stimson, Henry L., and McGeorge Bundy. *On Active Service in Peace and War*. New York: Harper, 1948.

Stossel, Scott. *Sarge: The Life and Times of Sargent Shriver*. Washington, D.C.: Smithsonian Books, 2004.

Sullivan, William C. *The Bureau: My Thirty Years in Hoover's FBI*. New York: Norton, 1979.

Tifft, Susan E., and Alex S. Jones. *The Patriarch: The Rise and Fall of the Bingham Dynasty*. New York: Summit, 1991.

————. *The Trust: The Private and Powerful Family Behind* The New York Times. Boston: Little, Brown, 1999.

Trohan, Walter. *Political Animals: Memoirs of a Sentimental Cynic*. Garden City, N.Y.: Doubleday, 1975.

Troy, Thomas F. *Wild Bill and Intrepid: Donovan, Stephenson, and the Origin of CIA*. New Haven: Yale University Press, 1996.

Tugwell, Rexford G. *The Democratic Roosevelt*. Garden City, N.Y.: Doubleday, 1957.

Vidal, Gore. *The Last Empire: Essays 1992–2000*. New York: Doubleday, 2001.

Voorhis, Jerry. *Confessions of a Congressman*. Westport, Conn.: Greenwood Press, 1970.

Waldrop, Frank C. *McCormick of Chicago: An Unconventional Portrait of a Controversial Figure*. Englewood Cliffs, N.J.: Prentice-Hall, 1966.

Ward, Geoffrey C. *A First-Class Temperament: The Emergence of Franklin Roosevelt*. New York: Harper & Row, 1989.

Watkins, T. H. *Righteous Pilgrim: The Life and Times of Harold L. Ickes, 1874–1952*. New York: Henry Holt, 1990.

Watson, Mark. *Chief of Staff: Prewar Plans and Preparations*. Washington, D.C.: Center of Military History, 1991.

Wedemeyer, Gen. Albert C. *Wedemeyer Reports!* New York: Henry Holt, 1958.

Weil, Martin. *A Pretty Good Club: The Founding Fathers of the U.S. Foreign Service*. New York: Norton, 1978.

Welky, David. *The Moguls and the Dictators: Hollywood and the Coming of World War II*. Baltimore: Johns Hopkins University Press, 2008.

Wheeler, Burton K. *Yankee from the West*. Garden City, N.Y.: Doubleday, 1962.

Wheeler-Bennett, Sir John. *Special Relationships: America in Peace and War*. London: Macmillan, 1975.

White, David Fairbank. *Bitter Ocean: The Battle of the Atlantic, 1939–1945*. New York: Simon & Schuster, 2006.

Winchell, Walter. *Winchell Exclusive*. Englewood Cliffs, N.J.: Prentice-Hall, 1975.

Worthy, James C. *Shaping an American Institution: Robert E. Wood and Sears, Roebuck*. Urbana: University of Illinois Press, 1984.

Wright, Bradford W. *Comic Book Nation: The Transformation of Youth Culture in America*. Baltimore: Johns Hopkins University Press, 2003.

INDEX

Page numbers in *italics* refer to illustrations.

ABOUT THE AUTHOR

LYNNE OLSON is the author of *Citizens of London: The Americans Who Stood with Britain in Its Darkest, Finest Hour; Troublesome Young Men: The Rebels Who Brought Churchill to Power and Helped Save England;* and *Freedom's Daughters: The Unsung Heroines of the Civil Rights Movement from 1830 to 1970,* and co-author of two other books. She lives with her husband in Washington, D.C.

www.lynneolson.com

———

Lynne Olson is available for select readings and lectures. To inquire about a possible appearance, please contact the Random House Speakers Bureau at rhspeakers@randomhouse.com.

ABOUT THE TYPE

This book was set in Bembo, a typeface based on an old-style Roman face that was used for Cardinal Bembo's tract *De Aetna* in 1495. Bembo was cut by Francisco Griffo in the early sixteenth century. The Lanston Monotype Company of Philadelphia brought the well-proportioned letterforms of Bembo to the United States in the 1930s